The Cinema of Sinatra

The Actor, on Screen and in Song

by Scott Allen Nollen

The Cinema of Sinatra

The Actor, on Screen and in Song

by Scott Allen Nollen

Luminary Press
Baltimore, Maryland

ISBN 1-887664-51-3
Library of Congress Catalog Card Number 2003116242
Manufactured in the United States of America
First Printing by Luminary Press an imprint of Midnight Marquee, Press, Inc., December 2003
Second Printing by Midnight Marquee, Press, Inc., September, 2008

for Thomas ("The BFG") Fortunato
and
Willy ("The Broom") Rizzo

The Cinema of Sinatra

Table of Contents

8   Preface

10   Introduction

17   Chapter 1: A Bum?

25   Chapter 2: Hoboken to Hollywood

42   Chapter 3: The Mogul, the Feet and the Voice

89   Chapter 4: The Lean Years

100   Chapter 5: Comeback Charley

148   Chapter 6: Quintessential Sinatra

175   Chapter 7: Sinatra at War

201   Chapter 8: The Summit, the Cold War and
                    Frank in Command

268   Chapter 9: Goodbye, Baby, and Amen

316   Filmography

340   Notes

353   Bibliography

357   Index

Preface

Music is either good or it isn't. It's not someone's opinion.
— Arturo Toscanini

It was "just one of those things" the first time I heard Frank Sinatra. I can't recall the exact date, but his voice was coming from my parent's console stereo sometime during the mid-1960s. A few years later, my mother bought *Sinatra: The Main Event*, and I spent hours destroying the LP's grooves, having no idea that it was a mediocre album recorded during a "comeback" tour when his voice wasn't in top form. Nevertheless, I was immediately attracted both to the sound of his voice and the unique finesse with which he performed the song.

My first knowledge of Sinatra as an actor must have been through one of the MGM musicals, as my parents never missed a television broadcast of anything in that genre. But the first Sinatra character that made an impression on my young mind was his Colonel Ryan in *Von Ryan's Express* (1965), which I was allowed to stay up and watch during a late-night broadcast during the early 1970s. Ryan was one of those admirable, intelligent, tough-guy leaders who always impresses a young boy. My lifelong interest in World War II was sparked by this powerful classic.

During my years as a weekend musician, 1978-84, in the Midwest lounge act "Together," I further developed an undying appreciation for jazz, and the night my bandmates and I backed a tolerable jazz singer (her name is forever lost to me; perhaps it never was known) was the highlight of six years of playing halls, clubs, restaurants and dives. The only Sinatra number that found its way into our book was "(The Theme From) New York, New York," but that was a gasser.

In 1984, while a film student at the University of Iowa, I directed a young, off-the-wall comic actor named Toby Huss in a short video production. At that time, Huss, who looked a bit like the youthful Ol' Blue Eyes, was developing a bizarre penchant for impersonating him. When he told me how he had sung along with a cassette of *Strangers in the Night* while driving to college, focusing on "Summer Wind," the album's best track, I replied I'd buy him and our pals as much pizza as we could eat *if* he would sing our order like Frank. He did—and 12 years later, turned up as a campy Sinatra impersonator on the TV show *I Want My MTV* and in the mediocre Kelsey Grammer film *Down Periscope*, in which he plays a Navy submarine electrician who inexplicably breaks into "You Make Me Feel So Young" while being shocked. (After such an inauspicious beginning in my little semi-autobiographical satire, Huss went on to roles in major Hollywood fare like *Jerry Maguire* [1996], *The Mod Squad* [1999] and *Bedazzled* [2000]).

Immersed in jazz music and American film, I think I have an insight into the connections between Frank Sinatra the singer and the motion picture actor. This book is the first to cover his film career thoroughly and prove that, indeed, he was one of America's finest screen performers. But it also goes beyond that, situating Sinatra's film work within the context of his entire career: His recordings are examined in detail to show how his musical and cinematic talents were inextricably linked. And not only did Sinatra sing in many of his films, he also waxed scores of songs that originally had been written for Hollywood productions. To appreciate Sinatra the actor, one first must grasp Sinatra the singer, for his talents in both areas evolved hand in hand. Moreover, this "dual career" must be situated within the context of his 82-year life: One cannot fathom Sinatra's talent either as a vocalist or actor without having a good handle on what made him tick—and most of the published biographies simply "don't grab it." His social and political values are covered at some length. To understand many of his films—particularly those he influenced, produced and directed—one must be aware of his beliefs and actions, particularly those during the mid-1940s and his later friendship and support of John F. Kennedy (which had effect on the production of *Robin and the 7 Hoods* [1964], here told accurately for the first time).

This book was written in many states of the Union—in several houses and apartments, in hotel rooms, on airplanes, in Italian restaurants and even in a health center. It was edited primarily on a hide-a-bed in Hollywood. (No, Sol Z. Steiner wasn't under it!)

I would like to extend a truly heartfelt thank you to the family of the late Jilly Rizzo, who were very kind in aiding me with various aspects of this project. Jilly's daughter, Abby, was generous in recalling her father's participation in Sinatra's late 1960s films, searching for rare photographs and putting me in touch with her brother Willy ("The Broom"), who managed Jilly's Bistro—"where the elite meet to eat"—on Chicago's legendary Rush Street. This Windy City establishment featured a piano bar, retro club and "An Italian Joynt" steakhouse—the finest of its kind. I was treated royally by The Broom and his staff while picking up a few nice tidbits for the book.

My gratitude also goes out to the following individuals, who shared their memories of working with Mr. Sinatra, provided information and materials, advice and suggestions, kind encouragement, or merely a place to flop: Bart Aikens, Milt Bernhardt, Nick Caruso, Sr., Nick Caruso, Jr., John Donaldson, Dave Eichhorn, Jack Elam, Dragi Filipovich, Rit Fuller, Chuck Granata, David P. Harmon, Nikki Harmon, John ("The Slack") Jensen, Sara Jane Karloff, Martin J. Kelly, Nancy Sinatra Lambert, Angela Lansbury, Harold N. Nollen and Shirley Nollen (who discovered Angelo's and Vinci's Restaurant in Fullerton, California, owned by Steven Peck, who twice tries to kill Frank in *Some Came Running*!), Anthony Potenzoand and Douglas Siegal.

Scott Allen Nollen
"On Da Road, Baby"
Autumn 2002

INTRODUCTION

I like films. —Frank Sinatra[1]

Frank Sinatra rightfully has been recognized as the greatest popular singer in American history, an achievement so enormous that it has overshadowed every other aspect of his life story, including the ubiquitous rumors and half-truths about his personal affairs that first surfaced during the mid-1940s. In particular, his incomparable vocal artistry—combining mastery of melody, rhythm, phrasing, breath control and dynamics with taste, understatement and an uncanny understanding of the meaning of lyrics—has overwhelmed his success as a motion picture actor. Even those who have written much about his achievements often have downplayed his work on the silver screen.

Sinatra's growth as a dramatic actor—beginning with his Academy Award-winning performance in *From Here to Eternity*—paralleled his musical career during the early 1950s, when he evolved from the romantic, youthful crooner of the Columbia years into the experienced, powerful swinger who, along with arrangers Nelson Riddle, Billy May and Gordon Jenkins, created a string of groundbreaking concept albums for Capitol that still reign supreme as the greatest recorded collection of popular American standards. Only Sinatra could attempt to match such a feat: as an *actor* who, from 1953 on, appeared in a remarkable variety of roles in nearly every film genre.

Jazz historian Will Friedwald noted:

> Sinatra's most appealing talent may be his capacity for emotional expressiveness. As time went on, Sinatra played an increasingly more finely tuned instrument, not only with a broader range at the bottom and top—sadder sads and happier happies—but with more degrees between the peaks.[2]

Sinatra brought the same natural talent for rhythm, phrasing and nuance to his film roles, whether in dramas, comedies, suspense films, crime thrillers or war epics. And following his landmark portrayal in *From Here to Eternity*, he still could revert to 1940s style for an old-fashioned musical, just as he could melt women's hearts with an impeccably sung ballad, only now with a deeper, sometimes world-weary, intonation. His complex, hard-hitting, occasionally cynical portrayals in *Suddenly* (1954), *Young at Heart* (1955), *The Man With the Golden Arm* (1955), *The Joker Is Wild* (1957), *Kings Go Forth* (1958) and *Some Came Running* (1958) are cinematic counterparts to his unique, emotionally engaging saloon-song performances on what he sometimes referred to as his "suicide" albums—*In the Wee Small Hours of the Morning* (1955), *Only the Lonely* (1958) and *No One Cares* (1958).

Sinatra's singing and acting both sprang from the same psychological font. While "The Voice," "The Chairman of the Board" and "Ol' Blue Eyes" exuded confidence, professionalism, perfectionism and sometimes tough-guy aggressiveness in public, the private Frank Sinatra was often lonely and depressed—a quality that pervades his enormous body of work, both recorded and filmed, hauntingly, relentlessly.

In her memoir *My Father's Daughter*, Tina Sinatra revealed:

> My father was a deeply feeling man who could not attain a meaningful intimate relationship. ...Raised a Catholic, Dad figured he had it coming when he was miserable. He settled for less because he thought he deserved no more. His perpetual unease was part and parcel of his nature—and, I maintain, an integral part of his art.

The Cinema of Sinatra

Had he been a healthier, less tortured man, he might have been Perry Como.[3]

Journalist and longtime Sinatra acquaintance Pete Hamill concluded:

As an artist, Sinatra had only one basic subject: loneliness. His ballads are all strategies for dealing with loneliness; his up-tempo performances are expressions of release of that loneliness. The former are almost all fueled by abandonment, odes to the girl who got away. The up-tempo tunes embrace the girl who has just arrived. Across his long career, Sinatra did many variations on this basic theme, but he got into real trouble only when he strayed from that essentially urban feeling of being the lone man in the crowded city. He is at his most ludicrous in the film clip [from *Till the Clouds Roll By* (1946)] where he sings "Ol' Man River" in a white tuxedo...[4]

There is no more ethereal recorded vocal performance than "Only the Lonely." This Sammy Cahn-James Van Heusen masterpiece waxed in 1958, together with dozens of other Sinatra saloon songs, may not have an exact cinematic equivalent, but many of Sinatra's dramatic—even comic—characters are filled with similar emotions of loneliness, longing , despair and regret. The man who laments his romantic state in "Only the Lonely," "Angel Eyes," "I Guess I'll Hang My Tears Out to Dry" and "I'm a Fool to Want You" is the same one who inhabits Angelo Maggio in *From Here to Eternity*, Charlie Reader in *The Tender Trap*, Frankie Machine in *The Man With the Golden Arm*, Joe E. Lewis in *The Joker is Wild*, Joey Evans in *Pal Joey*, Sam Loggins in *Kings Go Forth*, Dave Hirsh in *Some Came Running*, Tony Manetta in *A Hole in the Head* and Bennett Marco in *The Manchurian Candidate*.

Few film actors have appeared in such a large percentage of consistently high-budget, popular and critically acclaimed films. And not many have worked with top directors throughout their careers. Sinatra acted for a literal "who's who" of film direction, including Busby Berkeley, Gene Kelly, Stanley Donen, Fred Zinneman, Gordon Douglas, Stanley Kramer, Joseph L. Mankiewicz, Otto Preminger, Charles Vidor, George Sidney, Delmer Daves, Vincente Minnelli, Frank Capra, John Sturges, Lewis Milestone, Mervyn LeRoy, John Frankenheimer, John Huston, Robert Aldrich and Mark Robson. He also was a successful producer and directed a powerful, underrated anti-war film, *None But the Brave*, in 1965.

Sinatra enjoyed the collaboration and respect of a formidable constellation of star colleagues, including Montgomery Clift, whom he credited with teaching him the most about screen acting. And he once was coached by the equally unique Boris Karloff, who, in his finest roles, also was a master of understatement. Proving that Sinatra's thespian prowess has been eclipsed by his musical achievement, Karloff's daughter, Sara Jane, during a 1996 discussion about Frank, said, "You know, he really is an *excellent actor*," as if others need to be convinced.

Prior to Sinatra's film debut with the Tommy Dorsey Orchestra in 1941's *Las Vegas Nights*, Al Jolson and Bing Crosby had become major movie stars, and, although the latter developed into a very capable actor and light comic (as well as a television producer), no other vocalists had loomed very impressively on the screen for very long. Although it took Sinatra (who idolized Crosby and loved going to the movies as a youngster) 13 years to be given the opportunity to prove his dramatic mettle, his abilities evolved at a prodigious rate following his 1953 triumph as Private Maggio.

Very few artists have successfully crossed over into another medium with such overwhelming success. Many singers have been promoted by the Hollywood studios as sensational new screen stars, but who other than Sinatra has wrought such a lengthy and distinguished film career? Certainly not Elvis Presley, the only other singer whose fame can be compared to Sinatra's. Though a competent, naturalistic actor, Presley racked up an often embarrassing catalogue of cinematic fluff, with a few notable exceptions—particularly the Michael Curtiz-directed *King Creole* (1958), which "the King" considered his best screen effort. Though Colonel Tom Parker was partially responsible for these bad films, Elvis usually played a close variation on his own personality seasoned with influences from James Dean and Marlon Brando. Not an actor, but a movie star.

Interestingly, Sinatra's friend and colleague Dean Martin often created more impressive work as an actor than he did as a pop singer. Although he scored many novelty hits, his best singing occurred whenever he decided to swing (as when performing "Ain't That a Kick in the Head?" with Red Norvo's quintet in *Ocean's Eleven* [1960]) or croon lovely lullabies (under Sinatra's direction) on albums such as *Sleep Warm*. Even more underrated than Sinatra, Martin, who began his film career as straight man to Jerry Lewis (who admitted that his former partner was a genius of comic timing), essayed several outstanding performances, the best of which is arguably his brilliantly underplayed portrayal of "Dude," John Wayne's alcoholic deputy, in Howard Hawks' *Rio Bravo* (1959).

Excluding cameos and appearances with the Tommy Dorsey Orchestra, Sinatra enacted 45 major film roles and starred in one short subject, the Academy Award-winning *The House I Live In*, in 1945. He sings in only 25 of the major films, exactly half, and 15 of these were made prior to *From Here to Eternity*. After producing and starring in *Robin and the 7 Hoods* in 1964, he appeared in 11 more major roles, all of them non-singing characterizations, over a span of 16 years. Obviously, after he began to prove his dramatic abilities, the songs were not always integral in selling the films at the box office. Filmgoers now were buying tickets to see him solely as an actor. And, as Sinatra himself admitted, after the quality of his voice began to lessen with age, he still could rely on his dramatic talent to continue making his mark in show business. Interestingly, of his 45 major film characters, half incorporate that quality of loneliness, in some way.

At face value, a major technical difference between Sinatra the singer and Sinatra the actor was his endless retake perfectionism in the recording studio versus his reputation for being a one-take performer while on the film set. Why did he insist on cutting the same song more than 20 times, sometimes just to master one particularly troublesome note, yet refuse to redo a film scene that a director believed could be improved? He obviously thought his vocal performances should be as close to perfect as possible (he rarely listened to his records, feeling that he always could have done better), but did not push himself so much while acting. Perhaps the latter was easier for him; after all, though he was born with a talent for both, singing and acting are two different media.

Just as he did in the recording studio, Sinatra preferred to keep his film performances free of artifice, but the realities of film production (being limited by the director and screenplay [unless he was allowed to ad lib, he was expected to deliver his dialogue as scripted]) were quite different from recording a Cole Porter song, for instance. Although the arrangement of "I've Got You Under My Skin" for *Songs for Swingin' Lovers* (1956) was written by Nelson Riddle, Frank was still in control of all aspects of the performance, and his talent was such that, even on the 22nd take, his jazz-oriented approach kept his interpretation fresh (yet absolutely precise) on this ultimate Sinatra recording.

Actress Julie Harris remarked in 1996, "As long as an actor gets there, it doesn't matter *how* he gets there."[5] Regardless of the approach Sinatra used either to record an album or act in a film, the results were similarly impressive in both arenas. Friedwald writes, "With Sinatra, all vocal considerations—and even all musical considerations—come second to the fundamental mission, which is to tell a story in the most expressive way possible. His formidable musical and dramatic skills immediately blur together."[6] Sinatra was born with the natural talent to sing and to act. Just as he adopted and transformed the musical techniques he learned from his mentors Harry James and Tommy Dorsey during his "boy singer" days (1939-43), he further developed his dramatic skills by working alongside serious thespians like Monty Clift. But he already *knew* he could play Private Maggio, just as he predicted that he one day would be "the world's greatest singer."[7] After directing him in *From Here to Eternity*, Fred Zinneman recalled that Frank was a "'total rebel' who relied 'completely on his own spontaneity rather than careful rehearsing.'"[8]

When *Eternity* proved that Sinatra was an actor of range and subtlety, his audiences were witnessing his talent being communicated through a non-musical medium for the first time. Years later, he said:

> I never studied, you know. I never went to any of the schools or anything like that. I just felt that if you learn your words properly like you know your name—and first of all, if you believe when you've taken the job, you obviously believe in what you are about to do and then learn the words properly—that you're a cinch. If you have any brains at all, you should be able to do it very well.
>
> I thought that acting is play acting like we did when we were kids. But... suddenly, you're grown up and it's for real. And then you become immersed in what you're playing, too.... I made myself think that I was really that guy on any film I did; comedy or whatever it might have been.[9]

Sinatra revealed that his famous vocal diction and phrasing was born while watching 1930s movie stars in a Hoboken theater.[10] In fact, the cinema was integral to his overall success as an artist: After the films of his youth helped to create his unique vocal style, his singing later paved the way for his own stardom on the silver screen. Will Friedwald further describes Frank's vocal evolution, which applies equally to his acting:

> His ability to tell a story has consistently gotten sharper even as the voice grew deeper and the textures surrounding it richer. Generally, rhythm and dynamics are discussed as if they were two distinct qualities, but with Sinatra they're inseparable. They amount to the primary tools through which he affords varying degrees of weight to key phrases. The weight of emphasis can be applied in terms of both duration—the length of time that he holds the note (rhythm)—or in the volume level at which he chooses to hit it (dynamics). Before Sinatra, loud generally tended to mean long, but The Voice opened up a whole new world of rhythmic-dynamic thinking in which soft notes could be indefinitely extended for greater emotional effect.[11]

Sinatra did not always insist on numerous takes when recording, however. Orchestrator Claus Ogerman, who wrote the charts for the 1967 album *Francis Albert Sinatra and Antonio Carlos Jobim*, revealed that, after failing to complete an arrangement before a session at Los Angeles' Western Sound, he was astonished when he found Frank already in the studio: "He was rehearsing the tunes with [pianist] Bill Miller, which shows the reason why he's so professional and why he needs only one or two takes—because he works on all the stuff beforehand. I found it remarkable."[12]

Sinatra's live performances—during which he always improvised, never singing a standard the same way twice—were closely akin to his "one-take" cinematic style. His confident prowess on film sets was foreshadowed early in his musical career when, in 1939, he auditioned for Harry James. Arriving at New York's Lincoln Hotel with no written arrangements, he merely mentioned some song titles and their respective keys to the pianist before landing the gig. Saxophonist Arthur "Skeets" Herfurt later recalled that Frank "knocked everybody out. They were auditioning a lot of people that day, but the musicians said that when they heard Sinatra, that was it. There was no doubt about it."[13]

Frank Sinatra works his vocal magic. (Photofest)

     Sinatra's classic concept albums were deliberately sequenced to comprise a quasi-narrative, much like separate scenes that make up a film story. Longtime Sinatra associate Frank Military recalled, "He sat down and carefully planned his albums, and lyrically they had to make sense. They had to tell a story. He'd spend days and weeks just preparing this album. Each song would be handpicked, it had a reason for being in the album."[14] Just as he collaborated with filmmakers and fellow actors to tell a tale on film, Sinatra personally selected his musical colleagues to help him create an ambient narrative on tape. His utmost concern was getting the message across, regardless of the medium. In fact, the very structure of his vocal performances closely parallels the structure of good storytelling. Friedwald observes:

> Sinatra unfailingly triumphs in the development of devices that move the song
> forward on both the musical and dramatic planes. ...the most intense moment
> of a Sinatra performance is rarely the last line or note. Sinatra prefers to hit
> the big notes in the previous rhyme or line before the end, wherever it makes
> sense to him, and then bring it home on a surprisingly quiet note. He often

ends on a long note, but then it's almost never loud, just subtly and quietly extended. Even when the final note is of comparatively brief duration, he almost always diminuendos on it very slowly.[15]

Sinatra's vocal and acting abilities emanated from the same source, they were part of the same complex, powerful yet subtle approach to expression that first was nurtured by Tommy Dorsey, who taught him that the performer's main concern was to communicate *meaning*. Sinatra's innovative stylistic evolution was not only crucial to his emergence as popular music's greatest singer, but also integral in his development as an actor of nuance and understatement. Friedwald elaborates:

> Sinatra essentially built on the natural, as initially expounded by Crosby, Fred Astaire, Benny Goodman and Louis Armstrong, exploiting the idea that popular music — singing, dancing, or playing — should be an extension of conversation. He differs primarily from Crosby in that he favors the smooth, even lines of dance music from the mid-1930s, as opposed to the choppier, syncopated sound that Crosby grew up in and forever kept to some degree in his work.... Sinatra used longer phrases to achieve greater scope, a broader palette with which to communicate the dramatic underpinnings of a text. In conversationally singing the words of whatever song he was working on, Sinatra now had greater leeway to stress the words that were the most important in the context of the story. He could now emphasize key words or notes through a combination of choices related to dynamics (loud or soft) and rhythm (short versus long notes). ...In everything Sinatra does, he has faith in the idea that if you make telling the story your first priority, then musical values can't help but follow. This thinking affords a naturalness to his art that defies explanation...[16]

In his 1965 *Life* essay "Me and My Music," Frank, evaluating a few colleagues along the way, emphasizes the importance of storytelling over vocal pyrotechnics:

> Tony Bennett is the best singer in the business, the best exponent of a song. ...Take Lena Horne...a beautiful lady but really a mechanical singer. She gimmicks up a song... Judy Garland and Ella Fitzgerald... are technically two of the worst singers in the business. Every time I see Judy I fall down, and of course Ella is my all-time favorite, but they still sing wrong. I've heard Ella sing one word, then take a breath, then sing a word with two syllables in it and breath in between the syllables. This violates all the rules of singing. Judy does the same thing.
>
> They forget they're telling the story in the song lyric. It doesn't flow. ...It's just like reading poetry. And that's odd because poetry bores me. It always has. I'm one of the worst readers of poetry in the world. But when I do it in a song, I find that I enjoy it, and I find that I understand the distance necessary per phrase.... Sarah Vaughan... irritated me for a while... She was groping around, searching for a style, for a musical identity. She finally found it, and it was deceptively simple — just straight singing with very little of that wandering around in the upper stratosphere that she used to do. It's the hardest thing for any of us — to discover the art of straight, pure singing. It's easier to find a gimmick and hang onto it...
>
> Peggy Lee's pretty good with the lyrics. She sustains a little more than the other girls do. One of the great woman singers for technique is Jo Staf-

ford. She can hold notes for 16 bars if she has to. She's fantastic—perfect pitch, absolutely perfect pitch.[17]

Will Friedwald rightly claims, "Sinatra was never just a voice or even The Voice, he was always a musical auteur."[18] Indeed, he never would have had such a phenomenal effect as a singer in the 1940s and '50s, nor have endured for numerous decades had he not been. As an actor, he also often drove the content of his films, but he only could be described as a true cinematic auteur on a few occasions: in his conception of *The House I Live In* (1945), as the producer of several features in the late 1950s and 1960s and as the director and producer of *None But the Brave* (1965). Both *House* and *Brave*, his two truly "auteurist" works, deal eloquently with racism and hatred, calling for tolerance, equality and cooperation, aspects of his personal philosophy that often led conservative extremists to brand him a Communist. When confronted with such accusations, Sinatra, a lifelong crusader for human and civil rights, said that if concern for his fellow man made him a Communist, then he must be one. He also said, on many occasions, that the only label that fit him was "American."

Sinatra grew up in an environment populated with tough guys, some of them bootleggers who frequented his mother's saloon. Performing in clubs and casinos frequently brought him into contact with mobsters, a few of them becoming acquaintances. And sometimes he acted like a wiseguy himself. For more than four decades, the FBI, often working in collaboration with conservative journalists, tried to dig up any dirt they could, to prove he was a Communist or "affiliated with the Mob." Now the bureau's "secret file" has been made available due to the Freedom of Information Act, and it can be seen clearly that, though Sinatra did occasionally socialize with or perform for a mobster, no actual participation in their illegal activities was ever proved. The paranoid J. Edgar Hoover and his associates, who also surveiled Charles Chaplin, Errol Flynn and other Hollywood notables, often came to conclusions first and then attempted to find evidence that might fit into their preconceived schemes. Of all the film actors harassed by the press and the government, none was more pressed than Sinatra. Interestingly, his only cinematic wiseguy is the satirical "Robbo" in *Robin and the 7 Hoods*, and he never gave a serious performance as a mobster.

Regarding Sinatra's dual musical and cinematic talent, historian Chuck Granata concurs:

> Anyone who saw a Sinatra concert in person during his last 20 years can attest that whenever he sang it, he rarely failed to turn in a stunningly believable performance of his quintessential torch song, "One for My Baby." Are we to believe that each such performance (and there were thousands over several decades) is tinged with the singer's real sadness? Of course not. It's his ability as an *actor* that allows him to slip in and out of roles that enhance his vocal performance. But he needed to have learned the part.
>
> Of course, on record the singer needed to compensate for the visual effects that played a major role in his stage appearances. When all is said and done, Sinatra's genius, both as a vocalist and in the recording studio, is rooted in his considerable skill as a dramatic actor. The roles for which he garnered critical acclaim—*From Here to Eternity*, *Suddenly*, *The Man With the Golden Arm* and *The Manchurian Candidate*—are convincing examples of the breadth and seriousness of his talent. His ability to intuitively grasp a character's essence and identify the most meaningful elements of a plot helped Sinatra transfer his persuasive on-screen sensitivities to the lyrical interpretation required for his vocal performances.[19]

Frank Sinatra was the greatest singer who ever acted, and the greatest actor who ever sang.

Chapter One
A Bum?

Do you want to get a regular job? Or do you wanna be a bum?
—Marty Sinatra, to his son Frankie, 1931

In 1915, Hoboken, New Jersey, located across the Hudson from Manhattan, was not unlike other Eastern industrial cities, home to a diverse accumulation of European immigrants and their first-generation American offspring. More often than not, each ethnicity—whether Dutch, Swede, English or Scottish—formed its own tightly knit neighborhood.

A year earlier, the once prominent Germans were viewed suspiciously after their brethren in the fatherland escalated what came to be known as the Great War, leaving a void at the top of the social ladder to be filled by Irish keen to gain positions of authority. Beneath them both were Hoboken's Italians, a proud community in the downtown ghetto of Little Italy, where discipline was strict and youngsters were scrappy but well-heeled.

Any Hoboken resident with ties to the Old Country often had mixed feelings when he wandered into a motion picture theater that year. He may have laughed hysterically at one of Charles Chaplin's innovative "Little Tramp" shorts released by Chicago's Essanay company; but by September, the Hollywood film industry was focusing on the European conflict as a source for movie plots. Spurred by British government officials who distributed propaganda films to America's 21,000 theaters in the belief that the working class could be convinced to adopt a pro-Allied attitude, studio moguls jumped on the jingoistic bandwagon, using anti-minority issues as backgrounds for action stories. Even the show-biz bible *Variety* referred to Italian-Americans as "wops," reflecting the industry's depiction of them as "extremely dark" and being of "a lower type."[1]

Ethnic and race hate flourished in 1915 cinema, most blatantly in D. W. Griffith's paean to the Ku Klux Klan, *The Birth of a Nation*, the first film to be screened at the White House. Although the NAACP had protested it, President Woodrow Wilson enthused, "It is like writing history with lightning. And my only regret is that it is all so terribly true."[2] While his recently deceased first wife had tried to improve living conditions for blacks, Wilson sparked a series of race riots that impelled him to retract his insensitive statement. The racist content of *The Birth of a Nation* and the even more offensive film *The Nigger* foreshadowed the nativist and anti-immigrant images that flashed across movie screens throughout 1915.

Three decades later, Hoboken's most famous native son would receive a special Academy Award for speaking out against such prejudice, in the short film *The House I Live In*, when the world again was at war. But no cinematic drama could equal the real life-or-death struggle that ensued at 415 Monroe Street in Hoboken on December 12, 1915.

An inept physician had fumbled with forceps while delivering a huge, 13 1/2-pound baby from diminutive 92-pound Natalie Garavente Sinatra. Concerned with tending to "Dolly's" serious injuries, he set aside the child, who was quickly grabbed up by Grandmother Rose Garavente, an experienced midwife, and thrust under cold running water to shock air into his tiny lungs. (Twenty-five years later, Francis Albert Sinatra would repeat this act, spending long hours swimming to develop the extended breathing technique he learned from Tommy Dorsey.)

Though his face and neck had been scarred by the forceps, the ailing Dolly and her husband, Marty, were understandably excited about the birth of their only child. Born Anthony Martin Sinatra in Sicily, Marty had eloped with Dolly on Valentine's Day 1913, against the wishes of his parents, who disapproved of his desire to marry a girl from Genoa. Having immigrated to

New Jersey with her parents at age two, Dolly was an unusual Genoan: blond and blue-eyed, the latter trait being inherited by baby "Frankie." Nearly four months after the birth, on April 2, 1916, Dolly remained bedridden while Frankie was baptized at Hoboken's St. Francis Roman Catholic Church.

Frankie's parents worked at a variety of jobs: Marty fought blazes as a fireman and other people as professional boxer "Marty O'Brien," Dolly operated a candy store and, like her mother, worked as a midwife; and they jointly ran a saloon called "Marty O'Brien's" where illegal hooch was served. After the United States entered the war on April 6, 1917, and Hoboken was placed under military authority as the center of troop embarkation, President Wilson introduced federal Prohibition to the city. Although tough characters including bootleggers frequented their joint, Dolly held her own, and the bar was listed in her name, since firemen weren't allowed to own such establishments.

While Marty and Dolly were off making a living, Frankie often was cared for by Grandmother Rose and two aunts, Mary and Rosalie. But sometimes when he arrived home from school, the house would be empty with no supper in sight. Decades later, when recalling this period for his daughter Nancy, he admitted, "It was very lonely for me. Very lonely."[3]

The prejudice that permeated the cinema was a reflection of attitudes prevalent on the streets. Each ethnic group guarded its own ghetto, and an Italian wandering into an Irish sphere might find himself kissing the sidewalk. Even on his own turf, after his parents had moved to a home at 703 Park Avenue, Frankie was ridiculed as "Scarface." He remembered, "The funny thing about the Park Avenue neighborhood was that the guys there were worse than the guys downtown. They were brighter, more insidious; well mannered, with good clothes—and deadly."[4]

In 1928 Frankie entered Hoboken's David E. Rue Junior High, where he received another nickname, "Slacksey O'Brien," mocking the many pairs of fancy pants made for him by Grandmother Rose. He later said,

> I'll never forget how it hurt when the kids called me a dago when I was a boy.
> It's a scar that lasted a long time and which I have never quite forgotten. It
> isn't the kids' fault. It's their parents'. They would never learn to make racial
> and religious discriminations if they didn't hear that junk at home.[5]

As an adult, Frank spoke further of the circumstances that fostered stereotypes of Italian-Americans in general and, at times, himself in particular:

> Prohibition was the dumbest law in American history. It was never gonna
> work, not ever. But what it did was create the Mob. These dummies with
> their books and their investigations, they think the Mob was invented by a
> bunch of Sicilians in some smoky room someplace. Probably in Palermo.
> Bullshit. The Mob was invented by all those self-righteous bastards who
> gave us Prohibition. It was invented by ministers, by Southern politicians,
> by all the usual goddamned idiots who think they can tell people how to live.
> I know what I'm talking about on *this* one. I was there.[6]

As an only child in an environment populated by large families, Frankie continued to develop the qualities of a self-reliant loner. Not having to compete with siblings, he became used to doing things his own ruggedly individualistic way, a trait that would affect his behavior for the rest of his life. In his book *Why Sinatra Matters*, Pete Hamill notes:

> Against the cynical backdrop of Prohibition, Frank Sinatra was on his own.
> On the street the most admired men were tough guys. The bootlegger could
> be seen as a glamorous rebel, one who reaped the rewards of fine clothes,

shiny cars and beautiful women. At the movies the heroes were often cow-boys, silent men, handy with guns, who rode in and out of town alone. Each taught the lesson that one solution to perceived injustice was violence. The outlaw, the desperado, the good man who was dealt a bad hand by life: They were central to the emerging American myth, as defined and spread by the new technology of mass culture.[7]

Rather than always knocking about with his pals, Frank became interested in popular culture, going to the movies and listening to singers and comedians on the radio. He began to imitate his favorite stars, and particularly liked the way his voice mixed with that of his emerging hero, Bing Crosby, whose photographs adorned the walls of his bedroom. Hamill observes that, at this time, Frank, influenced by the cinema, "began to live a split life":

> On the street he donned the mask of the wise guy, an image fed by the gang-ster films that had taken the place of Westerns in creating the myth of the American outsider. He posed like Cagney, like Edward G. Robinson. He dressed "sharp." He jingled change in the pockets of his slacks. He cursed. He talked tough. He showed his friends he would fight if he had to, and what he lacked in street-fighting talent, he made up for with courage. On the street he was developing an act, a disguise that would protect him from the world while asserting his presence in his own small piece of that world.[8]

In 1930 Frankie joined the glee club at A. J. Demarest High School, where he impressed other students with his developing vocal prowess. But he hated the formality of studying, often played hooky, and finally quit school altogether. To satisfy New Jersey educational requirements, he attended the Drake Business School for one semester. He admitted,

> At one point I said I wanted to be an engineer, to go to Stevens Institute in Hoboken, number two after MIT when I was a boy — a great school — because I love the ideas of bridges, tunnels and highways. It was my great desire until I got mixed up in vocalizing.[9]

Still living at home in 1932, Frankie moved with his parents to a house "they really couldn't afford" at 841 Garden Street. Worried that his only son was destined to be a "bum," Marty insisted that he find a "real job" having nothing to do with music.[10] Frightened out of a position catching white-hot rivets while perched over a four-story shaft at the Teijent and Lang shipyards, he tried unloading book crates for Lyons and Carnahan in New York City, repetitive work he called "stupid."[11] He then quit another dock job after nearly freezing to death helping clean ship condenser units for the dago-baiting United Fruit Lines. Fed-up, Marty threw him out of the house. Following a brief period looking for work in New York, he returned to Hoboken.

At the height of the Great Depression, perhaps Frankie shouldn't have been so choosy about jobs, but he thought his talent was being wasted. Forget manual labor; performing was his kick. While there were any number of avenues, he knew which one he wanted to take:

> You find that there are just as many angles to figure in being honest as there are in being crooked. If what you do is honest and you make it, you're a hero. If what you do is crooked and you make it, you're a bum. Me — I grabbed a song.[12]

By this time, Dolly was more supportive of her son's singing aspirations but was not averse to slapping him in the head when he talked back to Marty. Although she knew very little about the local music scene, she tried to find clubs where Frankie might be given a chance. And when the old man finally came around, he agreed to loan $65 for a small sound system and some sheet music.

On weekends and evenings, 17-year-old Frankie, armed with his microphone, amplifier and charts, performed in Hoboken nightclubs. He explained, "If the local orchestras wanted to use my arrangements, and they always did, they had to take the singer, Sinatra, too."[13] He sang at school dances, for the Hoboken Sicilian League and at Democratic Party meetings, where Dolly was a welcome supporter.

Dolly and Marty actually were impressed and amazed by their son's marvelous voice. Though he had learned to sing along with Bing Crosby, whom he also loved to see on the screen, Frank made an important decision. He was developing his *own* style:

> Bing was on top, and a bunch of us... were trying to break in. It occurred to me that maybe the world didn't need *another* Crosby. ...I decided to experiment a little and come up with something different. What I finally hit on was more of the *bel canto* Italian school of singing, without making a point of it. That meant I had to stay in better shape because I had to *sing* more. It was more difficult than Crosby's style, much more difficult.[14]

The precise vocal diction and phrasing for which Frank would become known began to develop; and though he spoke with a Jersey accent, this quality disappeared when he "grabbed a song." From whom did he receive his first voice lessons? He later revealed:

> I'd go to the movies, and hear the leading men speaking English—not just Cary Grant, but Clark Gable and all the other guys—and I knew that my friends and I were talking some other version of the language. So I started becoming, in some strange way, bilingual. I talked one kind of English with my friends. Alone in my room, I'd keep practicing the other kind of English.[15]

During the summer of 1934, Frank was a guest of Dolly's sister, Aunt Josie Garavente Monaco, who lived in Long Branch on the Jersey shore. Now 18, and possessing an ever-developing romantic voice, he became enamored with a 17-year-old girl he spied at a house across the street. Also on summer vacation, Nancy Barbato was trimming her fingernails when Frank sauntered over with a ukulele for an impromptu serenade. Equally infatuated, she became his first serious girlfriend but thought that the romance would end with the summer.

After Nancy returned to Jersey City with her father, Mike, she continued to see Frank, since Hoboken was only a few miles north of the Barbato home. By spring 1935, Frank was working for Mike, a plasterer known as "The Chief." Paired with Nancy's brother Bart, he contributed very little to the craft and sometimes fell asleep after a late-night gig. Again he wanted to avoid manual labor, but Mike insisted that he keep plastering if he wanted to be Nancy's beau.

But Frank quit anyway, managing to see his best girl in secret. That summer the two attended a Bing Crosby concert at Jersey City's vaudeville theater, the Loew's Journal Square, and Frank left yearning to be a professional singer. Nancy recalled:

> It was a very exciting evening for both of us, but for Frank it was the biggest moment of his life. Bing had always been his hero... but watching him perform in person seemed to make it all come alive for him. ..."Someday," he told me on the way home, "that's gonna be me up there."[16]

On September 8, 1935, Frank auditioned for the radio show *Major Bowes and His Original Amateur Hour* at the Capitol Theater in New York. Teamed with another Hoboken act, the

Three Flashes, he went on to perform "Shine," a former hit for Crosby and the Mills Brothers, on an actual broadcast. Renamed the Hoboken Four by Bowes, the quartet appeared on several weekly shows and were featured in two short films, *The Night Club* and *The Big Minstrel Act*, shot at Biograph Studios in the Bronx the following month. In the former, Frank made an inauspicious film debut as a waiter, and was required to wear blackface and a gaudy minstrel's costume as a chorus boy in the latter. A standard show-business element of the era, the mocking of African-Americans had been carried over into the cinema primarily by Al Jolson during the late 1920s. Frank later lamented, "We didn't realize that we were hurting anybody at the time, until the mid-forties when the NAACP made us all aware. We were insensitive."[17] (Marty had preceded his son on the silver screen, appearing as an extra in some early films shot at studios in nearby Fort Lee, New Jersey.)

The Hoboken Four hit the road with Bowes late that year, opening their tour on the West Coast with dates in San Francisco, Los Angeles and Seattle, followed by stops in Pueblo, Colorado, and Chicago, among other cities across the nation. Backed by local theater bands, they continued to perform "Shine" for enthusiastic audiences. "The radio program was such a hit that people wanted to see what we looked like, like animals in a cage," claimed Frank.[18] By the spring of 1936, the three backing singers—Pat Principe, James Petrozelli and Fred Tamburro—became jealous of Frank's powerful effect on young females. Considering their attitudes ridiculous, and hating being one voice in four, he quit the tour. He wanted to perform only as a solo act; and he did, back in Hoboken, setting up his $65 system at small clubs, weddings and political meetings. Having left yet another paying job, Frank again was called a "quitter" and a "bum" by Marty, although the old man's patriarchal disappointment was leavened by Dolly's retort of "Jesus Christ, let him sing, will ya?"[19]

Late in 1936, Frank began singing for free on local radio stations WAAT in Jersey City and WNEW in Manhattan, where he eventually did 18 spots per week. Soon he was making a whopping $4 per month. Walking the streets of New York, he acquired more charts in Tin Pan Alley and listened to professional singers in the nightclubs on 52nd Street. He also studied voice and diction with John Quinlan, a vocal coach who charged him $1 per lesson and helped him work the Jersey accent out of his style.

A few months later, Frank's cousin Ray Sinatra, a member of NBC's house orchestra, told him about a 15-minute daily radio show that paid 70 cents per week. Landing a featured spot, he performed for radio peanuts during the next year. On May 12, 1937, he also fronted "Frank Sinatra and His Four Sharps" on *The Town Hall Variety*, hosted by Fred Allen. After discussing current music, he sang "Exactly Like You." Then, in 1938, he accepted a job as singing emcee at the Rustic Cabin, a roadhouse in Englewood Cliffs, New Jersey. Paid nothing, he shared tips with a blind pianist, pushing the half-piano around the floor as he sang, but was pleased that the show was broadcast live from 11:30 to midnight five nights a week on the WNEW *Dance Parade*.

Gained through Dolly's contacts with local politicians and union leaders, and with the help of Henry ("Hank") Sanicola, a strong-arm song promoter of Sicilian parentage who became Frank's unofficial manager, the Rustic Cabin gig earned him $15-$30 in weekly gratuities. Aside from graduating from 70-cent radio shows, Frank occasionally was overwhelmed by the clientele at the roadhouse. One evening, Cole Porter stopped in, causing Frank to fumble embarrassingly through "Night and Day" in an attempted tribute to the great songwriter.

Not long after Frank opened at the Rustic, members of the house band noticed that most of the female patrons had their eyes fixed squarely on him. Saxophonist Harry Schuchman, who had told Frank about the job, claimed:

> [H]e had more broads around than you ever saw. I used to sit there and watch
> the gals with him and think to myself, "What do they see in him? He's such
> a skinny little guy?" But when he opened his mouth, you knew. He had that
> charisma that went right out to every gal in the room.[20]

The Actor, on Screen and in Song

The youthful Frank Sinatra in the early 1940s (Photofest)

On November 26, 1938, "that charisma" landed Frank at the county court house in Hackensack on a "breach of promise" charge. A local woman, Antoinette Della Penta, claimed that she had sex with Frank, who had proposed marriage and then reneged. He was released on $1,500 bond and the complaint subsequently was dropped when the court learned that the woman already was married. On December 22, she again tried to railroad Frank, this time for "committing adultery," a charge dismissed by a jury on January 24, 1939.

Though his legal problems were over, Frank still had to contend with a devastated Nancy, whom he assured of his intentions, going so far as to marry her at the Church of Our Lady of Sorrows in Jersey City on February 4. Soon after the wedding, Frank scored some additional radio gigs and, with Nancy's financial aid, had some publicity photos delivered to trumpeter Harry James, who, having left Benny Goodman's big band, now was forming his own.

After hearing Frank on the radio, James dropped in at the Rustic Cabin. Listening to him croon Porter's "Begin the Beguine," Harry, impressed with his voice and phrasing technique, asked him to audition at the Lincoln Hotel in New York. Arriving without a chart, Frank merely told the pianist the song title and key and then nailed it. Leveling the competition, he was signed to a two-year, $75-per-week contract, but when James asked him to change his name to "Frankie Satin," he refused. Having offended his parents when he had considered a stage name ("Frankie Trent") during the run at the Rustic, he now knew better. He later admitted, "Changing my name, man, that was the best thing I ever *didn't* do."[21]

In late June, Frank debuted with Harry James and his Music Makers at New York's Paramount Theater and then dashed off to Baltimore's Hippodrome to sing "Wishing" and "My Love for You." A tour then took them through the East, including several dates at the Roseland Ballroom in Manhattan, where Frank attempted to build his confidence before joining his new colleagues in the recording studio. On July 8, his somewhat weak vocal on "Stardust" was nearly blown off the stage by James' stratospheric soloing as the band swung into the final chorus. Occasionally he would open a song a bit shakily, missing a few pitches, but then smoothly segue into a groove; and hints of the swinger to come could be heard in the up-tempo "Wishing Will Make It So."

On July 10, an appreciative crowd helped Frank sing more confidently on "If I Didn't Care." Three days later, he made his first professional recording, a 78-r.p.m. release of "From the Bottom of My Heart" backed with "Melancholy Mood," credited to "Harry James and his Orchestra; Vocal Chorus: Frank Sinatra." Neither song made the charts, but "Heart" demonstrated that Frank's voice lessons had paid off: His diction and phrasing were already quite refined, particularly for a 23-year-old who previously had done a few radio spots and crooned while pushing a piano at a Jersey roadhouse. (James was three months younger than Frank.)

On July 24, the band played the Marine Ballroom on the Steel Pier in Atlantic City. Frank sounded even more assured, impressively holding a climactic high note on "My Love for You," which was broadcast by a local radio station. Back at the Roseland on August 10, his voice displayed greater maturity on "Moon Love," a song incorporating a melody from Tchaikovsky's Fifth Symphony; and he again was hitting unusually high notes a week later, while recording "My Buddy" at another James session in New York. Having attended several of the Roseland gigs, jazz critic George Simon was impressed by Frank's "pleasing vocals" and "easy phrasing."[22]

Amidst performances at the 1939 New York World's Fair in late August and early September, the band returned to the recording studio. An August 31 session yielded versions of "Here Comes the Night" and "All or Nothing At All." The latter, when released the following summer, sold only 8,000 copies, but later became a smash hit. The song includes a very gentle, sensitive performance by Frank, who atypically crescendos to a high note on the ending (a style he would forsake for quieter, more dramatic concluding notes sung in a lower register). Having written four of the songs recorded by Frank and the James band, Jack Lawrence later said, "It's interesting to listen to that young voice... the way he attacked that song, and what he did with breath control, with all of the wonderful phrasing that he did even in those early days."[23]

Frank cut two sides with the band on October 13, before they packed up for Los Angeles, playing venues in Chicago and Denver en route. On November 8, James arranged a session at Columbia, recording two additional songs, including an uneven rendition of "Ciribiribin," which had been recorded by Bing Crosby in his first collaboration with the Andrews Sisters, in September and released a month later. While the Crosby-Andrews arrangement is a typically bubbly affair, the groove of the James version is bogged down by Frank's uncertain vocal until Harry kicks in with his solo, driving the band to a hard-swinging conclusion.

After being stiffed and subsequently fired in mid-song by the owner of Victor Hugo's restaurant, the band motored East, playing dates in St. Louis and Chicago before returning to New York. Having spoken with Tommy Dorsey, whose orchestra had played on the same bill with the James band at Chicago's Hotel Sherman, Frank was eager to replace vocalist Jack Leonard, who recently had split with "the Sentimental Gentleman of Swing." Offered a long-term contract at $100 per week, an increase that pleased the now-pregnant Nancy who had joined Frank on much of the James tour, he accepted without considering the cut-throat conditions Dorsey had included in the agreement, an oversight that later would haunt him. Conversely, he benefited greatly from James' good-heartedness: Harry merely tore up the two-year contract he had signed six months earlier. Frank remembered:

> I wanted to do it in the worst way. I watched all of the orchestras, and in those days one band was as good as another, but they had different styles. ...Tommy handled the singers with such finesse. ...The singer was featured and Tommy was simpatico about vocalizing. Because the instrument that he played had the same physical qualities as the human voice.[24]

Frank's swansong with the James band occurred at Buffalo's Shea Theatre in January 1940. Dorsey's manager had sent him a train ticket, and he was scheduled to depart from Grand Central Station to catch up with the tour in Rockford, Illinois. As his former bandmates headed for their next gig in Hartford, Connecticut, Frank got the blues:

> I stood in the snow with my two bags and the bus was pulling away and I had lived with those guys and they were fun and I stood there like a schmuck and I'm in tears as I see the red lights going away. And I figure to myself I ain't never gonna make it, and I'll never get home and it'll be terrible. I'm going to die up here in the Buffalo snow.[25]

On February 1, he recorded two songs, "The Sky Fell Down" and "Too Romantic," with Dorsey at the RCA studios in Chicago. He recalled, "It was like going from one school to another... and I was really kind of frightened."[26] But his performance on "Sky" betrayed any butterflies he experienced; opening with Dorsey's warm, welcoming trombone, the song, though offering Frank only a brief vocal, proved that he deserved a featured spot with a premier big band. The following week, they played Indianapolis' Lyric Theatre, where he was billed as "Frank Sinatra, the Romantic Virtuoso." Dates in Michigan, New Jersey and at New York's Paramount followed. Dorsey songbird Jo Stafford, recalling her first encounter with Frank's voice, said:

> After four bars, I thought, "Wow! This is an absolutely new, unique sound." In those days, most male singers tried to sound as much like Bing as possible. Well, he didn't sound anything like Bing. He didn't sound like anybody else that I had ever heard.[27]

Not only did Frank join the established Stafford, but also cocky drum wizard Buddy Rich, alternately a friend and foe, and ace arranger Axel Stordahl, who would become one of his most significant collaborators and a major player in his future success. However, it was the time he spent standing next to Dorsey, in rehearsal and on stage, that proved the most profound element of this new musical experience, "one of the most remarkable opportunities for artistic growth ever afforded a popular performer."[28]

Chapter 2
Hoboken to Hollywood

> I think my appeal in those days was due to the fact that there hadn't been a troubadour around for 10 or 20 years, from the time that Bing had broken in and went on to radio and movies. And he, strangely enough, had appealed primarily to older people, middle-aged people. When I came on the scene... I think the kids were looking for somebody to cheer for. Also the war had just started. They were looking for somebody who represented those gone in their life. —Frank Sinatra[1]

"I was cold shouldered by that whole band," Frank said of his first days with Dorsey.[2] But while the veteran members of the orchestra were remarking, "Well, let's see what he can do," audiences at the Paramount were finding out, offering the most applause the 24-year-old singer had received. On February 26, 1940, he recorded "Shake Down the Stars," combining the natural beauty of his voice with superb phrasing that perfectly fit the Dorsey style. Whereas many big band leaders played two basic types of material, up-tempo swing numbers (then known as "flag-wavers") and pop ballads, Dorsey put an effortless swing pulse into everything, even love songs. During the same session, they also cut "I'll Be Seeing You," a sublime version that segues from Frank's lovely vocal, to out-and-out swinging brass, and back to a soft melody played on muted trombone by Dorsey. On March 12, Frank's recording of "The Fable of the Rose" provided solid proof of why he captured the hearts of so many young women. Two weeks later, singing "Hear My Song Violetta," he powerfully foreshadowed his later development as a swinger, brilliantly phrasing the lyric over the driving groove of Sy Oliver's sweet sax arrangement and Buddy Rich's incomparable drums. On May 23, he recorded the exquisite "I'll Never Smile Again," his first major hit, which remained at the number one spot on the *Billboard* chart for 12 weeks. Opening with vocals by Frank and the Pied Pipers, Fred Stulce's arrangement benefits from Dorsey's otherworldly muted trombone virtuosity.

Will Friedwald describes the Dorsey style that had begun to influence Frank's interpretive approach even before he joined the band:

> Dorsey can best be appreciated as one appreciates a singer: He leaves the substance of the original melodies intact but remolds it to his own image. He doesn't dramatically reshape a tune... as if he were spontaneously composing the song or rewriting it. Instead, the tune is a friend of his that he wants you to meet, and to make a good impression he's dressed it up in one of his good suits. ...Since Dorsey essentially sang with his trombone, it's easy to see how someone who sang with his own vocal instrument would have much to learn from him... If Harry James instilled in Sinatra a greater feeling for jazz, Dorsey imparted to the young singer something more meaningful than his own prodigious technique: The concept of stating a melody so that it could instantly be recognized, yet at the same time personalizing it so that it sounded like a creation completely by or for the performer.[3]

Of his early success with Dorsey, Frank revealed, "I began to work harder than ever. The audience reaction meant they liked me. I didn't know what was causing the reaction exactly. I was experimenting with singing and different forms of phrasing and picking songs better."[4]

Frank's experimentation with phrasing resulted from his close analysis of Dorsey's "singing" technique:

> He would take a musical phrase and play it all the way through seemingly without breathing, for 8, 10, maybe 16 bars. ...How in the hell did he do it? ...I discovered that he had a "sneak" pinhole in the corner of his mouth—not an actual pinhole, but a tiny place where he was breathing. In the middle of the phrase, while the tone was still being carried through the trombone, he'd go shhhhh and take a quick breath and play another four bars with that breath. Why couldn't a singer do that too?[5]

Though Frank realized that Dorsey incorporated a circular breathing technique, he still pushed himself to gain more lung power, attempting to match vocally the continuous bowing of violin master Jascha Heifetz, whose technique "carried the melody line straight through, just like Dorsey's trombone":

> It was my idea to make my voice work in the same way as a trombone or violin—not sounding like them, but "playing" the voice like those instruments. The first thing I needed was extraordinary breath control, which I didn't have. I began swimming every chance I got in public pools—taking laps under water and thinking song lyrics to myself as I swam, holding my breath. I worked out on the track at the Stevens Institute... running one lap, trotting the next. Pretty soon I had good breath control, but that still wasn't the whole answer. I still had to learn to sneak a breath without being too obvious. It was easier for Dorsey to do it... because the horn's mouthpiece was covering up his mouth.[6]

In *Sessions with Sinatra*, Charles Granata elaborates:

> Often Sinatra is referred to as a "crooner," like Bing Crosby or Russ Colombo and Rudy Vallee before him. The crooner hits a note above or below the desired note, and then shifts up or down into that note, producing a distinctive, pleasing warble. Sinatra, however, used a subtler technique known as portamento; in which the vocalist glides gradually from one tone to the next, effecting what amounts to a vocal glissando between notes. Portamento is surely what attracted Sinatra to Heifetz's fluid violin bowing and Dorsey's billowy trombone slides. The circular breathing that Sinatra learned from Dorsey is probably what makes his portamento so completely effective.[7]

Dorsey historian William Ruhlmann pinpoints "I'll Never Smile Again" as a forerunner to the genre of vocal pop music that superseded the big band sound during the early 1940s, a development for which Sinatra was largely responsible:

> The result... was a recording that bore little or no relationship to the music of the Swing Era. The slow tempo, the prominent vocals that turn up right at the beginning of the song, the restrained band parts, and most of all Sinatra's feel for the lyric, all mark "I'll Never Smile Again" as a precursor to the vocalists' era that would follow the big bands. It was the biggest hit that Tommy Dorsey and his Orchestra ever had, but it was really Frank Sinatra's hit. From now on, people would come to see Sinatra as much

as to see the band. And of course, Sinatra's days with Dorsey were now numbered, just as the days of the Swing Era were.[8]

Frank's continuing musical evolution was matched by a major development in his personal life on June 8, 1940, when Nancy gave birth to a daughter, Nancy, Jr., at Margaret Hague Hospital in Jersey City. In Hollywood with the band, Frank made up for his absence with sheer enthusiasm. Jo Stafford recalled, "He was so excited that all he did was talk about his new baby girl."[9] Many years later, Nancy, Jr., wrote, "Already I was being prepared for having to share him with the rest of the world. It was the start of one of the themes of my life: a father who was always going away."[10]

Returning home as soon as possible, Frank (who chose Dorsey as little Nancy's godfather) then re-joined the band to begin a Saturday-afternoon summer radio series at New York's Astor Hotel. Dorsey also was hired to replace Bob Hope as host of an NBC variety show sponsored by Pepsodent, broadcast at 9:30 p.m. on Tuesdays from June 20 through September 17. Increasing the network's ratings, the band then was signed to perform on *Summer Pastime*, broadcast from New York on Tuesday nights from July 2 through September 24, resulting in unprecedented national exposure for Frank. Three weeks after *Pastime* finished its run, NBC, in conjunction with its music publishing company (in which Dorsey had a piece of the action), retained the band for *Fame and Fortune*, a radio program that awarded a $100 prize and a publication opportunity to an amateur songwriter each week.

Back in the RCA recording studio on July 17, Frank layered incredible phrasing over a relentlessly driving big-band beat on "Love Lies" and cut his first Sammy Cahn song, "I Could Make You Care," which his future collaborator cowrote with Saul Chaplin. Cahn later said:

> I'd never heard a popular singer with such fluidity and style. Or one with his incredible breath control. Frank could hold a phrase until it took him into a sort of paroxysm: He actually gasped, and his whole being seemed to explode, to release itself. I'd never seen or heard anything like it.[11]

The *Fame and Fortune* radio show—which opened with the introduction of "that star-maker of the music world, Tommy Dorsey"—gave Frank and his colleagues an opportunity to inject a little more passion into their performances, making them hotter than the recorded versions. On October 17, the band played a rendition of "Marie" that swung much harder than the majority of their up-tempo studio numbers. Incorporating more of a jazz style into his vocal, Frank was beautifully complemented by the solos of Ziggy Elman on trumpet and Don Lodice on sax. At this point, his radio performances already were proving that he often performed better when given only a single take: Although the voice might crack on rare occasions, the fresher, more improvisatory nature of the performance conveyed more real emotion than a careful recording captured after several takes.

That same month, Tommy Dorsey, planning to open the Palladium, a new Los Angeles dance club, signed a contract with Paramount to lead the band in scenes for *Las Vegas Nights*, the studio's new musical comedy starring Phil Regan and Bert Wheeler. Scheduled to sing one number, Frank was guaranteed an extra's wage, $15 per day. But due to extensive re-takes, everyone in the band had to work overtime to complete his scenes; then they all struggled to play the nightly gig before rising for the daily 5 a.m. call at the studio. As part of their pay, Dorsey and each musician received an official studio portrait, which also were printed into a composite publicity photo.

A plotless hodgepodge of songs, dull gags and obtrusive mugging, *Las Vegas Nights* attempts to tell the tale of four broke vaudevillians who, after being stranded in Sin City, hit it big at the tables but are menaced by a shyster and their own ineptitude, particularly that of Stu Grant (the ever-obnoxious Wheeler). Contemporary critics faulted Ralph Murphy's direction and Phil

Regan's weak romantic lead, noting that the beauty of the three female vaudevillians—played by Betty Brewer, Virginia Dale and Lillian Cornell—provided "plenty of optical relief but not much else."[12]

Frank—whose "I'll Never Smile Again" vocal is primarily drowned out by dialogue—is merely one of many faces in the band. *Variety*'s "Odec," however, praised the musicians for contributing some palatable moments:

> It's Tommy Dorsey's first try at a feature picture. His orchestra makes pleasant listening so long as it remains in a familiar groove. Such cases in point are "Song of India," "I'll Never Smile Again" and "On Miami Shore." Once the aggregation turns to the film's original tunes [by Frank Loesser, Burton Lane, and Louis Alter], the going is ordinary. Dorsey also reads lines and proves that he is still a good trombone player.[13]

Frank's affect on audiences, particularly the females, began to increase dramatically by late 1940. Dorsey was both dumbstruck and gratified:

> I used to stand there on the bandstand so amazed I'd almost forget to take my solos. You could almost feel the excitement coming up out of the crowds when that kid stood up to sing. Remember, he was no matinee idol. He was a skinny kid with big ears. And what he did to women was something awful. And he did it every night, everywhere he went.[14]

Though Frank's non-acting role in *Las Vegas Nights* lasted a mere three minutes, he spent hours on the stages of movie theaters like the Paramount, singing with the band before films such as Hope and Crosby's *The Road to Singapore* (1940) flashed onto the screen. And his radio appearances did give him a chance to "act" a bit, sharing shtick with Tommy on *Fame and Fortune* and *The Fred Waring Show*.

In January 1941 Dorsey returned to the Paramount, where, seven months later, they played another sold-out series of dates. At this point, though Dorsey was considered the greatest big-bandleader in the business, the musicians knew that Frank had become the top drawing card.

On January 6, Frank, joined by Connie Haines and the Pied Pipers, recorded Sy Oliver's memorable arrangement of "Oh, Look At Me Now," another number that demonstrated his growing emergence as a swinger, his smooth phrasing benefiting from the lyrical improvisation that would become one of his trademarks. A prime example of Dorsey's ability to merge driving swing with the popular "sweet band" sound, this fascinating hybrid of jazz (Haines' vocal is reminiscent of Billie Holiday and Ella Fitzgerald) and straight-ahead big band harmonies spent six weeks at number two on the charts. Nine days later, the band cut four Johnny Burke-Jimmy Van Heusen songs from *The Road to Zanzibar*, another of the popular Hope-Crosby vehicles, which was scheduled for release in April. Two of the sides, "You Lucky People, You" (arranged by Sy Oliver) and "It's Always You," feature Frank.

On January 20, Dorsey cut four more numbers, including the classic "Without a Song," which provides a fine example of Frank's evolving long-breath technique, and a Sinatra-Pied Pipers collaboration on Frank Loesser and Louis Alter's "Dolores," from *Las Vegas Nights*, which was released on March 24. On May 28, Frank recorded Axel Stordahl's arrangement of "This Love of Mine," a song he had brought to Dorsey's attention, for good reason. He had written the lyrics, set to music by Sol Parker and his pal Hank Sanicola. By the end of June, "Dolores," its sales bolstered by the release of *Las Vegas Nights* and the *Hit Parade* radio show, reached number one on the charts. Two other chart toppers for the Dorsey organization also occurred: Frank was named number-one male singer by *Billboard*'s College Music Survey on May 20, and his colleagues displaced the Glenn Miller Orchestra as the favorite big band on Martin Block's Make Believe Ballroom Poll during the summer.

In August, Dorsey published a book, *Tips On Pop Singing*, that featured contributions from Frank and his operatic vocal coach, John Quinlan. Following the August-September gigs at the Paramount, the band played Washington, DC, where Frank summoned up the courage to walk into Dorsey's dressing room and drop a bomb. He said he was giving one year's notice that he would be leaving the band to begin a solo career. (Two weeks' notice was customary among musicians.) The taskmaster was not amused.

"What for?" Dorsey asked. "You know you're doing great with the band and we've got a lot of arrangements for you."

Frank calmly thanked him for the all the opportunities to perform and develop his style and technique, but tried to explain his need to break out on his own before popular crooners like Bob Eberle and Perry Como beat him to it.

"I don't think so," fumed Dorsey, reminding his singer that he had signed a contract guaranteeing his employer 43 percent of *all* his future earnings.

"I had a contract with Harry," Frank said, "and he took the contract and tore it up and wished me luck."[15]

A great musician, yes; but as a man, Tommy Dorsey was no Harry James.

After this tense exchange, the band again headed for Hollywood to appear as the big band attraction in MGM's musical comedy *Ship Ahoy*, another studio potboiler with unfunny gags. Shot in November and December 1941, the film features an inane spy plot seemingly tailor-made for the wartime environment raging at the time of its release five months later. (In fact, the cast and crew were working on the film when Pearl Harbor was attacked on December 7.) Structured around the labored shenanigans of Red Skelton and the music of the Dorsey band, the espionage angle involves Axis saboteurs who pose as U.S. government agents to dupe pretty Tallulah Winters (Eleanor Powell) into transporting a secret mine to Puerto Rico during a pleasure cruise. En route, she becomes involved with pulp-fiction writer Merton K. Kibble (Skelton), whose story "The Exploits of Olga" has provided the impetus for the enemy scheme!

Like a familiar Dorsey number, the film opens with Tommy on trombone, cutting to Ziggy Elman on trumpet and Buddy Rich pounding the skins on a furious swing tune. In fact, the band never seems to stop playing, and either is shown on screen or heard in the background of dialogue scenes. At one point, Tommy even lays some "hep" talk on Skelton, who is unfamiliar with such swing jive. "Groovy," says Dorsey.

For his second feature-film appearance, Frank performed two songs, "The Last Call for Love" and "Poor You." As in *Las Vegas Nights*, he did not receive a separate screen credit, but this time was mentioned in major reviews. In an April 1942 issue of *Variety*, "Scho" wrote:

> Dorsey's band is... given plenty of latitude, and at times the film looks like a full-length juke-pic. However, considering Dorsey's popularity with the jitterbugs and the poor quality of the story, perhaps it's just as well for the b.o. that the band gets all that prominence and staging. Dorsey's own tromboning, Ziggy Elman's trumpet, Buddy Rich's drum work and Frank Sinatra's singing, latter doing 90% of the vocalizing in the film and doing it well, stand out. ...Performances, with the exception of Lahr, the restraint of Dorsey, Sinatra's singing and the swell playing and delivery of Buddy Rich at the traps, are hardly flattering to anybody in the cast.

In fact, the entire Dorsey organization was viewed as the only bright spot in an expensive but unbelievably dull production:

> It doesn't seem probable that four writers... have come up with something so hare brained and so lacking in even the bare essentials of a smooth-running plot. This may have been Buzzell's chief handicap, but the direction doesn't

show any ingenuity, regardless, and the cutter appears to have whacked out pieces of film without regard to their relation to subsequent business.[16]

Frank does very little during his two numbers. After rising from his chair on the bandstand, he slowly walks to the microphone and croons into it while keeping his hands folded in front of him. Connie Haines and the Pied Pipers join him on "The Last Call for Love," while he only is allowed to sing one verse of "Poor You," the remainder of which is butchered by Skelton and the deliberately stiff Virginia O'Brien, a frigid chick constantly accosted by the ever-annoying Bert Lahr. The "Bal Caribbean" costumes worn by Dorsey and the band during the latter number are like something from a Disney cartoon, and the skinny Frank nearly is swallowed up by his enormous, absolutely ludicrous jacket. The absurdity of this sequence is capped off by the choreography of two embarrassingly stereotypical black hoofers. In a later scene, Frank can be heard reprising "Last Call" off-camera. (Two months after the film wrapped, Frank recorded studio versions [which, during the era, always were recorded separately from those cut for movie soundtracks] of "Poor You" [without the Skelton interruption], "The Last Call for Love" and "I'll Take Tallulah" [which he did not sing in the film]. "Tallulah" originally had been titled "I'll Take Manilla," but was changed after the Japanese captured that island.)

Frank's most pleasant experience while shooting *Ship Ahoy* was an opportunity to watch his idol perform at another studio. Yank Lawson, a former Dorsey trumpeter who currently was playing with the Bob Crosby band, recalled:

> Frank had never met Bing. We were doing the music for a picture called *Holiday Inn*, and he asked me if he could go out and see the filming. He wanted to watch Bing work... Crosby was the big star of that time and Sinatra was still just the singer with the band. Frank met me at the Paramount lot and I took him in. He just loved it, watching Bing.[17]

(Six months later, Frank and Tommy recorded "Be Careful, It's My Heart," one of the numbers Irving Berlin wrote for *Holiday Inn*.)

Aside from most of the Dorsey scenes, *Ship Ahoy* is an excruciating viewing experience. The young Skelton had yet to develop as an effective physical comedian (later he would learn a great deal about subtlety from Buster Keaton), and his performance is on par with Harry Clork's bad dialogue. Not even Powell's ultra-leggy dancing can save a film that features the bizarre Bert Lahr as a language-mangling, would-be Casanova. An 85-minute collection of cobbled-together nonsense, *Ship Ahoy* is one of the worst musicals MGM ever made, and it did little for Frank's career other than earn him a mention in *Variety* and other trade publications. At this point, his recordings and radio appearances were far more important than films listing only "Tommy Dorsey and his Orchestra" at the bottom of the end credits. But after making another major career move, that was soon to change.

While in Hollywood, Frank was approached by Columbia Records producer Emmanuel ("Manie") Sacks, who wanted to record him as a solo act. Although he replied with great enthusiasm, Frank had to decline for the moment. However, two months later, at a January 19, 1942, session in Los Angeles, Frank cut four Axel Stordahl arrangements for Bluebird Records, an RCA subsidiary—"Night and Day," "The Lamplighter's Serenade," "The Night We Called It a Day" and "The Song Is You"—without the Dorsey Orchestra but with Tommy's permission. Emphasizing lush strings over the Dorsey big-band sound (arrangements that anticipate the Columbia solo recordings), this quartet of songs, recorded in just three hours and 15 minutes, features more genuine passion from Frank, who is not reigned in by the bandleader's formula. On the ending of "The Song Is You," a number that would become one of his trademarks, he hits an incredible high note; and the beautiful, gently swinging ballad version of "Night and Day" features phrasing that prefigures his incomparable performance on the Nelson Riddle arrangement of 1956 (on the Capitol album *A Swingin' Affair*).

His intention to go solo was bolstered when *Down Beat* published its January 1942 issue, naming him top vocalist of the year, an honor that had been held by Bing Crosby for the previous six years. The Dorsey band also rated highly, reaching the number-two spot in both the "swing" and "sweet" categories. After playing several dates in the Midwest, they began another month-long stint at New York's Paramount on April 1. Fearing a strike by the American Federation of Musicians, Dorsey decided to record a large number of singles to stockpile in case the threats became reality. Four months later, the AFM struck, placing a ban on studio recordings by instrumental musicians that would last two and one-half years.

Frank's admission to Dorsey that he would leave before his contract expired was emphasized by his performing occasional weekend solo gigs, some of which were being agented by Manie Sacks, who was anxious to sign him. When Dorsey's lawyers demanded a 43-percent "cut" from the solo performances, Sacks hired high-powered entertainment attorney Henry Jaffe, who told the bandleader that he had better release Frank Sinatra or risk losing his NBC radio contracts. (Later, Sinatra detractors spread rumors that Dorsey was visited by mobsters who tried to strong-arm him into tearing up the contract. Frank commented, "That's so far afield it's scary. It's incredible."[18])

The intractable trombonist still refused. Meeting with MCA's Jules Stein, Sacks offered to persuade Frank's current agents, Rockwell-O'Keefe, to release him if the new talent agency could induce Dorsey to capitulate. After a serious negotiation with Dorsey, Stein agreed to pay him $75,000 (one-third of which would come from Frank) and secure a few additional bookings for his band.

For the rest of the summer, Frank felt a cool wind from Dorsey as he stood up to sing his numbers, but his style and technique were better than ever. On June 17, he performed one of his most impeccable Dorsey-era vocals on "In the Blue of the Evening," another beautiful Axel Stordahl arrangement. Following standing-room-only dates in the East and Midwest, he gave his farewell performance at Indianapolis' Circle Theater on September 3, 1942. Ridiculously introduced by Tommy as "the Hoboken Broncho Buster," Frank replied by calling him "Mack" before mentioning his successor, Dick Haymes, who agreed with Dorsey that Frank would "knock them dead" as a solo act. After the show, the last comment Frank heard from his former mentor was, "I hope you fall on your ass."[19]

The following month, Frank headlined the 15-minute radio show *Reflections*, broadcast by CBS on Tuesdays and Thursdays. To orchestrate his new career, MCA hired George Evans, who had paid a group of teenage girls to scream and swoon over him when he opened with Benny Goodman's big band at the Paramount on December 30. One of Manhattan's largest movie palaces, the Paramount drew many of its crowds, not with its namesake studio's currently popular films, but on the popularity of the live bands and singers who appeared there. Paramount manager Bob Weitman asked Jack Benny to emcee Frank's debut, but the master comedian had not heard of the starring act:

> [T]hey introduce me to this skinny kid called Frank Sinatra. I shook hands with him and said hello, and he said, "Hello, Mr. Benny." Now it's time for the introductions, and first Benny Goodman went on and did his act. And then he says, "Now, ladies and gentlemen, to introduce our honored guest, we have Jack Benny." I certainly didn't think Sinatra would get much of anything 'cause I never heard of him. So I did two or three jokes, and they laughed, and then I realized there were a lot of young people out there, and they were probably just waiting for Sinatra. So I introduced him as if he were one of my closest friends. And then I said, "Well, anyway, ladies and gentlemen, here he is, Frank Sinatra." And I thought the god-damned building was going to cave in. I never heard such a commotion, with people running down to the stage screaming and nearly knocking me off the ramp. All this for a fellow I never heard of.[20]

The Actor, on Screen and in Song

Evans' stunt was proved unnecessary when huge throngs of adoring females unleashed high-decibel fan fury every time Frank took the stage. Some of them waited in line outside the theater for 12 hours just to see the first show at 11 a.m. Initially contracted for two weeks, Frank stayed at the theater for 10, breaking a record Bing Crosby had set 15 years earlier, fronting the orchestras of Goodman and Johnny Long. Having made $150 per week with Dorsey, his starting salary at the Paramount was $750; by the time the engagement was over, he was making $25,000.

To take his solo act nationwide, MCA landed Frank a role in Columbia's *Reveille with Beverly*, a musical-comedy starring Ann Miller that offered him a repeat of his *Las Vegas Nights* experience. Sharing the musical spotlight with the Mills Brothers, the Radio Rogues, and the orchestras of Bob Crosby, Freddie Slack, Duke Ellington and Count Basie, he was relegated to a single three-minute scene in which he croons "Night and Day." But when the film was released in April 1943, after his smash success at the Paramount, he was given star billing on the advertising materials, many of which were kissed by "bobbysoxers" as they waited outside movie theaters.

Directed by future Abbott and Costello collaborator Charles T. Barton, *Reveille with Beverly* is a clumsily edited visual jukebox strung together by a nearly nonexistent plot concocted by Howard J. Green, Jack Henley and Albert Duffy. Scenes of an early morning disc-jockey show hosted by Beverly Ross (Miller) are interspersed with musical performances of the acts whose records she spins. Two additional "steaming jive" acts—the Mills Brothers and the Radio Rogues—are part of a camp show at a local Army base where the radio program is a hit. Intended as wartime escapism, the film was labeled as only for the "hepcat" crowd by major reviewers, including *Variety*'s "Hobe":

> [A]lthough Frank Sinatra, on the strength of his present popularity, gets top marquee billing on this New York showing, he also has only one number, lugubrious, clumsily directed and photographed vocal of "Night and Day"... introduced via phonograph recording. ...It's all painfully inept in the writing, production and, with few exceptions, in performance. The single excuse, the hot swing by the various bands and the Sinatra vocal, will be good for box office, but won't satisfy even the jitterbug customers...[21]

The New York Times reported that even hepcats "seemed to have stayed away in large numbers," due to the "noisy demonstrations which resemble nothing so much as the left-over numbers from some old musical short subjects...all equally depressive."[22]

Following his shattering performances at the Paramount, Frank began his long association with *Your Hit Parade*, CBS's Saturday night radio show that highlighted a countdown of each week's most popular songs. Due to his ever-increasing fame, he began to influence the general musical taste of listeners who switched their focus from the orchestra to the vocalist. In March, he scored a major hit with a re-issue of Harry James' 1939 "All or Nothing At All." Although he now was able formally to sign with Columbia Records, the musician's strike prevented him from recording any new material.

During May 1943, Frank, unable to serve in the armed forces, began actively supporting the war effort, singing at bond rallies and military hospitals. While continuing his appearances on *Your Hit Parade*, he also began a long-term association with *Broadway Bandbox* on May 14, two days before he entertained a massive audience at a Central Park war-bond rally dubbed "I Am an American Day." Swing stars Louis Armstrong, Count Basie, Benny Goodman and former Sinatra colleagues Harry James and Buddy Rich (who later served overseas) had been signed by Captain Bob Vincent of the U.S. Army to produce a series of "V-Discs" to be shipped monthly, in boxes of 25, from Special Services headquarters in New York to servicemen in Europe and the Pacific. Like those who performed for the USO, all artists donated their services, many of them appreciating the opportunity to get back into a studio during the AFM's commercial recording

Sinatra became the idol of bobbysoxers in the 1940s. (Photofest)

ban. Truly excited about contributing as many songs as possible, Frank agreed to allow radio performances and live rehearsals to be recorded through Columbia for V-Discs, the only Sinatra records featuring instrumental accompaniment that would be produced over the next 18 months. The first of these sides would be gleaned from an appearance on *Broadway Bandbox*, a show he initially headlined with bandleader Raymond Scott but soon took over himself, supported by Axel Stordahl, whom he had hired away from Dorsey.

On May 16, he sang "(I Got a Woman Crazy for Me) She's Funny That Way" on *Texaco Time with Fred Allen*, during which the host mentioned the riot at the Paramount. Ten days later, he again set the bobbysoxers screaming when he began another month-long series of daily shows at the famous theater. By this point, record-industry executives burned by the musicians' strike

The Actor, on Screen and in Song

Sinatra with Michele Morgan in *Higher and Higher*

had discussed releasing commercial discs featuring lead vocalists backed only by a cappella accompaniment, but Frank considered such an idea artistically dubious and wanted to hold out until the ban ended and full arrangements could be used. However, when Decca Records began cutting a cappella sessions with Bing Crosby and Dick Haymes, Manie Sacks hired Alec Wilder to write arrangements for Frank and the Bobby Tucker Singers. Frank later recalled, "I got a lot of pressure from the people at Columbia Records to do them. I didn't want to cross the lines, in a sense."[23] Tucker had arranged the choirs on both the *Reflections* and *Broadway Bandbox* programs, but here gave way to Wilder, along with Stordahl, who contributed but waived credit, due to his membership in the AFM. The first Columbia side, "Close to You," was waxed on June 7, 1943. Copyrighted by Barton Music Corporation, a new publishing company formed by Frank, Hank Sanicola and Ben Barton, it was followed in the session by "You'll Never Know." Both songs feature Frank backed by 12 voices.

On June 17, Frank contributed to an ABC armed forces radio show broadcast from New York's Stage Door Canteen. Five days later, he was back at Columbia, cutting two more a cappella numbers, "Sunday, Monday or Always" and "If You Please," which benefits from a more instrumental-sounding arrangement. Having sparked the "era of the vocalist," he then went one step further by planning a short tour during which he would sing with various symphony orchestras. After fronting the Cleveland Philharmonic on July 14, he performed with the Philadelphia Philharmonic for an audience of 5,000 "highbrow" music fans at Lewisohn Stadium. One week later, as he headed for Los Angeles, police escorted him through a fanatical crowd at the Pasadena train station. On August 8, he added two songs from the stage hit *Oklahoma!*, "People Will Say We're In Love" and "O, What a Beautiful Mornin'!," to his a cappella catalog.

I COULDN'T SLEEP A WINK LAST NIGHT

Lyrics by HAROLD ADAMSON   Music by JIMMY McHUGH

As sung by

FRANK SINATRA

IN THE RKO RADIO PICTURE

Higher & Higher

Starring

**FRANK SINATRA
MICHELE MORGAN
JACK HALEY**

with

LEON ERROL · MARCY McGUIRE
DOOLEY WILSON · PAUL and GRACE HARTMAN
PRODUCED and DIRECTED by TIM WHELAN

R K O
RADIO

A LOVELY WAY TO SPEND AN EVENING
I COULDN'T SLEEP A WINK LAST NIGHT

T. B. HARMS COMPANY, N. Y.
By Arrangement with
ROBBINS MUSIC CORPORATION

Michele Morgan

Jack Haley

Marcy McGuire

Although promoters at the classical-only Hollywood Bowl had been reluctant to book him, Frank joined the Los Angeles Philharmonic for an unforgettable concert on August 14, enrapturing 10,000 fans whose tickets literally saved the troubled venue from bankruptcy. After film favorite Constantin Bakaleinikoff conducted the orchestra on Russian classics such as Mussorgsky's "Night on Bare Mountain" and Rimsky-Korsakov's "Flight of the Bumblebee," Frank and maestro Morris Stoloff emerged with "Dancing in the Dark," "Night and Day," "You'll Never Know," "The Song is You," "Ol' Man River" and his hit "All or Nothing At All." A standing ovation at this landmark led to another Hollywood triumph when he signed a seven-year contract with

RKO-Radio in September, to begin with a featured role as "himself" in the Michele Morgan-Jack Haley musical *Higher and Higher*.

Originally a 1940 Gladys Hurlbut-Joshua Logan Broadway show featuring an excellent Rodgers and Hart score, *Higher and Higher* was completely overhauled by Jay Dratler and Ralph Spence, with additional dialogue by William Bowers and Howard Harris and "special songs" by Jimmy McHugh and Harold Adamson. Incorporating nine numbers, the film tells the silly but entertaining tale of Drake (Leon Errol), a wealthy man on the brink of bankruptcy, who, at the behest of Mike (Jack Haley), his valet, chooses another of his servants, Millie (Michele Morgan), the scullery maid, to pose as his lovely daughter, hoping that she can be married off to a rich suitor. After fumbling about as the beautiful debutante and attempting to back out of the deal, Millie nearly is wed to an incognito criminal (Victor Borge) whom they think is titled aristocrat "Sir Victor Fitzroy Victor." But in the nick of time, love-struck Mike, discovering rare vintage wines and a priceless antique harpsichord in the cellar, saves the day. Amassing a fortune from the treasure trove, Drake transforms the cellar into a swinging nightclub.

The film opens in Drake's kitchen with an adolescent-looking Mel Torme leading off an energetic musical number that eventually includes all the household servants. Waking with a massive hangover, Drake learns that it is actually 7 *p.m.*!

Frank plays a neighbor whom Millie imagines as her first suitor, though she really is in love with Mike and, in her role as debutante, is forced to consort with "Sir Victor" at the "Butler's Ball," a local society wing-ding. Frank's initial dialogue scene shows him appearing at the front door of Drake's mansion as Mickey (Marcy McGuire), one of the maids, opens it.

"Good morning. My name is Frank Sinatra," he quietly announces, causing her to faint dead away. Fortunately, he catches her before she hits the tile. Will Friedwald believes that this scene "remains the single most important moment in Sinatra's cinematic career...the world at last could see that "The Voice" also had a face...seeing it across a 50-foot screen was guaranteed to send his young female fans into apoplectic spasms."[24]

Given a respectable amount of screen time, Frank sings five songs, including "I Couldn't Sleep a Wink Last Night" (accompanied by Dooley Wilson) and "The Music Stopped," which he croons to Michele Morgan and Barbara Hale at the ball. "Wink" is a musical and visual highlight: Whelan shot the entire performance in a single long take, panning back and forth between Frank and Michele, then cutting in her close-up profile near the end of this exquisitely romantic performance.

"Who was that singing down here?" Drake asks as he descends the stairs. "Bing Crosby?"

"Bing Bang Sinatra," replies Sandy (Mary Wickes).

"Well, he'll never get any place," adds Drake.

Later, Morgan joins Frank for "A Lovely Way to Spend an Evening" (which is blended with Sergei Rachmaninov's "Rhapsody on a Theme of Paganini"), and he duets with Marcy McGuire on "I Saw You First," which begins with him riding a bicycle and "smoking" a pipe! Arriving with a box of flowers for Millie, he claims that his old man is a florist (which was probably news to Marty Sinatra). The maid hops on the bike with him, but he eventually sends her crashing to the concrete, causing her to threaten to "listen to *Crosby*" thereafter. In the concluding scene, when he is paired off with Hale, several of the cast chime in on "When It Comes to Love, You're On Your Own."

When *Higher and Higher* was released on December 1, 1943, the tag "The Sinatra Show" was included above the title on the posters, a strategy given extra punch by a final scene depicting Frank singing in a cloud-shrouded, heavenly setting. Including an outlandish plot that links together a host of songs (but far better than *Las Vegas Nights*, *Ship Ahoy* and *Reveille With Beverly*, due in part to Tim Whelan's brisk direction), the film was well-received by major critics, including *Variety*'s "Char":

> Light in vein but rich in comedy and song values, plus having very fine
> pace, the picture is destined to rank high at the box office. Among other

things, it's as escapist as they come. The lads and lassies in the service are bound to take to it warmly. There may be some folks who can't figure out the reasons for Sinatra's meteoric rise, or might be wondering whether he's here to stay or not, but in his first starring role on the screen he at least gets in no one's way. Though a bit stiff on occasion and not as photogenic as may be desired, he generally handles himself ably in song as well as a few brief dialogue scenes.[25]

While *The New Yorker's* David Lardner praised Frank's acting, *The Hollywood Reporter* noted how "the camera captures an innate shyness in the singer."[26] In his *Los Angeles Times* review, John L. Scott wrote:

> The crooner certainly doesn't fulfill the cinema's traditional idea of a romantic figure which may be a break for him eventually. He... appears more at ease than we expected and should find his place as a film personality with careful choice of subjects. Crosby did, didn't he?[27]

Interestingly, in casting Frank in his first actual role, RKO had followed the lead of Paramount, who had debuted Crosby as himself in *The Big Broadcast* (1929). In addition to the positive criticism, the film also earned an Academy Award nomination for Best Song, Frank's rendition of "I Couldn't Sleep a Wink."

On the August 31, 1943, *Burns and Allen Show,* Frank made one of several radio guest appearances with the comedic couple. Trying to prove the singing prowess of her beloved husband "Sugarthroat," Gracie instigated a contest with the Voice, whose voluminous fan mail had been weighing upon "the Happy Postman" (Mel Blanc). On the September 9 *Sealtest Village Store*, the brilliant comedienne Joan Davis, playing a love-starved man hunter, attempted to land a date with him. Back in New York, he sang at more war benefits before beginning an eight-week run at the luxurious Wedgwood Room of the Waldorf-Astoria on October 1. Again singing to "high-class" crowds, he further broadened his appeal beyond bobbysoxers and radio fans, although he certainly did not ease up on his bread-and-butter audiences. Three songs recorded at the dress rehearsal for the October 17 *Broadway Bandbox* (the final installment of the program) marked his initial contribution to the V-Disc program. These for-soldiers-only numbers included "I Only Have Eyes for You," "Kiss Me Again" and "(There'll Be A) Hot Time In the Town of Berlin," a propaganda flagwaver cowritten by Johnny DeVries and former Dorsey pianist Joe Bushkin, both of whom were now in uniform. Frank, grabbing "Berlin" for his Barton Music Corporation, enjoyed Stordahl's arrangement, which punctuates his smoothly swinging vocal with powerful blasts of brass.

One week later, Frank debuted his own 15-minute radio show, *Songs By Sinatra*, broadcast by CBS in the old Sunday-night *Bandbox* slot. He also sang "Stardust" in a Lucky Strike-sponsored film short, "Your Hit Parade Extra," featuring the Hit Parade Orchestra conducted by Mark Warnow. On November 3 and 10, Alec Wilder conducted a cappella arrangements (incorporating up to 20 backing voices) of three songs from *Higher and Higher* — "I Couldn't Sleep a Wink Last Night," "A Lovely Way to Spend an Evening" and "The Music Stopped" — which became the final voice-only recordings Frank cut for Columbia. With *Songs By Sinatra* fully established, Frank now was able to support the V-Disc program in earnest, contributing numbers from the broadcasts of November 14 and 21. Axel Stordahl took the same three *Higher and Higher* numbers and reworked them into superior, fully orchestrated versions that only the troops were lucky enough to hear after the initial radio airings. Although the band arrangements spurred Frank to be a bit bolder with his performances, he used an identical long-breath technique on the impressive final choruses of both versions of "The Music Stopped," recorded only four days apart. Other V-Discs taken from these broadcasts included "The Way You Look Tonight" and a lovely version of "She's Funny That Way."

In December Frank was called up by Local Draft Board #19 in Hudson County, New Jersey, and told to report for a physical. On the 11th of the month, he was declared 4F due to "chronic perforation [of left] tympanum" and "chronic mastoiditis," a condition caused by the doctor's forceps when he was born, and "emotional instability." Later, when he fell afoul of reporters who accused him of being a draft dodger, the FBI investigated the matter, concluding that a "civilian physician at the Armed Forces Induction Station...indicated that he was certain that it was absolutely necessary to reject Sinatra in the induction."[28]

During January 1944, Frank joined Bob Hope, Bing Crosby, Ginger Rogers and other musical stars for some USO gigs, including the first Hollywood Canteen extravaganza for servicemen on leave. Troops at the Canteen were so impressed by Frank's performance that they called for several encores, keeping him on stage for more than an hour. On January 5, CBS traded in *Songs By Sinatra* for *The Frank Sinatra Show*, a 30-minute radio program emceed by comedian Jerry Lester and featuring an eclectic mix of guest stars. Also known as the "Vimms Vitamins Show," due to its sponsorship by that division of Lever Bros., it was his first long-term series. While he was broadcasting live from Hollywood five days later, Nancy gave birth to a second child, Franklin Wayne Emmanuel Sinatra, at Margaret Hague Hospital in Jersey City. In naming his son, Frank honored two of his heroes, Franklin Delano Roosevelt and Emmanuel Sacks.

On January 12, he cut Harold Arlen and Johnny Mercer's "My Shining Hour" during the dress rehearsal for "Vimms Vitamins" (making this V-Disc his only recording of the song until 1979's *Trilogy*). At the end of the month, he participated, via a Hollywood remote, in the radio program *America Salutes the President's Birthday*, singing "Speak Low (If You Speak Love)" with Axel Stordahl's Orchestra. A benefit for polio victims, the show also featured Mary Pickford, Paul Whiteman, Garry Moore, Jimmy Durante, Frances Langford and military bands performing in various locations across the nation. On February 9, he waxed another V-Disc during rehearsal, introducing himself in Jersey-speak before crooning Jerome Kern and Ira Gershwin's "Long Ago and Far Away": "Gentlemen of the armed forces. This is the hoodlum from Hoboken. I'd like to sing a tune for ya. My name's Sinatra, and I hope youse like it, hey."

But Frank was back in tinsel town ostensibly to star in his second film for RKO, *Step Lively*, in which he would play his first top-billed role. Based on the John Murray-Allen Boretz play *Room Service*, which had been filmed by RKO and the Marx Brothers in 1938, the film re-teamed him with director Tim Whelan and house cinematographer Robert de Grasse. As Glen, Frank is an aspiring playwright who mails one of his efforts and $1,500 to Miller (George Murphy), a fly-by-night Broadway producer. Upon reaching Manhattan, Glen discovers that the bum is holed up in a hotel, unable to pay his bill and rehearsing a different production with 22 deadbeat actors. Soon after, Jenkins (Eugene Pallette) arrives with Miss Abbott (Anne Jeffries), a beautiful protégé, and $50,000 from an unnamed backer. Discovering that the investment is worthless, Miller and his partners, Harry and Binion (the low-rent comedy team Alan Carney and Wally Brown), attempt to open the show before the check bounces. All's well that ends well when they also discover that the troublesome Glen is actually a lady-killing crooner ("a singing Shakespeare"); given the lead in the show, he saves the day and wins his girl, Christine Marlowe (Gloria DeHaven).

In *Step Lively*, Frank plays a naive innocent who soon learns the ways of the world, particularly discovering trouble, his talent and his attraction to the opposite sex, visually demonstrated when he receives his first screen kiss, from the drop-dead gorgeous DeHaven. (Later, he also locks lips with the equally luscious Jeffries.) Although, at 28, he did exude a certain amount of boyish, vulnerable charm, this character, that he would vary in several subsequent films, was very different from his own self-assured, sometimes cocky persona, not to mention his apparent prowess with the ladies. His legendary penchant for making on-set demands began during the production of this film: Sensitive about his height, he asked that DeHaven remove a very tall hat she was wearing.

The innocent nature of Frank's character is tempted and tried throughout the film. At one point, Miss Abbott crowds into a narrow phone booth with Glen; and while trying to seduce him, firmly grabs the mouthpiece. Apparently overwhelmed by this Freudian display, Glen beats the retreat. Later, he proves as oblivious to alcohol, when a single glass of beer lays him low. But

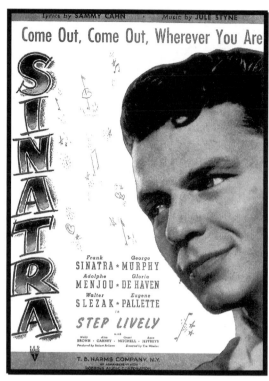

there are several references to the "real" Sinatra, including dialogue about his skinny frame, innate singing ability and "golden voice."

Not only was *Step Lively* the first film to give Frank top billing, but also the first Sinatra picture to feature songs written by the formidable team of Sammy Cahn and Jule Styne (with arrangements for "Mr. Sinatra" by Axel Stordahl). Unfortunately, due to the AFM ban, his performances of "Some Other Time," "Come Out, Come Out, Wherever You Are," "Where Does Love Begin?" and "As Long As There's Music" would not be heard outside movie theaters, except by the men in uniform who received the V-Disc versions of all four numbers, which were waxed during "Vimms Vitamins" rehearsals. Manie Sacks had decided against recording any further a cappella versions of the movie songs.

The visual highlight of *Step Lively* occurs during the closing production number, when Glen's "play" finally is staged to thunderous applause. Opening in long shot, the scene shows a spotlight on Frank's face, which is surrounded by complete darkness. Against this pitch-black backdrop, the light widens to show him attired in elegant white tie and tails, book-ended by dancing and harmonizing female backing singers. Creating an incredible image, Frank (in the bottom right of the frame) raises his right arm to "cast" a ray of light (into the top left of the frame) onto which Gloria DeHaven walks, all the way down to him. The stark contrast of the entire sequence, posing white-clad, celebratory performers against the uncertain darkness of night, concludes the film, hopeful in the embrace of Glen and Christine, yet ambiguous—an interesting way to end an uneven and often unfunny cinematic remake.

Noting the film's well-trodden content and characters, but rating it a "pleasant enough celluloid divertissement," *Variety*'s "Abel" wrote that "Sinatra... handles himself with ease but still needs some camera assists,"[29] while *The New York Times'* resident curmudgeon Bosley Crowther was clear about his cynical contempt for Frank's popularity, a sentiment that was beginning to build in the press:

> The onward and upward advancement of Frank Sinatra as a motion-picture star, which presumes a minimum of acting and a maximum of voice, has been rather neatly accomplished by RKO-Radio in the prodigy's latest screen effort... The trick has been to hitch Frankie to the rapidly moving tail of a highly dependable farce comedy... and let him drag it precipitately into stellar space. In that undemanding position, Frankie can burble his songs and generally attract attention while others do most of the work. ...The frequent injections of Frankie, as the yokel playwright who now can sing (a matter, that is, of opinion), perceptively hobble the farce, for the crooner is no Eddie Albert, but they seem to inspire his fans. When the

Alan Carney, Frank, George Murphy, Gloria DeHaven and Wally Brown

modestly grinning young heart-throb gave voice (as you might say)... the voltage worked up... was as tingling as that of Boulder Dam.[30]

Other New York critics were kinder to Frank. While Howard Barnes of *The Herald Tribune* believed the film "demonstrates that he has far more performing range than many might have suspected," *The Post*'s Archer Winston noted both the pros and cons of his appeal:

> Sinatra... is better than in his previous movie efforts. He looks better, acts better, and sings in the manner that has made him famous. If it were not for the rampant demonstrations of his fanatics, there would be little to hold against him. ...Apparently the Voice is here to stay, and if the progress continues, the experience will not be as trying as anticipated, providing the incidental squeals can be tuned out.[31]

Was Frank personally, *morally* responsible for the behavior of the bobbysoxers?

While performing a benefit concert at Los Angeles' Jewish Home for the Aged, Frank was closely observed by MGM mogul Louis B. Mayer, who was moved by his rendition of "Ol' Man River," which originally was performed by Paul Robeson in the 1927 Broadway version of *Showboat*. One of the aspects of Frank's interpretation that Mayer appreciated was his refusal to sing the racist lyric, "Darkies all sing on the Mississippi," instead changing it to "Here we all work on the Mississippi." Frank recalled, "I guess the way I sang it made him cry. But L. B. turned to an aide and said, 'I want that boy.' Let me tell you something. Mayer was a giant. When he said, 'I want that boy,' he got that boy."[32] In February 1944, through MCA, Frank signed a $1.5-million, long-term Metro-Goldwyn-Mayer contract, to run concurrently with his RKO agreement.

The Actor, on Screen and in Song

Chapter 3
The Mogul, the Feet and the Voice

When I arrived at MGM, I was a nobody in movies. ...Because I didn't think I was as talented as some of the people who worked there, I went through periods of depression... It was Gene [Kelly] who saw me through. ...Movie-making takes a lot of time, and I couldn't understand why. He managed to calm me when it was important to calm me... he taught me how to move and how to dance. ...He taught me everything I know. He's one of the reasons I became a star. —Frank Sinatra.[1]

Every aspect of Frank's life had not been onward and upward over the past two years. His 4-F military status had plagued him, both as a personal disappointment and as easy exploitation for Sinatra-bashing journalists. His frequent touring and trips to Hollywood, where he was showered with, not only the adulation of bobbysoxers, but the attention of beautiful young starlets, also complicated his personal life and made journeys home to see his family few and far between.

After signing the lucrative contract with MGM, Frank moved Nancy and the children to Los Angeles during the spring of 1944. While waiting to move into their new San Fernando Valley home, a Mediterranean-style house once owned by Mary Astor, they stayed at Hollywood's Castle Argyle. Having been besieged by crazed fans who peered into the windows of their Jersey City home, they made certain that the estate had adequate security, namely a surrounding wall.

To reflect his new status in tinsel town, Frank decided to join a posh club, but the Los Angeles Country Club had allowed only one show-business personality—Fred Astaire—to join its exclusive ranks. And when he discovered that Lakeside was totally anti-Semitic, he signed up at Hillcrest, a Jewish club where he ate lunch at the "round table" with Al Jolson, Eddie Cantor, George Burns and Milton Berle.

Prior to reporting to MGM for a screen assignment, he vocally dueled with Bing Crosby on the second anniversary installment of *Command Performance* on February 1. Produced by the Armed Forces Radio Service (AFRS), the program, which ran from 1942 through 1949, was the most elaborate offered by the U.S. military. Three weeks later, he starred as singer Eddie Kane in *Wake Up and Live*, adapted for *The Lux Radio Theatre* by Sanford H. Barnett from the 1937 film featuring Jack Haley and Alice Faye. The supporting cast was impressive, including Bob Crosby, James Gleason, Marilyn Maxwell and James Dunn. In his introduction, legendary producer-director Cecil B. DeMille said:

> There's a pot of gold at the end of the Hollywood rainbow for the right answer to the question, "What makes a star?"
>
> Nobody has found out yet, and I don't think they ever will. No two stars are alike, but each has a certain indefinable power—a power that draws people like a magnet draws bits of metal. I've watched that power at work for 50 years—in a lovely face, in a pair of dancing feet, in a voice. And it has come again this year—in the voice of Frank Sinatra.
>
> When a star is born overnight, there are always the cynics who say, "He won't last." But he will last if that mysterious power is there. And it is my belief that, in Frank's case, it is there. For his first appearance in the dramatic end of radio, we picked a delightful comedy that made a hit on the screen for 20th Century-Fox...

In this story, an aspiring singer, initially scared of the microphone, became a huge radio hit as "The Phantom Troubadour." Frank sang "I Don't Want to Walk Without You," "I've Heard That Song Before," "Embraceable You," "Dancing in the Dark" and "Wake Up and Live."

Two weeks later, on March 6, he was reunited with Gloria DeHaven in *The Gay Divorcee*, a radio version of the 1935 Astaire-Rogers film, on *The Lady Esther Screen Guild Theatre*. As Guy Holden, a popular American singer mistaken for a correspondent intended to trick Mimi Glossup's (DeHaven) husband into a divorce, Frank crooned "Night and Day," "I'll Follow My Secret Heart," "Time on My Hands" and "The Continental."

Warner Bros. released *The Road to Victory* (aka *The Shining Future*) on May 18. Featuring an all-star cast directed by LeRoy Prinz, this short included Frank singing "(There'll Be) A Hot Time in the Town of Berlin" with an orchestra conducted by Leo Forbstein.

To continue his participation on *Your Hit Parade*, he was allowed to broadcast his performances from KFWB in tinsel town but, according to the *Hollywood Citizen News*, Lucky Strike required him personally to foot the weekly $4,800 fee for studio rental, the orchestra and the AT&T feed to Manhattan. Although the program paid him $2,000 less, "he thought the exposure was still worth whatever it cost."[2] He also guested on *The Lifebuoy Show* on May 25, singing "South of the Border" with Spike Jones and the City Slickers and discussing popular singers, including Crosby — who reportedly walked onto the stage to hand him a $1 bill — with host Bob Burns.

Director George Sidney began shooting Frank's first MGM film, *Anchors Aweigh*, a Technicolor musical-comedy extravaganza pairing him with dancing dynamo Gene Kelly, on June 15, the morning after he completed his final "Vimms" broadcast of the season. Of his initial experience at the legendary studio, Frank recalled, "I used to... get terribly embarrassed at myself. After all, what was I then? A crooner who'd been singing for a big band for seven years and whose only claim to fame was that girls swooned whenever I opened my mouth."[3] He also said, "I... walk[ed] around the lot, looking at Hepburn, Tracy, Lionel Barrymore — all people who, a year before, I was paying to see."[4]

Though he had been given his own director's chair emblazoned with "The Voice," he almost refused to report to the studio. Apparently, during pre-production, producer Joe Pasternak had asked him for suggestions regarding a composer for the film's songs, expecting a reply of Rodgers and Hart, the Gershwins, Jerome Kern or another top contender.

"Sammy Cahn," Frank said. Pasternack was neither impressed nor amused. Later, Cahn, who actually referred to himself as Frank's "alter ego," recalled:

> It came to such an impasse that Lew Wasserman of MCA came to me and said, "Unless Frank gives in, he will lose the picture." Would I talk to Frank? I, of course, went to Frank and said, "Frank, you've done me more honor than I can handle. Why don't you pass on this one, and there will be others." He looked at me and said, "If you're not there Monday, I'm not there Monday."[5]

Frank may not have had trouble standing up to Joe Pasternak, but Gene Kelly was another matter. With him, Frank had difficulty *standing up*, period. The great choreographer had to teach the Voice to dance, and the rehearsals were so taxing that the skinny kid from Hoboken actually began to lose weight. Of his first meeting with Kelly, Frank nostalgically recalled:

> Gene flashed that twinkly Irish smile and said, "I've got a five-tube radio, so I know you can sing. The important thing is, can you dance?"
> I pointed at my feet and issued a pronunciamento:
> "These here babies can do anything I tell 'em to do!"
> "Good," said Gene. "Tell 'em to do this!"
> He hopped straight up like a champagne cork, did a mid-air somersault, came down in a leg-split, and segued into a tap routine that sounded like a nest of angry machine-guns.
> Suffice it to say, I was impressed, and fool that I was, when Gene volunteered to be my dance instructor, I accepted—and with humble gratitude yet![6]

Though he was truly grateful for Kelly's patience and willingness to teach a non-dancer a very complicated routine, Frank quickly became "one of the first victims of Gene's mania for perfection."[7] He remembered, in exaggerated fashion:

> Cut to eight weeks later. I've got seven hundred torn ligaments, compound fractures in every bone in my body, and I've lost vitally needed weight. In fact, I'm down to 116 1/2. ...But my wild Irish slavedriver paid me the ultimate compliment.
> "Francis," he said, "you've worked your way up from lousy to ad-equate—I'm ready to dance on camera with you."[8]

During the filming of their hotel room song-and-dance number, Frank felt like he might collapse from exhaustion. Citing extreme fatigue, he asked for the day off, an unacceptable request at MGM. After several studio suits demanded that he continue working, he ducked into his dressing room, where Louis B. Mayer—who rarely ventured out of his office—soon arrived to raise some executive hell. Knocked out by Kelly's workaholic pace and refusing to be told off by the boss, Frank went home. Although the incident would not affect the way he devised and directed his choreography, Kelly, realizing "that singers did not have the same stamina as dancers," supported Frank's decision.[9]

From that moment on, Frank always would respect and appreciate Kelly:

> [A]fter working with Gene, who always saw me through my depressions and encouraged me to do a little better than I thought I was capable of doing, I felt I actually had some talent. I was born with a couple of left feet, and it was Gene and only Gene who got me to dance. Apart from being a great artist, he's a born teacher. I felt really comfortable working for him and enjoyed his company, in spite of his insane insistence on hard work.[10]

Kelly later said, "I showed him the steps and he copied me. I taught him when to join in and he joined in. It was the same technique he used to sing. It was his timing." [11]
George Sidney later commented on Frank's work habits:

> It took the cameraman about twelve minutes to light a scene, and after that he'd be playing around for another thirty, lighting the walls. You know

the expression, follow the money, follow the star? No wall ever won an Academy Award...

Sinatra didn't originate the whole thing of getting it in one or two takes. Spencer Tracy... with Spence you'd do it in one or two takes and that was it. Look, Frank knows he's good, and he goes on, and he gives it, and he lets go. ...It's like anything... like rehearsing when you're blowing a trumpet. If you know the conductor's gonna keep on rehearsing it, you're not gonna hit that high C, you're gonna lay off. But if you know: This is the money... then off you go!

Gable was the same way. At one minute to nine, he was in front of the camera. If he was supposed to have a hat on and be carrying a glove and a flower, he was ready to go, and God help you if you weren't ready. ...If the girl was late, he would scream and yell. And if she was late by two or three minutes, he'd be up at the front office. And that, I think, is part of being an artist.[12]

Anchors Aweigh opens with a stunning production number on the deck of an aircraft carrier. Fading in on military drums, the sequence cuts to separate close-ups of trombones, saxophones and trumpets (all in impeccable formation) before the entire band is shown on deck, forming an anchor and spelling out N-A-V-Y. Only a few seconds in, this composition must have inspired overseas servicemen like no other shot in 1945.

After "Anchors Aweigh" is performed, two sailors, Joe Brady (Gene) and Clarence Doolittle (Frank), are being decorated with the Silver Star, for bravery they both exhibited when the former saved the latter from drowning. Soon after, while interacting with their shipmates, the relationship between Joe and Clarence—and Gene and Frank as a musical-comedy team—is firmly established. Joe appears to be the worldly, experienced man who enthralls the other sailors with his tales of dames—in fact, they call him "the Sea Wolf"—while Clarence is so shy and naive that he refuses to ask a woman for a date; instead, he asks Joe to help. But this time, after listening to his friend's descriptions of "Lola Laverne" who awaits ashore in Hollywood, he no longer wants to spend his four-day leave at the library. He wants to "go out with girls."

At the head of a line of sailors waiting to use a pay phone, Joe makes a sexy call to "Lola," impressing all his mates. Clarence then takes his turn, pretending to ask for a date but actually speaking to an operator who tells him to buy war bonds. As Joe walks off toward his apparent date, Clarence follows him—and here, Frank was given his first chance to demonstrate the natural acting ability that easily matched his musical prowess. Although he seldom spoke about particular actors during the infrequent interviews he gave (Montgomery Clift and Laurence Harvey were two he mentioned), he loved to watch the films of others, including golden-age greats Laurel and Hardy. Being an instinctive actor who liked to perform with as much improvisation—and as little rehearsal—as possible, his style and technique were similar to those of classic comic performers such as Chaplin, Keaton, and Laurel and Hardy. (In fact, he earned his nickname "One-Take Charley" during the making of this film.) Watching Frank in this scene, as he follows Gene, is literally like seeing Stan Laurel: the rail-thin, naive, childlike innocent trying to emulate his more mature, experienced friend. Whether or not he appropriated them intentionally, his movements and gestures are straight out of Stanley's comic bag. At one point, Clarence, desperately wanting a date, even makes a Laurel-like statement: "What's the use of having your life saved if you can't have any fun with it?" Later, when Clarence is nervous during a discussion with "Aunt Susie" Abbott (Kathryn Grayson), Frank adjusts his collar, exactly matching the way Laurel did it in countless films. Other connections to the Laurel and Hardy films (most of which were distributed by MGM from 1927-38) are Joe's attempt to teach Clarence pick-up methods by acting "like a dame" and incurring the stare of a male passerby, Clarence's cozying up to Joe as he speaks to Lola on Susie's phone, and the presence of Stan-and-Ollie foils Edgar Kennedy and Billy Gilbert in small character roles.

Sinatra dances too! It's a top toe-tapping twosome with inimitable Gene Kelly.

Frank and Gene Kelly's comic timing is near-perfect throughout *Anchors Aweigh.*

Not only is their singing and dancing brilliantly integrated, but Frank and Gene's comic timing is near-perfect throughout the film. (Unfortunately, due to Frank's later firing by MGM, they only had the opportunity to make two more films together.) The wholesome, all-American boy image established by RKO in *Step Lively* is solidified in *Anchors Aweigh* and would continue to be Frank's on-screen persona through *On the Town* (1949). Although both sailors play with Donald Martin (Dean Stockwell), the small boy who wants to join the Navy, Joe first wants to ditch the kid so he can pursue willing dames. Clarence returns to the Abbott household because of his infatuation with Aunt Susie, but he genuinely enjoys the lad's company, going so far as to sing him to sleep with "Brahms' Lullaby" (a beautiful performance by Frank). Later, Clarence reinforces his boyish wholesomeness by drinking chocolate milk at a soda fountain and only barely fondling a glass of beer at a bar. As the brew sits in front of Clarence, merely an object of contemplation, Joe guzzles several shots of Scotch, thinking his chances are over with Aunt Susie, whom *he* is now in love with. (By this point, Clarence has become smitten with "Brooklyn" [Pamela Britton], a hometown girl now working as a Hollywood waitress.)

Macho Joe's tales of conquest and liquor-drinking abilities are only two of the qualities that set him apart from neophyte Clarence. As in all of the musicals he either choreographed and/or directed, Gene Kelly works in as much erotic symbolism as possible (without raising the ire of Production Code censors, who rarely had enough artistic sense to notice such things). Joe's "history" with women and their notice of him (several buxom lasses whistle at his backside as he walks through MGM studios) are obvious, but Kelly's own choreographic (often Freudian) touches are a bit more subtle. In one scene, after Clarence takes Aunt Susie on a date—during which Joe does all the dancing with her while his buddy becomes interested in "Brooklyn"—he practically embraces a wooden lamp post while the naive bumbler kisses the girl he's fallen for. Near film's end, during the *Romeo and Juliet*-like Latin dance number, Kelly performs amazing dancing and athletic feats: scaling a wall, a tree and a rooftop, and swinging from one building to another (a là Douglas Fairbanks, Sr.). But as a preface to these seemingly effortless acts, he tosses a blood-red rose to Grayson

Lucky songstress Kathryn Grayson — with two such guys as Sinatra and Kelly after her heart!

Sinatra, Kathryn Grayson and Gene Kelly

(which she slowly slides between her exquisitely attired breasts) and then slowly inserts his sword into his red cape and draws it out again. And he does all of this just for a *kiss*, which, throughout the film, is the one thing he wants from a girl. The scene culminates with the final shot dissolving to one showing the real Joe and Susie kissing (the entire sequence was a romantic fantasy Joe had described to her—a production number anticipating Kelly's tour de force in his later masterpiece *An American in Paris* [1951]).

Though Kelly is billed third, he dominates the film, both with the nature of his character and the power of his production numbers. Top-billed and making his actual debut in a major acting role, Frank is thoroughly believable throughout. And whereas he had to dance with "the Feet," as Kelly affectionately was called on the set, Gene had to sing with the Voice, which is aptly demonstrated on Sammy Cahn and Jule Styne's excellent songs, which helped the score win an Academy Award. *Anchors Aweigh* is one of MGM's "realistic" musicals, in which actual explanations are given as to why the characters break into song now and then (Clarence was a choirmaster in Brooklyn, and Susie is an aspiring singer-actress who finally gets an audition with pianist-conductor Jose Iturbi. Less realism is connected to the dancing, however; though the Latin number is played as Joe's fantasy, his dancing talent is never explained.) Rather than dramatically singing libretto to one another, as in operetta-style musicals, the "realistic" style involves characters *performing* a song and/or dance. (Most of Sinatra's musicals feature realistic elements; some are completely so, but many combine realistic with fantastical elements.)

As in many musicals, characters break into song like a Shakespearean actor performing a soliloquy, alone and engaging in deep expression. Clarence sits alone at a nightclub table, thinking of "Brooklyn" while Joe dances with Susie; as silhouettes of the band play on the wall behind him, he speaks to an imaginary companion before breaking into "The Charm of You." Later, after he and Joe sneak into the Hollywood Bowl to tell Iturbi about Susie, Clarence sits alone at the maestro's piano when everyone else has left the band shell. With the expanse of the Bowl behind him, Frank sings the lovely "I Fall in Love Too Easily," a 1:30 performance captured in two long takes: one a frontal close-up and the other a profile medium shot almost unnoticeably held together by two unobtrusive cuts. It is a textbook musical sequence that provides a calming coda to the rousing Iturbi multi-piano arrangement of Lizst's "Hungarian Rhapsody No. 2" that precedes it. (Both this Iturbi performance and an earlier one feature innovative cinematography [by Robert Planck and Charles Boyle] and editing [by Adrienne Fazan], including images showing the musicians reflected in the maestro's mirrored piano and his nimble fingers shot from beneath transparent keys.)

Sammy Cahn always had his partner compose the music for a song before he wrote the lyrics. Referring to the ultimate fate of their collaborations, Jule Styne recalled:

> [Y]our completed score... is taken away from you and you lose all contact with it. Either they edit it to bits in the cutting room — and you can go drop dead — or it comes out altogether different from what you had in mind. In *Anchors Aweigh* we wrote "The Charm of You" for Frank Sinatra to sing to winsome Kathryn Grayson on first meeting her. Instead, he wound up crooning it to Pamela Britton, a Brooklynese character. "I Fall in Love Too Easily"... intended as a tender, intimate tune for Frank, he ended up singing in the Hollywood Bowl to a piano.[13]

One of Frank's most humorous scenes involves Clarence's meeting with Iturbi, whom he desperately has been trying to contact. Continually ejected from the MGM studio gate, Clarence, with Joe's expert aid, finally gets in but falls asleep on a soundstage and has no idea who Iturbi is when the great musician arrives to practice Tchaikovsky's "Piano Concerto." (The two had met briefly during the decoration ceremony on the aircraft carrier.) Clarence thinks Iturbi is a piano tuner and has never heard of Tchaikovsky (attributing the piece to "Freddie Martin"), but tells him that he plays well. Hearing him sing along, Iturbi replies that he sings "pretty good."

The most famous sequence in *Anchors Aweigh* does not involve Frank, but is another of Kelly's innovative fantasy sequences. While visiting little Donald and his classmates at the Hollywood Day School, Joe spins the yarn of a mythical kingdom wherein he interacted with a host of cartoon characters, including Jerry the Mouse (of the *Tom and Jerry* series), who had banned dancing because he could not cut a rug himself. In the flashback scene, which is filtered through Donald's imagination (a widescreen-like image is superimposed "inside" Stockwell's forehead), Joe rectifies the problem, teaching the mouse to dance as formidably as he does. More than a half-century later, this marriage of live action and animation, beautifully devised and executed by Kelly, choreographer Stanley Donen and director George Sidney, remains cinema at its most magical. (Donen had conceived the sequence as a dance with *Mickey* Mouse, but Walt Disney characteristically informed them that the character "will never be in an MGM picture. He works for me."[14])

While most military-related Hollywood films produced during 1944-45 now are seriously dated by their blatant propaganda content and images of barbarous Nazis and "Japs," spies, saboteurs and screen icons such as Laurel and Hardy, Tarzan and the Invisible Man ludicrously joining the fight, *Anchors Aweigh* is timeless. It is a marvelously entertaining, superbly made musical comedy that brought joy both to servicemen and those on the home front while avoiding the conventionalized trappings "suggested" by the Office of War Information. In fact, neither the war nor the enemy are mentioned, and the film generated its flagwaving appeal simply by depicting the Navy in a powerful, glamorous light (particularly through the opening and closing production numbers and little Donald's obsessive quest to join at any cost). Aside from the war bonds plug, the only reference to the conflict was a title card placed after the final cast listing:

TO FAMILIES AND FRIENDS OF
SERVICEMEN AND WOMEN:
Pictures exhibited in this theatre
are given to the armed forces for
showing in combat areas
around the world.
WAR ACTIVITIES COMMITTEE,
MOTION PICTURE INDUSTRY

For soldiers and sailors, *Anchors Aweigh*, like the V-Discs, may have brightened some dark days.

Frank had recorded his songs for the film on June 13, two days before Sidney began rolling the cameras. During the shoot, he had continued his contributions to *Your Hit Parade*, as well as several AFRS radio shows. In coordination with Columbia and V-Disc producer Morty Palitz, he also organized a special session at Los Angeles' KFWB Studio Theatre to wax some professional records for the troops, rather than continue to offer what he considered second-rate dress rehearsals. Performing as well as he would have at a paying session, Frank cut eight songs, seven of which were issued. After a lovely long-breath performance on Jerome Kern and Oscar Hammerstein's "All the Things You Are," he swung "All of Me" before cutting a new song written by his friends Phil Silvers and Jimmy Van Heusen, a tender ode to his little daughter, "Nancy (With the Laughing Face)," as well as "Mighty Lak' a Rose," his first recorded version of Rodgers and Hart's "Falling In Love With Love" (in a waltz tempo), "Cradle Song," the pop version of Johannes Brahms' "Lullaby" that he had sung in *Anchors Aweigh*, and Noel Coward's "I'll Follow My Secret Heart."

With *Anchors Aweigh* in the can, Frank was scheduled to return to Manhattan for an engagement at the Rio Bamba club, but instead decided to join his family in their new home. Needing a replacement for the dates, the nightclub hired Dino Crocetti, a new, young Italian crooner who went by the stage moniker "Dean Martin."

On the August 9, 1944, AFRS program *Mail Call*, Frank joined Fred Allen, Mary Livingstone, Gloria DeHaven and host Rudy Vallee in a tribute to Maine servicemen, singing "Begin the Beguine" and (with DeHaven) "Come Out, Come Out." Six weeks later, on September 28, he was a tea-time guest at the White House, where he spoke with his hero, President Roosevelt, to whose third re-election campaign he had donated $7,500. "He was very nice," Frank said. "I told him how well he looked. He kidded me about making the girls faint and asked me how I do it. I said I wished to hell I knew."[15]

Back in New York in October, Frank prepared to open another series of dates at the Paramount, this time with the Raymond Paige orchestra. He also guested on *The Lucky Strike Program Starring Jack Benny*, during which the notoriously penurious comedian settled for listening to the Voice sing "All the Things You Are" over the radio. On the 11th, after impatiently sitting through *When Our Hearts Were Young and Gay*, 5,000 screaming teenagers rushed the stage during Frank's show and then refused to make way for the next audience. Soon, the 30,000 fans outside stampeded the building, attempted to break in the doors and blocked traffic for hours. Called in just after noon, police were still at the scene when darkness fell. Dubbed the "Columbus Day Riot," the incident gave more ammunition to those who considered "Frankie" a bad influence on America's youth.

The day before the riot, more V-Discs were waxed during a radio dress rehearsal, including a version of the Gershwins' "Someone to Watch Over Me" that was issued with Frank making a rare mistake: Confusing the word order, he repeated the same one twice. More V-Discs followed, on October 18 and 23, cut during dress rehearsals for "Vimm's Vitamins" and NBC's *For the Record*, respectively. The latter date included an autobiographical parody, "Dick Haymes, Dick Todd and Como," written by Johnny Burke, Jimmy Van Heusen and Sammy Cahn, in which

Frank mentioned his skinny physique, the bobbysoxers, Crosby and his contract with RKO. At one point, referring to the precarious nature of a solo career, he speculated, "It will mean the end of me, and good news for T. D." On the 20th, he also performed for the military on *G.I. Journal*, playing opposite Roy Rogers as "Two-Gun Sinatra." When asked by Edgar Bergen why he wore two shootin' irons, he replied, "One gun would tilt me."

Columbia finally came to an agreement with AFM president James Petrillo on November 11, 1944. Three days later, Frank was in the studio, cutting his first legitimate records, with Axel Stordahl at the helm. For the initial number, "If You Are But a Dream," the music of which had been adapted from Arthur Rubinstein's "Romance," the arranger pulled out all the stops, using a full chamber orchestra and eight of the Bobby Tucker Singers to create a quasi-classical piece with an exquisite vocal. Five songs were recorded, but only one, Cahn and Styne's swinging "Saturday Night (Is the Loneliest Night of the Week)," was new to Frank, since he had performed the others on the radio and V-Discs. "White Christmas," featuring the Bobby Tucker Singers, was released just in time for the holidays; charting on December 30, it reached number 7. Backed by Stordahl, Frank also sang "These Foolish Things" via a remote from Buffalo, New York, on the November 16 *The Kraft Music Hall Starring Bing Crosby.*

Joining Crosby, Bob Hope and Harpo Marx, he then briefly re-teamed with Harry James, singing "Saturday Night" in *The All-Star Bond Rally*, a short made by the U.S. Treasury Department and released by 20th Century-Fox the following May. As Frank finishes the final chorus, an earmuff-wearing Bing, looking up from a newspaper, yawns and then returns to his reading.

Anchors Aweigh was the first film for which Frank was able to record 78-rpm releases. On December 1, he cut the swinging "I Begged Her," which he had sung as a duet with Kelly, the Latin-flavored "What Makes the Sunset?" and an extended orchestral version of "I Fall in Love Too Easily." Two days later, he added "The Charm of You" and his first commercial recording of "Cradle Song" to his list of *Anchors Aweigh* sides. The latter date also produced legitimate releases of "Nancy" and "Ol' Man River," which features one of the most accomplished vocal performances of his early career. Frank's technique of "acting" a lyric is never more apparent than in this recording, when he uses an incredibly long breath to join the phrases "You get a little drunk and you land in jail" and "I gets weary and sick of tryin'" Completing the first phrase by extending the "l" in "jail," he then segues immediately into "I gets weary," first suggesting the rock-bottom, demeaning experience of incarceration, with its long hours of boredom; and then sounding truly exhausted when singing of being weary (by this point in his breath, he *must* have been weary!). Here, Frank's unique style not only impresses with its technical quality, but also in the drama it conveys.

On December 12, Gracie Allen attempted to slip Frank a mickey on *The Burns and Allen Show*, so her tone-deaf, would-be-vocalist hubby could be "discovered" at a war bond rally. To add realism to the skit, the program was staged at an actual E bond rally held at the Warner Bros. Theater in Hollywood. In a bizarre *Command Performance* broadcast five days later, Frank chatted with actor Frank Morgan, who played a Peeping Tom at Greta Garbo's house and claimed that he had been "the Frank Sinatra of my day." Following a bluesy "One Meatball" by the Andrews Sisters, the Voice swung "Saturday Night."

Frank cut his final recordings of 1944 two days later, superbly crooning Stordahl's light swing arrangements of "When Your Lover Has Gone," "She's Funny That Way" (which he dedicated to his wife) and the Gershwins' "Embraceable You." Shortly after the New Year, he played his first bona-fide villain, Howard Wilton, a paranoid, psychotic handyman, on the popular radio program *Suspense*. "I'm not in the service like your boys," he said at one point. "They wouldn't let me in. …They said there was something wrong with my mind." Ten days after this dramatic broadcast, on January 28, 1945, he guested on one of radio's most absurd programs, *The Charlie McCarthy Show*, hosted by Edgar Bergen's famous ventriloquism dummy! In this episode, the wooden one, aspiring to be Frank's agent, vows to make the girls flock to him. Backed by Ray Noble and His Orchestra, Frank sang "There's No Use." The next day, he again was in the recording studio waxing several sides, including his first version of Rodgers and Hart's "Where or When." Two days later, during *The Frank Sinatra Show*, V-Disc recorded his performance of "None But the Lonely Heart," the melody of which was borrowed from Tchaikovsky.

Continuing to focus on commercial recordings, Frank completed a dozen singles in the next few months. Future Sinatra collaborator Gordon Jenkins contributed a song, "Homesick—That's All," to the repertoire, and Stordahl received a cowriter's credit (with Sammy Cahn and Paul Weston) on "I Should Care." Frank cut works by Johnny Mercer ("Dream"), Rodgers and Hammerstein ("You'll Never Walk Alone," from *Carousel*) and Harold Arlen and Y. A. Harburg ("Over the Rainbow").

On March 1, 1945, he guested on the *Abbott and Costello Show*, during which the Voice and the "short, fat and stupid" one traded barbs and vocal riffs. The skinny jokes were in full force, with Lou telling Bud, "That guy looks like a stand-in for a dust mop" and "Just slip him under the door." One week later, he hosted *Command Performance*, singing "The Trolley Song" and taking flak from a group of child stars, including Elizabeth Taylor, Margaret O'Brien, Roddy McDowall, Peggy Ann Garner, Bing Crosby's children and his own daughter, Nancy! On March 20, he was a memorable guest on *A Date With Judy*, starring Louise Erickson. In this episode, Judy, after going to a Sinatra movie with her boyfriend, Oogie Pringle (Richard Crenna), dreamed that the males' roles were reversed.

After hearing her recount the nocturnal experience, Oogie admitted, "It's mighty tough for a fella to live in the same world with Frank Sinatra. ...It's mighty sad to think that a whole generation is doomed like that."

Referring to Sinatra the actor, Judy revealed, "He is a girl's dream of the utter acme of ideal love, and when he stands before you on the screen, you see something absolutely beautiful."

During the episode, Frank recited dialogue from a bogus film and sang, "Night and Day." Louise Erickson recalled, "I suggested the idea for the episode. Since Judy lived in a small town, it was unlikely that Sinatra would ever visit, so I suggested that she could dream that Frank was her boyfriend and that Oogie was the movie star I had the crush on."[16]

On April 14, Frank recreated his "Ol' Man River" long-breath wizardry for *The Frank Sinatra Show* and a V-Disc, and then crooned "I Can't Give You Anything But Love" on *Mail Call*, a radio tribute to New Jersey servicemen, on the 25th. Hosted by Betty Hutton, who sang "I Want Some Huggin'," the program also featured Vivian Blaine, the King Sisters and William Demarest. Stressing that New Jersey must be recognized, Frank told Hutton, "I promised those guys I'd put this thing over, even if I had to wrestle the emcee to do it."

"Now, Frank, don't do anything foolish. I weigh more than you do," she countered.

"Who doesn't?" he asked. "And besides, it wouldn't be cricket. Men don't wrestle with girls. What am I sayin'?"

"They don't wrestle with girls?" she replied, her voice growing stern. "Have you ever been up in the balcony of the Paramount?"

Back in the studio, he waxed "Put Your Dreams Away (For Another Day)," which features a Dorsey-like trombone solo, during a May Day Columbia session. He joined Dinah Shore on radio's *Birds Eye Open House* on May 10, singing "That's You, That's You" and "fighting" with Harry Von Zell.

The following week, he made the unusual move of recording with a small group of musicians, including legendary trumpeter Red Nichols and black gospel group The Charioteers, on some light swing numbers ("Lily Belle," featuring Louis Armstrong-style blowing by Nichols, and "Don't Forget Tonight Tomorrow") and traditional spirituals ("I've Got a Home In That Rock," which sounds like it was lifted from the soundtrack of a John Ford film, and "Jesus Is a Rock in the Weary Land"). Eight days later, he was joined by the Xavier Cugat Orchestra for a Latin-flavored session that produced "Stars In Your Eyes" and "My Shawl."

The general release date for *Anchors Aweigh* had been set for August 15, 1945, but apparently Frank had jeopardized its box-office success by making a rash statement sensationalized by the newspapers. After he made the off-the-cuff remark that "Pictures stink. Most of the people in them do, too. I don't want any more movie acting. Hollywood won't believe I'm through, but they'll find out I mean it," MGM issued the following "apology," supposedly written by Frank:

> It's easy for a guy to get hot under the collar, literally and figuratively, when he's dressed in a hot suit of navy blue and the temperature is 104 degrees and he's getting over a cold to boot. I think I might have spoken too broadly about quitting pictures and about my feelings towards Hollywood...[17]

Distrustful of and often angered by journalists who interrupted his personal affairs, Frank, in an effort to fend them off, sometimes was his own worst enemy, playing into their hands by remarking sarcastically about his work. But the feared imbroglio did not affect either the popular or critical success of *Anchors Aweigh*. After it was tradeshown in Los Angeles on July 14, *Variety*'s "Brog" used such superlatives as "solid," "zingy" and "outstanding": "It's a showmanly package of entertainment cut to order for hefty box-office returns."[18] Even the anti-Sinatra Bosley Crowther begrudgingly began to warm to the Voice, though he gave credit to the film's producer:

> [T]hat agile young fellow, Gene Kelly, conclusively proves to be the peer, if not the superior, at rigadooning, of Fred Astaire. But, indeed, Mr. Pasternak—a champion at making such films with youthful stars—has accomplished an even greater wonder in this one. He has made Frank Sinatra look good.
> Well, maybe that word is misleading. He has put the fabulous "Voice" in his place, but he has done it with such charming candor that even Sinatra fans squeal with glee. ...he is not the best thing in the show. That distinction is plainly Mr. Kelly's. ...But bashful Frankie is a large-sized contributor to the general fun and youthful charm of the show, and through him—or through his characterization—is transmitted a genial touch of ridicule.[19]

Apparently having no axes to grind about his appearance or affect on bobbysoxers, the *Motion Picture Herald's* Thalia Bell wrote, "All the world knows Frank Sinatra can sing; now it turns out that he can act, too. His characterization of Kelly's shipmate is delightful."[20] Millions of Americans agreed, and the success of *Anchors Aweigh*, as MGM had hoped, made Frank a bankable film star.

An established star Frank admired as much for attitude as acting was Humphrey Bogart, whom he had met at Players Restaurant on the Sunset Strip just prior to filming *Anchors Aweigh*. Bogie always had spoken his mind rather than pandering to his publicist and the press, and sometimes made matters worse when trying to ditch a reporter. As their friendship grew, Frank would borrow a few "tough-guy" movie mannerisms (including Bogie's confident yet subtle swagger) as well as reinforce his personal nose-thumbing at the hypocrisy of tinsel town, including a tendency to go out nightclubbing with those who could in no way advance his reputation and career. Nancy, Jr., wrote:

> Bogie liked Dad's cockiness and his irreverence toward the Hollywood establishment. Both would become increasingly evident as FS ignored the advice of publicist George Evans and movie-industry bigwigs to be more discreet about conducting his personal life in public. During this heady period of newfound stardom, he was allegedly seen around town squiring starlet Marilyn Maxwell and "sweater girl" Lana Turner, among other women. It would only be a matter of time until the gossip columnists began to report on his "extracurricular activities."[21]

The Actor, on Screen and in Song

Journalists also began to turn up the heat on Frank's non-military status, accusing him of being unpatriotic, a slacker, a Communist. Due to the Red-baiting, his application for a visa to entertain the troops overseas had been denied. Much of the furor had been drummed up by *New York Daily Mirror* columnist Lee Mortimer, who fancied himself an expert on everything from Hollywood films to international politics. Nancy, Jr., suggested:

> Dad felt that the bad blood began when Mortimer sent him a song he'd written and wanted the singer to record. But after Frank voiced his blunt opinion that the song was no good, Mortimer broke out the brass knuckles of his trade and embarked on a relentless campaign of innuendo and gossip about Sinatra's personality, performances, politics, and friends.[22]

Just prior to the release of *Anchors Aweigh*, Frank finally had been cleared to perform for the troops in Europe, but they no longer were fighting. Hitler's "Thousand Year Reich" had fallen and V-E Day had passed, but he and his friend Phil Silvers traveled through Italy (where he met Pope Pius XII) and North Africa, entertaining servicemen still waiting to return Stateside. Dissatisfied with the pianist chosen to accompany them, Frank opted for Saul Chaplin, who had to be loaned out by Columbia's Harry Cohn. As payback, Frank agreed to record a song for the film *A Thousand and One Nights*.

Back home, Frank's hero, President Roosevelt, was dead, and the fact that he had campaigned for FDR's fourth term so publicly also lent fuel to conservative fires about his "leftist" activities, including his views on prejudice, a topic he often spoke about to public groups. On July 20, 1945, Columbia released *A Thousand and One Nights*, in which Aladdin's sidekick (Phil Silvers) makes a wish that he be able to sing like Sinatra. Directed by Alfred E. Green and starring Cornel Wilde and Evelyn Keyes, it includes a scene featuring "All or Nothing at All" and a crowd of hysterical females shouting, "Oh, Frankie!"

On August 24, Frank announced, "For the first time in four weeks, I'm going to do the skinny jokes" on *The Ray Bolger Show*, whose star pleaded with the Voice to set him up with a date. After hearing Bolger's terrible "opera singing," Frank agreed to let him impersonate "Sinatra" at Mrs. Woodford's School for Girls. After trying to pass himself off as "Vladimir Sinatski," the Voice's Russian manager, Frank sang "Autumn Breeze" and "Someday." The following week, he hosted *Command Performance*, costarring with Humphrey Bogart and Lauren Bacall. *Anchors Aweigh* was mentioned and, after he sang "What Makes the Sunset?" he acted in a skit in which Bogie tried to hire him as Betty's bodyguard.

"That's the kind of body I'd like to guard," Frank replied. After Bacall repeated her whistle act from *To Have and Have Not* (1945), Frank admitted, "I'm wild about you, Lauren."

Following "Mr. Lauren Bacall"'s exclamation of "Darn it!" Frank told Bogie he was carrying her off to his mountain hideout! He then closed the program with "Nancy (With the Laughing Face)."

On September 6, he joined Bob Hope, Judy Garland and Bing Crosby for another *Command Performance*, singing "All the Things You Are," a medley of "You Are My Sunshine" and "Sunny Boy" with Crosby, and "You're the Top" with Bing and Bob. But his concerns about American society were voiced most effectively on the cinema screen, when RKO released the 10-minute propaganda short *The House I Live In* on September 11. Conceived by Frank and Mervyn LeRoy, who had directed Warner Bros.' gritty urban classics *Little Caesar* (1930) and *I Am a Fugitive from a Chain Gang* (1932), during a chance meeting aboard a train, the film was written by Albert Maltz (who became one of the "Hollywood Ten" during the House Un-American Activities Committee [HUAC] hearings two years later). As part of Frank's subsequent agreement with RKO, all those involved in the project worked for free and the profits were donated to programs combating juvenile delinquency.

Axel Stordahl selected the 1942 Broadway revue number "The House I Live In" as the title song for the film. (In 1944, the vocal group The Golden Gate Quartet had sung it in the film *Follow the Boys*.) The lyrics, by leftist writer Lewis Allen (who also penned "Strange Fruit," one of Billie Holiday's classics), proved the perfect complement to Maltz's script. The music was also by a left-wing composer, Earl Robinson, whose later works include "Black and White." The film can't be accused of subtlety, but hits hard with Frank's personal punch. During a recording session with Axel Stordahl, he sings the beautiful love song "If You Are But a Dream" and then steps out into an alley for a five-minute cigarette break. Interrupting a group of boys who are taunting one defenseless young lad, he casually asks, "Somebody in for a licking?"

"You bet," one of the boys replies. "We're gonna smear 'im!"

"Yeah, but 10 against one," Frank observes. "That's not very fair. What's it all about?"

"None of your business!"

"Scared to tell me?"

"No, I'm not a-scared," replies the young ringleader. "I'll fight you, even."

"Not if I can help it," Frank replies. "I just wanna know—why the gang war?"

"We don't like him! We don't want him in our neighborhood or going to our school."

The persecuted kid tries to defend himself: "I've been living here as long as you!"

"What's he got? Smallpox or somethin'?" Frank asks.

A tiny lad speaks up: "We don't like his religion!"

Frank is puzzled. "His religion?"

"Now look, mister, he's a dirty..."

"Now hold on!" Frank interrupts. "I see what you mean. You must be a bunch of those Nazi werewolves I've been readin' about."

"Mister?" the tiny one asks. "Are you screwy?"

"Not me," Frank insists. "I'm an American."

"Well, what do you think we are?" asks a boy dressed in a suit and tie.

"Nazis," Frank replies with a slight smirk.

"Don't call me a Nazi!" threatens the most obnoxious boy in the bunch. "My father's a sergeant in the Army. He's been wounded, even!"

"Wounded, huh?" Frank contemplates. "Say, I bet he got some of that blood plasma."

"He was wounded so bad, he had to get it three times," the kid replies.

Turning to the persecuted one, Frank asks, "Son, anybody in your family ever go to the blood bank?"

"Sure, my mother and my father both."

"Uh-huh. You know what? I'll bet you his pop's blood helped save your dad's life. That's bad."

"What's bad about it?"

"Well, don't you see? Your father doesn't go to the same church as his father does. That's awful! Do you think maybe if your father knew about it in time, he would rather have died than to take blood from a man of another religion? Would you have wanted him to die? Would your mom have wanted him to die?"

"No!"

Frank then explains why the boys should be tolerant of all races and creeds:

> Look, fellas, religion makes no difference, except maybe to a Nazi or somebody as stupid. Why, people all over the world worship God in many different ways. God created everybody. He didn't create one people better than another. Your blood's the same as mine. Mine's the same as his. Do you know what this wonderful country is made of? It's made up of a hundred different kinds of people, and a hundred different ways of

talking, and a hundred different ways of going to church. But they're all American ways. Wouldn't we be silly if we went around hating people because they combed their hair different than ours? Wouldn't we be a lot of dopes? My dad came from Italy, but I'm an American. Should I hate your father 'cause he came from Ireland or France or Russia? Wouldn't I be a first-class fathead?

You guys remember Pearl Harbor? Why the Japs socked us so it looked like we could never do anything about it. But a couple of days later, something very important happened. Close your eyes, and let me tell you about it. Go on, close your eyes, all of you.

There was a Jap battleship—the *Haruna*—and one of our planes spotted it. Do you know what it takes to bomb a battleship? It takes guts, know-how and teamwork. And our boys sure needed plenty of it, because that Jap was throwing up enough flak to get out and walk home on. But the pilot had only one thing on his mind: to get over that ship, and he did. And then the bombardier pushed a button and a 500-pound tomato smacked that Jap right in the middle.

Yep, they sank it, and every American headed back and felt much better. The pilot of that ship was named Colin Kelly, an American and a Presbyterian. You now who dropped the bombs? Myron Levin, an American and a Jew. You think they should have called the bombings off because they had different religions?

Ending his lecture, Frank advises, "So think about that fellas. Use your good American heads. Don't let anybody make suckers out of you." Patting one of them on the head, he adds, "Well, gotta go to work" and walks to the studio door.

"What do you work?" the tiny lad asks.

"I sing," Frank replies.

"Ah, you're kiddin'!" the kid scoffs, but when Frank says, "Now, you all stand here, and no hissin' allowed," and tells them to draw close, they all run to hear his voice, which segues into "The House I Live In." After Frank finishes this ode to the American Dream, a variation on the melody of "America the Beautiful" fades and the boys walk away, one of them stopping to pick up the persecuted lad's school books and welcome him into the group.

Maltz's dialogue for Frank is both bold and careful, addressing the problem of ethnic intolerance while tying it to a reinforcement of dominant American values: church, country and a wartime sensibility. Prior to the preachy section, Frank engages the boys in a realistic conversation that could have occurred between the off-screen Sinatra and a group of youths. In his lecture, although he equates all bigots with Nazis, Frank is speaking to children, so he avoids patronizing more mature characters. Italy—which had been an Axis power—is mentioned, but then neutralized with the word "American." Then three of the Allies—Ireland, France and Russia—are included.

Cue magazine, filled with the same wartime gusto, was quite enthusiastic:

The picture's message is tolerance. Its medium is song. And its protagonist is Frank Sinatra, who has, amazingly, grown within a few short years from a lovelorn microphone-hugging crooner to become one of filmdom's leading and most vocal battlers for a democratic way of life. Mr. Sinatra takes his popularity seriously. More, he attempts to do something constructive with it. Millions, young and old, who will not or cannot read between the lines of their daily newspapers and are blind to the weed-like growth of

bigotry and intolerance planted by hate-ridden fanatics, will listen carefully to what Mr. Sinatra has to say in this short film.[23]

Frank delivers Maltz's sometimes heavy-handed dialogue beautifully. His performance of "The House I Live In" remains powerful and moving, even if some of the lyrics are simplistic and naive. Though World War II had ended by the time the film was released, its effectiveness remained sharp.

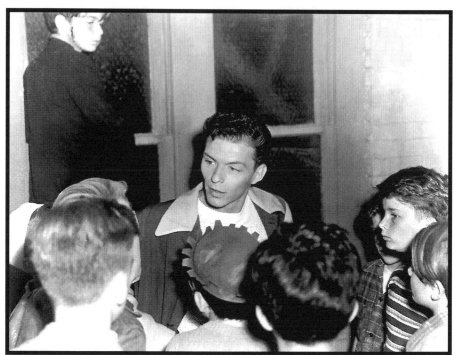

Frank stops the "gang" from persecuting the lad whose religion they "don't like" in *The House I Live In*.

A radio "sneak preview of the picture" was broadcast on September 19, 1945. The previous month, Frank had recorded a single version of the song, which eventually reached number 22 after its release on January 19, 1946. Perhaps to provide a counterbalance to the "radical" message of "The House I Live In," Columbia also had him cut two reverent versions of establishment songs, "America the Beautiful" and "Silent Night." And his renewed activity in the V-Disc program also re-shined his patriotic gloss. From September 26 through November 14, he contributed nine sides, recorded during *Frank Sinatra Show* and *Songs By Sinatra* broadcasts and dress rehearsals, to the troops still overseas. He duetted with Dinah Shore on "The Night is Young and You're So Beautiful," demonstrated his tendency toward a more improvisational approach on the swingers "Aren't You Glad You're You" and "You Brought a New Kind of Love to Me," and was reunited (for patriotic purposes) with Dorsey and the Pied Pipers on "I'll Never Smile Again." On September 27, he "sued" Rudy Vallee after being "bitten by his Doberman" on the crooner's *Dream Show*. Following a hilarious skit involving a judge and a jury who are all Sinatras save one, Frank sang "Slowly."

Interestingly, two radio shows broadcast in October projected Frank's life a half-century into the future. Costarring as substitute hosts, he and Judy Garland helmed *The Danny Kaye Show* on October 4, featuring "My Romance," a fictitious look at their 50-year love affair from the retrospective vantage point of 1995. On an even more absurd note, asking "Where will I be 50 years from now?" on the October 21 broadcast of *The Fred Allen Show*, Frank was told to "go hillbilly."

On November 1, less than two months after *The House I Live In* hit American screens, CBS executive William S. Paley asked Frank to visit campuses across the nation to lecture about racial tolerance. During the tour, he stepped into a "strike" by white teenagers at Froebel High School in Gary, Indiana, where a recently hired principal had integrated the student body, mixing 270 blacks with 1,000 whites. At his lecture, Frank addressed an audience of "rough, tough steel workers and their kids." As they hooted and heckled, he stood firm for two minutes and, after silence fell, stepped up to the microphone and threatened, "I can lick any son of a bitch in this joint!"[24] Asking the students to return to class, he mentioned the purpose of the recently ended war, the reputation of their hometown and the experiences he had growing up as a "dirty wop" in Hoboken. The unenlightened teens remained on strike, but Frank subsequently was honored by educational, religious and ethnic organizations across the country, receiving awards from the Bureau for Inter-cultural Education, the National Conference of Christians and Jews, and American Unity. Now that he had become one of the world's first celebrity activists, the conservative press had all the more reason to attack him. And the FBI, in an effort to brand him a Communist, began to keep an extensive file containing reports of any speeches, performances or monetary donations he gave in support of "leftist" causes.

In New York on November 7, Frank opened another three-week stint at the Paramount and then again traded a bobbysox audience for one in evening attire at the Waldorf's Wedgwood Room. Three days after Christmas, he sang "Nancy" on *The Ginny Simms Show*, paying back the big band canary for her previous guest spot on his *Old Gold Show*.

Broadcasting from a live NBC remote in New York, Frank received a special award on *The Bill Stern Colgate Sports Newsreel* on November 23. Speaking from Indianapolis, Stern said:

> [W]e're about to present him with a very, very fine silver plaque… that bears the following inscription: To Frank Sinatra, not because he's a great artist, but rather through his unselfish devotion to the cause of tolerance in America, he has upheld the highest ideals of good sportsmanship.

Accepting the honor, Frank replied, "Thank you, Bill. I shall always treasure this plaque and what it stands for. I'm not going to make any speeches about this country or about tolerance, but I'd like to tell you a little story that illustrates exactly how I feel"; then he described the plight of a family who emigrated to the United States from Germany because of religious persecution: the Eisenhowers. "However," Frank added, "there are two words on this plaque that please me immensely…'tolerance' and 'sportsmanship,' because to me they mean the same thing."

On December 5 and 10, he ventured into new musical territory with the Columbia String Orchestra for the album *Frank Sinatra Conducts the Music of Alec Wilder*. Having discovered some of Wilder's compositions while playing radio transcription discs between shows at the Paramount, he phoned the composer and proposed they record some legitimate sessions. Though "the orchestra players first looked upon him with an ill-disguised cynicism…Frank knew this music by heart, knew what he wanted, told them in a straightforward way what he expected of them, made intelligent suggestions and, in short, really conducted the orchestra."[25]

Back on the West Coast at the beginning of the New Year, he cut his first recordings at Columbia's Hollywood studio and more V-Discs on *The Frank Sinatra Show*. Another duet with Dinah Shore, Rodgers and Hart's "My Romance," from the January 23 broadcast, was followed by a February 13 recording introduced by a fellow entertainer: "Hi ya, men. This is Bob ("V-Disc") Hope. You know, when Bing Crosby was 14, he had his adnoids removed, and here is one of them now, Frankie Sinatra…" Performing one of his signature numbers, "The Song Is You," Frank wowed his listeners by holding the concluding high note for an amazing duration.

Frank also guested on the January 29 *Bob Hope Show*, playing the skinny shtick to the hilt as "The Original Thin Man." Described as a "bone with a bow tie on it" gone unrecognized by Hope's dog, he told fellow guest Frances Langford that she should see more of him.

"I'd like to," the songbird replied. "Where'd you leave it?"

Hope plugged *Anchors Aweigh*, and the Voice sang "Nancy" and starred in "Weird and Chilling Ghost Story: The Life of Frank Sinatra," a fictionalized satire in which the stork leaves him to a father who mistakes him for spaghetti.

The charge that Frank was a "front" for Communists was voiced by America First hardliner and outspoken anti-Semite Gerald L. K. Smith during his testimony at a HUAC hearing in January 1946. Based on no evidence whatsoever, his accusations were ludicrous but began an even more vociferous anti-Sinatra campaign among right-wing groups. On the other hand, big-name Hollywood stars were beginning publicly to note his effect on their own box-office potential. In *Road to Utopia* (1946), the current installment in the popular Hope-Crosby series, the former, ending their routine, looks at his partner and states, "Next time I get *Sinatra!*" Now he actually had become part of the self-reflective content of films starring fellow singer-actors. And a well-known comic actor tried to keep him away from a prospective date on the February 13 episode of *Starring Jack Carson*, during which the Voice sang "Brahms' Lullaby" and (with eight-year-old Norma Jean Nillson) "Onesie-Twosie."

Frank's first album, a 78-rpm collection titled *The Voice*, was released on March 4, 1946. Songs for this first "concept" album—including "These Foolish Things (Remind Me of You)," the Gershwins' "Someone to Watch Over Me" and Cole Porter's "Why Shouldn't I?"—had been waxed at two separate sessions, on July 30 and December 7 of the previous year.

On March 7, Frank, Mervyn LeRoy and producer Frank Ross won Oscars for *The House I Live In* at the 18th Academy Awards ceremony at Grauman's Chinese Theater. Since this short film didn't fit into any established category at the time, a "special" designation was created.

Frank took part in one of the longest recording sessions of his career three days later, completing seven issuable sides, including Harold Arlen and Johnny Mercer's "That Old Black Magic," Irving Berlin's "How Deep Is the Ocean (How High Is the Sky)," a gorgeous studio version of "The Song Is You," and the traditional folk song "Home on the Range" (which, demonstrating the maturity of his voice, sounds no more incongruous than Crosby's "cowboy songs").

Two weeks after *The Voice* hit the streets, Frank contributed a cameo to *Till the Clouds Roll By*, MGM's all-star tribute to Jerome Kern, before setting off on a nationwide tour including concerts in San Francisco, Philadelphia, Detroit, New York and Chicago. On May 28, he recorded the ambitious Rodgers and Hammerstein piece "Soliloquy (Parts 1 and 2)" from *Carousel*, in which he, as narrator of the song, twice refers to himself in terminology that would become an indelible part of Sinatra jargon: "A *bum*, with no money... brought up in slums with a lot of *bums* like me!" At the same session, he cut "Five Minutes More," which begins as a ballad and then picks up into a driving up-tempo number. On August 3, the song began a 22-week stint on the charts, eventually reaching number 1; but beyond its commercial appeal, it demonstrated the importance of Sammy Cahn and Jule Styne in Frank's development as a swinger. A novelty number dealing with wartime shortages and rationing, "The Coffee Song (They've Got An Awful Lot of Coffee in Brazil)," recorded at a July 24 session, provided a hint of Frank's later "nice 'n' easy" swing style.

But it was during a July 30, 1946, Columbia session that Frank really began to swing in earnest. Though he had recorded a few songs at faster tempos since beginning his solo career, he

Frank's cameo of "Ol' Man River" in *Till the Clouds Roll By*

really did not feel comfortable doing them, preferring to stick with ballads. But, seemingly out of Irving Berlin's "Blue Skies," the ability to swing, unencumbered by stylistic concerns, allowing the phrasing consistently to float out and above Stordahl's pulsing, bouncy beat and given wings by a catchy, sexy saxophone arrangement, simply *hit* him. Frank had recorded the song as a big-band number with Dorsey, and had sung it with Louis Armstrong on an AFRS program the previous year, but now it became what Will Friedwald accurately calls "one of Sinatra's fiercest up-tempos ever."[26] (Eight more years would pass before he started to swing similarly on a regular basis.) At the same session, he also cut his first version of Styne and Cahn's masterpiece "Guess I'll Hang My Tears Out to Dry."

On August 8, Frank made the first recording of "Lost in the Stars," Kurt Weill and Maxwell Anderson's song about racial persecution. Cutting records by day, he began a return engagement at the Hollywood Bowl during the evenings. On August 20, comic "Rags" Ragland, who had played a policeman in *Anchors Aweigh*, passed away, leaving his partner Phil Silvers alone to perform some scheduled dates at New York's Copacabana. On September 9, about an hour before show time, a distraught and nervous Silvers answered a knock at his dressing room door, only to find Frank outside.

"Hi, what do we open with?" asked Frank, who had performed Rags' routines with Silvers during their USO tour.

"Well, I'll do a few minutes first," Silvers calmly replied, "and when I touch my tie you appear and we'll do our routines. You know them all." Out on stage, Silvers joked, "Scram, kid, I work alone," much to the surprise of the audience. Silvers recalled:

> We proceeded to do an hour and three quarters of material, and at our con-
> clusion received an ovation. But gratitude embarrassed Frank. I looked
> for him to thank him for this expression of love and friendship, and he was
> gone—back to Hollywood, where he had caused a two-day delay because
> of his gesture.[27]

The delay had affected production of his next vehicle, *It Happened in Brooklyn*, costarring Kathryn Grayson, Peter Lawford and Jimmy Durante. Louis B. Mayer had been concerned about all the negative publicity, and others at the studio were not sure what to expect when the Voice returned for his first new picture in two years. The shoot did not begin well, due to his jaunt to New York, as well as his insistence (over George Evans' objections) that he fight back against all the reporters and columnists who took shots at him. But he enjoyed working with Peter Lawford, an MGM contract player, whom he had met at a Mayer-hosted party during the spring of 1944. Lawford later said:

> He took direction beautifully, listened, contributed, and was generally
> extremely professional about the whole operation. In other words, he was
> a joy to work with, which surprised everyone from the prop men to L. B.
> Mayer, because of his reputation, which preceded him, of his being dif-
> ficult to get along with.[28]

Frank's reputation for having a short fuse also inspired practical jokes among his coworkers at MGM. Stanley Donen recalled:

> We used to play nasty, mean tricks on Frank Sinatra, because he was always
> a pain in the neck. He didn't want to work and was always very quixotic
> and quick to anger, so we used to take great pleasure in teasing him. ...The
> MGM commissary had square tables with blue plastic tops, pushed against
> the walls, like in a cafeteria. Every table was square, except one, and that
> belonged to Gerry Mayer. ...So one day, mean bastards that we were, Gene
> [Kelly] and I said to Frank, "Wouldn't it be wonderful if we could have a
> round table? It's so much nicer that way, because then we could sit closer
> together." As soon as Frank heard us say that, he said, "You watch. I'll get
> us a round table." ...There was no way Frank was going to get us a round
> table. We knew that. Then, when he was told to forget it, he got into this
> *huge* argument. He steamed and he fumed and threw fits and said he was
> going to quit. All this for a round table.[29]

On October 1, 1946, Frank was back in New York to perform at a tribute to Al Jolson. The following day, he returned to Hollywood to attend an emergency meeting of the Screen Actors Guild at American Legion Stadium. One week earlier, actors had begun to form picket lines at the major studios, and threats of a strike were voiced. Joining 3,000 of his fellow actors, including Boris Karloff, Gene Kelly, Red Skelton, Walter Pidgeon and Jane Wyman, Frank listened to Ronald Reagan, vice-president Franchot Tone, and legal counsel Laurence Beilenson, who "stressed that if the Guild as an organization voted to respect picket lines... it would be voting to strike."[30] The walk-out eventually was averted.

Frank sang "September Song" on the November 7 *Maxwell House Coffee Time Starring George Burns and Gracie Allen*, during which the comedienne insisted that her husband was "twice the singer" that Sinatra was. Gracie revealed that Clark Gable had been dropped from the cast of MGM's *The Hucksters*, which now required a singing performer. Attempting to convince Frank to go to Africa or India, she claimed that George's casting would result in the studio changing its name to Metro-*Burns*-Mayer. After George himself baited Frank with baby clothes, convincing him that Gracie was pregnant, the Voice capitulated.

In December, MGM released *Till the Clouds Roll By*. Frank performed an abridged version of "Ol' Man River" in the film's closing Jerome Kern medley, and was held personally responsible for the way he looked on screen—the political opposite of how he had appeared in *The House I Live In* and the way he really was. Bosley Crowther, who considered the film "phoney... hackneyed and sentimental," even hated the way the Voice sang the song: "the picture... concludes in a bath of blazing light with a pale, prim and pedestaled Frank Sinatra hymning 'Ol' Man River' horribly."[31] The film is a dreadful, plotless parade of songs stiffly performed by an all-star cast (Lena Horne is a notable exception), but Frank's all-too-brief contribution, which finally appears during the closing seconds, after 135 minutes have dragged by, is its finest moment.

A half-century after its release, while performing at Frank's 80th birthday bash, musician Ray Charles humorously said:

> You know, Frank, I understood that you were out there in your *white* suit, with your *white* orchestra, in your *white* set, singing a *black man's* song. I just want to know, "What kind of *snow job* is that?"
>
> You know, I must say, though, 50 years later, tonight I'm going to sing "Ol' Man River," and Frankie, if you don't mind, I'm gonna do it *my* way.[32]

Frank's interpretation is a far cry from Paul Robeson's prototypical, quasi-operatic version, but "Ol' Man River," by Kern and Hammerstein, was a song written by two white men to be performed by their *image* of a black man; and for the film, the composers wanted Frank in the role. Kern said, "My idea with that song was to have a rabbitty little fellow do it—somebody who made you believe he was tired of livin' and scared of dyin'."[33]

When referring to this scene, Charles and others have taken it out of context: Frank's excerpt from *Till the Clouds Roll By* is not an isolated scene, but the climactic element in a lengthy production number set in a dreamy, heavenly white atmosphere among the clouds (reflecting the film's title). MGM's tribute to Kern paints him as a near-angelic talent who contributed much to American culture, the sort of whitewashed "biography" that classic Hollywood gave to composers (Cary Grant's fictitious turn as Cole Porter in *Night and Day* [1948], for example). Frank's reading of the song is as good as ever, and the viewer, after suffering through a truly grueling film, is able, at the very end, to see him perform one of his most famous long-breath feats. (Early in the film, during a scene depicting excerpts from *Showboat*, an African-American singer performs a much more typical, melodramatic and bombastic version of the song.)

On December 15, Frank recorded a beautiful Stordahl arrangement of Irving Berlin's "Always," but Columbia was dissatisfied. From the same session, three other songs were issued: the bluesy "That's How Much I Love You," with Al Viola on guitar, "You Can Take My Word for It, Baby"; and "I Want to Thank Your Folks," in which he emphasizes the line, "But darling, to be perfectly *frank*, I really have to thank your folks." Two days later, the Voice met the "King" as he teamed with the incomparable Nat Cole and the *Metronome* All Stars for a superb Sy Oliver arrangement of "Sweet Lorraine," which the pianist had been performing with his trio for several years. Giving life to a great saxophone chart were two members of Duke Ellington's band, Johnny Hodges on alto and Harry Carney on baritone. Also in the All Stars were Coleman Hawkins on tenor sax, Charlie Shavers on trumpet, Frank's old Dorsey mate Buddy Rich on drums, and another Ellingtonian, Lawrence Brown, on trombone. Swung by such formidable talent, the song was one of the first to display Frank's more improvisatory jazz side. Three days after Lorraine was sweet, things turned bitter when the Hollywood Women's Press Club voted him "Least Cooperative Star of 1946," due primarily to the stories about his personal conduct that continued to circulate.

Frank enacted another dramatic role on the airwaves, as Lieutenant Joel Scott, for the December 19 *Radio Reader's Digest*. Ordered to report for duty on Christmas Day, Scott managed to get the train to stop in Rockford Junction, Illinois, so he could visit his girl in nearby Belport. Learning that a connecting train didn't run on the holiday, the lieutenant and his girl were picked up by locals and taken to a party, where he sang "Silent Night."

On January 9, 1947, Frank's re-take of "Always" was accepted by Columbia, along with "My Love for You" and Cole Porter's "I Concentrate on You," an exquisite model of dramatic storytelling in song form, his final long-breath note masterfully fading down into the brass and strings.

The following month, Frank planned to vacation with Nancy in Mexico City, but first gave a "command performance" for military personnel in Miami and then layed over in Havana to gamble for two days. There he made the huge mistake of palling around with two Jersey acquaintances, Rocco and Joe Fischetti, who had ties to organized crime. Following a day at the casino and racetrack, Frank was introduced to exiled La Cosa Nostra boss Charles ("Lucky") Luciano in the dining room of the Hotel Nacional, an even bigger faux pas. In fact, a literal convention of mobsters was occurring in Havana at the time, and an entire group of Mafiosi clamored to get the Voice's autograph. Big shots like Frank Costello, Joe Adonis, Willie Moretti and Albert Anastasia were in town—and so was Frank, who was surprised by the turn of events but did not overly concern himself with how his presence at the "convention" would look when he returned to Hollywood. Later, Luciano, who liked to boast about his "association" with famous Italian entertainers (he even wanted Dean Martin to play him in a biopic he supposedly had written), spread rumors that the Mafia had put up money to start Frank's solo career.

In any event, journalists crucified him when his trifle in Havana was discovered. Zealous reporters began to search for possible connections between Frank and the Mob, any inconsequential or trivial meeting, introduction or chance encounter during childhood, at a nightclub while performing, or in Hollywood. Anxious to prove he was a mobster *and* a Communist, they feverishly searched for "facts" to fit their conclusions. In a March 14, 1947, letter to conservative columnist Westbrook Pegler, Robert C. Ruark of the Scripps-Howard Newspapers syndicate wrote:

> Nice to hear from you, and I'm glad you concur on Frankie boy. In the last day or so, I have turned up a surprising number of sins in the dear fellow's cloistered background... My stuff...will show a definite tie-up with the fact that he is still being cut by an Italian named Morietti [sic]... a proven hoodlum, a former associate of Luciano's, and a current employee of our Mr. Frank Costello...
>
> I got a guy over in Jersey stirring up some evidence in a quashed charge of either rape, adultery, seduction, or a combination of all three, and I'm running down to Miami myself to try to document the fact that we both know—that the soupspoon spent a week with the freres Frischetti...
>
> My tiny feet are pattering down to the ever-loving Selective Service Board #180, which, the FBI tells me, will reveal that Mr. Sinatra was willing to brand himself as a psycho-neurotic in order to escape the fate to which I and some million other American [sic] were subjected... please keep Larry Larrea and the Hotel Nacional out of the mess. Larry is a hell of a nice guy, and he was very helpful to me while I was down there, and he asked me if it were possible to keep him and the Nacional as far away from the odor as I could.
>
> As I said before, I'll ring you when I get the mess nailed down sufficiently to clear my skirts of any possible libel. If you have any astounding truths on the charming young man that I don't, we can hosstrade.[34]

Here, Ruark proves that agents of the press were concerned, not with reporting the news, but with going to any lengths to nail Frank, as long as they and their informants were kept clean. According to Ruark, it was fine to conduct a smear campaign against Sinatra, but not acceptable to drag Larry Larrea, who provided accommodations for the Mob convention, into the "mess." Of the entire incident, Frank later admitted, "It was one of the dumbest things I ever did."[35] He also elaborated:

> Did I know those guys? Sure, I knew some of those guys. I spent a lot of time working in saloons. And saloons are not run by the Christian Brothers. There were a lot of guys around, and they came out of Prohibition, and they ran pretty good saloons. I was a kid. I worked in the places that were open. They paid you, and the checks didn't bounce. I didn't meet any Nobel Prize winners in saloons. But if Francis of Assisi was a singer and worked in saloons, he would've met the same guys. That doesn't make him part of something. They said hello, you said hello. They came backstage. They thanked you. You offered them a drink. That was it. And it doesn't matter anymore, does it? Most of the guys I knew, or met, are dead.[36]

Many years later, Tony Bennett, recalling a similar career, admitted:

> In those days, there wasn't a business or industry that wasn't connected one way or another with the underworld or nightclubs that were run by unsavory characters. It was understood by everyone in the business that if you wanted to play the big clubs, if you really wanted to make it, sooner or later you'd run into one of these guys. There was nothing you could

do to avoid it. The underworld also ran the jukebox operations across the country, and it's no secret that they built Las Vegas.[37]

While Robert Ruark was planning his journalistic assault, Frank was back in the recording studio on March 11, cutting "Ain'tcha Ever Comin' Back," "Stella By Starlight" and a heart-breaking "Mam'selle" (written for *The Razor's Edge* by director Edmund Goulding), which hit number one that spring. *It Happened in Brooklyn*—a quasi-realistic musical-comedy that was a product of the "coming home" genre of the postwar years—was released on the same day Ruark outlined his scheme for Pegler. Opening "Somewhere in England," the film introduces Frank as the "wounded" Danny Webson Miller, who sulks in his room, his head wrapped in a bandage, as other homeward-bound G.I.s enjoy music and dancing downstairs. In fact, Danny is such a wallflower that he tries to avoid girls entirely; for he is really in love with his hometown, and carries a picture of the Brooklyn Bridge to prove it. When a beautiful young, blonde nurse (Gloria Grahame) tells him that his stand-offish attitude belies his Brooklyn roots, he is forced to join the soiree, where he meets Jamie Shellgrove (Peter Lawford), a handsome but stodgy English "square" whose grandfather (Aubrey Mather) is trying desperately to inject some enthusiasm (particularly involving women) into his life. Since Jamie is a talented musician, Danny befriends him, telling his grandfather (who, it turns out, is actually the wealthy Duke of Dunstable) that he will receive proper tutoring if ever visiting Brooklyn.

Returning Stateside, Danny is awestruck to find himself again standing face-to-face with the landmark he has dreamed about since he shipped out. Filmed on location, this scene, showing Frank singing Styne and Cahn's "Brooklyn Bridge," is a superb blend of musical performance and urban realism. Danny is alone on the bridge, sharing a truly intimate moment with his "girl-friend," while vehicles pass beneath, receding into the background of the shot. The sequence is paced and edited beautifully, with the song opening at one end of the bridge and closing at the other. Delightfully atmospheric, it is a memorable piece of postwar cinema that predates Gene Kelly and Stanley Donen's use of New York locations in *On the Town* by two years. (The crew and equipment were transported to Brooklyn in several railroad cars, and Frank masterfully lip-synched the vocal to a pre-recorded track.)

Now a civilian, Danny is required to re-register for the draft, which he plans to do at New Utrecht, his old high school. Given a lift by pretty Anne Fielding (Kathryn Grayson), he later discovers that she is the school's current music teacher. He also runs into Nick Lombardi (Jimmy Durante), a veteran janitor who lives in an apartment just off the school's gymnasium. Except for a high-pitched voice tick that he occasionally incorporates, Durante is less stylized and more subdued here than in his earlier films, and he proves a good partner for Frank, both seriocomically and musically. Their rhythmic teaming (with young singer-dancer Bobby Long) on Styne and Cahn's "I Believe" is a treat, as is their duet on "The Song's Gotta Come from the Heart" when Danny applies for a job as a sheet-music peddler. The latter number includes Frank and Jimmy singing in Russian, as well as the Voice doing a Durante impression. ("You can sing as well as Bing," Jimmy growls to him at one point.)

"Time After Time," perhaps the best song written for Frank by Styne and Cahn up to that point, is heard in various arrangements. The first version (recorded in seven takes on September 17, 1946) is the most intimate, featuring Danny at the piano in Nick's apartment, singing the words he has married to music by Jamie. The aspiring songwriter, who tells Nick that he "freezes up" when singing for strangers, then gets up to wash the dishes. Later, Danny asks Anne to sing it to Jamie as he plays the piano, thereby contributing to his friend's enamorment with the girl he assumes is his own squeeze.

Frank's other songs include "It's the Same Old Dream," which he performs as a light swing ballad as Danny attempts to interest a music-store gathering of young people, who then swing it in four-part harmony, big-band style. Taken aback by their insensitive performance of the material, Danny finally croons it as a romantic ballad, backed by the harmony of the "kids" (actually

the Starlighters) as surrounding young females squeal in bobbysoxer style. But his duet with Grayson is the film's most unusual number: While in an Italian restaurant, Danny joins Anne in a performance of "La Ci Darem La Mano" from W. A. Mozart and Lorenzo Da Ponte's *Don Giovanni*, an integration of opera and pop styles that *Variety*'s "Stal" considered "amusing."[38]

Other classical material is performed by the ever-exquisite Grayson, in her obligatory operatic fantasy sequence, singing "Lakme," accompanied (on the soundtrack) by Andre Previn, whose

The Actor, on Screen and in Song

"He came to Brooklyn to 'get hep'. Let's show him how it's done!"

Peter Lawford, Sinatra and Jimmy Durante

piano solos are mimed by young Billy Roy, who plays Leo Kardos, a penniless prodigy awarded a five-year scholarship after Danny, Jamie, Nick and Anne organize a concert on his behalf. The only musical scene that director Richard Whorf could have left in the cutting room features a performance of "Whose Baby Are You?" a stiff boogie-woogie number ludicrously sung and hoofed to by *Peter Lawford*. Although Jamie ultimately gets the girl, Danny's attempts to loosen him up with Brooklyn pluck obviously have not paid off as well as the Duke had hoped!

As in *Anchors Aweigh*, Frank is thoroughly believable as a wholesome and naive young serviceman, but Danny is a better developed character than his earlier Clarence Doolittle. Here, he not only becomes interested in girls but also sincerely seeks employment, helps his friends and does charitable work for the son of an impoverished immigrant. His concern for Jamie is such that he actually forgets his feelings for Anne after realizing they are really in love (instead, he vows to find his fellow Brooklynite, the lovely blonde nurse he met in England). Simply put, MGM was doing its job in creating a positive cinematic image for Frank, one that perhaps would go some way in balancing the trouble he seemed to attract outside the studio.

Though *Brooklyn* presented fewer opportunities for physical comedy than did *Anchors Aweigh*, Frank again worked in some (less noticeable) Stan Laurel mannerisms, including the "collar grab" and a hilarious dance-floor maneuver. In its promotional trailer, MGM billed Frank and Kathryn Grayson as "the Singing Sweethearts from *Anchors Aweigh*," but, as in the previous film, they don't end up together.

Most major publications published enthusiastic reviews, noting that Frank improved with every cinematic outing. *Variety* of course focused on his appeal at the box office:

> Much of the mure will result from Sinatra's presence in the cast and the
> Voice presumably exerts as much pull now as he ever did... he emerges in

this one as a smooth, confident thesper. Guy's acquired the Crosby knack of nonchalance, throwing away his gag lines with fine aplomb.[39]

In his *PM* critique, John McManus wrote, "Sinatra seems to have loosened up and got into the swing of things as a film player and even as a comedian. Things look promising for Frankie-boy in films even if his wooing notes should one day peter out."[40] And *The Los Angeles Examiner*'s Sara Hamilton echoed the opinion that the quality of his acting was catching up to his musical prowess: "Frank... thrills the customers with his vocalizing, but it's his naturalness and easy-going charm that begets applause. It just seems like all of a sudden it's spring and Frankie is an actor."[41] Even Bosley Crowther, warming up a bit more since *Anchors Aweigh*, half-praised Frank this time, though he considered the film a "capricious assortment," a "hodgepodge":

> Maybe you won't believe this... but Mr. Sinatra turns in a performance of considerable charm. He acts with some ease and dexterity, he speaks as though he's thought of what he says and sings without too much suggestion of having a stomach-ache. ...[he] appears in one scene, arising from his bed in a nightshirt, and no one in the audience passed away. Two years ago, such desecration of his glamour would have been hooted from the screen. It looks as though Mr. Sinatra — and "the kids" are growing up.[42]

Crowther's New York colleague, Lee Mortimer, in the *Daily Mirror*, did the opposite, lauding the film but predictably maligning the performer: "This excellent and well-produced picture... bogs down under the miscast Frank (Lucky) Sinatra, smirking and trying to play a leading man."[43] Only a true axe-grinder could write such an erroneous review: Frank is not miscast, nor does he smirk at any time in the film; his character is not a "leading man," but part of an ensemble cast; and assigning him the nickname of a notorious gangster is outrageous.

On October 9, Frank was declared "Most Popular Film Star of 1946" by *Modern Screen* magazine. On *Songs By Sinatra*, Louis B. Mayer, accompanied by the screams of a bobbysox horde, said to the Voice:

> [T]he honor bestowed last year on Van Johnson. ...The award is this bronze bust of yourself done by the great American sculptor Joe Davidson, the artist who has sculpted Franklin Roosevelt, Madame Chaing Kai-Shek, Premier Clemenceau and other famous people. ...You can be proud, Frank, as proud as we are of you. Remember, we at MGM can only choose the personalities to present to the public, and they let us know whether or not we have chosen wisely. It is the fans who make the stars. And such a tribute as this voted by them is an honor indeed.

Two weeks later, Frank recorded four of the Styne-Cahn *It Happened in Brooklyn* songs for Columbia release. The ballads "Time After Time" and "It's the Same Old Dream" were followed by the swingers "The Brooklyn Bridge" and "I Believe" a week later. Gliding above Stordahl's medium swing tempo, Frank delivers "Brooklyn" with such confidence that the listener might be persuaded to buy the bridge from him. The latter session also yielded a formidably swinging novelty song, "I Got a Gal I Love (in North and South Dakota)."

On March 27, 1947, two weeks after *Brooklyn*'s release, Frank played the San Francisco Paramount, joining Bob Hope and Jack Benny to raise money for the Damon Runyon Cancer Fund. Four days later, he cut two Lerner and Loewe songs from *Brigadoon*, "There But for You Go I" and "Almost Like Being in Love." Ending the latter, (perhaps referring to Ava Gardner) he states, "In fact, I *have* fallen in love."

By this time, the FBI, who investigated any entertainer accused of having "Communist connections," was keeping its eye on Frank, and this surveillance was compounded by Lee Mortimer who continued to gather any rumors, half-truths and innuendoes he could find, repeatedly lambasting "Frankie" in the *Daily Mirror.* All of this upset Frank, who mentioned to George Evans that he eventually would get back at the reporter.

At midnight on Tuesday, April 8, 1947, while dining at Ciro's in Hollywood, Frank accidentally ran into Mortimer and punched him out. Arrested and released on $500 bail, Frank claimed that he had retaliated for being called "a little dago bastard," which Mortimer denied. The following day, the editors of all Hearst newspapers were sent an official "roundup" of the criticisms Mortimer had made of Frank since 1944. The press release referred to the reporter's status as a former G.I., describing him as "breezy," "witty" and "pungent," while Frank was a 4-F "bobby-sox swoonmaster," a "leftist," "Communist" and "Red Fascist."[43] Red Fascist?

An Associated Press article sensationalized the Ciro's incident as "a midnight flurry of fisticuffs on fashionable Sunset Strip" during which Mortimer, jumped by four men, saw "a face that looked like Sinatra's above me."[45] On April 14, two syndicated articles appeared in newspapers across the nation: one reporting that Frank, during a New York ceremony, had received the Jefferson Prize from the Council Against Intolerance in America for his "outstanding interpretation to America for the need for fair play for all races and religions"; and another mentioning his Havana hobnobbing with the Fischettis and the loss of his gun permit after the Mortimer incident.[46]

Meanwhile, Mortimer met with Clyde Tolson, J. Edgar Hoover's closest associate at the FBI, to learn what the bureau had compiled on Frank. Though Tolson reported to Hoover that "we could not be of any official assistance to him," they had engaged in a lengthy discussion during which the reporter asked about the Cuban trip, the 1938 Bergen County, New Jersey, "seduction" incident and several Sinatra acquaintances who had ties to the Mob.[47] Mortimer left with some "unofficial" dirt—and subsequently would pass on to Tolson any further information he could drum up on Frank.

On April 21, Frank costarred with Bob Hope and Lucille Ball in "Too Many Husbands" on *The Lady Esther Screen Guild Players.* Hope ad-libbed throughout, and Frank sang "Time After Time." Four days later, he again was paired with Dinah Shore in the recording studio, this time to cut "Tea for Two" and Rodgers and Hart's "My Romance," during which, backed by a chorus and Stordahl's orchestra, they harmonize in rhythmic perfection.

The following day, in his syndicated column "As Pegler Sees It," Westbrook Pegler began another campaign with the piece "Discusses Sinatra's Brawl With Newsman." Rather than outlining the events that transpired at Ciro's, Pegler attacked Frank personally, focusing on his wartime activities, though never mentioning that he officially had been declared 4-F (as had Ronald Reagan and John Wayne):

> Mortimer was a soldier in the war. Sinatra, though robust, active and pugnacious, ill-tempered, intemperate and profane, was a vicarious though ferocious warrior against the Nazi like Charlie Chaplin. ...Other young men, slightly maimed or blind in one eye, managed to get into the war. Some who couldn't get into the armed services went to sea as merchant sailors or joined the American field service. Some joined foreign armies.[48]

Pegler didn't mention Frank's numerous charitable contributions to the USO, AFRS and V-Disc programs, all of which benefited servicemen. He did, however, malign him further by mentioning an upcoming film project, which eventually became RKO's *The Miracle of the Bells*:

> Plans are currently afoot to present Sinatra in a moving picture in the role of an idealistic priest. Of course, this would be only make believe, but the public has an emotional tendency to endow eminent ham-fats with the virtues of the characters which they portray. In recognition of this tendency, Sinatra and the movie industry might more honestly dramatize his own life as it is lived and his influence on the cult of the bobby-sox.[49]

Columnists often demonstrate nothing more than egotism by setting themselves up as the arbiters of knowledge, taste and morality. Here, Pegler not only shows his contempt for Frank but patronizingly proves that he regarded the American public in much the same way. How could a person be so concerned about America and hold its citizens in such disregard?

In May, Frank played New York's Capitol Theater for the first time since his 1935 gigs with Major Bowes. For his opening act, he passed on the Nicholas Brothers, asking manager Sidney Fairmont to hire another dance group, the Will Mastin Trio, whose youngest member was Sammy Davis, Jr., an amazing hoofer who first had met Frank several years earlier at a Tommy Dorsey concert. Becoming reacquainted with his idol, Sammy revealed that he, proudly wearing his Army uniform, had attended several of the Voice's radio shows during the war. Later, Davis admitted, "Frank was giving us twelve-hundred and fifty dollars a week! We had never seen that much money in our lives."[50]

During the late spring and summer, Frank led "The Swooners," a softball team that challenged other celebrity outfits to weekend games at Hollywood Bowl Field and Gilmore Stadium. Joined by Hank Sanicola, Sammy Cahn, Jule Styne, Anthony Quinn, Barry Sullivan and others, he played second base and was spurred on by a group of starlet cheerleaders: Virginia Mayo, Marilyn Maxwell, Shelley Winters and Ava Gardner, whose siren spell he quickly fell under (in fact, prior to meeting her, he had waxed romantically over her picture on a magazine cover).

Faced with a June 3 trial date in the Mortimer affair, Frank, admitting that the journalist had not actually provoked him at Ciro's, settled out of court for $9,000, far short of the $25,000 Mortimer originally wanted. But with his legal fees added, the punch cost Frank about $20,000. Many years later, he said, "I actually only had one physical bout in my lifetime with anybody in the press. That was Lee Mortimer, and if he [were] alive today, I'd knock him down again." Pete Hamill notes:

> In almost four decades in the newspaper business, I have never met anybody who liked or respected Lee Mortimer; he was a nasty, mean man, a poor reporter, a worse writer and the king of the "blind item." But it was a critical mistake to belt him. Newspaper people who despised Mortimer suddenly started getting much tougher about Frank Sinatra; as contemptible as Mortimer was, he was part of their Guild, not Sinatra's.[51]

The day after the affair was settled, the final installment of *The Frank Sinatra Show* was broadcast on CBS. Soon after, Frank headed north for Sonora Township to shoot location scenes for his next MGM musical-comedy, the thoroughly absurd *The Kissing Bandit* costarring Kathryn Grayson and J. Carrol Naish. This time around, rather than being forced to learn dancing skills, Frank had to look convincing in Western-adventure action scenes, handling weapons and performing derring-do aboard stagecoaches while speeding through Sonora's Stanislaus National Forest. Shedding his comic-operetta outfit back in Los Angeles, Frank briefly visited Yuletide in July when, on the day before his nation's nativity, he recorded unique, extremely melancholy renditions of "Christmas Dreaming (A Little Early This Year)" and "Have Yourself A Merry Little Christmas," which Judy Garland had debuted in *Meet Me in St. Louis* (1944).

On August 5, *Look* magazine published a feature titled "What Will Sinatra Do Next?" by E. J. Kahn, Jr., author of the book *The Voice: The Story of an American Phenomenon*. Outlining Frank's recent "range of activities," Kahn outlined the events leading up to the Ciro's brawl:

> Mortimer had been heckling Sinatra for quite a while in his columns. Sinatra on his part had indicated a readiness to take direct action in retaliation for the journalist's severely critical remarks. The columnist's comments had hit at Frankie's singing, at his non-singing activities and at the general intelligence level of his fans, which Mortimer had appraised as moronic.

Then the two ran into each other in a Hollywood night club and Mortimer took it on the chin.[52]

Kahn also noted the number of journalists and broadcasters who were pro-Sinatra, including Ed Sullivan, Jimmy Fidler and Walter Winchell (who accentuated the positive about Frank but covertly provided information to the FBI). And one of his observations put a common-sense perspective on the Lucky Luciano meeting:

> A few progressive friends of [Sinatra's] made much of a photograph taken at a Hollywood party not long ago. It showed Sinatra in a seemingly amiable pow-wow with that eminent spokesman of the right—Colonel Robert R. McCormick, publisher of *The Chicago Tribune*. But, to judge by Sinatra's past performances, this brief encounter can hardly be taken as meaning Sinatra approves of McCormick. There seems to be no more reason for taking his brief encounter with Luciano as showing his approval of the gangster.[53]

On August 1, Frank "pinch hit" for the vacationing host on *The Bill Stern Sports Newsreel*, featuring Dwight Eisenhower's baseball career, President Truman's stretch as an umpire, John L. Sullivan, and a Frenchman who was executed by the Nazis for playing the great American pastime. He returned to the recording studio on August 11 to cut "That Old Feeling," "The Nearness of You" and his first version of Harold Arlen and Johnny Mercer's "One for My Baby (And One More for the Road)," the ultimate saloon song, to which he would return time and again. Here, it is a bit sprightlier than his legendary 1958 "suicide" rendition on *Frank Sinatra Sings for Only the Lonely*. The following week, he waxed "A Fellow Needs a Girl," "So Far" and Johnny Burke and Jimmy Van Heusen's "But Beautiful," which Will Friedwald calls "quintessential Sinatra, who expresses mountains of emotion without so much as even raising or lowering his voice."[54]

Having finished *The Kissing Bandit* at MGM, Frank was back at RKO, making *The Miracle of the Bells* on August 19. Executives at both studios were concerned about his image: As a form of "discipline," Louis B. Mayer agreed to loan him out; while RKO's Jesse Lasky and Walter MacEwen, as well as George Evans, believed that the role of Father Paul would cast him in a positive, Crosby-like light (although Frank would perform only one song in the film). Before production began, Lasky met with representatives of the Catholic Church, both to ensure their approval of Frank as the priest and offer the subsequent donation of his $100,000 salary to the church. In late August, *Screen Album* magazine published an "update" on Frank's career, identifying him as "No. One Target for all the yellow journals in the country," listing the "slanders" involving his 4-F status, the Mortimer incident, his "underworld" connections and Communism before noting his recent accomplishments:

> They've accused Frank of nearly everything but beating Frank, Jr., with a horse whip. But maybe they're saving that one for next time Frank stumps around the country talking his guts out for some worthwhile American cause. No, we're not whitewashing Frankie. Sure, he shouldn't have taken a poke at that columnist—and he admitted it. Sure, he shook hands with Lucky Luciano. So did a lot of respectable citizens. People in show business meet a lot of undesirable characters. It's part of the game. The trouble with Frankie is, he'll never stop doing what he thinks is right. He made a short called *The House I Live In*, turned all the proceeds over to charity and won an Oscar. Most guys would stop there. Not Frank. As soon as he's finished making *The Kissing Bandit*, he'll play Father Paul

in *The Miracle of the Bells*—and once again every cent he earns will be turned over to a worthy charity. He was the only performer, too, who contributed his talents to all three of the major Damon Runyon Cancer Fund shows—in Los Angeles, San Francisco and Miami. We're not surprised that the members of his 5,000 fan clubs have agreed to boycott the newspapers that attacked Frank so maliciously. They may miss their favorite comics, but at least it'll keep their minds clean of gutter journalism.[55]

On September 1, Mortimer, writing from his office at the *New York Mirror*, sent a copy of the article to Pegler, arming him for another round of Sinatra-bashing:

Jack Lait suggested I send you the enclosure. It is from the Fall 1947 issue of *Screen Album*, a Dell Publication. Jack says there is a concerted campaign to whitewash Sinatra for the priest role in *Miracle of the Bells*. Sinatra completes his assignment in it next week, and it will be released shortly. Jack believes money may have been passed for some of these sickening fan mag blurbs; similar ones are appearing in many other publications.

This one goes pretty far—talking about a boycott and "gutter journalism."[56]

The letter is signed, "Faithfully, Lee Mortimer." The $9,000 settlement paid by Frank apparently had not settled the reporter for long.

While shooting *The Miracle of the Bells*, Frank was visited by an old pal, George ("Bullets") Durgom, who had brought his European mother to meet the Voice. But when the pious woman, having no knowledge of American popular culture, knelt down to kiss his ring, Frank resumed his "Father Paul" persona to avoid embarrassing her.[57] *Miracle* was the first of his films that didn't require him to cut studio recordings for the soundtrack; directly for the camera on August 19 and 20, he performed an a cappella rendition of Styne and Cahn's "Ever Homeward."

On September 6, Frank resumed his appearances on NBC's *Your Hit Parade*, this time costarring with the incomparable Doris Day, who proved an excellent female match for the Voice. Frank said, "She has something wonderful about her style. It kind of bubbles. I love working with her."[58] Maintaining a relentless schedule of recording, broadcast and film work, he returned to Columbia on the 9th to cut a bizarre bar-mitzvah-style version of "It All Came True" with Alvy West and the Little Band.

Beginning another wholehearted smear campaign, Westbrook Pegler, in his September 10 column, wrote, "A campaign of propaganda has been running in some areas of our press, including magazines, and on the radio, to rehabilitate the reputation of Frank Sinatra."[59] Had Pegler and cronies like Mortimer actually destroyed Frank's reputation so thoroughly that it had to be "rehabilitated"? Rehashing the same tired material, Pegler then criticized those who had been level-headed or positive about Frank, including Kahn and Sullivan, whom he said, "impugned the professional integrity of legitimate journalists."[60] The next day, "Peg" was at it again, reviling "Frankie And Some of His Pals" by calling Kahn names, dredging up the "sexual offense" of 1938 for which Frank had been cleared, and blaming the "Far Left" for the Voice's popularity. (First, his success was due to the Mob, then morons and now Communists.) Not surprisingly, the column ended with the endorsement, "Read another forceful, *factual* [author's italics] article of significant comment from the pen of Westbrook Pegler in Saturday's *Journal-American*."[61]

But most Americans who appreciated Frank's talents were not affected by the viewpoints of newspaper columnists. In fact, an ABC radio poll conducted during 1947 named him Second Most Popular Living Person, falling between Bing Crosby and Pope Pius XII on the list. Though the FBI made numerous attempts to connect Frank with the Communist Party, J. Edgar Hoover, in an official memo, finally concluded that "the investigation failed to substantiate any such allegation."[62] As stated by Tom and Phil Kuntz, editors of *The Sinatra Files: The Secret FBI Dossier*, "In the end [the bureau] had nothing on him but the ordinary activities of a liberal celebrity."[63]

In New York on October 19, 1947, Frank began a series of five Columbia recording dates, cutting Styne and Cahn's "Can't You Just See Yourself?" and "You're My Girl," and a laid-back but kicking swing version of "All of Me" featuring improvisation he would use again (on the 1954 Capitol album *Swing Easy!*): "All of me! Why not take *all* of me? You know, I'm *just a mess* without you!" From October 22-29, he waxed 15 songs, including the ethereal "Laura," a new arrangement of "Night and Day" (which was not issued), "The Night We Called It a Day," yet another version of "The Song Is You" and an unforgettable "None But the Lonely Heart," showcasing his incomparable dynamic range, moving from high emotion to a whisper at the conclusion (a quality that was becoming a Sinatra trademark). The session on the 29th also produced an exquisite version of "The Music Stopped," which he had sung in *Higher and Higher* but only in a cappella form on disc, and a Nacio Herb Brown-Edward Heyman song from *The Kissing Bandit*, "(I Offer You the Moon) Senorita."

On October 30, accompanied by Dolly, Marty and Nancy, Sr., he received the key to the city of Hoboken, where "Sinatra Day" was announced by the mayor and chief of police, before returning to New York for six more recording sessions and another series of dates at the Capitol. He cut "Mean to Me," "Fools Rush In (Where Angels Fear to Tread)" and Rodgers and Hart's "Spring Is Here" on Halloween, and began his November efforts with gorgeous readings of Rodgers and Hart's "It Never Entered My Mind" (another song from *Higher and Higher*) and the Gershwins' "I've Got a Crush on You," featuring trumpet solos by Louis Armstrong disciple Bobby Hackett, on the 5th. Hackett joined him again on the 9th for an exquisite "Body and Soul" before he opened at the Capitol four days later.

From November 13 through December 3, Frank maintained a grueling schedule, sometimes performing eight shows a day. On November 25, he needlessly returned to the studio to record two of the worst songs he ever sang, the contemporary swinger "I Went Down to Virginia" and the perfectly dreadful "If I Only Had a Match," which, at only 3:10, is harder to sit through than *The Kissing Bandit*! The day after he closed at the Capitol, he cut another song from that film, "If I Steal a Kiss," as well as his first versions of perhaps the best song ever written about the Big Apple, "Autumn in New York," and a romantic ballad, "Everybody Loves Somebody," which later was transformed into boozy kitsch by Dean Martin. On December 8, he waxed a curious pair of songs, a fully orchestrated version of the *Miracle of the Bells* number "Ever Homeward," which Styne and Cahn had based on a Polish folk melody by Kasimierez Lubomirski, and a two-part comedy-blues song, "A Little Learnin' Is a Dangerous Thing," by Sy Oliver and Dick Jacobs. While he sang in both English and convincing phonetic Polish on the former, he engaged in constant bluesy ad-libbing with Pearl Bailey on the latter. Thought to be the first interracial duet released on a commercial record, "A Little Learnin'" was also little known among Sinatra fans: Many shop owners refused to stock it.

And the witch-hunters out to burn Frank at the stake did not give up easily. On December 10, Westbrook Pegler still was browbeating him for not serving in the military, campaigning for Roosevelt and palling around with another leftist slacker, Orson Welles—though his "seditious" activities actually involved singing for a group of sick children at a Los Angeles hospital on Christmas Day.[64]

The following afternoon Frank was back at Columbia's Hollywood studio, where only a pair of songs were recorded; but two days later, he cut a total of seven, four of which were Yuletide favorites, though there was no potential to release them at that time of year. The same day, he performed "Great Day" and "You'll Never Walk Alone" with Stordahl to plug U.S. Savings Bonds on radio's *Guest Star*. On the 29th, he costarred with Gene Kelly and Kathryn Grayson in an abridged *Anchors Aweigh* on the *Lux Radio Theater* program, during which *The Kissing Bandit* was plugged. On the penultimate day of 1947, he waxed

three more songs before taking an enforced recording respite that would last nearly three months. The American Federation of Musicians again had called for a recording ban, effective at midnight on New Year's Eve.

In February 1948, Frank, while performing at the Copacabana in New York, became actively engaged in politics, and this time involving foreign affairs. After meeting Teddy Kollek, a leading figure in the Israeli independence movement, who had established a Haganah headquarters above the Copa at Hotel 14, he agreed to act as a courier of arms money between the hotel and the Manhattan docks, thereby beginning a lifelong support of Jewish causes. "It was the beginning of that young nation," Frank later told Nancy, Jr. "I wanted to help. I was afraid it might fall down."[65]

With the AFM ban still in effect, Frank could not record with live musicians, but Columbia had a trick up its corporate sleeve. On December 8, 1947—three weeks before the ban was enacted—orchestral arrangements, sans vocals, of two Irving Berlin songs from *Easter Parade* had been recorded. (A little more than a week earlier, the company had experimented with the possibilities of multi-tracking during a session with Dinah Shore.) So, on March 16, 1948, Frank sidestepped the ban, tracking his voice over the instrumentals for "It Only Happens When I Dance with You" and "A Fella with an Umbrella," on which he swings as effortlessly as he would have with a live band. He also was to have provided a vocal for the main theme from *The Miracle of the Bells*, but declined. Will Friedwald observes, "With a typical concern for what was quality rather than what would help him most, Sinatra elected to dub on the vocal part only to the two Irving Berlin songs and skip the tune intended to plug one of his own pictures."[66]

Frank plugged *Miracle* during a March 18 radio spot in which he returned to *House I Live In* ground, blending wartime patriotism with religious tolerance. Philadelphia's Chapel of the Four Chaplains was the focus of a contest presenting listeners the following challenge: "We had religious unity during the war, but how can we maintain it during the peace?" Representatives

Sinatra, Alida Valli and Fred MacMurray in *The Miracle of the Bells*

of the Jewish, Protestant and Catholic faiths chose 100 winners to meet the stars at Jesse Lasky's premiere of the film in KYW radio's auditorium.

During the celebration of another "Sinatra Day" a week later, Frank served as guest DJ on New York's WINS radio, helping to spin 24 continuous hours of his music. Two days later, *The Miracle of the Bells* was released nationwide. One of the strangest films ever to emerge from golden-age Hollywood (Frank reportedly called it "a silly picture"[67]), it is an uneasy hybrid of the styles of Frank Capra and Billy Wilder, featuring a quasi-religious story and *Double Indemnity*-like noir narration by Fred MacMurray

Predating the moribund beginning of Wilder's *Sunset Boulevard* (1950), the film opens with a close-up of a sign on an undertaker's van: "Nick Orloff, Funeral Director." As Bill Dunnigan's (MacMurray) voice-over recollections begin, he identifies himself as a Hollywood talent agent and a coffin in the back as containing the corpse of a young actress, Olga Treskovna (Alida Valli), who is being returned for burial in Coaltown, Pennsylvania. Unable to do so when she was alive, he admits to himself (and presumably to her spirit) that he loves her. Essentially reprising his *Double Indemnity* (1944) characterization, MacMurray is more sympathetic here, a hard-boiled hero who eventually overcomes emotional obstacles and, aided by Father Paul, makes a difference in the lives of others by waging a four-day church bell-ringing campaign to induce Marcus Harris (Lee J. Cobb), a Hollywood producer, to release *Joan of Arc*, Olga's only completed film. During the flashback sequences, in which he recounts his experiences with Olga, the actor refers to his companion as "baby," just as he had for Barbara Stanwyck in the earlier film.

Though the Capra-esque plot is bizarre and often outlandish, the mood created by director Irving Pichel and RKO house cinematographer Robert de Grasse, and the performances of MacMurray and Valli compensate. The message of the film is spiritual rather than religious, with Ben Hecht and Quentin Reynolds' screenplay providing an admirable balance between supernatural and secular beliefs. Well-played by Frank in a humble and quiet manner, Father Paul is a rational and cool-headed man who refuses to lead the parishioners of St. Michael's with blind dogma. Late in the film, when a crack in the ground caused by mine tunnels shifts the foundation of the church, making two stone statues "look" toward Olga's coffin, he speaks to the congregation, focusing on the "miracle" wrought by Olga's return to Coalville (the coming together of the previously schismatic populace), rather than a "supernatural" occurrence. (Reflecting the quality of the dialogue undoubtedly written by Hecht, Harris, finally persuaded to release *Joan of Arc*, tells his assistant, "Do you think that for one moment, that *God* is interested in selling pictures for me?")

Despite the cacophony wrought by five churches incessantly ringing bells, *Miracle* is a very quiet film, its somewhat disjointed parts held together by MacMurray's atmospheric narration and intense yet relaxed acting style. (Somehow this man, once the highest-paid performer in Hollywood, combined the styles of Clark Gable and Henry Fonda!). A sequence in which Olga "auditions" for Bill as Joan of Arc is a visual and dramatic highlight, featuring stylized chiaroscuro lighting and a medieval setting as the two characters work out the scene. Mentioning St. Michael, she provides a spiritual link between Joan, the saint and Father Paul. Valli's death scene as Joan of Arc also has an otherworldly, dreamlike quality, as the smoke from the consuming flames wafts around her sublime face. (Olga, diagnosed with tuberculosis, passes away the morning after the scene is shot.) The spiritual component of the film is introduced in an earlier, intimate scene in which Bill and Olga accidentally meet "in the heart of Iowa," where they are treated to a splendid meal by Ming Gow (Philip Ahn), the kind owner of a Chinese restaurant.

Frank nearly whispers his role, and, despite the barbs of journalists who were outraged at the very thought of the bad boy playing a man of the cloth, created a completely convincing Paul. His a cappella reading of "Ever Homeward" is another high point, performed as Paul and Bill visit the graveyard high on a hill above St. Michael's and Coaltown.

Variety's "Brog" was impressed with every aspect of the film:

> The Miracle of the Bells comes to the screen as a tremendously moving drama. Told with compelling simplicity and great heart, it will rate audience acclaim... Jesse L. Lasky and Walter MacEwen have strung their production on a chord of simplicity that registers with the widest appeal. The characters, locale and theme ring true. ...Sinatra, the poor priest, is outstanding. It's a human, thoughtful portrayal. ...Leigh Harline's musical score... is an ace job... other credits are equally outstanding in measuring this one for attention.[68]

While some publications, such as *Photoplay*, noted that filmgoers, before seeing the film, might suspect that Frank had aped Crosby's *Going My Way* character, none could accuse him of it after leaving the theater. In his *Los Angeles Times* review, Philip K. Scheuer noticed the naturalistic approach that Frank immediately brought to his first dramatic role: "Sinatra wisely doesn't attempt to 'act' at all. His portrayal has the virtue of simplicity."[69] But Frank was disappointed, echoing *The New York Times*' Bosley Crowther by admitting that the film "turned out less well than we had hoped."[70]

On April 10, 1948, Frank momentarily reverted to a cappella recording, an atmospheric version of "Nature Boy" cut a week before Nat Cole's definitive, haunting version was released. Guesting on *The Jack Benny Program* eight days later, he joined producer Samuel Goldwyn and silent star Charlie Farrell for the comic whodunit "Mystery at the Racket Club." And on May 31, he reprised his Father Paul role, joining MacMurray and Valli for a *Lux Radio Theatre* "Miracle of the Bells." At the end of the broadcast, Frank mentioned having returned from the sold-out Chicago premiere, where the proceeds had been donated to the National Cancer Drive.

Three weeks later, during the evening of June 20, Frank abandoned his guests, the Jule Stynes, and frantically ran a host of red lights as he sped Nancy, Sr. to Cedars of Lebanon Hospital, where their third child, Christina ("Tina") was born. A local radio station announced, "Frank Sinatra got a terrific Fathers' Day Present today—a brand new baby girl."[71]

The Colgate Sports Newsreel "with Frank Sinatra pinch-hitting for Bill Stern" on July 9 was the second installment in a month of programs that also featured John Garfield, William Holden and Errol Flynn as "the foremost spinners of sports yarns." Broadcast nearly three years after World War II, this episode uncomfortably had Frank speaking of "Japs" and affecting a "Japanese accent" while telling the tale of how opera singer-movie star Lawrence Tibbett traded in his Navy boxing gloves for a golden voice. He actually stuttered through his narration a few times, (again) covering Dwight Eisenhower's "baseball career" and the writing of the song "Take Me Out to the Ball Game."

Prior to the general release of *The Kissing Bandit* (which Frank perhaps wished would never see the light of day), production began on his next MGM musical, *Take Me Out to the Ball Game*, on July 28, 1948. Two years earlier, MGM had expressed interest in a Sinatra-Kelly follow-up to *Anchors Aweigh*; and after Stanley Donen had completed work on the musical numbers for a Broadway show, *Call Me Mister*, Kelly asked his collaborator to help him write an original story for the film. Joe Pasternak had his own idea for a screenplay, and Kelly thought it was terrible: After demobilization, two ambitious sailors (again) convert a dilapidated aircraft carrier into a floating nightclub. This ridiculous, hoary premise simply would not do, so Kelly and Donen, during a train trip from New York to Hollywood, devised the tale of two professional baseball players who become vaudeville performers during the off-season. At MGM, they accepted $25,000 for their seven-page scenario from Arthur Freed, who hired radio writer George Wells to pen a full-length treatment and Harry Warren and Ralph Blaine to compose the score. Eventually all three would be replaced, with screenwriter Harry Tugend, composer Roger Edens and lyricists Betty Comden and Adolph Green. Although Kelly and Donen, keeping *Anchors Aweigh* in mind, had suggested Kathryn Grayson as the female lead, Freed cast Judy Garland, who in turn was replaced (due to her various marital and substance abuse problems) by Esther Williams. In typical Hollywood fashion, the co-creators, having been paid for their outline, also temporarily lost out on their dream of directing the film: Freed hired Busby Berkeley, but when

Esther Williams, Gene Kelly, Jules Munshin and Frank in *Take Me Out to the Ball Game*

the formerly formidable genius of the Warner Bros. musical quit, Kelly and Donen directed most of the picture themselves. "He didn't know what he was doing," Donen recalled. "He couldn't remember anyone's name."[72] Sadly, Berkeley had been plagued by a number of psychological and alcohol-related illnesses and their related legal problems.

Kelly told Freed he wanted to pair Frank with a real baseball player, Leo Durocher, who would play the role of Shaughnessy: "I've worked out an Irish jig that Sinatra and Durocher will be able to dance and which will carry on the myth of Frankie's dancing ability (and believe me, this will top any of our joint numbers in *Anchors Aweigh*)."[73] Eventually, the Shaughnessy role was rewritten as "Nat Goldberg" for Jules Munshin, and a different song, "O'Brien to Ryan to Goldberg," was penned for Gene, Frank and Jules. Actress Betty Garrett recalled that the Sinatra acting technique again was in evidence on the set: "Frank was quick but hated to rehearse... saying that if he did a scene more than once, he'd get stale."[74] She later said:

> The first shot was over my shoulder, a close-up of Frank. And they finished the shot, and the director said, "Okay, let's move on," and Frank said, "Hey, wait a minute. How about a close-up of my girl here?" And he made them turn the whole shot around, over his shoulder, and get a close-up of me. And don't think that didn't make me feel good, the very first day of working with him.[75]

On August 5, a little more than a week into production of *Take Me Out to the Ball Game*, Frank performed at another benefit concert, "Music for the Wounded," in Hollywood. He also guest starred on radio shows, including the American Tobacco Company's *Let's Talk Hollywood* (September 26), *Spotlight Review Starring Spike Jones* (October 1) and *Duffy's Tavern* (October 24). Kelly and Donen finally wrapped *Ball Game* on October 26.

Less than a month after Frank hung up his "Wolves" baseball uniform, *The Kissing Bandit* opened on November 19, more than a year after director Laslo Benedek had wrapped it. Was the film so bad that MGM had withheld its distribution? In 1995, Nancy, Jr., wrote, "I remember visiting my father on the set... He may make jokes about this movie and equate sitting through it to a sadistic form of torture, but I think it's adorable."[76]

The term "adorable" probably was not in the mind of Frank nor any other performer who worked on *The Kissing Bandit.* Unfortunately, Benedek wasted excellent production values, beautiful locations stunningly captured in Technicolor by Robert Surtees, good songs and the choreography of Stanley Donen on an atrocious script by Isobel Lennart and John Briard Harding.

Frank plays Ricardo, a Boston business school graduate who returns to his ancestral home in California to manage his late father's inn. There, the locals, led by Chico (J. Carroll Naish), expect him to be the very image of his rip-roaring, romantic and rebellious progenitor, known far and wide as "The Kissing Bandit." Coached by Chico, Ricardo is hopelessly inept, both on and off a horse, particularly where women are concerned, but he eventually, bumblingly wins the heart of Teresa (Kathryn Grayson), daughter of Don Jose (Mikhail Rasumny), the territorial governor.

Frank is introduced in the first scene, riding through a verdant valley toward the inn, where Chico and his amigos await Ricardo's surely stunning arrival. (They even have tacked up an old wanted poster picturing his father.) As the horse nears the building (and Frank gets closer to the camera), the animal bolts, tossing him through the front wall and into the room. Frank then emerges from beneath a table and into a medium shot, his face becoming visible for the first time. It is the most absurd cinematic entrance he made in a four-decade acting career.

Contrary to Chico's expectations, Ricardo wishes to create a comfortable inn for travelers. He has brought cookbooks from Boston and wants to build windowboxes filled with "pretty flowers." The bad dialogue adds to his milquetoast persona: "Oh my. Oh me. Son of a bandit. That's terrible." And when Chico speaks of him filling his father's boots, he replies, "Look at me. If I held you up, would you give me your money? I'm practically afraid of everything." Ricardo is an absurd costume version of the character Frank had played (and would continue to play) in the MGM films: a naive, inexperienced innocent who has no interest in the opposite sex until a seemingly worldly companion spurs him on. Here, however, he is a virgin in every sense of the word: Though he is expected to take up the family profession of kissing bandit, he has yet to plant even one peck on the lips of a lovely senorita. In fact, he has no interest in kissing, especially female strangers! When first meeting Teresa, after fumbling atop her runaway stagecoach during a botched hold-up, he actually backs up when she expects him to kiss her. Later, after serenading her with "If I Steal a Kiss," he attempts to climb up to her balcony but falls off, landing on his guitar, as the don's troops shoot at him.

Although Frank and Kathryn Grayson do what they can with ridiculous characterizations, J. Carroll Naish gives one of the most stereotypical "ethnic" performances of his career. Saddled with an outrageous prosthetic nose and a furry black wig, Naish does not improve matters with a bad "Hispanic" accent, screaming "Aye-eeeee!" when confronted with *any* situation. (The absurdity of some scenes puts *Bandit* on a par with some of Elvis Presley's worst films, including *Stay Away Joe* [1968], in which both the King and Burgess Meredith play offensive stereotypes of Native Americans.) At one point, Grayson asks Frank, "How can you be so *horrible*?" Years later, Frank mentioned Naish:

> You know what radio show I hated the most? It was called *Life with Luigi*, with J. Carroll Naish—there's a good Italian name for you—and it was all about Italians who spoke like-a-dis, and worried about ladies who squeeze-a da tomatoes on-a da fruit stand. The terrible thing was, it made me laugh. Because it *did* have some truth to it. We all knew guys like that growing up. But then I would hate myself for laughing at the goddamned thing.[77]

Aside from the Technicolor location footage, Brown and Heyman's songs and Donen's choreography are the only saving graces. "The Whip Dance" is the most interesting production number, with the exotic Irish-Japanese Sono Osato menacing Frank with a six-foot bullwhip. "My main function was to be sexy and entice Frank," the dancer recalled. Though she studied on the set with a cowboy to learn whipping techniques, she drew the line after Donen's creative vision became dangerous: When asked to "jump to the floor from the top of a six-foot armoire," she told him, "You must be crazy. You've been working with Gene Kelly too long."[78] Another elaborate instrumental number by Nacio Herb Brown, "Dance of Fury," is gratuitously performed late in the film by Ricardo Montalban, Ann Miller and Cyd Charisse.

Contemporary reviews of *The Kissing Bandit* ranged from lukewarm to very positive, although audiences were not as enthusiastic, as predicted by *Variety*'s "Brog," who faulted Benedek's lackluster direction but gave credit to Frank for contributing much of the film's interest:

> Title role is the exact opposite of the usual derring-do hero and casting of Frank Sinatra to play it sharpens the physical contrast. ...Sinatra plays the role broadly as well enough. His clumsiness on horseback, his shyness at amour, and the general incongruity of his gauntness and lack of heft gives to the hero character a natural for laughs but it doesn't always come off.[79]

Not surprisingly, *The New York Times*' Bosley Crowther found the film very pedestrian, noting that Benedek "has done little" and Frank "contributes little," an assessment shared by Cue: "Mr. Sinatra is further handicapped by a weak script, silly dialogue and uncertain direction."[80] The more trade-oriented publications, however, characteristically put a positive spin on Frank's contributions; while *The Hollywood Reporter* called him "just wonderful," *Box Office* praised his "ingratiating" performance.[81] Frank summed up the entire production: "I hated reading the script, hated doing it and, most of all, hated seeing it. So did everyone else."[82]

Just as bizarre as *Bandit* were Frank's next "gigs": a guest spot on the December 2 *Spotlight Revue Starring Spike Jones*, during which the new film was plugged, and a recording session, held in Hollywood on the 6th, producing only one side, a hillbilly number called "Sunflower" (the melody of which later was revamped for the famous "Hello, Dolly"). Eight days later, he waxed "Once in Love with Amy" with pianist Henry Rowland; and, without his presence, a full orchestra conducted by Mitchell Ayres was added the following day. For several reasons—for better or worse—technology was changing the way records were made. On December 15—the same day Ayres' orchestra laid down their track—Frank was on a separate coast, recording two cuts, Cole Porter's ballad "Why Can't You Behave?" and the challenging, uncharacteristic "Bop! Goes My Heart," with a small Nat Cole-style group at Columbia's New York studio. Sessions on December 19 and January 4 produced five more tracks, including Styne and Cahn's "Kisses and Tears," a song written for the soundtrack of "It's Only Money," which had begun shooting on the RKO lot the former month.

Depressed by the current state of his career—bad press, miscasting in the *Bandit* role and the loss of some of his fans (*Down Beat* soon would rate him as the fifth favorite male singer in the United States)—Frank told Manie Sacks that "he felt like he was all washed up." Sacks replied. "In a few years, you'll be on top again."[83] The truth was that the bobbysoxers who had swooned five years earlier were no longer impressionable teenagers; they now were adults, many of them married, with children to raise. But during the early months of 1949, Frank's attention began to be arrested even more by Ava Gardner, whom he ran into on several occasions, including a color photo shoot in January, to commemorate MGM's Silver Jubilee. While Ava sat dead center, between Clark Gable and Judy Garland, among a formidable group of stars, Frank was poised toward the back right, flanked by Ginger Rogers and Red Skelton. The next month, their relationship became serious after they visited "a little yellow house in Nichols Canyon." "Oh, God, it was magic," Ava recalled, "We became lovers eternally."[84]

The gay finale to the dancing, singing, Technicolorful all-star picture!

Esther Williams, shown with Frank, Betty Garrett, Jules Munshin, and Gene Kelly, who would reunite in _On the Town_.

Frank went Broadway on the final day of February, cutting Rodgers and Hammerstein's "Some Enchanted Evening" and "Bali Ha'i" from _South Pacific_. On March 3, he recorded "The Right Girl for Me" from _Take Me Out to the Ball Game_ while simultaneously working on his role for _On the Town_. MGM released _Ball Game_ one week later. Frank received top billing above the title, but again was upstaged by Kelly, who, though billed third, did conceive the film, direct portions of it and (with Donen) choreograph and design all the musical sequences.

The film opens in Sarasota, Florida, where the old-time professional baseball team the Wolves is holding spring training. After posing for a group photo, the absence of two star players, Eddie O'Brien and Denny Ryan, is noted; after all, they still are performing their off-season vaudeville act, on the road in Pottstown, Illinois! These two Irish-American athlete-performers are very similar to Gene and Frank's characters in _Anchors Aweigh_: While the former absolutely adores dames and habitually will break curfew to do so, the latter knows nothing about them and prefers to play checkers in his room; however, lately he's "been thinking a lot about girls."

The plot of _Ball Game_ is simple, yet far more engaging than its underrated reputation suggests. When the Wolves fall into the hands of the owner's management-bound descendant, members of the team begin immediately to berate "K. C. Higgins." After O'Brien tries to pick up an elegant dame (Esther Williams) at the hotel, he is humiliated to discover that _she_ is the new owner. Following a series of machismo-driven mishaps, fines imposed by Higgins and romantic attempts and entanglements, O'Brien helps the team win the pennant (after being victimized by crooked gamblers led by Morgan [Edward Arnold] and fired by K. C.) and wins the hand of Higgins, while Ryan ends up with Shirley Delwyn (Betty Garrett), former consort of the crooks.

Running a mere 90 minutes, _Ball Game_ is loaded with musical sequences that emphasize Kelly's often over-the-top characterization. Two of the numbers, Albert Von Tilzer and Jack

Norworth's "Take Me Out to the Ball Game" and Roger Edens' "Strictly U.S.A.," performed on the vaudeville stage (the latter also features Williams and Garrett), frame the baseball story, while the remainder (written by Edens, Comden, and Green) emerge from it. The entire film is a backdrop for Kelly's dancing prowess, most obviously during a clambake scene that exists only for him to perform a lengthy "Irish" dance. Another number, "Boys and Girls Like You and Me," featuring Frank and Betty, was shot but edited out of the scene. Dropped from Rodgers and Hammerstein's *Oklahoma*, this number was acquired by Arthur Freed for MGM's *Meet Me in St. Louis* (1944); when Judy Garland didn't sing it in that film, it was re-assigned to her projected *Ball Game* role but finally given to Frank, who ultimately was robbed of it, too! At one point early in the film (after O'Brien and Ryan sing "Yes, Indeedy" to their teammates), Frank (anachronistically) gets a shot in at Gene when he uses the popular 1940s phrase "You swing like a rusty gate." The musical highlight is "O'Brien to Ryan to Goldberg," sung and danced wonderfully by Gene, Frank and Jules Munshin.

The trio of friends provides amusement throughout the film, particularly when poking fun at Ryan's naiveté and unmanliness. When he first falls for K. C. (later revealed as Katherine Catherine), he needs to be coached in amour by O'Brien and Goldberg, who more than once engage in the type of innocent "gay" humor that Kelly often utilized. Once more doing his Stan Laurel collar-grab, Frank descends a balcony to sing, in lovely long-breath style, "She's the Right Girl for Me" before practicing a little baseball with Katherine! (This "seduction" sequence is prompted by an obligatory but brief Esther Williams swimming scene. Berkeley was asked to re-create one of his famous synchronized underwater routines, but failed to do so.) Later, Shirley pursues *him* to the point of sexual harassment while singing "It's Fate, Baby, It's Fate" at the ball park. But Frank's size bears the brunt of most of the film's humor: On numerous occasions, he or others mention his skinniness, and several times he is knocked out by a single swat to the head.

After the opening "Take Me Out to the Ball Game" number, as Ryan attempts to stand up to a burly stage hand, O'Brien asks, "Why don't you pick on somebody your size?"

"There ain't nobody my size," Ryan replies.

As baseball players will do on deck, Ryan attempts to swing three bats while warming up, but nearly knocks himself down. Later, after he has been swatted unconscious, Shirley carries him off the field and into the stands. And an entire montage sequence shows him trying to fatten up, stepping on the training scale only to realize he has *lost* weight.

In his *Variety* review, "Kahn" hit the film right in the strike zone:

> *Take Me Out to the Ball Game* has fundamental box office. Musical, backgrounded by an early-day baseball yarn, is short on story, but has some amusing moments—and Gene Kelly. Kelly is one of the most exciting examples of oldtime song-and-dance showmanship, linked with a mixture of the new. ...Aided by Technicolor, Miss Williams is an eyeful, and Sinatra cavorts pleasantly... there is no pretense that *Ball Game* is anything more than a romp for Kelly's virtuosity. There is, for example, a late production sequence in which his dancing, brilliantly staged, is as exhilarating as anything seen in a filmusical.[85]

Despite the positive reception of audiences across the country, and its inclusion of his best cinematic dancing to date, Kelly pointed out what he considered a major flaw: "The fact that we'd totally ignored the foreign market and blissfully refused to realize that few people outside America knew or cared about what a ball game was was irrelevant. We thought it a funny idea and that's all that mattered."[86] Certainly, by 1949, foreign (as well as many American) filmgoers would have had difficulty understanding the shot in which a portentous, smiling, heavily mustached Wolves fan (Ed Cassidy) is asked to "pose with this big stick."

On April 10, a session producing the rhythm hit "The Huckle-Buck" was spoiled by the subsequent, tragic death of saxophonist Herbie Haymer as he crossed the street in front of Columbia Studios. On May 6, Frank cut two Irving Berlin numbers from *Miss Liberty*, including a duet with Doris Day on "Let's Take an Old Fashioned Walk." Antiquated indeed, the song unfortunately is their only studio collaboration, "not quite up to what one would expect from an encounter between two gods."[87]

During the spring of 1949, Frank again was attacked by various syndicated columnists, this time female, who criticized his taste for extramarital affairs. Reading articles by Hedda Hopper, Louella Parsons and Sheilah Graham, George Evans advised him to clean up his act, including staying faithful to Nancy, easing up on his alcohol intake and steering clear of individuals with any ties to the Mob. Frank was not thrilled about his agent's paternalism, but was much more excited about his next film project, although it again involved wearing a sailor suit and dancing with the slave-driving Gene Kelly. During the late spring and early summer, he worked at MGM and on location in New York to shoot *On the Town* under the direction of Kelly and Donen, whom Joe Pasternak hired legitimately this time.

At the behest of Kelly, Arthur Freed had convinced L. B. Mayer to pay $250,000 for the rights to Betty Comden and Adolph Green's successful Broadway show *On the Town* in 1944, but after perusing the material, which had been adapted from the Jerome Robbins ballet *Fancy Free*, the MGM mogul objected to a scene featuring a dance between a black girl and a white man. The show was "smutty" and "Communistic," Mayer alleged.[88] When the war ended, any chances of the film being produced died with the "service picture" genre. But by the winter of 1949, Freed, Kelly and Donen had persuaded Mayer to go ahead with the project, and, with Comden and Green's screenplay completed in late January, budgeted the picture at $1.9 million. The production would take 20 weeks, half for rehearsal, a prospect unheard of for Frank, who (based on his five-year contract set to expire on January 1, 1950) was guaranteed a flat salary of $130,000. By comparison, Kelly received only $42,000 to costar *and* co-direct, while Donen, under the terms of an earlier contract, was paid a paltry $8,400. Comden and Green each received $42,000 for their work on the screenplay, plus an additional $12,000 for new songs. (Leonard

Bernstein's score for the original stage show was scrapped, but he was paid to compose music for the elaborate "Lonely Town" ballet.) The other principals' guarantees were as follows: Jules Munshin, $20,250; Ann Miller, $16,833; Vera-Ellen, $8,875; and Betty Garrett, $6,250.

Rehearsals for *On the Town* began February 21, 1949. Five weeks later, shooting commenced at MGM, breaking briefly on April 13 for the company to celebrate Donen's 25th birthday. (Frank sang while Ann Miller and Vera-Ellen cut the cake.) On May 5, the principal cast and crew packed up for New York. Also having hired some East Coast crewmen, Donen carefully planned the shooting schedule to allow for city regulations and permits, and especially to hide the cameras from curious passersby. Nonetheless, no matter where the company filmed, scores of New Yorkers stopped to gawk at the Voice. Donen later recalled, "At that time, Sinatra was as popular as all four Beatles put together."[89]

The opening dance montage, beginning in the Brooklyn Navy Yard, took two full weeks to shoot. Initially, L. B. Mayer's production

The Cinema of Sinatra

manager, J. J. Cohn, wanted the entire film shot in Hollywood, but through the efforts of Arthur Freed, Donen had been allotted five days in the Big Apple. Eventually, the location work would stretch to 18 days, raising the final budget to $2,111,250. Much of the time was necessary to shoot at all the landmarks Kelly and Donen wanted to showcase: the Brooklyn Bridge, Wall Street, Chinatown, the Statue of Liberty, Greenwich Village, Central Park, Columbus Circle, Rockefeller Center and Grant's Tomb. But other delays were caused by Jules Munshin's severe acrophobia, which required the invention of various "safety devices" to be used on ledges and rooftops, and—Frank.

On the Town Belgium poster

The ending of the film was to be shot on the same battleship appearing in the initial scene. Conferring with the admiral of the Brooklyn Navy Yard, Donen admitted that he knew nothing about "nautical shit," and "picked the exact minute" when the weather and tide would be perfect for the captain to sail out of the harbor. The shot was to be captured at precisely 1:30 p.m. on a particular day, with Donen 300 feet off the ground on a huge crane. Shouting through a bullhorn, the pressured co-director ordered, "Okay, it's time to bring everybody in!"

Kelly, Munshin and the rest of the actors performed flawlessly, but the Voice was nowhere to be seen. Donen remembered:

> An assistant said, "Frank got tired of waiting." Frank got hungry and decided he wanted to have lunch at Toots Shor's, in Manhattan. Here we were, in Brooklyn, the cast, the crew, and the ship. And between Manhattan and Brooklyn was this bridge to cross. I knew we couldn't make the shot after lunch. The sun wouldn't hold. It was now or never.[90]

But just as Donen was about to explode from his high perch, One-Take Charley came breezing in, jumped out of his limousine and slid into the shot. Donen added, "Only thing, we had to cut it out of the movie. The admiral had told me the ship would pull away and sail into the harbor. What he didn't tell me was that it would take fifteen minutes to do that."[91]

On the final day of shooting, Frank became very angry when one of his songs, "Lonely Town," was dropped. Having been promised this exceptional ballad as an incentive to do the film, he was outraged that Kelly and Donen's egos led them to look down on him as a "second-stringer" who didn't deserve such a musical highlight.[92] (On May 16, Frank, Gene, Betty Garrett and Jules Munshin sang "Strictly U.S.A." on *The Savings Bond Show*.) After location work on the film was wrapped on the 23rd, a two-week rehearsal for the ballet sequence began back at MGM three days later. Requiring four shooting days, the sequence was created by Kelly solely to showcase his dancing prowess (a gratuitous parallel to the Irish dance scene in *Take Me Out to the Ball Game*). To compensate for the "limited abilities" of Frank, Jules Munshin, Betty Garrett and even the formidable Ann Miller, Kelly hired four highly accomplished hoofers to ballet with him and Vera-Ellen. When the scene was completed on July 2, *On the Town* was in the can. Although previous MGM musicals had combined realistic with fantastical elements, this film presented Kelly with his biggest challenge to date: how firmly to ground an entirely dance-oriented musical within a real urban space. He recalled:

Jules Munshin, Sinatra and Gene Kelly explore "New York, New York" in *On the Town*.

> I really believed it would be a milestone, because I set out to try to make it so. Everything we did in the picture was innovative from the way we flashed the time of day across the screen, as if it were a news flash... to the way we cut the picture, which was pretty revolutionary for its time, and which was greatly admired by the French. The fact that make-believe sailors got off a real ship in a real dockyard, and danced through a real New York was a turning point in itself.[93]

A week after *On the Town* wrapped, Frank became a bit more improvisational in the studio while cutting "It All Depends On You," and also recorded his first version of "Don't Cry, Joe (Let Her Go, Let Her Go, Let Her Go)." On July 14, while Axel Stordahl enjoyed a vacation with his songbird wife, June Hutton, he went under the baton of Hugo Winterhalter while waxing "Every Man Should Marry" and the Dorsey-like "If I Ever Love Again." The following week, he cut three numbers with Hollywood conductor Morris Stoloff before taking a two-month recording hiatus, returning to the studio on September 15 to perform the passionate, spiritual-like "That Lucky Old Sun (Just Rolls Around Heaven All Day)," "Mad About You" and, with Barney Kessel on guitar, a superbly powerful "(On the Island of) Stromboli," the theme for the Roberto Rossellini film that infamously created the scandalous extramarital affair between the director and star Ingrid Bergman. Sessions on October 30 and November 8 yielded five songs, including two from *Riding High* by Johnny Burke and Jimmy Van Heusen, "(We've Got a) Sure Thing" and "Sunshine Cake," a bouncy swing duet with the Modernaires' Paula Kelly. On Halloween

Frank, Betty Garrett, Jules Munshin, Ann Miller, Gene Kelly and Vera-Ellen "Going on the Town."

eve, he also guested on *The Jack Benny Program*, singing "You Must Have Been a Beautiful Baby" and playing the father of Benny's sidekick in "The Don Wilson Story."

On the Town dynamically crescendoed onto screens across the nation in early December. Opening with a shot of the New York skyline and a graphic indicating "5:57 AM," a lone dock worker performs a quiet a cappella song just before a whistle blows and a throng of sailors frantically disembark from their ship. Launching into "New York, New York," Chip (Frank), Gabey (Kelly) and Ozzie (Munshin) appear in a breathtaking montage of familiar New York locations. Having musically expressed their joy for 24-hour shore leave, Gabey and Ozzie immediately want to cruise for dates, but Chip prefers to sightsee in the Big Apple. Demonstrating that this character is more mature than his earlier MGM innocents, Frank-as-Chip agrees to pick up dames *and then* view the sights. "Who you got waitin' for you in New York? Ava Gardner?" Ozzie asks.

Soon, Gabey falls in love with Ivy Smith, a.k.a. "Miss Turnstiles" (Vera-Ellen), a poster girl he sees tacked up in a subway car and subsequently fantasizes about (via a dream sequence). Reading that she is studying at New York's museums, the trio is taken to the Museum of Anthropological History by cab driver Brunhilde Esterhazy (Betty Garrett), who immediately puts the moves on Chip: When asked to show him all the landmarks, she counters, "Why don't you come up to my place?" At the museum, Ozzie impresses Claire Huddeson (Ann Miller), a man-crazed anthropologist who notices his resemblance to Pithecanthropus Erectus! A high point of the film and one of the most entertaining sequences ever to hit the screen, the innuendo-ridden number "Prehistoric Man," includes the sex-starved Miller dancing up a whirlwind, Frank, Gene and Jules making guttural "caveman" sounds, and the collapse of a Apotosaurus skeleton. When informed of the tumbling of the fossil of a dinosaur, a New York cop laments the loss of his "favorite singing star—that Dinah Shore."

Moreso than many musicals, the plot of *On the Town* is nearly superfluous. The sailor story exists only to provide a 24-hour window within which the three gobs pursue pleasure in New York, dancing and singing all the way. Kelly and Donen's use of the single-day scenario and the on-screen hour-and-minute graphics almost give the film a feeling of real time.

Unlike the earlier Sinatra-Kelly collaborations, here their characters are on somewhat more equal footing with the opposite sex. Gene is not the lone wolf this time, and wants only Ivy (their shared home town of Meadowville, Indiana, is a broad contrivance in grand Hollywood fashion), while his two shipmates also look for companions. But Frank's "Chip" (hailing from Peoria, Illinois!) still possesses many of the traits indelible to his MGM image, including his cowering from the image of a live "nude" model at an art session, and tendency to accept the protection of Gabey (who, at one point, tells him he loves him). However, Chip has a bit more machismo than Frank's virginal innocents in *Anchors Aweigh*, *It Happened In Brooklyn*, *The Kissing Bandit* and *Take Me Out to the Ball Game*: Here he actually accompanies Brunhilde to her apartment and makes out until they are interrupted by her roommate, the klutzy and clueless Lucy Schmeeler (Alice Pearce).

Aside from "New York, New York" and "Prehistoric Man," "Come Up to My Place" and "You're Awful," both duets between Frank and Betty Garrett, are the film's song highlights. The beautiful pacing established by Kelly and Donen, culminating in a superb chase sequence—in which the three sailors dress in drag to escape from the police (at Coney Island, where Gabey discovers Ivy is really a "cooch" dancer), who escort them back to their ship, just in time for another trio to disembark for 24-hour leave—is broken only once. Unfortunately, Kelly could not check his ego at the studio door; instead, late in the film, inserting a superfluous ballet sequence (fantasized by Gabey) recounting the entire plot up to that point. Although the scene is brief compared to the "Irish jig" in *Take Me Out to the Ball Game*, and contains some of Kelly's trademark eroticism, it detracts from the near-perfection of the rest of the film. The ballet did receive some criticism in contemporary reviews, but the film was accorded near-universal acclaim for its exuberance, memorable songs and dancing, luscious Technicolor and, as reported in *Time*, tendency "to bounce right off the screen."[94]

Though it was a major critical and popular success, *On the Town* proved to be the swansong of Frank's MGM contract. Evidently, his tendency to express his witty opinions caused trouble again. One day, while eating lunch in the MGM commissary, he overhead someone remark that Mayer was seriously injured after a nasty fall from a horse.

"Nah," Frank broke in. "He fell off Ginny Simms."

Having engaged in many a "father-and-son" style conversation with the mogul since his arrival at the studio five years earlier, he was not expecting such a harsh response to this crack about a singer who had appeared in some films at RKO and Universal but never really made the big time. (The fact that Simms was a real beauty, a superb vocalist and capable actress was beside the point. Mayer subsequently fired her after she rebuffed his marriage proposal.)

Three days later, Mayer called Frank into his office. Evidently, word around the MGM lot traveled fairly quickly, and the old man was quick to react, although apparently ailing. "I want you to leave this studio here," said L. B., "and I don't ever want you to come back again."

Frank later admitted, "My face dropped. I knew I was sunk."[95]

After he walked out of Mayer's office, Frank's contract was terminated a year early and he was paid off with $85,000.

Without film work, Frank tried to land the role of a young New Jersey man being sent to the electric chair for murder in Columbia's *Knock on Any Door* (1949). However, his repeated calls did nothing to persuade studio chief Harry Cohn, who considered him too old for the role. The part of the accused man eventually went to beefcake star John Derek.

Chapter 4
The Lean Years

I wasn't paying enough attention to my job at the time. I think I was tired. That's not an excuse. It's a fact. I think I was weary, because I had worked tremendously for the years preceding that period. Working constantly three hundred days a year or more, in many instances. And I was traveling constantly, and just doing all kinds of work, and I had a personal problem which I will not go into. When I was ready and I'd had enough rest...I took time to have all the cobwebs blown out of my head, I went back to work... — Frank Sinatra[1]

Manie Sacks resigned from Columbia Records in January 1950, and Frank lost his staunchest ally in the music business. The company's new artists-and-repertoire man, Mitch Miller, was primarily interested in producing flavor of the day singles for the widest commercial appeal, a policy that created problems for the Voice, who was devoted to masterful, sensitive interpretations of standards and only the best new songs. In fact, Miller had no idea what to do with Frank, and was more comfortable with new bloods like Frankie Laine and Tony Bennett.

On the January 8 *Jack Benny Program*, Frank was involved in a crime investigation headed by "Captain O'Benny of the Beverly Hills Police." In this episode, he was mistaken for "a broom leaning against the table" and a bone being continually buried by the dog. Having eaten a raisin for lunch, Frank admitted, "Boy, am I stuffed!" Also guesting, Gene Kelly danced his replies to Benny's questions and then plugged *On the Town* and mentioned *Take Me Out to the Ball Game*, *The Pirate* (1948) and *Anchors Aweigh*.

Like his studio sessions of the previous year, Frank's 1950 waxings began with a mixed bag. On January 12, he cut three songs, including the bluesy gospel number "God's Country" by "Lucky Old Sun" composers Beasley Smith and Haven Gillespie, which features fine trumpet work by Ziggy Elman, and the Crosby-style boogie-woogie "Chattanoogie Shoeshine Boy," the type of silly song favored by Miller.

Exasperated by the new A&R guru, Frank was not faring any better with George Evans, who, tired of running interference, refused to represent him any longer. The following day, on January 27, Evans, aged 48, dropped dead of a massive heart attack. Saddened by the loss of his friend, Frank flew to Houston on the 28th, to open the Shamrock Hotel, where Ava Gardner surprised him. After his show, while dining at Vincento Sorrentino's Restaurant, Frank and Ava were approached by a photographer who, though advised to scram, would not back off. Frank exploded verbally but kept his fists to himself; however, over the next few days, newspapers across the country reported an embellished version of the incident, the beginning of a downhill career slide that he had sensed a year earlier.

Since moving to Hollywood, Nancy, Sr., had endured both rumors and her own personal suspicions about Frank's extramarital affairs, but the press generated by the Houston imbroglio was too much for her. On Valentine's Day 1950, she filed for a separation and announced an official split with her husband, who had moved into a Coldwater Canyon home with Ava, whom journalists were portraying as an insidious homewrecker. And as "adulterer" was added to the list of terms attached to him, Frank carried on with recordings on February 23, when he cut another version of "Kisses and Tears" from *It's Only Money* (later released as *Double Dynamite*) on which he is joined by a very competent Jane Russell and the Modernaires. Three days later, he performed at a fundraiser for the Jewish Home for the Aged at the Biltmore Bowl and then flew to New York to record and begin a series of dates at the Copacabana.

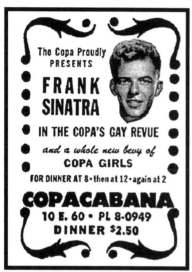

The Copa Proudly
PRESENTS

FRANK
SINATRA

IN THE COPA'S GAY REVUE

and a whole new bevy of
COPA GIRLS

FOR DINNER AT 8 • then at 12 • again at 2

COPACABANA

10 E. 60 • PL 8-0949
DINNER $2.50

On March 10, under Miller's direction, Frank cut "American Beauty Rose," a bouncy Dixieland-style swinger in which he breezily equates attractive girls with various kinds of flowers. Miller wanted Frank to record more "rhythm numbers," and this one hit the mark but charted only for a brief time. Opening at the Copa on March 23, he performed five shows each night. Having signed to play the female lead in MGM's *Pandora and the Flying Dutchman*, Ava flew to Europe after watching him perform for 10 nights.

Back in the studio on April 8, Frank was teamed with recent Columbia signee Rosemary Clooney for "Peachtree Street," a song he cowrote and published through Sinatra Songs, Inc. Rosie and her sister Betty had admired the Voice since 1943, and she was in the audience at several of the Copa shows, but remained thoroughly professional at the session: "I didn't even tell Frank I was a big fan. Nothing. Oh, I didn't want to be un-hip!"[2]

Encouraged by the sound of "American Beauty Rose," Miller, deciding to have Frank record an entire album of rhythm songs, scheduled additional April sessions. Understandably, the Voice was nervous. He had preferred ballads while at Columbia, and although he had proved he could swing with the best of them, rarely was given the opportunity. Moreover, *Sing and Dance with Frank Sinatra* would be his first album in the 33-rpm format.

The Copa engagement was his first nightclub gig in some time, but the long run and number of shows (three each evening) began to take a serious toll on a constitution already troubled by overwork (recordings, five radio performances each week, benefits, and additional daytime shows at the Capitol), the stress caused by a new relationship and the break-up of an old one. Plus the usual drinking, smoking and sleep deprivation. During the sessions, his voice was so ravaged that Miller often turned off his mike and then had him dub the vocal later. No one could tell: On April 14 and 24, Frank produced seven issuable takes in which he demonstrates the evolving swing style that would take him to new heights four years later. Beginning with a driving rendition of "Should I (Reveal)," he then cut Cole Porter's "You Do Something to Me," a superlative version of Rodgers and Hart's "Lover," "When You're Smiling (The Whole World Smiles With You)," E. Y. Harburg and Harold Arlen's "It's Only a Paper Moon," a stand-out "My Blue Heaven" and "The Continental." In short, Frank, buoyed by George Siravo's arrangements, sounded damned good for being a washed up crooner. Released with an eighth track, "It All Depends On You," recorded in July of the previous year, the excellent *Sing and Dance* unfortunately failed to hit the *Billboard* charts.

Two days after the final *Sing and Dance* session, during a Copa show on the evening of April 26, Frank reached for a note and nothing came out of his mouth. The voice was gone:

> I was never so panic-stricken in my whole life. I remember looking at the audience, there was a blizzard outside, about seventy people in the place—stunning, absolute silence. I looked at them, and they looked at me, and I looked at Skitch Henderson, who was playing the piano. His face was ghastly white. Finally I whispered at the audience, "Good night," and walked off the floor.[3]

After coughing up blood, he was diagnosed as having suffered a submucosal hemorrhage, and his doctors ordered him to remain silent for a week. Somehow managing not to speak, he then canceled an upcoming engagement at Chicago's Chez Paree before flying to Tossa del

The Cinema of Sinatra

Mar, Spain, where Ava was filming on location, on May 10. Though he had spared his voice the rigors of another lengthy club engagement, he would unleash it in a far less positive fashion when confronting his new lover about her torrid affair with toreador Mario Cabre. (Ava frankly admitted her insatiable desires, later writing, "I didn't understand then and still don't why there should be this prurient mass hysteria about a male and a female climbing into bed and doing what comes naturally.")[4]

Frank soon left the Mediterranean, angry and depressed. Back in New York, he made his television debut on the May 27 broadcast of Bob Hope's *Star Spangled Revue*, playing Bing Crosby in a skit and singing "Come Rain or Come Shine." From May 29 through June 2, he made his final appearances with Dorothy Kirsten on the *Light Up Time* radio series: His contract was not renewed.

On June 28, he made a truly ludicrous return to the recording studio when Miller had him cut the Leadbelly folk song "Goodnight Irene," which was released as a single with "Dear Little Boy of Mine" on the B-side. Arranged and conducted by Miller, "Irene" was on the charts for 12 weeks, eventually reaching number five, but Frank hated it.

In early July, he flew to London to open a two-week series of standing-room-only dates at the Palladium on the 10th. Unlike the current "backlash" in the States, the engagement was an English version of the 1943 Paramount experience: "Two tall red-headed girls nearly got my tie. One was actually pulling it off my neck. I pulled back."[5] Ava attended one of the concerts but, avoiding photographers, left before the conclusion.

On August 2, Frank was back in New York, recording Jimmy Van Heusen and Johnny Burke's "Life Is So Peculiar" with Helen Carroll and the Swantones. When he played Atlantic City later in the month, the Sinatra hysteria seemed to have sailed back home, when huge crowds demanded that he sing (of all things) "Goodnight Irene." On September 18, he cut two more songs, "Accidents Will Happen," another Van Heusen-Burke collaboration, in which he proved that the hemorrhage had done nothing to diminish his long-breath phrasing technique, and "One Finger Melody," a perfectly dreadful novelty number published by his own Barton Music. Three days later, his material was much more consistent, including the lovely "London By Night" and the in-joke swinger "Meet Me at the Copa," with music by Axel Stordahl and lyrics by Sammy Cahn that were "an accommodation for [club owner] Jack Entratter."[6] And on October 7, he debuted his own television variety series, *The Frank Sinatra Show*, broadcast on Saturdays at 9 p.m. by CBS, who also began airing a radio equivalent, *Meet Frank Sinatra*, on Sunday afternoons.

Frank waxed quasi-operatic on October 9, giving full range to his recovered voice on "Come Back to Sorrento (Torna a Surriento)" for Columbia. Performing a portion in phonetic Italian, he gave an impressive, powerful performance, and then geared down to provide a more characteristically romantic vocal on Vernon Duke and E. Y. Harburg's "April in Paris," featuring the sublime trumpet soloing of Billy Butterfield, who also contributed to "I Guess I'll Have to Dream the Rest," a straight remake of the Dorsey classic, and "Nevertheless (I'm In Love With You)," one of the most passionate, ethereal recordings of his career.

The next day, Frank guested on *Life with Luigi*, a radio show featuring broad caricatures of Italian-Americans. Even in 1950, the producers, thinking that such stereotypes might offend some listeners, included the announcer's claim that their depiction was "a typically American radio program—a friendly, enjoyable show that sort of symbolizes the American spirit of tolerance and goodwill." In this episode, Luigi Basco (J. Carroll Naish) wins a trip to New York after identifying Frank on the radio. The timid little man is overjoyed by the Voice's offer to be his tour guide in the Big Apple, but rather than hitting Toots Shor's, the Stork Club, the Copa and El Morocco, Luigi wants to see all the typical tourist sites. "Maybe I've been seeing too much of my New York, anyway," Frank admits. Caricatures aside, the show provided an interesting look at a different side of (a somewhat fictionalized) Frank.

On November 5, he cut an obligatory Yuletide number, a swinging rendition of Styne and Cahn's "Let It Snow! Let It Snow! Let It Snow!" and moved back into ballad territory the following week with Cole Porter's "I Am Loved" and "You Don't Remind Me," and "Take My

Love," the first classically based piece (with a melody by Brahms) he had done in some time. And on December 11, he was reunited with Rosemary Clooney for two songs, "Love Means Love" and "Cherry Pies Ought to Be You," a comedy number in which Orson Welles and Errol Flynn are mentioned.

One day in December 1950, at 4 a.m. in the Rockefeller Center office of Joseph Nellis, an attorney for Senator Estes Kefauver's Special Committee to Investigate Crime in Interstate Commerce, Frank was questioned about his "ties" to the underworld. Replying that, on occasion, he only had "said hello or goodbye," he was not recalled to testify at any committee hearings.[7]

Before taking over as Columbia A&R man, Mitch Miller, an accomplished instrumental musician, had been a friend of Frank's; but his insistence on churning out faddish commercial material continued to annoy the Voice. Hired to play on "You're the One" at Frank's January 16, 1951, session, pianist Stan Freeman remembered, "I only remember Sinatra being very aware of what he wanted, and getting it! If he thought a flute part or an oboe part should be left out of one section, he would say so. He never took charge, but nominally he was in charge—everybody knew that."[8] Seeking a theme for his television series, Frank had commissioned the music for "You're the One" from film composer Victor Young.

On February 2, Frank recorded two Rodgers and Hammerstein songs, "Hello, Young Lovers" and "We Kiss In a Shadow," from *The King and I*. Drummer Johnny Blowers recalled that 22 takes were required to nail "Lovers," an excruciatingly long time to wait before the musicians could break at a bar next to the studio.[9] At Frank's next session, on March 27, a third *King and I* song, "I Whistle a Happy Tune," was recorded, comprising a trilogy that "represents the [Sinatra-Stordahl] collaboration at its Olympian zenith."[10] The latter session also yielded one of Frank's most magnificent performances, his powerfully heartbreaking "I'm a Fool to Want You," a Jack Wolf-Joel Herron song that he dramatically imbued with his own personal experiences, improvising the lyric in a manner that earned him a writing credit. (His Barton company then published the song.)

Apparently, Frank's tempestuous relationship with Ava, and the fact that his career was lost in the shadow of hers, created the angst that he released while recording the song. Will Friedwald wrote:

> In getting into the bridge, the Voice really socks it to us, and when he utters the phrase "time and time again" twice, he skillfully extracts totally different meanings each time, musically and dramatically, following the melody optimistically up on the first and depressingly downbeat on the second. At the end of the bridge, Stordahl amplifies the singer's sturm-und-drang with an a cappella crying violin. Supposedly, after packing an opera's worth of pathos in a single 32-bar chorus, Sinatra became so overcome with grief that he bolted from the studio in tears.[11]

From April 25 through May 8, Frank again returned to New York's Paramount, to front the orchestra of former Dorsey-mate Joe Bushkin in a two-week engagement. Two days later, he was back in the studio with the Teutonic, tone-deaf "singer-actress" Dagmar, cutting the ludicrous "Mama Will Bark," a Miller production that became the worst single he ever recorded. Although Frank could have refused to wax the number, he gave in to Miller, who reduced the Voice to barking, growling and whining like a dog in this abysmal travesty. On June 3, he opened a weeklong series of shows in New York's Latin Quarter, finishing on the 9th, when he also broadcast the final *Frank Sinatra Show* of the television season. And the following month, *Meet Frank Sinatra* ended after a nine-month radio run.

During June and July, Frank worked at Universal for the first time, in *Meet Danny Wilson*, a film written by his friend Don McGuire and directed by Joseph Pevney. On June 6, he joined costar Shelley Winters to record "A Good Man Is Hard to Find" under the baton of studio music director Joseph Gershenson, who led another session a week later to cut "She's Funny That Way,"

"Meet DANNY WILSON"

Starring

Frank SINATRA
Shelley WINTERS
Alex NICOL
with RAYMOND BURR

which Frank originally had waxed in 1944. On July 17, he accompanied Ava to the premiere of MGM's lavish Technicolor triumph *Showboat*, but they avoided the party at Romanoff's so he could report to the *Danny Wilson* set early the next morning.

Two days later, Frank was reunited with his old boss, Harry James, for the first time since 1944, to cut three sides, "Castle Rock," "Farewell, Farewell to Love" and "Deep Night." But times were decidedly different: Frank and the band did not perform together; he dubbed his vocals after the orchestra recorded Ray Conniff's arrangements. Harry later said that "Castle Rock" was "the worst thing that either of us ever recorded."[12] (Perhaps he never heard "Mama Will Bark"!)

Since their separation more than a year earlier, Nancy, Sr., had believed that Frank might return home to her and the children; but, by the summer of 1951, realizing that he was inescapably in love with Ava, who kept demanding that he free himself, allowed him to get a quickie divorce in Mexico. Soon after, Frank took Ava to Hoboken to meet Marty and Dolly, who, although planning to dislike her, eventually warmed to her charm. On August 4, Frank flew to Acapulco, where Ava had gone to work on a film, and after returning to Los Angeles, announced their engagement.

From August 11 through 24, Frank headlined a two-week engagement at the Riverside Inn and Casino in Reno, the first Nevada gambling-resort gig of his career. Though madly in love with Ava, who also professed reciprocal feelings, the relationship continued to be tempestuous. During the Labor Day weekend, while drinking too much at a rented house on Lake Tahoe, they had a lengthy argument, during which Frank "made an offhand remark."[13] After Ava stormed out and headed back to her home in Pacific Palisades, he apparently took enough Phenobarbital to feign suicide. Hours later, Hank Sanicola phoned Ava, frantically asking her to hurry back because Frank had overdosed. Returning to Tahoe, she knew he had faked it. Soon after, Frank told *Time* magazine that he was "allergic to sleeping pills" and that "I had drunk two or three brandies and broke out in a rash."[14] Less than a month later, he played his first show in Las Vegas, at the Desert Inn, and in October, opened the second season of *The Frank Sinatra Show*, this time on Tuesdays at 8 p.m.

The Actor, on Screen and in Song   **93**

In Santa Monica on October 30, 1951, Nancy, Sr., was granted an interlocutory divorce decree, which would be finalized in one year. On November 1, Frank, having established a five-week residency in Nevada, obtained a divorce; and the next day, he, Ava and Manie Sacks flew to Philadelphia, where they picked up a marriage license. Five days later, they were married at the home of Manie's brother, Lester, in suburban Philadelphia. Axel Stordahl was best man.

Shelved for nearly three years, *It's Only Money* became Frank's first new film since *On the Town* when RKO finally released it as *Double Dynamite* during the first week of November. Currently without a studio contract or even freelance film work, the Voice made a brief, thoroughly inauspicious "return" to the screen. But, at least for the moment, acting was the last thing on his mind. He was on a honeymoon with Ava Gardner. Besides himself, only Mickey Rooney and Artie Shaw had been able to do that.

Having lost interest in the film during their December 1948-January 1949 production hiatus, RKO made a curious move in deciding to release *Double Dynamite* when Frank was taking such a drubbing in the press. Perhaps his firing by Mayer prompted the company to fill a cinematic void by screening their one unreleased Sinatra product, but reviews of the film were lukewarm at best, with *Variety*'s "Brog" assessing it as "a lightweight hodgepodge with comedic intentions... for the double bill market":

> Intentions are apparently good but the fluffy story framework runs its course at a mild pace with no strong gags or situations to bolster it. ...Marx provides some lift with facile wit in handling a line, but, overall, the effect is not enough. Sinatra comes off okay as a sort of simple-simon type of hero.[15]

The New York Times concurred, noting, "Even the most ardent devotees of Frank Sinatra, Jane Russell and Groucho Marx will find meager Christmas Cheer in *Double Dynamite*... strictly a wet firecracker."[16] But critics could not fault Frank for the overall quality of the film; while the *Times* called him "completely natural," *The Los Angeles Daily News'* Howard McClay noticed that he "displays quite a knack... in getting rid of some funny tag lines."[17]

When *Double Dynamite* played at New York's Paramount in December, it opened for the up-and-coming Tony Bennett, who was headlining a series of dates with the Art Mooney Orchestra. At least Frank's two songs in the film were good Styne and Cahn numbers, "It's Only Money" and "Kisses and Tears," duets with Groucho and Jane, respectively. In fact, the film actually is much better than its reputation: "lightweight," yes; but also funny and consistently entertaining.

As Johnny Dalton, a $42-per-week bank teller who is falsely suspected of robbing from his employer after he wins $60,000 from a bookie (Nestor Paiva), Frank is in fine comic form, building on the "innocent" persona that had been created for him at MGM: In the scene set in the gambler's office, he strongly objects to betting on horses! Other gags poke fun at his diminutive size, including an incident when he "saves" the bookie from two toughs: Hopping onto the back of one of the thugs, he provides just enough of a diversion; and, in return, he is "loaned" a thousand bucks that eventually grows into the $60,000 won at the track.

As Emile J. Keck, a waiter at the Napoli Cafe (Johnny's Italian restaurant hangout), Groucho is characteristically good. Delivering Mel Shavelson's dialogue and reciting English Renaissance poetry with equal aplomb, he is as comfortable with Frank as he was with any of his famous brothers, compensating somewhat for Jane Russell's typically stiff performance

as Mildred ("Mibs") Goodhug, Johnny's girlfriend. Groucho's introduction sets the stage for the ensuing robbery plot, as Emile, referring to Johnny's unwillingness to marry Mibs for financial reasons, suggests, with deadpan earnestness, "Why don't you rob the bank?"

Double Dynamite is not a great comedy, nor a good musical, and some of its in-jokes (one indirectly referring to Groucho's *You Bet Your Life* program) and self-reflective humor (a cop remarking that the skinny Johnny "resembles Frank Sinatra" and that Miss Goodhug is "extremely well distributed" [hence the film's title change]) might be a little too campy, but it is exponentially better than the tedious and absurd *The Kissing Bandit*. "It's Only Money," which actually makes sense, would have been a far better title for a film that marked the last performance Frank would make before beginning his more mature, substantial career as a screen actor. While *Double Dynamite* played theaters during December, Frank gave a command performance for Prince Philip and Princess Elizabeth at the London Coliseum. During their stay in London, Frank and Ava's suite at the Washington Hotel was burglarized by a thief who absconded with $17,000 worth of jewelry, including a stunning diamond necklace.

While staying at Manie Sacks' New York apartment during the autumn of 1951, Frank went out one evening and overindulged in his favorite libation, Jack Daniels bourbon. Returning inebriated, he leaned over to light a cigarette on one of the stove burners and decided to really end it all this time. After turning up all four burners, he pulled up a chair and inhaled the gas fumes. If Manie had walked in only a few minutes later, Frank would have been dead.

At this time, he publicly began criticizing Mitch Miller, stating that he would not renew his contract with Columbia when it expired a year later. However, on January 7, 1952, in Hollywood, he was in top form on Rodgers and Hart's "I Could Write a Book" from *Pal Joey*, "I Hear a Rhapsody" and "Walking In the Sunshine." But it was only a matter of time before the conflict would become unbearable: Frank had started to order Hank Sanicola to remove Miller from the recording booth if the producer intruded to instruct the band or fiddle with the controls. On February 6, Frank again was knee-deep in bad Miller material, particularly "Feet of Clay," which rivals "Mama Will Bark" for sheer inanity. Absurdity also had been rampant on the radio when he guested on the January 18 *Dean Martin and Jerry Lewis Show*, which featured the three as boyhood pals in Ed Simmons and Norman Lear's "Summer Days."

In early 1952, Frank was having difficulty landing substantial gigs, settling for dates at lesser nightclubs and saloons. Depressed that Ava had left to film *The Snows of Kilimanjaro* in Kenya, he became angry when she was held over an extra day by director Henry King's difficulties in shooting an epic scene with thousands of extras. But she was back by February 8, when they attended the premiere of *Meet Danny Wilson* at San Francisco's Orpheum Theatre.

Frank called Danny Wilson "the first role I could ever get my teeth into."[18] He understandably appreciated the dramatic opportunities the character afforded, but he also performed more songs than in any previous film, most of them great standards he had polished over the years: "All of Me," "How Deep Is the Ocean?" "She's Funny That Way," "That Old Black Magic," "When You're Smiling," "You're a Sweetheart," "Lonesome Man Blues," "I've Got a Crush on You" and "A Good Man Is Hard to Find."

A month before its release, the film had been previewed for the press, including *Variety*'s "Brog," who immediately noted the "autobiographical" material created by Don McGuire:

> The resemblance to Frank Sinatra's own career is more than passably noticeable... in a yarn about a nobody who rose from the streets to a top crooning position. As a result, it is believable entertainment, told with a sense of humor most of the time... Title role is tailor-made for Sinatra and he plays it to the hilt with an off-hand charm that displays the various facets of his personality. Character even goes so far as to show the cocky, pugnacious side the real-life crooner demonstrates on occasion...[19]

On March 26, the film played the Paramount as the opening attraction for the Buddy Rich Orchestra and vocalists Frankie Fontaine, June Hutton and—the Voice himself. The next day, *The Times* reported:

> The restraining hand of time may have had its effect on the Sinatra set, who devotedly turned up at the Paramount for a double-helping of their hero on the stage and on the screen...But the sighs and screeches that greeted the crooner heretofore were somewhat subdued yesterday morning. *Meet Danny Wilson*, oddly enough, could not have been the cause since this yarn... is tailored to Mr. Sinatra's talents and is pleasantly tune-filled and amiable. Perhaps it is the beginning of the end of an era. ...Sinatra is charming, natural and casual as he breezily portrays the cocky Danny Wilson... Sinatra fans should find nothing wrong with his rendition of [the] standards... If a jaundiced viewer can ignore that disturbing lyric in "She's Funny That Way"—the one that goes: "I'm not much to look at, nothin' to see"—chances are he will find *Meet Danny Wilson* a simple and satisfactory entertainment.[20]

Despite favorable reviews, the film was not a big hit with audiences, who shared the indifferent opinion of New York critic Wanda Hale: "Let us kindly say that the star has looked, acted and sung better before. And, in fairness, that he has had better stories to back him up."[21] Although, on October 16, Columbia had assigned a matrix number to Frank and Shelley Winters' Universal recording of "A Good Man Is Hard to Find," the track was not released commercially; and plans for a soundtrack album were scotched by the film's poor box-office returns.

Subsequent critics have appreciated *Meet Danny Wilson* for Frank's dramatic development and the self-reflective content of the screenplay. While John Howlett has called Danny "his most underestimated piece of acting,"[22] Ethan Mordden wrote:

> This is the Sinatra most people know, casual, underplaying, sharing his jokes with the audience as well as the other characters, and director Joseph

Pevney underlines the new natural Sinatra in a dark underworld setting. *Meet Danny Wilson* even touches on *verite* in Sinatra's occasional rudeness or hostility when performing; at one point he calls himself "the King." Is this *Meet Frank Sinatra*?[23]

Indeed, a great percentage of the film is "Meet Frank Sinatra," although its makers denied having based it on the Voice's own career. The truth is that Don McGuire used Frank's story as the framework for the entire screenplay, which provides an interesting fictionalized chronicle of his career up to "the fall" of the early 1950s. In fact, if the film had been more successful at the box office, it could have created a renewal of interest in Frank's music: From his first successes in nightclubs to the bobbysoxer swooning and then romantic devastation resulting in melancholic boozing, it is all there, albeit in a superficial way. Tommy Dorsey is present, too, exaggerated in the form of shady Nick Driscoll (Raymond Burr), a character who covers two bases: By giving Danny his first big break, he demands 50 percent of his income for life, casting him in a Dorsey-like light; but his status as a criminal with a couple henchman (not exactly a "gang") also addresses the subject of Mob-operated nightclubs. Through McGuire's inclusion of the framework of Frank's musical history, *Meet Danny Wilson*, during its initial release, may have been intended both to resurrect his faltering career and clear up the public's misconceptions about it. In retrospect, the film makes this very clear, giving the viewer a fascinating look not only at how a performer, in general, can affect the content of his work, but also a specific document of how Frank, even while supposedly on the skids, could command such a story (even though Universal and director Joseph Pevney may not have been the top of the cinematic heap).

Throughout the film, Danny and his piano-playing partner, Mike Ryan (Alex Nicol), make references to Frank's persona and performance style. In an early scene, after they have been bailed out of jail by Driscoll, Danny melodramatically jokes about their situation.

"Take it easy," advises Mike. "You're overacting."

"How can you tell?" Danny asks.

Later, during his first date with Joy Carroll (Winters), whom Driscoll also pursues, while discussing his cocky behavior, he admits, "I'm not tough. I'm just a little *nervous*."

When Danny "makes it," newspapers announce his "fab" record deal with Columbia, and, as the bobbysoxers go wild, a cop complains that all the excitement has been generated by "a freak with a frog in his throat." Just prior to a show at a Paramount-like theater, he recalls Jack Benny's comment about "the god-damned building [about] to cave in" when he tells Joy, "Come on with me and watch the building fall down." But, unlike the real Frank, Danny was not turned down by the draft board, and served with his pal during World War II before coming back to pound the pavement searching for gigs.

Danny also signs a lucrative movie contract with "Majestic" Pictures and holds up the filming of a feature when he attempts to contact Joy by long distance. (She tries to avoid him because she actually loves his partner.) In the end, Danny discovers their "affair," shows up inebriated at a Damon Runyon concert benefit and hits the skids before facing down Driscoll (who has returned from hiding) at Wrigley Field. (The shootout on the baseball diamond is a bit incongruous but provides a rousing conclusion to the story.)

Frank's songs are a definite highlight, and provide the best filmed document of the style he developed during the Columbia years, blending his long-breath ballad phrasing with moments of swing. Danny's audition for Driscoll is unforgettable as Frank croons "She's Funny That Way" accompanied only by piano and sexy trumpet soloing. Not only is the gangster enamored by his talent, but so is every employee in the joint, down to the janitor and the scrub woman. During Danny's first club gig, Frank flawlessly bridges the ballad and swing styles in "That Old Black Magic," moving the crowd from casual indifference to total captivation within moments. And during "When You're Smiling," Joy ignores Driscoll's attempts to give her an engagement ring. "Let's listen to him!" she demands. (Later, "Smiling" provides a powerful counterpoint when it emanates from a saloon jukebox as Danny is hunched facedown on the bar.)

In 1952 Frank and Columbia parted ways. (Photofest)

Two musical sequences lose the *cinema verite* atmosphere and tread closer to the MGM quasi-realistic style. While lounging in the slammer early in the film, Danny's vocalizing of the 12-bar "Lonesome Man Blues" (a style rarely attempted by Frank) is accompanied by the harmonica playing of a fellow inmate and some off-screen guitar strumming. But the most fantastical sequence occurs at the Los Angeles airport, when Danny tries to persuade Joy not to return to New York and her singing career. As four African-American porters harmonize beautifully, he croons "I've Got a Crush on You," creating a wonderfully entertaining sequence (and what could have been an equally romantic one, had Joy been played by an actress other than Shelley Winters; not once do we get the feeling that Danny could possibly be in love with her).

Shelley as a sort of fictionalized Ava is the film's major flaw. While her singing is acceptable, her "tough broad" style simply does not convince in a romantic-lead role. In fact, although both Frank and Alex Nicol give convincing, realistic performances, they simply do not adequately convey that they both love Joy. Not only did Universal miscast Winters, but, to make matters worse, she and Frank reportedly could not stand working with each other. (And their duet "You're a Sweetheart" is not one of the musical highlights.) Another interesting bit of casting is noticeable in the benefit scene, when the drunken Danny stumbles off the stage and into a nearby table, knocking a very young Tony Curtis out of his seat. (Seven years later, the two actors would be reunited, much more substantially, in *Kings Go Forth* [1958].)

The film ends with Danny making a successful comeback, singing "How Deep Is the Ocean?" at the London Palladium—a dramatization of Frank's own triumphant 10 dates at the venue in July 1950. (Eventually this concluding sequence would prove accurate in terms of his renewed success, but he would have to make stylistic changes in both his music and acting for this to occur.) Although some contemporary critics thought he could do better, Frank gives an outstanding performance in the film, and is supported ably by Nicol, whose Ryan has enough street smarts and common sense to reign in Danny's exuberance and cockiness. As the imposing Driscoll, Raymond Burr is a commanding presence, a figure who needs no goons to back him up when he makes a subtle suggestion to his crooning meal ticket; the actor is so good that his malevolent character is actually appealing.

Following the success of *Singin' in the Rain* (1952), MGM planned a screen adaptation of the 1935 Broadway circus musical *Jumbo*, to be produced by Arthur Freed and directed by Stanley Donen. Freed's first choice for the lead roles were Judy Garland and Frank, but neither was under contract, so Doris Day and Donald O'Connor were substituted. But when O'Connor's contract lapsed, the project was shelved. (Ten years later, *Jumbo*, pairing Stephen Boyd with Day, was directed by Charles Walters.)

Frank guested with George Burns, Groucho Marx and Danny Kaye on the March 2 *Jack Benny Program*, singing the host's infamous number, "When You Say 'I Beg Your Pardon,' Then I'll Come Back to You," which Benny had written to be performed by whomever he could convince to suffer through it. In this radio broadcast from Palm Springs commemorating the Tamarisk Country Club, "Jackson" slammed Eddie Cantor, called conductor Phil Harris a drunk, and was told to "shut up" by Kaye when he began to butter them up. The song, a melange of barber shop quartet, swing, contemporary pop and music hall mayhem, was a complete mess.

After two seasons on CBS television, *The Frank Sinatra Show*, consistently having lost ratings points to Milton Berle's program, was canceled on April 1, 1952. Later that month, Frank flew to Hawaii for a series of dates, including an appearance at the Kauai County Fair that Nancy, Jr., has called "a turning point not only in his career but in his personal life."[24] *Honolulu Advertiser* reporter Buck Buchwach was there:

> Frank went on and sang, song after song, hit after hit, maybe twenty. I was stunned. It was fantastic; it was one thousand percent for several hundred small-town ticket holders with big hearts and hands that grew red from clapping. Afterward, Frank had tears in his eyes. "Buck," he told me, "I sang the best I know how. Those people deserved it. It's a night I'll never forget. Tonight marks the first night on the way back. I can feel it in every bone." From that moment, everything seemed to go right for him.[25]

Well, not *everything*. He had to endure one last Columbia recording session on June 3, when he mixed blues (including an excellent version of "The Birth of the Blues" that has been called perhaps "the first great recording of the mature Sinatra"[26]) with two more absurd novelty songs, "Bim Bam Baby" and the washboard-driven "Tennessee Newsboy," which ranks with "Mama Will Bark" and "Feet of Clay" as the worst of the Miller-produced singles. Worse yet for Frank, while his recent sublime interpretations of the great standards had not done much business, fodder such as "Bim Bam Baby" actually charted (four weeks, reaching number 20).

In June the bottom dropped out. Beating Frank to the punch, Columbia announced they would not renew his contract, and MCA refused to represent him any longer. MGM had fired him. His television show had been canceled. He no longer had a radio program. And now he discovered that he owed an enormous amount of back taxes to the I.R.S. Frank was sans gig, but he could still work for free: On June 21, he joined Bob Hope and Bing Crosby in a telethon to raise money for the United States Olympic Committee.

On September 17, 1952, he cut his final Columbia side, the apropos "Why Try to Change Me Now?" a "miraculously tender and sensitive" performance, a "moving piece of self-analysis."[27] Around that time, pianist Bill Miller, who had joined Frank's touring rhythm section a few months earlier, heard him call Dolly and tell her, "I just fired Columbia Records."[28]

Chapter 5
Comeback Charley

I lost a great deal of faith in human nature because a lot of friends I had in those days disappeared. I don't say it begrudgingly because I [learned] something about human nature after that. I found out, or at least I think I understood, that some people don't know how to help. They want to, but they don't quite know how to do it. They're either shy or afraid they'll louse it up and make it worse than it is, because later on, when things got better for me, I just came back and kept working. I did lay down for a while and had some large bar bills for about a year, I think. But after that I said, "Holiday's over, Charley, let's go back to work."

—Frank Sinatra[1]

One day in early November 1952, Frank finished James Jones' best-selling novel *From Here to Eternity*, which had been published the previous year. As he put it down, he thought, "For the first time in my life, I was reading something I really had to do. I just felt it—I just knew I could do it. I just couldn't get it out of my head."[2] Knowing that Columbia's Harry Cohn was developing a screenplay based on the book, he told the infamously hard-headed studio chief that he was perfect to play scrappy Brooklynite Angelo Maggio, but Cohn replied that his past work as a song-and-dance partner to Gene Kelly hardly suited him to such a dramatic role. Undaunted, Frank kept up his campaign, going so far as to send telegrams signed "Maggio" to Cohn and producer Buddy Adler.

Cohn wanted *big stars* for his film. The monumental, 850-page novel, based on Jones' own experiences in the Army prior to the 1941 attack on Pearl Harbor, had not only racked up impressive sales but was praised by every major critic in the country. When Cohn, defying the wishes of Columbia's New York office, bought the screen rights from Jones for $82,000, he announced a big budget production, an atypical move for the notoriously tight-fisted minor-league mogul.

Why was Frank so adamant about playing this character? He revealed, "I knew Maggio. I went to high school with him in Hoboken. I was beaten up with him. I might have been Maggio."[3]

Then Ava entered the picture. Living in the Cohn's guest house at the time, her friend, artist Paul Clemens, invited her to dinner, where she asked Harry if her "son of a bitch husband" could be considered for the role.[4] Cohn's wife, Joan, agreed that he was right for the part, and lobbied her husband after Ava flew to Nairobi to costar with Clark Gable and Grace Kelly in John Ford's *Mogambo* on November 7. Frank accompanied her, but disliked being treated like "Mr. Ava Gardner" during the shoot. A week later, his spirits were lifted by a telegram from Bert Allenberg of the William Morris Agency asking him to return to Hollywood to shoot a screen test for *From Here to Eternity*. Ava gave him the money for an airline ticket. Less than two days—and 13,500 miles—later, he was on a Columbia soundstage.

Now he had a shot at a legitimate film role, if only he could pull off two test scenes—one set in a saloon and another in a hotel garden where he is discovered AWOL and drunk—which was not all that likely, considering that his competition was lauded stage actor Eli Wallach. Frank recalled:

That was an amazing afternoon because the director, Fred Zinnemann, said, "Well, what do we do here?" There was nothing in the script. He then said I should ad lib for two pages. I can't ad lib for a quarter of a page. And he said, "Well, do something. You know, what does a drunk do at the bar?" "Well, drunks do a lot of things at bars," I said. So I worked out some pieces of busi-

Frank and Donna Reed peruse the script of *From Here to Eternity*.

ness with a couple of olives with the dice, and all that. And that was the test. And then I went to Africa. I heard that Eli Wallach, my dear friend, had also tested and I said, "Forget it!" I thought I was dead.[5]

The day after the test, he flew back to Nairobi. To celebrate Christmas 1952, he bought presents for all the *Mogambo* principals and John Ford, who continued to cajole him about his size and weight in typical "Fordian" fashion. Grace Kelly, whose performance in the film made her a major star, later recalled:

I think we were all a little glum and gloomy about being away from home and loved ones, so Frank decided to take Christmas in hand....He...returned from Nairobi with, I think, just about every Christmas ornament the city contained and the one Santa Claus suit. I think they tried to offer him a few capes for Father Christmas, but he wouldn't accept that. And he came back to the bush,

The Actor, on Screen and in Song **101**

where we were on safari. And Christmas Eve, we gathered in the clearing, under a starry African sky, and there in the center was a huge, big mantel piece. Frank even talked John Ford into reciting "The Night Before Christmas" to us, and this wonderful evening ended with 60 Congolese Africans, barefooted, with their blankets around them, singing French Christmas carols. It was a wonderful Christmas, thanks to Frank.[6]

Following another month in the African heat (and allowing Ava to get an abortion [the second during their marriage] in London; she felt they never would have "a sane, solid lifestyle," but he sat "next to the bed with tears in his eyes"[7]), he was back on stage, playing a series of dates at Boston's Latin Quarter club. In early February 1953, he began a 10-day stint with the Bob Harrington Orchestra at Montreal's Chez Paree, where he received a call from Harry Cohn, who miraculously ordered, "Come back, you've got the part." The fact that he would receive only $8,000 for his work was beside the point.

Cohn actually had preferred Wallach, but the actor's refusal to sign a seven-year contract and demands for too much money ($20,000, when the part had been budgeted at $16,000) sent him back to Broadway, where he starred in Tennessee Williams' *Camino Real* under the direction of Elia Kazan. But common sense also led to Cohn's acceptance of Frank, who better represented the scrappy, wiry character; and—most importantly—was Italian, while the more robust Wallach shared the mogul's own Jewish ethnicity. After watching Frank's test again, Cohn turned to Adler and said, "This is a thin little guy with a caved-in chest but with a great heart."[8]

Eventually, rumors of Frank's use of his "Mob ties" to land the job began to circulate, as they had when he left Dorsey many years earlier. (Two decades later, some assumed that the singer character in Mario Puzo's *The Godfather* was based on Frank's quest for the Maggio role.) However, Frank was not the crooning actor in question. Richard Quine, a young Columbia executive when *Eternity* was made, later told Sinatra biographer Michael Freedland:

There was a great deal of talk of Mafia heavy boys trying to make a deal on behalf of an Italian-American singer. The only thing was Cohn didn't care. He had his own mob who could deal with any such disturbance. ...It was Dean Martin. ...He came begging. But nobody at Columbia would take him seriously. When the Mob moved in, Cohn told them to move out again—and they did. Perhaps Dean hadn't paid all his dues![9]

The Cinema of Sinatra

From Here to Eternity began shooting on March 2, 1953. Cohn had rejected several drafts of Daniel Taradash's screenplay, preferring to retain Jones' hard-edged thematics and profanity (which *had* to be watered down to meet Production Code standards); and the schedule had been delayed further by the Army's objection to the author's unflattering portrayals of military men. A former lieutenant with the Signal Corps, Buddy Adler secured the cooperation of top brass. When Cohn, seemingly wanting to cut back on the budget, had suggested a Columbia contract player (Aldo Ray or John Derek) to play Robert E. Lee Prewitt, director Fred Zinnemann was aghast. He would not make the picture unless Montgomery Clift was cast in the role, and the temperamental and troubled genius actor landed it at $150,000. Intense leading man Burt Lancaster had been signed to play Sergeant Milton Warden for $120,000, followed by Deborah Kerr (who had to lose her English accent to play Karen Holmes, the unfaithful wife of Captain Dana Holmes [Philip Ober]), Donna Reed (as Alma Lorene, a dance hostess [prostitute in Jones' novel]) and Ernest Borgnine.

On March 13, after being rejected by RCA, Frank signed a seven-year contract with Capitol Records' Alan Livingston, who had invited him and his aides Hank Sanicola and Frank Military to lunch at Lucy's in Hollywood. The terms were a far cry from what he had enjoyed at Columbia for nine years, namely that he would have to pay the musicians as well as all fees for arranging and copying, while receiving no advances. It was a lousy deal, but he had no alternative. At Capitol's subsequent annual convention, Livingston's announcement of the signing was greeted with pessimism, but Voyle Gilmore, who agreed that "Frank is the best singer in the world," became his record producer, suggesting that he work with the up-and-coming Nelson Riddle rather than Axel Stordahl.

Frank had never heard of Nelson Riddle. At the KHJ radio studios in Hollywood on April 2, 1953, he cut four sides with Stordahl at the helm, but only "Lean Baby" and "I'm Walking Behind You" were released. Although the arrangements differed little from those Stordahl did at Columbia, Frank sang with great confidence, lending a toe-tapping drive to Heinie Beau's arrangement of the former. But the Voice's insistence on sticking with Axel was cut short when the conductor accepted the position of musical director on *Coke Time*, Eddie Fisher's television series. Shot in New York, the lucrative job would prevent Stordahl from working on further Hollywood sessions. With this initial Capitol date in the can, Frank reported back to Columbia to prepare for the location scenes of *Eternity*. Burt Lancaster recalled the cast's flight to film in Hawaii:

> Deborah Kerr and me and Frank and Monty are sitting up in front of the plane. And he and Monty are drunk. Monty, poor Monty, was this kind of a drinker—he'd chug-a-lug one martini and conk out. And Frank was, I believe, having a few problems, and so, when we arrived, these two bums were unconscious. They were gone! Deborah and I had to wake them up.
> ...This is the way they arrived, and Harry Cohn is down there with the press and everything. Well, we got through that, and now we start to do the picture.

Every night, after work, we would meet in Frank's room. He had a refrigerator and he would open it and there would be these iced glasses. He would prepare the martinis with some snacks while we were getting ready to go to an eight o'clock dinner. We'd sit and chat about the day's work... When you finished your martini, he would take the glass from you, open up the icebox and get a fresh cold glass, and by eight o'clock he and Monty would be unconscious. I mean really unconscious. Every night. So Deborah and I would take Frank's clothes off and put him to bed. Then I would take Monty on my shoulders and we would carry him down to *his* room, take *his* clothes off and dump *him* in bed. And then she and I and the Zinnemanns would go out and have dinner.[10]

The Hawaiian exterior work involved the use of several locations represented in the novel, including Schofield Barracks (to which the Army initially had objected), Diamond Head, Waikiki Beach, the Royal Hawaiian Hotel and the Waialea Golf Course. After returning to the mainland, the cast and crew filmed some outdoor sequences at the Columbia Ranch. Lancaster vividly recalled the problems encountered during the shooting of Maggio's late-night death scene:

It's 38 degrees... We're doing the scene where I'm sitting in the road with Monty and at the end of the scene in comes Frank, who has been beaten up by Borgnine, and he dies in Monty's arms. ...The crew gave us coffee and they laced it with brandy. After about two sips Monty was unconscious. And they had to call off the shooting for an hour or two. Monty got up, we walked him around, and then Frank and I went with him to a little tent and he lay down on a cot.[11]

When Jack Fier, Harry Cohn's head of production, rushed into the tent, paranoically ranting that a doctor must be called to get Clift back in action, Frank flew at him, ready to strike, but was contained by Lancaster. Just as Frank tried a second time, Clift regained consciousness and calmly settled the matter, frightening himself in the process. Lancaster added that Fier "didn't know how to deal with this sort of nonviolent approach to things," while Daniel Taradash claimed, "I think everybody had good reason to be grateful to Frank. Without him, it [the scene] might not have happened."[12]

Cast as Maggio's nemesis, Fatso Judson, Borgnine had difficulty treating his "idol" with brutality:

I loved him in everything he did. And I said, "How can I, a mere nothing, come on here?" But I knew I had to play this part as the meanest SOB that ever existed, otherwise the part won't play. ...I'm just shaking... And Fred suddenly looked up and said, "OK, begin the scene!" So we started. I'm playing the piano and it came to the point where Frank says, "Come on, why don't you stop this banging on the piano, will ya? Give us a chance with our music." And I stood up to say my first line. I said, "Listen you little wop." He looked up at me, and as he looked up at me, he broke out into a smile and he said, "My God, he's ten feet tall!" Do you know the whole thing just collapsed. His laughter broke the tension. It was so marvelous. I've never forgotten Frank for that. He was the most wonderful guy to work with that you ever saw in your life. He knew how I must have felt... And because of it, he took the time to break that tension. That's something that I have done with everybody that I've worked with since. I break the ice for the other people. And I think it's nice because it reverberates all down the line.[13]

With Axel Stordahl out of the picture, Capitol wanted Billy May to arrange the next Sinatra recording session, but the popular bandleader (who had several swing instrumental hits to his credit) was out on the road. Therefore, it was up to Nelson Riddle to nurture Frank's new swinging sound by writing two charts, a lá May, "South of the Border" and "I Love You," as well as penning two in his own style. On April 30, Frank was back at KHJ studios, where he sang Harold Arlen and Ted Koehler's "I've Got the World on a String" and *meant* it. What a way to begin the collaboration with Riddle, who had started his career as a big-band trombonist before graduating to arranger-conductor for the likes of Nat Cole (including the superlative "Mona Lisa," a perfect pop recording). Backed by Riddle's pulsing tempo punctuated by powerful brass kicks, Frank swings with a newly found assurance, a declaration of confidence from a musician who obviously understands *what* he is singing as well as how to sing it. He had performed the song during concerts the previous year, but now he and his new colleague (whom he apparently met just moments before cutting the song [in 10 takes]) made it a transcendent work of musical art. Will Friedwald (in his usual hyperbolic fashion) wrote:

> It would be remarkable if it were their third project or even if it were their twelfth, but the fact of it's being their first makes it yet more incredible. ...the partnership has already reached a pinnacle — it almost has nowhere to go, every element is already there and in place. ...It's more than the new arranger-relationship that's established here, but the entire new Sinatra persona is herewith launched. This is the dynamic, hard-swinging, hell-bent for leather Sinatra of the Eisenhower years, and it too is here fully formed, as if it had sprung from the head of Zeus. ...When he sings "if I should ever let it go," he's clearly speaking with the knowledge of someone who knows what it's like to let go, to let go of his career, as he had in the past few seasons, and now to let go of his inhibitions, and to dive into a bold new direction, as he does here.[14]

At KHJ on May 2, Frank cut four more songs for single release, all Riddle arrangements of ballads, including the wonderfully romantic "My One and Only Love" and "From Here to Eternity," a song not written for the film but pitched to Harry Cohn as a way to promote it. Frank Military recalled, "Frank made a great record of that song, but he never really liked it"[15]; though it reached number 15 on the charts, he never performed it again.

On May 10, *The New York Times* reported James Jones' own observations about the filming of *Eternity*:

> He said he'd been watching the shooting up until the day the crew departed for Hawaii to film the outdoor stuff, and it all looked absolutely right, even to the shoes under the foot lockers. Montgomery Clift, he went on, had hovered around him for days at a time trying to pick up clues and insights into Prewitt. He and Burt Lancaster... were wonderful. Mr. Jones didn't qualify it. He also didn't qualify his silence on Frank Sinatra... He said he was told, and he himself had the feeling, that all hands down (or up to) the grips and gaffers had caught the excitement. Was Mr. Jones excited? "Well," Mr. Jones declared, "it was kind of weird in a way — seeing those faces you'd seen before playing people that had come out of your own head."[16]

Zinnemann was consistently impressed with Frank's professionalism during the shoot: "He was very, very good — all the time. No histrionics, no bad behavior. He always took direction."[17] While Adler said that "He dreamed, slept and ate his part," Zinnemann added, "He played Maggio so spontaneously we almost never had to reshoot a scene."[18] Both Lancaster and Clift were impressed with the rushes they viewed each day. After seeing one of Frank's close-ups, Clift responded, "He's going to win the Academy Award."[19] Later, Frank admitted, "I learned more about acting from [Clift] than I ever knew before."[20] Later, Frank, comparing the arts of singing and acting, elaborated on how One-Take Charley had adapted himself to this particular role:

> As a singer... I rehearse and plan exactly where I'm going. But as an actor, no, I can't do that. To me, acting is reacting. If you set it up right, you can almost go without knowing every line. But if you're not set up right, if the guy you're acting with doesn't know what he's doing, forget it, the whole thing's a mess. If I rehearse to death, I lose the spontaneity I think works for me. So... it's a problem for me sometimes working with a guy, or girl, who has to go over something 50 times before they get it right. I wanna climb the wall. I wanna say, "Jesus Christ, just do it, and let's move on." With Montgomery, though, I had to be patient, because I knew that if I watched this guy, I'd learn something. We had a mutual-admiration thing going there.[21]

With *Eternity* in the can, Frank set off on a lengthy concert tour of Europe. Ava took a hiatus from shooting *Knights of the Round Table* (1954) to join him on a "second honeymoon," but during a performance in Italy, audience members angered over *her* failure to appear booed him off the stage before shouting, "Ava!" over and over again.

Back in the States, *From Here to Eternity* was released "in stereophonic sound" on August 23, 1953. The film repeated the success of the novel, grabbing both critical raves and huge box-office receipts, raking in a total of $19 million during its initial run. Appropriately, Taradash's screenplay opens with a scene involving Monty and Frank, as bugler, former boxer and future whipping boy Prewitt arrives at Schofield barracks while Maggio is doing grounds work. Referring to Clift as "arguably the most sensitive male actor in movie history," Sinatra aficionado Stan Britt noted his influence on Frank:

> You can see Sinatra's debt to the short-lived Clift in *Eternity* itself, as well as in many of Sinatra's acting assignments during the Fifties and Sixties. The hunched shoulders, the sometimes clenched fists, and the haunted look—they were all physical trademarks inherited from Monty Clift by Sinatra, who used them, intelligently and naturally, to his own advantage.[22]

The "great heart" noticed by Harry Cohn is what makes Maggio tick as he stands up for the abused Prewitt. Early on, when "Prew's" billiard game is interrupted by other enlisted men who accuse him of being scared to box, the scrappy Italian is the only one who gets in his corner, explaining, "I just hate to see a good guy get it in the gut." Soon after, when he again supports Prew's refusal to give in to coercion, he joins his new friend on the track, running seven laps while carrying his rifle.

In his first dramatic role sans vocalizing, Frank demonstrates his innate magnetism. Though he was not required to perform a song (several of the other enlisted men harmonize "Reenlistment Blues" on two occasions, and Prew rips into a swinging bugle ride at the Congress Club), he does work in some musical material, including singing some trumpet riffs while standing in the pay line, humming and "trumpeting" "Chattanooga Choo-Choo" while preparing for a night on the town, and criticizing the bad piano stylings of Fatso at the Congress Club. Ordering him to stop playing his "stinkin' noise," Maggio sparks a conflict that inevitably culminates with his death (Fatso is sergeant of the guard at the stockade).

Maggio possesses a large degree of the innocence and naiveté of Frank's earlier screen characters, combined with a tendency to lash out against what he views as injustice and unfairness. He not only stands up for a fellow mistreated G.I., but also seeks a little pleasure, wearing flashy Hawaiian shirts ("my sister sends them to me") and seeking solace in inebriation. But his

Sinatra makes the most of his first dramatic role in *From Here to Eternity*.

naive views on the military eventually lead to his ruin, when, deprived of a pass after getting ready to leave the base, he goes AWOL and later is discovered, unconscious and half naked on a hotel bench, by Prew, who is unable to rescue him from two MPs. Ultimately, Prew sacrifices his own life to avenge Maggio's death, killing Fatso in a savage knife fight behind the Congress Club before attempting to reach the base after the Japanese attack on Pearl Harbor. Unlike Jones' novel, which harshly criticizes the military establishment, the film telescopes the brutality and inhumanity into the lone figure of Captain Holmes and some of the enlisted men who follow his twisted orders.

Although the Maggio role is a supporting one, giving Frank far less screen time than the leads and even some of the other "second stringers" like Philip Ober, his performance is the best in the film. Lancaster is his usual intense self, Kerr sometimes can't mask her English accent and Donna Reed goes a bit over the top when the seriously wounded Prew decides to return to the base. Clift is excellent, yet he does not match Frank in the scenes involving drunkenness. Never once does Frank appear to be acting, and the natural quality of his performance combined with his magnetism are what led Clift to mention the possibility of an Oscar win. Frank is at turns likable, powerful, naive and humorous, particularly in the initial scene set at the Congress Club, where he again reveals the influence of Stan Laurel in his gestures and facial expressions, as he and Prew prepare to get loaded.

Despite some of the story's soap-opera elements, *From Here to Eternity* is an unforgettable film, with many of Zinnemann and cinematographer Burnett Guffey's indelible close-up images perfectly capturing the nuances created by Reed and Clift, the latter's most effective moment, sans dialogue, occurring as Prew tearfully plays taps the morning after Maggio's tragic death. Contemporary reviews stressed the contributions of Zinnemann and Guffey, as well as Monty and Frank, as in "Brog's" *Variety* critique:

Clift, with a reputation for sensitive, three-dimensional performances, adds another to his growing list... Sinatra scores a decided hit... While some may be amazed at this expression of the Sinatra talent versatility, it will come as no surprise to those who remember the few times he has had a chance to be something other than a crooner in films.[23]

While *Time* noted that Frank "does Private Maggio like nothing he has ever done before," *The Los Angeles Examiner*'s Ruth Waterbury wrote, "He is simply superb, comical, pitiful, childishly brave, pathetically defiant. ...Sinatra makes his death scene one of the best ever photographed."[24]

Truth to tell, the plummeting of Frank's career is more legend than fact. In retrospect, Sinatra historians concur that, in the words of Leonard Mustazza, "reports of the death of [his] career in 1952 were certainly premature, for it reached staggering heights beginning the following year and never bothered to come down."[25] And the assertion that *From Here to Eternity* completely jump-started his career is also slightly exaggerated. Capitol signed him four months *before* the film's release and earned subsequent widespread critical praise, and Frank already had shifted into his more confident, mature and harder swinging style with Riddle before completing his *Eternity* assignment. So, while the film, which became a hit prior to the release of his first Capitol albums, did put the Voice back on top, now as a serious and powerful actor, the rejuvenation of his musical career (freed from the commercial meddling of A&R men like Mitch Miller) was already under way. Fortunately for Frank, in March and April 1953, he was introduced to both Fred Zinnemann and Nelson Riddle, who helped him simultaneously to create second, more successful stages in his film and musical careers, respectively. Now his acting and singing, which sprang from the same font of natural talent, would develop hand in hand even more spectacularly.

Following his last European date, Frank and Ava returned to the East Coast in September 1953. He had accepted an offer from Skinny D'Amato to play the 500 Club in Atlantic City, where he was introduced to Chicago mobster Sam Giancana, a figure who, like Lucky Luciano, would plague him in the future. "Momo" loved good singing, and was a big fan. When Ava asked Frank why he treated such a hoodlum with respect, he replied pragmatically, "That hoodlum is responsible for giving me a job."[26] Before flying to Los Angeles, where Ava departed for Palm Springs, they attended the premiere of *Mogambo* in New York on October 2.

Four days later, Frank began starring in the radio noir series *Rocky Fortune*, which ran 26 weeks (October 6, 1953-March 30, 1954). In the opening episode, "Oyster Shucker," his "footloose and frequently unemployed young gentleman"—his first detective role—found a dozen pearls, got held up and discovered a smuggling racket. The second installment, "Steven in a Rest Home," broadcast on March 13, depicted him cracking a double indemnity scam and revealing his real name as "Rocco Fortunato."

He then returned to Las Vegas, where he began a week of concerts at the Sands on October 19. On the day following his final show, he and Ava—only 11 months after their wedding—claiming irreconcilable differences, announced their separation and impending divorce. But a month later, still hoping to patch things up, Frank intended to accompany his estranged wife to Europe, where she would be shooting *The Barefoot Contessa* with his pal Humphrey Bogart. However, the stress of performing in *Rocky Fortune* and another weekly New York radio show, *To Be Perfectly Frank* (which ran November 3, 1953-July 2, 1954), overwhelmed him. Rushed to Mount Sinai Hospital, he was diagnosed with "complete physical exhaustion, severe loss of weight, and a tremendous amount of emotional strain."[27] In her memoir *My Father's Daughter*, Tina Sinatra wrote:

> Dad's days with Ava were numbered, even before he made his comeback in *From Here to Eternity*. ...To reinvent himself and revive his career, my father had to focus on his work. He couldn't do that and hold on to Ava, too. The stronger he got, the less responsible she felt for him."[28]

Two weeks after his illness, the Voice was back again, joining Riddle in Hollywood to cut material for his first Capitol "concept" album, *Songs for Young Lovers*, a work that Stan Britt has labeled "a milestone in the history of recorded music."[29] Recorded with a small jazz ensemble in just two days (November 5-6, 1953), all eight songs (seven of which were George Siravo arrangements Frank had been using on his road dates) became superlative Sinatra classics, particularly the Gershwins' "A Foggy Day" and "They Can't Take That Away from Me," Rodgers and Hart's "My Funny Valentine" and Cole Porter's "I Get a Kick Out of You," perhaps the finest version of the 1934 standard. By far the best of his five recordings of the song, "Kick" is a perfect combination of bouncy swing and long-breath phrasing, exquisitely rendered on the lines, "Flying so high with my gal in the sky,—*issss*—my idea of nothin' to do." For the only time, Frank also included Porter's reference to cocaine, drawing out the composer's rhyme with a brilliantly long-phrased "sniff riff" that suggests a drug abuser snorting the narcotic powder: "Some may go for cocaine, but if I took even one sniff, it would bore me terri*ffffff*-fically too. But I get a kick out of you." (Later he would substitute "the perfume in Spain" or "the bop-tight refrain" for cocaine.) The *Young Lovers* album contains many such examples of Frank "acting" the lyrics for maximum effect, further proving that his singing and screen talents were linked inextricably.

At KHJ on December 8 and 9, Frank cut several additional sides with Riddle to be released as singles. Some—"Take a Chance," "Why Should I Cry Over You?" (adding "Frankisms" to the lyrics like "all of my love was a *big fat* waste of time" *and* simultaneously improving the rhythm) and "Ya Better Stop" (a bluesy number issued only in Great Britain)—were moderate swingers, but it was a beautiful, winsomely orchestrated balled, Johnny Richards and Carolyn Leigh's "Young at Heart," that emerged as the sessions' top number, hitting number one on the *Billboard* chart and remaining there for 22 weeks. Frank insisted on 27 takes before he was satisfied, and the resulting masterpiece offers another example of the "reborn" Sinatra, one who is confident, positive and imparting an upbeat message to others: Regardless of one's circumstances, "you have a head start, if you are among the very young at heart." During the final phrase, Frank, demonstrating how he used musical performance to narrative effect, holds the word "young" for additional emphasis. Two more ballads, "I Could Have Told You" and "Rain (Falling from the Skies)," benefited from Frank's long-breath phrasing and Riddle's lush, atmospheric string arrangements.

Having amassed enough capital to make a $54,000 investment, Frank's bid to buy two percent of the Sands was approved by the Nevada Gaming Commission in January 1954. Having re-established at least a tentative foothold in the music and film industries, he decided to increase his business interests beyond publishing and chose the playground of his old friend Jack Entratter, who had owned the Copacabana during the Voice's first gigs there.

Back as *Rocky Fortune* on February 16, Frank was offered $5,000 to bump off one of "Too Many Husbands" by southern belle Lulu Ann (Betty Lou Gerson). In his noir narration, he recounted:

You know, there's an old saying, "Never look a gift horse in the mouth." With pen in cheek, I now write me a new saying: "Never look a gift blonde in the eyes." She was blonde, 'cause her hair told me so. That was the only proof I had. She didn't walk; she insinuated. She was from New Orleans and her name was Lu; and believe me, brother, Lu was no lady. When I saw her, I said to myself, "I dig this babe." She almost dug me, too—right into a grave.

While waiting for Sergeant Hamilton J. Finger (Barney Phillips) to answer the phone, Rocky sang a bit of "From Here to Eternity."

"Don't tell me. Let me guess: Frank Sinatra?" the cop asked.

"Oh, you are a *funny* man," replied the Rock.

At the top of his form with an Oscar nomination dancing around in his head, he cut three gorgeous ballads at KHJ on March 1. Riddle had rearranged Axel Stordahl's version of Rube Bloom and Johnny Mercer's "Day In, Day Out," which surrounds a dramatic Frank with a dynamic duel between Kathryn Julye's flowing harp and the playful yet subtle flourishes of the string section, all of it crescendoing into a climax underpinned by Frank Carlson's percussion. (Unfortunately, the track was withheld from U.S. release and issued only in Europe.) Harold Arlen and E. Y. Harburg's superb "Last Night When We Were Young," also opening with Julye's harp, and Jule Styne and Sammy Cahn's "Three Coins in the Fountain" were sung so well that it seemed the orchestra had stolen Frank's voice and was not about to give it back.

On March 21, he guested on *The Bing Crosby Show*, singing "Young at Heart" and duets with the old man on "Among My Souvenirs" and "September Song" with John Scott Trotter's Orchestra. Four days later, his professional dream really came true when he was joined by Nancy, Jr., and young Frankie for the 26th annual Academy Awards ceremony at the RKO Pantages Theatre in Hollywood. On the eve of the festivities, he received a gift from his family, including Nancy, Sr.: a gold St. Genesius medallion featuring a bas relief of the Oscar statuette on the reverse. Good luck then ensued, for *From Here to Eternity* won six Academy Awards, including best picture, director, screenplay, cinematography and supporting actress (Donna Reed). When Mercedes McCambridge stepped up to the podium to open the best supporting actor envelope, she read

'From Here To Eternity' Named Year's Best Film

HOLLYWOOD (UP) — A story considered useless as movie material, a big-eyed Hollywood newcomer, a veteran actor William Holden, won coveted Oscars last night at the 26th Academy Award ceremonies. "From Here to Eternity" reached the rank of a film music by winning eight separate awards including the "best picture" Oscar—honors that equalled those for old favorite "Gone with the Wind." Miss Hepburn won the best actress award for her first picture, "Roman Holiday." Holden won his first Oscar for his portrayal of the cynical hero in "Stalag 17." Song and dance man Frank Sinatra, to the shouts and applause of 2800 celebrities and fans in the Pantages Theater here, collected the best supporting actor award for his first serious role, that of tragic GI in "From Here to Eternity."

One of his co-stars, pretty Donna Reed, shouted "hurray" and raced to the stage to take an Oscar for the best supporting actress of 1953, also an "Eternity" role. "From Here to Eternity," James Jones' lusty barracks-room novel of Army life in pre-Pearl Harbor days, had been turned down by many major studios before Columbia bought it for the screen. Jones' earthy dialogue and plot had been considered unsuitable for film fare.

Yet it swept the Academy Awards categories, equalling "Gone with the Wind," and passing "The Best Years of Our Lives" which won seven Oscars.

Fred Zinneman won for best director and Daniel Taradash for best screen play with "Eternity." The movie also scored in the black and white photography and film editing divisions.

the names of Eddie Albert in *Roman Holiday*, Robert Strauss in *Stalag 17* (for which the superb William Holden beat out a devastated Monty Clift for the best actor award), little Brandon de Wilde in *Shane* and Frank, who was poised to run up the aisle before she broke the seal.

Accepting the statuette with humility and great shyness, Frank said:

Ladies and gentlemen, I'm very thrilled and deeply moved, and I really, really don't know what to say, because this is a whole new kind of thing. You know, I've done song and dance man type stuff, and I'm terribly pleased, and if I start thanking everybody, I'll do a one-reeler up here, so I better not. And I'd just like to say, however, that they're doing a lot of songs here tonight, but nobody asked me. But I love you, though. Thank you very much. I'm absolutely thrilled. Thank you.

Later, Frank avoided any congratulatory gestures. "Talk about being 'born again'," he said. "I couldn't even share it with another human being. I ducked the party, lost the crowds and took

The Cinema of Sinatra

a walk. Just me and Oscar. I think I relived my entire life as I walked up and down the streets of Beverly Hills."[30]

Three days after taking the statuette home, he sang "Take a Chance" on *The Bing Crosby Show*, joining the host on "'Til We Meet Again," "Meet Me Tonight in Dreamland" and "There's a Long, Long Trail." On March 30, he gave his final performance as *Rocky Fortune*, claiming he was Julius LaRosa after being mistaken for a thief. The following day, he re-recorded "Three Coins in the Fountain" for the opening credits of the 20th Century-Fox film starring Clifton Webb and Dorothy McGuire. Two days later, he waxed a syrupy novelty, "The Sea Song," with a chorus and orchestra conducted by Riddle, for release only in Australia.

But from April 7 through 19 at KHJ, he cut eight magnificent Riddle arrangements of standards for an album titled *Swing Easy*, a superb follow-up to the previous year's *Songs for Young Lovers*. Opening with Cole Porter's tale of a burned-out love affair, "Just One of Those Things," this collection of moderate rhythm songs became Riddle's favorite project with Frank, who had been using George Siravo's arrangements of some of the numbers on stage, as he had with the material recorded for *Young Lovers*.

"Just One of Those Things" is a truly sublime Sinatra recording, one of the very finest of his career. Throughout the song, he perfectly blends his unique phrasing and dynamics with a subtle, beautifully controlled tremolo that rides just above Riddle's bouncy swing. The song begins with a lightly driving pulse created in equal parts by brass and the rhythm section before Frank smoothly comes in on two elongated pick-up notes, initially laying back while the band swings along, a sprightly piano punctuated by tasteful saxophone riffs. After completing the first verse and chorus, the band begins to swing a bit harder, with Frank alternately driving them and getting behind the beat, subtly holding a note, then allowing a pause before letting loose of the lyric: "A trip to the m*ooooonnnnnn* on gossamer wings—Just one those things." But it is the second time through the chorus that Frank unleashes one of his most amazing feats of rhythmic phrasing (even he would never repeat it in future versions of the song). Demonstrating the improvisational quality that made him a great jazz musician as well as the supreme interpreter of popular songs, he doubles the time it takes to sing a single line, swinging Porter's original lyric "So goodbye, baby, and amen..." something like this: "So good-bye, goodbye, bye—bye, goodbye, ba-by, and a-me*nnnnnn*..." weaving a charismatic musical trance for the listener. Sinatra scholar Ed O'Brien agrees: "It is the verbal and melodic improvisations of Sinatra and Riddle on 'Just One of Those Things' that deliver a Cole Porter song from popularity to perfection."[31]

Everything is light and upbeat (hence the album's title), with the punchy sound of a small combo rhythm section enhanced by tasteful brass arrangements and soloing on "I'm Gonna Sit Right Down and Write Myself a Letter," "Sunday," "Wrap Your Troubles in Dreams," "Taking a Chance on Love," "Jeepers Creepers" and the ultimate feel-good standard, "Get Happy," which features a dramatic, crescendoing instrumental bridge that would become a trademark of the Riddle-Sinatra collaborations. Of all eight, "All of Me" was the only song Frank had cut previously, first as a V-Disc and then for Columbia and *Meet Danny Wilson*. Here, he again improvises, "I'm just a *mess* without you" and then ends the album on an emotional high note with "Why not take *all* of me?" By this time, he indeed was giving the public everything he had in his entertainment arsenal.

At this time, Frank was accepted into an elite group of show-business people who gathered at Romanoff's Restaurant in Beverly Hills. "Led" by his former Holmby Hills neighbor Humphrey Bogart, this group of "nonconformists" included David and Hjordis Niven, Judy Garland and her husband Sid Luft, Jimmy Van Heusen, Swifty Lazar, Mike and Gloria Romanoff, and Bogie's wife, Lauren ("Betty") Bacall, who was quite fond of Frank. When they weren't imbibing at Romanoff's, they partied in the Bogart's "butternut" room or during trips to Vegas. Upon observing the extremely dissipated state of the Holmby Hills mob at the end of a four-day, Frank-"sponsored" binge, Bacall exclaimed, "You look like a goddamn rat pack."[32] Not long afterward, the press latched onto the term. Bogie said, "Frank's a hell of a guy. He tries to live his own life. If he could only stay away from the broads and devote some time to develop himself as an actor, he'd be one of the best in the business."[33] While Bogart was the "public relations" man, Frank was "packmaster," Luft "cagemaster," Garland "first vice-president," Lazar "recording secretary and treasurer" and Bacall "den mother." Nathaniel Benchley, dubbed pack "historian," drew their insignia depicting a rat gnawing on a human hand. (A few years earlier, when Betty was pregnant, Frank, Romanoff, Paul Douglas and others had thrown a baby shower for Bogie. "His shower was bigger than the one I had," Bacall said.[34])

On May 6, Frank discussed his latest film work on the *Talk with Louella Parsons* show. "You wouldn't say anything behind my back that you wouldn't say to my face, would you?" he asked at one point. And on August 15, he took some shots at Bing on *The Gary Crosby Summer Show*, a radio program hosted by the old man's son. "I believe that John Scott Trotter has already hacked down my arrangement of 'Half as Lovely' to summer show size," he claimed, afterward telling young Crosby, "In order to put across a song like that, you've got to suffer."

With another satisfying album ready for release, Frank needed a successful dramatic follow-up to prove that *From Here to Eternity* was no fluke. Claiming that he had been promised the lead role in *On the Waterfront*, which is set in Hoboken, he was crushed when this seemingly tailor-made character was given to Marlon Brando. Unable to persuade Budd Schulberg and Columbia to budge, he sued for $500,000 but settled out of court.

Instead—just as he had surprised the public with Maggio—he again opted for a character different than those he had played previously. After a proposed role in the musical *Pink Tights* fell through due to a tempestuous walk-out by Marilyn Monroe, he shifted 180 degrees, accepting independent producer Robert Bassler's offer to play psychotic killer John Baron in *Suddenly*, a suspenseful and intense film about presidential assassination, a topic that only had been depicted by D.W. Griffith, with respect to the United States' 16th chief executive, in *The Birth of a Nation* (1915) and *Abraham Lincoln* (1930). Frank was taking a risk with such a heinous role, but knew that, if he pulled it off, it could greatly advance his acting career. And this time, he would be top-billed, above the title with Sterling Hayden, who was signed to portray Tod Shaw, the rock-jawed Sheriff of Suddenly, California, a formerly wild frontier town that now has been quiet for a half-century.

Although it was not shot in an anamorphic "scope" process, *Suddenly* was filmed to compete with the widescreen films that currently were attracting audiences away from their living room television sets. Director Lewis Allen and cinematographer Charles G. Clarke composed their shots in the standard 1.33:1 ratio, but then masked the final cut to be projected in the aspect of 1:66:1, giving it a pseudo-scope appearance. Although it is not a true widescreen film, it was the first such production Frank took part in.

During the shoot, *New York Times* Hollywood correspondent M. A. Schmidt was allowed on the set to watch Frank work:

> He tenses, like a fighter going into the first round, when he has a job to do.
> But the tension is caused by concentration, not by uncertainty. ...When the action was over, his whole body seemed to melt into relaxation.[35]

As usual, Frank approached the filmmakers to suggest ways he could improve his character and "benefit the film." Robert Bassler recalled, "I steeled myself, for there is nothing more disturbing than the celebrations of an actor. But Frank wasn't making demands to exploit himself at the expense of the picture. The suggestions he offered made sense."[36]

Scripted by Richard Sale, a veteran novelist and screenwriter whose previous credits included the original story for MGM's eerie *Strange Cargo* (1940), *Suddenly* consistently examines the role violence plays in American society, making the film, however generalized and simplistic, seem prophetic when viewed decades later. Opening with a tourist being told about the town's old days of hell raising, the initial scene includes Sheriff Shaw and young Pidge Benson (Kim Charney) discussing the boy's desire to have a cap pistol. "Mom won't let me see war pictures," Pidge tells him. "She doesn't like guns." Although Ellen Benson's (Nancy Gates) aversion to violence was bred by his father's death in World War II (making it impossible for Pidge to remember him), he still wants to be "a sheriff like Tod" when he grows up. After trying to make a date with Ellen in the supermarket, Tod is reprimanded for buying the boy the cap pistol.

"Guns aren't necessarily bad," the sheriff explains, adding, "It depends on who uses them," trying to emphasize that even a child needs to acknowledge the reality of the outside world, that shielding Pidge will only make it more difficult for him later in life. Here, Allen's verite visual style, aided by shooting on location in a small California town, perfectly complements Hayden's dialogue as the couple and the boy walk out onto Suddenly's main street.

Sinatra as the psychotic killer in *Suddenly*

Sale's script is carefully structured, with each event subtly foreshadowing those to follow. At the beginning, a citizen's use of the word "hangover," which then is reinforced by the Secret Service's choice of "Operation Hangover" for its investigation of the town, where the president is soon to make a stop, indicates that some residue from Suddenly's violent past remains, though it ultimately arrives from outside its environs in the form of hit man Baron and his two accomplices, Benny Conklin (Paul Frees) and Bart Wheeler (Christopher Dark).

The remainder of the plot is presaged when Shaw meets the feds. After agent Dan Carney (Willis Bouchey) tells Shaw, "You're a careful man, Sheriff," Shaw replies, "Not always. Thought this was a good time to be, though." Learning that a house on the hill is owned by his "old boss," "Pop" Benson (James Gleason), Carney grins from ear to ear, perhaps becoming a bit overconfident. Meanwhile, just as state troopers begin to roll in, the three criminals led by Baron arrive at the scene, driving to Benson's house, where they introduce themselves as FBI agents. Prior to their arrival, "Pop," proud of his son who sacrificed his life during the war, and echoing Shaw's earlier warning to Ellen, mentions the "cruelty, hatred and tyranny in the world."

John Baron's attire includes the first cinematic appearance of Frank's famous Cavanaugh hat, a visual aspect that immediately suggests an attitude of toughness and subtle swagger. Telling the Bensons that he and his men need to secure the house to protect the president, Baron gazes out the window to the train yard below, allowing Frank to register the first of many subtle, naturalistic facial expressions that barely mask the character's psychosis. Here, he demonstrates a great performer's talent for expressing so much by doing so little. Though Baron gets more talkative, revealing details about his plan, as the film progresses, Frank's nonverbal acting is just as effective: Nuance, particularly in the way he uses his eyes, and the controlled violence he exhibits through hair-trigger gestures are masterfully combined.

Promised $500,000 to kill the president "for absolutely nothin'—that politics jazz, it's not my racket," Baron, becoming increasingly agitated and psychotic, explains to Shaw, Pop, Ellen and television repair man Jud Hobson (Jim Lilburn) that he learned to enjoy killing during the war. "I killed 27 men all by myself," he repeats, proudly stressing that he won a Silver Star for his murderous efforts. He views working for an independent operation as an extension of killing for the United States government: The work is the same; the employer different. Baron does not have to reveal much before Shaw can tell he is a megalomaniac. When the sheriff mentions previous assassinations, including those of Lincoln and McKinley, Baron joins in, adding Garfield and boasting that his will be different, because it has never been tried before. Baron's weakness is his egotistical bravado, but he eventually needs to keep talking to release the tension that is building up inside him; to avoid sensory overload, he orders the others to be quiet so he "can *think*." Later, he says, "I have to think of everything!" He also unleashes stress by reveling in others' pain, as when he punches the Sheriff's broken arm, which one of his cohorts earlier had shot and he had "reset" by yanking the bones back into place.

After the inept Benny, who complained about having to reconnoiter the town, is gunned down by the authorities, Baron's mission is jeopardized. When an officer arrives at the house, he orders Ellen to tell them that Carney, Pop and the boy had left. To his remaining henchman, he commands, "If anybody gets brave, kill 'em all. You can only hang once." After Shaw taunts him about being a Section Eight during the war, killing innocent people and being court-martialed, Baron admits, "Without the gun, I'm nothin'." Having wired the metal table holding the gun with high voltage from the television set, Jud is killed but electrocutes Bart, leaving only Baron, who, attempting to fire the gun himself, is driven over the edge when the train speeds through the station. Having grabbed Pop's old Secret Service pistol from a bedroom drawer (it resembles his own cap gun), Pidge fires a shot before sliding it to Ellen, who, along with Shaw, drops the cold-blooded assassin. Shortly before his death, Baron had displayed a split second of humanity by allowing Pidge to retrieve his grandfather's heart pills from the bedroom, but also (accurately) accused the old man of faking it, as well as allowing the boy to hasten his destruction.

The first independent production by former 20th Century-Fox executive Bassler, *Suddenly* is by no means a perfect film. Some of the acting, particularly that of Hayden in the early scenes, is wooden, and a few plot contrivances detract from the realistic atmosphere, but the low budget actually enhances the claustrophobic ambiance of the scenes set in the town and especially at Pop Benson's after the criminal trio arrives. Working with an intelligent script, Allen makes the most of its potential for drama, suspense and intensity, all of which are carried primarily by Frank's performance.

After being previewed for the press in late August 1954, the film went into general release on September 24. *Variety*, as always, noted the box office appeal the film's star would generate:

> Frank Sinatra's name will be a valuable asset in boosting the b.o. chances of this slick exploitation feature... Sinatra as a professional gunman... is an offbeat piece of casting which pays off in lively interest. Thesp inserts plenty of menace into a psycho character, never too heavily done... Lewis Allen's direction manages a smart piece where static treatment could have prevailed, and Charles Clarke's fluid photography is a further assist in maintaining attention.[37]

Of course, *The New York Times*' Bosley Crowther, again could not resist adding tongue-in-cheek sarcasm to another (positive) critique of a Sinatra performance:

> Who would have dreamed, this time ten years back, when Frank Sinatra was making sweet moan as the current fascination of the bobby-sox brigade, that he would ever be cast in a movie to play the repulsive role of a fellow grimly

intending to assassinate the President of the United States? Not by singing to him, either, but by shooting him with a pistol! The suggestion would probably have occasioned the heart-failure of several thousand fans.

Yet such is the role that Mr. Sinatra plays in *Suddenly!*, a taut little melodrama... And, what is more he plays it not only repulsively but well. Indeed, he plays it so well — and the film is so adroitly contrived — that *Suddenly!* shapes up as one of the slickest recent items in the minor movie league. ...we think that Mr. Sinatra deserves a special chunk of praise for playing the leading gunman with an easy, cold, vicious sort of gleam. His memorable playing of Maggio in *From Here to Eternity* served fair notice that the singer could act a dramatic role. In *Suddenly!* he proves it in a melodramatic tour de force.[38]

On a critical level, Frank had proved what he set out to do by accepting the assassin's role in a B film. Belying the fact that he had become known on film sets as One-Take Charley, *Cue* magazine ethused, "He holds the screen and commands it with ease, authority and skill that is, obviously, the result of care, study, work and an intelligent mind."[39] A half century later, his John Baron remains an indelibly powerful and frightening character, one who is repulsive yet curiously engaging, and not only because Frank Sinatra is playing the role. In an age when violence has become chic, in all forms of media, reflecting how it has saturated American society, this character still can be examined as a cultural archetype. Did Baron's service in World War II make him a killer, or was he, in the words of Sheriff Shaw, "a born killer" before he went overseas? The question is not answered, but what is certain is that Baron liked to kill and would not stop even when the president was the target. In 1987, film historians Jay Robert Nash and Stanley Ralph Ross wrote that Frank achieved "one of the most powerful portrayals of a psychopath ever committed to film." (A decade after its initial release, *Suddenly* would haunt Frank after a real-life incident in  Dallas, Texas, bearing striking similarities to the film's plot, led to the assassination of his friend, President John F. Kennedy. Even more frightening was the fact that, just a year before JFK was shot, Frank would make another film focusing on political assassination, the classic *Manchurian Candidate* [1962].)

During the making of *Suddenly*, Frank cut three singles at KHJ on May 13. While the swinging "The Gal that Got Away" opens with a Riddle roar and ends with a Sinatra swoon, "Half as Lovely (Twice as True)" takes Frank back to his earlier Stordahl-Columbia ballad style, and "It Worries Me" further indicates the new late-night lover sound that he and the arranger were developing. He also had considered several film roles, accepting Stanley Kramer's pitch to costar with Robert Mitchum and Olivia de Havilland in *Not As a Stranger* and Warner Bros.' offer to team him with Doris Day in *Someone to Watch Over Me*, a faithful, though more musical, remake of the hugely successful *Four Daughters* (1938). He also discussed potential projects with MGM, including the possibility of costarring with Ava in *St. Louis Woman* and Gene Kelly

Sinatra as the troubled composer in *Young at Heart* (Photofest)

in another Technicolor musical, and 20th Century-Fox, to concoct a substitute for the canceled *Pink Tights*.

Someone to Watch Over Me, re-titled *Young at Heart*, was the first film to hit the soundstages. Producer Henry Blanke had hired Liam O'Brien to adapt Julius J. Epstein and Leonore Coffee's 1938 screenplay, based on Fannie Hurst's novel *Sister Act*, for the new Warnercolor version, to be directed by Gordon Douglas and shot by Charles Lang for release in the 1.66:1 ratio. What emerged was a scene-for-scene revamp, punctuated by vibrant color and sound, greater character development, wonderful songs and a more believable relationship between the two major romantic interests, here played by Frank and Doris Day (John Garfield and Priscilla Lane in the original).

The story of *Four Daughters* and *Young at Heart* involves a music-professor father and his beautiful daughters (only three in the remake), all of whom are on the verge of romantic relationships. Soon, the young women, although some already have beaus, are smitten by a handsome and witty composer (Jeffrey Lynn in the former; Gig Young in the latter) who eventually asks one of them (the Lane/Day character) to become his wife. When the composer's fatalistic orchestrator (Garfield/Sinatra) expresses his love for her (Lane/Day), and the fact that one of her sisters, also in love with her fiancé (Lynn/Young), is heartbroken, she marries him instead. The plot climaxes with a terrible car crash deliberately engineered by the depressed musician, who dies in *Four Daughters* (the Lane character then reunites with the Lynn character) but survives in *Young at Heart* to experience happiness with his wife, new baby and a hit song he finally has completed.

Doris Day recalled working with Frank:

> Our reunion on *Young at Heart* was the first time I had seen Frank since those *Hit Parade* days. He seemed a bit more querulous now, more reactive to his situation, less inclined to accept things as they were. In *Four Daughters*

John Garfield had died at the end, giving his performance and the film a sharp poignancy, but Sinatra refused to die. He put his refusal on a take-me-or-leave-me basis, so after many hectic conferences, the producers caved in and changed the ending to satisfy Frank. I thought it was a mistake, because there was an inevitability about the character's death that would have given more dimension to Sinatra's performance. And enhanced the film.[40]

Apparently, Frank's reputation for being difficult dramatically reared its head during production. Though his Barney Sloan did not require the intensity of *Suddenly*'s John Baron, instead needing pent-up frustration and angst, he may have been working more of "the Method" into his performance than he realized (and his current depression over Ava certainly added fuel to the fire). He particularly disliked Day's husband, agent Marty Melcher, and made no bones about it, as she revealed:

> [F]rom the very beginning Frank displayed an open hostility toward Marty. I remember one meeting that Frank attended during which he sat with a newspaper in front of his face, reading, for the entire time. I was the only person he talked to. He read through the paper at that meeting, rustling the pages as he turned them, never taking the paper away from his face, and when he finished it he got up and left without a word to anyone.
>
> Before the picture started, Frank sent word that he would not step onto the set if Marty Melcher was anywhere on the lot. I really have no idea what caused Frank to be so hostile to Marty. There must have been some basis for it. Marty said he didn't know. That they'd never had a quarrel.[41]

Frank was prepared to sing "Someone to Watch Over Me," "Just One of Those Things" and "One for My Baby" in the film, but apparently Melcher had attempted to influence the musical content. Music publisher Sam Weiss claimed:

> Marty tried some hustle having to do with some of the songs in the show— Marty was always trying to work little angles for himself—and whatever pitch Melcher made to Sinatra, it was something that really set Frank off. Frank threw Melcher out of his dressing room, and then he put out an order that if Melcher was anywhere on the studio lot—and the studio was nine miles long he, Sinatra, would walk off the movie.[42]

Having received an urgent call from Henry Blanke, Jack Warner rushed to the set. "What the hell's going on down here?" he asked.

"What's going on is I refuse to work on the picture if that creep Melcher is anywhere on the Warners lot," Frank replied. "I've heard too many rotten things about him and I don't want him around. Now I'm just as much to this picture as Doris and if she can't get along without him then I walk." Perhaps Frank believed that having his costar's husband around would detract from the strong on-screen chemistry they were achieving.

Back in his office, Warner returned Blanke's call: "Now here's an order and I want you to get it straight. Frank Sinatra does not want Marty Melcher around, and I want you to find the lousy bum and run him off the lot and be sure he *stays* off until this picture is in the can. That's it, period! An order. You got it?"[43]

Although he had succeeded is getting Melcher banished from Warners, Frank still was not happy with the production. In the middle of a scene, he came to a dead stop, telling the cast and crew that the cameraman, Charles Lang, was not operating up to standard and had to go. Day said:

It may be that Lang took too long in his setups for Frank's tastes. Lang was a very careful, methodical man who was very fussy about lighting, and it might have been that Frank, who is a very impatient, impulsive actor, couldn't abide the long waits between takes. Frank didn't like to rehearse. He didn't like doing a scene over and over. He liked to come on, do one take, and have it printed. That was all right with me. I think that repeating a scene makes a performance mechanical...

After Frank made his point about Charles Lang, he walked off the set. The message was clear: it was either Lang or Sinatra. Of course, Frank had no right to do what he did but when a picture is in production, with all of its overhead in operation, there is no right and wrong; there is only that old devil, expediency. [Lang's replacement, Ted McCord] never had a minute's trouble with Frank.[44]

But the trouble continued, with Frank often arriving hours late, sometimes not until noon, as Day recalled:

I was of two minds about Frank's tardiness. On the one hand, I sympathized that perhaps he was feeling down, hungover perhaps, or just plain not feeling up to the demands of the camera that day; perhaps he looked in the mirror and didn't like what he saw there. On the other hand, I am a compulsive performer. I am too aware of all the people on the set whose jobs rely on my being there on time. ...I don't think Frank was concerned with what his absence meant to the other people on the picture. It caused the director, Gordon Douglas, some anguish, and Harry Blanke, the producer, fretted and fumed, but as for me, despite Frank's sure and rather cocky exterior, I always felt there was a sad vulnerability about him. Perhaps that's why I always had understanding and compassion for what he did. I liked him. We had a fine relationship. There were many lovely things about him that I admired.[45]

On July 12, 1954, Frank, with Ray Heindorf at the podium, recorded "Someone to Watch Over Me," his first waxing of the Gershwin classic in 10 years. Portions of the following two days were spent recording "Just One of Those Things" with Heindorf and Bill Miller at the piano; and after Frank again worked his magic on this Porter masterpiece, he re-cut "Young at Heart" for the film's soundtrack. Although it would not be used in the actual narrative, this lovely number, which Frank originally had recorded with Riddle seven months earlier, now was conducted by Heindorf for use during the opening and closing credits. Frank already had landed a major hit with the song, and this success led to the film's title being changed. Also on July 14, he cut a solo rendition of Jimmy Van Heusen and Mack Gordon's "You, My Love," which he would redo as a duet with Day (the version that ultimately was used in the film) the following month.

On August 11, Heindorf and Previn were back to record "One for My Baby" with Frank, who, for the first time, gave the Harold Arlen-Johnny Mercer standard the noir treatment he would stick with thereafter. Four days later, he threw a surprise 75th birthday party for Ethel Barrymore, who gave a scene-stealing performance as Aunt Jessie, the longtime aide to Mr. Tuttle (Robert Keith) and his three daughters, Laurie (Day), Fran (Dorothy Malone) and Amy (Elisabeth Fraser). Now the legendary actress often was confined to a wheelchair, as her brother Lionel had been for many years, and could only work on her feet for short periods of time. When the host toasted his guest of honor, she gently kissed him on the cheek, declaring, "Frank is a livin' doll."[46] Thinking it might be Ethel's final birthday, Doris began to tear up.

"Hey!" shouted a crewman. "Doris needs a Kleenex!" Then a box came flying across the set, striking the actress on the forehead. She remembered:

Doris Day and Sinatra in *Young at Heart*

It stung a little and I gasped more in surprise than in pain. Frank sprang at the man who had flipped the box at me and grabbed the front of his shirt, pulling the fabric up tight under his chin. "Don't you ever do that!" he shouted at the man. "You don't throw things at a lady, you understand?"

"It's all right, Frank," I said. "I'm not hurt."

"That's beside the point! You bring the box, you creep, and you offer a Kleenex — you got that? You *offer* a Kleenex!"

Frank let the man go and came over to me to be sure that I was all right. Often, over the years, whenever I pulled a Kleenex out of a box, I thought of Frank.[47]

A week after Barrymore's party, on August 23, Frank was back at KHJ to cut three Capitol singles with Riddle. His perfect vocal on the ballad "When I Stop Loving You" unfortunately is marred by a bombastic choral arrangement, but his fourth and final version of Berlin's "White Christmas" and initial take on Styne and Cahn's charming "The Christmas Waltz," also with choruses, are better balanced Yuletide fare. Exactly one month later, he returned to the studio to cut three additional singles, including "Don't Change Your Mind About Me," which grouped him with June Hutton and his old collaborators the Pied Pipers, showcasing how much he had progressed as a vocalist since his Dorsey days: Rather than simply crooning the lyrics, as the Voice would have a dozen years earlier, he combines respectful phrasing with the masterful rhythmic maturity he had developed while swinging via Siravo and Riddle. He also cut yet another sublime version of "Someone to Watch Over Me," his longing voice beautifully backed by Riddle's subtle string arrangement and a beckoning French horn (either John Cave or Vincent de Rosa), and a lush version, sans Doris Day, of *Young at Heart*'s "You, My Love."

Young at Heart, *Suddenly* and *From Here to Eternity* all were mentioned on the September 15 *Amos 'n' Andy Music Hall*, the popular program featuring white actors Freeman Gosden and Charles Correll impersonating the black "Amos Jones" and "Andy Brown." This later version of the original radio series was a disc jockey program: Accompanying the duo's spinning of "The Birth of the Blues" was their attempt to have Frank pay them to guest on the show.

On December 13, the day after Frank's 39th birthday, his Capitol session at KHJ included some new faces, arranger Dick Reynolds and conductor Ray Anthony, who collaborated on two singles, the romantic waltz "Melody of Love" and the hard-driving, Latin-flavored "I'm Gonna Live Till I Die," which anticipates some of his later "show-stopper" style.

Released on January 15, 1955, *Young At Heart* was sold on the strength of its two stars. For several weeks, the Warnercolor trailers had boasted:

> Doris Day is listening to the voice that thrills half the world... and Frank
> Sinatra is listening to the voice that thrills the other half!

In his *Variety* review, "Brog" also focused on the musical angle, but obviously had forgotten most of *Four Daughters*, which he probably had not seen since its release 16 years earlier:

> The Henry Blanke production has been smoothly fashioned so there is not too
> strong a resemblance to the *Four Daughters* production on which it was based.
> ...The writing for this version is first-rate, being well-dialoged and plotted.[48]

Again, the redoubtable Bosley Crowther contributed his Sinatra review to *The New York Times*, giving the film credit for its "nicely warmed up" sentiments and Frank's performance that is "well-acquitted" but lacking in the "bite and sharpness that Mr. Garfield had."[49]

Remakes have existed ever since Hollywood was put on the map. Few of them are very good, and hardly any improve on their originals, simply because they usually have so much to live up to. Since the release of *Young at Heart*, the critical consensus has followed conventional wisdom in championing *Four Daughters* as the better of the two; when in reality, each film has its own particular merits and shortcomings. But the most obvious improvement made by *Young at Heart* is the Laurie Tuttle-Barney Sloan relationship — the chemistry created by Doris and Frank. Although the lovely Priscilla Lane and the classically brooding John Garfield (very effective in his film debut) give good performances in the earlier film, this chemistry does not exist. Garfield's Mickey Borden does not have any remotely positive or likable qualities; he simply is a fatalistic person who attracts little empathy, and the "love" that Lane's Ann Lemp expresses for him fails to convince. His death at film's end makes sense in this version — the darker world of director Michael Curtiz — whereas Barney's survival in *Young At Heart* works equally well: He has a truly loving wife and a baby to look forward to. It is not only the possibility of a hit song that saves Barney from "the fates," but the promise of a future with a real family. Naive Hollywood narrative? Perhaps, but also optimistic and, within the world of *Young at Heart*, believable. Could a film with such a title really end with a suicide?

The more positive atmosphere of *Young at Heart* is heralded by Frank's voice, which croons onto the blank screen before the opening credits sequence begins, billing Doris Day and him above the title. The early scenes, visually resembling all those from *Four Daughters*, are distinguished by greater character development, particularly between Laurie and Amy, who discuss marriage while lying on their beds. Day's performance here is one of the finest examples of her naturalistic, convincing style, one that instantly draws in the viewer.

Frank's introduction is stunning, indicative of the improvements he made on Garfield's original. Similar to Boris Karloff's first appearance as the Monster in James Whale's *Frankenstein* (1931), Barney is shown with his back to the camera as Alex Burke (Gig Young), the composer, opens the Tuttle's front door. The audience recognizes the Cavanaugh hat, the suit and the skinny

In the remake *Young at Heart*, Sinatra's character survives a serious car crash. (Photofest)

frame, but does not get to see the face (framed in close-up) until he turns around. (Perhaps Frank came up with the idea himself, as Karloff was one of his favorite actors and a future collaborator.) Entering the house, speaking essentially the same dialogue as did Garfield, Frank instantly exudes more charisma than his predecessor, signaling to the viewer that, no matter how cynical he may be, he also will gain empathy. In an expanded scene about how "the fates" have affected Barney's life, Frank improvises a bit, tossing in the term "lady luck." He also mentions that his birth name was "more Italian," so he changed it to "throw [the fates] off track." Another moment of ad-libbing has him transforming a motif about being struck by lightning into some classic Sinatra-speak: "Pow! D—E—D, dead!" he exclaims.

"Just One of Those Things," performed during the day in a lonely bar as Barney broods over losing Laurie to Alex, and "One for My Baby," sung as a noisy nightclub crowd ignores him, punctuate the narrative and are two of the best musical sequences Frank performed on film. (Barney's constant desire both to write music and to perform also sets him apart from the earlier Mickey Borden, who really is little better than a complaining bum.) "Things" involves Frank performing a slow introduction before kicking into the lightly swinging version he had recorded a few months earlier for *Swing Easy*, and here he again magnificently plays with the rhythm of the phrase "So goodbye, baby, and amen..." This take is equally as good as, and a little more intimate than, the Capitol arrangement. The latter scene features a subtle element of eroticism, as Laurie pulls down a glove to show Barney her naked wrist as he plays "Baby." Earlier in the evening, he had told her to get rid of a charm bracelet given to her by Alex, and now she smiles as she proves the deed has been done. Later, Barney buys it back for her, but she turns it over to Alex when the family gets together for Christmas (the night that Barney decides to take his own life).

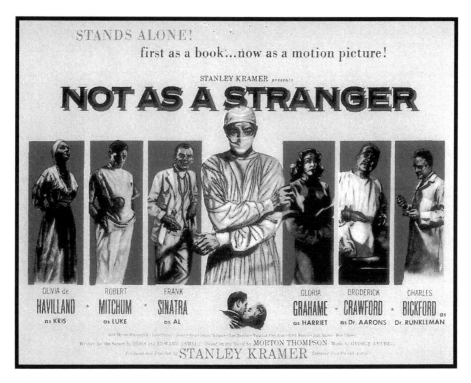

Another major project involving Frank, *Finian's Rainbow*, also went into production during 1954. Intended as an animated feature version of Burton Lane and E.Y. Harburg's 1947 Broadway hit, the film was to feature a soundtrack also including Louis Armstrong, Ella Fitzgerald, Sonny Terry and Brownie McGhee, Oscar Peterson and Red Norvo. Though Frank recorded nine tracks—including a scat duet with Satchmo on "Ad Lib Blues" and a pairing with Fitzgerald on "Necessity"—they remained unheard when the film was scrapped by Walt Disney, who apparently objected to its left-wing political content.

Stanley Kramer's *Not as a Stranger*, a melodramatic tale of medical interns based on the best-selling novel by Morton Thompson, had begun shooting the previous October. Having worked as a producer since 1941, and primarily interested in serious drama, this project marked Kramer's directorial debut, an aspect that attracted Frank, who admired a filmmaker whose credits included *Home of the Brave* (1949), *High Noon* (1952) and *The Caine Mutiny* (1954), starring Bogie.

Screenwriters Edna and Edward Anhalt did what they could to adapt a 1000-page novel into a 135-minute film, but aside from some impressive, groundbreaking documentary detail, *Not as a Stranger* is little more than an overlong soap opera containing primarily underplayed performances uncomfortably offset by George Antheil's bombastic and syrupy musical score and Kramer's overwrought and heavyhanded direction. Containing the kind of preachy dialogue that the producer-director often favored in his later films, the story involves Lucas Marsh (Robert Mitchum), a young intern who believes that doctors should be infallible, demonstrating his struggles to get through medical school and establish his own practice. Along the way, he marries Kristina Hedvigson (Olivia de Havilland), a Swedish nurse, who has enough money to pay for his tuition, and befriends Alfred Boone (Frank), a fellow intern who eventually exchanges a flippant attitude for that of a serious physician. After becoming a "country doctor" in the small town of Greenville, Marsh has an affair with sexy widow Harriet Lang (Gloria Grahame) and experiences a falling out with his partner, Dr. Runkleman (Charles Bickford). Becoming pregnant, Kristina withholds the truth, realizing that her obsessional husband will not accept her choice to give up the medical profession to raise a family. Alfred attempts to reason with his old friend, but ultimately the death of Dr. Runkleman at his own hands (due to his mistake during open-heart surgery) makes him realize that he is only a man, not a god. Pleading for Kristina's help, he is welcomed back into his home.

Kramer's attention to detail in depicting hospital, particularly surgical, procedures is an admirable element, but it fails to gain audience interest in and empathy for the characters, who are often badly written and portrayed with apparent boredom by many of the actors, particularly Mitchum, whose trademark stoicism simply does not fit the role. The film incessantly makes the point that a doctor needs to be as much of a human being as he does a font of medical knowledge and skill, but his attempt to purge all emotion out of the character makes it nearly impossible for the viewer to care about him. In fact, the overall atmosphere of the film is merely an extension of Mitchum's characterization: Beginning with an autopsy, it concludes with the death of his friend and partner. While the theme of "doctors are not gods, they make mistakes" is a valid one, perhaps Kramer could have directed a more balanced narrative. When the film was released in June 1955, critics praised the clinical detail, having just seen such footage for the first time, but uniformly panned Mitchum.

Again, Frank provides the finest moments in a major Hollywood film, here injecting some warmth, good will and humor into a chilly and dark world. Olivia de Havilland, too, tries her best, but often fails to convince with a phony Swedish accent (Harry Morgan's is worse) and several overplayed scenes (which seem all the more histrionic due to the film's funereal mood). While *Variety* noted that Frank "comes close to doing a little picture stealing,"[52] Crowther called him "light-hearted" and "credible."[53] In his *Hollywood Reporter* review, Jack Moffitt wrote, "the spectators are thoroughly entertained during the first half of the film by Frank Sinatra in the role of a lovable young cynic to whom the study of medicine is more or less a lark. Sinatra, who seems to become a better actor with each successive part, is simply terrific."[54]

Frank's Al Boone isn't really that cynical. When the film opens, he, unlike his driven friend, simply is unsure of what to do with his life (as are so many college students). After engaging in some shenanigans for his fellow classmates, performing a Danny Kaye-like demonstration of an autopsy before being "caught" by the stern Dr. Aarons (Broderick Crawford), he whispers to them, "Anybody for law school?" Al is likable, levelheaded, consistently in good spirits and willing to help others, and it is these qualities that eventually make him a good doctor—traits that Luke does not understand.

Frank's naturalistic acting style is developed further in *Not as a Stranger,* during which some of his trademark mannerisms and facial expressions can be seen—the head "shiver," the assuring wink or nod to another character, and rubbing his index finger on his cheek, neck, chin or nose as he is thinking about something—techniques that he had begun to experiment with (with the help of Montgomery Clift) during the making of *From Here to Eternity.* He also again wears his familiar suit, tie and hat. (The first appearance of the hat, early in the film, is offset by his pouring a cup of coffee from a boiling beaker in the medical lab!) Similar to the impeccable dynamics he used while singing, he demonstrates how quiet an actor he could be while still delivering the full dramatic impact of his dialogue. In a scene wherein Al informs Luke of the death of his alcoholic father, Job (Lon Chaney, Jr., in a brief but moving performance), Frank does so with his back to the camera and a whispered voice, yet wringing believable emotion out of the circumstance.

Perhaps it was Kramer's sense of humor (displayed rarely in the film) or merely Frank working in some of his own suggestions, but two Sinatra in-jokes are included. The first involves a close-up on artwork of Ava Gardner, who is featured on a movie poster advertising *The Barefoot Contessa,* as Luke and Kristina exit a theater after a date. Discussing the film, Kristina mentions the incomparable beauty of the female star. The second reference is made by Frank himself, when, after being bawled out by his friend for making a misdiagnosis and endangering the life of a patient, Al remarks, "Sometimes I wish I had 75 more pounds. I'd belt you one!" (Earlier, Mitchum performs his only real physical action in the film when Luke grabs Al, who has criticized his reason for wanting to marry Kristina, and pins him against a dresser.)

Though Kramer did make some strides in filmmaking with *Not as a Stranger*, allowing visual detail (shot in widescreen, but in an unembellished, straightforward style by Franz Planer) and some previously taboo content (the use of the word "pregnant," for example) into the cinema, this material is lost amongst a tide of heavyhanded symbolism (particularly when the [supposedly] aroused Luke frees Harriet's raging white stallion before "taking" her) and painfully stereotypical characters: the naive, innocent and faithful wife; the "slutty" widow who corrupts a "good" man; the Swede (named "Oley," of course); the unbending, conservative authority figure at the hospital; and the goodhearted, down-to-earth country doctor.

During February 1955, Frank began working on songs from Rodgers and Hammerstein's *Carousel*, including "Soliloquy," which he had recorded previously for Columbia, with the intention of appearing as Billy Bigelow opposite Shirley Jones in 20th Century-Fox's lavish film adaptation. However, the production hit a serious snag when he learned that he would have to perform some scenes *twice*, to accommodate two versions of the film, one to be shot in Cinemascope and another in the new Cinemascope-55 ratio. Regardless of the fact that the rest of the cast and crew would have to put in the same amount of time, Frank threw $150,000 and what could have been one of the greatest roles of his career to the four winds. "You're not getting two Sinatras for the price of one," he said.[55] Fox sued him for $1 million, but he settled with the studio by agreeing to appear in another film at a later date. The more personally and professionally predictable Gordon McCrea was hired to play Bigelow. One song, Rodgers and Hammerstein's "If I Loved You," was completed by Frank, who apparently also took a stab at "Soliloquy," but became frustrated after a number of unsuccessful takes.

Shirley Jones remembered:

> Frank kept saying, the whole time we were doing all of this, how lucky he was to get to play Billy Bigelow, and how excited he was to be singing the score of *Carousel*. And it was just amazing to everybody that this would be the reason that he left. We had done all the pre-production on *Carousel* here in Hollywood. He had rehearsed. We had done the pre-recording, which you do ahead of time, and the costume fittings, and everything.
>
> He claimed that, when he got to the set, he saw two cameras...and some of the time—not all of the time—we would have to shoot twice. And Frank is known for doing one take. His philosophy—that's the way he feels—and he feels that's his best, is his first take. So, when he saw the two cameras, he said, "I signed to do one movie, not two," and back in the car he got, and back to the airport. And it was astounding—and we may never know the real truth, but that's what he said.[56]

(The fate of the recordings also remains a mystery. No documentation of Frank's work on the film exists, and his recordings remain unavailable due to contractual restrictions.)

In February and early March 1955, Frank completed 19 sides during six sessions at KHJ, 15 of which, along with the previously recorded "Last Night When We Were Young," became the utterly sublime, late-night masterpiece *In the Wee Small Hours*, his first 12-inch concept album, a work demonstrating his increasing ability to convey a sustained and deeply nuanced artistry to his audience. In 1991, critic Pete Welding wrote:

> An album of unparalleled beauty and unfeigned emotional sincerity... It is a well nigh perfect album in every respect. ...the performances... comprise something

of a personal statement, a pain-etched commentary on lost love, of love gone wrong, for Sinatra is no songwriter himself but rather the interpreter of songs written by others, he is never merely or simply an interpreter. No, his artistry is such that he literally makes these songs and the sentiments they articulate his and his alone. In voicing them he transforms them, leaves his mark on them, personalizes them and, through this, makes them newly real to us, no matter how many times we may have heard them before. And that's his power as a singer; it's what has made him the single greatest interpreter of popular song we've ever been privileged to hear.[57]

The song on which the album's mood is based, "In the Wee Small Hours of the Morning" had been brought to Frank and pianist Bill Miller by writers Dave Mann and Bob Hilliard, adding impetus to his evolving interest in creating solid concepts to link recordings together. This tale of a forlorn, insomniacal lover is followed by five more torch songs, including Rodgers and Hart's aching "Glad to Be Unhappy." "Can't We Be Friends?" then picks up the pace a bit with a lightly swinging rhythm section and one of Frank's jazziest vocals ever (interestingly done on a ballad album rather than on an up-tempo swinger) before he revisits a number from a decade earlier, "When Your Lover Has Gone," here devastatingly haunting. Before "Last Night When We Were Young" brings additional lamentation, Frank, accompanied by a sexy clarinet, engagingly asks (in another of his finest performances) an eternal question in Cole Porter's "What Is This Thing Called Love?" and offers his services to a lady with romantic problems in Alec Wilder's "I'll Be Around," which he first had cut as a V-Disc in 1943. Legendary Basie trumpeter Harry "Sweets" Edison, instrumentally matching Frank's economical style and vibrato, lends a muted solo to Harold Arlen and Ted Koehler's "Ill Wind"; Rodgers and Hart's "Dancing on the Ceiling" brings back the motif of lovelorn sleeplessness to lightly swing with the rhythm section including a sparkling jazz guitar; and finally "This Love of Mine," which Frank had cowritten with Sol Parker and Hank Sanicola during the Dorsey period, ends the album on an upbeat note: Although the singer laments lost loves, he admits, "This love of mine goes on." Looking like his Barney Sloan character in *Young at Heart*, Frank appears, via a watercolor painting, dressed in his dark suit and fedora, somber and smoking a cigarette, on the album's noir front cover.

During the final session for *Wee Small Hours*, on March 4, Frank also cut the "Not as a Stranger" single, which incorporates the title theme from the film. Three days later, he picked up the tempo, on four singles conducted by Riddle but arranged by Dave Cavanaugh in a style combining swing elements with standard 1950s pop. "Two Hearts, Two Kisses (Make One Love)" and "From the Bottom to the Top," in particular, offer a "rockin'" Sinatra that must have sounded embarrassingly out of place even at the time. Not since his days with Mitch Miller had he been subjected to such ridiculous, commercially driven material. When he sings the lyric "You can pet my dog, you can tease my cat" on the latter song, one wonders how he managed to suffer through a usable take. Moving from *Wee Small* to this had to be a shocking affair, but his historic recording of "Learnin' the Blues" on March 23 must have buoyed his musical spirits. Dolores Vicki Silvers, a young Philadelphian, had written the song for a local singer, Joe Valino, who made a record that she managed to get to the Sinatra camp; arranged by Riddle, it pleased Frank after 31 takes, became his first number-one hit since signing with Capitol, and remained on the *Billboard* chart for 21 weeks.

That same month, Frank learned that fellow actor Bela Lugosi had checked into a hospital to receive treatment for drug addiction. Though his substance abuse problems began during the mid-1930s, when he began taking morphine for back pain, Lugosi now was nearly bankrupt, managing to land only humiliating roles in grade-Z horror films directed by schlockmeisters like Edward D. Wood, Jr. Perhaps admiring the former star's courage in being the first Hollywood figure to make his addiction public, Frank sent him "a kind note and a basket of gourmet deli-

SAMUEL GOLDWYN
Presents America's Own Musical

GUYS AND DOLLS

STARRING

MARLON BRANDO · JEAN SIMMONS
FRANK SINATRA · VIVIAN BLAINE

with ROBERT KEITH · STUBBY KAYE · B.S.PULLY · JOHNNY SILVER

and THE GOLDWYN GIRLS Written for the Screen and Directed by JOSEPH L. MANKIEWICZ

Book and Lyrics by FRANK LOESSER · Choreography by MICHAEL KIDD

IN CINEMASCOPE Photographed in EASTMAN COLOR · Distributed by M-G-M

cacies." During a press interview, Lugosi admitted, "It was a wonderful surprise. I've never met Sinatra, but I hope to soon. He was the only star I heard from."[58]

Irritated at being stuck with the supporting role of Nathan Detroit, Frank began working on Samuel Goldwyn's screen version of Jo Swerling, Abe Burrows and Frank Loesser's Broadway hit *Guys and Dolls*, in which the plum role of Sky Masterson went to Marlon Brando. Rather than singing and wenching his way through the film, he was relegated to managing "the oldest established floating crap game in New York," and Brando got to romance Jean Simmons, who, contrary to the opinions of past critics, played Sister Sarah Browne of the Save-a-Soul Mission brilliantly, sexily heating up the screen when the film shifts to Havana, where Sky gets her drunk to tango the night away.

Frank later referred to his Detroit performance as "the only part I was ever very disappointed with. ...I was pressured into doing it. I wanted to play Masterson. I mean nothing disparaging about Marlon Brando, but Masterson didn't fit him and he knew it."[59] Truth to tell, Frank and Marlon each disdained the other's approach to acting: the former being One-Take Charley and the latter chained to "the Method" (much as Frank was when he cut his songs). While Frank is occasionally stiff and uninspired in his role (perhaps due to his dissatisfaction with the part, but also from having to speak dialogue that disallows contractions), Brando is a passable Sky, even singing his many songs up to film musical standard, hitting all the notes and phrasing acceptably. Frank unquestionably would have sung Masterson's songs better, but he probably would not have played the character better than Brando, whose realistic approach to the gambler lends credibility to the film's stagy atmosphere. He even makes Masterson's knowledge of the Bible believable, the character having learned scriptural passages simply by spending so much time in hotel rooms during gambling trips. Frank's friend and colleague Henry Silva, who ran into Brando at a friend's house, revealed that the actor "started talking about [his costar]": "He got very quiet and seemed to be very, very far away and all of a sudden he sat back, and Brando, the great actor, said—you could barely hear him—'Boy, to be able to sing like that.'"[60]

As Detroit's love interest Adelaide, Vivian Blaine is the film's treat, delivering pages of lyrics with wonderful phrasing, often in duets with Frank, whose songs are not the highlights but still command attention. (As his later Reprise recording would prove, Sky's "Lucky Be a Lady" would have been better in his throat rather than that of Brando, who appears to be aping James Cagney.) As directed by Joseph L. Mankiewicz, the "Lady" scene is too claustrophobic, the choreography unfortunately cut into separate shots that only sporadically capture the dice game held in the sewer. The lack of convincing musical numbers detracts from the overall effectiveness of the film, which is a plotless melange of Detroit's attempts to keep his crap game afloat and Masterson's budding romance with Sarah. Frank's most successful song is his Yiddish-tinged "Sue Me, Sue Me" duet with Blaine.

Guys and Dolls finally hits its stride two hours in, during the scene in which Sky tricks all the gamblers into attending a meeting at Sarah's mission. Detroit begins to loosen up at this point, as the "bums" are domesticated and Nicely Nicely Johnson (Stubby Kaye) leads the group in the film's best song, "Sit Down, You're Rockin' the Boat." Both Masterson and Detroit then are married, to Sarah and Adelaide, respectively, in Times Square, where the musical whimsy began.

Contemporary critics found little to fault in the film. In his *New York Times* review, Bosley Crowther praised the "fine cast," though he did note that Frank was a bit "bland" and Brando "has some trouble with his never quite untangled tongue."[61]

Brando and Sinatra in *Guys and Dolls*

Shot immediately after *Guys and Dolls*, *The Tender Trap* directly tied into the Sinatra persona, introducing his self-assured, worldly, hip, swinging yet vulnerable protagonist to film audiences. Whereas previous productions had featured him as a character in the screenplay, *Trap* became the first *Sinatra film*, its plot focusing squarely on the activities of theatrical agent Charlie Y. Reader, although several other strong characters, played by a wonderful ensemble cast, also receive their due. *The Tender Trap* allowed Frank to demonstrate his effortless comic ability, beyond what he had been able to do within the confines of the naive characters he had played at MGM. His Stan Laurel-like comedy often stands out against the more scripted efforts of his cohorts in the earlier films, but here the talents of David Wayne, Celeste Holm and Debbie Reynolds beautifully coalesce with his own.

Now 39 years old, Frank developed a sort of "older brother" relationship with Reynolds. She later recalled:

> Frank took me under his wing. I was only 23. It was during the filming that Eddie Fisher and I announced our engagement. Frank took me to lunch. He said, "You know, Debbie, your life may be very difficult if you marry a singer. It's not the individual necessarily, it's the singer's way of life. You have to think very hard about this, Debbie. Please give this very deep and serious thought." I didn't. I should have![62]

The opening sequence of *The Tender Trap* is brilliant, fading in to a long take showing a man's silhouette in the Cinemascope distance. When Frank's voice begins with Cahn and Van Heusen's words, "You see a pair of laughing eyes, and suddenly you're sighing sighs...," his figure walks forward, looming larger until the camera depicts him from the waist up. Here, the title lands on the screen, Frank *scats* a bit and the credits take over. The level of charm already has been set, but the initial post-titles sequence entices the viewer even more: Fading in on a close-up of an end table, the camera pans across to a full ashtray, where a woman's hand picks up a lit cigarette; as the scene widens, "Poppy" (Lola Albright), an absolutely sumptuous female, puts the smoke in Charlie Reader's mouth. As they neck on the couch, Charlie admits "something I've wanted

to tell you for months": "You are the *softest* girl." A sexier opening scene, particularly in 1955 terms, cannot be imagined. MGM's pressbook actually reported that Frank "began his role…by spending an entire day kissing Lola Albright. …'A perfect way to begin,' he declared."[63] (The red socks worn by Frank in this scene were a costume requirement intended to show off the rich color achieved by cinematographer Paul C. Vogel. Reportedly, when actor Van Johnson, who was famous for wearing dazzling red woolen socks with tuxedos, learned that Frank was to sport a pair in the film, he sent a half dozen as a gift.)[64]

Just as they begin to turn up the heat (the chemistry between Frank and Lola is tangible, even in its brevity), Charlie's old pal, Joe McCall (David Wayne), arrives from Indiana to interrupt the Manhattan menage. When Poppy retires to freshen up, Charlie tucks in his silk shirt (Frank's favorite, orange), welcomes his friend, and the two slap each other silly. After Poppy bids Charlie a sensual adieu, another femme, buxom Southern belle Jessica (Jarma Lewis), arrives, bearing a gift of cheese and rounding up all the apartment's cigarette butts. "And that couch!" she exclaims. "What *have* you been doin' on that couch?"

Joe cannot believe his eyes. While he's been back in Indiana, married to "Ethel" for 15 years and playing faithful father to a brood with braces on their teeth, Charlie has lived the bachelor's high life. A blonde, then a brunette; now a redhead enters, walking a dog named Joe. But this dish, Helen (Carolyn Jones), is mysterious and beautiful but perhaps a cold fish.

"I've got dames I haven't even called yet," Charlie tells Joe. One woman he has been seeing is Sylvia Crewes (Celeste Holm), an accomplished violinist for the NBC television orchestra, who eventually is courted by Joe. (The actress took violin lessons prior to filming.) When first meeting Sylvia, Joe comments about Charlie's *lack* of musical ability, to which she replies, "Oh, he's not such a tin ear. I've been working on him." (This in-joke is not the only "Frank-ism" in the film; the blending of his own traits with those of the scripted character is what brings Charlie to life, as when he gives David Wayne the Sinatra "neck rub and wink" before Joe and Sylvia leave for a date.)

Debbie Reynolds' introduction is a memorable moment, her 22-year-old "Julie Gillis" innocently half-stumbling onto a stage to audition for Reader and his cohorts. She is the *ultimate* ingenue facing Charlie's predatory keep-them-on-a-string playboy. Just after her nervous appearance, she flabbergasts Charlie, Sylvia and Joe with her marriage "plan," a meticulous schedule of events formulated in the absence of any kind of suitor. Julie's extreme views on morality and propriety do not stop Charlie from trying to add her to his roster; however; but when he asks her for a date, she refuses, telling the 39-year-old lothario, "You're even attractive in an off-beat, beat up sort of way."

Charlie is unfazed by Julie's behavior, and instead finds himself uncharacteristically attracted to her. Donning the now-mandatory Sinatra suits and hats (the bands are outrageously wide here), Charlie appears ultra-confident, particularly in a scene containing the cinema's first moment of "Sinatra quintessence": When asked about Julie's refusal to sign a "run of the play" contract, he motions off his associates with a right-handed gesture that was unique to him. Equally his own, of course, is the Sinatra way with a song, here Cahn and Van Heusen's "(Love is the) Tender Trap," which Reynolds performs first as Julie auditions a dance number. While her version is straight ahead and stiff—as Charlie describes, "a throwaway"—his, performed solo at the piano as she looks over his shoulder, lays back into light swing, nice and easy. "It's gotta have more warmth," he explains. Here, the film demonstrates the Sinatra style for the audience and then follows with a scene of Julie's vastly improved version, which segues into a montage of their budding romance.

Julie's attempts to cure Charlie of his womanizing ways provide some humorous moments. In a scene set in her parents' apartment (she still lives at home), as he attempts to "nibble," she finds various ways to divert his attention from amour, including television and Renaissance art, but they all contain images involving sex. While they are embracing, she discovers a large bundle of mail and telephone notes written by Joe, all from members of his harem. Incensed, she lays down the law about their relationship, including thoughts of marriage, in which Charlie claims he has no interest. Earlier, as they had observed Helen, tethering little Joe, enter his apartment, he explained, "She's a professional dogwalker. She walks my dog every day."

The Tender Trap originally was written by Max Shulman and Robert Paul Smith and produced on Broadway by Clinton Wilder. The screenplay by Julius Epstein (one of the brothers who wrote *Casablanca*) sparkles with dialogue timed perfectly by Frank and David Wayne. At one point, Joe, fed up with his friend's insensitivity, accuses, "You're one of the few really indecent men I've ever met!" When played so well, even the following exchange still seems fresh:

> Charlie: "I'm a pretty broadminded fella."
> Joe: "That's putting it mildly."

After being rebuffed by Julie and dressed down by Joe for his cavalier treatment of Sylvia, Charlie proposes to the 33-year-old fiddler. "There's too much gloom around here. Let's get *blind*!" he exclaims, picking up the telephone to invite all his pals to a party. Realizing that the booze is nearly gone (his apartment features hot and cold running martinis), he then steps out to hail a cab and, meeting Julie, also agrees to marry *her*. Carried back into the building, he holds up two fingers to a doorman who asks about the "engagement."

Cleverly (like a good romance scene showing no actual sex, but only what leads up to the act and what follows), the party itself is not depicted; rather, the audience is treated to the aftermath, which is far more devastating and entertaining. (A notable precursor is the premise of *Helpmates* [1932], an excellent Laurel and Hardy short.) Fading in on a close-up of bottles, the sequence offers brilliant, near-silent comedy, played without dialogue by Wayne, who first appears, attempting to drink tomato juice, and then Frank, who struggles to retrieve only his necktie from the midst of the ravaged living room. (Earlier, Charlie offers another Sinatra in-joke when, after attempting to knot his necktie, he asks, "I don't know why I don't wear bow ties, anyway.") As described, the uninhibited behavior resulting from the drunken soiree—the cutting of the telephone cord, toppling of furniture, draping of clothing over lampshades, a woman giving a man a crewcut—is both funny and accurate in demonstrating how people act under the influence of alcohol. Earlier, Charlie orders some good turkey to serve his guests. Finally able to speak, the severely hungover Joe asks, "Who was the girl in the turkey shoes? I think I'm engaged to her." The most insane moment occurs when Charlie and Joe fold up the hide-a-bed unexpectedly to discover Sol Z. Steiner (Joey Faye) *and* his trombone underneath; banging the instrument into the floor, the manic musician pours himself some hair of the dog. This moment is one of the film's most hilarious.

Charlie (now wearing an orange sweater) loses both of his "fiancees" when Julie arrives without warning and Sylvia returns to the scene of the crime. After Joe explains, Charlie, having been searching for an earring, emerges just above the bar top, a white rag signaling his defeat. Losing her prospective husband and turning down another (Joe, who offers to leave his wife for her), Sylvia then is reacquainted with Charlie's neighbor, Mr. Loughran (Tom Helmore), as she departs. One year later, they are married, and Charlie, having returned from abroad, is reunited with Julie at the wedding. The film culminates with the fifth arrangement of the title song, reprising the opening scene, with Wayne, Holm, Reynolds and finally Frank forming a quartet, and Albright, Lewis and Jones providing vocal backup.

Though its stage origins are obvious, *The Tender Trap* is a delightful cinematic experience kept moving by MGM studio director Charles Walters and enhanced visually by Vogel's Cinemascope lensing. The acting is picture perfect, with Frank hitting his stride, surrounded by Wayne's deft and subtle touches (both of them displaying Stan Laurel nonverbal influences), Holm's sophisticated and endearing comic charm and Reynolds' alternating innocence and indignation. Frank's charisma clicks with all the women (except, of course, Carolyn Jones), but the strongest chemistry between a couple is demonstrated by Wayne and Holm, whose scenes together are dramatic highlights.

Following its general release on October 17, 1955, *The Tender Trap* became the highest-grossing American film of that year. Audiences loved what MGM's advertising hyped as Frank's switch from drama to "riotous comedy," but what did critics think? Usually on the mark regarding box office prospects, *Variety* believed the "overlong" film could "hit a satisfactory level in the regular runs," but conceded that the cast was excellent, particularly the women: "There's quite a bit of sizzle in that opening couch scene between Sinatra and Miss Albright."[65] Reaction was primarily positive, with *Films and Filming*'s Peter G. Baker noting, "Frank Sinatra sings only one song and it is a pleasant surprise to find him such an accomplished comedian,"[66] and Bosley Crowther, becoming even fairer to Frank as time went by, perhaps offering the most perceptive view:

> Sinatra... and... Wayne...have a capacity to turn the crisp, idiomatic lines of Julius Epstein's adaptation into cheerfully sparkling repartee. And when it comes to such a thing as conveying the immensity of a celebrating brawl through the gloom and debris of the morning after, you'll not get it better than from these boys. ...Charles Walters' direction is smooth and lively, the settings and costumes are chic and the whole thing looks very delicious in color and Cinemascope... a thoroughly diverting show.[67]

Four decades later, Nancy Sinatra, Jr., wrote, "In my opinion they [Frank and Debbie Reynolds] should have made more movies together because they made a good team. They were funny and romantic, and it's too bad nobody saw the potential."[68]

On July 11, 1955, Frank and Humphrey Bogart, accompanied by Dean Martin and Sammy Davis, Jr., who recently had lost an eye in an auto accident, made a "Rat Pack" jaunt to Long Beach, where Judy Garland was performing. After their fellow "rat" finished the show, the gang all joined her on stage for a bow.

Frank recorded a number of Capitol singles during the summer and early autumn of 1955. On July 29, bouncing "Same Old Saturday Night," he continued with the pop style he and Riddle

"You're the softest, prettiest thing," Frank Sinatra tells Lola Albright. He tells that to all the girls!

M-G-M's CinemaScope "THE TENDER TRAP" in Color

Copyright 1955 Loew's Incorporated

Frank and Lola Albright turn up the heat in *The Tender Trap*.

had adopted a few months earlier, but "Fairy Tale" took him back into romantic balladry just in time for a legitimate performance in a September 19 television broadcast—on NBC in "living color"—of Thornton Wilder's *Our Town* in which he portrayed the Stage Manager opposite Paul Newman and Eva Marie Saint, who recalled:

> Frank didn't rehearse with us at all for the whole three weeks before the broadcast because he had some contractual problem going on. We had a stand-in, and until the dress rehearsal, we didn't know if the stand-in would come on for the show or whether Frank Sinatra himself would. But when the music came up, suddenly around the corner came Frank. He was wonderful, and I remember thinking, "How does he do that? How does he just come on and do that?" I think he was a little embarrassed about not having been there all that time, and I think he was concerned that he do as good a job as everyone who had been rehearsing all those weeks. He was very dear with all of us. I had known him as a sexy, wonderful singer, and the quality he brought to the role of Stage Manager was wonderful. He's an incredible performer. I don't think many people could have done what he did; just do the dress rehearsal and go on live.[69]

On August 15, Frank recorded single versions of Cahn and Van Heusen songs from the *Our Town* soundtrack: "Look to Your Heart," "The Impatient Years," "Our Town" and "Love and Marriage," which would win an Emmy Award and remain on the *Billboard* chart for 17 weeks, peaking at number five. (More than 30 years later, the song would grace the opening credits of the Fox domestic satire *Married...with Children*.)

The Actor, on Screen and in Song

During that month, the spurious tabloid *Confidential* published an article about the "Wrong-Door Raid," which had occurred the previous November. Frank had been asked by his friend Joe DiMaggio to drive to a certain Hollywood address, where the baseball great reportedly believed his estranged wife, Marilyn Monroe, was carrying on an illicit affair. Though he testified under oath that he had waited outside, smoking a cigarette by the car, Frank again was made the object of a smear campaign, which claimed that he had joined DiMaggio and some detectives in breaking down the apartment door of Florence K. Ross, who had no connections to Ms. Monroe. When one of the detectives, Philip Irwin, was beaten by thugs after the article was published, he told police that he thought Frank had hired them. Years later, Frank's longtime friend, music publisher Frank Military, who attended the hearings, said, "Frank was totally innocent. He got suckered in by Joe."[70] Though he did not see Marilyn Monroe during this incident, he would do so in the future.

On September 13, Frank and Nelson Riddle cut yet another arrangement of "The Tender Trap" for the Capitol single, combining the singer's insouciant swing style with a chugging sax chart and intermittent brass punctuation left off the film soundtrack. And none of the five versions in the film include the improvised lyric, "You're hooked, you're *cooked*, you're part of the tender trap." Retaining the same tempo, they moved on to "You'll Get Yours," one of Frank's first bluesy romantic retribution songs, and "Weep They Will," which was not released. Two cuts from the next session on October 17, "You Forgot All the Words" and "Love Is Here to Stay," also remained on the shelf, but he finally was pleased enough to let a version of "Weep They Will" hit the streets, as the B-side of the "Tender Trap" single.

A recent issue of *Time* magazine, sporting his face on its cover, reported that, "In the movies, Frank Sinatra is currently more in demand than any other performer."[71] And *The Man with the Golden Arm* provided the next silver-screen role that he desperately desired, second only to his quest for Maggio; but this time he won the lead, and the film's theme symbolized a subject as subversive as Communism during the height of the Cold War: drug addiction, something that was utterly *un-American*. Years earlier, John Garfield had bought the rights to Nelson Algren's novel, but the blacklisted actor had no chance of filming it. After his death, director Otto Preminger acquired it from Garfield's estate, hiring Algren to cowrite the screenplay. But after Preminger ensconced the recovering heroin addict in a nice hotel near Columbia Studios, he checked out and "moved downtown to a disreputable, broken-down, flea-ridden hotel full of pimps, addicts, and drunks."[72] Preminger admitted, "He was an amusing, intelligent man, but he couldn't write dialogue or visualize scenes."

Showing Algren the door, Preminger hired Walter Newman and Lewis Meltzer to write the screenplay, ordering them to transform the novel into his own personal vision, being quite cold toward the integrity of the original work:

> Algren was furious when he saw the result. He felt I had done violence to the book. ...When a producer buys the rights to a book or a play he owns it. The property rights are transferred, as in any sale. The writer gives up control, as the word "sell" implies.[73]

When only 70 pages were completed, Preminger sent copies to two performers: Frank and Marlon Brando, "actors [he] thought most suitable for the lead."[74]

In no way was Frank about to give another plum role to Brando. He already had read the novel, at the suggestion of sportswriter Jimmy Cannon, who, like Frank, "was afflicted by insomnia and bouts of personal loneliness [and] read widely and intelligently, deep into the night."[75] Frank's agent immediately phoned Preminger to accept for his client.

"Fine. As soon as the script is finished, I'll send it to you," Preminger replied.

Frank's agent made himself *very* clear. "You don't understand. Sinatra is ready to sign the contract right now. He doesn't need to see the rest of the script."

As he had persevered with *Eternity*, Frank scored a major triumph. Elsewhere in Los Angeles, Brando's agent was very "upset," having been unable even to give his client the 70 pages of script.[76]

But Preminger still had a long road ahead to bring the story to the screen:

> *The Man with the Golden Arm* was my second fight against the absurd censorship that Hollywood still tried to impose. [In 1953, difficulties arose over *The Moon is Blue*.]
>
> When I read the novel by Nelson Algren about a heroin addict I decided to make the film, although I was aware that the Hays Office code expressly outlawed even the mere mention of drugs on the screen.[77]

Frank was so dedicated to the project that he eventually overcame his one-take tendency, putting as much single-minded effort into his performance as he had done on his finest recordings. Preminger, revealing that Frank thought little of his thespian abilities, recalled:

> When I notified Sinatra that we were starting rehearsals of the film, he said, "Ludvig," — which is what he always calls me, mispronouncing my middle name — "I am not an actor. I can't rehearse. I try to do it the best I can and that's it."
>
> "Anatole," I told him, using the name I inexplicably call him, "come at ten tomorrow morning and I will teach you how to rehearse."
>
> He was surprised to discover that he loved rehearsals. He could not get enough. When I wanted to quit, he would ask, "Let's do it again, just once, please!"[78]

To capture the documentary realism he sought, Preminger initially planned to shoot the film in Chicago, but budgetary restrictions did not permit such location extravagance. Forced to film on backlot sets, the director instead benefited from the stark reality of Frank's performance, arguably the best he ever gave on celluloid and one that may be difficult to watch for Sinatra fans who view him as the essence of "cool." It is the best pre-Nicolas Cage (*Leaving Las Vegas*) portrayal of an alcoholic/addict on film, one that makes Ray Milland's Oscar-winning turn in *The Lost Weekend* shiver in its shadow.

Frank's impeccable taste in all things cultural steered him in the right direction with *Golden Arm*, as it had with his attempts only to sing the best material with Dorsey, at Columbia and in his first sessions at Capitol. Perhaps he was pressing his luck calling Preminger "Ludvig" or "Herr Doktor," but the bizarre "Anatole" (after a character in an Arthur Schnitzler play) appellation did not bother him. (Preminger, like many film directors, was a *very* strange man.)

Stranger still was Frank's willingness to rehearse endlessly before shooting the scenes. He thought so much of the film that he gave every fiber of his talent to the role, much as he did his music at the time, working for 12 hours each day. Never before, not even during the *Eternity* shoot, did he dedicate so much energy to creating a character for the camera. Observing that he even had given up late-night drinking and smoking, Preminger said, "I never believed these stories about Frank not wanting to work in the morning."[79]

However, the director admitted that one particular incident set off Frank's temper:

> We had just finished a very difficult long scene to my satisfaction. The head electrician approached me and told me that one of his men had made a mistake. We would have to do it again. When I told Sinatra he blew his top and said he wouldn't. He had done it right, I had okayed it, and as far as he was concerned, that was it.

Robert Strauss, Sinatra and Arnold Stang (wearing glasses) in *The Man with the Golden Arm*

I followed him as he stormed into his dressing room. "Look, Anatole, what do you want me to do? Kill the electrician? He's entitled to make a mistake, the same as you or I."

He came out with me and apologized to the electrician and we did the scene again.[80]

Working with Kim Novak for the first time, Frank was very understanding and helpful, just as her "Molly" is to his "Frankie" in the film. Preminger said:

> He was compassionate about Kim Novak's extreme nervousness in front of the camera. She was terrified, and though she tried very hard she had great difficulty delivering her lines believably. Sometimes we had to do even very short scenes as often as thirty-five times. Throughout the ordeal Sinatra never complained and never made her feel that he was losing patience.[81]

Novak admired Frank and socialized off-camera, going out to dinner and discussing all sorts of subjects with him and his pals. She revealed:

> The only way I could work with him on *Man with the Golden Arm* was to know him as the man he was playing. That way I could feel sorry for him and give him the sympathy which was needed. As soon as I walked on the set each day, I purposely forgot we were friends.[82]

Novak's Molly is an old flame of Frankie's whose feelings are readily apparent when he returns from rehab, even though she now is seeing "Drunky" (John Conte), a pushy and occasionally violent (but totally ineffectual) alcoholic. Frankie attempts to go straight by using his recently developed talent for jazz drumming, but no one in his old neighborhood will leave him alone, particularly his wife, Zosch (Eleanor Parker), who feigns disability, and the seedy gamblers for whom he used to deal. Again hooked on heroin by Louie (Darren McGavin), who taunts him constantly, he first is suspected of the gambler-pusher's murder (Zosch accidentally kills him), but then is saved by Molly, who convinces him to go cold turkey and locks him in her apartment.

The emotional highlight of the shoot occurred during the cold turkey incident, when Molly piles a stack of quilts on the shivering Frankie before finally climbing on top to warm him with her body. Novak actually began to cry spontaneously and, as Frank gave a truly chilling performance, Preminger moved in for a close-up as the scene was done in a single take. When the director called, "Cut," the stage remained in an awesome silence for some time as the crew remained dumbstruck. Frank later said, "It was great to watch [Kim] emerge as an actress for the first time. She had so much empathy for this character."[83]

To make the withdrawal scene as realistic as possible, Frank did some firsthand research. He recalled:

> [F]or about 40 seconds, through a peephole, I was allowed to see what happens to people when they try to kick heroin cold turkey—a youngster climbing a wall. It was the most frightening thing I've ever seen. I never want to see that again. Never.[84]

Before he performed the extended withdrawal that precedes Molly's covering him with the quilts, he told Preminger not to ask him to rehearse or to cut during the filming. "You'll get what you want," he assured "Ludvig." "Trust me."[85] Preminger not only got what he wanted, but more than anyone could have expected.

Composer Elmer Bernstein, a neophyte at the time, actually participated in the production, watching the filming and the dailies, and discussing the score with Preminger. Eventually the two agreed on music that would combine incidental dramatic material with a bebop-style leitmotif that emerges each time Frankie heads to the beer joint or takes a fix from Louie. Preminger appreciated Bernstein's willingness to "become part of the film," noting, "This system eliminates most well-known, sought-after composers because they are not willing to devote all that time to one picture."[86]

The score was a brilliantly haunting stylistic choice, in that the heroin-addicted bebop pioneer Charlie ("Bird") Parker had died at 34 the previous April. In an essay on bebop, author Al Young revealed:

> A former babysitter of Charlie and Chan Parker has described to me the Parkers' affection for Frank Sinatra's singing, which Pres [John Coltrane] also adored. "'Listen,' he would say. 'Just listen to this,'" Joyana Brookmeyer told me. According to her, Bird might spend an entire Saturday afternoon carefully taking in a brand-new Sinatra album, studying the singer's phrasing, reviewing or mastering the lyrics.[87]

Elmer Bernstein said:

> Actually, *The Man with the Golden Arm* started a very long relationship I had with Sinatra. Curiously enough, during the filming... I only got to know Frank at that point. I was closer to and working with the director, Otto Preminger.
> I was present at the first reading, when they all sat around a table, all the actors, and I stayed with that project all the way through—so I did get

to know Frank at that point. And he *loved* the score. And from that time on...I was his guy.[88]

The film opens as Frankie exits a bus back in his old neighborhood, making his first mistake by gazing into the window of the tavern where his lowlife friends congregate. (Here Preminger uses a striking close-up of Frank's face, shot from inside as he peers around the word "beer" on the window.) A touching scene with Zosch follows, as she makes a pathetic attempt to celebrate his return from six months' incarceration and treatment. Although she gains Frankie's sympathy by presenting him with a cake (with a single candle) and a homemade cardboard sign, she soon proves to the audience that her "handicap" is only being used to manipulate him.

Frankie tries to stay clean but is blackmailed by Louie into returning to dealing the illegal poker game after he is arrested for shoplifting clothes that his buddy, Sparrow (Arnold Stang), actually filched for him. After returning to his old profession, his relationship with Zosch, who is seen perusing her bizarre keepsake "My Scrapbook of Fatal Accidents" (a foreshadowing of her later unintentional killing of Louie), worsens and he soon seeks out Molly. Discussing his upcoming drum audition with a local big band, he asks her (in a line tailor-made for Frank), "Tell me something, Molly. Do you think those bobbysoxers will really fall for me?" But tragically, Frankie's inability to escape his old environs, particularly Louie's insistence that he deal a game that continues for several days, ruins his tryout. At this point, the term "Man with the Golden Arm" refers to three components of Frankie's personality: the poker dealer, the heroin addict and the aspiring jazz drummer.

One of the film's highlights occurs when Frankie, devastated by his embarrassing audition and subsequent heroin fix, stumbles into the burlesque club where Molly works as a hostess. As Preminger cuts to a close-up of Frankie's dilated eyes, she instantly knows he's back on the junk, and a brawl with Drunky ensues. After Molly runs into the street to hail a taxi, Frankie follows and is nearly run down by a car, its squealing tires providing an effectively jarring moment.

The tender relationship that develops between Frankie and Molly reaches its apex when she forcefully persuades him to quit using heroin and then offers to help him. As she tells him to accept responsibility for his own actions and fight back against his demons (criminals, police, drugs), Kim Novak comes into her own as a capable and powerful actress. Following Frankie's harrowing withdrawal, he, Molly and the police captain all witness Zosch rise from her wheelchair. Terrified, she jumps to her death, allowing Frankie to begin a new life with his real love; but still the mood is one of uncertainty as they stroll away from the old neighborhood.

On Halloween 1955, Frank cut the Cahn and Van Heusen song "The Man with the Golden Arm," like "From Here to Eternity," a publicity number to coincide with the film's release. However, after Capitol made a test pressing, the single was shelved. Lyrically the song reflects the content of the screenplay: "He's following the devil's plan...The hopeless need for it that makes him plead for it."

In mid-November, Preminger completed a rough cut of the film for United Artists, who agreed to distribute it, pending approval from the Production Code Administration. However, when the completed print was viewed by the PCA, whose regulation that "neither the illegal drug traffic nor drug addiction must ever be presented" certainly applied in this case, the Motion Picture Association of America refused to issue its seal of approval. Ironically the Catholic Legion of Decency did pass the film; according to Preminger, "most likely want[ing] to avoid another battle after *The Moon is Blue*."[89] (The Legion tangled unsuccessfully with the Supreme Court over its charges of "obscenity" against *Blue*.) Although Frankie is shown taking several injections from Louie in the film, the word "heroin" is never mentioned, and any shots depicting the actual preparation of the drug were cut by the director.

As the company had done with *The Moon is Blue*, United Artists released *The Man with the Golden Arm* regardless of any censorship blockades, going so far as to resign from the MPAA. Much to Preminger's delight, 1,100 theaters booked the film, which became the ninth-highest grossing feature of the year and one of the most successful releases in the history of UA.

Swansea Central Library

Items that you have borrowed

Title: Lyrics
ID: 60004063382

Due: 30 July 2022

Title: The extraordinary life of A. A. Milne
ID: 60003133326

Due: 30 July 2022

Total items: 2
Account balance: £0.00
Borrowed: 6
Overdue: 0
Hold requests: 0
Ready for collection: 0
09/07/2022 14:46

Items that you already have on loan

Title: Somewhere becoming rain : collected
writings on Philip Larkin
ID: 60003668812

Due: 22 July 2022

Title: The odd couple : the curious friendship
between Kingsley Amis and Philip Larkin
ID: 60001408880

Due: 22 July 2022

Title: The Cinema of Sinatra ; the actor, on
screen and in song
ID: 00013667559

Due: 28 July 2022

Title: The Ipcress file
ID: 60004036661

Due: 28 July 2022

Thank you for using the bibliotheca SelfCheck
System.

Kim Novak, John Conte and Sinatra in *The Man with the Golden Arm*

Variety's "Gene," assuming that the average Joe in the mid-1950s would have no conception of drug abuse or addiction, wrote:

> Otto Preminger's second open defiance of the Production Code is expressed... a feature that focuses on addiction to narcotics. Clinical in its probing of the agonies, subject matter will seem forbidding to sensitive elements of the populace. Fortunately this is a gripping, fascinating film, expertly produced and directed by Preminger and performed with marked conviction by Frank Sinatra as the drug slave. ...This reviewer suggests the screen characters are too remote to make such personal identification with the spectator. ...The dope kick is beyond the ken of the general public and as a result there can be little sense of participation in the story and not much sympathy with the characters.[90]

When *Golden Arm* was released in December 1955, were only musicians and moral degenerates susceptible to drugs? Hardly, but even Preminger depicts addiction in this manner, having little choice during an era when drug addicts were placed in the same "subversive" category with homosexuals and Communists. Frank, like Preminger, stayed true to form in trying to push the boundaries of artistic expression and was successful in bringing a new viewpoint to the American public.

Bosley Crowther, who considered the film a "cleaned-up version" of the novel, favored *The Lost Weekend*, calling Frank "plausible,"[91] but fellow Big Apple journalist John McCarten, in his *New Yorker* review, wrote, "Frank Sinatra, who has continually amazed me with his acting ability, continues to amaze me."[92] Other publications were more specific, praising Frank for the remarkable depth and power of his performance. While *Cue* magazine noted his "run[ning] the shaky gamut from quiet confidence, uncertainty, bravado, fright, apprehension, and terror, through the range of the junkie's need, desire, satisfaction and ecstasy—and then the private hell reserved for all such," *The Saturday Review*'s Arthur Knight elaborated on his "truly virtuoso" characterization:

> The thin, unhandsome one-time crooner has an incredible instinct for the look, the gesture, the shading of the voice that suggests tenderness, uncertainty, weakness, fatigue, despair. Indeed he brings to the character much that has not been written into the script, a shade of sweetness, a sense of edgy indestructibility that actually creates the appeal and intrinsic interest of the role. But he is also an actor of rare ability. His scene in the jail with a junkie screaming for a fix in the same cell, the scene of his own first fix in Louie's room—both played in huge, searching close-ups—and the terrifying writhing agony of the "cold turkey" treatment are conveyed with clinical realism.[93]

The Man with the Golden Arm

Called an "extraordinary man" by Preminger, Frank truly had immersed himself into Frankie Machine, realizing that the film's success was more important than maintaining his usual lifestyle and cinematic work habits. And there is only one moment in *The Man with the Golden Arm* when the characteristic "Sinatra style" shows through: appropriately when Frankie enters the tavern after taking his first fix from Louie; approaching the bar, he speaks with confidence and a slight hint of swagger—qualities that soon are buried beneath the weight of the monkey on his back.

During the summer of 1955, Frank agreed to perform a brief cameo during a stint at the Sands in Vegas. Shot on location in Sin City, with interior work done at the Sands, MGM's *Meet Me in Las Vegas* was intended as an entertainment extravaganza; and, as produced by Joe Pasternak and directed by Roy Rowland, it delivered just that in stunning Cinemascope. Starring Dan Dailey as a gambling-addicted rancher and Cyd Charisse as a ballet dancer who becomes his good luck charm at the casinos, the film also features Paul Henreid, Agnes Moorehead, Lili Darvas, Jim Backus, Jerry Colonna and cameos by Debbie Reynolds, Peter Lorre, Vic Damone, Tony Martin, Elaine Stewart and Frank, who provides a nice comic touch: Immediately after Dailey and Charisse test their "magic handholding" at the Sands, they insert a coin into a slot machine for a man with his back to the camera; as it pays off, he turns around to do a very familiar head nod and facial expression.

The true highlights of *Meet Me in Las Vegas* are the ever-amazing Charisse's dance numbers, including a ballet by Hermes Pan and Eugene Loring, and a reworking of "Frankie and Johnny" with additional lyrics by Sammy Cahn. Although he is not shown, Sammy Davis, Jr., sings the number, marking the first time he was involved in a production in which Frank also had a hand. Variety's "Brog" wrote:

> Entertainment is delivered in bountiful measure in this sock ...production. Excellent comedy and romance, great music, songs and dances are skillfully

blended into a show that merits top playing time. ...Miss Charisse's versatility... is well established. This role... puts her over as an actress as well as a dancer... Pasternak's showmanly reining of the production makes the most of the entertainment ingredients. There are credited and uncredited guest stars wandering in and out for surprise visits.[94]

Frank, along with his cameo cohorts, all were in Vegas for other reasons, and were not billed in the credits. Only Vic Damone, who actually performs a song, was identified on screen.

Having established a credible reputation as a versatile screen actor, Frank formed his own company, Kent Productions, in December 1955 and set out to make his first independent film, a Western called *Johnny Concho*. As Nancy, Jr., recalled, "A bunch of the boys—Sinatra, McGuire, Riddle, Sanicola—got together to make a cowboy movie."[95]

Frank had known David P. Harmon since 1944, when the CBS writer had penned dialogue for the Voice to use between songs on the *Reflections* radio show. "They hit it off very well," recalled Harmon's daughter, Nikki:

> Over the years [they] spent some good times together—a drink here and there in New York, walks in the desert in Vegas after the show, etc. Dad and Mom would go in to see him when he was playing the Sands. I remember sitting at Jilly's table, myself, as a teenager.[96]

Frank's pal Don McGuire (who wrote *Meet Danny Wilson*) was signed to direct and collaborate on the screenplay with Harmon, whose original version, "The Man Who Owned the Town," had been performed on the *Studio One* television show. Sharing the production responsibilities with Hank Sanicola, Frank took the title role and cast Keenan Wynn, William Conrad, Phyllis Kirk and Wallace Ford in the major supporting roles. (Apparently, Gloria Vanderbilt originally had been chosen for the role of Mary Dark, but was replaced by Kirk after only a few hours of shooting.)

Nikki Harmon recalled:

> Dad... did go out on the set when they were shooting, but doesn't remember very much about that—writers pretty much stay in the background—except for one thing. There was a crew member whose wife was ill and in the hospital, and it was going to cost a great deal of money. And when Frank heard about it, without letting anyone know, he paid the hospital bill.
>
> I asked Dad how he would describe Sinatra and, without hesitation, he said, "Loyal. If you were his friend, you were his friend for life. And vice versa."[97]

Set in Cripple Creek, Arizona, in 1875, *Johnny Concho* tells the tale of the arrogant younger brother of a famous gunslinger who is shot down by two men, Tallman (Conrad) and Walker (Christopher Dark). When residents of the frontier town ask Concho to drive out these killers who have taken over the community, his cowardly ways force him to flee. However, after meeting Barney Clark (Wynn), a gunman turned preacher, and Mary Dark (Kirk), who bolster his courage, he returns to avenge his brother's murder. After rallying the townspeople, he is wounded in the ensuing showdown but lives to gain their respect.

On April 5, 1956, Frank recorded "Johnny Concho Theme (Wait for Me)," a promotional single to accompany the theatrical release. Distributed by United Artists, the film opened at the New York Paramount on August 15, and, as was the custom at the venue, was followed by a live stage show. The performers: The Tommy Dorsey Orchestra (combined with that of brother Jimmy) reunited with their erstwhile boy singer, Frank Sinatra. Not satisfied with his initial attempt at film production, Frank constantly took cheap shots at *Concho* throughout his week of shows. On

opening day, long lines poured into the theater at 9:50 a.m., with some of the teenagers carrying signs reading, "We love Frankie" and "Sinatra for President." One evening, after concluding his concert, he attended a party at Toots Shor's, where the guests were given "Vote for Johnny Concho" buttons and the bartenders and waiters wore cowboy hats.

Indeed, Frank was right about *Concho*, its script being far too wordy to sustain the interest of an audience who found it difficult to accept an urban New Jerseyite as a Western gunman. (Actually Frank seems no more out of place than does the Tasmanian Errol Flynn in his many oaters.) *Variety*'s "Brog" wrote:

> Passable for a first try. Could possibly have clicked strongly with surer direc-
> tion and scripting. The uncertain handling is reflected in Sinatra's own work
> and in the performance [sic] of some other cast members... It's a western which
> inclines toward talkiness. ...Mood is stressed in the lensing by William Mellor
> and in the excellent background score by Nelson Riddle.[98]

Bosley Crowther, however, thought that Frank had been let down by his material:

> Credit Mr. Sinatra with impressive dexterity. Credit him also with ability
> as his own producer to pick a good yarn. ...Mr. Sinatra does a pretty good
> job of making the chicken-livered tin-horn fairly credible. Outside of his
> dude-rancher get-ups, he looks the punk he plays and he ranges well from
> swaggering arrogance to sweating pusillanimity. It is something to see Mr.
> Sinatra swallow that Adam's apple of his.
>   But unfortunately, the finished screenplay and Don McGuire's direction...
> are not up to the quality of the story or of Mr. Sinatra's job. ...Mr. Sinatra,
> the actor, might mention to the producer of this film, who happens to be Mr.
> Sinatra, that he needs better writing and direction than he gets here.[99]

And Crowther was echoed by *The Los Angeles Times*' Philip K. Scheuer:

The film apparently represents two wish fulfillments of every Hollywood star—to boss his own company and to play a cowboy. Sinatra has, on the whole, done better with the second wish than the first: Performing competently if never brilliantly, he at least causes one to dislike him at the start and pull for him at the finish, which is what one is supposed to do. And his modesty has charm.[100]

Although a mediocre film and a disappointing production experience for Frank, *Johnny Concho* allowed him further to demonstrate his versatility as an actor and to branch out into another non-musical genre, proving that he was not satisfied to return to the same material time and again. Just as film acting had provided an artistic outlet to complement (and, for a time, nearly to replace) his singing, now attempting to produce his own pictures added another element to his talents as an entertainer. While appearing on *The Bob Hope Show* in 1957, Frank told the comedian, "I didn't see [*Johnny Concho*]. I was too busy making a comeback."

"It occurred to me that maybe Frank Sinatra could give me some advice," thought struggling singer Tony Bennett, while *Concho* was making its brief run at the Paramount:

> I went over to the theater and asked permission to see him. He said yes, and they led me back to his dressing room. The door opened, and there was Mr. Sinatra. He looked at me and without batting an eye, said, "Oh, hello, Tony, come on in." ...I told him about...how nervous I was. He said not to worry about that...If you don't care about what you're doing, why should the audience? ...I learned that anxiety is a very essential part of performing."[101]

Nelson Riddle had continued to work his magic while preparing arrangements for Frank's next Capitol album, *Songs for Swingin' Lovers*. (To fill the gap between the release of *In the Wee Small Hours* and the new effort, Capitol also issued *This Is Sinatra!*, a compilation of singles recorded from 1953-55.) On January 9, 1956, Frank had begun a series of four sessions considered by many to be his finest, waxing lightly swinging versions of "You Brought a New Kind of Love to Me," Jimmy Van Heusen and Johnny Mercer's "I Thought About You" (which he had recorded but abandoned six months earlier), "Memories of You" (left unreleased) and the superlative "You Make Me Feel So Young," which opens the album with Riddle's sprightly four-bar introduction  to Frank's unforgettable declaration of youthfulness. Recorded the next day, "Pennies from Heaven" (which had been a number one hit for Bing Crosby in 1936) opens with Riddle's dramatic approximation of a rain shower before Frank enters over the light groove; while Johnny Burke's lyric "James Durante's looks give me a thrill" on "How About You?"—sung with total earnestness by Frank—adds some unique humor. "You're Getting to Be a Habit with Me," written for the 1933 Warner Bros. film *42nd Street*, rounded off the session, featuring the buoyancy that distinguishes so many of Riddle's swing ballads.

Two days later, on January 12, 1956, lightning had struck during a truly magical session that produced the Latin-flavored swinger "It Happened in Monterey," "Swingin' Down the Lane," the chorus-backed ballad "Flowers Mean Forgiveness" (released as a single), and a track that

Frank approved after only 22 takes, in this instance the number required to attain absolute musical perfection and a landmark in popular music history. Ironically, the inclusion of Cole Porter's "I've Got You Under My Skin" was an afterthought necessitated by Capitol's A&R department, who wanted three additional songs for the album. Rushing out the arrangements at the eleventh hour, Riddle reputedly finished "Skin" in the back seat of his car as his wife drove to the studio. Opening with the laid-back Riddle bounce, the song continually builds behind Frank's vocal, then crescendos into an instrumental explosion led by the trombone solo of Milt Bernhardt; eight bars of brass then settle the groove back down a bit until Frank re-enters with the chorus, eventually hitting a peak with "*Do−n't* you know, little fool..." and then brilliantly matches each dynamic shade of the orchestra as it returns to the introductory vamp. No one describes this apex of Sinatra better than Will Friedwald:

> Was there ever a more perfect, more powerful or goose-bump-raising record...? After Sinatra's first chorus, swinging and passionate enough for any six crooners... Milt Bernhardt emerges from the ensemble as Sinatra's wordless alter ego. ...For half a chorus the trombonist plumbs depths of emotion that... we tell ourselves that no mere words could ever reach. But then Sinatra returns for an outchorus to end all outchoruses: He starts by using Bernhardt's highest emotional peak as his own lowest note and builds from there to a musical dramatic climax that fully exploits Cole Porter's lyric as meaningfully as his melody, combining pure swing with caveman machismo, capable of grabbing even the most Frank-resistant listener way down at the bottom of his soul.[102]

The final session for *Swingin' Lovers* was held on January 16, yielding "Makin' Whoopee" (featuring the Frank-altered lyric "A *mess* of shoes, a *gang* of rice"), a sexily swinging, punchy "Old Devil Moon," Cole Porter's masterful "Anything Goes," "Too Marvelous for Words" (another Crosby number one, with the Jimmy Dorsey Orchestra in 1937) and the beautiful ballad "We'll Be Together Again."

Not long after completing *Johnny Concho*, Frank returned to MGM to costar with Bing Crosby and Grace Kelly in *High Society*, a musical remake of *The Philadelphia Story* (1940). Producer Sol C. Siegel already had the two (alphabetically billed) stars on board and wanted to add Frank, who was thrilled at the prospect of starring with his boyhood idol. Musical director Saul Chaplin recalled:

> Bing would always come on time and do his rehearsing and Frank would every now and again show up late. ...I'd continue with the rehearsal with Bing, and when it came to Frank's turn, he'd say, "Come into the next room and show me what my part is. ...It was the first time he felt self-conscious. He was embarrassed at not doing things right−in front of Bing. ...They adored each other.[103]

Paired with Celeste Holm (as a magazine reporter and photographer, respectively), Frank again appreciated working with the talented actress, who later said, "A woman doesn't have to be in love with Sinatra to enjoy his company. I wasn't and I did. He's a stimulating talker on any subject: books, music, cooking, his children, whom he quotes oftener than most fathers, and sports."[104]

Commissioned for $250,000 to write the score for the film (Frank and Bing each were paid $200,000), Cole Porter invited the three costars to his home to listen to the songs. After Frank walked in the door, the composer recalled the ancient 1938 performance at the Rustic Cabin.

Porter said to Frank, "Gee, it's been a long time since we met. I don't know if you remember an evening with me at some nightclub where you worked."

"Oh, yeah," Frank replied. "I remember very well."

"So do I," Porter assured him. "That's about the *worst* performance I ever heard."[105]

Though Porter wrote nine new songs for the film, Chaplin added an extra number, the composer's "Well, Did You Evah?" which originally had been written for the 1938 Broadway show *Dubarry Was a Lady*, for a Frank and Bing duet scene. Updating the lyrics for a 1956 audience, Chaplin added one of the film's most humorous moments. After Bing's C. K. Dexter-Haven warbles some classic Crosby "Ba, ba, ba, ba, bah," Frank's Mike Connor sings, "I don't dig that kind of croonin', chum." In a line added by Crosby himself, would-be songwriter "Dex" counters with "You must be one of the newer fellas."

Throughout the *High Society* production, Frank and Bing referred to each other as "Dexedrine" and "Nembutal," respectively. Years later, Frank recounted a story—undoubtedly embellished by his wicked sense of humor—about Crosby's off-camera drinking. Apparently, Bing

A NEW HIGH IN THE MOVIE SKY. M-G-M PRESENTS IN VISTAVISION AND COLOR
A SOL C. SIEGEL PRODUCTION

**BING GRACE FRANK
CROSBY KELLY SINATRA**

in the hilarious low-down on high life

HIGH Society

CELESTE HOLM · JOHN LUND
LOUIS CALHERN · SIDNEY BLACKMER
and LOUIS ARMSTRONG and His Band

Story by JOHN PATRICK
Music and Lyrics by COLE PORTER

would duck into his trailer for a few shots of Scotch before reporting back to the set. Sinatra friend Nick Caruso, Jr., recalled, "Frank said that there was a group of nuns on the set who genuflected whenever Crosby went by. 'When I passed by,' Frank said, 'They spit at me!'"[106]

On January 17, 1956—the day after the *Songs for Swingin' Lovers* sessions were completed—Frank began recording his four numbers for the film: Cutting "Well, Did You Evah?" with Crosby, he waxed "You're Sensational," "Mind If I Make Love to You?" and "Who Wants to Be a Millionaire?" (with Holm) three days later. Other than his occasional tardiness and rehearsal problems, Frank blankly refused to re-record "You're Sensational" (his personal favorite in the score), which Connor sings to Kelly's Tracy Lord during a very effective love scene near the end of the film. When Chaplin's assistant Johnny Green told him that the original take was not acceptable, Frank replied that he thought it was perfect and was done working for the day. After conferring with Siegel, however, he agreed to do another take (on April 5) to be released on the soundtrack album. Green recalled, "It was just a small matter of professional disagreement. We sorted things out quite happily."[107]

At one point during production, Frank flew to Vegas to fulfill a singing engagement at the Sands. Aware that he was exhausting himself with overwork and too many late-night outings, Bing and Jimmy Van Heusen visited him in an attempt to slow him down. Crosby recalled, "[W]e were told he was on the verge of a complete physical collapse... Jimmy and I went over... to see Frank backstage, and I offered to go on for him so he could give his throat a rest and recover."

"No thanks," Frank refused. "I can handle it all right. But Bing, there's something I want to talk to you about. Can you meet me at Luigi's after the show?"

Later, at the Italian restaurant, Crosby joined Frank for a drink and to discuss the matter on his friend's mind.

Frank revealed, "Bing, we've got to do something about Van Heusen. He's not taking very good care of himself!"[108]

Bing Crosby ,John Lund, Grace Kelly and Sinatra in *High Society*

High Society features a simple story about ice-cold young divorcee Tracy Lord, who plans to marry stiff suitor George Kittredge (John Lund), has a drunken evening's "fling" with reporter Mike Connor and finally re-marries Dex, who has returned to Newport for the jazz festival featuring Louis Armstrong, who acts as the musical narrator. Having scored brief, often demeaning roles in earlier Hollywood films, "Satchmo," fronting his All Stars, reported to the MGM set for 23 days. Cinematically segregated throughout the film, Armstrong and his cohorts interact only with Crosby in a few scenes, most memorably during a party in which the two musical giants perform "That's Jazz," a swinging number that greatly enlivens the proceedings whenever "Pops" launches into one of his incomparable trumpet solos. (The fact that Crosby calls him this beloved moniker speaks to their shared understanding of the genre.) Armstrong, whose personality literally jumps off the screen, opens the film as his band bus snakes its way to "Dex's" mansion, his rendition of "High Society Calypso" providing a charming introduction to the wonderful Porter score.

As Mike arrives at the mansion with Liz, Frank again makes a cinematic entrance with his back to the camera, his comic style and timing again to the fore after serious roles in *The Man with the Golden Arm* and *Johnny Concho*. "I'm scared," Mike tells her. "I want to go home." This innocent quality, indicating Mike's discomfort at being ordered to cover the society wedding, is made even more humorous by Frank's casting in the role: After all, he is playing the very sort of journalist he loathed in real life (though the likable Mike is a far cry from the vitriolic Lee Mortimers of the world).

Two particular scenes effectively demonstrate the respective on screen charismas of Crosby and Sinatra. In a flashback sequence set aboard the yacht *True Love*, Dex's crooning of the song of the same name appears to enthrall Tracy (Kelly's hand movements are perhaps the most romantic in film history) but may not have had a similar effect on females in the audience. However, Mike's less formalized wooing of Tracy with "You're Sensational" in the library of the closed-down Lord mansion is a romantic highlight. In a beautifully photographed and edited sequence, director Charles Walters (who had helmed *The Tender Trap*) allows Frank to sing an entire verse and chorus before cutting from a two-shot to alternating over-the-shoulder close-ups of the characters. But the Sinatra-Kelly chemistry truly beams during a later scene set by Dex's pool, where she again does an erotic hand ballet as her suitor sings (this time Frank, crooning "Mind If I Make Love to You?").

The next morning, Mike and Tracy's "tryst" is followed by his best attempt to carry her across the lawn from the pool to the house. After Dex and George witness the bathrobed figures, Mike admits (in classic "Sinatra speak"), "We put away a gang of wine last night." Soon after, he adds, "You know how I feel about my grandmother, but I'd sell her for a drink." Having been exposed to how the "other half" lives, Mike and Liz both decide to resign from *Spy* magazine,

"What a Swell Party this is..." Frank and Bing in *High Society*

and the former reveals even more about his personal morality by declaring he couldn't "take advantage of [Tracy] because she was a little worse for the wine."

"Dexedrine" and "Nembutal" are paired magnificently in the "Well, Did You Evah?" sequence, each getting his due while refusing to upstage the other (unlike Frank's attempts to deal with Brando during the filming of *Guys and Dolls* the previous year). Frank's timing (rhythmic and comic) is honed to seemingly effortless perfection, providing one of the most effective and entertaining musical scenes of his cinematic career. *Variety*'s "Abel" considered the film "a solid entertainment every minute of its footage":

The original Philip Barry play, *The Philadelphia Story*, holds up in its transmutation from the Main Line to a Newport jazz bash. ...casting of Satchmo Armstrong for the jazz festivities was an inspired booking...

Porter had whipped up a solid set of songs with which vocal pros like the male stars and Miss Holm do plenty. Latter and Sinatra have a neat offbeat number with "Who Wants to Be a Millionaire?"; Crosby makes "Now You Has Jazz" (aided by Armstrong) as his standout solo... The romantic scenes are capitally done in every sequence...[109]

Noting the film's narrative and logical weaknesses (which can in large part be attributed to Barry's play), Bosley Crowther was astute in identifying Frank and Satch's performances as the true strong points:

> *High Society*... is as flimsy as a gossip-columnist's word, especially when it is documenting the weird behavior of the socially elite. ...To be sure, there are moments of amusement in this handsomely set and costumed film... One... is when Frank Sinatra... plies the haughty heroine with wine and somewhat unhooks her inhibitions. Mr. Sinatra makes hay with this scene. ...In the musical line, Mr. Sinatra and Bing Crosby also sing some fetching songs... Their best is "Well, Did You Evah?" a spoof of the haughty and blasé...[The] tedious stretches in this socially mixed-up affair... are due in the main to slow direction and the mildness of Miss Kelly in the pivotal role. ...And... Mr. Crosby seems a curious misfit figure in the role of the young lady's cast-off husband... having fun with Mr. Armstrong and his boys and viewing the feminine flutter with an amiable masculine disdain. He strokes his pipe with more affection than he strokes Miss Kelly's porcelain arms.[110]

Soon after completing *High Society* on April 19, 1956, Miss Kelly, called "Gracie" by Frank, would forsake her film career to become Princess Grace of Monaco. She recalled:

> I'd always wanted to do a musical and, of course, working with Bing and Frank was simply marvelous. They create a certain excitement and are two very strong personalities. So it was fascinating for me to be in the middle—watching the tennis match go back and forth from one to the other with tremendous wit and humor—each one trying to outdo the other... Frank and I did two numbers. He has an endearing sweetness and charm.[111]

That "sweetness" is an integral trait of Mike Connor, a combination of his earlier MGM musical characters and the less naive, more worldly Charlie Reader of *The Tender Trap*. In this respect, *High Society* represents a slight digression in Frank's ever-developing film career, but a thoroughly entertaining one nonetheless.

Entertainment, however, was the last thing on Frank's mind when, during the making of *High Society*, he had received some absolutely devastating news. Bogie was dying of throat cancer.

Though Bogart had survived a nine-and-one-half hour operation to remove the cancer, the disease continued to attack him, eventually leaving him bedridden in Holmby Hills, where friends like Spencer Tracy and Katherine Hepburn constantly dropped in to cheer him up. But it was difficult for them to see the once-virile "tough guy" wasting away, gradually shrinking to 90 pounds. Poor Bogie became jealous of the way Frank and Betty Bacall looked at each other, but he appreciated his pal's humorous attempts to cheer him up.

Chapter 6
Quintessential Sinatra

> People often remark that I'm pretty lucky. I don't think luck has much to do with it. You've got to have something more substantial. The competition is too fierce. Luck is only important in so far as getting the chance to sell yourself at the right moment. After that, you've got to have talent and learn how to use it.—Frank Sinatra[1]

Since March 1, 1956, Frank had been concentrating on another groundbreaking musical project, *Close to You*, an LP of love songs arranged for string quartet by Nelson Riddle. Not since his days with Axel Strodahl had he sung comparable arrangements, and never an entire album's worth. Though Riddle admitted that "the structure of popular songs does not lend itself to arranging in the true string quartet style of the classics," he worked his magic on more than a dozen great standards performed beautifully by the Hollywood String Quartet, featuring Frank's good friends Felix and Eleanor Slatkin, on violin and cello, respectively, and several soloists, including Mahlon Clark on clarinet and Harry "Sweets" Edison on trumpet.[2] Frank became even more of a musical perfectionist while recording this album, rejecting the version of Harold Arlen and Truman Capote's "Don't Like Goodbyes" cut during the first session. And the extra effort certainly paid off. Will Friedwald writes, "This is surely Sinatra's most intimate and delicate singing ever, and he imbues every track with an attention to nuance remarkable even for him."[3]

Gathering for a second session on March 8, Frank and the musicians, conducted by pianist Bill Miller, recorded a somewhat typical version of "If It's the Last Thing I Do" (which was cut from the album release) and a superb second stab at "Don't Like Goodbyes," featuring a very "classical" introduction eventually met by Frank's bluesy note-bending and long-breath phrasing. The most unusual arrangement cut during the *Close to You* sessions, it concludes with two dramatic choruses bracketing a lovely French horn solo by Vince De Rosa. Two other songs, "P.S. I Love You" and "Love Locked Out," also were laid down.

Still busy on the *High Society* set, Frank was unable to return to the recording studio until April 4, when he waxed a magnificent arrangement of "I've Had My Moments," in which he enters boldly after being beckoned by De Rosa's French horn and Edison's muted trumpet. Following an instrumental section featuring De Rosa beautifully backed by the strings, Frank leads the entire ensemble into a light Latin groove before they retreat to the original tempo. On his sole recording of Oscar Levant and Edward Heyman's "Blame It on My Youth," he instantly warms the song's tone when he steals the spotlight from Clark's clarinet, but becomes one with the instrument as he quietly holds his final note on the ending. A masterful interpretation of

"Everything Happens to Me" also made the grade, but Rodgers and Hart's sublime "Wait Till You See Her" unfortunately did not.

The following day, four more potential *Close to You* songs were recorded. The first, "The End of a Love Affair," which was chosen to conclude the album, demonstrates how Frank could *act* lyrics and music, when he sings the phrase, "I'm lonely and low," drawing out the final word and tonally descending simultaneously. And at the end, phrasing the song's title, he hits a "big" note on "Love," lowers the dynamic on "a-" and finally issues a quiet, superbly sustained tone on "-fair," making the last syllable all the more dramatic by first setting it up. "It Could Happen to You," with Frank warmly caressing the French horn, and "With Every Breath I Take" also met with his satisfaction, but one last string-quartet number was a bit mysterious, to say the least.

"There's a Flaw in My Flue" was first performed on the Philco *Radio Time* show by Bing Crosby and Ethel Merman seven years earlier. As usual, having selected all the songs for his album, Frank reportedly decided to record Johnny Burke and Jimmy Van Heusen's absurd novelty number with complete conviction and a straight Riddle arrangement in order to pull a gag on the Capitol A&R department. Producer Voyle Gilmore, not noticing anything *musically* different about the number, was ready to include it on the album. After this ridiculous charade was cleared up, *Close to You* became a perfect recording during which the beautiful arrangements and expertly conducted ensemble never overwhelm Frank's incomparable performances. (One additional session, yielding "I Couldn't Sleep a Wink Last Night," Rodgers and Hart's "It's Easy to Remember" and the title song, was held on October 1, 1956.)

Two singles and Frank's re-recording of *High Society*'s "You're Sensational" were also cut at the April 5 session. The elegant, gently swinging "(How Little It Matters) How Little We Know," kicking into high gear just before Frank concludes with a low a cappella note, eventually reached number 13 on the *Billboard* chart, where it remained for 14 weeks; while "Wait for Me" was Riddle's rearrangement of the theme he and Dok Stanford had written for *Johnny Concho*.

Close to You does more than demonstrate the growth of Sinatra the singer and musician. It represents a peak in his overall artistry. By the spring of 1956, Frank's musical collaborations with Riddle and his varied cinematic experiences, particularly his success in dramatic roles, had coalesced to create one of the most accomplished and versatile performers of the 20th century. In four short years, he had shed the weight of public criticism and personal self pity to become the nation's greatest jazz-pop vocalist and one of the movies' top box-office draws.

While recording the material for *Close to You*, he also led sessions for *Frank Sinatra Conducts Tone Poems of Color* in February and March 1956. "Greatly intrigued" by the "color poetry" of Norman Sickel, who had written for the *Perfectly Frank* radio series, he chose eight composers to provide instrumental interpretations of various colors and conducted 60 musicians in an inauguration of Capitol's new recording facility. Will Friedwald notes, "Most musicians agree that Sinatra... wielded the baton at least as skillfully as any of his arrangers (with the exception of Stordahl), if not more so."[4] Included on the album are once and future collaborators Gordon Jenkins, Billy May and Nelson Riddle; his longtime favorite Alec Wilder; cinematic scorers Victor Young and Elmer Bernstein; and Jeff Alexander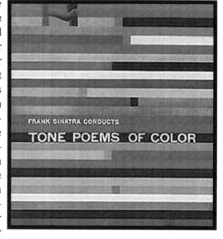
and Andre Previn. The selections range from Young's Yuletide "White" and moody, passionate "Black" to Alexander's playful, adventurous "Yellow" and Riddle's sweeping, epic "Gold" and sensual "Orange" (Frank's favorite color).

Turning his attention from Capitol back to the cinema screen, he accepted two roles that utilized his own charismatic persona, but first played his most atypical character since the Kissing Bandit. Before flying to Spain to begin the arduous filming of *The Pride and the Passion*, his second collaboration with producer-director Stanley Kramer, Frank cut two quasi-rock 'n' roll singles on April 9, "Five Hundred Guys" and "Hey, Jealous Lover," and the swinging "No One Ever Tells You," which he would save for his next album. Kramer had been involved in eight solid months of conferring with screenwriters Edna and Edward Anhalt, planning his VistaVision camera setups and scouting appropriate locations in the vicinity of Madrid. Armed with a 100-day shooting schedule, Kramer wanted to make good use of the time he had spent traveling over 1000

miles with production designer Rudolph Sternad, choosing 18 spots within a 75-mile radius of either Madrid or Avila.

Set in 1810 during the Peninsular Wars, *The Pride and the Passion* tells the tale of a group of Spanish guerrillas who discover an enormous, 6000-pound cannon abandoned by Napoleonic troops. Epic in scope but simple in story, the film focuses on the efforts of the soldiers to drag the gun across their war-ravaged nation to liberate the citizens of Avila. Prior to completing the screenplay, which was based on C. S. Forester's novel *The Gun*, Kramer met with the fascist Generalissimo Francisco Franco to rule out any chance of offending those who were allowing him to shoot in Spain. Since non-Spanish history books always had credited the English for defeating the French, Kramer decided to depict "exclusively... the bravery and battle-winning ingenuity of the Spanish guerrilla fighters."[5]

After arriving in Madrid, Frank joined his costars, top-billed Cary Grant, and Sophia Loren, who was preparing for her American film debut. As Captain Anthony Trumbull, Grant clashes with Frank's guerrilla leader, Miguel, both in terms of battle strategy and the romantic feelings they develop for Loren's Juana. The citizens of local villages were thrilled when the company moved through; and, at one point, Kramer enlisted 5,000 extras to appear as soldiers retreating from the French over Hoyo de Manzares, a mountain top 40 miles outside Madrid.

While the elegant Grant and Loren were not averse to sleeping in tents on location, Frank insisted on staying in a nice hotel in Madrid, which required long morning and evening commutes in the Mercedes-Benz Kramer had provided. Under a great deal of tension, he made matters worse by attempting to make the estranged Ava jealous: One of the reasons he returned to Madrid each night was 24-year-old singer Peggy Connolly, whom he had brought with him for the four-month shoot. Prior to his arrival, Ava had reserved a suite for him at the La Bruja hotel, only to be outraged, stating that she now would file for divorce. (Several attempts at reconciliation had proved tumultuous at best.) Though Frank was very unhappy, Kramer remembered his determination:

> [H]e worked hard and he insisted on doing a lot of things you'd normally expect a star to leave to a double. He ran through explosions and fires. I had him trudging up and down mountains, wading in rivers, crawling in mud from one end of Spain to the other, and he never complained once."[6]

But it was the ever-present One-Take Charley who caused some problems. Kramer added, "Frank is a tremendously talented man, intuitive and fast, which is good for him but not always good for the other actors. During the filming... he didn't want to rehearse. He didn't want to wait around while the crowd scenes were being set up."[7]

Eventually, Kramer and crew decided to film Frank's scenes back-to-back: "He wanted all his work done together. ...He couldn't stand it; he wanted to break loose. Eventually, for the sake of harmony, we shot all of his scenes together, and he left early. The rest of the cast acquiesced because of the tension."[8] Certainly the Ava-Peggy Connolly situation accounted for much of that stress, but he only added fuel to the fire. Having completed scenes four weeks ahead of schedule, he flew back to the States on July 31, 1956. After directing him in two films, Kramer concluded, "I don't know him well enough to be able to say I understand him. I've never discussed personal affairs with him. Actually I didn't see too much of him all the time we were in Spain."[9]

Not surprisingly, the most pleasant aspect of the filming had been his off-camera time with Loren. Much to his delight, he was able to slip some Sinatra-speak into the "English lessons" he gave her. She recalled:

> Before he came to Spain, I hear all sorts of things. He is moody, he is difficult, he is a tiger, he fights. Here he is kindly, friendly. He has even helped me with my English, has taught me how people really speak in Hollywood. He is a regular gasser. I dig him.[10]

Cary Grant later said:

> Frank is a unique man. Utterly without hypocrisy. Bluntly yet loyally opinionated. Unaffected and, to me, uncomplex despite everything written. It's almost frightening to some, to be faced with honesty. Frank fascinates the curious: the writers who try to analyze an enigma that is not an enigma; perhaps hoping to discover those qualities responsible for the man's personal appeal. Well, I think I know the quality. It's truth. Simple truth. Without artifice. I remember reading somewhere that in a world of lies a truth seems like a lie. I've read more nonsense about Frank Sinatra than about possibly anyone else in our time.[11]

A truly monumental undertaking, *The Pride and the Passion* would not be released for nearly another year.

The film opens with a powerful establishing shot depicting hundreds of retreating Spanish peasants slowly marching toward the camera. As Kramer cuts closer, individuals are seen hanging their heads as they go. It is an effective opening and one of the best moments in a production that could have been called "Slow Gun to Avila," as the majority of its 139 minutes are dedicated to the Spaniards', particularly Miguel's, relentless quest to bombard the walls of their ancient city and drive out the French, who have been hanging 10 of their countrymen each day. The locations, including vast panoramas of mountains, castles and cathedrals, are stunning, and the plotting does demonstrate the Spaniards' grim determination and love for their homeland, but the film *literally* is a long haul as the giant cannon undertakes all manner of accidents and disasters as it is pulled 1000 miles. (When the end credits roll, the viewer may feel that he or she, too, helped drag it to Avila.)

There are some highlights that break up the cannon's long journey, however. During a rainstorm, as Captain Trumbull strains to move one of the cart wheels out of a hole, the viewer may be thrilled by the sight of Cary Grant falling into the mud. And Loren, who adds nothing but a lukewarm love interest (not one scene with either Cary or Frank generates any real passion), shines only during her sensual dance scene. Considering that her acting in English was rudimentary at this point, the sequence benefits from what the filmmakers were really interested in showing: her pouting lips, ample breasts and equally lovely derriere, which, in all its pantied glory, may be viewed as her skirt flies up several times. There also is a spectacular scene of French troops being blown to the four winds on a bridge dynamited by Trumbull and Jose, a young Spaniard who is shot; a suspenseful sequence depicting their attempt to sneak the cannon through a guarded pass during the night, only to be foiled by a stubborn mule that sets off French fusillades from both sides; a truly epic scene set in a magnificent cathedral in which the cannon is hid beneath a rolling icon of the crucified Christ; and a lengthy section placing Trumbull in a *Don Quixote*-like position as he rides a donkey amidst windmills turning on the windswept plains. This quixotic overtone of noble futility is driven home when Trumbull, during a knife fight, kills a man he has backed against one of the windmills. When Trumbull is anguished by the incident, Miguel reveals that he intended the duel as a harmless entertainment.

The excitement finally begins during the last 15 minutes, when the intrepid band reaches Avila. A munitions expert, Trumbull has the cannon placed just within range of the walls and plans his strategy for the following morning. When the battle begins, an overhead long shot of the Spanish masses charging as the wall is breached is a thrilling reprise of the establishing shot: Originally seen pulling the gun, now they are able to fight their enemy because of it. But the most powerful image in the film occurs after the smoke has cleared, most of the Spaniards are seen slaughtered on the field, and Juana has died in Trumbull's arms. Discovering the dead Miguel just outside the wall, Trumbull carries his body into Avila and places it below a monument of Santa Teresa. Playing the straight-backed English officer throughout the film (and providing a stark contrast to the illiterate, emotional Miguel), Grant remains so as he effortlessly carries Frank, framed in another magnificent overhead long shot.

The Pride and the Passion is most effective when Kramer uses the 1.66:1 VistaVision ratio to create sweeping long shots depicting the struggling people against the awesome power of their environment. As in the best silent cinema, they convey content and meaning without using dialogue. In fact, *Pride* is often better when dialogue is kept to a minimum or avoided altogether: Loren is limited by her knowledge of English, Grant's drawing-room demeanor is out of place in dusty Spain and Frank is held back by his faux accent. And there is very little humor in the script, another aspect that adds to the lagging pace.

As usual, Frank's character is introduced in a memorable manner, subtly as Trumbull arrives in Spain to consult with "the general" about the cannon. Shown cutting a piece of leather (he presumably is a shoemaker, as he later finishes a pair of sandals for Juana), Miguel sits in a chair, focused on his work, as Kramer frames him in an overhead shot that keeps his face hidden. After Trumbull speaks, he slowly raises his head, beginning the low-key performance Frank maintains throughout the film. Though he always practiced subtlety and restraint, here he may have been further forced to do so by his accent. This requirement undoubtedly added to his frustration during the location shoot; but, regardless of the dialect and wig (an obviously synthetic rug which must have looked absurd to many Sinatra fans), he contributed a characterization more believable than most of *Pride*'s other elements.

Frank's one truly dramatic moment occurs when Miguel speaks to a huge crowd of Spaniards who have joined their French occupiers at a bullfighting arena. Displaying great conviction and patriotism without a hint of melodrama or maudlin pleading, the little leader of the resistance inspires the horde to foil the French and storm out of the city to join his ranks. Here, Kramer's effective use of long shots showing hundreds of people on the move is reminiscent of similar Cecil B. DeMille compositions in *The Ten Commandments* (1956), which was released as *Pride* was wrapping.

Perhaps one could argue that Frank's unwillingness to rehearse made it difficult for Grant and Loren to appear believable in their scenes with him, but they are just as stilted in their unconvincing "love" scenes. The majority of Kramer's $3.8 million budget undoubtedly was spent on the battle scenes, including thousands of extras, special effects and the enormous gun. Unfortunately, the rest of the film is not as interesting or exciting as these sequences involving mass violence. But Kramer always depicts these events in long shot (never resorting to the gory, close-up "realism" preferred by many subsequent filmmakers). No other depiction of Miguel's death would have been more effective than Trumbull carrying his body to the shrine. Additional

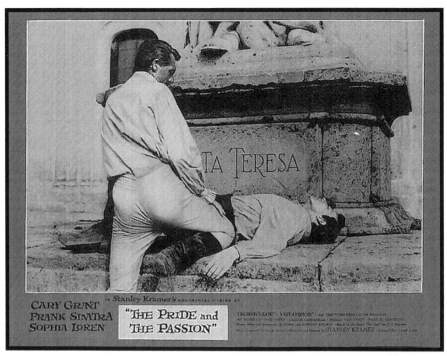

realism may have helped the actors to be more convincing, however: As in most films of the period, the lead male characters are clean shaven throughout; and Loren looks as made-up and fresh at the storming of Avila as she does in her first scene. But, after all, she was not cast for her dramatic abilities. What male filmgoer wanted to see her caked in dirt, with grease dripping from her hair? (Perhaps only a few.) While clowning on television with Bob Hope, Frank said, "It wasn't too tough pushing a cannon around, because Sophia was in the back, pushing all the time."

Most critics thought very highly of the film, including Frank's characterization, when it was released in June 1957. Apparently awestruck by the grandeur of the production, *Variety*'s "Gene" wrote:

> A big one, this is Stanley Kramer's powerful production of C. S. Forester's sweeping novel... The scope is immense, the impact forceful, the box office socko.
>
> *Pride and the Passion* has been highly touted. The publicity... came out of Spain without letup during the year and a half the picture was in preparation and production in that country. All leading to great expectations, it now can be stated, with justification, that this one is an epic that figures to be among the industry's top grossers.
>
> *Passion* is heavyweight with those cinematic elements that stir audiences. In addition to the size and importance of the physical production, it has a story that moves with excitement and suspense, and a provocative, highly attractive cast headed by Cary Grant, Frank Sinatra and Sophia Loren.
>
> They make for an engaging trio, imparting depth to the characters they portray. Grant is a strong figure. He reflects authority all the way through... Sinatra is more colorful... He looks and behaves like a Spanish rebel leader, earthy and cruel and skilled in handling his men in the primitive warfare. His is a splendid performance.[12]

The Actor, on Screen and in Song

153

Unconcerned with box-office appeal, *The Saturday Review*'s Hollis Alpert wrote that "Mr. Sinatra must be commended for his restrained and appealing *guerrilla* leader," while *Time* opined, "Sinatra—despite spit-curl bangs and a put-on accent—expectedly works hardest, acts best."[13] But Bosley Crowther, in his *New York Times* review, truly managed to breach the walls of Kramer's publicity campaign:

> Some heavy dramatic artillery... and a mighty bombardment of theatrics is showered upon the VistaVision screen. In his choice of a subject and in its treatment, Mr. Kramer, once a realist, now seems bent upon being a historical romancer in a class with Cecil B. DeMille.
>
> Not since the latter's *The Ten Commandments*... have we seen such a vast pictorial effort, such a fast flow of big activity, such a casual disregard for plausibility and such an obvious appeal to popular taste. ...What he is offering precisely is a turgid adventure yarn...
>
> Frank Sinatra as the Spanish leader is possessed of an evident inner fire that glows but fitfully on rare occasions, and Cary Grant as the English naval chap behaves with dignity but little sincerity. Both are stilted heroes in a stiffly heroic show. ...Mr. Kramer has spread a mighty canvas but it has virtually no human depth.[14]

During the autumn of 1956, producer Michael Todd released his weighty all-star epic *Around the World in 80 Days*, adapted from the Jules Verne novel by S.J. Perelman, who had written some of the Marx Brothers' best material, John Farrow (father of Mia) and James Poe. Starring David Niven (as Phileas Fogg), Cantinflas, Robert Newton and Shirley MacLaine, the film also includes cameos by John Carradine, Ronald Colman, Noel Coward, Sir John Gielgud, Sir Cedric Hardwicke, Trevor Howard, Buster Keaton, Peter Lorre, Victor McLaglen, George Raft, Red Skelton and

Marlene Dietrich, who appears as the hostess in a honky-tonk bar sequence. While thumping out a turn-of-the-century tune, the piano player turns around to reveal himself as Frank Sinatra! Dietrich was very enamored with her cameo colleague—"He is the gentlest man I have ever known, the Mercedes-Benz of men"[15]—while MacLaine later became a friend.

Around the World in 80 Days would win the Best Picture

David Niven, Marlene Dietrich and Sinatra as the piano player in *Around the World in 80 Days*

Academy Award the following spring. *Variety*'s "Hift" was very astute in identifying the film's genre, calling it "perhaps the most entertaining global story-travelog ever made":

Credit Todd with going all-out in giving the customers their money's worth. *80 Days*, lensed by Lionel Lindon with Kevin McCrory doing the foreign locales, is a bouncy, riotous, action-packed picture that still takes time out for hearty laughs and the magnificent scenery. ...This picture was made with showmanship in mind and the customers are guaranteed to eat it up. ...Todd, wisely, hasn't relied on just names. They're all well integrated. And the names must compete with the effects...[16]

Always a bit more critical than his trade-oriented *Variety* counterparts, Bosley Crowther essentially agreed:

This mammoth and mad picture... is a sprawling conglomeration of refined English comedy, giant screen travel panoramics and slam-bang Keystone burlesque. It makes like a wild adventure picture and, with some forty famous actors in "bit" roles, it also takes on the characteristic of a running recognition game. It is noisy with sound effects and music. It is overwhelmingly large in the process known as Todd-AO. It runs for two hours 55 minutes... And it is, undeniably, quite a show.[17]

Having purchased the rights to the galley proofs of Art Cohn's then-unpublished *Life of Joe E. Lewis*, a biography of the erratic nightclub entertainer, Frank began preparing *The Joker Is Wild* as the next Kent Production. Persuading Hollywood veteran Charles Vidor to direct, he then offered all three men a partnership in the enterprise, which would be financed and distributed by Paramount. By developing the project himself, Frank earned a guarantee of $120,000 plus 25 percent of the profits, proving he was one of the most popular stars in American cinema. But he was not just a *star*: As reported in *The New York Times*, "The Voice is now more securely on top than ever — as The Actor."[18]

The entire Sinatra family came to love Joe E. Lewis, who had sung in a Capone-owned speakeasy in 1920s Chicago until he accepted an offer from a rival club owner. Soon after, his throat was slashed by thugs employed by Machine-Gun Jack McGurn of the Capone gang, but after a time working in cheap burlesque shows, he made a miraculous comeback as a popular standup comedian. His alcoholism took its toll, but he eventually got sober and shared the bill with Frank in many nightclubs. With Lewis as a partner, Frank had the perfect story advisor and acting coach — two benefits that added gritty realism to the film. With Samuel L. Briskin producing for Paramount, Oscar Saul was hired to write the screenplay.

A selection of songs, both old and newly adapted, were chosen for the all-important soundtrack: Rodgers and Hart's "Mimi"; Fred Fisher's "Chicago," which became a leitmotif in Nelson Riddle's score; and Jimmy Van Heusen's "Swinging on a Star," with new lyrics by Harry Harris (who altered the verses of several other numbers). But the most important song in the film had to be a new one by Van Heusen and Cahn, who, after writing the lovely ballad "All the Way," went to Vegas to audition it. Having performed the previous night, Frank agreed to listen to it before breakfast, approximately 4 p.m.

Shuffling out of his bedroom, Frank looked at Cahn and grumbled, "You before breakfast? Yechh."

"Hey," Cahn replied, "from where I'm standing, I'm not sure who's being punished more."

Following a brief piano introduction by Van Heusen, Cahn sang the ballad, one of the finest collaborations of their careers. After hearing the final note, Frank simply said, "Let's eat," and they all sat down for an excellent breakfast.

Leaving the room, Cahn's agent, Lillian Small, with tears in her eyes, asked, "How could he not like that song?"

"Oh, he loved it," Cahn assured her.

"How do you know?"
"Because he loves them all."[19]

Italian poster for *The Joker Is Wild*

The autumn 1956 shooting of *The Joker Is Wild* began at noon and ran until 7 p.m. each work day. Musical director Walter Scharf enjoyed collaborating with Frank, who sang live in a real nightclub, to add to the realistic atmosphere and avoid the lip-synching techniques usually employed in musicals. But because of problems inherent with live sound, some of the material had to be re-recorded in the studio. On October 3, he cut two versions of "All the Way."

Though his dressing room was like Grand Central Station, with friends, other entertainers and various members of his entourage coming and going, Frank not only knew every word of his dialogue, but was aware of any troubling matters his coworkers were facing. When the script clerk's father became ill, he asked for updates each day; and when another cohort's wife had to travel to New Orleans to visit her ailing mother, he bought her a roundtrip airline ticket.

Scharf revealed that "the joker was never wild. He did everything to make me happy."[20] Occasionally he would miss a line, necessitating another take, but Vidor was aware that Frank instinctively knew when a scene was being played properly. The director later admitted, "Sinatra is the greatest natural actor I've ever worked with"; while Lewis said, "Frankie enjoyed playing my life more than I enjoyed living it."[21] Considering the hardships Lewis suffered, Frank undoubtedly did.

Beverly Garland recalled:

> "My first take is my best take." Sinatra is very much that way. I mean, "That's it, babe," you know. "You got me to stand in here, so you know where we're gonna light, and we're going to do it and we're not going to futz around with it." He just wouldn't do that.
>
> Eddie Albert was much more—"I think we should, and if we could, and I could just try that one more"—and we're all going, "Oh, come on, Eddie. It's all right, already."[22]

Eddie Albert said:

Marilyn Monroe, Joe E. Lewis and Sinatra

Now that I think of it, they asked me, "Would you mind meeting with him two weeks before and rehearse? It would be helping to him."

I said, "Yeah."

And they said, "Would you do it without any recompense?"

I said, "Well, what the hell, sure," and he never showed. So, for two weeks, I'm all ready there, with the piano and that kind of thing. And he never showed. He's a very admirable, independent man and he knew what he was doing.[23]

Joker opens with an atmospheric overhead long shot of nighttime Chicago, its speakeasies surrounded by the glare of dim lights reflecting off the rain-soaked streets. As the camera moves closer, the sign of the "777" club can be seen and a familiar voice can be heard emanating from within. After a man, having been observed through the door's peephole, is admitted, the scene cuts straight to Lewis performing on stage. Here is another classic Sinatra introduction, both gradual (like his entrances in *Young at Heart* and *Pride and the Passion*, but here done on the soundtrack only) and powerful, as the shot begins with him belting out a prominent note in a popular 1920s number. After Joe is threatened by Tim Coogan (Leonard Graves), the 777's resident head hatchet man, longtime pianist Austin Mack (Eddie Albert) quits, leaving his erstwhile partner to perform alone at his new engagement. Here, Vidor cuts to another overhead long shot, this time showing the loneliness Joe feels as Austin walks across the wet, empty street.

But Austin does show up on opening night and, as Coogan and his boss stare at them during "All the Way," Vidor uses stark counterpoint to foreshadow the inevitable event to come. While Joe tenderly sings a beautiful love song, the iniquitous gangsters glower with hatred and want of retribution in their eyes. A week later, as Joe is listening to his first record, again "All the Way," on his Victrola, three men, including Coogan, arrive to attack him inside his apartment. The throat cutting and skull bashing occur off-screen as Daniel L. Fapp's camera lingers in the hall. After the scene cuts to the gangsters walking down the lobby stairs, the switchboard operator receives a call from Joe's room, but hears nothing on the phone. Cutting back to Joe's door, the sequence then shows his injured hand creeping along the floor as he attempts to crawl for help, streaked with blood and his shirt cut to ribbons.

At this point, Frank's performance becomes as impressive as his *Golden Arm* heroin withdrawal. After six hours of surgery, Joe, his head thickly bandaged, awakens in a hospital bed as Austin sleeps in a chair. At first unable to make a sound, he manages to emit increasingly louder shrieks of pain as he feels the bandages and attempts to walk over to his friend. Austin wakes up in time to stop him from bashing his head into the door. Among the most harrowing moments of his acting career, this scene provides quite a contrast to the opening sequence showing the confident Joe at the 777 club.

When the physically and emotionally scarred Joe is released from the hospital, he "escapes" to New York, rather than return to his friends. When asked if "he will ever get his voice back," Austin (in a reference to Frank himself) forcefully replies, "He's more than a *voice*. He's a *human being*. He's a *man*." Austin and his colleague Swifty Morgan (Jackie Coogan) eventually find Joe, who is hesitant to resume old friendships, due to his current status as a clown in a humiliating burlesque routine, but is inspired by his success as a standup comedian, which is strongly bolstered by the stunning Letty Page (Jeanne Crain). During a romantic scene set behind a stage backdrop, Joe and Letty are backgrounded by silhouettes of dancers and a Crosby-like crooner before they begin swaying to an instrumental version of "All the Way."

Frank's performances in the burlesque and nightclub scenes display his considerable talent for both physical and verbal comedy. Using subtle mime, he creates just the right amount of

Sinatra's performance in *The Joker is Wild* displays his talent for comedy.

pathos as the abused clown, while his impeccable timing, even while acting drunk, puts him on a par with the finest standup comedians (then or now). Late in the film, when Joe has developed a severe dependence on alcohol, Frank begins a standup routine already considerably drunk, but brilliantly gets more inebriated as the routine continues. Perhaps the most effective image of Joe's alcoholism occurs in a scene during which he passes out after his wife, Martha (Mitzi Gaynor), leaves him: As he slumps backward onto his bed, his left hand, grasping a whiskey bottle, lands on her mattress.

Joker ends where it begins, on a wet, dark Chicago street, where the 777 club now is boarded up. In a series of flashbacks, Joe first hears a ghostly version of "All the Way" emanating from the club and then imagines seeing people from his past appear in store windows, recalling past events. Finally he sees an image of himself that attempts to advise him on how to kick his alcohol problem. Having been all alone, he now walks off into a street crowded with people, his future uncertain, providing an ambiguous and realistic conclusion for a film based on true-life incidents.

Though Angelo Maggio and Frankie Machine are impressive characterizations, they allowed Frank only to demonstrate certain aspects of his acting talent. With Lewis on board the

Joker project, Frank really gave his all, creating a full spectrum of moods, emotions, physical actions, nonverbal techniques (including mime), beautifully played dialogue and comic timing—all blended together by an incomparable, naturalistic style, which retains its subtlety even when he depicts Joe lunging into a fight. His adoption of the Jolson-like 1920s stage performance style also is flawless, as is his phrasing of the songs, in which the first influences of African-American jazz on the classic Tin Pan Alley sound can be heard. And his interpretation of Lewis during his alcoholic years is one of the cinema's most convincing depictions of a drunk. (While most actors overplay inebriation, Frank never loses his naturalism.) Over the past four years, he had proven his versatility in a group of films, but now he accomplished the same feat in a single picture, in which he appears in nearly every scene.

Though Maggio won him an Academy Award, and Machine garnered him a nomination, this performance, among his very best, was completely overlooked. (Not surprisingly, the epic-loving Academy awarded the 1957 Oscar to Alec Guinness for his performance in *The Bridge on the River Kwai*. While it is an outstanding performance, it does not include the depth demonstrated by Frank.)

The supporting cast is superb, particularly Eddie Albert, a vastly underrated character actor whose natural talent adds to the film's realistic atmosphere, a quasi-documentary look created primarily by Fapp's black-and-white noir cinematography. In their scenes together, Frank and Eddie display a chemistry rarely present in male friendships on the screen. All three major female roles are handled expertly by Jeanne Crain, Mitzi Gaynor and Beverly Garland (as Austin's wife, Cassie).

After *Joker* was previewed in San Francisco, Frank asked Walter Scharf to work the melody of "All the Way" into more scenes. He also told him, "I think we have an Academy Award in this picture."[24] Though Frank was passed by for a nomination, the song won an Oscar for Cahn and Van Heusen.

When the film was released the following August, Variety's "Gene" noted:

> Sinatra obviously couldn't be made to look like Lewis; any thought of a reasonable facsimile, appearance-wise, is out of the question. And Lewis' style of delivery is unique and defies copying (although some of his onstage mannerisms are aped by the film's star quite well). But these are minor reservations in light of the major job Sinatra does at being an actor. He's believable and forceful—alternately sympathetic and pathetic, funny and sad...[25]

In *The New York Times*, Bosley Crowther wrote, "[P]erhaps the brightest thing about this picture is the excellent dialogue—peppery, amusing and sensitive in turn. Add, certainly, the consistently fine acting of Mr. Sinatra, on view virtually every minute, armed to the hilt with period songs."[26]

During the second week of November 1956, Frank was back with Riddle and a full big band, to record a follow-up to *Songs for Swingin' Lovers*, the equally magnificent *A Swingin' Affair*. He opened the initial session with the 1934 standard "Stars Fell on Alabama" and the Dubose Heyward-Gershwin brothers *Porgy and Bess* number "I Got Plenty o' Nuttin'," but wasn't satisfied with any of the takes. On November 15, he tried it again, this time smoothly maintaining the incredible artistic ride he began with the previous two albums and his multifaceted performance in *The Joker is Wild*, jazzing the melody of "Alabama" with incomparable phrasing, altering the lyrics in fine Sinatra style: Soaring above Riddle's ebullient brass arrangement, he emphatically sings, "And stars *fractured 'bama* last night," then changes "My heart beat like a hammer" to a syncopated "My heart beat *just like a hammer*," acting the lyric, emphasizing the thump of a smitten lover's ticker.

"I Won't Dance," a 1933 Jerome Kern-Oscar Hammerstein collaboration that was adapted by different composers for several productions, including the Astaire-Rogers classic *Roberta* (1935), is one of Frank's swing masterpieces, in which he elongates certain words to create yet another variation on the original song. (It also includes his first recorded use of the legendary term "Ring-a-Ding-Ding.")

On November 20, Frank cut four supreme tracks, each featuring the playful, elongated jazz phrasing he now was favoring. Riddle's band, employing powerful brass and rhythm-section kicks, supported Frank's soaring interpretation of Cole Porter's lyrics on "At Long Last Love" like it never had done, but would continue to do so during the remainder of the *Swingin' Affair* sessions. "I Guess I'll Have to Change My Plans" was followed by Rodgers and Hart's "I Wish I Were In Love Again" and the Gershwins' "Nice Work If You Can Get It."

On November 26, Frank recorded Rodgers and Hart's "The Lady is a Tramp," but it was cut from the album. Three other numbers, however, made the grade. The first, Riddle's arrangement of Cole Porter's "Night and Day," rivals the same composer's "I've Got You Under My Skin" as the ultimate up-tempo Sinatra recording. Arranged in the same key, rhythm and tempo, the body of the song matters little, when Frank makes the entire production his own, pouring out every ounce of emotion he has, yet maintaining the incomparable restraint that made him the greatest interpreter of American song. As he bounces Porter's lyrics off Riddle's brass riffs, he drives every musician in the band yet stays with them in a spiritual bond, never soaring outside the framework that ultimately ends with a "big" brass and rhythm section cut-off. He sings with ultimate confidence, with no hint of vulnerability. Following the big instrumental break (the equivalent of Milt Bernhart's trombone solo in "Skin"), his phrasing of "In the ro*aaarrrr*ing traffic's boom" is one of the most effective emotional moments in all his recordings.

Next, Frank cut "Lonesome Road," a quasi-spiritual written in 1929 by Gene Austin and Nathaniel Shilkret (a studio composer-conductor who waxed many tunes for Laurel and Hardy), and "If I Had You," composed the same year and previously recorded with Axel Stordahl at Columbia in 1947. On November 28, the *Swingin' Affair* sessions were wrapped with usable takes of every song Frank had chosen. Duke Ellington and Paul Webster's "I Got It Bad (and That Ain't Good)" was followed by an outstanding version of Cole Porter's "From This Moment On," in which Frank hits the same magical orchestra-driving stride he reaches in "I've Got You Under My Skin" and "Night and Day"; a laid-back yet ebullient version of his former Dorsey colleagues Joe Bushkin and John De Vries' "Oh. Look at Me Now"; and perhaps the best ever version of the Gershwins' "You'd Be So Nice to Come Home To," making the listener feel the burning embers when he sings, "You'd be so nice by the fire."

During the waning days of 1956, Frank's star kept rising. In November, he was voted Musicians' Musician of the Year by a *Metronome* poll of the nation's jazzmen; and the following month, he made the list of "Top Ten Money-Making Stars" published in *The Motion Picture Herald*. On December 3, he recorded two singles with Riddle at Capitol Studios, the winsome light-swing ballad "Your Love for Me" and another pseudo-rock cut, "Can I Steal a Little Love?" (although the rhythm section sort of swings, the saxophone arrangement is undeniably 1950s rock), in which the only interesting element is his characteristic alteration of the lyrics, here adding a bit of machismo with "Can I *grab* a little love?"

On January 14, 1957, Humphrey Bogart mercifully passed away. Though he knew that death was imminent, Frank, scheduled to perform at the Copa in New York, announced that he "wouldn't be coherent."[27] Friends such as Marlene Dietrich and Joe DiMaggio, having bought tickets for the sold-out show, instead saw Sammy Davis, Jr., and Jerry Lewis, who filled in for him. Though he wanted to attend the funeral, at which John Huston gave the eulogy, Lauren Bacall told him to honor his contract at the Copa. Described by Bogart's son, Stephen, as "an anesthetic to the pain of losing Bogie," Frank turned up the heat on his relationship with Betty.[28] She later wrote:

> The last few months of Bogie's illness, a part of me needed a man to talk to, and Frank turned out to be that man. ...By the time Bogie died, my dependence on him became greater and greater. We continued for several months as good friends.[29]

Frank was back in the recording studio on March 14, 1957, to cut two singles with lyrics by Sammy Cahn, the swinger "So Long, My Love" and the swing ballad "Crazy Love." Arranged by Riddle, both punctuate Frank's easygoing vocals with bright brass and percussion kicks. His upbeat performances of these songs are indicative of the confident '57 version of Frank Sinatra. Jazz historian Pete Welding has agreed that the man was "at the absolute pinnacle of his artistry," and he now consistently demonstrated this fact both as a singer and actor:

> As an interpreter of song lyrics Sinatra, by this time, had no equal. He had the uncanny ability to "read" a lyric as though through the eyes of its writer and arrive at a perfect understanding of its intent. And as a performer he knew exactly how to bring this to bristling life—how to draw out and animate its dramatic potentials in such a way that the listener was engaged, fully and in some cases for the first time, by what Sinatra had found in the song and revealed in his interpretation. "He was phrasing the lyric, not just the music, which is the right way," said acclaimed songwriter Jule Styne. "He was finding the right tempo, the right kick for the music... Before Sinatra's great rise in the late '50s, songs were just sung—straight and without much panache. Crosby had a little sense of style, but Sinatra was the one who went the whole way."[30]

Teaming with veteran arranger Gordon Jenkins, Frank stunningly demonstrated his artistic peak—the ultimate in dramatic yet subtle singing running the entire gamut of human emotion—the following month, when they began recording numbers for the album *Where Are You?* Having served as musical director for many of the finest jazz and popular vocalists, including Ella Fitzgerald, Louis Armstrong, Billie Holiday, Bing Crosby and the Andrews Sisters, Jenkins used his expertise in arranging luscious string-dominated soundscapes that envelop but never overwhelm Frank's perfect singing. Unfettered by the commercial concerns that previously forced him to compromise his art, Jenkins wrote 12 orchestrations that, together with Frank's incomparable phrasing and interpretation of the lyrics, create an almost mesmerizing mood maintained from the first song through the last. And to add another dimension to the album, Capitol and producer Dave Cavanaugh chose it as Frank's first stereo recording, one that would astound listeners with its naturalistic reproduction of a live performance. (In fact, early two- and three-track stereo recordings are among the finest ever made, due to the intentions of producers who wanted to capture a real performance with natural acoustics, rather than the approach of later technicians who, working with multi-track machines, began to process natural sounds and over-produce projects, literally burying or destroying the original performance [if such a thing had been recorded].)

As usual, Frank handpicked the songs, and with his mature, warm voice sounding like a masterfully played cello, he contributed a record number of long-breath phrases, projecting meaning and emotion, to a single album. On April 10, Jenkins opened the first *Where Are You?* session with his beautiful orchestration of Alec Wilder and Edward Finckel's "Where Is the One?" which Frank first had recorded with Axel Stordahl nearly 10 years earlier. Delivering the song's most optimistic line on two separate occasions, he achieves the same long-breath triumph each time: "Some lucky day, I'm bound to find he*rrrrrr-aannnn*d when I do, I'll find love."

He did it again on the next arrangement, "There's No You," a lightly swinging torch song, in which the brokenhearted narrator believes that in "our favorite nook in the wa*llllll-inn*n spring, we'll meet again." And on one of *the* classic torch songs, "The Night We Called It a Day," Frank blended powerful long-breath phrasing with a bit of melodic improvisation. He had waxed the song twice previously, first with Dorsey in 1942 and five years later at Columbia (though this recording remained unissued and undocumented for 46 years). The session concluded with his first and only recording of Joseph Kosma, Johnny Mercer and Jacques Prevert's ethereal "Autumn Leaves," which he ends with an exquisite decrescendo that blends into the strings, the vocal and instrumental parts becoming one—a technique he uses throughout the album and a testament to the expert collaboration of singer and arranger.

Another set of four songs was recorded on April 29. The first number, "I Cover the Waterfront," eventually was omitted from the stereo release (due to the larger space required for the format), but was included on the monaural LP. "Lonely Town," the Bernstein, Comden and Green song from *On the Town* that was dropped from the 1949 film, features dynamic alternations between lonesome whisperings and emotive, longing-for-love crescendos. The introduction, which includes a brief nod to the film's "New York, New York," was suggested by Frank. Jenkins later said, "For many years, [Frank's] and my favorite were the same. He thought that 'Lonely Town' was the best record he ever made, and I did, too. Now I think it would be a toss-up for me between 'Lonely Town,' 'Laura' and 'Send in the Clowns'."[31]

As interpreted by Frank, David Raksin's haunting theme from Otto Preminger's *Laura* (1944) (with lyrics by Johnny Mercer) becomes utterly entrancing, and includes one of his most astounding feats of long-breath singing: "The laugh that floats on a summer night that you can never quite reca*llllllllll-ann*d you see Laura on that train that is passing through." Here, he accomplishes a remarkable musical feat while making it sound natural, never allowing the technique to surface. And he again beautifully sustains the final note, actually sounding like part of the strings while completing the phrase "only an incredible dr*eeeaaamm*m." The April sessions closed with a chamber orchestra-style arrangement of the 1919 blues standard "Baby Won't You Please Come Home."

The final four songs were recorded on May 1. The title track, Jimmy McHugh and Harold Adamson's "Where Are You?" again demonstrates brilliant phrasing and dynamic crescendos and decrescendos surrounded by lovely strings and spare woodwinds; "I Think of You," the Rachmaninov-inspired ballad he had recorded with Dorsey 16 years earlier, features a number of resplendently sustained quiet notes that float just slightly above the strings; "I'm a Fool to Want You," though less unabashedly emotive than his Ava-affected recording of 1952, is equally splendid, offering a more mature performance of a heart-wrenching torch song; and "Maybe I'll Be There," capping off the sessions, includes more longing-for-love, almost whispered vocals.

In February, a theater chain executive had speculated about Frank's recent triumphs as an actor:

Sinatra and Rita Hayworth in *Pal Joey*

He shocked the public in *Eternity* because he had never reached them before. He was always a personality. Personalities come and go at regular intervals in the movie business, but the actors stay on. Cooper, Taylor, Gable and several others were personalities before they proved themselves as actors. Sinatra, the actor, is exciting and unpredictable. People have confidence in him.[32]

Ironically, his next film, *Pal Joey*, features the truly defining role of his cinematic career, a character who is essentially Frank Sinatra. Now that he was an accomplished actor, he was able to bring that multifaceted personality vibrantly to the screen. Though he had played some remarkable roles since 1953, Joey preserved for all time the public persona, shades of the private man, the vulnerability, the indelible charm and the incomparable musicianship. No other film in his canon offers the viewer such an opportunity: While those who saw him perform live got a feel for Sinatra the performer, *Pal Joey* offers a look at him on stage and off. And, in all respects, it is a very fine motion picture.

During the late 1930s, writer John O'Hara had published a series of fictional letters, telling the tale of a small-town chorus boy, in *New Yorker* magazine. Signed, "Your Pal, Joey," they caught the eye of Broadway producer George Abbott, who asked that O'Hara adapt the short sketches into a libretto that could be paired with the songs of Rodgers and Hart. The resulting musical drama, set in a Chicago nightclub and starring Gene Kelly as Joey Evans, now depicted as a womanizing dancer, opened at the Ethel Barrymore Theatre on December 24, 1940, and ran for 198 performances.

Harry Cohn soon snapped up the film rights to the play, but was faced with watering down the sexy story to appease the Production Code. James Cagney and Cary Grant were considered for the title role, while Bebe Daniels, Gloria Swanson, Gladys Swarthout, Grace Moore, Ethel

Pal Joey

Merman and Irene Dunne were thought appropriate for Vera Simpson, the stripper-cum-socialite. But when the screenplay was rejected by the PCA, Columbia shelved it (perhaps fortuitously, considering some of the casting possibilities).

In 1944, Cohn achieved a great success with the Technicolor musical *Cover Girl*, which paired Gene Kelly with Rita Hayworth. As a proposed follow-up, he dusted off *Pal Joey*, but when MGM raised its loan-out price on Kelly, Cohn again tossed it aside. Eight years later, after the play was revived on Broadway, Columbia tried a third time, again mentioning Kelly and Hayworth (to portray Linda English), but a passable script still could not be written.

Finally, during the autumn of 1956, George Sidney (who had directed Frank in *Anchors Aweigh* and Ava in *Show Boat*) took over, hiring musical veteran Dorothy Kingsley to tone down the sexual references by masking them with the sort of double entendres that sailed right over the heads of PCA censors. Incredibly, Columbia now announced that the film would star Marlon Brando and Mae West!

Hearing of the now-approved screenplay, Frank jumped at the chance of playing Joey, remarking, "This is the only role I've dreamed of doing for many years outside of Maggio."[33]

The Actor, on Screen and in Song

RITA HAYWORTH
FRANK SINATRA
KIM NOVAK

LA BLONDE ou LA ROUSSE
"PAL JOEY"
DE BLONDE OF DE ROODHARIGE

Through his production company, Essex Productions, he cut a deal with Columbia grabbing the title role, a $150,000 salary, 25 percent of the net receipts and 100 percent of the soundtrack album profits. He also scored Rita Hayworth, who agreed to play Vera Simpson in exchange for Cohn's cancellation of her studio contract, and Columbia's rising star, the sumptuous Kim Novak. Frank insisted that Hayworth receive top billing, admitting, "She *is* Columbia Pictures."[34]

Since *The Joker Is Wild* is set in Chicago, Frank asked that the locale be changed to San Francisco and that Joey's profession be, not dancer but, of course, singer. While Hart's sexually suggestive lyrics were abandoned, Rodgers' melodies were incorporated into the score and a host of the team's standards were substituted, adding another irresistible element to the role tailor-made for Frank, *the* standard singer.

Location shooting began in San Francisco on April 15, 1957. One week later, the company returned to Columbia, where the $2.7 million production was wrapped on June 21. Though she had worked with Frank on *The Man with the Golden Arm* two years earlier, Novak was very uncomfortable throughout the production. After lengthy rehearsals, which Frank didn't mind because of his love for the part, she became depressed and, at one point, passed out in her dressing room, forcing Sidney to shoot around her until she was well enough to return.

Frank performed all his songs flawlessly, cutting "The Lady is a Tramp" and "I Didn't Know What Time It Was" on May 23, "I Could Write a Book" and "There's a Small Hotel" on June 14, and his brief rendition of "Bewitched" on July 25. "What Do I Care for a Dame?" which he sings in the film's surrealistic dance scene, was waxed during the soundtrack album sessions on September 27. Hayworth's singing was dubbed by Jo Ann Greer, and Novak's (including a beautifully lip-synched "My Funny Valentine") by Trudi Erwin.

Pal Joey features perhaps the best opening scene in all of Frank's films, beginning *in medias res* as a siren is heard wailing behind the Columbia logo. The pre-titles sequence then depicts a police car arriving at a railroad station, where two detectives pull Joey Evans from the back seat and drag him toward the train. Accused of consorting with a girl who is "underage" and "the mayor's daughter," Joey replies, "How did I know she was jailbait? She looked like she was 35." The cops disregard his excuses and toss him into the train just as it leaves the station. As he hits the floor of the car, the title seems to emanate from his body before filling the screen in vibrant yellow Technicolor.

The action continues throughout the credits, showing Joey (attired in the classic Sinatra jacket, tie and hat) arriving in San Francisco to seek a job at one of its "dump" nightclubs. Dorothy Kingsley's talent for maintaining some of the Broadway show's sexual references is already well in evidence as an elderly woman sitting at the station ticket window asks Joey, "Aid? Can I give you aid, young man?"

"What did you have in mind?" he replies.

Walking from one club to another, Joey either finds them closed by police or run by owners who have no need for a singer. "Legs — not tonsils," he is told. After getting soaked in the rain, he reaches the Barbary Coast Club, where he finds his old pal, pianist and trumpeter Ned Galvin (Bobby Sherwood), leading the house band, the Galvinizers.

Galvin, believing none of Joey's tall tales of great success, refuses to hire him. But when Joey winces at the terrible off-key warbling of the dancing girls, excepting "the mouse with the built" (Novak's Linda English), and learns that the evening's emcee has not shown up, he grabs a microphone, jumps onto the stage, launches into some shtick that no one laughs at, and sings

"I Didn't Know What Time It Was." (Frank does an excellent take as Joey notices a huge mirror ball above his head.) Knowing about some of Joey's earlier escapades, club owner Mike Miggins (Hank Henry) hires him, but argues over salary and billing, calls him a bum, and warns, "One false move and you're out on your Francis." This in-joke equating Frank with an ass is indicative of the ad-libbing that occurs throughout the film.

Frank's method of reading a script "about 50 times" and then delivering his own naturalistic paraphrasing of the dialogue is given full reign. There are many moments of Sinatra-speak, as in a scene depicting Joey being kissed by all the dancing girls except the whiny Gladys (Barbara Nichols) and Linda; walking toward the stage, he happily says, "I've got plans for this girl. Ring-a-ding plans!"

Following a ritzy gig at a Nob Hill society party, where Joey recognizes and embarrasses Mrs. Prentice Simpson (Rita Hayworth), formerly a stripper known as "Vera with the Vanishing Veils," he becomes enamored with her, as well. Later, while attempting to impress Vera and two male companions who have arrived at the club, he is rudely snubbed. Tired of Joey's exaggerations and outright lies, Mike fires him, but then gives in to the singer's wager that she will return by Saturday. Always the operator, Joey visits Vera's home, where the butler informs her, "He seemed to speak a vernacular I simply couldn't understand." Interrupting her solitary lunch, Joey orders, "Get rid of the pallbearer" and mentions, "Yeah, I got the old bounceroo." Of course, he is careful to tell her that Saturday is his final night at the club. On that evening, just as Mike is ready to fire him, she arrives, alone, inquiring, "I was told you have a singer."

Calling for Joey, Mike tells him to "surprise the lady." And he does more than surprise Vera: She is positively startled, perhaps offended for a second, when he serenades her with "The Lady is a Tramp." Finishing the song, Joey escorts her out the door as the band follows, playing an instrumental reprise. At Vera's yacht, they discuss opening their own nightclub, but Joey insists that the arrangement be a true business partnership. Making another statement reflecting Frank's own personality, he says, "No one owns Joey but Joey."

The next morning, Vera, awakened by her French maid, is radiant with the afterglow of lovemaking. Singing "Bewitched," she moves about her room and then undresses for a shower. Here, as she ends her song, George Sidney pressed his luck with the PCA by showing Hayworth's breasts behind the shower's frosted glass. (Again, not all of the Broadway show's eroticism was sanitized for the film.)

During preparations and rehearsals for the opening of "Chez Joey," Vera orders Joey to fire Linda, whom she considers a threat to her control over him. Inducing Linda to quit by assigning her a striptease number, he leaves the club while she drinks bourbon. Now living with Vera, Joey is not welcome to attend a dinner party. "Well, I wouldn't eat with those creeps, anyway," he replies, heading for the yacht. Later, while lounging on his bed, sporting monogrammed slippers, an expensive robe and a cigarette holder, he is interrupted by the drunken Linda, who talks about her body ("I'm stacked") before kissing him passionately. The amour is ended, however, when she passes out in his arms. (The skinny Frank attempting to drag the buxom, limp Novak over to the bed is one of the film's funniest moments.)

As Joey is making breakfast the following morning, Linda emerges, decimated by her first killer hangover. At this point, Joey realizes that all his bravado has accomplished nothing and, more importantly, that he is in love with her. He stops himself from telling her, however: Feeling ashamed of his previous behavior, he declares that "a bum is a bum." Later, at the club, to which Linda has returned, he stops the striptease, echoing his earlier statement: "A nice girl is a nice girl anywhere. And a bum is a bum." He then leaves for the yacht, where he begins to pack his clothes. Vera arrives and proposes marriage, but learns that he is in love with "the mouse."

Joey returns to the club one last time, finding it desolate. Thumping out a few notes on the piano, he experiences a daydream in which, tormented by both Vera and Linda, he sings "What Do I Care for a Dame?" As he leaves Chez Joey, he is met by an expensive convertible driven by Vera, who has brought the mouse to him. Though he describes the difficult life she will experience as a singer's wife, Linda counters everything he says, and they (accompanied by "Snuffy," the Cairn Terrier she had tricked him into buying) walk off toward the Golden Gate Bridge.

Frank's screen charisma saturates *Pal Joey*, reaching its peak during the musical numbers, which now are historical records of an entertainment phenomenon during the height of his artistic career. The combination of his performances and the work of director Sidney, cinematographer Harold Lipstein, and editors Viola Lawrence and Jerome Thoms created two of the finest scenes in all musical films: those in which he sings "I Could Write a Book" and the unparalleled "The Lady is a Tramp." Beautifully shot and edited, the former features a simple, straightforward style that enhances Frank's performance, at one point showing him in profile from a low angle so that a luminous stage light can be seen (in the upper left of the frame). Then, when Kim Novak joins him, the style changes, with the camera moving to the front of the stage to capture both of them, and a bright spotlight making them stand out against the curtain in the background. As in the best musical scenes, the cinematic technique never draws attention to itself.

Incorporating the same approach, "The Lady is a Tramp" is a perfect musical scene and the finest filmed performance of Frank Sinatra. Though the studio arrangement he had cut during the *A Swingin' Affair* sessions (and subsequently would be included on the *Pal Joey* soundtrack album) is one of his best recordings, this version (also done by Riddle) is so immediate and intimate that the viewer is transported to that darkened room with Vera and Mike as the former is mesmerized and the latter is mortified. The structure of both versions is identical (two verses, chorus; same two verses, chorus), but here Frank mimes the lightly swinging piano introduction as he sings the first verse and plays more with the phrasing than with the lyrics, adding an extra dynamic to the song. On the studio version, he took the Hart verse,

> She don't like crap games with barons and earls
> Won't go to Harlem dressed in ermine and pearls
> Won't dish the dirt with the rest of the girls
> That's why the lady is a tramp

and transformed it into the more personal

> She doesn't like crap games with sharpies and frauds
> Won't go to Harlem in Lincolns or Fords
> Won't dish the dirt with the rest of the broads
> That's why the lady is a tramp

This alteration obviously was done so he could use the word "broads" instead of "girls." In the film, concluding her first number, "Zip," which includes Hart's most intellectually dense lyrics, Rita Hayworth (although dubbed by Jo Ann Greer) sings, "I'm a broad with a broad, broad mind!" Curiously, Frank uses the word "girls" in the filmed "Tramp."

The scene is a masterpiece of what film theorist Andre Bazin called "pure cinema." The event seems utterly real and there are no techniques that disturb the atmosphere created by the fusion of Frank's peerless performance and Sidney's direction. Lipstein's moody nightclub lighting and the work of the editing duo also are superb. Though there are 20 cuts, only 10 separate shots appear.

After Joey is told to "sing the lady a song," Frank and Hayworth look at each other with the perfect combination of wanting and suspicion. Then, as Joey tells Ned to back him up with "number 26," Hank Henry can be seen (at far frame right) shaking his fist at Frank. The tension at this point is palpable.

Initially, the camera, in a medium long shot, tracks to the left, a little behind Frank as he and the band begin the song. Then a close-up of Frank in profile, singing "That's why the lady is a tramp," cuts to a 2-shot of Hayworth registering her brief surprise and Hank Henry in the throes of utter disbelief. The same close-up of Frank is then alternated with frontal close-ups of Hayworth and Henry.

Rising from the piano bench, Frank, in the coolest manner, finishes his cigarette, stomps it out and kicks it off the stage with his left foot. With his right foot, he then gently kicks the piano to the back of the stage as he faces Hayworth. This medium long shot, depicting a stage light (at upper left) creating a "halo" effect on Frank, and the band (at lower right) is one of the indelible Sinatra images. A medium close-up then shows only the light and Frank, as he continues his dynamically and rhythmically evolving, impeccable rendition of the song. Then the earlier close-up of Hayworth, now showing her very pleasant reaction, thrice alternates with this shot.

As Frank leans toward her table, the scene cuts to the earlier 2-shot of Hayworth and Henry as the singer circles around her. A medium shot of Frank and Hayworth shows him miming the end of a line—instead of "She's broke, and it's oke," he sings "She's broke" and then substitutes a silent "Who cares?" gesture with his arms and shoulders—before hitting his emotional peak, singing, "Haaaaaates California. It's cold and it's damp." A close-up shows him assuredly concluding, "That's why the lady. That's why the lady. *That's* why the lady is a tramp."

Sinatra admirer Stan Britt agrees about this scene. In his book, *Sinatra: A Celebration*, he notes that it "remains, forever, his single most exhilarating musical performance of all his 25 motion-picture appearances containing any kind of musical content."[35]

Other Sinatra-isms include his penchant for emphasizing certain words and then misspelling them outloud (as he had done in *Young at Heart*), constantly wearing his hat, even inside Chez Joey during rehearsals, and working some Stan Laurel comedy into Novak's blackout scene. Utterly frustrated, Joey walks onto the deck, leans over the rail slightly and twiddles his thumbs, interlocking his fingers to wiggle one on each hand, exactly as Stanley does in *The Devil's Brother* (1933). Even when Joey is cocky and putting on airs, Frank maintains his subtle, convincing style. Joey is both egocentric and irresistibly charming, qualities that Frank achieved in part by sticking to his paraphrasing method. George Sidney recalled:

> If he only wanted one or two takes, what's wrong with that? Horowitz played an hour and a half in concerts without going back and correcting a note or a passage he thought he could do better. He was a natural personality. No matter what he played, he was always Frank Sinatra, just as Clark Gable and Spencer Tracy were always themselves. His secret was complete concentration on what he was doing. There were no heights he couldn't reach, not much he couldn't do if he put his mind to it.[36]

Hayworth, too, gives an excellent performance, tempering haughtiness with admirable restraint and innate sensuality. Though Novak was nervous while shooting her scenes, this reality contributed the right quality to the meek mouse Linda, who is trying to establish a career, yet is suspicious of others' intentions. Her performance of "My Funny Valentine" during the rehearsals at Chez Joey is another effective musical sequence, beautifully photographed by Lipstein, whose extreme close-up of her face is one of the film's most unforgettable images. (The dubbed voices of Greer and Erwin are flawlessly synched.)

Pal Joey was previewed at Loew's 72nd Street Theatre in New York on September 5, 1957, and went into general release the following month. Noting that the film watered down little of the original show's "spice," *Variety*'s "Gene" wrote:

> [T]here are no efforts to obscure the basics; Joey is still the constant lover. Dialog [sic] is highly seasoned and bits and story situations are uncamouflaged boudoir played for laughs. In other words, Joey is still another reflection of Hollywood's return to "adult" material...
>
> Sinatra is potent. He's almost ideal as the irreverent, free-wheeling, glib Joey, delivering the rapid-fire cracks in a fashion that wrings out the full deeper-than-pale blue comedy potentials. ...Kim Novak... rates high as ever in the looks department but her turn is pallid in contrast with the forceful job done by Sinatra.
>
> Miss Hayworth, no longer the ingenue, moves with authority as Joey's sponsor and does the "Zip" song visuals with such fiery, amusing style as to rate an encore.
>
> Standout of the score is "Lady is a Tramp." It's a wham arrangement and Sinatra gives it powerhouse delivery. His "Write a Book" is another of the big plusses...[37]

New York Times critic A. H. Weiler agreed:

> There is no doubt that this is largely Mr. Sinatra's show. As the amiable grifter with an iron ego, he projects a distinctly bouncy likable personality into an unusual role. And his rendition of the top tunes, notably "The Lady is a Tramp" and "Small Hotel," gives added luster to these indestructible standards. He gets a professional assist from Rita Hayworth, who undoubtedly will be the envy of all women. ...
>
> The blonde Miss Novak is decorative, too, as any red-blooded American boy will attest, but her subdued histrionics and singing are not nearly as convincing as her robust competition.[38]

Obviously, at least one critic was fooled by the expert sound dubbing.

On May 3, Frank helped sell U.S. Treasury Department series E defense bonds on radio's *Guest Star*, singing "Why Try to Change Me Now?" and a superb version of "The Birth of the Blues." On the 20th, he joined Nelson Riddle to cut four more singles at Capitol Studio A. Cy Coleman and Carolyn Leigh's "Witchcraft," given a laid-back, "cool" reading, eventually became exclusively associated with Frank, who, punctuated by Riddle's dynamic brass, snaps his fingers during the final chorus, keeping straight time while simultaneously singing behind the beat. Joe Bushkin and John DeVries' lovely ballad "Something Wonderful Happens in Summer" followed, with Frank again lingering on supremely sustained quiet notes, and genuine emotion on the elongated phrase "when the moon makes you fe*eellllll* all aglow." "Tell Her You Love Her," a moderately swinging romantic ballad, features the trademark brass backing of Riddle and a nice, jazzy saxophone solo during the instrumental break. Then, for the last number, "You're Cheatin' Yourself (If You're Cheatin' on Me)," Riddle created a Billy May-style hard-swinging arrangement that begins with beckoning brass blasts before highlighting smooth saxes and punch-in-the-gut kicks.

From June 7 through 9, 1957, Frank, who rarely performed in a concert setting, played three dates in the Pacific Northwest, hitting Vancouver, Portland and Seattle. Accompanied by Bill Miller and an excellent orchestra conducted by Riddle, he served up an incomparable program of songs. Legendary recording engineer Wally Heider, who often captured big bands on the road, taped the Seattle gig on the 9th. Opening with *A Swingin' Affair*'s "You Make Me Feel So Young," Frank, his voice a bit raspy, kept swinging with "It Happened in Monterey," playfully toying with the lyrics, and a Cole Porter trilogy: "At Long Last Love," "I Get a Kick Out of You" and "Just One of Those Things." Injecting some shtick into "Kick," he joked about buying a case of booze and, after singing the "perfume in Spain" lyric, alluding to his recent experience with Ava, sarcastically added, "Spain—Holy geez!" During "Things," Frank admitted that "it was just, just—it turned out to be one of those mothery nights" before he *really* transformed Porter's "Goodbye, baby, and amen" line—into "So, goodbye, goodbye, so long, ta ta, goodbye, and you might even add an amen." The Gershwins' "A Foggy Day" included some Italian-American slang, while "The Lady is a Tramp" became a blend of his *Pal Joey* and studio versions, with a little extra improvisation: California was now "*God-damned* cold and damp." Another Gershwin number, a brief rendition of "They Can't Take That Away from Me"—also with Frank-ish humor—preceded the bouncy "I Won't Dance" (in which his partner is a "gasser" and—"ring-a-ding-ding"—a "grabber") and a five-minute monologue during which he borrowed from *The Joker is Wild*, calling Joe E. Lewis a "Greek philosopher," mentioned the Canadian whiskey Crown Royal and (perhaps taking another comic page from Stan Laurel) said of Bill ("Suntan Charley") Miller: "He gets so drunk, sometimes I can hardly see him. It's terrible."

Frank followed the swingers and comedy with a selection of love ballads and saloon songs: "When Your Lover Has Gone," "Violets for Your Furs," "My Funny Valentine," "Glad to Be Unhappy" and, accompanied only by Miller's "late-night" piano, "One for My Baby." After "Valentine," commenting on his somewhat strained vocal chords, he unleashed his famous line, "I think I swallowed a shot glass." Thanking the group "of highest caliber musicians in the United States today," Frank, claiming the short tour has been "a mothery ball from the beginning to the end," then grooved into "a little song that came from a motion picture that I loved making at MGM that turned out to be pretty great—it was a kind of fun picture, and the song is unusual": "The Tender Trap." Following a four-bar introduction to the silly "Hey, Jealous Lover," Frank interjected, "I absolutely and unequivocally detest this song!" deliberately butchered it, and then redeemed himself with "I've Got You Under My Skin," proving his respect for the song by performing a faithful reprise of his *Songs for Swingin' Lovers* masterpiece. Waxing nostalgic about Tommy Dorsey and pianist Joe Bushkin, he closed the show with "Oh, Look at Me Now."

Five days later, Frank's lawyers filed a divorce petition in Mexico City, finally ending any hopes of a reconciliation with Ava. (A decree for her divorce was granted on July 5.) On June 16, he performed an additional concert at San Francisco's Cow Palace.

After dropping in and out of Lauren Bacall's life, as he often did with others, Frank asked her to marry him. "I must have hesitated for at least 30 seconds," she admitted. "I was ecstatic—we both were."[39] One evening, before leaving for a singing date in Miami, he told the news to Swifty Lazar, but by no means were either he or Betty to inform anyone else of the impending nuptials. Confronted by Louella Parsons a few days later, Betty told the pushy reporter to ask Frank any questions about marriage, but unfortunately Lazar opened his mouth. Mobbed by the press he so disliked, Frank couldn't stand it and, after another period of silence, phoned his fiancee to break off their engagement. Tina Sinatra speculates, "I think he woke up one morning and looked at his future—two new stepchildren and a formidable, take-charge, no-bullshit wife—and he thought to himself, 'What the hell am I doing?'"[40]

Though devastated at the time, Bacall later wrote, "Actually, Frank did me a great favor—he saved me from the disaster our marriage would have been. He was probably smarter than I: He knew it wouldn't work."[41]

Retaining Gordon Jenkins for his next album project, Frank chose to celebrate Christmas in blistering July by recording 12 respectful arrangements of classic carols, popular contemporary songs and one original number that he cowrote with Hank Sanicola and Dak Stanford. This time, Jenkins chose to include lush choral parts, making his orchestrations less string-dominated. The initial session on July 10 yielded four beautifully performed traditional carols teaming Frank with

Sinatra began to build performances based on his own personality. (Photofest)

the Ralph Brewster Singers, with whom Jenkins often worked. The 1850 American carol "It Came Upon a Midnight Clear," which he originally had recorded in 1947, was followed by "O Little Town of Bethlehem" (waxed twice in 1945, for a V-Disc and a Columbia single), "Hark! The Herald Angels Sing," the 1855 hybrid of music by Felix Mendelssohn and lyrics by John Wesley, and the 1740s English-French Carol "Adeste Fideles." All feature sensitive dynamic changes, soaring Jenkins strings and Brewster harmonies, as well as dramatic entrances and subtle exits by Frank.

The second session, on July 16, brought a blend of Yuletide songs, and Frank continued to prove that he truly could get into the spirit even during the worst heat of summer. The perennial winter classic "Jingle Bells," arranged in a 1940s style by Jenkins, features the Brewsters in Pied Piper mode; originally waxed by Frank in 1946, it was followed by the sublime power of "The First Noel," orchestrated in a quasi-classical style expertly merging the singers, Frank and low strings on the familiar, monumental chorus. Throughout this traditional carol, Frank gives each note just the right touch, never overdoing a single emotion, as so many singers have, before and since. He then returned to more contemporary material, but made it sound just as timeless: Gently driven by a pulsing bass and light drums, "Have Yourself a Merry Little Christmas," which he first cut in 1947, contains some of the album's most emotive and dramatic singing, all wonderfully restrained; while his second recording of Jule Styne and Sammy Cahn's lovely "The Christmas Waltz" (the first was a 1954 Capitol single) is *the* incomparable version.

Frank concluded the Yuletide project the following day, opening with what he, Sanicola and Stanford must have intended for younger listeners, "Mistletoe and Holly," the least serious and, along with "Jingle Bells," the merriest song in the set. Requiring an opening phrase to rhyme with the title, they chose "Oh, by gosh, by golly," hardly an expression used frequently by Frank or his pal Hank. First recorded definitively by Nat Cole in 1946, Mel Torme and Robert Wells' "The Christmas Song" was recorded next, with Jenkins tossing in an unnecessary violin pizzicato of the "Jingle Bells" melody, but saved by Frank's sincere and at times slightly bluesy subtlety. One of the most famous carols, "Silent Night," written in 1818 and first recorded by Frank in 1945, returned the session to elegant traditional reverence, while Jenkins backed Frank with a brilliant blend of angelic vocals, gorgeous strings and pulsing bass on "I'll Be Home for Christmas." Very pleased with the results, Frank threw a lavish Christmas party for everyone who worked on the album. When it was released, the cover featured a painting including a close-up of Frank's looking-over-the-shoulder portrait from *Pal Joey*, but now he was sporting a heavy coat, scarf and winter gloves.

On August 13, Frank not only cut "I Could Write a Book," "Bewitched, Bothered and Bewildered" (which he doesn't sing in the film) and "There's a Small Hotel" for the *Pal Joey* soundtrack, but also two of the greatest singles of his career, "Chicago" and "All the Way," which he had performed in *The Joker is Wild*. While the former opens with an ebullient 1920s jazz style and then segues into full swing, alternating graceful saxes and trumpet-percussion kicks (Frank's opener, "*Chii*cago, Chicago, that toddlin' town" is unforgettable), the latter is one of his indescribably beautiful ballad triumphs, setting his combination of romantic longing and potent assuredness against Riddle's muted trumpets, flowing strings, pulsing bass and lovely flute obbligato.

After completing the *Pal Joey* soundtrack with "I Didn't Know What Time It Was" and "What Do I Care for a Dame?" on September 25, Frank concentrated on his next concept album, one of the most important in his career. For *Come Fly with Me*, he teamed with the great Billy May, who was known for his hard-swinging arrangements highlighting glissando unison saxophones and powerful brass blasts. But the new album was not be to an all-swinger like *Songs for Swingin' Lovers* or *A Swingin' Affair*, but a first-time mixture of bold big-band swingers laced with humor and luminous romantic ballads, all devoted to the theme of international travel.

At the initial session on October 1, 1957, Frank opened with a unique number, a 1907 Oley Speaks composition incorporating Rudyard Kipling's 1892 poem "Mandalay." Titled "The Road to Mandalay," the song begins with a robust gong and Frank's first line, "By the old Moulmein pagoda, lookin' eastward to the sea, there's a Burma broad a settin' and I know she thinks of me." Originally performed as an opera house piece, it becomes an exotic spiritual in the hands of May, who shifts the orchestra into a bright swing mode as Frank soars into a driving big-band break. After a decrescendo, Frank hits a pick up note, "*Come* you back to Mandalay, where the old flotilla lay," before the song ends abruptly with another strange gong tone. Recorded just 20 years after Kipling's death, this version, in which Frank improvises with words such as "broad" and "cat," was considered sacrilegious by the author's estate and thereafter banned in Great Britain, where the track was replaced with "Chicago."

Frank also tossed some "cool" substitutions, such as "grab" and "dig," into "Let's Get Away From It All," which he originally recorded with Dorsey in 1941. A jaunty swing number with Mediterranean flourishes, "Isle of Capri" blends mandolin, snare drum rolls and May's trademark hard-swinging brass as Frank overlays the arrangement with impeccable phrasing. (This song was cut from the stereo release, but included on the monaural album.)

On October 3, Frank recorded some of his most sublime singing, on four gorgeous ballads, Vernon Duke's "Autumn in New York" and "April in Paris" (lyrics by E. Y. Harburg), "London By Night" and the peerless "Moonlight in Vermont." He uses his lower register to great effect and feels "pain" as he sings the word in "Autumn," but switches from melancholia to romantic recollections in "London." "April," opening with Frank in full throttle and then settling into ballad mode, features a superhuman long-breath phrase, "Holiday tables under the treeeeeeeeeeeees" (lasting two full measures at a crawling tempo), which is outdone only by his next line, lasting just a wee bit longer, and coupled with a decrescendo: "This is a feeling that no one can ever repreeeeeeeeeeeeeeees." "Vermont," one of his very finest ballad performances, includes a line to which he gives the long-breath treatment twice, expressing even greater emotion the second time: "People who meet in this romantic setting are so hypnotized by the loveleeeeee-eeevening summer breeze..."

The final session included three geographically specific songs: "Blue Hawaii," the ballad first made popular by Bing Crosby in the 1937 film *Waikiki Wedding*; "Around the World" from *Around the World in Eighty Days*; and the lively marimba-up-tempo swinger "Brazil," featuring May's unison saxes and potent brass punctuation. But the highlights on this day were two numbers written especially for the album by Van Heusen and Cahn.

The first song ever penned expressly for a Sinatra concept project, "Come Fly with Me" is one of his most popular and finest swingers, opening with swirling strings and beckoning muted trumpets that draw in the listener before Frank summons young ladies with "Come Fly with me. Let's fly, let's fly away!" The easygoing swing tempo picks up dynamically during the chorus, May's saxes suggest a smooth flight, and then—pow!—an injection of solid brass as powerful as jet propulsion provides an instrumental break. Invited back in by the saxes, Frank sings the second chorus with smoother, more elongated notes, as in "it's such a luuuuuuvly day," and orders "Pack up, let's fly away!" on the dramatic ending.

Filled with Cahn wittiness, "It's Nice to Go Trav'ling" is a jaunty, moderate swinger with May brass blasts and a full big-band instrumental section broken by an effective string passage. Prior to a humorous brass and percussion finale, Frank speaks the following lines (each of which is preceded by a trumpet "sneer"):

> No more customs.
> Burn the passport.
> No more packin',
> and unpackin'.
> Light the home fires.
> Get my slippers.
> Make a pizza.

Working with May, particularly on the two Van Heusen-Cahn songs, allowed Frank to express musically what he had just done cinematically in *Pal Joey*: build a performance based to a large degree on his own personality. His previous Capitol albums, all of them superb, had showcased his unique and matchless style, but on *Come Fly with Me*, he transferred the hip and humorous qualities of Joey Evans into the lyrics he sang. All of the songs demonstrate that he now was at the top of his profession as a singer and actor, but "Come Fly with Me" and "It's Nice to Go Trav'lin," specifically tailored for him, prove that he could go anywhere he wanted, whenever he wanted. The sheer number of recordings and film projects he had completed in 1957 also proved that he was an incurable workaholic. And he just kept on going.

Chapter 7
Sinatra at War

I think I get an audience involved personally in a song—because I'm involved. It's not something I do deliberately. I can't help myself. If the song is a lament at the loss of love, I get an ache in my gut. I feel the loss myself and I cry out the loneliness, the hurt and the pain... Being an eighteen-carat manic-depressive and having lived a life of violent emotional contradictions, I have an over-acute capacity for sadness as well as elation.
—Frank Sinatra[1]

During the autumn of 1957, Frank joined Tony Curtis and Natalie Wood to begin working on *Kings Go Forth*, an unusual World War II film incorporating a subplot about miscegenation. Teaming with producer Frank Ross, Frank made a distribution deal with United Artists and hired Merle Miller to adapt a screenplay from Joe David Brown's novel. Once again he chose cinematographer Daniel L. Fapp, to create a documentary-like style in black and white (this time in the standard 1.33:1 ratio), and Elmer Bernstein to compose a powerful score.

In late November and early December, Frank, again teaming with Nelson Riddle, recorded seven tracks for inclusion on another compilation album, *This is Sinatra, Volume Two*. Three of four songs cut on November 25 were rearrangements of Jule Styne-Sammy Cahn numbers from *It Happened in Brooklyn*: "I Believe," which he had performed with Jimmy Durante, is given a more robust treatment as his solo vocal drives the hard-swinging orchestration; "It's the Same Old Dream" is a perfect ballad with Frank in peak form; and the lovely "Time After Time" (which also was released as a single) again is given long-breath phrasing and a dramatic climax ending on a quiet note. The remaining song, "Everybody Loves Somebody," which he also had recorded in 1947, opens as a light swing ballad, then builds with a sexy tenor sax solo and a punchy brass instrumental before Frank sails back in with a powerful, beautifully flowing reprise of the initial verse; the tenor then reenters for a jazzy coda.

Held on the eve of Frank's 42nd birthday, the December 11 session produced excellent versions of "You'll Always Be the One I Love" and "If You Are But a Dream," both 1940s crooner-style ballads that recall his earlier collaborations with Axel Stordahl. (In fact, he originally recorded "Dream" as a V-Disc in 1943 and as a Columbia single the following year.) Frank previously had used the final number, "Put Your Dreams Away," to close his '40s radio programs, and had recorded it for a V-Disc in 1944 and as a Columbia single in '45. This 1957 version, wonderfully arranged to highlight strings and woodwinds, is a fine example of his ability to combine superb enunciation with calming dulcet tones. "You'll Always Be the One I Love" also was released as a single, while the 16-track album incorporated nine previous singles, recorded in 1954-57. Though the seven new numbers were recorded in stereo, *This Is Sinatra, Volume Two* was released only in monaural, as the two formats were never mixed.

The great Peggy Lee also released a Riddle-arranged Capitol album, *The Man I Love*, in 1957, a collection of 12 sensual songs conducted by Frank himself. "I wouldn't call it a routine matter for the mature Lee to top Sinatra, but she does it often enough... for it not to be an event each time it happens," noted Will Friedwald.[2] Also influenced by one of Frank's favorites, Mildred Bailey, Lee, called "the Queen" by Duke Ellington, recorded these particular sessions during a hiatus from the Decca label. Though a beautiful album, *The Man I Love*—according to Friedwald—suffers from the overriding influence of conductor and arranger:

> [Y]ou get the idea that another's sense of order is being imposed on Lee... where Sinatra is an actor as much on a recording as on a picture and works best with a director—be he musical or visual—Lee loses interest when she

FRANK
SINATRA
•
TONY
CURTIS
•
NATALIE
WOOD

In
The
Most
Challenging
Love
Story
Of
Our
Time!

The FRANK ROSS Production

*Kings
Go
Forth*

··· LEORA DANA

From the novel "Kings Go Forth"
by JOE DAVID BROWN
Directed by DELMER DAVES
Screenplay by MERLE MILLER
Music by ELMER BERNSTEIN
A ROSS-ETON Production
Released thru UNITED ARTISTS

Sinatra and Tony Curtis in *Kings Go Forth*

subjugates her vision to someone else; her conductors do best when they execute or supplement her ideas. Lee has got to be her own auteur.[3]

The highlight of the album is the closer, Jerome Kern and Oscar Hammerstein's moving "The Folks Who Live on the Hill."

For several weeks, Frank treated the *Kings Go Forth* cast and crew to a "pre-Christmas" party catered by the Villa Capri. One day during the Hollywood portion of the shoot, Frank shut down production and flew to Philadelphia, where Manie Sacks was dying of leukemia. Though the doctor had forbidden visitors, Frank, paying the entire cost for the two-day layoff, rushed to the hospital and spoke with his dear friend. First Bogie, and now Manie, he thought to himself. After Manie passed away, Frank, with tears in his eyes, said, "When I holler for help, he ain't gonna be there anymore. There's a little bit of Manie in everything good that has ever happened to me."[4]

On January 6, 1958, *The New York Times* published a special report on Hollywood's "corporate stars," those who left behind all vestiges of studio contracts and formed independent production companies. Describing the old studio system, which had been broken up by a Supreme Court decision, as "benevolent despotism," the article revealed that high personal income tax rates, which topped at 92 percent, were the reason for the "rise of the 'small business man' within the framework of the motion picture industry."[5] By incorporating, a star paid personal income tax only on a salary drawn from the business, while he was required to pay no more than 52 percent on corporate earnings.

Among the galaxy of incorporated stars, which included Burt Lancaster, John Wayne, Kirk Douglas, Alan Ladd, Bing Crosby, Bob Hope, Jerry Lewis and Gregory Peck, Frank was among the brightest, having grossed about $4 million from his films, records and television programs during the previous year. The partnership agreements he had been making with the studios were much better than the 5-10 percent of box-office receipts many stars earned.

In February, the *Kings Go Forth* company flew to the south of France to shoot the location scenes. Much to Frank's delight, one of his favorite actors, Boris Karloff, also was there on holiday with his wife, Evelyn. Agreeing to serve as Frank's unofficial acting coach, Karloff ironically informed the century's most accomplished popular singer, "You must learn to act with your *voice* as well as your face."[6] In 1997, Nancy Sinatra, Jr., wrote that Karloff "was a sweet, dear man and a profound influence on my father."[7]

A month later, Frank was back in Los Angeles, recording more singles: two duets with Keely Smith, "Nothing In Common" and "How Are Ya Fixed for Love?," both Van Heusen-Cahn swingers given the unison sax and punchy brass treatment by Billy May, who created an even heavier arrangement for "The Same Old Song and Dance" (also Van Heusen-Cahn, with Bobby Worth). A fourth song, May's quick-tempo, hard-swinging arrangement of "Here Goes," mysteriously disappeared for 22 years (in 1990 it finally was released on the 3-CD compilation *The Capitol Years*). Written by an unidentified composer, it features one of Frank's most driving vocals.

On May 5, Frank and Nelson Riddle held the initial session for *Frank Sinatra Sings for Only the Lonely*, which originally had been planned as another Sinatra-Gordon Jenkins saloon song collaboration, but this time even more melancholy and arranged in a semi-classical style for a large orchestra. For this project, Frank referred to such numbers as "Guess I'll Hang My Tears Out to Dry," "Ebb Tide" and "Angel Eyes" (all of which were recorded during the session but left unreleased) as "suicide songs." Postponing the *Lonely* project, he then cut the *Kings Go Forth* theme song "Monique" on May 24. Backed by Felix Slatkin's "French-tinged" arrangement incorporating an accordion, Frank melds Elmer Bernstein's soaring melody and Sammy Cahn's romantic lyrics into one of his finest Capitol love ballads — quite the opposite of the "downer" songs he had cut three weeks earlier.

But on that same evening, he effortlessly shifted back to saloon mode, cutting six incomparable tracks for *Only the Lonely*, making the session one of the most amazing of his career. With Riddle away on tour with Nat Cole, Frank was pleased to have Slatkin, who was a much better conductor, at the podium. The results were simultaneously breathtaking and heartbreaking. This time Robert Maxwell and Carl Sigman's "Ebb Tide" was an unqualified success, Riddle's eerily atmospheric introduction leading to Frank's caressing interpretation of a lyric equating a woman's embrace with the sweep of the sea. Next came the unforgettably haunting "Angel Eyes," written for the 1953 film *Jennifer* by Matt Dennis and Earl Brent: Opening with a flourish and a lyric that at first sounds positive, the arrangement soon descends into a brooding recollection of a rejected lover whose woman has left him for an unidentified beau. Ending with the lyric "Scuse me while I disappear," Frank holds the final syllable and decrescendos, sonically suggesting the narrator's gradual exit, perhaps from a bar at which he's been drowning his sorrows. This performance ranks among his greatest dramatic achievements.

Though one might think Rodgers and Hart's "Spring Is Here" is about happy times, this song from the 1938 Broadway musical *I Married an Angel* tells the tale of a man whose loneliness only increases with the onset of this supposedly bright and hopeful season. Frank used this lovely lament (which he had recorded for Columbia in 1947) as a warm-up for the next song, Styne and Cahn's "Guess I'll Hang My Tears Out to Dry," which he also had cut for his former label. This version is simply one of the most sublime recordings ever made: Opening with Al Viola's quiet guitar and the gentle declaration, "The torch I carry is handsome..." the arrangement then soars on Riddle's strings and Frank's glorious interpretation of the line "When I want rain, I get sunny weather," indicating this poor soul's unfulfilled need to wallow in the depression precipitated by an affair gone bad. Every second of the song is equally ethereal, a towering achievement in an already unparalleled career. If only a film producer had been capable of offering him a cinematic equivalent. This recording inspired Ed O'Brien to write:

> A Sinatra recording session had become theater. The lead actor and his supporting cast performed for an elite group of invited guests. Sinatra enacted three- and four-minute soliloquies not unlike Shakespearean dramas. He was combining great musical intellect with raw emotion. The stage was a recording studio and the actor/singer was working his way inside each song to illuminate every moment of it. Translated onto disc, the results were startling. A song of joy jumped out of the speakers and a hymn to despair touched the listener. Recording artistry had moved to a higher plane.[8]

Remarkably, Frank then cut the exquisite title track, written for the album by Van Heusen and Cahn, collaborating with Harry Sukman to approximate a romantic-era cello and piano duet backed by another sweeping string arrangement. Though he next took a stab at Billy Strayhorn's "Lush Life," it eventually was dropped from the album; but the final track of the session, the 1932 standard "Willow Weep for Me," fortunately made the cut. Featuring a somewhat more discernible tempo than the other Slatkin-conducted songs and some bluesy muted trumpet soloing by Pete Candoli, the latter conjures up visions of cloudy skies threatening rain and willow branches caught in a gale.

Following this prolific evening, Frank took another month-long break from the *Only the Lonely* project. Meanwhile, *Kings Go Forth* premiered in Monte Carlo on June 14, 1958. Opening with a long establishing shot, the film shows a line of U.S. Army troops walking down a curved road in France's Maritime Alps. As the title and credits appear, the soldiers enter a village they have liberated from the Germans, and as a grateful old Frenchwoman (Marie Isnard) stands at the side of the road, holding out a wine bottle and glass, Lieutenant Sam Loggins (Frank) stops to accept a drink. After exchanging a few supportive comments, Loggins takes the bottle from her and rejoins his comrades. When the troops reach their colonel's (Karl Swenson) command post, the lieutenant begins to narrate the story, indicating that the events depicted are a series of personal flashbacks. Here, as in the rest of the film, Frank narrates with a very gentle, well-enunciated voice, perhaps indicating Karloff's influence. But the veteran actor's "coaching" also appears to have affected Frank's nonverbal techniques. A short time later, after a new replacement in Loggins' platoon, Corporal Britt Harris (Tony Curtis), disobeys an order, and the lieutenant demotes the shifty soldier, the Colonel reminds him of his own past inability to "hear an order a couple of times." As Loggins responds silently, Frank registers a very subtle Karloff-style facial expression.

Kings Go Forth consists of two interesting subplots—one depicting the company's attempts to reconnoiter and capture from the Germans a valley five kilometers from Italy, and another dealing with Loggins and Harris' feud over Monique Blair (Natalie Wood), a beautiful young woman whom they discover is half African-American—that are combined somewhat unconvincingly. Though the Allies have liberated the Riviera from German occupation (as Loggins narrates, "the Army had made it a rest area"), it is unlikely that a group of American soldiers could obtain passes every weekend to visit Villefranche while simultaneously being so crucial in nearby operations against the enemy. The overemphasis on the romantic-racial angle, although a noble one that was dear to Frank, trivializes the efforts of the real men who gave their lives to stop Hitler's war machine.

During his first visit to the Riviera, Loggins is approached by a little French boy who calls him "my first American" and hands over a small top, a toy that the lieutenant gives to Jean Francoise (Jackie Berthe), another lad seated on a pier with Monique, whom he desperately wants to meet. After three meetings with her and lengthy discussions with her ailing mother (Leora

Dana), Sam declares his love but is rebuffed. When he becomes confused and aggravated, he is asked to sit down, but merely rests against the arm of the sofa. Reiterating a comment that her father was "a great man," Monique adds (as the camera tracks into a tight close-up), "He was also a Negro." As the scene cuts to a close-up of Sam, he merely closes his eyes for a second and then slightly moves his head to the side. Following Monique's impression that "'nigger' is one of the first words you learn in America," her mother explains how she and her husband chose to move from Philadelphia to France when she became pregnant.

The following scene shows Loggins, back in the concrete bunker his troops had taken from the Germans, narrating how he "fought two wars" after learning the truth about Monique. Stating that the racist term was not the first word learned in America, and that "some people never learned it at all," he also admits that he "learned it early and used it often...A lot of people need someone to look down on, or think they do." Though he wrestles with the dilemma, he ultimately gets a pass and returns to see her.

Taking Monique to the Le Chat Noir club, Sam is surprised to see Harris sit in on trumpet with a jazz combo (the Red Norvo quintet, whom Frank had hired for the scene) and then concerned by his quick hit on the smitten young lady. After Monique asks Sam to "tell Britt about me," he does so in the bunker, where Harris responds, "Well, what do you know?" just as a German bombardment lands around them.

During their next trip to see Monique, Sam realizes that he has lost her to Britt, whose "sophisticated" ways appeal to her. When she tells Sam how to drink wine properly, he replies, "Yeah, I'm a slob." In this scene, as Sam's anger builds, more of the archetypal Sinatra begins to show, as it does briefly in the earlier sequence when he is told about Monique's heritage. After Sam pays the bill at the Chocolat Cafe, the scene builds to a powerful climax: Having exited, Britt and Monique kiss in a tight close-up, which cuts to a close-up of Sam's face as he walks out, and then an atmospheric two-shot of the couple embracing, the glistening water in the background and her skirt sensually blowing in the breeze. Turning down an invitation to join them on a late-night excursion, Sam instead wanders the lonely streets (accompanied by a haunting saxophone in Elmer Bernstein's score) and gets loaded in a bar.

Early the next morning, Britt arrives at the hotel, tells Sam that he is in love with Monique and that they plan to marry. Mentioning the seriousness of the situation, Sam walks toward the seated Britt, appearing like he may hit the prospective bridegroom but instead shakes hands. Frank's ability to create palpable tension simply with his posture and gait is well demonstrated here.

Though Monique is overjoyed, Sam suspects that the womanizing Britt will not honor his promise. After checking with Corporal Lindsay (Edward Ryder), he is told that Harris admitted the entire venture was only a "gag." Here, Frank again uses a subtle closing of his eyes (in close-up) to indicate Sam's discomfort. Forcing Britt to go into town and see Monique, he threatens, "You touch her and I'll *kill* you!" before forcing him to tell her the truth. Revealing that he has been engaged a number of times, but never married, he adds, "With the exception of your daughter, Mrs. Blair, all of them were white." Turning to Sam, he explains, "It was like a new kick for me," sending Monique shrieking from the room. In a beautifully shot and edited sequence, Sam punches Britt with such force that his head whiplashes to the side and he groans audibly while falling to the floor.

Searching the streets, Sam eventually finds Monique near the water, from which she has been rescued by local residents. Devastated, she pleads for him to leave her alone before she is placed in an ambulance. While looking down at Natalie Wood, Frank registers (in close-up) another Karloff-like facial expression, conveying strong feelings with subtle movements of his eyes and mouth.

The following scenes feature Frank back in his powerful yet perfectly restrained mode, reflecting not only the influence of Karloff, but Bogart as well. On his self-devised mission to reach a tower in a German-held village, in order to radio all enemy positions back to their artillery battalions, he refuses to shake hands with Britt, his only aide, admitting, "I'm going to *kill* you," a threat he repeats several times. After reaching the tower and ordering several successful bombardments, they escape when their radio signal is detected. While running out of the village, Britt is shot down and dies in Sam's arms. Threatened by heavy fire, Sam orders that the village be bombed immediately and his image is lost amidst the smoke, flames and debris.

Having survived a seven-month hospital stay, Sam is released, minus his right arm, and returns to Villefranche, where Monique is now teaching. After her mother passed away, she explains, their spacious house was transformed into a school for refugee children, who give the film's ending an upbeat tone by singing a song in tribute to him.

Though the screenplay is uneven, the battle scenes are given short shrift and Natalie Wood is physically miscast (the photograph of Monique's father is never shown), *Kings Go Forth* still packs moments of great substance and drama, created in part by Frank's excellent performance. By choosing to portray a character who first experiences racist feelings, then wrestles with them and defeats them, he was presenting a different take on his lifelong crusade for acceptance of all races and creeds (a more subtle approach than in *The House I Live In*, for example, the content of which was driven by wartime concerns). Tony Curtis also delivers a fine characterization, of the spoiled rich boy who wangles whatever he wants by preying on others, particularly innocent women who fall for what appears to be worldly charisma. His believable miming of the trumpet solo with Norvo's quintet is particularly impressive. Though unconvincing as an African-American, Wood, speaking both French and wonderfully accented English, contributes a moving portrayal of the lovely and innocent Monique. And Leora Dana gives a noble and unforgettable performance as the obviously dying Mrs. Blair, whose disappearance from the drama after Sam knocks out Britt diminishes the film's impact. (When Monique merely mentions her death as a side note, Miller's screenplay definitely lacks the emotional impact it could have had.) The scene in which Sam gently kisses her forehead is a nice moment between Frank and Ms. Dana.

Frank made an additional appearance in the film's trailer, mentioning the popular literary adaptations in which he already had appeared—*Eternity* and *Golden Arm*—and then began to describe the new project as dealing with "a question... a question almost never talked about in films." As the trailer ends, *Kings Go Forth* is boldly referred to as "The Most Challenging Love Story of Our Time."

In early July, the film played across the United States to mixed reviews. *Variety*'s "Hift" believed it had strong box-office potential and a powerful racial subplot, but an unconvincing script and some characters who "aren't very consistent in their attitudes":

> Film's strongest exploitation asset, apart from the top names, is the race angle, which is played to the hilt. ...It leaves Sinatra stunned for a while and produces a rather cynical attitude in playboy Tony Curtis. Neither reaction rings particularly true, as the script puts it, and the gravity of the whole issue therefore appears overemphasized.
>
> Still, the mixed-marriage question gets a thorough — and positive — going-over in the dialog, particularly on the part of Leora Dana, the mother, who movingly recounts the fullness and happiness of her marriage to her Negro husband, and the penalty of exile from the U.S. which she had to pay for it. It's in these sequences that *Kings Go Forth* takes on an adult shape and deviates from the otherwise routine pattern.
>
> Sinatra... turns in a capable performance... and creates sympathy by underplaying the role. Miss Wood looks pretty, but that's just all. She is best when the script gives her a chance to say out loud what she feels. Curtis has had experience acting the heel, and he does a repeat, though his is a tough character to swallow. He's best when acting the charm boy. Miss Dana gives stature to the role of the mother who takes pride in what others see as her "shame."[9]

Serious racial problems still exist in the United States more than four decades after *Kings Go Forth* was released. Published in 1958, this *Variety* review indicates a very respectful, "enlightened" view on part of its critic, who was writing at the dawn of the modern civil rights movement. Despite its flaws, *Kings Go Forth*, released less than three years after Rosa Parks inspired the Montgomery Bus Boycott led by Martin Luther King, Jr., and Ralph Abernathy, was one of a few contemporary Hollywood films to deal positively with civil rights, a topic that already had concerned Frank for 20 years.

By contrast, *The New York Times*' Bosley Crowther, giving Frank a less-than-glowing review for the first time in many years, hated the film:

> It is some war that Frank Sinatra, Tony Curtis and, occasionally, the American Army fight in *Kings Go Forth*... the heroes seem free to go whenever they aren't sniping at the Nazis or wandering around the pretty hillsides on casual patrols. ...On the basis of the screenplay Merle Miller has fetched from the novel of Joe David Brown, it should be easy for any halfway student of movie mores to catch the drift quickly and go home.
>
> That way, we promise, you'd miss little, for the whole thing is so opaquely done that it only multiplies the banality of its romantic and war-movie clichés. Even the business of having the girl a Negro is brushed with the easiest kind of dismissal, after the sensation of it has been used.
>
> The performances, too, are sticky, under the direction of Delmer Daves. Only Mr. Sinatra occasionally acts halfway real. Mr. Curtis is bumptious and boorish, Miss Wood is affected up to here and Leora Dana plays her mother like something arisen from a grave. A couple of soldiers are funny and the Riviera scenery is good. But the sum of it makes a travesty of the atmosphere of war.[10]

Publishing this critique on the Fourth of July, Crowther is on target about the warfare subplot, but his harsh attitude toward the romance-racial angle makes one wonder if he really paid much attention to it. There are some Hollywood clichés, to be sure, but the new twist of the African-American love interest is not "easily dismissed" nor used merely for "sensational" purposes. It becomes a major thematic element and is handled with sensitivity. As to the characterizations, Curtis is supposed to be a boor, Wood handles her accent as well as any American actor could at a time when personal dialect coaches weren't a permanent fixture on film sets and Dana is terminally ill: During her first meeting with Sam, Mrs. Blair mentions that there are some things she wants to do before dying, including "jumping out of a parachute."

"You jump out of a plane," Sam corrects. "You hold on to the parachute." Alas, she never gets to try.

Dorothy Manners, in *The Los Angeles Examiner*, wrote, "The thin singer has never had a more difficult role and he has never more completely mastered a characterization. Might as well admit it, he's a great actor."[11] Later in July, Monte Carlo also was host to a special concert given by Frank, both to promote the film and raise money for the United Nations Refugee Fund, which was supported heavily by his friend Princess Grace.

Just as *Kings Go Forth* was opening at theaters across the world, Nelson Riddle recaptured the *Only the Lonely* baton from Felix Slatkin and completed the sessions on June 24 and 26, during which six additional numbers were recorded for inclusion on the album. "Blues in the Night," Harold Arlen and Johnny Mercer's 1941 classic vamp song, was followed by Bob Haggart and Johnny Burke's "What's New?" Telling the tale of erstwhile lovers who meet again, the latter, which features some gorgeous trombone work by Ray Sims, is, in the words of Pete Welding, "the finest, most powerful reading... ever recorded. Sinatra's slow, stately emotion-wrenching vocal framed by one of the most exquisite orchestrations Riddle ever devised... this is perfection."[12] A song of a "romance that has flown away," "Gone With the Wind" was followed by a recorded rehearsal take of Arlen and Mercer's "One for My Baby (And One More for the Road)" featuring only Frank and Bill Miller. (Thought destroyed, this intimate rendition eventually was issued on the 1990 3-CD *Capitol Years* collection.) On the 26th, Gordon Jenkins' 1935 ballad "Good-bye" and the positively eerie 1930 chestnut "It's a Lonesome Old Town" (also featuring Ray Sims on wonderfully warm trombone) were cut before the album version of "One for My Baby" was completed in a single take. Opening with Miller's late-night saloon piano, the song is saturated with noir atmosphere even before Frank enters with "It's quarter to three," describing his character's situation to an imaginary bartender as he creates perhaps the loneliest vocal of all time. As the song reaches its climax, Frank's mellifluous melody is joined by the sensual alto sax obbligato of Gus Bivona. It was the perfect number to end the album. Will Friedwald noted, "'One for My Baby' is the finest piece of musical acting Sinatra has ever turned in. He has never sounded closer to the end of his rope, and he makes the lyric come alive, word by painful word, in an intimate reality that's as frightening as it is believable."[13]

Actually *Only the Lonely*, taken as a whole, is arguably Frank's finest performance as an actor as well as a crowning achievement by the greatest pop singer in history. "For my money, this is the greatest blues album ever made," Frank Sinatra, Jr., has remarked. "This album should be available in drugstores by prescription only—because this is death, this record."[14]

For *Some Came Running*, filmed in August and September 1958, Frank returned to MGM, now headed by Sol C. Siegel, who chose the adaptation of James Jones' popular novel as his first personal production. Having scored such an amazing success in his first Jones role, Frank was anxious for another hit. Adept at depicting the effects of societal repression on "misfits," Jones had taken the title of his novel from the gospel according to Mark, which "is construed to mean that some have come running to find the meaning of life, but are prevented from finding it by obsession with materialism."[15]

Though Siegel hired Vincente Minnelli to direct, Frank, cast as writer-disillusioned war veteran Dave Hirsh, insisted that Dean Martin play Hirsch's friend, alcoholic and professional gambler Bama Dillert. Martin already had appeared in 20 films, but this one offered his first

Sinatra and Dean Martin as misfit adventurers in *Some Came Running*

non-singing dramatic role. He said, "[Bama] was a snap for me. I just played cards and talked Southern."[16]

Dave and Bama are two misfits in conservative Parkman, Indiana. Joining them in their gambling and boozing adventures is Ginny Moorhead, a naive Chicago party girl with a heart of gold, who travels to Parkman after Hirsh, in a state of complete inebriation, asks her to join him on the bus. Frank recalled how the role of Ginny was cast:

> [O]ne night when we were watching the *Dinah Shore Show*, we saw our Ginny dancing toward us, wearing a tight black leotard and belting out a song in an off-key voice best described as a clamor. It was Shirley MacLaine, but the cuteness, the strength, the humor—everything we wanted in Ginny—was wrapped up in that one package.[17]

Madison, Indiana, which would represent 1948 Parkman, had been chosen for much of the location shooting. (Other sites included Hanover, Indiana, and Milton, Kentucky.) While the cast and crew lodged in a nice hotel, Frank and Dean rented a nearby house so they could maintain their habits of staying up all night, playing cards and drinking Jack Daniels, which of course led Frank to suggest that Minnelli shoot from noon until 7 p.m. each day. MacLaine, who received a $15,000 salary, already was angered by the way MGM was treating her, and arrived in Madison only one day before filming began.

Frank and Dean, both naturalistic actors, occasionally balked at the meticulous Minnelli's direction, particularly during the filming of a scene set at a summer carnival. With the great William Daniels at his service, Minnelli insisted that the cinematographer keep moving the camera until the ferris wheel was captured at exactly the "right" angle in the background of a particular shot. Still dissatisfied, the director ordered the wheel itself moved, and Frank, who had been waiting about two hours, walked off the set. After shutting down production, Minnelli and Siegel had to coax him to return.

Some Came Running, though shot in Metrocolor and Cinemascope, opens with a scene reminiscent of Frank's entrance in *The Man with the Golden Arm*. Passed out on a Greyhound bus apparently containing only him, the driver and one another unconscious passenger, Dave Hirsh is roused when reaching Parkman. Wanting to tip the driver, Dave can't find his wallet. Did he lose it in a Chicago bar fight? No (as Frank reaches down into the crotch of his pants!), he put it where no one would look. Outside the bus, he is joined by an unfamiliar redheaded floozy who recounts the previous evening's events, including an invitation to accompany him to Parkman, but he hands her some money to catch a later ride.

Though his brother Frank (Arthur Kennedy) lives in town, Dave books a room at the Parkman Hotel and surveys the businesses on unchanging Main Street, including the family jewelry and gift store. Rather than deposit his large bank draft at the savings and loan where his brother is a board member, he asks the hotel clerk to run it over to the competing financial institution. Through the small-town grapevine, brother Frank finds out in short order.

As Dave unpacks his suitcase, he pulls out two of his favorite things: bottles of whiskey and books by Faulkner, Steinbeck and Wolfe. Then he tosses his own manuscripts into the trash can, but retrieves one to store in a dresser drawer. When his brother visits, Dave asks about their father, who "passed on about four or five years ago."

"Booze, eh?" Dave asks rhetorically. "Pshew, what a family."

While discussing Dave's current situation, brother Frank admits, "News sure gets around fast here."

"It's about the only thing that does," Dave replies.

Soon, Dave has a drink at Smitty's, where he meets Bama Dillert, who is seated in an adjacent booth. First seen in profile with his face obscured by a cowboy hat, Martin's introduction is similar to those enjoyed by Frank in several films: First he lifts his head and then turns slowly before speaking; and his unique, naturalistic manner of conveying charismatic personality traits with the movements of his hands begins here and continues throughout the portrayal (as this acting technique does in most of Martin's subsequent roles).

Accepting a dinner invitation from his brother and sister-in-law, Agnes (Leora Dana), Dave grows more uncomfortable as he is asked questions about his "former occupation" of writing. When his niece, Dawn (Betty Lou Keim), asks him if valuable experience can be gained from

Italian poster for Some Came Running

"bumming around... Didn't that help to make you a good writer?" he replies (in the film's first use of this familiar Sinatra-ism), "Bumming around can only make you a bum." Soon, his embarrassment is increased by the inquisitiveness of lovely English teacher Gwen French (Martha Hyer), who, along with her professor father (Larry Gates), has been asked to join them on their dinner date.

"I'm an admirer of yours, Mr. Hirsh," Gwen reveals.

"People usually are," Dave answers, "until they get to know me."

At the supper club and afterwards in Gwen's car, Dave gets too fresh and asks to be dropped at Smitty's, where he joins Bama's backroom poker game. During the card contest, which is soon disbanded by the sheriff, Dave says to Bama, "Ain't that a kick in the head?" (Two years later, Frank would commission Van Heusen and Cahn to write a song with this title for *Ocean's Eleven*. In that film, Dean sings it with the Red Norvo quintet, but he also recorded a studio version with the Nelson Riddle orchestra in May 1960.) A worse kick, however, occurs when Ginny takes up with Dave, Bama and Bama's girl, Rosalie (Carmen Phillips), in a booth that is accosted by Raymond Lanchak (Steven Peck), the abusive Chicago cad who had been punched out by Dave the night before. Though Bama persuades him to leave, he attacks Dave when the party leaves Smitty's. Dave defends himself by using martial arts techniques learned in the Army, but the fighting gets ugly when Lanchak brandishes a broken booze bottle. Called by a neighbor at Ginny's request, the police arrest both Dave and the cad and take in the floozy as a witness.

Dave moves in with Bama the following morning, and as his host shaves while wearing boxer shorts and ever-present cowboy hat, he argues with his brother, who has smoothed over the legal problem. When the elder Hirsh reveals he acted to protect his own reputation, Dave, sick from a hangover, orders, "Get the hell out of here!" Apparently, not only Rosalie, but Ginny, after serving as a witness, also spent the night at Bama's: Leaning over the sofa, Dave pulls out a long stole made from who knows what kind of animal, observing, "Hey, Bama? Looks like something died back here."

Later, Dave visits Gwen, who has expressed interest in reading the story he left unfinished. Behind the French home, Dave (backed by Elmer Bernstein's beautiful love theme that opens with solo piano and then segues into a full orchestral arrangement) awaits her verdict as she reads in the guest house. Informed that his tale, featuring outstanding characters, is indeed finished, Dave kisses Gwen, who initially pulls away but returns for more. Shot in silhouette, this scene is a visual and dramatic highlight: When Frank effortlessly tosses away Martha Hyer's proper "school teacher" hairpins and takes down her gorgeous blonde locks, the viewer sees a true master at work.

The subplot involving the Frank Hirsh family now comes into play more strongly. Telling her husband that she "has a headache" and completely ignoring her daughter, Agnes sends both of them into the night to seek greener pastures. Stopping off at his jewelry store, Frank Hirsh discovers Edith Barclay (Nancy Gates), his comely secretary, apparently working overtime but looking far too sexy (in the classic raised-arms-while-wearing-a-sleeveless-top pose that has melted the resolve of many a male) to be doing anything else but turning on her boss. (In an earlier scene, he tells Dave he's never noticed Edith's beauty, but his nonverbal behavior has always indicated otherwise.) Though he tells her to go home, he then asks her if she's seeing anyone and if they can "drive around for awhile." They soon park at a popular teen make-out point and (as Gates strikes that steamy pose again) kiss. Having pulled up behind them, Dawn and her boozing, hormone-raging boyfriend, Wally Dennis (John Brennan), argue before she spies her old man about to make hey-hey with a woman young enough to be her sister. Dawn then demands to be taken home.

Having waited for Gwen to call, Dave returns to the French home, but she confusedly tells him that their escapade may have been a mistake. She does not care for his lifestyle and, in particular, his "violence." In an effective use of musical foreshadowing, Gwen turns off the radio, which had been playing Bernstein's love theme, just after Dave rings the doorbell. Aggravated by this rebuff, he decides to join Bama on a gambling tour to Terre Haute and Indianapolis, accompanied by Ginny and Rosalie. As Dave packs for the trip, Shirley MacLaine enacts a nice comic bit, following Frank into the closet each time he grabs some clothes off the rack.

The following scene, set in Terre Haute, is filled with the type of well-played nightclub humor for which the "Rat Pack" became famous. When the totally fractured Rosalie is unable to find their table, Bama sits her down, lights a cigarette, and puts it in her hand. "Here, smoke up. Force yourself to have fun." Ginny's terrible singing ("To Love and Be Loved," written for the film by Van Heusen and Cahn) is then stopped by Dave at the insistence of the management. A self-reflective line follows, through which a purveyor of atrocious vocalizing asks the master of popular song, "You appreciate my singing, don't you, Dave?" As Rosalie gets truly stiff, Dave dances with Ginny, who asks that he buy her a soft pillow from a rack on the dance floor. (Continuing to give fellow musicians bit roles in his films, Frank asked guitarist Al Viola to appear briefly in this sequence.)

Sinatra, Shirley MacLaine, Dean Martin and Carmen Phillips

Soon, Dave notices a drunken Dawn living it up with a middle-aged man at a corner table. Informed by his niece that the gent is a "traveling salesman," Dave intimates that the party is over.

"Are you leaving?" the salesman asks.

"No, *you* are," Dave explains. "Walk." Discussing the situation with Dawn, he then puts her on a bus to Parkman.

Meanwhile, back at Bama's table, the amiable Southerner is placing ice on the comatose Rosalie's neck; but when she pops back up, he asks, "How 'bout another drink?"

Moving on to Indianapolis, Dave and Bama play a high-stakes game with some local poker players who are a bit too suspicious of their actions. After speaking with Gwen on the phone, Dave returns to the table to find one of the men talking about a player who had secretly received telephoned information about others' hands.

Much of this scene was improvised, allowing Frank and Dean to add realism to the escalating conflict. When Dave is asked what he would call a man who received such tips, he replies, "I'd say he was a dishonest bum." Accused of such, he threatens, "Now look, Charley..." And when the man begins scrutinizing Bama's hat, Dave adds that it transmits "radio signals that tell us what you bums are holding."

When the sore loser knocks off the sacred hat, Bama punches him and Dave orders, "Pick it up and put it on his head." Pulling a knife, the man stabs Bama before Dave chases him and the others out of the room. The next morning, while playing solitaire in a Catholic hospital, Bama receives the terrible news that he is suffering from diabetes and must stop drinking. Stubborn to the end, his hat atop his head and having no intention of giving up whiskey, he demands his clothes so he can leave.

In Parkman, Dave is once more bawled out by his brother, who in turn is informed that the adulterous affair with Edith, who also is present, is known to him. But unbeknownst is Ginny's visit to Gwen, who then believes that Dave had been romantically involved with her during the gambling trip. When he later goes to see Gwen, the professor talks to him, but he instead intrudes into her upstairs bedroom. In one of William Daniels' best uses of the Cinemascope image, Gwen is seated at her dressing table (screen left), Dave stands inside the door (screen right), and his reflection is seen in a full-length mirror (mid-screen), visually juxtaposing Dave as reflected in her mind against the person he actually is. Daniels then tracks in as their argument heats up.

As written, Dave Hirsh is a character who shares certain qualities with the real Sinatra, which gave him leverage to add his own distinct touches and ad-libs to the film. Dave is certainly a man who displays manic-depressive behavior, one minute doing his utmost to attain what he wants, and the next grabbing a glass of whiskey or taking out his frustration on someone else, as he does on Ginny in the next scene. Frank, in describing his approach to singing, spoke about his tendency to move from one intense emotion to another—but his remarks about being an "18-carat manic-depressive" also can be applied to his naturalistic acting. (His reference to his bipolar behavior reflects a question asked by Walter Cronkite during a televised interview a few years later. His reply was that he had needed help with a "personal problem" at one point.[18])

Back at Bama's, Ginny is reading Dave's story, which Gwen had gotten published in *Atlantic* magazine. When Dave tells her she isn't intelligent enough to understand it, she responds, "Just because that schoolteacher doesn't want you, you have no right to take it out on me!" She then pleads with him, revealing, "I love you so awful much... I'll do anything for you."

Having noticed the appalling state of Bama's house, Dave apologizes and asks, "Would you clean the place up for me?"

"Oh, could I?" she replies.

But soon Dave humiliates her again. After reading his story out loud, he accuses her of being too stupid to know what it's about.

Stating a truism about human thought (and gaining audience empathy), she says, "Just because I don't understand it doesn't mean I don't like it!"

Tired of being lonely, with his life devoid of direction, Dave asks Ginny to marry him, but her joy is temporarily interrupted when Bama refuses to be best man. "Even she knows she's a pig," Bama adds.

Disgusted by his friend's use of this term to describe "loose" women, Dave is not dissuaded and the two are married by a local judge. In the absence of Bama, an elderly couple serve as witnesses. A dynamic scene, set at the Parkman summer carnival, follows, expertly combining Daniels' roving camera with the movement of the actors and amusement rides within the frame. Reminiscent of Hitchcock's *Strangers on a Train* (1951), the sequence first shows Edith and Dawn preparing to leave Parkman on the same train, and then the return of the brutish, drunken, now totally psychotic Raymond Lanchak, who is out to kill Dave. Though Bama spots the lunatic, drives to the carnival and runs to the rescue, Lanchak shoots Dave once and then moves in for the kill. Throwing herself in front of her new husband, Ginny is murdered instead. As the townspeople, including the other principal characters, run to see what has happened, Dave rests Ginny's head on the pillow he had bought her in Terre Haute. At the subsequent funeral, Dave stands motionless as Gwen and her father watch from a distance. Indicating that stubborn attitudes can be changed, the formerly recalcitrant Bama removes his hat.

Giving another fine performance, by turns moody and intense, searching for something but not knowing what it is (qualities shared by many writers), Frank is effortlessly matched by Dean Martin, whose utterly *real* characterization surprised critics who had viewed him solely as a singer and straight man for the loon-faced scenery chewing of Jerry Lewis (though he already had proved himself in *The Young Lions* [1958], holding his own with Brando and Clift). The following year, Dino would give arguably the best dramatic performance of his career, alongside John Wayne and Walter Brennan, in Howard Hawks' masterful *Rio Bravo* (1959).

Shirley MacLaine's Ginny is way over the top, but she's supposed to be: a naive, goodhearted, goofy, childlike young woman who probably grew up on the "wrong side" of Chicago's tracks. (The following spring, this performance earned her an Academy Award nomination for best supporting actress.) All of the female supporting roles are played superbly: Martha Hyer is as frustrating (both to Dave and the viewer) as she is gorgeous; Betty Lou Keim's would-be rebellious teen is

Sinatra and Shirley MacLaine

admirably restrained; Carmen Phillips is fine as the clueless but caring doll (Rosalie's terrified reaction to Bama's stabbing is quite effective); Nancy Gates smolders enough to heat up the aging Arthur Kennedy; and the versatile Leora Dana as his unremittingly argumentative wife creates a character completely unlike her quiet and dignified Mrs. Blair in *Kings Go Forth*. Kennedy recalled the One-Take Charley technique: "Frank is gracious because he keeps you on your toes—unexpected sallies and original twists. That characterizes his style. And it's fun to play against."[19]

Though known for his lavish musicals, Vincente Minnelli fashioned an effective dramatic film, balancing John Patrick and Arthur Sheekman's script, which at times veers into melodrama, and the un- predictability of actors who loved to improvise. He uses counterpoint throughout the film, offsetting love with rejection, humor with violence, and boisterousness with tragedy—thematic elements reflected in all the major characterizations. Dave is not alone in his tendency toward inner turmoil, as Bama, Ginny, Rosalie and each of the major Parkman characters are also battling their demons. It is a film loaded with manic-depressive behavior.

Although visually interesting, the ending seems hastily tacked-on. But Minnelli ultimately didn't have as much control over the final product as did Frank, who at one point excised some scenes because the company was running behind schedule. (Some reports claim the delay was caused by his own complaints about how the film was being shot.) Though Dave Hirsh is killed in Jones' novel, Frank decided to let him live and instead give MacLaine the big, showy sendoff. (One of her major scenes had been among those removed from the script.) The funeral epilogue, however, indicates that these people may come to terms with their conflicts and disallusionments.

On October 15, 1958, Frank again cut a Capitol single to promote his latest screen effort: Cahn and Van Heusen's "To Love and Be Loved," conducted by Nelson Riddle and released on December 1. *Some Came Running* premiered at the Hollywood Paramount on December 18, and at New York's Radio City Music Hall one month later. Critics were very positive, and about equally divided over the ending. *Variety*'s "Powe" wrote:

> *Some Came Running*, despite some minor flaws, is certainly one of the most exciting pictures of the season... It has been brilliantly directed by Vincente

Minnelli, with fine performances by Frank Sinatra and Dean Martin and a shattering one by Shirley MacLaine that could only have been surmised from her previous work.

Sinatra gives a top performance, sardonic and compassionate, full of touches both instinctive and technical. It is not easy, either, to play a man dying of a chronic illness and do it with grace and humor, and this Dean Martin does without faltering.

With her performance, Miss MacLaine moves into the front row of film actresses. She isn't conventionally pretty. Her hair looks like it was combed with an eggbeater. But it doesn't make any difference, because she elicits such empathy and humor that when she offers herself to Sinatra, she seems eminently worth taking.[20]

There was very little Powe didn't admire about the film. He lavished equal praise on the performances of Hyer, Kennedy, Gates and Dana, Minnelli's direction, Elmer Bernstein's score ("one of his best") and Franklin Milton's "natural" sound recording.

Bosley Crowther found the characters to be drawn a little too ambiguously, but lavished high praise on the performers:

> Frank Sinatra is downright fascinating — or what the youngsters would call "cool" Engaging, too, is Dean Martin (you're no more surprised than we were!)... His comical way of indicating hard-boiled simplicity, with the suitable lines to go with it, reveals a character. And his boisterous pot-walloping with Mr. Sinatra and with a garishly bedizened Shirley MacLaine, who plays a pick-up from Chicago, makes for the best fun in the film. ...Arthur Kennedy does a crisp and trenchant job... Leora Dana conveys... pettiness... and Betty Lou Keim is quite touching...[21]

Other critics praised Frank, and most agreed that his costars either matched or outdistanced him. In *The Motion Picture Herald*, James M. Jerauld wrote, "Sinatra moves with impressive speed and precision in every situation, with occasional flashes of humor. It's his picture, but he has distinguished support"; while Dick Williams, in his *Los Angeles Mirror-News* review, noted, "Frank Sinatra and Dean Martin punch over two of their best performances. But the surprise hit is Shirley MacLaine's touching, unforgettable portrait of the crude, pathetic little floozy." *Cosmopolitan*'s columnist agreed: "Sinatra, as usual, gives a polished performance; but it is Shirley MacLaine... that might well win an Academy Award next year, and Dean Martin who walk off with the acting honors."[22]

On September 11, Frank had recorded three singles with Riddle at Capitol Studio A in Hollywood: "Mr. Success," a straight-ahead swing collaboration between Frank, Hank Sanicola and Ed Greines; the lovers' lullaby "Sleep Warm"; and an unequaled ballad rendition of Rodgers and Hart's "Where or When" on which he is accompanied only by Bill Miller's piano until the orchestra enters for the final chorus, crescendoing along with Frank as he soars to a dramatic conclusion. (Unfortunately, this last track was not released until 1978, when it was included on the Capitol collector's album *The Rare Sinatra*.) On September 30, three more songs were cut, this time with Billy May: While "Just in Time" and "The Song Is You" were shelved, Capitol fully intended to release "It All Depends on You." None, however, were issued at the time. ("The Song" and "It All Depends," too, were later included on the 1978 *Rare Sinatra*, as was Van Heusen and Cahn's "I Couldn't Care Less," one of three Riddle-conducted tracks from an October 15, 1958, Studio A session.) The other two recordings were different arrangements of "To Love and Be Loved" (the first released as the promo single, and the second, longer version held over for inclusion on the 1961 Capitol collection *All the Way*).

For his next film project, Frank joined forces with another famous Italian-American, Frank Capra, to produce an adaptation of Arnold Schulman's Broadway smash *A Hole in the Head*. Naming their partnership Sin-Cap Productions, they hired Schulman to write the screenplay; and, having worked with William Daniels on *Some Came Running*, Frank chose him to create Cinemascope magic once again. Cahn and Van Heusen also were salaried to write two songs, "All My Tomorrows," which would be heard during the opening credits, and "High Hopes," to be sung by Frank (as hotel owner Tony Manetta) and young Eddie Hodges (as his son, Ally). Shooting began in Miami on November 10, 1958, with costars Edward G. Robinson, Eleanor Parker, Carolyn Jones and Thelma Ritter, as well as Hodges and other supporting players.

Robinson had been one of Frank's cinematic heroes since 1930, when the Hoboken teenager had seen Warner Bros.' gangster classic *Little Caeser*, which brought great stardom and some degree of typecasting to the former Emmanuel Goldenberg, born in Bucharest, Rumania, and raised in New York. Though he was Jewish, Robinson became famous for portraying Italians, and continued to do so throughout his career, which makes his casting perfect in *A Hole in the Head*, a Jewish play "Italianized" for the screen. As Tony Manetta's conservative brother Mario, Robinson worked with Frank in many scenes, and though a mannered, extremely professional actor, he was able to adapt somewhat to the One-Take Charley approach. Frank explained to Robinson, "I don't believe exhausting myself before the take. On the other hand, I read the script fifty times before I ever go to work. So you can't say I'm unprepared."[23]

One evening during the shoot, Carolyn Jones went to dinner with Frank. She recalled, "There were a lot of good-looking young girls, yet he was most attentive to an old lady who could have been his grandmother. How she beamed!"[24] And Eleanor Parker, who attempted to coordinate Christmas shopping with the busy shooting schedule, really benefited from her acquaintance with him:

> In conversations on the set about children and toys, I remember that a favorite
> of all my kids was a toy pinball machine which had long since been sent on

its way to toyland Valhalla... I was determined to move upward and onward: a real, store-bought professional superflasher of a pinball machine. But how? Well, never fear—Frank Sinatra is here! The machines are manufactured in Chicago and readily available by means of a catalog which would be brought to me at once, if not sooner. Action. What a relief. All I had to do was wait for the catalog, place my order. However, waiting for the catalog became an ordeal. Each passing day brought a reminder from me that time was getting short and each reminder was met with the cool assurance. He would bring the book the next day. Finally I was forced to the conclusion that the conversation was charming, but the pinball machine was *tilt*.

A week before Christmas, the doorbell rang. I opened the door and there—fully grown and gaily bedecked with a patchwork of color papers and ribbons—was the machine, a gift from Santa Sinatra, whose card complained, "I couldn't get the catalog, so here's the machine instead. I wanted to surprise you for Christmas but you're such a nag!"[25]

Having closely worked with Frank, Capra later said:

He's a great singer and he knows it. The excitement of moving and reaching the hearts of live audiences with his lyrical virtuosity makes his blood run hot. Sinatra is also a great actor, and he knows that, too. But he cannot bewitch an audience of dispassionate cameramen, soundmen, script girls, makeup people, deadpan electricians who have seen it all before. If directors keep him busy, he maintains any easy truce, for having started something, Sinatra's next goal is to finish it—but fast. He bores easily; can't sit still or be alone; must be where the action is.[26]

As the *Hole in the Head* shoot was wrapping up, Frank re-teamed with Billy May to take another stab at a new upbeat album, one that later would inspire Pete Welding to write, "Music just doesn't get any better than this."[27] Temporarily abandoning lush string arrangements and doom-and-gloom torch songs, Frank intended *Come Dance with Me* to be a collection of (as noted on the back cover) "vocals that dance." And indeed every number selected for the project ended up hoofing along at a driving clip, thanks to May's brass and rhythm section charts and Frank's most impressive hard swinging yet perfectly relaxed singing to date. As Welding noted:

The bracing, witty and, above all, deliciously imaginative orchestrations Billy May devised for the songs exposed much more fully a facet of the singer's gifts, his resiliently swinging way with uptempo songs, that largely but not wholly had been scanted, or at least downplayed, in his earlier collaborations with Nelson Riddle. Now, it's true that Sinatra and Riddle had evidenced a bright and effortless handling of rhythm... but this had been tempered by other considerations, chief among them a generally sophisticated, romantic approach to song selection and setting in which rhythmic incisiveness was held to be of lesser importance. The effect desired was an urbane, reserved kind of swing, easy and unforced, even elegant in character... But with May, Sinatra let fly.[28]

As he did with his cinematic projects, Frank preferred to alternate "serious" concepts with those he considered more entertaining and fun, and his depth as a performer continued to be in evidence both on the screen and on the fabulous LPs Capitol continued to release.

On December 9, 1958, Frank and May re-recorded "The Song Is You," his first uptempo version of the Kern-Hammerstein classic. And swing it does, opening with an explosion of brass and Alvin Stoller's driving drums; and here, May already demonstrates his expert use of the stereo format, bracketing Frank's effortless phrasing with punchy brass kicks on the right and his trademark flowing saxophones on the left. Johnny Mercer's "Something's Gotta Give" was cut next, the orchestra creating instant excitement increased by Frank's unerring capability to remain firmly in the driver's seat. Then May decreased the tempo a bit but maintained the electric interplay between the horns and the saxophones on Jule Styne, Betty Comden and Adolph Green's "Just in Time," another track wonderfully propelled by Frank and Alvin Stoller. Two days later, a version of "Day In, Day Out" was recorded but ditched, and singer and conductor took up exactly where they left off on December 22, completing no less than five excellent tracks. "Day In, Day Out," which opens with a surprise brass blast that is a portent of sounds to come, features one of the most powerful moments in the history of swing vocals. Following a Count Basie-like piano solo by Bill Miller, May's saxes rise to the fore and then the horns and drums return to set up Frank's glorious, rhythmically and lyrically improvisational return: "*Come* rain!" (thunderous kick by the entire band) "*Come on*, shine!" (saxes and trombones) "I—meet you and, to me, the day is *fiiine*." (trumpets) "*Then* I kiss those lips, and the pounding becomes—" (saxes) "—a large ocean's roar." (trumpets) "*Nine* thousand drums." (trumpets) "*Can't*—you see that it's love?" (trumpets) "Can there be any doubt?" and then weaving his way through a full-band crescendo until the final "Day in, *Daaaay Ouwwwt!*" Here Frank combines natural acting talent with the graceful prowess of a fine athlete—definitely dancing. And every other cut during the session followed suit: the ultimate swing version of "Baubles, Bangles and Beads" (impeccable phrasing, finger snapping and ending with "Baubles, bangles—and them *coo-coo* beads!"); "Dancing in the Dark," written by Arthur Schwartz and Howard Dietz for the 1953 Fred Astaire film *The Bandwagon*; a smoking resurrection of Cahn and Styne's "Saturday Night (Is the Loneliest Night of the Week)"; and an equally exciting arrangement of Irving Berlin's "Cheek to Cheek" (another number made famous by Astaire, in *Top Hat* [1935]).

The *Come Dance with Me* sessions were completed the following evening, making this project one of Frank's greatest successes before it ever hit record stores: Nine of the 12 tracks were cut in two days! Now it seemed that perhaps One-Take Charley could even venture into the recording studio as well as onto a movie soundstage. Though the songs actually required about three to 10 takes, Frank's ever-fresh performances continued to achieve the effect of effortless perfection. Featuring a great Heinie Beau arrangement, "Too Close for Comfort" was followed by Lerner and Loewe's "I Could Have Danced All Night" and two Van Heusen-Cahn numbers commissioned for the album: the opening title track and the closer, "The Last Dance." "Come Dance with Me" introduces the driving, heavy brass style of the album, with Frank insouciantly inviting a young lady onto the floor ("Hey there, cutes, put on your dancin' boots, and come dance with me. Come dance with me—what an evening for—some—terpsichore [mispronouncing terps*icore* in a clever rhyme]) and explaining that (in a slight improvisation on Cahn's lyrics), "And while the rhythm swings, what *coo-coo* things I'll be sayin'. For what is dancin' but makin' love set to music—*playin?*" The only slow song on the album, "The Last Dance" approximates the way in which 1940s orchestras bid adieu to their evening's dancers. And the album's excellence wasn't lost on anyone: It not only became a best seller but also won three 1959 Grammy Awards, for Album of the Year, Best Arrangement and Best Male Vocal Performance, allowing Frank to place the musical equivalent next to his Oscars for *The House I Live In* and *From Here to Eternity*.

On December 29, 1958, Frank and Riddle cut four singles, including "All My Tomorrows," Van Heusen and Cahn's tranquil title song for *A Hole in the Head*. As the number fills the soundtrack, the film opens with a unique title sequence in which a Goodyear blimp, flying over Miami Beach, pulls a train of credits behind it. Immediately, the talents of Frank, Nelson Riddle and William Daniels set the stage for a film both funny and bittersweet (two Capra trademarks). Narrating the background of Tony Manetta, Frank introduces his character's primary interest—broads—two of which are shown flanking him in a photo taken outside his garish

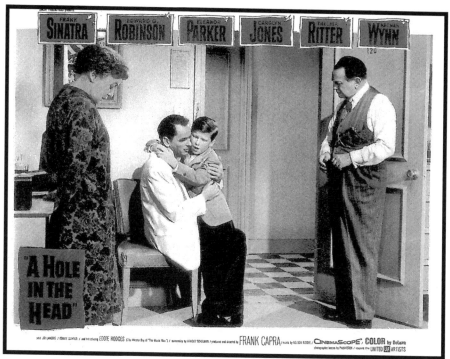

Thelma Ritter, Sinatra, Eddie Hodges and Edward G. Robinson

hotel, the Garden of Eden. Currently, only one lodger—a middle-aged woman who undergoes a blackout drunk every night, yelling, "Geronimo!" each time she returns—is in residence.

This brief establishing scene cuts to Tony's night on the town with a live one, Shirl (Carolyn Jones), whom he refers to as a "*kooky* broad"—and for good reason. How can a man drive his Cadillac convertible with a half-drunken, amorous woman in his lap? After reaching the hotel, Tony attempts to "guide" Shirl up the stairs, but she runs off, strips down to her underwear and rushes into the surf. Here, Frank and Ms. Jones engage in some excellent physical comedy as he (being much smaller than the curvy Carolyn) cradles her in his arms while using his rump to struggle his way toward the second floor, one step at a time and *backwards* to boot. As he reaches a landing, he, not being able to see what lies behind, moves onto a step stool and topples over the back, with Carolyn landing hard on top of him. One-Take Charley certainly couldn't have tolerated too many takes here.

Having quickly established Tony's tribulations with wild women, the film immediately shows the "other side" of the man, a caring father who, after the death of his young wife, created a special relationship with his son. While his dad had been out carousing with Shirl, Ally had fallen asleep with an eviction notice in his hand. Leaving Shirl to her frolic in the ocean, Tony retires to the bedroom he shares with the boy, who soon brings up their dire financial situation; though he attempts to divert Ally with questions about sports, the subject eventually turns to ways of scraping together enough bread to pay the landlord. Tony mentions Uncle Mario, but Ally wants nothing to do with *that*. The scene then includes a moment unique in Frank's films: a tender shot of him holding the boy as he describes what they'll have when he strikes financial paydirt (to be brought about by building a "Disneyland" in Miami Beach). As Ally finally turns in, Tony's lamentations about being a "loser" are interrupted by the appearance of the tipsy, half-naked Shirl at the window. The scene concludes with a fade-out on the smiling boy.

The next day, Ally's efforts to help his father are demonstrated when he argues with a laundry delivery man who refuses to leave clean towels; as the boy struggles, Tony arrives in time to swipe bundles of Fontainebleau towels from the truck. Having exhausted all other financial avenues, Tony is forced to phone Mario in New York, telling tall tales about Ally's "stomach trouble." Frank is excellent as Tony lies to his brother and motions his son out of the room. This scene also introduces Mario's "nerd" son, Julius (Jimmy Komack), who spends all his time attempting to master the hula hoop and "runs into the toilet" whenever a customer enters their store. After Mario and his wife, Sophie (Thelma Ritter), agree to fly to Miami Beach, Tony spots his old pal, now the rich and famous Jerry Marks (Keenan Wynn), roll into town amidst a full-scale parade. Thinking he now can pitch his Disneyland idea, he sings a bit of "All My Tomorrows" and advises Ally to "put up a front" whenever pitching a entrepreneurial plan: Honesty, he says, can only elicit the response, "Scram, bum!"

Just as Tony attempts to leave for the airport, Shirl announces, "I'm checking out," distracting him enough to drive to a make-out point along the beach. She describes the differences in their personalities and attitudes, comparing her unfettered spirit and sense of fun (a "free bird") to his stuffy seriousness (a "kiwi bird"). This time, she strips behind a bush, tossing each article of clothing at his head before running to the ocean with her surfboard.

Infuriated at being stood up at the airport, Mario takes a cab to the hotel, where he tips the cabbie with an entire dime, a lavish gratuity the hard-working man hasn't received "since '32." Inside, he and Sophie witness the arrival of the inebriated lodger, who receives her key from the obviously well Ally. "I won't say nothin'," Mario remarks as Robinson makes his first of four hilarious forays into a low-seated rocking chair: While others have no problem relaxing in it, Mario is slammed in the back each time he sits down. Meanwhile, Sophie refers to Ally's environment as being populated by "drunken bums, dope fiends [and] gamblers," all the while looking at Fred (Dub Taylor), the kindhearted desk clerk.

The inevitable brotherly argument begins as soon as Tony returns. Having seen him kiss Shirl outside, the utterly conservative Mario harshly observes, "I don't have a Cadillac car, you bum!"

"Bum?" Tony responds in bewilderment.

"You're happiness crazy," Mario accuses. "You're a bum!"

"Bum?"

"Bum! Bum!" Mario insists, also remarking that Ally, forced to eat hotdogs, has been living like one, too. "Bum! Did you meet us at the airport?"

Now Ally comes to the rescue. "He's not a bum. He's my pop, and he's a champ!" (The Sinatra "bum" motif reaches its peak in this film.)

Capra and Daniels make the most of the 2.35:1 ratio, using a three-shot encompassing the entire room that depicts the space dividing each of the characters: The frame shows Tony at far screen left, Sophie in the middle and Mario at far screen right—an image possible on a theater stage, but not in a film shot in the standard 1:33 ratio. However, here the cinematic image is superior to a theatrical one: While the stage is a large area that often includes distractions, widescreen cinema allows Capra to create the same physical space while intimately focusing in on the three characters. The physical image reinforces Sophie's dilemma of acting as arbitrator in the war between her husband and brother-in-law.

Ally wretches as Mario firmly pinches his cheek and kisses him. "Bum," he whispers as his uncle walks off to bed.

Outside the hotel, the boy cries, but Shirl, sitting in her window and playing bongos, mocks him. Joining his son, Tony shifts back into loser mode: "I could be walkin' right past a solid block of gold and if I touched it—psssht—spaghetti, right in my hand." But the remark has the desired effect on Ally. "Pop, you got a hole in the head," he says, asking to hear "the ant song." Here, Frank and young Hodges launch into "High Hopes" which the boy mangles with a deliberately off-key ending. (Frank's cringing is a highlight.) Reconsidering Sophie's earlier offer to introduce him to "Mrs. Rogers," a local widow, Tony tells Ally, "We'll tell 'em to bring over the broad, and we'll have a look at her."

Soon after, when Tony discusses the matter with his brother and sister-in-law, some improvisation occurs as Frank works in some Sinatra-speak: "Sophie, you're a gasser."

"Did you hear that, Mario?" she asks her husband.

"Gasser," he replies facetiously.

Just before Mrs. Rogers is scheduled to arrive, Tony speculates to Ally that she is probably "some old, dried-up tomato" and then asks him if he expects her to look like Marilyn Monroe. The latter is the boy's prediction, which rings true when he walks out of the bedroom and is stunned by the gorgeous redhead (Eleanor Parker) who winks at him.

Attempting to make small talk, Mario speaks of another son, a doctor who has advised him about problems he experiences with his feet. "It's 'psychophematic'," he informs her. "My feet are in my head."

Capra's allowance for ad-libbing is also obvious when Ally, literally hypnotized by Mrs. Rogers' beauty, stumbles into Mario, knocking his cigar out of his hand. Here, Hodges looks off, screen right, with a laughing expression on his face. The director left it in the final cut.

Attired in nothing but a blue button-down shirt and panties, Shirl first decides to confront them but fortunately reconsiders. Meanwhile, Mrs. Rogers demonstrates that her beauty is matched by her intelligence, impressing both Tony and Ally with her knowledge of sports trivia. But the merriment is soon broken by the clumsy Mario, who attempts to run their matchmaking like a business. Mrs. Rogers scurries out, Mario again is attacked by the chair and Ally tries to smooth things over with the shocked lady, who is persuaded by Tony to join him for coffee at a nearby cafe. Later, when Shirl cries at the sight of Tony leaving in his convertible with Mrs. Rogers and a bag of groceries, Ally takes her a bouquet of flowers that is quickly rejected.

Tony demonstrates great sincerity at Mrs. Rogers' cramped home, discussing the premature demises of their former spouses and what they had done in the past. (Frank again plays with the dialogue, saying, "We had a store. *A* store. We had a gang of 'em.")

Back at the Garden of Eden, Mario still hasn't stopped complaining, going so far as to point out the absurdity of putting holes in ice cubes. Capra and Daniels again use the widescreen camera to good effect, tracking backward through the halls of the hotel as the two brothers argue over Tony's request for "a couple thousand to tide [him] over." This technique again is used after Tony sees the lipstick goodbye that Shirl has left on the mirror in her room. Forcefully strutting to Mario's door (here Frank shows how well he could nonverbally project strong emotion), he kicks it open and tells off his brother.

Invited to Jerry Marks' self-laudatory pool party at the Fountainebleau, Tony repeatedly attempts to spring his Disneyland idea but, forced to accompany his old pal to the local dog races, sells his Cadillac for betting money. First winning enough to pay off his debtors, he then tries to impress Marks by matching a $5,000 wager but loses it all. Realizing that Tony has been exaggerating his position as a hotel bigwig, Marks patronizingly hands him a roll of bills, but he (in classic Sinatra style) swats the cash to the ground and is sucker punched by two goons.

Back at the hotel, Mario, having heard that Tony raised the dough, ironically laments that he hadn't been allowed to help his own brother. Sullenly walking in on a party organized by Ally, Tony escapes to a bedroom. "You're absolutely right, Mario," he admits. "I'm nothing but a bum. Never have been anything but a bum... a cheap, chiselin', connivin' bum."

"What do you mean, you're a bum?" Mario counters. "How can you be a bum? You're my brother. ...You're not a bum. Nobody in the family's a bum."

Tony then tries to persuade Ally that he would be better off with Mario and Sophie. "I need you like a hole in the head," he tells him, doing his best to appear uncaring, but when the boy talks back, he slaps him hard in the face. Later, despondent on the beach, Tony is hugged by his brother, who concludes, "You crazy roughneck bum." Ally begins his cab ride to the airport with his uncle and aunt, but his love for his father is too strong. The film then closes with Tony,

Ally and Mrs. Rogers being joined in the tide by Sophie and Mario, whose outlook on life has passed beyond emotional repression and rigid penny-pinching. When he yells, "Geronimo!" the classic Capra happy ending is in full force.

Every performance in *A Hole in the Head* is superb, from Frank's convincing mixture of playboy, unrealistic dreamer and loving father to Dub Taylor's faithful and funny desk clerk. The film is somewhat constricted by its stage origins (as are many adaptations of plays), but these moments are balanced by the fluid camerawork, excellent widescreen compositions and wonderfully timed ensemble acting. Though Frank is the star, he is matched every step of the way by the versatile Robinson, who had been demonstrating his great comic talent since the mid-'30s, in a series of Warner Bros. gangster parodies and John Ford's *The Whole Town's Talking* (1935), in which he created one of the most convincing drunk scenes in cinematic history. Working with his childhood hero was a great learning experience for Frank, whose Tony Manetta again proved that he could play a variety of multifaceted characters. And portraying a struggling and essentially decent common man who is looked down upon by the decadent rich put him in the Capra pantheon with Gary Cooper, James Stewart and Spencer Tracy.

As the worried but sensible Sophie, Thelma Ritter is perfect, her flawless timing effortlessly blended with that of Frank and Edward G. Eleanor Parker is absolute beauty and gentle sophistication as Mrs. Rogers, Carolyn Jones provides a 180-degree contrast to her frigid dog-walker in *The Tender Trap* and, aside from an overplayed weeping scene, Eddie Hodges is touchingly effective as Ally.

Frank recorded two promo radio spots for the film, one featuring "All My Tomorrows," and the other including him singing an excerpt from "High Hopes" and naming all the   principal actors, claiming they all had holes in their heads. Contemporary critics loved the   film. Following a May 14, 1959, preview at United Artists' New York office, *Variety*'s "Gene" wrote:

> Sinatra... works with conviction. Robinson, bewildered by the behavior of his brother and not savvy to the ways of the unconventional Miami, turns in a cleverly funny job in a subdued way.
>
> Hodges, the carrot-topped boy and a newcomer, is an appealing performer, drawing top sympathy as he shows unalterable devotion to his father. Miss Ritter is the understandable aunt all the way. Carolyn Jones is Sinatra's somewhat goofy girlfriend and provides laughs unerringly. ...Capra has given the proceedings sufficient pace to avoid criticism about that 120-minute running time.[29]

When the film was released in July, the critic for *The New York Times* couldn't find enough superlatives to include in his review:

> The picture... is a perfect entertainment... Anyone who remembers [Capra's] great pictures... will find a most gratifying kinship in this sparkling *A Hole in the Head*, which chased a big money-making picture (*Some Like It Hot*) out of Loew's State yesterday. For this is another of those wonderfully colloquial American comedies that has the recklessness, the sentiment, the flavor and the stabbing pathos of what we like to reckon as average American life... Mr. Capra might well have done a single take-out on a lovable fumbler and a cornball sentimentalist. But that isn't his disposition, and it certainly would not be in the line of Mr. Schulman's aggressively incisive and brilliantly dialogued script.
>
> Their fellow, performed by Frank Sinatra, is a faker and a fraud in many ways; he's a chiseler and a cheap conniver. To a Babbitt, he might well seem a bum. But he is, deep down, a decent, wistful fellow, a fugitive

from the order to conform and a pathetically lonely individual who kids no one more thoroughly than himself. ...

As the brother, a narrow-minded dullard, Edward G. Robinson is superb—funny while being most officious and withering while saying the drollest things. Excellent, too, is Thelma Ritter as his compassionate wife, and Eleanor Parker is touchingly responsive as a widow lined up to wed the rollingstone.

As the son, Eddie Hodges is rugged and straightforward, too. Carolyn Jones gives a fine, off-beat performance as a vagrant border who keeps uttering siren calls.

But the prize goes to Mr. Sinatra, who makes the hero of this vibrant color film a soft-hearted, hardboiled, white-souled black sheep whom we will cherish, along with Mr. Deeds and Mr. Smith, as one of the great guys that Mr. Capra has escorted to the American screen.[30]

And *Newsweek* concluded:

Sinatra manages to arouse sympathy without employing sentimentality; Robinson... displays such finesse as a broad-comedy foil... that he almost steals the show from Sinatra. Not quite, of course. No one these days ever completely steals the show from Sinatra.[31]

Not only had Frank benefited from a variety of roles during the past five years, he had worked with some of Hollywood's finest directors: Fred Zinnemann, Stanley Kramer, Otto Preminger, Vincente Minnelli and Frank Capra. Though he maintained his One-Take Charley approach to a great degree, he respected good directors who helped him to develop further his dramatic, comic and cinematic skills.

While *A Hole in the Head* was in post-production, Frank conducted 12 songs for the Capitol album *Sleep Warm*, Dean Martin's "beguiling set of lullabies for moderns." Arranged in the new "full dimensional stereo" format, these intimate collaborations recorded on January 2, 1959, feature Dino at his peak. The title song, waxed by Frank a few months earlier, is Dean's most beautiful ballad, his gentle vibrato enveloped in shimmering strings and celeste.

Frank recorded tracks for his next album, *No One Cares*, on March 24-26, 1959. On May 8, he cut two singles, "High Hopes" and "Love Looks So Well on You," and then returned for additional *No One Cares* takes six days later. The album cover, which won a Grammy, depicts Frank sitting alone with a drink at a nightclub bar and is one of the most blatant visual examples of the essential loneliness that permeates his art. Frank opens the album with a haunting long-breath performance on Cahn and Van Heusen's "When No One Cares," another title song expressly written for him by his favorite tunesmiths. "A Cottage for Sale" offers another ethereal arrangement and vocal, followed by the classic "Stormy Weather," the first of the album's three "rain songs," during which the listener may actually feel the cool precipitation resulting from the combination of Gordon Jenkins' strings and Frank's longing voice. The pleasant humidity continues on "Where Do You Go?" and only briefly bows out during "I Don't Stand a Ghost of a Chance Without You" before again dousing the listener on "Here's That Rainy Day," during which Frank beautifully acts the lyric, achieving true vocal chilliness when phrasing "cold rainy day" as "*coooolllld* rainy day." "I Can't Get Started," "Why Try to Change Me Now?" which he previously had cut just before leaving Columbia in 1952, and "Just Friends" are followed by a "lonely" version of "I'll Never Smile Again," the Tchaikovsky-inspired "None But the Lonely Heart," during which Frank adds a classic crescendo on the last line, descending down into his lower register, and "The One I Love (Belongs to Somebody Else)," the only song on the album with a distinct light-swing tempo.

More than a decade had passed since Frank and Sammy Davis, Jr., had become good friends. By the late '50s, Davis was a full member of his "inner circle" and the "Rat Pack," the leadership of which was taken over by Frank after Bogie's untimely death. Now the group, which Frank preferred to call "The Summit," not only included some of the old members, but primarily Dean Martin, Davis, Peter Lawford, comedian Joey Bishop and "mascot" Shirley MacLaine, who was a "dame" they treated like one of the boys. Rather than carrying on the "nonconformist" format of Bogart's days, they got together simply to have fun, devise comedy material and drink (not that Bogie's leadership advocated teetotalism, by any means), sometimes bringing this potent combination to the stages of Las Vegas.

Davis revealed:

> I was the only black person that traveled in that sort of circle. Frank and I would talk about prejudiced people, and he'd say, "Aah, they're full of shit! Pay no attention to it." I can handle it all because of that learning experience, early in my life, with Frank. He forced me to learn. I was doing a gig at this nightclub in L.A., Ciro's. And Frank would bring all the heavyweights to see me. And then he started taking me around, introducing me to Gary Cooper, Judy Garland — all those people. I wanted to be like him so bad.[32]

Now using the name Canterbury Productions, Frank made another movie deal, this time with MGM, to distribute *Never So Few*, a World War II tale set in the Pacific, in which he would costar with Peter Lawford and Davis, who was offered a tailor-made role that would add a racial theme. Shooting was to begin in July 1959, but before the company left Hollywood for location work in the Phillipines, Davis had been replaced by up-and-coming Steve McQueen. Several speculative reasons have been given for his removal from the cast, including one suggesting that Davis' mild criticism of Frank during a Chicago radio interview enraged his "boss," but none were proved conclusively. In his autobiographical book *Hollywood in a Suitcase*, Sammy wrote:

> Frank and I did fall out over... *Never So Few*. Our fight was about how my part should be played, and we had entirely different concepts of it. As usual, Frank was in charge of everything that went on and definitely had the last say. We both realized that neither of us was going to change his opinion, so Frank pulled me out of the deal and put in Steve McQueen.[33]

Frank got along well with McQueen. At one point he told director John Sturges to "give the kid close-ups."[34] For his love interest, Frank had chosen Gina Lollobrigida; and when MGM had balked at paying the $75,000 Peter Lawford asked for, Frank made certain he got it. Davis, too, was to earn $75,000 but, in the end, MGM got McQueen for a mere $20,000.

Some of the location shooting was unpleasant. Once, a gun exploded too close to Frank's face, scorching the cornea of his left eye. Temporarily blinded, he was led off the set by Lawford and examined by a doctor, who said he was lucky not to have lost one of those baby blues.

Never So Few opens with a prologue in which Sir Winston Churchill's famous wartime words are paraphrased. As soldiers run onto a beach to collect supplies parachuted from an American cargo plane, Captain Tom C. Reynolds rushes into the action (providing Frank with another unique cinematic introduction). The reworked racial element occurs almost instantly, when Sergeant John Danforth (Charles Bronson), a Navaho, objects to another soldier's reference to him as "Hiawatha," yet in turn calls the Kachins, whom the Allies are protecting from the Japanese, "gooks." Danforth steps in and denounces the bigotry. (Here Frank's own concerns about civil rights lend his characterization great believability.)

This social component also is briefly included in the subsequent warfare scene in the Burmese jungle, where Japanese troops savagely attack the Kachins and their Allied supporters. Frank's favorite cinematographer, William Daniels, again was on hand to create the stunning widescreen

compositions, some of which depict the enemy's point-of-view. After the Japanese are fought off, Reynolds chooses to honor the request of a trusted Kachin aide who now lies dying from a severe belly wound. Against the objections of his Caucasian comrades, who call him a murderer, the Captain relieves the poor man's misery with a single pistol shot.

Having earned a pass out of his months in the jungle, Reynolds and his English counterpart, Captain Danny De Mortimer (Richard Johnson), fly to Calcutta for a little drinking and carousing. As the American standard "Easy to Love" plays in the background, they enjoy cocktails in a posh club, where Danny demonstrates how he can hold in his monocle while being dealt a brutal blow to the head by Tom. After they fall to the floor, the shapely legs of Carla Vesari (Lollobrigida) enter the shot and, as they look up, the camera tilts to show her gorgeous chassis accompanied by the domineering presence of Nikko Regas (Paul Henreid). Though she has draped a scarf over her chest, she pulls it off after sitting down, giving Tom a good look at her ample cleavage. (In medium close-up, Frank's peepers register great interest in this visual delight.)

Tom and Danny are offered a two-week leave, which they accept after being granted their request for Bill Ringa (McQueen) as their driver. Prone to piloting his jeep like a maniac, fighting both with MPs and Indian officers, and distilling his own rotgut gin that he peddles to the natives, Ringa easily fits into their devil-may-care lifestyle. Unfortunately, the tension developed in the film's early scenes disappears at this point, and the intensity of warfare is replaced with unrealistic romance. However, the stunning Ceylon location work compensates to some extent (and Tom's referral to the "Road to Mandalay" creates a pleasant Sinatra in-joke).

Further character development does occur at the home of Regas, where Tom devotedly cares for Danny, who has been stricken with malaria (conveniently ending his own romantic plans while giving his friend full reign). Here Lollobrigida offers a sexy bathtub scene, as Carla begins to break down her earlier resistance to Tom's advances. Frank may have insisted on doing only one take in this scene, since the word "damn" is simply dubbed out of his phrase "you damn well know it," obviously not the line that appeared in the script.

After declaring his head-over-heels love, Tom returns to the jungle, where his comrades are celebrating Christmas. In a physical representation of Tom's emotions (and of Frank's characters in earlier films), he has a real monkey on his back as he talks to Sergeant Danforth about a

Japanese woman they have captured. Just as Tom decides to let her go, the camp is besieged by a surprise attack and, during a powerful scene, he is wounded and airlifted to the base hospital.

While recuperating, Tom again witnesses racist attitudes that are adversely affecting the operations of the Allied-Kachin forces. After speaking with the Kachins (one of whom is played by a young George Takei) about the unsuitable food they have been served, he leads them in protest to the colonel, who agrees to make their diet more culturally appropriate (replacing such American staples as cornbread with rice, peppers and monkey brains).

Tom recovers and is assigned to lead an attack on a Japanese ammo dump and airstrip at Ubachi. When Carla visits him, he, knowing that the mission is a suicidal one, tells her that their relationship won't work. The remainder of the film shifts back into the tense and dramatic mood of the opening scenes and the Christmas attack, leaving the intrusive romantic shenanigans behind. The nighttime scene at Ubachi, where Tom, Danny, Danforth, Ringa and the rest of the men use scores of large gasoline cans to torch the dump and airstrip, is a tremendous battle scene depicting both the valor and futility of war.

Tom, discovering that some renegade Chinese have killed U.S. and British troops in order to loot their weapons and supplies, leads his drastically reduced force on a harrowing mission to fight them in their own camp. When he discovers a warrant from the Chungking warlord that authorized the vultures to prey upon the Allies and then sell the stolen supplies to the Japanese, he requests but is denied a go-ahead from his superiors to move farther. Ignoring the political implications of his plan, Tom asks, "What's the use of fighting a war if you don't do what's right?" After Danny is killed by a Chinese soldier they presumed dead, Tom orders that all the prisoners be executed and sends a message back to his commanding officer: "Go to Hell."

Still refusing to play the political game, the stubborn Tom faces a court-martial, but after proving the existence of the Chungking warrant, receives the support of General Sloan (Brian Donlevy), who has been inundated by Nautaung (Philip Ahn), a Chinese diplomat, for an official apology. Instead, Tom tells him, "You go to Hell." Having run his subordinate over the coals, Sloan then produces a note written by Chiang Kai-Shek, fully exonerating Captain Tom C. Reynolds for the offense. All is well and the two lovers face the future together.

Never So Few is, in many ways, a remake of *Kings Go Forth*, a film comprised of two nearly unrelated plots. In both films, Frank plays a protagonist who, on the one hand, may die at any moment in the heat of battle, yet can safely travel out of the war zone to drink and fall in love with gorgeous women. Both films also contain a subplot dealing with racial prejudice, although this aspect is not as developed in *Never So Few*. Curiously, though Carla Vesari actually visits Tom at the military hospital, Monique Blair never crosses the line between her civilian environment and the war zone in which Sam Loggins operates (when he isn't away on a pass, that is), yet the latter develops a more believable relationship with her soldier boy. While the statuesque Gina Lollobrigida is stilted and unconvincing—never once making her character appear to be in love—Natalie Wood, not only a great beauty but also a fine actress, demonstrates some real emotion while paired with Sam, even though she does not love him.

Never So Few's war scenes are infinitely more impressive and powerful, thus more suspenseful and emotionally effective, than their counterparts in *Kings Go Forth*. Although the film places the viewer on the side of the Kachin-U.S.-British alliance, it does not unfold its story in black-and-white terms: Even in their brevity, the subjective point-of-view shots from the Japanese perspective show that the enemy are actually human soldiers and not monsters; and Tom's struggles with various moral dilemmas—bigotry, euthanasia, mixing personal comfort with professional duty, the severe treatment of enemy prisoners and disobeying an order one believes is wrong—are the most interesting aspects. The love interest in *Never So Few* is no better than its predecessor in *The Pride and the Passion*, and both films would be better if this subplot was included only briefly, to add emotional depth to Frank's character. In the jungle and on the battlefield, *Never So Few* is an effective film, though it bogs down when featuring elegant cocktail parties and stilted buxom beauties. In 1959, not only war stories sold tickets; so did exotic European dames. But even Gina's physical attractions couldn't save this film, as it fairly died at the box office.

Chapter 8
The Summit, the Cold War
and Frank in Command

I am very happy to have been asked to appear briefly tonight in aid of this most important charity. And I'm particularly proud to have the opportunity of introducing to you a man who, in my opinion, is one of the great artists of our time. As an actor, his taste is impeccable—and in all the varied and different parts I've seen him play, I've never yet known him to strike a false note. As a singer of songs, we all know he has brought happiness to millions of people all over the world—not only because of his light, charming voice an his incomparable technique, but because when he sings, he sings from the heart.

— Noel Coward, United Nations Fund for Children, 14 June 1958

The filming of Frank's next film, *Can-Can*, took place at 20th Century-Fox during late August and September 1959. After the studio purchased the screen rights to Abe Burrows' Broadway smash, which had run for two years and 894 performances, Executive Head of Production Buddy Adler, who had worked with Frank on *From Here to Eternity* at Columbia, chose Jack Cummings as producer.

When Cummings offered Frank the role, he replied enthusiastically, agreeing to back the project with one of his own companies, Suffolk Productions. By the time director Walter Lang wrapped, *Can-Can*, budgeted at $6 million with a 71-day shooting schedule, had become the most elaborate film Fox had produced. Cole Porter's score, arranged and conducted by Nelson Riddle, also was a major drawing card.

Cast as Parisian lawyer Francois Durnais, Frank was supported by Maurice Chevalier, Louis Jourdan and Shirley MacLaine as Simone Pistache, a cabaret owner attempting to fight local authorities who regularly shut down the "lascivious" dance known as the Can-Can. Frank had asked Cummings to hire MacLaine, whose work on five other films had to be rescheduled before she could commit to the role. Prior to Lang's first day behind the camera, the actress, supported by Juliet Prowse and several other dancers, had to rehearse for six weeks with celebrated choreographer Hermes Pan.

About as French as "french fries" or "french toast," *Can-Can* unconvincingly places Frank and Shirley in 1890s Paris, and the presence of Chevalier and Jourdan merely makes their American traits stand out even stronger. Perhaps the fact that Charles Lederer, who penned the screenplay with Dorothy Kingsley, rewrote during production added to the confusion. Though Frank originally planned to attempt a French accent, MacLaine advised against it, noting the difficulty he had experienced playing a Spaniard in *The Pride and the Passion*. Her strong-willed nature began to show itself even more during this shoot, as she strived to get the best of One-Take Charley. Jack Cummings said:

> Mr. Sinatra thinks that he can only shoot a scene his way—and without what most people would consider an adequate amount of rehearsal. She let him know that that wasn't good enough. He had to rehearse. And as for only working from noon 'till the evening, she told him not to be an S.O.B.[1]

Frank also asked that new lyrics be written for "Let's Do It (Let's Fall in Love)," but Porter protested, eventually telling Saul Chaplin, who served as associate producer, to write them himself.

Sinatra and Shirley MacLaine in *Can Can*

After Chaplin brought in Ira Gershwin to do a rewrite, Frank rejected the lyrics and had his pal
Sammy Cahn provide the final version used in the film.

One day, when Frank failed to report to the set, Chaplin, flanked by cast and crew members,
turned on a television set to catch some of the 1959 World Series (in which the L.A. Dodgers
were playing for the first time) and spotted One-Take Charley in the stands. The following day,
Frank arrived with his agent, who claimed, "Mr. Sinatra didn't like the scene you thought he was
going to shoot yesterday."[2] After asking for another scene to be rewritten, Frank still avoided
performing the new material. Chaplin recalled, "He made up his own lines—and they worked
just as well."[3]

On August 27, Frank began recording the soundtrack album for the film, cutting "It's All
Right with Me," which Ed O'Brien called "probably the most intimate singing Sinatra has ever
done,"[4] and "C'est Magnifique." "Montmart" was completed the following week, while additional sessions, for "Let's Do It" and "I Love Paris," were scheduled for September 22 and
October 13, respectively. Though Chevalier joined Frank for the latter number, it eventually
was dropped from the film.

On September 19, 20th Century-Fox president Spyros P. Skouras welcomed special guests
Mr. and Mrs. Nikita Kruschev to the studio, where a luncheon and four hours of discussion and
entertainment were held as a goodwill gesture toward the Soviet Premier. While eating, Nina
Kruschev spoke through an interpreter with Frank, Bob Hope and David Niven. To conclude the
festivities, the Kruschevs were escorted to the *Can-Can* soundstage, where a scene was performed
and filmed especially for them. Frank served as master of ceremonies and his comments were
translated for the Premier and his party, who sat in a private box above the stage.

Announcing the opening number by Chevalier and Jourdan—"Live and Let Live"—Frank
explained that the movie is "about a lot of pretty girls and the fellows who like pretty girls."

Kruschev smiled and applauded enthusiastically as the song began. Next, Frank introduced the Can-Can piece: "Later in this picture, we go into a saloon. A saloon is a place where you go to drink." Now the Premier laughed as Frank performed Porter's "C'est Magnifique" and MacLaine, in broken Russian, thanked him for sending so many great artists to the United States. Finally, 16 dancing girls, all of whom Frank called his "nieces," took to the floor. Led by MacLaine and Juliet Prowse, they performed the dance Kruschev later called "immoral" and indicative of decadent Western society. (Ten days later, on the September 29 *Bing Crosby Show*, Frank was more in his element, guesting with fellow master swingers Peggy Lee and Louis Armstrong.)

To keep Frank on the charts, Capitol released another compilation album, *Look to Your Heart,* which features three songs from the 1955 NBC television production of *Our Town* and eight singles cut between 1953 and 1955. The highlights of this release include "Same Old Saturday Night" and "Not as a Stranger," the sole film-oriented number.

Can-Can reflects Hollywood in March 1960 as much as "Monmarte 1896." Though the film opens with a dynamic street scene in which Frank sings with Chevalier (as corrupt court magistrate Paul Berriere), the tone shifts to a swinging Vegas style during the subsequent number set in Simone's nightclub. MacLaine's introduction is a highlight as she enters the Todd-AO frame by draping her left leg across the table where Durnais and Berriere are sitting, but these brief moments of sensuality become lost amidst an unconvincing and overlong battle between those seeking "artistic freedom" (bribers of the police), those pretending to uphold an archaic 1790 law declaring the dance "lewd and lascivious" (the police who accept graft) and those who actually attempt to enforce the law (represented by Louis Jourdan's Phillipe Forestier). (Curiously, the innocuous Can-Can is considered immoral, but the misogynistic, abusively violent Apache dance is totally acceptable.) The romantic triangle between Simone, Francois and Phillipe also is awkward: No chemistry exists between the miscast Frank and Shirley; and poor Jourdan, though giving an entertaining performance, is left without real support whenever Chevalier disappears.

Frank occasionally demonstrates his comic expertise, as when he sings "C'est Magnifique" to a bevy of young beauties he has successfully defended in court, but his Stan Laurel-like performance is belied when he simply allows Durnais to slip into a parody of *Pal Joey*, adding "Ring-a-ding-ding-*ding*" to the lyrics. (Sinatra-speak can be fun, but here it is inappropriate; however, it becomes even more ridiculous when Jourdan reprises this shtick later in the film!) Frank does have some good dialogue: At one point, Durnais calls himself "a lousy lawyer and unreliable lover," and later tells Simone that he considered solving his romantic predicament (he has an aversion to marriage) through "murder, suicide, chronic alcoholism—but none of those things satisfy me."

There are some effective musical set pieces, including the silly yet sensual "Adam and Eve" ballet that has nothing to do with 1890s Paris nor could be staged within the walls of Simone's club. (Though it does not soar to the fantastical heights of 1930s Busby Berkeley or 1950s Gene Kelly.) The musical high point of Frank's performance occurs during a scene in which he sings the ballad "It's All Right with Me" to Juliet Prowse, with whom he began a serious relationship during the production. On the rebound after Simone tells him that she plans to marry Phillipe, Durnais pours his heart out to the leggy Claudine (allowing Frank to play a cinematic scene with one of his real-life lovers).

Variety's "Holl" faulted the film for its jarring juxtaposition of "authentic Parisians" and actors not even pretending to be such, noting, "Even if you accept *Can-Can* as a tongue-in-cheek offering, the basic premise is still hard to swallow."[5] Not surprisingly, Bosley Crowther had a field day flaying the film, referring to MacLaine as "foot-heavy... groping and galloping" and crediting Prowse with providing the real terpsichorean talent:

> It is not only in the dancing that this effort is dismally remiss. The story is also a downright foolish pastiche, cut to Frank Sinatra and Miss MacLaine,

Sinatra, Shirley MacLaine and Maurice Chevalier in *Can Can*

who look about as logical in Paris of the 1890s as they would look on the Russian hockey team.

He... and she... behave, under Walter Lang's direction, as if they were companions in a Hoboken bar, slightly intoxicated and garrulous with gags...[6]

Unfortunately, even worse than the awkward Sinatra scenes is a sequence in which Chevalier performs a stiff French cabaret version of Porter's "Just One of Those Things," a song not written for *Can-Can* and definitively performed by Frank on *Songs for Young Lovers* and in *Young at Heart*.

Not taking the film seriously, Frank walked through *Can-Can* playing himself. For his next film, however, he had a blast portraying Frank Sinatra, an approach perfectly suited to the material, which was not intended to be taken too seriously by anyone. Prior to the making of *Never So Few*, Frank and Peter Lawford had planned to work together on another film, to be based on a fascinating story the latter had heard from Gilbert Kay, a Hollywood assistant director, in 1955. Lawford explained:

> He had acquired it from a gas station attendant, who was one of 25 men to dismantle some valuable radio equipment in Germany during the war and carry it piece by piece out of the country. We thought the idea could be applied to a fictional story for a movie [about a group of war veterans who] rob six gambling casinos simultaneously in Las Vegas on New Year's Eve when the lights go out.[7]

However, when Lawford couldn't promise Kay the director's chair, the idea was tossed around tinsel town for the next four years. Unsuccessful, Kay returned to Lawford, who, with his wife, Pat, purchased the story outright for $10,000.

After Lawford pitched *Ocean's Eleven* to his friend, Frank chose the lead role of Danny Ocean and envisioned members of the Summit, both major and minor, in all the supporting parts. Still under contract to Warner Bros. for one picture, Frank hired Harry Brown and Charles Lederer to write the screenplay. After reading it, Jack Warner reportedly replied, "Let's not make the movie. Let's pull the job," but bought it for $50,000.

The Lawfords were reimbursed their $10,000 and Peter's agent, Milt Ebbins, began to negotiate for one third of the film's profits and a prominent role for his client. Neither Warners nor Frank's agent, Burt Allenberg, were obligated to give Lawford anything, but, by this time, Frank was running the show. Lawford's original request was cut in half—to one sixth of the profits—though he also was guaranteed a $50,000 salary for acting in the film. Peter suggested the director, as well: Lewis Milestone, famed for his powerful adaptations of Erich Maria Remarque's *All Quiet on the Western Front* (1930) and John Steinbeck's *Of Mice and Men* (1939). Now, decades later—having been victimized by the HUAC blacklist—he took what he could get and helmed a project having absolutely *nothing* in common with his earlier classics. In fact, his patience during the January 26-February 16, 1960, location shoot proved miraculous as he somehow tolerated the casual and impromptu antics of Frank and his cronies: Dean, Sammy, Peter, Joey Bishop, Henry Silva, Richard Conte, Shirley MacLaine, Cesar Romero and Angie Dickinson, who revealed, "It wasn't that it wasn't professional, but you'd have to look hard to find a camera to prove to you that they weren't playing. They really had fun together. The director was very easy. He knew exactly who was signing his check."[8]

The man "signing the check," according to Sammy, "was very easy to work with":

> He was always at the helm, and we kept it that way. He made the actual filming as painless as possible because he got bored easily and couldn't bear hanging around the set. When we worked together, there was a feeling of camaraderie, and we seemed to move as one force. We managed to carry that onto the screen. None of us... had ego problems with the others.[9]

Lawford, however, recalled that One-Take Charley occasionally got out of hand:

> [H]e would tear handfuls of pages out of the script and allow the director only one take of a scene, unless there was a technical difficulty of some kind. I remember once the sound man kept complaining about an unusual number of low flying airplanes, which he was picking up through his earphones, and which were constantly being heard on the track. Well, after the fourth take, which was unheard of for Frank, he said, "Aw, fuck it! Everyone knows they're airplanes." Indeed! But flying through a bathroom? Which was where the sequence was being shot.[10]

Having given powerfully intense yet eminently controlled interpretations of complex characters in a string of serious films, Frank now wanted to cash in on Lawford's idea and produce

something lighthearted. According to Sammy, Frank admitted, "We're not setting out to make *Hamlet* or *Gone With the Wind*. The idea is to hang out together, find fun with the broads and have a great time. We gotta make pictures that people enjoy seeing. Entertainment period. We gotta have laughs."[11]

But Milestone found little amusement. Least of all, he had to make sure the $2,800,000 budget wasn't being tossed around too cavalierly. Frank often went over the director's head, suggesting new lines for his pals or creating new bits in order to work another friend into the script. "When he wasn't actually acting himself," Milestone recalled, "he would say, 'Get him to do this' or 'Make sure he does that.' Ask me which was my least favorite film that I ever made and it has to be *Ocean's Eleven*."[12]

Each night, some or all of the five major Summit members would perform in the Sands Copa Room to 1,200 people who couldn't get enough of their irreverent, sarcastic and self-deprecating humor, as well as Frank, Dean and Sammy's "altered" versions of great standards such as "When You're Smilin'" and "The Lady is a Tramp." Following two evening performances, Dean, Sammy and Peter would be induced to stay up until the wee hours to party with Frank. At 5 a.m., they finally would collapse in their respective rooms before reporting to Milestone's set at about noon. "They were taking bets we'd all end up in a box," Lawford recalled.[13] Only Joey Bishop was spared the all-night carousing: Though some of the stage show was improvised, the quick-witted comedian spent many a night writing material for the gang. Bishop said:

> Originally we were supposed to draw straws. The one with the shorter straw was supposed to perform that night. I drew it, prearranged, the first night, but the guys jumped up on stage and that's when we started to have so

much fun. But the people were under the impression that there was going to only be one each night.[14]

However, the Vegas night sequences actually had to be shot during the wee hours of the morning, from about 2:15 to 6:00 a.m., utilizing two camera crews to complete as many scenes as possible. On these days, the Summit schedule had to be altered a bit.

While Frank tended to all of the business arrangements and details, the others just lived it up. "He always had a brilliant business mind and an excellent set of advisers," Sammy wrote. "When he showed me the contract, I saw my salary was to be $100,000, which was then extremely good money, unless you were a leading star. In 1960 I needed it."[15]

Frank not only provided Sammy with a role and salary, but also taught him basic acting and cinematic techniques:

> Frank humored me when I tried to learn how certain scenes should be played. He had an instinct about how some things would look on the screen. In fact, he was very much an instinctive actor in every sense of the word. That's why he became known as One-Take Charley. Frank figured he had to play it straight off the cuff. ...He also gave me practical advice about camera angles: how to keep in range even when the camera is concentrating on someone else, perspective, catching the light, and framing a shot. I had picked up something from my visits to film sets, but Frank was the only one who had ever bothered to take me to one side and give me the benefit of his experience.[16]

One of the difficulties Sammy experienced while making *Ocean's Eleven* was worrying about what to do with his hands. The chain smoker suggested that a cigarette would keep them occupied, but Frank said the prop would cause more problems.

"Okay, *Mr. Sinatra*," Sam fired back. "How would you do it?"

"Simple," Frank replied as he lit a king-size, acted Sammy's part and then put out the smoke. "You can't take one of these from shot to shot unless you're Bob Mitchum."

Angie Dickinson recalled her One-Take Charley experience:

> Frank was notorious for not wanting to do a scene again. I've never known a man who knew exactly what was right for him at almost all times. He was so levelheaded. And so when he felt he had a scene right, he didn't have to

question it. And we got to the end of this scene, and he gets up to go and he went out... kept right on going—didn't wait for "Okay, that's good" or "Let's try it again." ...And I said, "Frank! Maybe I wasn't very good. We need another one." He was beyond earshot. He was gone.[17]

Creating Las Vegas' most successful draw of the season, Frank and Dean, both Sands investors, each received $75,000-$100,000 per week, while the other three Summiteers grabbed about $25,000 apiece. Though Lawford often had little to do while on stage, his status as John F. Kennedy's brother-in-law guaranteed his continued participation. Having announced his candidacy for president in January 1960, Senator Kennedy attended one of the shows on February 7. After Frank introduced young Jack to the audience, Dean called the senator "one of my best buddies," then turned to his colleague and asked, "What the hell is his name?"

On the evening before the Vegas filming was wrapped, Frank hosted a *Timex* television show during which he interviewed his old friend Eleanor Roosevelt. The performers included Lena Horne and new squeeze Juliet Prowse, who had appeared on another episode of the show, with Ella Fitzgerald, Nat Cole and Peter Lawford, the previous month.

Frank returned to Capitol on March 1-3 to record tracks for his next major album tentatively titled "The Nearness of You," a collection of popular ballads that he had previously waxed during his days at Columbia. Now he wanted to create definitive interpretations of some of his favorites, using Nelson Riddle and—in the words of Pete Welding—"the vastly increased, poised command of technical and expressive means he had arrived at in the decade-and-a-half that had elapsed since he first recorded [them]."[18]

The *Ocean's Eleven* shoot was completed in Hollywood on March 23, 1960. While still in its post-production phase, colorful publicity insured a box office success. Sammy, a classic film aficionado, explained:

> It was not unlike what was done years ago when Hollywood teamed stars like Katherine Hepburn and Spencer Tracy, Walter Pidgeon and Greer Garson, William Powell and Myrna Loy, Cagney and Raft; and although each had been tremendous on their own, when they came together in a picture it virtually exploded at the box office. In the last 10 or 15 years the studios had stopped doing it, but now Frank's idea had so captured the public's imagination that movie theaters all over the world were ordering a picture that wasn't even finished. Recognizing the potential in our combination he formulated what he called "The Five Year Plan": Assuming things continued as it seemed they would, we'd make five pictures together, one a year.[19]

During the filming, Frank, Sammy, Peter Lawford, Joey Bishop, Richard Conte and Cesar Romero contributed cameos to Columbia's *Pepe* (1960), directed by *Pal Joey*-veteran George Sidney and starring the Mexican comic Cantinflas, Dan Dailey and Shirley Jones. While the Summit contributions were shot at the Sands (where Jack Entratter also appeared in a scene), additional bits include Bing Crosby, Jimmy Durante, Greer Garson, Ernie Kovacs, Jack Lemmon, Kim Novak, Donna Reed, Debbie Reynolds, Edward G. Robinson and many others. This 195-minute extravaganza about an alcoholic film director (Dailey) who is saved from ruin by the intercession of Pepe, a Mexican stallion groomer who is brought to tinsel town along with his equine charge, was considered uneven and overlong by the major critics.

On April 13, Frank bumped "The Nearness of You" from his new album in favor of a new, lightly swinging song by Lew Spence and Marilyn and Alan Bergman, re-titling the release *Nice 'n' Easy*. At Capitol that day, he also cut three singles, "River Stay 'Way from My Door," "I Love Paris" and "It's Over, It's Over, It's Over."

Nice 'n' Easy opens with the title track, providing a finger-snapping introduction to one of his finest albums. Beginning with muted brass, "Nice 'n' Easy" builds in intensity to a kicking swing section with Frank turning up the heat as he sings, "W*eee*'re on the road to romance. That's safe to say. But let's make all the stops [finger snap] along the way." Continuing to play his percussive digits, he leads the orchestra back into a relaxed groove and concludes the song with one last snap.

The remainder of the 12-song album is a nonstop ballad masterpiece performed by a consummate actor. Plas Johnson's sexy tenor sax introduces "That Old Feeling," and is matched by Frank's flawless vocal. He enhances his long-breath, fluid phrasing by dipping into his lower register, and then descends to one of the most impressive low notes of his career on Irving Berlin's sublime "How Deep Is the Ocean," here given its definitive reading by Frank: Descending down an octave on "*How deep…*," his timbre is echoed by George Roberts' bass trombone solo; in true Sinatra style, he doesn't repeat the low note the last time around, soaring to an emotive climax.

The Gershwins' "I've Got a Crush on You" follows: the sensual, long-breath "Could you c*oooo—oo—*Could you care?" impeccably offset by his staccato pull-off on the final word of the phrase, "The world will pardon my mu*sh*" on this brief yet perfect 2:13 performance. The ultra-romantic "You Go to My Head," featuring yet another masterful phrase—"You intoxicate my s*oooooooooo*le—With your eyes"—leads to a lightsome arrangement of Johnny Mercer and Rube Bloom's "Fools Rush In" and a slightly grooving version of the sexy, bluesy love song "Nevertheless," featuring an ethereal trumpet solo by Carroll Lewis. Frank's fourth recorded version of "She's Funny That Way" also includes a superb Lewis solo and another octave descent, on "But why should I leave her and *why should I go…*" Felix Slatkin contributes a lovely violin solo on "Try a Little Tenderness," and "Embraceable You" provides another incomparable Gershwin interpretation before the violinist returns on "Mam'selle," the beautiful ballad written for *The Razor's Edge* (1946) by director Edmund Goulding and lyricist Mack Gordon. As Nelson Riddle's slumberous strings fade in, the album then concludes with Johnny Mercer's "Dream."

With *Nice 'n' Easy*, Frank created a ballad album graced by an upbeat outlook, the first in this genre devoid of the "suicide" trappings of his previous saloon-song efforts. Back on the cinematic front, *Ocean's Eleven* premiered at Las Vegas' Freemont Theater on August 3, 1960, and one week later at the New York Capitol, where ticket sales broke records set by *From Here to Eternity* seven years earlier. Cahn and Van Heusen again provided the songs and, arranged by Riddle, they drew in audiences as soon as the titles began, the melody of "E-O-Eleven" being varied for each performer as his or her name appeared on the screen.

Danny Ocean (Sinatra) cases The Sands casino in *Ocean's 11*.

The film opens in Las Vegas as "Mushy" O'Conners (Joey Bishop), providing a bit of expla-
nation in a voice-over, meets with Spyros Acebos (Akim Tamiroff), the frustrated, neurotic boss
behind the proposed caper. Here the scene crosscuts between these two characters and Jimmy
Foster (Peter Lawford) and Ocean in their San Francisco hotel room, contrasting the mounting
impatience and anger of Acebos and the relaxed, devil-may-care attitude of the former members
of the 82nd Airborne Division. (The shirtless Foster receives a massage from a leggy beauty
while Ocean, wearing an orange mohair sweater, enjoys a large cocktail.)

Another former 82nd man, Roger Carneal (Henry Silva), then enters a San Francisco shop,
asking the owner (George E. Stone) about the status of former comrade Tony Bergdorf (Richard
Conte), who, unfortunately, is "in San Quentin... doing one to five." Carneal then runs into Mrs.
Bergdorf (Jean Willes), who is divorcing her husband and has sent their son to a military school.
However, she also reveals that, as luck would have it, Tony will be released from prison the fol-

lowing morning. This initial sequence, crosscutting between various parties with no establishing narration, adds both realism and a bizarre atmosphere of haziness to the plot, which doesn't jell until the 11 former soldiers group together to receive their "orders." Prior to heading to Vegas, Ocean and Foster have trouble recruiting Vincent Massier (Buddy Lester), who finally gives in after he is fired from a club where he and "Honeyface," his "dancer" wife, had been working. (An instrumental version of "The Tender Trap" is used as Honeyface's stage number.)

When Sam Harmon (Dean Martin) is met in Vegas by "Curly" Steffens (Richard Benedict), he doesn't recognize his old buddy until seeing his severely balding head; but Carneal has a much rougher time with the freshly sprung Bergdorf, who turns down the offer to join the heist. Only after visiting a doctor who confirms that he soon will enter "the Big Casino" does he throw in with them (to score enough dough to send his son through college). (While examining an X-ray that indicates Bergdorf's heart disease, the "doc" doesn't realize it's upside down!)

The following scene opens at a Vegas dump ground where a group of trash haulers have congregated beside their trucks. (One of Warners' greatest pre-production hurdles had been convincing Clark County Disposal to let them use an official vehicle. Then wood blocks had to be affixed to the foot pedals so Sammy could drive it!) Accompanied by a harmonica-playing pal, Josh Howard (Sammy) croons into a superb blues version of "E-O-Eleven," with Riddle's rhythm section kicking in as the sultry vocal crescendos in vintage Sammy style. (His cohorts in the sequence were all top Vegas musicians.) Arguably giving the film's best performance, Sammy is able briefly to mention the racist attitudes that have kept Josh from achieving success in his chosen field. (This content also indirectly addresses the double standard followed by Vegas casinos that welcomed black artists but refused to accept them as patrons. Fortunately, Frank was able to make Sammy and other blacks who worked with him exceptions to the rule.)

"A one-eyed third baseman in Mobile?" Josh rhetorically asks Vince Massier, demonstrating a friendship unaffected by race. "Trash is where you find it," he adds. While *Ocean's Eleven* may be a lighthearted caper comedy, there also are moments that illustrate Frank's more serious concerns.

The next musical offering is served up by Dino, crooning his way through a bit of "Ain't That a Kick in the Head?" while playing the piano in his hotel room. Several chambermaids are enthralled by Sam's spell, but after they depart, Danny's wife, Beatrice (Angie Dickinson), arrives. Sam asks Bea about the state of the Ocean marriage; and after revealing that she favors stability over "a floating crap game" and Danny's "love of danger," she is whisked off to the closed restaurant at the top of the hotel, where her husband asks, "What's wrong with a little hey-hey?" A subsequent scene involving Jimmy on the phone, schmoozing his mother for money, establishes his persona as an Oedipal idler who is tired of her numerous trips to the altar, this time to marry smalltime operator Duke Santos (Cesar Romero). During Jimmy's conversation, Sam attempts to distract him (with Dean performing some subtle physical comedy). Soon, Adele Ekstrom (Patrice Wymore), a broad Danny picked up at the Biltmore Bar, arrives to browbeat him about his wife's visit. Reminding her that he promised nothing, he throws her out.

Now, halfway through the film, the characters finally are developed and the pace picks up with the caper getting under way. As the 82nd Airborne reunion begins, Danny, Sam, Josh and Jimmy voice their opinions on various subjects. (Here the four main Summiteers, improvising on the script, create a cinematic vignette resembling their stage performances.)

Offering a bold Lawford in-joke, Jimmy admits, "I think I'll buy me some votes and go into politics."

Sam calls him "our latest senator" (referring to Jack Kennedy), while Danny suggests that he become an ambassador (a reference to Joseph P. Kennedy). Then Sam expresses his desire to repeal the 14th and 20th amendments and "turn women into slaves."

"Yes, and stamp out mental health," Jimmy adds.

As Danny describes the operation to the men, William Daniels' widescreen camera captures all 11 as they stand over the table. Ocean informs them that they will use their war experience to engineer and execute the simultaneous robberies of the Sahara, Riviera, Desert Inn, Sands and Flamingo casinos.

Though the 82nd Airborne would not have included a black soldier among its ranks during World War II, Danny appoints Josh as the caper's "main cog," the man who will be entrusted to get the stolen millions out of town. Then the skeptical Sam, the only one to voice dissent, asks, "What about you, Josh? You got brains." (Here the film again focuses on the abilities of the African-American character.) Realizing that Josh approves of it, Sam adds, "When do we blow this mausoleum?"

"Coo-coo," Josh replies.

At the Sands, where Danny Thomas and Red Skelton are sharing the bill, Ocean cases the joint, only to see a casino cashier refuse to cash a check for Skelton, who is escorted out by two security guards. At the Desert Inn, "Learnin' the Blues" is playing in the background, while at the Sahara, Sam performs "Ain't That a Kick in the Head" with the Red Norvo quintet (marking the vibraphonist's third collaboration with Frank).

"Red—ain't that a kick?" Sam sings at one point. (This is one of the best that Dean Martin ever performed; on May 10, 1960, he recorded a single release with Riddle's orchestra.)

Contrary to Frank's advice, Sammy does smoke in the subsequent bowling alley scene, when Josh confers with all his pals about the status of the "mission." Afterward, the heist begins, and the intercutting of the five casinos' respective New Years' Eve shows provides very entertaining viewing. But at the Sahara, the timing of the caper is almost thrown off when a drunken redhead (Shirley MacLaine, in an unbilled, ad-libbed cameo) accosts Sam. When she asks him if he is Ricky Nelson (Dean's costar in *Rio Bravo* [1959]), he replies, "I used to be Ricky Nelson. I'm Perry Como now."

Making an ironic gesture, Jimmy, just as "Auld Lang Syne" begins (in a nice touch, the tune is played in a different key at each casino), leaves a tip on the bar as the heist gets under way. Then, as he walks outside the casino, he is startled by a mechanical Santa Claus that "grabs" his waist. After Josh and Louis Jackson (Clem Harvey) knock out the power to Vegas, all five casinos are robbed without a hitch and the scrappy little trash man-singer-demolition expert pilots his truck to collect a million bucks from a garbage can at each site. However, just as everything appears kosher, Tony Bergdorf, who labored to re-wire the security devices at the casinos, suffers a heart attack and drops dead in the street.

Jack Strager (George Raft) brokers a meeting with the other four casino owners to devise a way to recover the $5 million. Enter Duke Santos, who claims he will do so for a finder's fee: He wants a third but "will accept 30 percent." After assuring the owners he is working for them, he tells the sheriff (Robert Foulk) a similar lie, all the while planning to play both sides against the middle: Discovering (through the comments of Jimmy's mother) that Ocean and his pals from the 82nd have pulled the heist, he calls Danny, who replies, "You're talkin' to a dead phone, Charley." Santos then visits Danny and Sam, demanding *50* percent to keep his mouth shut. (Romero's characterization is as greasy as his slicked back hair.)

Retrieving the cash from Josh's hiding place at the landfill, the gang dumps it in Bergdorf's coffin at the Cohen and Kelly's mortuary (an in-joke referring to the early 1930s radio and film series). In a macabre scene reminiscent of an expressionist horror film, the men place the bundles of bills around the corpse, but Josh keeps 10 grand to send to Bergdorf's wife. (Milestone's choice of showing the men and the coffin in silhouette harkens back to his earlier black-and-white films, but here is captured wonderfully by the widescreen color work of Daniels.)

Soon the film's style shifts from horror film to vintage Western, as some of the men wait at the station for the train that will take Bergdorf's body to San Francisco. Cutting from a medium shot to a long shot depicting more of the nervous gang, Milestone creates an atmosphere recalling similar scenes in *My Darling Clementine* (1946) and *High Noon* (1951). But "Operation Pinebox" goes awry when Ocean learns that Tony is going "to be planted right here in Vegas"; even worse, all the men, now seated at the American Legion service, hear the sound of flames as the funeral begins, then increasing as the eulogist unleashes one platitude after another. To save

Mrs. Bergdorf any unnecessary funerary and transportation costs, Tony is being cremated! In an excellent left-to-right pan across the pew, the widescreen image powerfully shows the faces of the men, then cuts closer and pans back left as each of them turns to look at the one beside him. Finally, the scene cuts to a medium-long shot depicting all of them, whose despondency culminates with Mushy placing his head in his hand. The credits then roll as they walk down the Vegas strip and Sammy sings a lament version of "E-O-Eleven" on the soundtrack. For this closer, Cahn and Van Heusen combined the lyrics of the film's two major songs: "Once I had a dream, but that dream got kicked in the head." (Indeed, but the film had to end this way: The Production Code could not allow the gang to get away with $5 million in stolen loot.)

The original ending involved all 11 dying when their chartered plane crashed. Jack Warner instead chose to leave them broke on the street, and—according to Frank—the director devised the ultimate way of burning up the bread:

> Lewis Milestone…came up with the idea for the ending. …In the temple, the crematorium is tied in with the temple. …He said, "I saw that happen once, and we were shocked…because, while the rabbi was doing all the prayers…they could hear this noise." Consequently we put it in the picture, which was a marvelous switch.[20]

Though he basically plays himself, Frank interestingly does not sing in the film, allowing Dean and Sammy to grab that spotlight. (With his excellent characterization, Sammy definitely increased his clout as a truly capable actor.) Did Frank's portrayal of a cool Vegas criminal increase the public's perception of him as having "ties to the Mob?" And what did the Kennedys think of "Brother-in-Lawford's" similar characterization? What is certain is that moviegoers loved these characters and the film. But *Ocean's Eleven* could have benefited from a tighter script and better pacing in its first half. Though Milestone's leisurely direction of Brown and Lederer's somewhat confusing script actually adds an unusual atmosphere of realism to the early scenes, this approach is proved unnecessarily expository after the film shifts into the far more exciting caper plot. The entire screenplay is fantastical, but the unique story of old war buddies hitting the hot spots of Vegas is fascinating.

During August 1960, audiences packed theaters across the country, but critics were understandably lukewarm. *Variety's* "Tube" wrote:

> *Ocean's Eleven* figures to be a moneymaker in spite of itself. …Laboring under the handicaps of a contrived script, an uncertain approach and personalities in essence playing themselves, the Lewis Milestone production never quite makes its point, but romps along merrily unconcerned that it doesn't. …Set in motion on the doubtful premise that 11 playful but essentially law-abiding wartime acquaintances from all walks of life would undertake a job that makes the Brink's heist pale by comparison, it proceeds to sputter and stammer through an interminable series of scrambled expository sequences. …Acting under the stigma of their own flashy, breezy identities, [the] players… never quite submerge themselves in their roles, nor try very hard to do so.
>
> At any rate, the pace finally picks up when the daring scheme is set in motion. …There is a plentiful amount of humor in the film, but much of it is largely for its own self-conscious sake and not consistent with or vital to the characterizations.[21]

"Tube" is dead on the mark, but at the time this review was written, he could not have known that the performers had no intention of "submerging themselves in their roles." The script, a lot of which was changed with on-set rewrites and improvisation, only existed to provide a suitable vehicle for the Summit, who all were appearing together on screen for the first time. Frank never intended the film to be anything more than that. Bosley Crowther, who originally had lambasted Frank but grew to admire his acting prowess, now continued to revert back to his earlier attitude, climbing on his high horse to write his August 11 *New York Times* review:

> A surprisingly nonchalant and flippant attitude toward crime—an attitude so amoral it roadblocks a lot of valid gags—is maintained throughout *Ocean's Eleven*...no dishonor, no moral misgivings, no sweat, outside of the normal, natural tension that occurs while the crime is being done. ...[T]he substance is...very funny in spots—the dialogue is cleverly written and the roles are deftly and colorfully played.[22]

Apparently Crowther had forgotten about earlier Hollywood films that took a "nonchalant and flippant attitude toward crime." When the gangster genre literally was killed by censorship after three major successes—*Little Caesar* (1930), *The Public Enemy* (1931) and *Scarface* (1932)—any films dealing with gang activities either had to (1) feature criminals who become remorseful before they are annihilated or (2) totally satirize the Mob boss, such as in the Edward G. Robinson comedies *The Little Giant* (1933), *You Can't Get Away with Murder* (1938) and *Larceny, Inc.* (1942). Frank loved Robinson and undoubtedly enjoyed following in his footsteps. Regardless of its flaws, *Ocean's Eleven* is an entertaining comedy, not a serious, "amoral" depiction of criminality.

Following this self-indulgent romp, Frank wanted to return to serious filmmaking, and for source material bought the rights to *The Execution of Private Slovik*, a powerful novel about the only U.S. deserter put to death since the Civil War. On February 10, 1960, *The New York Times* reported that Frank was slated to produce and direct the film, with Steve McQueen in the title role. In an interview with author William Bradford Huie, a reporter discovered that President Eisenhower would be depicted "as the military commander who signed the death certificate."[23] Eisenhower had been the World War II general who ordered Slovik's execution, and now Republicans worried that such a portrayal would tarnish the waning days of his administration and have a negative effect on the upcoming campaign of Vice President Richard Nixon.

Less than six weeks later, *The Times* ran a headline announcing, "Sinatra Defying Writer Blacklist—Hires Albert Maltz for His Filming of *The Execution of Private Slovik*." In 1947, Maltz had refused to give in to HUAC witch hunters and subsequently was jailed for contempt of Congress; but, upon his release, wrote screenplays under pseudonyms while living in Mexico. Following the lead of two of his erstwhile directors—Otto Preminger and Stanley Kramer—Frank decided to hire a blacklisted writer but also give him proper screen credit, something Maltz had not received for 13 years. Frank had greatly appreciated Maltz's screenplay for *The House I Live In* 15 years earlier, and now looked forward to making his directorial debut with a faithful adaptation of an excellent novel, following in the tradition of *From Here to Eternity* and *Some Came Running*. When he announced his plan to begin shooting *Slovik* in Italy or France during January 1961, many believed he was delaying the production to avoid casting any adverse publicity on the Kennedy presidential campaign. When phoned on March 21, 1960, by *New York Times* reporter Murray Schumach, who asked if he "was fearful of the reaction in Hollywood," Frank replied, "We'll find that out later. We'll see what happens."[24]

Shortly after, the Sinatra-bashing Westbrook Pegler received a clipping of the story from a colleague, who wrote, "Please do a piece on this bum. No writer does a more patriotic ethical job than you do."[25] Once again, the First Amendment tramplers were after Frank, who, rather than "criticizing" the Eisenhower-Nixon administration, now appeared to be "protecting" his man, Jack Kennedy.

One week later, the *Slovik* affair again was mentioned in *The Times*, in an article about how the current Screen Actors Guild strike had induced Universal-International to resign from the

Association of Motion Picture Producers and sign with the union—telltale proof that independent producers were gaining more strength in tinsel town:

> Frank Sinatra defied the position of the major studios by signing with the Screen Actors Guild and continuing to make his latest movie, *Ocean's 11.* Since then, he has shown his indifference to studio authority once more by hiring Albert Maltz, a blacklisted writer, to do his next movie...[26]

On that same day, March 28, Frank ran large ads in *Daily Variety* and *Hollywood Reporter*, in which he explained:

> Since I will produce and direct the picture I am concerned that the screenplay reflects the true pro-American values of the story. This means that the picture must be an affirmative declaration in the best American tradition. I spoke to many screenwriters, but it was not until I talked to Albert Maltz that I found a writer who saw the screenplay in exactly the same terms I wanted. This is, the Army was right.
>
> Under our Bill of Rights, I was taught that no one may prescribe what shall be orthodox in politics, religion or other matters of opinion. I am in complete accord with the statement made earlier this week by J. D. Nicola of the Catholic Legion of Decency, who said, "The Legion evaluates films on the basis of art, not the artist." As the producer of the film, I and I alone will be responsible for it. I accept that responsibility. I ask only that judgment be deferred until the picture is seen.
>
> I would also like to comment on the attacks from certain quarters on Senator John Kennedy by connecting him with my decision on employing a screenwriter. This type of partisan politics is hitting below the belt. ...I make movies. I do not ask the advice of Senator Kennedy on whom I should hire. Senator Kennedy does not ask me how he should vote in the Senate.
>
> I am prepared to stand on my principles and to await the verdict of the American people when they see *The Execution of Private Slovik.*
>
> I repeat: In my role as a picture maker, I have—in my opinion—hired the best man to do the job.[27]

Tina Sinatra revealed:

> Both Joe and Bobby Kennedy told my dad flat out to fire Maltz. I suppose they expected him to do the expedient thing without a second thought—which was, after all, how the Kennedys had made their way in the world. They hadn't banked on my father's stubborn Sicilian streak. He was willing to compromise, but not to compromise himself in the process. And he resented being told what to do, even by the father of the next president of the United States. He told the Kennedys that he'd stick by Maltz, whether or not it jeopardized his role in the campaign.[28]

One newspaper, *The New York Post*, praised Frank's actions and referred to him as a hero for attempting to expose the truly un-American nature of blacklists and oppressive organizations like HUAC. But most papers launched philistine attacks: While *The New York Mirror* called Maltz "an unrepentant enemy of the country," *The Los Angeles Examiner* considered the film a vehicle for Communist propaganda.[29] By April 9, right-wing diatribes by Pegler and the Hearst newspapers, the American Legion and other veterans' groups, various anti-Communist organizations, and even fellow screen tough guy John Wayne proved too much for Frank, who had stood by Maltz as long as he could. He announced:

> In view of the reaction of my family, my friends and the American public, I have instructed my attorneys to make a settlement with Mr. Maltz and to inform him that he will not write the screenplay for *The Execution of Private Slovik*. I had thought that the major consideration was whether or not the resulting script would be in the best interests of the United States. Since my conversations with Mr. Maltz had indicated that he has an affirmative approach to the story and so, since I felt fully capable, as producer, of enforcing such standards, I have defended my hiring of Mr. Maltz.
>
> But the American public has indicated it feels the morality of hiring Albert Maltz is the more crucial matter and I will accept this majority opinion.[30]

Frank was denied his right to freedom of choice. Since the first round of HUAC witch hunts, Dalton Trumbo and Nedrick Young had written excellent Hollywood scripts (for Preminger and Kramer, respectively), but their pseudonyms had prevented public outcry. After attempting honestly to employ one of the "Hollywood Ten," Frank had to give up what may have been one of his finest films.

Albert Maltz had paid his "debt to society," one born of Cold War paranoia. (Some Hollywood elites, like director Elia Kazan, *had* provided lists to HUAC, and subsequently were cold-shouldered in tinsel town.) As Peter Lawford's ex-wife Patricia Seaton Lawford wrote, "While many commentators unfamiliar with the era or the intensity of the attack have used the incident to show Sinatra's 'weakness,' the truth is that it is doubtful that anyone else in Hollywood would have gone as far as he did."[31] Private Slovik had been executed again.

But Frank had carried on with other engagements during this controversy. On May 12, 1960, he hosted "It's Nice to Go Traveling: Welcome Home, Elvis," his final *Timex Show* of the season, welcoming the "King of Rock 'n' Roll" back from a two-year stretch in the U.S. Army. In Miami, two generations of singing phenomena were paired in an effort to grab millions of viewers. And tune in they did, to see a shy and stiff, tuxedoed Elvis standing next to Frank as they "jammed" an alternation of "Love Me Tender" and "Witchcraft." While the Voice did an acceptable job lightly swinging the former, the King awkwardly fumbled through a few lines of the latter. The remainder of the show consisted of Frank singing a few numbers (including an excellent full-length "Witchcraft"), Elvis performing two songs with his band, Joey Bishop and Nancy Sinatra aiding "the boss" and endless screams from young females in the audience.

At 44, Frank was recognized as the entertainment industry's biggest box-office draw. In a *Good Housekeeping* article published in July 1960, journalist Richard Gehman wrote that he was "not merely an entertainer and a personality, but an immensely powerful force—a law unto himself. He could spend the rest of his life making all the films offered to him in a single month."[32] But, despite all his silver-screen success, film work still took a back seat to singing and recording.

Nelson Riddle and Sinatra at a 1956 recording session

The Cinema of Sinatra

On August 22-23, Frank returned to up-tempo mode to record *Sinatra's Swingin' Session* with Nelson Riddle at Capitol. One week later, on August 31-September 1, he and the arranger cut the second half of the new album, which is a virtual, though high-octane, remake of the 1950 Columbia album *Sing and Dance with Frank Sinatra*. After Riddle had written the charts, Frank told him that he wanted to record the songs at much faster tempi, resulting in a short (approximately 26-minute) album but one that effortlessly swings like a well-oiled live Sinatra performance. Whereas Frank had meticulously crafted his last LP, *Nice 'n' Easy*, now he could relax, creatively improvising on both melodies and lyrics. Opening with "When You're Smiling," he then crafts a punchy swing — perhaps the most hip version — of Rodgers and Hart's "Blue Moon," an effortless "S'posin'," his third version of "It All Depends on You," bouncy renditions of "It's Only a Paper Moon" and a pseudo rock 'n' roll "My Blue Heaven." Nacio Herb Brown and Arthur Freed's "Should I" drives along at a frantic clip, while the more restrained, sensual "September in the Rain" sounds like an outtake from the *Songs for Swingin' Lovers* sessions.

A lightly honking bass trombone supports Frank and Nelson's "easy" swinging version of Irving Berlin's "Always," one of the most atypical arrangements of the song, particularly during the Voice's deliberate, behind-the-beat phrasings. "I Can't Believe That You're in Love with Me" is followed by a pair of Cole Porter standards — "I Concentrate on You" and "You Do Something to Me" — with Frank effortlessly outdoing his previous timing on the Berlin song: "You *do* — the voo-*doo* — that — you — *do* — so well." Three songs cut during the August 31-September 1 sessions — "Hidden Persuasion," "Sentimental Baby" and (incredibly) a swing version of "Ol' MacDonald" — were released as singles. In the midst of the *Swingin'* sessions, he was one of the headliners at the Urban League Jazz Festival held in Chicago's Comiskey Park on August 27. And to perform at this event, he had to take a respite from another occupation he recently had accepted: campaigning for JFK.

Following a walk down the aisle with Nancy, Jr., who wed singer Tommy Sands on September 11, 1960, he jumped at the chance to costar with one of his acting heroes, Spencer Tracy, in *The Devil at Four O'Clock*, the story of three hardened convicts who become involved with a priest and his followers during a savage volcano eruption. In mid-October, he flew to Maui to begin location shooting with Mervyn LeRoy, who had directed *The House I Live In*. In an effort to help offset Nixon propaganda in the Hearst newspapers, he performed at a Kennedy rally in Waikiki on the 12th. He said, "I've been campaigning for Democrats ever since I marched in a parade for Al Smith when I was a 12-year-old kid."[33]

Tracy recalled working with Frank:

> Nobody had his power. *The Devil at Four O'Clock* was a Sinatra picture. Sinatra was the star. Although we worked very differently, he knew what he wanted. Some people said there would be fireworks, but there wasn't.[34]

Though Tracy would have a cocktail or two in the bar, he would turn in early while Frank and his cronies characteristically partied all night. Sometimes, as the sun rose to find everyone else conked out, Frank would recharge his batteries to have breakfast with "the Grey Fox," as he called the 60-year-old Tracy. Displaying some of the curmudgeonly behavior of Father Doonan, the legendary star would ride Frank about not getting any sleep but, on December 12, joined in celebrating his 45th birthday. In an on-set interview with *The New York Times*, Tracy admitted, " I have thought about directing [but] I don't have the patience. I could never stand some of the things I have seen directors put up with from actors. I would kill the actors."[35] Could he indirectly have been referring to One-Take Charley?

As Frank conferred with Mervyn LeRoy, Tracy caught his attention with a friendly wave, telling *The Times'* Murray Schumach that Sinatra had more financial clout than any actor during the heyday of the Hollywood studio system: "I am getting a percentage of this picture. I could never have gotten a percentage at Metro. And I guess there were a few years when I was considered pretty good box office there."[36]

The Actor, on Screen and in Song

To what extent did Frank's relationship with the Kennedy family affect his decision to shelve *Private Slovik*? Joseph Kennedy previously had asked for Frank's help and got it. If the singer could ask a Mob boss like Sam ("Momo") Giancana to deliver, via 500 Club owner Paul ("Skinny") D'Amato, 120,000 West Virginia primary votes to his son, the matter of who should write a Hollywood screenplay seemed a mere trifle. (Frank told Giancana that the favor—muscling support in an anti-Catholic, union-organized region—was a "personal" one, and not to expect repayment from the Kennedys.) Persuaded by two Catholic cardinals—Cushing in Boston and Spellman in New York—that public support of Maltz could adversely affect JFK's chances with voting members of their flock, Joe had told Frank to dump the "Commie" scrawler. While Frank covertly arranged votes for JFK, his own dream was dashed. (In her book, Tina Sinatra claims that he finally caved in after a classmate asked her if she, like her father, was "a Communist."[37])

Frank carried on tirelessly stumping for JFK, singing a revamped version of "High Hopes," temporarily renaming his exclusive club "the Jack Pack," and arranging a $100-per-plate dinner to raise money for the campaign. The day after 2,800 people slapped down c-notes to support JFK, the Democratic National Convention was held at Los Angeles Memorial Sports Arena, where the Jack Pack, Tony Curtis and Janet Leigh all sang the "Star Spangled Banner." Shortly after the opening of the convention, an unfortunate event occurred that marked a sign of the times but also indicated that the Democrats might not be planning a brave new world for America. Many years earlier, upon first coming to the United States, young Peter Lawford lost a country club job after a member complained that he had been speaking to a black worker. That member was Joseph P. Kennedy. And now nothing was done about a portion of the convention crowd who booed and heckled Sammy Davis, Jr., as he attempted to perform with his colleagues. Deeply hurt, he couldn't take Frank's advice to ignore the "dirty sons of bitches," and walked off stage. And after JFK won the nomination, Joe Kennedy persuaded Sammy to postpone his upcoming marriage until after the election: The African-American phenomenon was engaged to Swedish actress Mai Britt. Nancy, Jr., revealed, "Sammy loved JFK and would do anything for him, no matter how hurt he was."[38] (In the end, JFK won the election against Richard Nixon, but by so narrow a margin that it can be argued that, without Frank Sinatra—whose request to Giancana also pulled in Chicago votes during the general election—he may have lost.)

After JFK squeaked by Nixon, the President-elect spent a weekend at Frank's home in Palm Springs, an event commemorated by the placing of a plaque reading, "John F. Kennedy slept here, November 6 and 7, 1960" on the guestroom door. One week later, Frank was best man at Sammy and Mai Britt's wedding in Vegas. In December, JFK asked Frank to organize and host the inaugural gala to be held in Washington, DC, the following month. But again his effort of good will had to cater to political hypocrisy: Though JFK already had won the election, the Kennedy family still didn't want Sammy to participate. In fact, they even refused to invite him to the gala. Fuming inside, Frank asked them to reconsider, but in this situation not even *Sinatra* could have any influence. Nancy, Jr., wrote, "He... told me it was one of the few times he ever felt at such a loss. In the past he'd always been able to help Sammy. He had been able to protest and bring about change. But now he could do nothing. Yes, he could have backed out of the inaugural, but Sammy never would have allowed that."[39]

Sublimating his aggravation, Frank created an incredible show starring a who's who of the musical, theatrical and cinematic worlds, including Leonard Bernstein, Bette Davis, Jimmy Durante and Joey Bishop. When Sir Laurence Olivier and Ethel Merman couldn't get out of their respective Broadway engagements, Frank bought all the tickets at both theaters and closed them down for a night. And even when a terrible blizzard threatened to shut down the whole shebang, he remained undaunted. To the Kennedys' credit, they did not object to the other African-Americans on the bill, including Nat Cole, Harry Belafonte and Sidney Poitier. (Cole had befriended JFK in October 1958; during the 1960 campaign, Kennedy asked him to appear with him in Wisconsin, but their respective schedules clashed.)

When the performances concluded, the freshly inaugurated President Kennedy announced to the gathering:

Since the time of Thomas Jefferson, the Democratic Party has been identified with the pursuit of excellence — and we saw excellence tonight. I know we're all indebted to a great friend, Frank Sinatra. Long before he could sing, he had to poll a Democratic precinct back in New Jersey.

Though the Sammy situation had troubled him, Frank truly liked and admired JFK, going so far as to ease off on his ideals somewhat to remain within the Kennedy sphere. After all, how many entertainers are given the chance to organize a president's inaugural, sit at his table and escort the new First Lady (especially Jackie Kennedy) to the festivities? But, as future events proved, this "sociopolitical" accommodation did not go both ways: Soon after being named Attorney General, Bobby Kennedy began to attack organized crime, including Sam Giancana, with a vengeance. Betrayed by the family he had helped to gain the White House, the mobster was enraged.

Tina Sinatra claimed that Frank "thought to himself, 'What have I done?'":"He'd gone to Giancana out of friendship for Jack Kennedy and expected nothing back. What he did not expect was to be set up like a blindsided innocent, like a fool to take the fall."[40] (Though one of his thugs wanted to whack the Voice, Giancana said he had "other ideas"; and Frank, Dean and Sammy eventually "settled the debt" by performing for free at the Mob-run Villa Venice nightclub in Wheeling, Illinois, a Chicago suburb, in November 1962.)

While preparing the inaugural gala, Frank also inaugurated Reprise Records, his own label, for which he would cut LPs alongside the two years' worth of recordings he still owed to Capitol. At this point, he believed that production and technology, particularly dubbing and multi-tracking, were beginning to encroach upon the purity of live performance and sound he worked for in the studio. After unsuccessfully attempting to buy the Verve jazz label from producer Norman Granz, he opted to create a brand new company. While he was shooting additional footage for *The Devil at Four O'Clock* at the Columbia Pictures ranch, Bill Miller drove arranger Johnny Mandel out for a meeting. Mandel recalled:

> Frank started telling me about how he was finished with Capitol, and he was starting this new label, and the records were going to be colored vinyl... all that sort of thing. He had a lot of ideas, and I remember just watching his eyes and he was talking about the company, you know, and they were *sparkling*.[41]

Frank cut his first recordings for Reprise on December 19-21, 1960, titling his debut album *Ring-a-Ding Ding!* Using Mandel, Skip Martin and Dick Reynolds as arrangers, he waxed 12 songs for the LP and four additional numbers, two of which were arranged by Nelson Riddle and released as singles. A drum roll crescendos into a powerful Mandel brass arrangement as Cahn and Van Heusen's "Ring-a-Ding Ding" opens the LP, introducing Frank's newfound musical freedom expressed through a driving swing style that differs from those of Riddle and Billy May. On Harold Arlen and Ted Koehler's "Let's Fall in Love," he roars in with the bridge and then he and the orchestra *stop* to pause for an entire measure before he impeccably leads his cohorts back in with "*Let's* fall in love..." A hard-swinging version of Cole Porter's "In the Still of the Night" features Frank in perfectly controlled high spirits and a Frank Rosolino trombone solo recalling Riddle's "I've Got You Under My Skin" arrangement.

The Gershwin's "A Foggy Day" includes a return of the chimes first heard on the title track and muted trumpet soloing by Don Fagerquist, while Irving Berlin's "Let's Face the Music and Dance" receives a driving arrangement with potent brass kicks, during which Frank alters the title's romantic request to a confident command: "*Face* the music and dance." "You'd Be So Easy to Love" is a more laid-back Cole Porter swinger, as is Jerome Kern and Dorothy Fields' "A Fine Romance." "The Coffee Song," which he originally had cut at Columbia in 1946, rhumbas along at a fine clip before he concludes with some classic Sinatra-speak: "Man, they got a *gang* of coffee in Brazil!" Two Irving Berlin swingers follow: "Be Careful, It's My Heart" and "I've

Got My Love to Keep Me Warm," during which Frank creates the album's most effective phrasing by dropping key words, singing "*Got* my love to keep me warm" behind the beats. "You and the Night and the Music" creates a noir atmosphere before Mandel introduces "When I Take My Sugar to Tea" with punchy brass and Frank enters all alone before the orchestra returns. Unreleased tracks included "The Last Dance" and "Zing! Went the Strings of My Heart" (due to its too-brisk tempo), while the Riddle-arranged "The Second Time Around" and "Tina" (Cahn and Van Heusen's song about Frank's younger daughter) were released as singles.

On January 27, 1961, Frank brought Sammy back into the fold for a Carnegie Hall benefit concert he organized for Dr. Martin Luther King's Southern Christian Leadership Conference. Dean Martin also contributed his time, helping to support a man Frank had admired since the Montgomery Bus Boycott. Over the next sixth months, he performed more benefits for a variety of causes, including shows in Los Angeles and Mexico City.

Capitol still strived to capitalize extensively on the rebellious Sinatra, issuing yet another compilation LP, *All the Way*, including 12 singles and movie hits, the most prominent being the title song, "High Hopes," "Witchcraft" and "All My Tomorrows." And Billy May once again provided high-powered big-band arrangements when Frank made one last new up-tempo release for the label, *Come Swing with Me*, recorded at the Hollywood studio March 20-22. To utilize fully the possibilities offered by the new stereo format, producer Dave Cavanaugh induced May to split the brass section in two; in the words of Pete Welding, "used antiphonally, in call-and-response fashion, one section positioned to the left, the other to the right, with the singer in the middle-center stage…"[42]

Twelve great standards were recorded in this "revolutionary" sonic process. Originally cut as a ballad in 1945, Axel Stordahl, Paul Weston and Sammy Cahn's "Day by Day" opens with May's heavy brass. Immediately, the stereo format proves perfect for the punchy arrangement, as the brass sections trade off chords from right to left and Frank, in dead center, naturally, effortlessly, provides the melody tying them together. Les Brown, Bud Green and Ben Homer's "Sentimental Journey" nearly lulls the listener off to sleep before Lerner and Loewe's "Almost Like Being in Love" hits like a May sledgehammer. "Five Minutes More"—beginning with May's "metal," settling down into a driving groove graced by Frank's effortless ebullience, and culminating with his incomparable behind-the-beat insouciance—is followed by a very familiar (though heavily brass enhanced) "American Beauty Rose," Sy Oliver's 1941 quasi-spiritual "Yes Indeed!" and a boisterous, improvisational "On the Sunny Side of the Street. Henry Nemo's "Don't Take Your Love from Me" made its first appearance in the Sinatra catalog, but "That Old Black Magic" received its third incarnation, here in a hard-swinging May phrased miles-behind-the-beat treatment.

Rodgers and Hart's "Lover" originally was written for the then-risque Ernst Lubitsch film *Love Me Tonight* (1932) starring Maurice Chevailer and Jeanette MacDonald—a song that seems let down by the rather pedantic light-shuffler "Paper Doll." Fortunately, the album ends with Jule Styne and Sammy Cahn's "I've Heard That Song Before, a 1943 Harry James hit that had been misused by the movies (*Pistol Packin' Mama* and *Shantytown*) but here swings hard in the best May fashion, it's finest recorded version.

Frank did double duty on March 20-21, also recording eight songs intended for the Reprise release *I Remember Tommy*, a tribute to his mentor and would-be nemesis, Mr. Dorsey, but they were left unreleased. On May 1-3, Frank was far more satisfied with the takes cut with arranger Sy Oliver and trombonist Dick Nash. "I'll Be Seeing You" is revised as an up-tempo swinger (with Frank getting groovy, improvising, "Yes, I will *dig* you in the early bright…"), but "I'm Getting Sentimental Over You" is given a more expected ballad treatment. Frank enjoys toying with the phrasing on Jimmy Van Heusen and Johnny Burke's "Imagination," waxes dramatic on "Take Me" and gently swings, then continuously builds in intensity along with the orchestra on "Without a Song."

Following a brief bluesy introduction, he returns to balladeer for the Van Heusen-Burke classic "Polka Dots and Moonbeams" and Ferde Grofe and Harold Adamson's "Daybreak."

Referring to the former, jazz critic Gene Lees noted, "[Y]ou will hear peerless phrasing for the meaning of the lyrics, you'll hear some remarkably controlled singing, with beautiful in-tune and well-sustained lines so long that you wonder if he's ever going to pause for breath."[43] Sy Oliver actually duets with Frank on Gus Kahn and Isham Jones' swinger "The One I Love Belongs to Someone Else," but his repeated long-breath phrasings on the ballad "There Are Such Things" are far more impressive. The remainder of the songs include Van Heusen and Burke's "It's Always You," "It Started All Over Again" and the classic "East of the Sun (And West of the Moon)," on which Frank sings the "ending" three times.

On May 18, 19 and 23, Frank, with Billy May, recorded another album's worth of songs. Originally titled *Swing Along With Me* but changed to *Sinatra Swings* after Capitol sued, claiming that Reprise was treading too close to their *Come Swing With Me* LP, this collection was actually released three months before *I Remember Tommy* hit the stores.

Rodgers and Hart's "Falling in Love with Love" is introduced by woodwinds and a lightly swinging groove, builds with May's familiar saxophone riffs, and finally kicks into high gear with brass and dynamic drums. "The Curse of an Aching Heart" explodes with hurricane force and driving percussion as Frank effortlessly glides over this *Come Dance with Me*-style arrangement. May then eases off the throttle for the bluesy ballad "Don't Cry Joe," but still brackets Frank's vocals with punchy horns and surging saxophones. "Please Don't Talk About Me When I'm Gone" returns to up-tempo territory before the Gershwin's "Love Walked In" provides a high point: Frank's a capella "Love" is followed by woodwinds and hi-hat cymbal before the song settles into an irresistible groove. Frenzied south-of-the-border sounds introduce "Granada," which opens in Broadway style, with Frank dramatically acting the lyric before the band jumps into mid-tempo swing.

"I Never Knew" shifts the album back into May overdrive, followed by the familiar Benny Goodman swinger "Don't Be That Way." "Moonlight on the Ganges" recalls Frank and Billy's "travel collaborations" on *Come Fly with Me*, blending light swing with exotic "Indian" elements. The bouncy "It's a Wonderful World" (ending with "It's a ring-a-ding world") is followed by Rodgers and Hart's "Have You Met Miss Jones?" (which Frank had attempted to record six months earlier for *Ring-a-Ding-Ding!*) and the superlative "You're Nobody 'Til Somebody Loves You." After lightly grooving the first time through, Frank carefully builds the second and third choruses ("the big *fat* world and its gold"), hitting a dynamic peak on the hard-swinging ending.

During the summer of 1961, Frank re-teamed with Summiteers Martin, Davis and Lawford to shoot their second cinematic collaboration, *Sergeants 3*, an Americanized "cowboys and Indians" spoof of MGM's *Gunga Din*-inspired *Soldiers Three* (1951). Rather than depicting the exploits of the British Army in Colonial India, this W. R. Burnett–scripted concoction focuses on the U.S. Cavalry fighting Native Americans in Utah. After filming in the desert at Kanab and Bryce Canyon during the day, the Summit repeated their *Ocean's Eleven* experience by performing in Vegas at night. Classic film fan Sammy also brought along his 16mm projector so he could show his favorite Laurel and Hardy shorts to the—often inebriated—gang.

Costar Ruta Lee, whom Frank had seen in Billy Wilder's *Witness for the Prosecution* (1957) and was involved with Peter Lawford at the time, recalled that One-Take Charley was in top form:

> He'd say, "Print it because I'm not going to do it again." And unless it really hit the fan, he wouldn't. But he was very correct. He'd come in at 11, but he'd say, "I'm giving you all the time in the world to set up the shot, I'll come in and do a walk-through. I don't want to hear after I've done a walk-through that there's a shadow here, that the sound isn't right there. Take all the time in the world, but when I walk in, I want it perfect."[44]

When Frank needed a landing strip for his new private jet (the interior of which was decorated in orange, of course), he had one of his press people make a deal with a local school to use an

FRANK SINATRA DEAN MARTIN IN SERGEANTS 3
PETER LAWFORD SAMMY DAVIS JR. JOEY BISHOP

athletic playing field in exchange for his financial support of an academic project. When he was unable to decide which one on the list to underwrite, he put up $5,000 to cover them all.

On June 17, to celebrate Dean's 44th birthday, Frank threw a party in Vegas, where Elizabeth Taylor and Marilyn Monroe were among the guests. And the good times generally carried over onto the Kanab set for the remainder of the shoot. According to Ruta Lee:

> *Sergeants 3* was one of the happiest experiences of my life, because I was the baby doll on the set with all of these guys. I had a wonderful time but, unfortunately, they all treated me like their kid sister. Dean was great fun to be around. They all sipped pretty good, but I never saw him sloshed. In fact, he taught me to drink beer on the rocks. And Frank taught me to drink champagne the same way.[45]

Lee also recalled that it was Sammy who smoothed over any conflicts: "If someone was upset, he'd go 'round and ask, 'Are you all right?'"[46] Sammy recalled, "*Ocean's Eleven* was a lot of fun, but I think *Sergeants 3* was the best film we ever did together. It was a good story with a lot of fine points, and we packed it with action." [47]

Though its promotion promised top stars, a major director and state-of-the-art special effects, *The Devil at Four O'Clock*, released on July 16, failed to reach its artistic and commercial potential. This tale of a once idealistic, now alcoholic, priest who regains his faith after three convicts aid him and his invalid flock during a volcano eruption never catches fire, seeming much longer than 126 minutes. During production, Tracy claimed that Frank was the star of the film, but none of the actors stands out above the (often unconvincing) volcanic backdrop. Frank's "Harry" is one character role among several, none of whom are developed to any extent. LeRoy and screenwriter Liam O'Brien tailored the part for Frank—he is introduced as a voice emanating from beneath a straw hat and, at one point, Father Doonan speaks of his Jersey accent ("You spit your Ts…")—but he actually is little more than an attitude in a light blue shirt and trousers. His few moments of real acting occur when LeRoy and

The Cinema of Sinatra

cinematographer Joseph Biroc's close-ups allow him to register some very subtle gestures and expressions: While getting to know Camille (Barbara Luna), a young blind woman at Doonan's hospital; or, later, when realizing that volunteering to aid the priest in evacuating the threatened patients might commute the sentence levied on him and his comrades, Marcel (Gregorie Aslan) and Charlie (Bernie Hamilton).

The dramatic potential of *The Devil at Four O'Clock* wasn't realized, yet it marked an interesting sidetrack in Frank's film career. Rather than portraying the lead role, he was relegated to a character part in an ensemble cast; and, aside from a few redeeming moments and his suicidal decision to stay with Doonan and Charlie as the island explodes (gazing at the priest, the former atheist makes the sign of the cross), Harry was the actor's most unappealing creation since John Baron in *Suddenly*. Much of the dialogue seems improvised, including a fair amount of Sinatra-speak: Harry constantly refers to authority figures as "cruds," and, during his romantic interlude with Camille—whom he later marries during their flight from the killer lava—admits, "I've been a bum most of my life."

Variety's "Whit" considered *Devil* "a strong entry," Tracy "colorful" and Frank "first-class but minor,"[48] while *The Los Angeles Examiner*'s Sara Hamilton enthused that this "picture worth seeing" featured a "strong performance" from Spence, with his costar, "in a less showy role... not far behind him. Sinatra is good, very good."[49] However, A. H. Weiler of *The New York Times* was less positive:

> Director Mervyn LeRoy may not have extracted memorable performances from his principals but his technicians did achieve a few spectacular effects... Tracy's delineation of the priest who has been driven to drink and to doubt his faith by the callousness of his parishioners is mostly physical. It is, largely, a composite of grimaces and angry looks. ...Sinatra's characterization of the convict from Jersey City (for no apparent reason)... is casual in the extreme and riddled with colloquialisms closer to Hollywood than Tahiti.[50]

On August 15, 1961, Frank, continuing to diversify his business ventures, inaugurated Park Lake Enterprises, Inc., a partnership with Hank Sanicola and Sanford Waterman, to reopen the Cal-Neva Lodge situated on the northern shore of Lake Tahoe. Not only did this legendary summer getaway offer first-class entertainment and gambling, but also outdoor activities such as sailing and waterskiing. He also increased his share in the Sands to nine percent, in order to be on par with other licensed shareholders. In an attempt to raise additional capital for the refurbishment,

Sinatra and John F. Kennedy

Frank and attorney Mickey Rudin applied for a $5 million loan from Jimmy Hoffa's Teamsters Union pension fund, but were denied. The FBI, who were investigating Hoffa's possible loans to Mob-run gambling operations in Nevada, also kept an eye on Frank's activities. One bureau memorandum stated, "Both Rudin and Sinatra advised they wished to go on record that there were no under-the-table payments of any kind involved, that this was a simple straight forward business transaction with sufficient collateral involved."[51]

To make the return to Capitol bearable, Frank re-teamed with Axel Stordahl to record the material for *Point of No Return* on September 11-12, 1961, when 12 usable album tracks were cut. Backed by the elegance he had enjoyed during his years at Columbia, Frank created a milestone, yet ultimately flawed, album—an uncomfortable blending of his modern swing style and the straightforward ballad crooning of the 1940s period. Pete Welding wrote, "The singer, there can be no doubt, was at peak vocal and expressive form on these performances which rank with the finest, most compelling achievements of his Capitol years."[52]

Frank, concentrating on his new record company, really didn't give a damn. Originally sung in English by Peggy Lee (lyrics by Johnny Mercer), the French song "When the World Was Young" opens the album in pseudo-Broadway style; then the record actually begins to sound like a Sinatra album, though the strings and percussion-only arrangements are jarring when paired with, not the 1944 voice, but that of 1961. First recorded with Stordahl in 1946, Weill and Anderson's "September Song" is a bit overwrought due to the maestro's dated string style, as is the rhythmically stilted "A Million Years Ago." Noel Coward's "I'll See You Again," the occasionally bombastic "There Will Never Be Another You," "Somewhere Along the Way" and "It's a Blue World" don't offer anything special; but Frank's reading of "These Foolish Things" provides an interesting comparison to the classic interpretations of Peggy Lee and Ella Fitzgerald.

Frank's version of Herman Hupfeld's "As Time Goes By" is a rare recording of the 1931 song made famous in Warner Bros.' *Casablanca* (1942). (Natalie Cole's later attempt also is a pleasant rendition.) The World War II-era song "I'll be Seeing You," by Sammy Fain and Irving Kahal, is given a superlative performance, before "Memories of You" closes the session.

Seven years after starring in *The Man with the Golden Arm*, Frank again contributed to an Otto Preminger film, *Advise and Consent*, for which he recorded the lightly swinging ballad "Heart of Mine," arranged and conducted by Jerry Fielding, on September 18. Though he had been disappointed by the Kennedys' attitude toward Sammy, Frank then spent the weekend of September 23-24 with the family at Hyannisport, Massachusetts—Joe Kennedy's way of thanking him for helping to swing the West Virginia primary and Chicago general-election votes for Jack. From November 20-22, he was back in Hollywood, recording material with arranger Don Costa for *Sinatra and Strings*, a new ballad album featuring love songs rather than those of the torch, saloon, "suicide" variety. A superb album, it became a triumph for Costa, who was working for the first time with Frank, who acted the lyrics and melodies as effortlessly as he ever had. As Will Friedwald writes, "Like a Joe Turner or Jimmy Rushing, Sinatra never tries to instill in listeners

The Cinema of Sinatra

the idea that he's actually creating music right now; rather, he's simply allowing it to come out of him—like molasses leaking slowly out of a crack in a barrel.[53]

"I Hadn't Anyone Till You" opens the album in lush romantic style, with Costa's sweeping strings accompanied by woodwinds, light percussion and solo trombone. A wholly original arrangement of Porter's "Night and Day" follows, with Frank, performing his fourth studio version of the song, combining long-breath phrasing with impeccably controlled vocal power. "Look at me…" Frank intones, leading the orchestra into his first recording of Errol Garner and Johnny Burke's "Misty." An exquisite "Stardust" follows, a rendition that apparently angered composer Hoagy Carmichael, who objected to Frank's inclusion of only the verse; but Costa's lovely introduction—which could have been used as the opening theme for a classic film—creates the atmosphere for the Voice's subtly dramatic performance and is utterly sublime. Harold Arlen and Johnny Mercer's "Come Rain or Come Shine" features the album's bluesiest vocal and a dramatic, brassy instrumental bridge, while "It Might as Well Be Spring," written for the 1945 film *State Fair* by Rodgers and Hammerstein, provides a lighter, sensual mood. "Prisoner of Love," the theme song of Frank's predecessor Russ Columbo, precedes "That's All," written by Dick Haymes' brother, Bob, and a reworking of his classic collaboration with Harry James, "All or Nothing at All" that opens in dramatic style, settles into the album's most melancholy vocal, and finishes in bravura fashion with a "big" vocal note and a brass crescendo. "Yesterdays," a Jerome Kern and Otto Harbach song from *Roberta*, a 1933 Broadway musical adapted for the classic 1935 Astaire-Rogers film, concludes the album.

"As You Desire Me" was the first song cut on November 20, but was dropped from the album release. Henry Nemo's "Don't Take Your Love from Me" also was deleted, due to a subsequent agreement prohibiting Frank from recording for Reprise any songs that he had waxed for Capitol over the previous five years. Two singles, both penned by Van Heusen and Cahn, also were cut: a "High Hopes"-like number, "Pocketful of Miracles," featuring a children's chorus, and "Name It and It's Yours." One week after the *Strings* sessions, Frank began a series of shows in Sydney, Australia, that ended on December 2.

Soon after New Years' Day 1962, President Kennedy told Frank that he would like to stay at the Sinatra home during an upcoming visit to Palm Springs. Already in the midst of building a new guest house, Frank ordered further remodeling to be done to most of the compound, including the construction of a concrete helipad for JFK's use.

Sergeants 3 was released in January, featuring Frank, Dean and Peter as Sergeants Mike Merry, Chip Deal and Larry Barrett, respectively. Assigned to the Utah Indian Territory in 1873, they are joined by Jonah Williams (Sammy), a freed slave, during a barroom fight and head out on the trail of a Sioux tribe. After Deal is captured by the Sioux, he is rescued by his three comrades and a potential massacre is averted when Jonah's bugle alerts the cavalry. As Barrett rides off to join his fiancee, Amelia Parent (Ruta Lee), he is declared a deserter, having been re-enlisted by his unscrupulous pals.

Director John Sturges and cinematographer Winton Hoch make the most of the Kanab and Bryce Canyon vistas, lending the film a pseudo-John Ford ambiance enhanced by Frank Hotaling's art direction and Vic Gangelin's set decoration. Though some of the action is dependent on slapstick humor (a lá Cary Grant, Victor McLaglen and Douglas Fairbanks, Jr., in *Gunga Din* [1939]), Sturges creates a fine pace, effectively backed by Billy May's score.

Gordon Jenkins again collaborated with Frank on sessions held January 15-17, 1962, for an album of songs originally titled "Come Waltz with Me" but eventually released as *All Alone*. Frank's voice remains a cappella for two full phrases when introducing Irving Berlin's "All Alone," the first of 11 quiet explorations of love and loneliness. A melancholy clarinet and oboe play a familiar melody in the introduction to "The Girl Next Door," written by Hugh Martin and Ralph Blane for the Judy Garland classic *Meet Me in St. Louis* (1944) and previously cut by Frank in 1953. Penned in 1926, Lou Handman and Roy Turk's "Are You Lonesome Tonight?" had been a huge hit for Elvis Presley two years earlier, but here Frank is given a lush setting, the waltz tempo suggesting the era in which the ballad was written. Wisely, Jenkins substituted an instrumental

bridge for Elvis' familiar narration. Adapted from a 1913 Hungarian waltz for John Ford's *What Price, Glory?* (1952), "Charmaine" injects some romance into the album before loneliness returns on Irving Berlin's "What'll I Do?" Another Berlin number, "When I Lost You," was penned by the composer in 1912 after his wife of five months passed away; Frank, who had been a pallbearer at Ernie Kovacs' funeral on the morning of January 15, recorded the song that evening. The "saddest" song on the album, the arrangement and vocal truly make one feel "all alone."

"Oh, How I Miss You Tonight" opens with harp, flute and pizzicato strings, supplements Frank's vocal with a beckoning French horn, and includes a minimalist, quasi-classical bridge. This song, cut on the final day of the *All Alone* sessions, arguably features Frank's best acting on the album. His old pals Van Heusen and Cahn had written "Indiscreet" for Stanley Donen's 1958 film starring Cary Grant and Ingrid Bergman, while "Remember" is a romantic Irving Berlin waltz, composed in 1925. Two additional 1920s songs, "Together" and "The Song is Ended" close the original album. "Come Waltz with Me," a Van Heusen-Cahn number penned for the sessions, was recorded but dropped by Frank, who thought it out of place. (It later was included on the 1992 Reprise CD release.)

On February 25, 1962, Frank and Dean joined Judy Garland on her NBC television show. Two days later, Frank cut two Reprise singles arranged by Neil Hefti, "Everybody's Twistin'," an absurd swing-rock 'n' roll hybrid, and "Nothing But the Best," a more appropriate swinger. On March 6, he waxed "The Boys' Night Out," a humorous Van Heusen-Cahn single left unreleased by Reprise (until 1995), as well as his last vocal track for Capitol, on Harold Arlen and Ted Koehler's "I Gotta Right to Sing the Blues," which wasn't released until the compilation album *Sinatra Sings of Love and Things* hit the stores later in the year. This "greatest hits" album also includes "Monique" from *Kings Go Forth* and "Chicago."

Veteran television writer George Axelrod, who recently had worked closely on the *Thriller* series with Frank's hero Boris Karloff, was collaborating on *Breakfast at Tiffany's* with director John Frankenheimer when the latter left the project. Soon after, Axelrod phoned his former colleague. "Have you ever read a book called *The Manchurian Candidate*?" he asked. Frankenheimer hadn't, so the two drove to a nearby book shop and bought two copies. That afternoon, they sat together, reading Richard Condon's gripping political thriller and immediately agreed that a film should be made. After all, every studio in Hollywood had turned it down. By the early evening, Axelrod's agent, Irving "Swifty" Lazar, using his client's and Frankenheimer's own savings, had purchased the screen rights. Axelrod had heard that Frank admired the novel and wanted to appear in an adaptation. The next day, the writer contacted him at the Fountainbleau in Miami. While flying to Florida, Axelrod advised Frankenheimer not to "get into any kind of prolonged discussion—anything that would make [Sinatra] think that he didn't want to do this movie."[54]

When the filmmaking duo arrived at Frank's hotel room, he opened it, a huge smile lighting up his face. "God, I just can't wait to do your movie," he enthused.

"We knew that anything we said from then on was going to hurt us," Frankenheimer later admitted.[55] After a friendly visit with Frank, the director and writer left, flew back to Los Angeles the following day; and, with their star in hand, began to make pre-production plans.

Returning to California, Frank chose tinsel town veteran Howard W. Koch, who currently was enjoying small-screen success with *The Untouchables*, to executive produce the film. Though Koch had no idea what Frank's offer would be, the excited actor assumed that the producer's very appearance at the Sinatra home ensured his participation. When Frank was told that other com-

The Cinema of Sinatra

mitments and specific economic issues needed to be considered, he guaranteed Koch $100,000 (250% more than the producer had made on any previous film) plus a limousine and chauffeur. Koch accepted and soon began to advise Frank to forego "The Rat Pack" and be much more particular when choosing his roles.

With *The Manchurian Candidate*, he definitely was moving in the right direction. After some time had passed, Frank, wanting to see a script, called Axelrod. "I want to see some pages," he said. Having completed about 20 pages, the writer frantically shuffled some material together, spending the following weekend cranking out an additional 60.

United Artists agreed to release the film, budgeted at $2.5 million on a 45-day shooting schedule, but executives were concerned that its content might create additional tensions between the Soviets and the Kennedy administration. Frank, however, had recently met with the president at Hyannisport, and when JFK asked about his old friend's next film project, *The Manchurian Candidate* was mentioned.

"Great," replied Kennedy. "Who's going to play the mother?"

Frank later added, "He was very interested in the facts of the project itself."[56] Tina Sinatra revealed that JFK "called Arthur Krim, the president of United Artists, and gave the movie his blessing."[57]

Casting the pivotal character of Raymond Shaw was a great challenge. Eventually, English Shakespearean actor Laurence Harvey, who previously had played an American, Colonel William Travis, in John Wayne's monumental *The Alamo*, was chosen. Frankenheimer said:

> We had thought of every possible actor who could have played Raymond Shaw, and we jointly decided that Laurence Harvey would be the best actor to do it. I think that Larry's American accent is quite good... but we always knew there would be a trace of accent, but John Kennedy was the president at the time; and with John Kennedy's accent, we thought that it justified any accent that Larry Harvey had.[58]

"I wouldn't have known how to play [it]," Frank said of Harvey's role. "Larry was a fine actor...a marvelous actor. ...He left us too soon."[59]

To achieve a realistic "documentary" style, Frankenheimer and cinematographer Lionel Lindon shot the film in black and white with wide-angle lenses in the 1:1.85 widescreen ratio (to achieve great depth of focus), utilizing as many locations as possible. 38 sets were built on two large soundstages in Hollywood, where shooting began on January 22. Some location work was done in Los Angeles (Franklin Canyon and the Olympic Auditorium, intercut with shots filmed later at New York's Madison Square Garden) and the Santa Monica Airport (which doubled for Washington, DC). Frank's private plane even made an appearance, as the "birthday gift" that the corrupt Senator John Iselin (James Gregory) receives from his supporters.

The first scene to be filmed involved Marco being placed on "indefinite sick leave" by his commanding officer. Frankenheimer admitted that both he and his star were quite nervous:

> I just decided that I would do it in the most economical type of camera set-up that I could. ...We rehearsed it very carefully—and it took only about two hours to film the whole scene.
>
> Sinatra really amazed me in this scene. He was just so good. He just came to it so full. And this was to characterize his performance throughout the movie. This was a delightful, glorious first day. We did this and another scene that first day. It was...after we filmed this first scene that I thought, "Wow, we have a real chance with this."[60]

On February 5-6, a few scenes were filmed in New York—where Central Park and Jilly's, as well as Madison Square Garden—were used. One evening, while shooting in 16-degree weather,

The Manchurian Candidate broke new ground in Hollywood.

Harvey, in a scene depicting Shaw bolting from Jilly's bar in a hypnotic trance, was required to jump into the lake in Central Park, where two dozen reporters and photographers captured the event. Frankenheimer didn't hire a double for Harvey, since several close-ups needed to be shot. One of the cameras actually froze and bulldozers had to work for hours to clear a spot for the actor to jump into, as the ice was a foot thick. Fished out of the freezing water, Harvey was rushed into the boat house for a wardrobe change and then back to the Plaza Hotel for a hot bath and toddy. 20 minutes later, he was dressed as a priest for his final scene set at the fateful presidential convention. Both Frank and Janet Leigh were impressed by their fellow actor's dedication to his craft.

Another scene, shot outside the Garden, also proved a cold one, as a large group of extras, portraying presidential conventioneers, nearly froze while cavorting in sub-zero temperatures wearing short-sleeved shirts. Warmed only by a power generator, they initially were unable to please Frankenheimer and Koch, who grumbled, "They aren't holding these posters right. I'll have to do it myself."[61]

The Manchurian Candidate also broke new ground by including the first karate fight ever included in an American film, one in which Marco fights Chunjin (Henry Silva). Frank, having taken weeks of karate lessons, sometimes using an artificial hand, was injured after slamming his actual right hand into a table top, which splintered:

> There was a moment when he knocked me down, and I said, "Kick at my face with your left foot." The scene started, and he came at me, and he kicked with the other foot. ...I never moved so fast in my whole life. I just shoved everything over to one side...and he caught it in the fist. I broke my finger in that thing...when I went for his head and hit the table. ...It was a solid table, and they cut into it. And there was a movement where I hit him and he fell against the table. In the rehearsal, I said, "That's the right position." Either he didn't hear well, or he didn't know left or right... but he moved into the area where I was going to bring my hand down.[62]

Frankenheimer clarified:

> Henry Silva... was actually left-handed; and we couldn't stage the fight with him being left-handed, so we had to make him do everything from the opposite side, which was a bit of a problem. ...It got criticized at the time of being very, very brutal. Looking at it today, it's hardly anything compared to what you see, even in just a family movie.[63]

Another scene proved interesting for Janet Leigh, who portrays Marco's girlfriend, Rosie. The actress spoke about the scene, noting the fact that she was 34 and Sinatra 46:

> They're in love. Not *falling-all-over-each-other* love. I mean, they're old enough to know how to *share* the knowledge of their love. *Everything* they

Sinatra and Laurence Harvey in *The Manchurian Candidate*

do is intimate. Frank and I play one six-minute sequence on a train, talking about Chinese railroad workers, college towns and girls' camps in Maine. But you know we're getting off that train together. Cast a younger girl in a part like that and it would just look silly.[64]

"We started this scene at four o'clock in the afternoon," Frankenheimer recalled. "We were finished with it at seven o'clock at night."[65] The scene in which Rosie follows Marco outside the dining car was completed in single take. The director added, "This is the kind of scene that could have taken three days if it didn't go well; because I just don't think it's the kind of scene that demanded a lot of intercutting. The scene plays so much better…in a two-shot."[66]

Later in the film, the two actors share a scene in a cab, which Frankenheimer also shot in one take. Leigh said, "I had one long, difficult scene in a taxi with Frank Sinatra where I talk and talk and after one take [the director] said, 'Fine, print it.' I asked if we weren't going to do it over, and he said, 'What for? What am I going to cut to?'"[67] Frankenheimer added, "There was no other coverage ever filmed. That was it."[68]

The Actor, on Screen and in Song

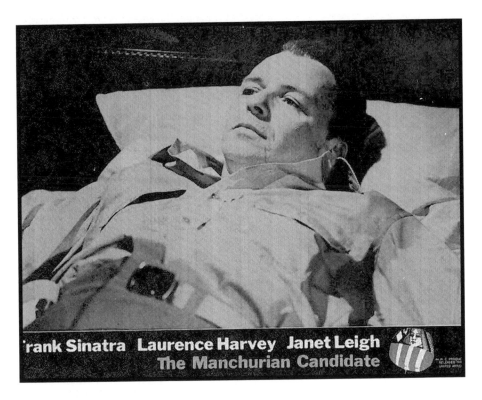

rank Sinatra Laurence Harvey Janet Leigh
The Manchurian Candidate

Of the entire crew, Frank recalled:

> I remember the wonderful enthusiasm on the part of everybody involved
> in the film. And I mean it sincerely. I'm talking about grips, the assistant
> cameraman, the cameraman—everybody was excited about doing the picture,
> which made, I think, 30 to 40 percent of the enthusiasm…from those people.
> And it helped. …It was a wonderful, wonderful experience of my life. …I
> think it only happens once in a performer's life. Once.[69]

Remaining in New York, Frank appeared at a February 10 benefit screening of *Sergeants 3* for
handicapped children at the Capitol Theater. Four days later, he was back in Beverly Hills to attend
an engagement party thrown in his and Juliet Prowse's honor at Romanoff's Restaurant. But by
the 22nd of the month, the proposed marriage was abandoned, due to the couple's disagreements
over her dancing and acting career. After another five days passed, a second "engagement" also
was ditched—that of JFK's visit to the Sinatra home. The Secret Service reportedly had realized that, being open on all sides, Frank's pad posed too much of a security risk and henceforth
decided that the President should stay with Bing Crosby instead. Forget that der Bingle was a
Republican; his place was built against a mountain and very secure. Although JFK phoned to
apologize, Frank became angry at both Peter Lawford and Bobby Kennedy (conflicting reports
suggest that the Attorney General was worried about Frank's "criminal connections" but that
he also attempted to persuade the Secret Service to stick to the original plan); though, according to Tina, "he didn't tear any walls down or take a jackhammer to the helipad, as the yellow
journalists would have it."[70] On a more pleasant, ridiculous, note, he and Dean Martin made
brief cameos as extraterrestrials in *The Road to Hong Kong* (1962), a latter-day entry in the
Hope-Crosby "Road" series.

To promote the release of *The Manchurian Candidate*, United Artists prepared a massive publicity campaign to coincide with the current election, running a special trailer on ABC during the network's broadcasting of the returns. And a full-page print insert, stating, "Don't *vote* for the Manchurian Candidate — *See* It!" was included in a dozen major newspapers.

The film opens in 1952 during the Korean War, as Major Bennett Marco leads a night patrol who are sold out by their translator, Chunjin, and flown by Soviet troops into Manchuria. For three days, the American soldiers are brainwashed to believe their mission was saved by the heroic efforts of Raymond Shaw, who receives the Congressional Medal of Honor upon his return to the States. Though they have been in the presence of Soviet and Chinese officers and psychiatrists, the men believe they had been guests of a women's hydrangea club in a hotel lobby in New Jersey. Stateside, Marco and Corporal Melvin (James Edwards), an African-American member of the patrol, have bizarre, shocking nightmares in which Shaw murders a member of the group.

Frankenheimer, Lindon and editor Ferris Webster's construction of Marco's dream is brilliant. Images of the Chinese psychiatrist, American women, Soviet and Chinese officers and the soldiers are intercut at random and, at one point, a 360-degree pan is used, during which they incorporated a Manchurian amphitheater set that was manually pushed in on train tracks. The effect is a constant alternation between what actually happened to the men and what they were brainwashed to believe.

Frank was very impressed by the masterful cutting of this sequence. "That knocked me out," he admitted. Frankenheimer said:

> The idea for this came right out of Richard Condon's book, which stated that the men thought that they were at a garden club party in a hotel in New Jersey. …We filmed this scene with about six different combinations…and we put the whole thing together in the editing room. …Now, by editing together all these unique combinations, the way we shot the scene…it takes on a very surrealistic quality.[71]

Unable to break away from directing, Frankenheimer asked Axelrod to join Webster in the editing room. Marking up a copy of his script, the writer decided how he would cut the scene. "Believe it or not, that's more or less what we ended up with," the director revealed.

The scene was varied later in the film, to depict a similar dream experienced by Corporal Melvin, who witnesses the same events attended instead by black female gardeners. "Again, this scene was edited…at random," Frankenheimer said, "with no thought to continuity whatsoever. Just to make it weird."[72]

Frankenheimer and Lindon's deep focus cinematography, which enhances the entire film, really shines in the press conference scene, in which Iselin makes spurious McCarthyite claims to the Secretary of Defense (Barry Kelly) and Marco. Three distinct planes of action can be viewed in many shots, with a character in the foreground at one side of the frame, a television monitor in the middle ground and another character in the background at the opposite side of the frame. Frankenheimer recalled:

> This scene was unique in the fact that we have live television and we have film. We have what's going on the monitor and we have what the film camera is seeing. …I was in the television truck, directing the live television cameras, so that what you see on the monitor, I was actually doing at the time the film camera was filming the scene. …It was absolutely, totally live action. You can see that the James Gregory character who is talking totally matches the image on the screen. And that's because it was obviously done at the same time. …All of this [was] ad-libbed…this was all take one…we never tried to go back and do this again — we couldn't have.[73]

The Actor, on Screen and in Song

Sinatra is superb in *The Manchurian Candidate*.

Just before the Secretary of Defense tears into Iselin's outrageous demonstration, Frank has a choice line as Marco advises him, "I don't think it's a good idea to speak to a United States senator that way—even if he is an idiot."

Frankenheimer appreciated Axelrod's depiction of Iselin's demagogical obsession with Abraham Lincoln, particularly the scene opening with the haughty senator's image reflected in a framed portrait of the 16th president. This sequence involves Iselin's pleading to his wife about "settling on" how many "card-carrying Communists" there are in the United States Senate. The scene ends with his dousing of a steak with Heinz ketchup, cutting to the subsequent sequence in which he preaches to his fellow senators about the existence of *57* Commies!

Shaw is consistently controlled by the Communists each time he draws the queen of diamonds while playing solitaire. After Yen Lo (Khigh Dhiegh), the Chinese psychiatrist, and Zilkov (Albert Paulsen), a Russian agent, arrive in the States, they stage a hit-and-run accident in which Shaw is supposedly injured. Placed in fake traction in a private sanitarium, he is "tested" when ordered to murder his journalist boss, Holborn Gaines (Lloyd Corrigan).

In the scene in which Marco is ordered on sick leave, the character reflects an actual aspect of Frank's own intellectual interests: The major is a voracious reader on a vast multitude of subjects. While heading for New York by rail, he then meets Rosie, who helps him light a cigarette after witnessing his profuse sweating, twitching and shaking. Frank's performance in this scene is one of his best on film. Following his reinstatement to active service, he is assigned to monitor Shaw, whom he tells about his dream—that it was "a real swinger of a nightmare." Another of the film's finest scenes occurs shortly after, when the drunken Shaw, in flashback, recollects his previous romance with Jocelyn Jordan (Leslie Parrish), an affair that was broken up by his mother, who had been waging a bitter political war with the girl's father, Senator Thomas Jordan (John McGiver).

Later, in an effort to manipulate the senator, Shaw's mother arranges a party for Jocelyn, who has returned from two years' schooling in Europe. She has decided that her son should marry the girl, which he does; and soon mother's terrible plan takes shape as she has him play solitaire: On the day following the elopement, he shoots and kills his wife and her father. After Senator Jordan and Jocelyn are shot, Marco feels at least partially responsible for their deaths; but Jocelyn, having married Raymond, had asked him to allow them a honeymoon. Frankenheimer said:

> Larry Harvey… just transforms Raymond Shaw into somebody really lovable, likable, and makes it possible for the Sinatra character to feel such compassion for him that he lets him go…when all sense would say, "Don't let him go," because there's just too much at stake.[74]

In Condon's novel, Bennett Marco orders Raymond Shaw to assassinate his mother and stepfather during the convention. Frankenheimer and Axelrod, however, fully aware of the Production Code, knew they couldn't get away with such an act in the film—so Frank was spared having to portray a character who makes such a murderous decision. Instead, his version of Marco has an innocence not in the novel. Having investigated Shaw, he still doesn't know what his orders are. While "deprogramming" him, he asks, "Now, Raymond, Why, why is all of this being done? What have they built you to do?"

Even Shaw doesn't know until the phone rings and he is given the final plan by the "American operator." "Yes. Yes, I understand, Mother," he says quietly just before hanging up the receiver. When Shaw leaves the hotel room, he still hasn't told Marco what he has been ordered to do, but the major assures him that "They can't touch you any more. You're free."

Referring to this important sequence, Frankenheimer said:

> It's important to know that Frank Sinatra was a man who really was better on the first take. It wasn't a question of the fact that he would only do one take, as rumor has it sometimes. He was just *better* on the first take. This scene…is his most dramatic scene in the picture. He had great anxiety about doing it. On his close-up…he did it magnificently, on take one. When we looked at the daily rushes the next day, Frank Sinatra was out of focus, and his major leaves were in focus. I was absolutely devastated. It was the longest walk I have ever taken, from that projection booth to Frank Sinatra's dressing room, to tell him this. He was in tears, because he knew how good he'd been in the scene.
>
> He said, "What do you want to do?"
>
> I said, "Well, we're going to have to re-shoot it."
>
> Well, the first time we went to re-shoot it, Frank got laryngitis. He was so nervous about having to redo it. We couldn't shoot. We scheduled it to re-shoot again. We did it. It wasn't good. We shot it again. …We did, like 10 takes. It was never good…and I didn't know what to do. And I was alone in that cutting room, putting this movie together. Tried all the other stuff, and finally, I said, "The hell with it. Put the out of focus shot in." And a lot of people, including the editor, argued vociferously not to do it.

I said, "His performance is much better in this shot. Put it in."

Well, I cannot tell you, the great reviews I got, as being a genius to use the brainwashed man's point of view of this out of focus man, Sinatra…de-brainwashing him. Everybody thought it was Larry Harvey's point of view. Everybody thought that this was on purpose, this shot. In reality, it was the assistant cameraman's fault.[75]

The following scene, during which Shaw's mother orders him to "shoot the presidential nominee through the head" so that Iselin can rise to the fore, features a terrifying performance by Angela Lansbury. Here, the viewer is given absolute proof who the *real* president will be should Iselin reach the White House—"with powers that will make martial law seem like anarchy." Initially, Frank wanted Lucille Ball to play the megalomaniacal, incestuous Mrs. Shaw, but Frankenheimer asked his star to watch his previous picture, *All Fall Down*, in which Angela Lansbury has a prominent role. Of Lansbury, Frank later admitted, "She was superb. Absolutely marvelous. And she was sinister, she really was. She was a heavy."[76] Though Condon is very explicit about the sexual contact between mother and son, Frankenheimer only subtly suggests it, having Lansbury kiss Harvey at the end of the scene.

Frank is outstanding in the scene in which Marco fears that Shaw will fail to call before carrying out whatever heinous act he has been ordered to commit. As he paces while blaming himself for not stopping Raymond, Frankenheimer and Lindon use the most extreme example of deep focus in the film, with the head of Marco's commanding officer (Douglas Henderson) filling the left foreground as the major frets in the right background.

"Okay, Milt. I blew it! I blew it!" Marco emotes. "My magic is better than your magic. I should have known better. Intelligence officer. *Stupidity* officer is better. If the Pentagon ever wants to open up a Stupidity Division, they'd know who they can get to lead it. Milt, Raymond was theirs, he is theirs, and he always will be theirs." When advised that "He may still call," Marco concludes, "Let's get the hell out of here" and they race to the Garden to stop whatever it is that may happen.

The following sequence, benefiting from Frankenheimer and production designer Richard Sylbert's research on the 1960 Democratic Convention, flawlessly juxtaposes images filmed at the Garden and L.A.'s Olympic Auditorium. "Some of these big crowd shots are stock shots," the director admitted.[77]

Frankenheimer also revealed that he stole from another prominent director:

> Now…the trick here is how does Sinatra find Laurence Harvey? And we could never come up with it. And, finally, one day, I said to George Axelrod…"*Foreign Correspondent*." And we both knew exactly what was meant by that. In other words, in *Foreign Correspondent*, Joel McCrea finds where the Nazis are, in this mass of windmills, because he looks out and all the windmills are going in one direction, except for the one where the spy's radio is, which is going the other direction, because that is electrically powered.
>
> Today, they call such a thing an homage, but in those days, I think I would have called it a *rip-off*. Anyway, I think I have to admit that I ripped off Hitchcock here. Because, what happens is that all the lights dim except the one. Raymond Shaw's light does not dim, and that's how Sinatra finds out where he is—which is why we use the "Star-Spangled Banner" as we do. …And I think everybody buys the fact that he knows.[78]

Interestingly, the names of two former presidents—Benjamin Harrison and Chester A. Arthur—are telescoped into "Benjamin K. Arthur," the presidential nominee whom Shaw is supposed to assassinate. One effective deep-focus shot features hats that Frankenheimer and

Sylbert based on those used by the Kennedy campaign. The assassination is the final beautifully edited sequence. Shaw first trains the gun on Arthur but then shoots Iselin and his mother. After Marco breaks into the room, he straps on the Medal of Honor and commits suicide.

Sound is used superbly, particularly when the scene, culminating with Shaw shooting himself in the head, dissolves from the rifle shot to the rumble of thunder in the final sequence (called an "epitaph" by the director[79]), featuring Marco's reading to Rosie of actual Congressional Medal of Honor citations. Frank delivers the concluding monologue—Marco's own "citation"—with just the right amount of respect and anguish:

> Made to commit acts too unspeakable to be cited here, by an enemy that had captured his mind and his soul. He freed himself at last—and, in the end, heroically and unhesitatingly, gave his life to save his country. Raymond Shaw. Hell. Hell.

As the major moves to the window, saying his final word, thunder again rolls. Frankenheimer said, "Like most scenes in this picture, Frank shot that in one take. We shot the whole picture in 41 days, and it was probably one of the most enjoyable experiences of my life."[80]

This "first film to take on McCarthy"[81] was both critically lauded and viewed as extremely controversial by several different groups with varying political ideologies. While it was attacked by Communist journalists as being vicious propaganda, according to Frankenheimer, the film "is not anti-Russian."[82] Conservative organizations in the United States, such as the American Legion, also offered negative criticism, stating that it is "a vivid example of an attempt to undermine Congressional committees."[83]

Variety's "Anby" raved about the picture:

> Every once in a rare while a film comes along that 'works' in all departments, with story, production and performance so well blended that the end effect is one of nearly complete satisfaction. Such is *The Manchurian Candidate.* ...Like all the best films, there probably has never been anything quite like [it] before, though in sheer bravado of narrative and photographic styles it shares the tradition of Hitchcock, Capra, Welles and Hawks. ...*Candidate* must inevitably come up for a bundle of Oscar nominations next spring. ...Sinatra who, after several pix in which he appeared to be sleep-walking, is again a wide-awake pro creating a straight, quietly humorous character of some sensitivity. ...One of the brilliant achievements of the film is the way Axelrod and Frankenheimer have been able to blend the diverse moods, including the tender and explosively funny as well as the satiric and brutally shocking.[84]

In his *New York Times* review, conservative Bosley Crowther—always inconsistent in his evaluations of Frank's performances—called the film a "wild... piece of fiction," criticizing its "fanatical" portrayals created by "the script of George Axelrod":

[T]he basic suppositions, which might be more tolerable in a clearly satiric context, are extremely hard to take... We are asked to believe that, in three days, a fellow could be brainwashed to the point that two years later, he would still be dutifully submissive to his brainwashers' spell. And the nature of the plot and its key figure here in this country... are so fantastic that one is suspicious of the author's sincerity.

With that said, however, it must be added that the film is... artfully contrived... the dialogue... racy and sharp... So many fine cinematic touches pop up that one keeps wishing the subject would develop into something more than it does. ...Frank Sinatra is slightly over-zealous and conspicuous with nervous tics to carry complete conviction...[85]

Other critics were effusive in their praise for Frank. "Sinatra, in his usual uncanny fashion, is simply terrific," reported *The New Yorker*. While *The Los Angeles Times'* John L. Scott noted that he "provid[es] one of his strongest portrayals," James Powers of *The Hollywood Reporter* wrote, "Sinatra gives a seasoned and in many ways more mature performance than he has ever done before."[86]

The Manchurian Candidate, later called (by critics) "the most poundingly suspenseful political thriller ever made" (*People* magazine) and "one of the best and brightest of modern American films (Roger Ebert), is a lasting testament to the true cultural significance and power of the cinema. Frank Sinatra and his compatriots realized that after reading the novel, before Axelrod's script was ever written. In 1988, Frank said, "I think it's a damn good film." [87]

Having arranged two singles for Frank, Neil Hefti was hired to create hard-driving arrangements for an entire concept LP, *Sinatra and Swingin' Brass*, considered the finest up-tempo Reprise album by many critics and fans. Incredibly, Frank recorded all 12 songs in only two sessions, on April 10 and 11, 1962. Johnny Mercer and Matty Malneck's "Goody, Goody" opens the album in a relatively laid-back jazz style as Frank alters the lyric, "And I hope you're satisfied, you rascal, you" by adding some Sinatra-speak: "And I hope you're satisfied, 'cause *you got yours!*" The Gershwins' "They Can't Take That Away from Me" receives a "cool" swing treatment featuring rhythmic saxophones and a muted trumpet solo, and is followed by a bouncy arrangement of Cole Porter's "At Long Last, Love." These two swinging versions of Broadway classics are followed by a true swing masterpiece, the Duke Ellington band's "I'm Beginning to See the Light," written by the maestro, Harry James, Johnny Hodges and Don George in 1944. Introduced by a single note played in unison on piano and triangle, "Light" then swings lightly, with Frank and the band both entering on the first beat of the second measure—a charming opening for a jazz number. The solo by tenor saxophone great Ben Webster is a highlight of the album.

"Don'cha Go 'Way Mad," a mid-tempo swinger, was adapted from "Black Velvet," an Illinois Jacquet instrumental, and features Frank impressively setting up a powerful, brassy bridge by singing a bluesy phrase that descends both melodically and dynamically. Cole Porter returns on "I Get a Kick Out of You," on which Frank alters his 1953 lyric, "Some people go for cocaine. I'm sure that if I took even one sniff, it would bore me terri*ffffff*ically, too" to the more socially acceptable "Some like the bop-type refrain. I'm sure that if I heard even one riff, 't'would bore me terri*ffff*ically, too." "Tangerine" is a 1942 Victor Schertzinger-Johnny Mercer swinger, while "Love Is Just Around the Corner," originally sung by Bing Crosby in the 1934 film *Here is My Heart*, opens with a muted brass riff resembling a theme from a 1960s television detective show. (Interestingly, Neil Hefti would go on to write the repetitious theme tune for the *Batman* TV series.) The 1927 Tin Pan Alley classic "Ain't She Sweet?" precedes "Serenade in Blue," a ballad written for *Orchestra Wives* (1942), starring Ann Rutherland, George Montgomery and the Glenn Miller Band. "I Love You," another Cole Porter number, from his 1944 Broadway show *Mexican Hayride*, and Jerome Kern and Dorothy Fields' "Pick Yourself Up," written for the Astaire-Rogers classic *Swing Time* (1936), close the album as Frank orders the band, "That's enough, now."

During the spring of 1962, Frank made plans to tour various parts of Europe, the Middle East and Asia on behalf of needy and ill young people. Admitting that it was time for "underpriviledged children" to be helped by an "overpriviledged adult," he organized The World Tour for Children, a series of 19 concerts to begin on April 18. Film footage shot at several venues eventually was edited into a 30-minute documentary titled *Frank Sinatra with All God's Children*. Never released commercially, the film, which emphasized his out-of-pocket expenses and featured many scenes of him (sans toupee) playing with visually and physically impaired youngsters, was the sort of obvious publicity that Frank traditionally avoided.

Frank visited children's hospitals and youth centers in Hong Kong, where he joined his band for two concerts at the new City Hall and a youth matinee, raising $95,000 for charity. In Israel from May 2-10, he broke ground at the Frank Sinatra International Youth Center for Arab and Jewish Children and played two shows in Nazareth, then on to Jerusalem to meet Prime Minister David Ben Gurion and perform two additional concerts. Following a week of rest cruising the Greek Islands, on May 18 and 19, he sang for enormous crowds at the Herodus Atticus, an ancient Roman ampitheater, in Athens, where actors first took the stage 2,500 years earlier. Introduced as "Frankus Sinatropopolous," he told the audience of his plans to repeat the children's tour once each year. Before leaving Greece, he received the Athens Medal of Honor. One week later, he performed in Rome and Milan, and was presented with the Italian Star of Solidarity.

On May 30, he played a superb show for Princess Grace and a capacity crowd at the Royal Festival Hall in London, where he and the band remained through June 4. Following a moving visit to the Children's Home for the Blind, he played additional shows at the Odeon and the Hammersmith Gaumont. From June 5 through 7, he sang at two venues in Paris, then concluded the tour in Monaco, where he again thrilled Princess Grace and her husband, Prince Rainier. Among his final honors were the dedication of the "Sinatra Wing" at the Summer Home of the St. Jean De Dieu for Crippled Boys at Bruyeres le Chatel, France, and his receipt of the Gold Medal of Paris, which previously had been awarded to Dr. Albert Schweitzer and John F. Kennedy.

Back in London, Frank recorded tracks for a new concept album on June 12-14, 1962. Collaborating with arranger-conductor Robert Farnon, he chose 11 songs by English composers, 10 of which were included on *Sinatra Sings Great Songs from Great Britain*. Unfortunately, the long, taxing tour had taken its toll on his voice, and the weariness came through as he sang over Farnon's slow, orchestral arrangements. (Frank disliked the album so much that it would not be released in the United States until 1990.)

Nevertheless, he opens the album a cappella, on Ray Noble's "The Very Thought of You," a song often associated with Nat Cole. The Voice is a bit rough, but he still manages to pull off his trademark long-breath phrasing. Ivor Novello's "We'll Gather Lilacs in the Spring" is one of the album's weaker tracks, and he had recorded the bluesy "If I Had You" more capably twice before, for Columbia and Capitol. A rather ancient song from New Zealand rather than England, "Now Is the Hour," written in 1913, actually allows Frank to use his weariness to bring just the right emotion to the lyrics. A Middle European-tinged oboe opens "The Gypsy," a track thought unsatisfactory by Farnon, who objected to some of Frank's phrasing choices.

One of the high points of the album, Eric Maschwitz and Sherwin Manning's "A Nightingale Sang in Berkeley Square," recorded just 18 months earlier by Nat Cole, finds Frank in somewhat finer fettle and a sublime solo from trombonist Harry Roche. "A Garden in the Rain" is another weak number that can be imagined being sung far better by the Sinatra of the Dorsey years, and "London By Night" is another ballad recorded more satisfactorily by Frank for both Columbia and Capitol. He sounds equally fatigued on "We'll Meet Again," while the concluding track, Noel Coward's "I'll Follow My Secret Heart," which he previously had recorded as a V-Disc in 1944, arguably features the most powerful voice he could conjure up on June 12, the first day of the sessions. One song, "Roses of Picardy," was dropped due to his "dislike" for the performance, but producer Alan Freeman, though he believed the Voice "wasn't holding his notes well," wanted to keep the track: "He sang it so beautifully, with tremendous *feel*."[88] (The song later was included on the CD release.)

From June 29 through July 5, 1962, Frank played to sold-out audiences at the Cal-Neva Lodge. Later in the summer, while he and Hank Sanicola were driving from Palm Springs to Las Vegas, his old colleague voiced his opinion that Sam Giancana had directly defied the Nevada Gaming Control Board's "Black Book," which listed persons who were forbidden access to gambling operations in the state. Sanicola knew that Giancana had gone to Cal-Neva to see his girlfriend, Phyllis McGuire, who performed at the resort, and was worried that his $300,000 investment in the Lodge was at stake. After also claiming that, due to the poor box office returns of Frank's recent films, his stock in Park Lake Enterprises was at risk—and rejecting a buyout offer—he chose to get out of the car in the desert. Although he had been a trusted pal for decades, he never spoke to Frank again, and Ermiglia ("Jilly") Rizzo became the Sinatra "right-hand man."[89]

Frank met Rizzo at a New York restaurant, one of six Big Apple establishments where the latter worked as a bouncer. "Frank saw my father handling a situation," recalled Rizzo's son Willy. "It impressed him and he said, 'I gotta meet this guy.' It started their lifelong friendship."[90]

On August 22-25, 1962, Frank joined Dean and Sammy for some free gigs to help Skinny D'Amato re-energize his 500 Club in Atlantic City, where business had been hit hard by the legalization of gambling in Vegas. Returning to Los Angeles, he sang at Samuel Goldwyn's 80th birthday party at the Beverly Hilton on the 26th and cut two singles, "The Look of Love" and "I Left My Heart in San Francisco" (which was not released), the following day before flying back to Atlantic City for another gig at the 500 Club with Dean and Sammy. The Newark Office of the FBI, surveilling Giancana, kept a close eye on the casino and the Claridge Hotel, where they claimed Frank had booked an entire floor of rooms. On September 1, Frank was back at Cal-Neva to perform two Labor Day shows with Dean.

SINATRA-BASIE

AN HISTORIC MUSICAL FIRST

"I've waited twenty years for this moment," Frank said as he prepared to record an album with one of his musical heroes, William ("Count") Basie, on October 2, 1962.[91] He often had hung out with Basie in New York, and the Count's legendary saxophonist Lester Young had admitted in 1956, "If I could put together exactly the kind of band I wanted, Frank Sinatra would be the singer. Really, my main man is Frank Sinatra."[92] In 1965, Frank recalled, "Basie, as we all know, epitomizes the greatest kind of tempo for swing, in jazz. It was a joy because all I had to do was just stay up on the crest of the sound and move along with it. It just carries you right through."[93]

Opening *Sinatra-Basie: An Historic Musical First*, Basie takes six measures to play his trademark minimalist introduction, on "Pennies from Heaven." Frank first lays back, then bows out for a tenor saxophone solo and brassy bridge, then dynamically soars "on the crest of the sound," but never over the peak, singing beautifully behind the beat before the song concludes with the stark dynamic contrast between the raging band and the Count's feather-touch piano.

Sammy Cahn and Saul Chaplin's "Please Be Kind" is another example of the superb sound created by the marriage of a great jazz band and Frank Sinatra. Like a lead saxophonist, Frank is a fine soloist, staying with the basic melody yet adding individual phrasing, melodic improvisation and endless dynamic invention. Though some Sinatra aficionados find "(Love Is) The Tender Trap" a curious choice, here it is not the meticulously crafted movie song, but a swinging interpretation replete with big band dynamics. "Looking at the World Through Rose-Colored Glasses," a breakneck swinger, is followed by Leslie Bricusse's "My Kind of Girl," a medium-tempo number featuring a familiar melody and lyrics, given a jump start by Neal Hefti's potent brass and percussion kicks. And the lyric, "She's sweet enough to eat" seems rather contemporary, timeless. The two "stars" attempt to upstage each other on the ending, although the Count gets the last word: After Basie plays his trademark three-note piano riff, Frank sings a bluesy, melodically descending phrase, yet Bill counters with an even more bluesy keyboard coda.

After performing "I Only Have Eyes for You" for V-Disc and Columbia, Frank took a lightly swinging stab at it this time. Though many people recall the pop version from the 1950s, the song actually was written in 1934 for the Broadway show *Dames*. Following a brassy instrumental bridge, Frank vocally crescendos above the band, driving the final verses home. Written by the Gershwins for the Fred Astaire film *Damsel in Distress* (1937) and first recorded by Frank in 1956, "Nice Work If You Can Get It" moves along like a movie chase, with Frank and the band alternating rhythmic "shots." A number-one hit, in fact the biggest success he ever had with Capitol, "Learnin' the Blues" is courageously rearranged here, in a straightforward style but also including a minimal amount of soloing by Basie.

"I'm Gonna Sit Right Down and Write Myself a Letter," written in 1935, was first cut by Frank in 1954, but now, with Hefti at the helm, he swung the song with a newly found swagger, cautiously crossing over into improvisational jazz soloing. Not only does he sing miles behind the beat, but his lyrical changes — "Gonna sit down, *knock out* a letter" — further alter the original rhythm. "I Won't Dance" — written by *five* major songwriters — and used in *Roberta* (1935), closes lyrically on a negative note. Leave it to Frank.

On October 22, Frank returned to the studio to record Dan Dreyer, Al Jolson and Billy Rose's 1927 novelty number "Me and My Shadow" with Sammy Davis, Jr., and Billy May. "You'll never get rid of your shadow, Frank. You'll never get rid of me," Sam sings, while Frank mentions Jilly's and Toots Shor's. The following month, the duo, joined by Dean Martin, finished "paying back" Sam Giancana at Chicago's Villa Venice, a nightclub surrounded by canals and gondolas. Over the course of a week, they performed 16 shows that attracted the high rollers expected by operator Jimmy Meo, who, according to the FBI, "fronted" for Giancana, known at the club as "Mr. Flood." The bureau compiled information about all the known wiseguys who attended the shows and a dive up the street that reputedly was used as an illegal casino.[94]) Though 10 songs and a great deal of improvised comedy were recorded on 59 reels of tape, the proposed album *At the Summit* was not released. (Eventually, two bootleg compact discs were distributed, prior to the release of a legitimate, 24-carat gold CD by Tina Sinatra's Artanis Productions in 1999.)

After scoring a triumph in *The Manchurian Candidate*, Frank walked through *Come Blow Your Horn*, playing himself. According to director Bud Yorkin, One-Take Charley "was terrific. I enjoyed working with him....He had a certain impatience, a certain desire to get moving."[95]

Prior to location shooting in New York, Yorkin wanted to discuss some concepts for the film, but Frank was unimpressed and left the studio. The following day, discovering a note asking him to meet with Frank in the latter's dressing room, Yorkin rapped on the door.

While putting on his makeup, Frank asked the director if he had heard that the actor was "difficult to work with... don't like to do a lot of takes... don't like to work past [five o'clock]?"

Responding affirmatively, Yorkin was told, "Well, if you've heard all that, why didn't you get Gordon MacCrea to play the part? He's a sweet guy. He'll cause you no problems." Laughing, Frank added, "Come on, pal. Let's get this thing over with."

Yorkin later said, "He broke the ice and we went ahead and did it. So, in a strange way, there are those good sides of him, which turn out to be better than those son of a bitch things."[96]

Though Norman Lear based his screenplay on Neil Simon's Broadway play, *Come Blow Your Horn* treads too uncomfortably close to both *The Tender Trap* and *A Hole in the Head*, both better films. Like *A Hole in the Head*, it is a barely disguised Jewish comedy, but this time the filmmakers didn't even bother to make Frank's character, Alan Baker, an Italian. *Come Blow Your Horn*, while very entertaining and funny at times, is often a maddening melange of styles.

Lee J. Cobb, hamming his Papa Baker to the hilt, is Edward G. Robinson redux, objecting to his son's playboy lifestyle, particularly his influence on younger brother, Buddy (Tony Bill, in his first of three films with Frank). Frank's Alan romances several beautiful women simultaneously (including Jill St. John and Barbara Rush) at his bachelor pad and, when the kid leaves Mom and Pop and moves in, buys him new clothes to befit his new swinging attitude.

An awkward but charming musical sequence depicts Alan singing "Come Blow Your Horn" as they search for the perfect ensemble on Madison Avenue. As the song ends, Frank improvises, "I tell you, chum. I tell you, *bum*! It's time to come blow your horn." Soon the two dapperly dressed brothers are quaffing martinis at Toots Shors. (Frank reprised his use of Jilly's in *The Manchurian Candidate* by using his other favorite watering hole.)

During the filming of the musical sequence (on the first day of the location shoot), Frank's impatience was at its pinnacle, particularly when cinematographer William Daniels was waiting for the sun properly to light the street. Yorkin recalled:

> I actually had Frank stashed in a store on Madison Avenue—because it's such a narrow street, you literally have sun at midday for forty-five minutes. After that, it's cast in deep shadows. In those days, films and lenses weren't as fast as they are today. You really had to wait for the light to be bright. ...We had cameras hanging out of the window on the second floor across the street. He had the music piped into his ear, so he could be mouthing the tune he was listening to. My assistant was on a walkie-talkie talking to another assistant director. I kept hearing, "How soon are we going to go? How soon are we going to go?" ...I knew these questions were coming from Frank to the other assistant director.[97]

Though Yorkin didn't want to pressure a cinematographic legend like William Daniels, he had to voice Frank's displeasure. The cameraman complained that the light wasn't right, which would necessitate another full take from the actor, but then finally gave the director the go-ahead.

According to Yorkin:

> We cued the music so that he could hear it in his earpiece as he came out of the door onto the street. People were walking by and didn't realize it was Frank Sinatra, singing. He walked the block, stepped off the curb, flagged the first taxi that came along—and was gone for the day. We didn't know whether we had [it] or not. We had one crack and that was it.[98]

The Cinema of Sinatra

Van Heusen and Cahn again wrote the title song for a Sinatra film, this time a charming light swinger. Conducted by Nelson Riddle, Frank recorded his actual soundtrack vocal on October 25, 1962, but waxed the Reprise single, again with Riddle at the helm, on January 21, 1963. He also cut a second Van Heusen-Cahn single, "Call Me Irresponsible," written for the Jackie Gleason film *Papa's Delicate Condition* (1963), on the latter date.

Continuing to work nonstop, Frank spent February 18-21 on a soundstage at Goldwyn Studios, accompanied by Nelson Riddle and a 73-piece orchestra (the largest ever to back up a pop singer) for *The Concert Sinatra*, an impressive collection of eight classic show songs. Having recorded albums of intimate ballads, small-ensemble swing numbers, big band classics and powerhouse hard swingers, he now added an impressive collection of eight famous show songs to his discography, an ambitious undertaking for his first Reprise LP with Riddle.

Rodgers and Hammerstein's "I Have Dreamed," written for *The King and I*, opens the set quietly and builds for the next three minutes, ending with Frank at his most majestic, combining sheer power with supreme vocal control. As Chuck Granata writes, "It may well be the most powerful performance of Sinatra's career."[99] "My Heart Stood Still," written by Rodgers and Hart for the 1927 musical *A Connecticut Yankee*, is another example of Frank commandingly playing his "reed," as is "Lost in the Stars," the Kurt Weill-Maxwell Anderson song about racial tolerance he originally recorded for Columbia in 1946. Frank produces one of his greatest vocal performances, which Chuck Granata describes as a "wide open" version of "Ol' Man River":

> Inspired by the powerful lyrics and Riddle's opulent textural setting, Sinatra ponders each syllable, searching to extract every gradation of color possible.
>
> Here his acting skills serve him well. Near the finale he reaches the line:"You get a little drunk and you lands in jaiiiiiiiiiiiilllllllllllllllll...,
> and without pause, slides into the next phrase:
> Ohhhhhhhhhhhhhhhhhhh...,then plummets way down, lower than you've ever heard him go, and then half an octave lower than *that*. Finally, without the slightest trace of vibrato, he smooths it out, seemlessly flowing into the finale:
> ...ohhhhhhhhh...I gets weary, and sick of tryin'...I'm tired of livin', but I'm scared of dyin'...
> As Sinatra blazes across the final notes, the strings soar, the brass screams, and the percussion pounds, bringing the vocal and instrumental crescendos to a dramatic close.
> This ending powerfully captures the breadth of Sinatra's vocal range and the strength of his voice...[100]

In 1955, Frank had recorded a Riddle arrangement of Rodgers and Hammerstein's "You'll Never Walk Alone" from *Carousel*, and here uses the same chart, beautifully supported by strings and woodwinds as he hits a dramatic peak and then ends quietly. On a less serious note, Frank sings another classic Rodgers melody (with Hart lyrics) on "Bewitched," which he briefly sang in *Pal Joey* and recorded for that film's soundtrack album in 1957. The Sinatra-Rodgers combination remains for "This Nearly Was Mine," which had been written (with Hammerstein) for the Broadway production *South Pacific* in 1949, and "Soliloquy," another *Carousel* number first recorded by Frank in 1946. "Soliloquy," a richly textured narrative vocal performance, is, as Will Friedwald writes, about balances:

> Sinatra striking the right mix of aggressiveness and tenderness, Riddle finding the border between Broadway and his own, less earthbound imagination. ...the only time the work has been completely successful outside of the show that spawned it.[101]

The Concert Sinatra arguably features Frank's best sonic acting since *Only the Lonely*, yet here he embraces a style 180-degrees away from the earlier album. He achieves dramatic excellence at both ends of the spectrum, controlling his delivery, phrasing and pitch—apparently effort-lessly—like a Laurence Olivier or Ralph Richardson at the height of his powers performing Shakespeare. But here, rather than the Bard, the album offers 75-percent Richard Rodgers.

Three additional songs, Van Heusen and Cahn's "California" and "America the Beautiful," both backed with a large chorus, and "You Brought a New Kind of Love to Me," were recorded during the *Concert* sessions. The first two were pressed as singles but not released, though "You Brought," which Frank previously had cut with Riddle in 1956, was issued by Reprise.

Bud Yorkin wrapped *Come Blow Your Horn* on February 23, one week early and $100,000 under budget. On April 8, Frank hosted the Academy Awards, broadcast by ABC.

Come Blow Your Horn is often as self-indulgent (and not an iota as inventive) as *Ocean's Eleven*. Frank does impressions of Humphrey Bogart and John F. Kennedy, wears orange sweaters and vests (and has Bill decked out in them, too), plays an entire scene with Bill while shaving in the bathroom (as he does with David Wayne in *The Tender Trap* and Kim Novak in *Pal Joey*), and the "bum business" *really* goes on forever.

Yelling, "Bum!" directly into Alan's face, Papa Baker criticizes his son's recent absence when he was supposed to be home, working in the family business, which is producing and sell-ing artificial fruit! "Did you have a nice weekend, Bum?" (Alan works two days and then takes five-day weekends.) "If I was in the bum business, I'd want ten of you!"

"Why am I a bum?" Alan asks.

"Are you married?" replies Papa.

"No."

"Then you're a bum!"

Later, Alan, becoming aggravated with his brother's total degeneration, calls him a bum; but after realizing that he is turning into his own father, mends his ways and marries Connie (Rush). To cap off the bum content, Dean Martin has a cameo in one scene, playing a panhandler on the street who is handed a raw steak by Alan. (Alan had been punched in the face by Mr. Eckman [Dan Blocker] after attempting to put the make on his wife, a prospective artificial fruit client.)

Perhaps the film's most entertaining self-reflective moment occurs when Connie reminds Alan that he had called her "a lousy singer."

"I said you had a lousy voice," he replies. "There's a difference, you know. Even the hockey players are making albums now."

Tony Bill is wooden in the early scenes, but loosens up as the film progresses. Lee J. Cobb and Molly Picon overact as the parents, while Jill St. John is effective as the luscious bimbo and Barbara Rush, giving the best performance, is her usual classy self. Norman Lear's dialogue, coupled with the ad-libbing of Frank, is often funny; and Yorkin's direction is unobtrusive.

Though there were some moments of tension on the set, Yorkin truly admired his star, particularly his penchant for literature: "He was a voracious reader, I suppose because he never slept much. There was never a book I used to talk to him about that he hadn't read." But when Frank asked him to work with him on another project, Yorkin bowed out: "I said, 'You and I are now friends. I would like it to stay that way.' I knew that the second time around, there would be trouble. I didn't want to get into a pissing contest."[102]

Paramount worked with Reprise Records to promote the film, which benefited from the heavy airplay given to the "Come Blow Your Horn" single. Nelson Riddle's complete score was issued on LP and an instrumental version of the title song also was released as a 45. The pressbook ballyhoo, not surprisingly, included some slightly exaggerated claims:

> *Come Blow Your Horn* is Frank Sinatra's most spectacular movie to date, and he plays the kind of role his fans like best. He is seen as a high-liv-ing, hard-drinking playboy who abhors work and loves to chase pretty girls.[103]

Reprise's Mike Shore, who managed the publicity, devised a slogan—"Art it ain't—Fun it is"—but Frank wouldn't approve it, indicating that he may have taken the film somewhat seriously. "I think that sort of complaint was a little far-fetched," Shore claimed, "but he didn't want to belittle what he did."[104] On June 6, 1963, he attended the world premiere at the Plaza Theatre in Palm Springs.

On April 29 and 30, Frank had cut 10 tracks for *Sinatra's Sinatra*, an album of his favorites newly arranged by Nelson Riddle for Reprise. Included with "I've Got You Under My Skin," "In the Wee Small Hours of the Morning," "The Second Time Around," "Nancy," "Witchcraft," "Young at Heart," "All the Way," "How Little It Matters How Little We Know," "Oh, What It Seemed to Be" and "Put Your Dreams Away" are "Call Me Irresponsible," the single recorded the previous January, and "Pocketful of Miracles," which had been waxed on November 22, 1961. Frank is in good voice throughout, and plays with the lyrics on several of the songs, but the performances, though not without merit, pale in the shadow of the earlier Columbia and Capitol versions. Milt Bernhart was busy with a film score gig, so Dick Nash, borrowing from the trombonist's legendary solo, substituted for him on "Skin."

During July 1963, Frank waxed a dozen songs for inclusion on the ambitious four-record set *Reprise Musical Repertory Theatre*, a collection of major songs from *Finian's Rainbow, Guys and Dolls, Kiss Me, Kate* and *South Pacific* conducted by Morris Stoloff and also featuring Bing Crosby, Dean Martin, Sammy Davis, Jr., Jo Stafford, Dinah Shore, Debbie Reynolds, Rosemary Clooney, the McGuire Sisters and Keely Smith. Dean and Sammy joined Frank on a Billy May arrangement of Cole Porter's "We Open in Venice" on July 10, when a Frank and Dino duet of "Guys and Dolls" also was attempted. Eight days later, a successful version of "Guys" (replete with "bums" and "broads") was laid down, followed by Nelson Riddle charts of "Old Devil Moon," "When I'm Not Near the Girl I Love" and "I've Never Been in Love Before."

Keely Smith effectively teamed with Frank and Riddle on July 24, for Porter's "So in Love" and Rodgers and Hammerstein's "Twin Soliloquies (Wonder How It Feels)." The following day, Frank cut two versions of "Some Enchanted Evening," a solo and a duet with Rosemary Clooney, and a smokin' Billy May arrangement of "Luck Be a Lady." Dino returned on July 29, joining Frank and Bing Crosby on two more *Guys and Dolls* numbers, "Fugue for Tinhorns" and "The Oldest Established (Permanent Floating Crap Game in New York)." Frank rounded out the month two days later, recording two singles—"Here's to the Losers" and "Love Isn't Just for the Young"—arranged by Marty Paich. In between the *Repertory* sessions, he recorded another song for a film in which he did not act, Carl Foreman's *The Victors*, on July 16. Heard during one sequence, "Have Yourself a Merry Little Christmas" paired him with the Wally Scott Orchestra and Chorus.

In August, Frank was joined by Kirk Douglas, Tony Curtis, Robert Mitchum and Burt Lancaster to contribute heavily disguised cameos to John Huston's bizarre adaptation of Philip MacDonald's mass-murder mystery novel *The List of Adrian Messenger*. Amidst a very tangled narrative—concerning a list of 11 names given to British intelligence officer Anthony Gethryn (George C. Scott) by Adrian Messenger (John Merivale) just before he is killed in a plane bombing—Frank is unrecognizable beneath a thick hide of gypsy stableboy makeup prepared by Bud Westmore. Even Mitchum (as a London shopkeeper), Curtis (an Italian organ grinder) and Lancaster (an old woman!) are easier to spot. Douglas appears in several disguises and actually concludes the film with a full-fledged characterization: the inheritance-seeking murderer, who meets his end impaled on a farm implement! Huston, who also makes a cameo appearance in a fox-hunting scene, exercises his strange sense of humor throughout the film.

Frank again joined his pal Dino for an Old West romp in writer-producer-director Robert Aldrich's *4 for Texas* (1963), a tale of banking and insurance fraud in post-Civil War Galveston. But this time Frank (as "Zack Thomas") and Dean (as "Joe Jarrett") were pitted against each other, vying for $100,000 also sought by banker Harvey Burden (Victor Buono) and hired gun Matson (Charles Bronson) while romancing their respective European voluptuaries, Elya Carlson (Anita Ekberg) and Maxine Richter (Ursula Andress). Having developed an idea to refurbish a river boat, Zack is initially outraged by Joe's moving in on the craft and its inhabitant, Maxine, but eventually forms a partnership when Matson and his gang start a murderous brawl on grand-opening night. When the smoke clears, Matson is dead at the bottom of the river, Burden is arrested by a Texas marshal, and the two heroes wed their women.

Though *4 for Texas* did not return Frank to his former cinematic glory, Aldrich's script required him to portray a personality other than his own. There are no "bums," "broads" or "ring-a-ding-dings" here; however, the film features one self-indulgent moment—this time, not for himself, but for his daughter, Nancy. After their stagecoach crashes, Zack holds a rifle on Joe, ordering him to walk back across the desert with the money-filled carpetbag he has stolen. As Aldrich cuts to close-ups of Martin's feet, Frank says, "They tell me those boots ain't built for walkin'." Soon after, Dino reassures, "And you're right about those boots. They ain't made for walkin'." This scene, filmed on location by Aldrich and cinematographer Ernest Laszlo, perhaps pays homage to John Ford when the left foreground of the widescreen image is filled with Frank's rear end, calling to mind "Pappy's" many similar compositions juxtaposing actor Ward Bond's posterior with such natural formations as the buttes of Utah's Monument Valley. (Ford hinted that these shots were his visual proof that Bond literally was a "horse's ass.")

Another in-joke involves the production partnership formed by Frank and Dean prior to filming. Naming their business entity "The Sam Company" (Sinatra and Martin), they had art director William Glasgow design a dockside warehouse sporting a sign with the same moniker. And though this off-screen bond does not appear on-screen until the last moments of the film, there are few surprises in the behavior of their characters: Both Zack and Joe are worshipped by beautiful women, handle lots of liquor and triumph over every adversary. Most of the audience sympathy is directed toward Joe until they join forces to battle the banker and gunslinger.

Elya and Maxine are very capable 1870 women, but the very title *4 for Texas* could just as well refer to their bulging breasts, which threaten to burst the bonds of their clothing at any moment. In fact, in his December 1963 review, *Variety*'s "Tube" noted, "The film is loaded with distracting cleavage, thanks to the presence of Anita Ekberg and Ursula Andress. (Stacked up alongside Miss Ekberg's stupendous proportions, even Mae West might seem anemic)."[105]

"Tube" also opined, "The Robert Aldrich production is a Western too preoccupied with sex and romance to enthrall sagebrush-happy moppets and too unwilling to take itself seriously to sustain the attention of an adult."[106] The film's humorous elements reach ridiculous proportions when workmen arrive at the riverboat to ready it for opening night. Among the delivery men are none other than the latter-day Three Stooges (Moe Howard, Larry Fine and "Curly Joe" DeRita), who recently had made a comeback via television reruns of their Columbia shorts and a series of awful new feature films such as *Snow White and the Three Stooges* and *The Three Stooges Meet Hercules*. At one point, Dino gives the trio the old "multiple face slap" formerly utilized by Moe, and is seconded by an old woman (Ellen Corby) who has objected to their delivery: a nude painting of Maxine scheduled to hang aboard the boat.

Several familiar character actors appear among the supporting cast, including the physically imposing and psychologically cowering Victor Buono, who previously had appeared in another Aldrich film, the classic *What Ever Happened to Baby Jane?* (1962). He recalled:

I always had fun with Frank. There was more drinking and dancing and laughing on the sets than there was working, which was a little strange to get used to, as I always liked to be able to concentrate on the work. It was like being in a Vegas nightclub. Frank and Dean and their friends turned

Sinatra, Dean Martin and Victor Buono

every place they went into a Vegas club. Everyone's eyes were bugging out at Ursula and Anita—who were really very sweet—and there were women hanging around hoping to get a look at Frank and Dean, and Aldrich would have to track them down half the time just so he could get a scene shot; it was madness. Bob was a disciplined director but he'd have to take a shot [of booze] now and then just to keep up with Frank and Dean—or because of them.[107]

Other familiar faces include Richard Jaeckel and Jack Elam, whose outlaw is gunned down by Matson in the opening, pre-titles, sequence. In January 1998, Elam recalled his experiences with Frank:

I have great respect for him personally....On *4 for Texas* I did a one day guest shot and I don't think he worked on my day. ...In the early '60s...at Warner Bros....I was doing the television series *Teple Houston*. Occasionally we would cross paths and it was always a warm greeting by name from him. Frankly, I was rather flattered that he knew me. There are damned few people who have the savvy and guts to get up in the morning and be Frank Sinatra all day! And besides all that, he can sort of sing, too. If I were king I'd knight him.[108]

One institution that definitely *didn't* want to knight Frank was the Nevada State Gaming Board, who, having learned that Sam Giancana had been spotted at Cal-Neva with Phyllis Mc-Guire, asked him to attend a hearing during the summer of 1963. Now Frank's gambling license was at stake. Not only did this situation threaten his investments in both Cal-Neva and the Sands in Vegas, but it also worried Jack Warner, whose company was in the process of buying Reprise from Frank, who in turn was to receive executive status at the movie studio. When Warner advised attorney Mickey Rudin to encourage Frank to attend the hearing or risk jeopardizing the business deal, Frank turned in his license rather than endure the publicity of a hearing. Frank admitted running into Giancana at the resort, but throughout the ordeal insisted that he had not been invited. But it wasn't only Jack Warner who helped Frank decide to dash his Cal-Neva dream; apparently he didn't want to cast any untoward light on President Kennedy, whose name surely would have become involved. (Ironically, while the FBI continued to investigate Frank's "relationship" with Giancana, the CIA hired the Mob boss and his associate Johnny Roselli to develop a plan to assassinate Cuban leader Fidel Castro.)

As Nancy, Jr., has written, "The sale of...Reprise to Warner Bros. gave [Frank] big money, real security for the rest of his life."[109] He not only gained a powerful position at the studio, where a new L-shaped building had been constructed as his base of operations, but "it was thought for a while that [he] might take over as head of the studio when Jack Warner retired."[110]

From September 6 through 8, Frank re-teamed with Dean and Sammy at the Sands for three evenings of Summit shows with the Tony Morelli Orchestra. Intending to release the September 7th performance as a Reprise album, Frank instructed Wally Heider to record it, but later changed his mind—an unfortunate decision, considering that he was in fine voice and sang his numbers seriously when not cutting up with his pallies. As always, Dino opened the show with booze-altered lyrics, including a parody of Cole Porter's "I Love Paris" re-titled "I Love Vegas." Frank delivered an excellent set including "I Only Have Eyes for You," "Call Me Irresponsible," "My Heart Stood Still," "Please Be Kind," "I Have Dreamed" and "Luck Be a Lady."

"It's your world. I'm just livin' in it," Dino told Frank at one point. Then Sammy literally landed in it by singing his own version of "The Lady Is a Tramp." The show closed with Dean and Frank dueting on *Guys and Dolls'* title song and "The Oldest Established (Permanent Floating Crap Game in New York)." The audience included Buddy Rich, Lucille Ball and Jimmy Van Heusen. (This show was released by Capitol as *The Rat Pack Live at the Sands* in 2001.)

For the meantime at Warner Bros., Frank made a three-picture deal, signing Gene Kelly as a partner to serve a different function on each: producer, actor and director, respectively. Planning

to appear in all three, Frank then asked Kelly to direct the first completed script, *Robin and the 7 Hoods*, an innovative musical spoof placing the Western world's most legendary populist hero within two of the United States' most shattering historical events: the gangland wars of 1920s Chicago and the early days of the Great Depression.

Having ordered an old-fashioned musical with an original score, Jack Warner received that and more. While cameraman William Daniels had experienced some trying moments while shooting *Come Blow Your Horn*, now he was hired as cinematographer *and* associate producer on a Sinatra project. To lead the cast, the Summit would return in even greater glory, minus the ousted Peter Lawford, but with the added attraction of Bing Crosby.

Kelly was ready to begin rehearsals in Hollywood, but Frank, busy with other professional and personal commitments, kept stalling. Kelly revealed:

[H]e kept telling Howard Koch... that he'd be arriving the next day, then the day after that and so on, until I decided the tension and the waiting wasn't doing any of us any good, and I told Jack Warner I was quitting. Warner kept reminding me how friendly I was with Frank, to which I replied that I was more than friendly. I really loved him and that was the reason I was walking out because it was my intention to remain friendly with him, and that if I stayed on, as a kind of paid laborer, our relationship would be over. I told Warner to call his public relations man and release the story that I wanted nothing more to do with the set-up, but I stressed to him that I didn't want Frank to come out of it badly. They could tell the press we had a difference of opinion and leave it at that. Which is exactly what they did, and I quietly withdrew. Most of the other fellows remained on except Saul Chaplin, who was doing the music. He left as well.[111]

Soon after Kelly's exit, versatile Gordon Douglas, whom Frank had worked with on *Young at Heart*, took over the director's chair; and, on October 15, 1963, David Schwartz delivered the final draft of the script to Howard Koch, who again executive produced for Frank. Since the story was a satire of events that actually occurred in Chicago, Warner Bros. research department head Carl Milliken, Jr., in an inter-office memo, reported to Koch his legal concerns on October 25, six days before filming was to begin. Though the film obviously would take place during the early days of the Great Depression, no specific date would be named. To avoid "possible lawsuits," Milliken advised:

> There is one matter of rather large importance, namely, your use of the Cook County sheriff as one of your criminal characters. This use, combined with the fact that you pinpoint—several times in the course of the script—1929 as the time of the story, sets up a clear case of libel against the sheriff at that time, JOHN E. TRAEGER.
> Not only was he sheriff, but his son was assistant sheriff and we find both "John E. Traeger" and "John E. Traeger, Jr." currently listed in Chicago directories. ...Since the humor involved is obviously not as great if you utilize a less important and identifiable individual, such as a deputy sheriff, the only solution apparent... would seem to be to fail *completely* to identify any given year during the Twenties.
> This would mean eliminating the dates from all the cornerstones, etc. It would also mean very careful attention to any other internal evidence (such as license plates) that would enable anybody seeing the film to pinpoint a year. ...[I]n the matter of the sheriff's office, there is—in Chicago—an office called "Chief Deputy Sheriff" as well as an "Assistant Sheriff." A second large problem arises with your use of the character, Deputy Crocker... who—having rubbed out his boss—promptly steps into his shoes. To increase this hazard, there was one single individual who served—almost throughout the Twenties—as Chief Deputy Sheriff, namely CHARLES W. PETERS. ...To a lesser degree, you are involved with three other public figures—the Governor of Illinois, the Mayor of Chicago and the Chief of Police in Chicago.[112]

Milliken went on to cite other specific names referring to individuals, places and events. In general, his concerns address the corruption that was rife in Chicago, as well as New York and other cities, during Prohibition, when young Frank Sinatra was exposed to similar goings-on in Hoboken, including the bootlegging and mobsterism that took place at Marty O'Brien's, his mother's own speakeasy.

Koch replied to Milliken on October 30:

> In order to protect our picture from having any legal problems we will not establish the exact year of our story. The cornerstones are not to be dated. The license plates on the cars are not to be dated. We will use large bills that went out of existence in July 1929.[113]

The Actor, on Screen and in Song

Copies of Koch's Sinatra Enterprises memo, in which he mentions 11 total changes to the script, were issued to 13 members of the production crew, including Frank.

Warners allocated a substantial budget for the film: Frank saw to it that Sammy's salary was increased to $125,000 and nearly $330,000 was spent on art director LeRoy Deane's impressive sets, including two lavish casinos that were to be wrecked on camera, a courthouse, orphanage, mission, penthouse apartment, soup kitchen and pool room.

Contrary to popular belief—including Nancy Sinatra's claim that "Dad brought the Summit to Chicago to film"[114]—no scenes for *Robin and the 7 Hoods* were shot there. Beginning on Halloween, Thursday, October 31, 1963, the entire film was produced on soundstages and the backlot at Warners, and a few locations in the Los Angeles area. Frank began working on the backlot late on the first day and then did not report back until Monday, November 4, to shoot "Robbo's" first confrontation with his rival, Guy Gisborne (Peter Falk), on stage 4, where Deane had constructed his "Nottingham Hotel Conference Room" set.

Schwartz's witty and wacky script (which underwent seven revisions between October 22 and December 6) includes Chicago versions of several characters from the Robin Hood legends: Robbo (also called Robin Hood at times); Gisborne; Little John (Dean); Will [Scarlet] (Sammy); Marian (Barbara Rush), the daughter of "Big Jim" (Edward G. Robinson); and Allen A. Dale (Bing). The Sheriff of Nottingham character also is present in the form of Sheriff Octavius Glick (Robert Foulk), described as a "schmendrick" (by gangsters and the public) on several occasions.

Douglas' 33-day shooting schedule was to end on December 17, with four additional days marked for recording two musical numbers, wrapping the day before Christmas. All told, Frank would work only five days strictly as producer. Despite two extremely traumatic events, he and the company had fun making the film.

Hunt Pushed
For Sinatra

STATELINE, Calif. (AP) —
Posses pushed a two-day hunt
today in the snowy mountains
ringing Lake Tahoe for singer
Frank Sinatra Jr., reported hostage of kidnapers.
His famed father kept an
around-the-clock vigil 65 miles
northeast in a Reno hotel. A
spokesman said FBI agents had
urged him to do it.
Sheriff Ernest Carlson of El
Dorado County, Calif., was
asked by newsmen Monday if
there was fear for young Sinatra's life. Carlson replied, "Certainly. There always is in every
kidnaping."
No demand for ransom has
been reported since the 19-year-
old Sinatra vanished Sunday
night from a motel, just before
he was to go on stage at a Lake
Tahoe night club.
But John Foss, a band trumpet player, told officers he was
with Sinatra Jr. when two gun-
men burst into the motel room
and that they demanded
"Where's the money?" before
gagging Foss and making off
with the young singer.
There was a brief flurry of
excitement Monday night when
FBI agents announced they had
seized six men and 18 guns 20
miles west of Lake Tahoe.
Two of the men were identified as Joseph James Sorce, 23,
of El Cerrito, Calif., and Thomas Patrick Keating, 21, of Riverside, Calif., wanted for two
bank robberies which netted
$13,000.
After Sinatra Jr. vanished, officers had put out an alert, saying these two men were known
to be in the area and might possibly be connected with the Sinatra case.
But arresting FBI agents said
the two and their four alleged
conspirators, seized in two cars
on U.S. 50, were held only for
the bank robberies.
Officers took Foss to view the
men but he could make no positive identification.
In Reno, the worried Sinatra
Sr. said:
"I've always had a fear of kidnaping, especially when the
children were much younger
than they are now.
"But I thought that was all
past, now that they're grown
up."
A spokesman in his suite said
Sinatra was "sleepless, nervous, tired, worried, concerned
— everything a father should
be."

The first tragic incident occurred on November 22, 1963, during the filming of a backlot scene involving Frank, Dean, Sammy, Peter Falk, Hank Henry (as Gisborne's goon "Six Second") and several supporting players. Contrary to an apocryphal legend—Frank was *not* involved in the location shooting of Big Jim's funeral scene (during which he supposedly stood next to a gravestone marked, in various accounts, "Kennedy, 1802-1884" or "John F. Kennedy, 1883-1940") when he was told that JFK had been fatally gunned down in Dallas. While that scene was filmed at Rosedale Cemetery on Thursday, November 14—eight days earlier—the sequence being filmed as the President was assassinated (as confirmed by the official Warners shooting schedule) involves the concrete cornerstone "ride" taken by Sheriff Glick courtesy of Gisborne as Robbo refuses to join his gang. Frank left the backlot on that fateful Friday afternoon, returned to his Palm Springs compound and confined himself to his bedroom for the weekend. After the cast and crew recovered from the shock, filming continued on the following Monday.[115]

Less than three weeks later, on Sunday, December 8, 19-year-old Frank, Jr., was abducted from a Lake Tahoe hotel and held by three men for a $240,000 ransom. Having planned the crime well in advance, the kidnappers were paid by Frank and an FBI agent three days later, but rather than delivering Frank, Jr., at the appointed time, one of them eventually released him at the drop-off point along the San Diego Freeway. Picked up by a security officer of the Bel Air Patrol, the terrified young man then was taken to the Los Angeles home of Nancy, Sr. Within 48 hours, the inept kidnappers were in police custody. The incident understandably hit Frank very hard, but he maintained an outwardly calm appearance, continuing to give a polished performance in the film. (Another myth is that Frank scrapped a scheduled kidnapping scene after his son was abducted. No such sequence ever appeared in the script.) While the result of this harrowing incident improved the relationship between Frank and the FBI, it did not stop the bureau from surveilling him.

Set during a time when government at the local level was corrupt and the federal bureaucracy seemed uninterested in the average Joe, *Robin and the 7 Hoods* offers its own updated version of the classic Saxon versus Norman motif. While the gang-influenced Sheriff of Chicago is the parallel of the Prince John-controlled Sheriff of Nottingham, the (unmentioned) President Herbert Hoover, whom many came to view as an absentee leader, could be the parallel of King Richard the Lionheart.

Adding Bing to the potent mix of Frank, Dean and Sammy, *Robin* reaches the level of smart social satire, simultaneously a wittily written parody of the gangster genre (including the appearances by Robinson and ubiquitous Warner Bros. side-kick Allen Jenkins [who, nearly 30 years earlier, had been named as one of the potential Merry Men in the studio's aborted James Cagney Robin Hood project, which eventually was made as *The Adventures of Robin Hood* (1938) with Errol Flynn]), a musical with memorable songs and dynamic dancing, and a bizarre Prohibition twist on the Robin Hood legend.

Frank's Robbo is one of the very few characters, perhaps the *only* mob leader, in the history of the gangster genre, to refuse to commit murder to achieve his ends (even though, early in the film, he utters the chilling line—to Peter Falk—"You come over there like George Washington, I send you back like Abe Lincoln," a comment that came to haunt him in the wake of the JFK assassination). When Marian offers to pay him $50,000 to eliminate Sheriff Glick, the man responsible for her father's murder, he turns her down; but when Gisborne has the untrustworthy lawman encased in concrete, Marian pays Robbo anyway. This act precipitates the Robin Hood angle, when Robbo orders Little John and Will to "dump" the $50,000 at "an old ladies' home" or "orphanage." The following morning, the newspapers herald, "Robin Hood in Chicago," and a radio announcer declares that the well-known mob boss is using "the gaming table and bootleg beer to aid the unfortunate." The only person Robbo and his men actually "take for a ride" is Gisborne, but the script intimates that the killing was committed in self-defense.

When all the Robin Hood publicity ensues, Robbo tells the press that the $50,000 gift to the Blessed Shelter Orphans Home was a one-time beneficence and that his "name is Robbo, not Rockefeller"; but soon, Little John, inundated with letters from unfortunates asking for assistance, informs his boss of the fallout. "How do you know they ain't chiselers?" John asks.

Giving his fellow man the benefit of a doubt, Robbo replies, "How do you know they are?" ordering Little John to send each of them "a couple hundred." Soon, the gang is visited by Allen A. Dale, an amanuensis from the orphanage versed in literature, who reveals that he made "the Robin Hood comparison." Robbo then appoints Allen head of charities, declaring, "Start this bum off with a c-note a week." (The line in the script reads, "Put him down for a 'C' note a week.") "Oh, gee. I'm a hood. I'm a hood!" the sheltered ex-waif joyously declares.

After the gang opens a free soup kitchen, a "project of the Robbo Foundation" (a parody of the actual fronts run in Chicago by Al Capone, who became a folk hero to many down-and-outers in the Windy City), they accept further charity donations during the debut of their new, elaborate speakeasy casino (built to replace Robbo's earlier joint that was hit by Gisborne's boys).

As comely waitresses in Lincoln Green leotards and feathered forest caps collect the money, Allen and Little John count it, sitting beneath a large banner advertising the "Robin Hood Foundation." Earlier, when one of the men is confused about who Robin Hood was, Little John replies, "He was some Englishman who wore long, green underwear and had an operation going for him in the forest." As head of charities, Allen opens a Robin Hood club at the orphanage, outfitting the boys with feathered caps and bows and arrows. And, apparently, they take the "robbing the rich to give to the poor" concept to heart; later, one of Gisborne's mugs complains, "I caught a kid stealin' a tire off my car the other day, and he pulled a bow and arrow on me!"

Interestingly, the film avoids a romantic interest for Robbo, who is not duped by Marian's attempt to regain her father's position as mob boss of Chicago. In its depiction

Frank poses for a studio publicity shot for _Robin and the 7 Hoods_.

of Marian, _Robin and the 7 Hoods_ ranks as the only film to cast the traditional lover of Robin in a villainous light. After she is unsuccessful in seducing Robbo, she manages to manipulate the less cautious and very amorous Little John, who eventually dumps her when he can't betray his boss and friend. But Marian never deviates from her plan, and before film's end, leads both Gisborne and Deputy Sheriff Potts (Victor Buono) to their demises in concrete cornerstones for new Chicago buildings.

When Robbo is framed by Guy and his mugs for the murder of Sheriff Glick, he is forced to listen to the "testimony" of a literal liars' parade. (Meanwhile, a Chicago headline reveals, "Robin Hood's a Hood!") During his time on the stand, Gisborne offers his alibi: Glick's murder occurred on a Tuesday afternoon, and each week at that time he always plays mah jongg quietly with some companions at the _Nottingham_ Hotel! Later, while trying to explain the public support Robbo has achieved, Guy tells Marian, "The fact that the man [Robin

Hood] has been dead for 600 years—it don't mean nothin'."

Frank is at the height of his *Pal Joey*-like self-assurance in *Robin and the 7 Hoods*, always in control, backing down to no one, entering rooms with the swagger he learned from Humphrey Bogart. In his only portrayal of a gangster, he was able to combine his "tough guy" persona with his considerable comic talent, not to mention the three opportunities to flex his reed. The Robin Hood angle also reflects his own qualities as both outlaw and lifelong contributor to charities across the globe.

Composed by Van Heusen and Cahn, and arranged by Riddle, the eight songs provide potent musical punctuation to Schwartz's script. Not surprisingly, Dean warmly solos on a sentimental crooner ballad, "Any Man Who Loves His Mother," while Sammy flies alone, tapdancing across a bartop and shooting up Gisborne's casino, as he belts out "Bang, Bang"; Bing, instructing a group of orphans, warbles the charming, laid-back "Don't Be a Do-Badder"; and Frank swings "My Kind of Town," the Chicago anthem that became one of his signature songs. The Van Heusen-Cahn contribution also includes collaborations between Bing, Dean, Frank and Sammy (the hilarious "Mr. Booze," performed during the "mission casino" scene) and Bing, Dean, and Frank (the excellent soft-shoe number "Style"), as well as a number sung by Peter Falk. The most utterly odd musical moment, "All for One" occurs at the beginning of the film, when the Chicago mobsters (including Allen Jenkins as "Vermin Witowski"!) become backing vocalists for Guy, who, in the wake of Big Jim's "demise," declares himself the new boss of the Windy City.

The "Mr. Booze" sequence, during which Robbo's joint is automatically transformed into an austere Skid Row mission adorned with temperance slogans, is a musical and comic highlight, with Crosby becoming "the Reverend Allen A. Dale." That the entire Summit had a marvelous time shooting the scene, some of which was improvised, is openly apparent: When Davis first testified that "sin" overtook him, then changed the word to "gin," Dean, attempting to mask his mirth, added, "Yeah, a little of that, too," before returning to character. (Gordon Douglas and editor Sam O'Steen left it in the final cut.) In fact, Crosby appears to be enjoying himself immensely throughout the film, giving a splendid performance. However, his offscreen relationship with Frank apparently was not as pleasant; although Frank was a lifelong fan of Bing's musicianship, still photographer Ted Allan later recalled that Ol' Blue Eyes, a very gentle father, repeatedly chastised his hero for the abusive way he treated the Crosby children.[116]

Other than the vocal performances (patterned after those in *Guys and Dolls*), the gangster scenes are played straight, with only a layer of expertly integrated comic exaggeration added for good measure (particularly served up by Falk, who demonstrates keen timing in his turn as the ambitious yet imbecilic Gisborne). Like Warner Bros.' "golden age" gangster parodies *The Little Giant* (1933), *A Slight Case of Murder* (1938) and *Larceny, Inc.* (1942), all starring Edward G. Robinson, who displays the same ineptly self-reliant quality, albeit in a more subtle style, the film (unlike the later parodies of Mel Brooks and others) eschews buffoonery, slapstick and sight gags for a more sophisticated style in which the comedy arises *naturally* from the absurd counterculture of gangsterism. The very nature of Robbo and Guy Gisborne's competing operations, not to mention the corruption of the Chicago police, provides the springboard for situations that are hilarious yet grounded in a historical setting. Even the violence, a staple element in gangster films, is downplayed. The only violent action is committed by the mobsters against inanimate objects, namely the two casinos owned by Robbo and Guy. And though Sheriff Glick and Deputy Sheriff Potts both get taken for rides, these crimes occur off screen; when the officers are again

mentioned, they have become part of the cornerstones. The only on-screen murder is that of Big Jim, who is gunned down by the singing mugs at his birthday party!

The entire "gang war" is a game pitting Robbo against Guy, who commits all the actual crimes usually associated with mobsters. Of course, the film does exactly what the early Warners gangster classics were accused of doing—romanticizing and glamorizing the ruggedly individualist criminal lifestyle—but these gang members are humorous, likable lugs whose violent acts are the adult equivalent of children breaking each others' toys.

Some of the humor is downright bizarre, including two running gags involving Potts' love of cocoa and one of Robbo's men who has a passion for knitting. In one scene late in the film, just before irate women break into the free soup kitchen (which Marian has transformed into a counterfeiting operation), the obsessive knitter is seen demonstrating his craft for Little John. The only truly weak comic element in the film is the ending, which depicts Robbo, Little John and Will reduced to working as bell-ringing Santa Clauses at Christmas, an abrupt and unsatisfying conclusion to a clever and funny story combining two seemingly incompatible genres.

Though noting the disappointing denouement and the "threadbare story," *Variety*'s "Whit" was very positive:

> Warner Bros. has a solid money entry... sparked by the names of Frank Sinatra, Dean Martin and Bing Crosby to give marquee power... Hefty laugh situations are afforded as pic unreels...
>
> Performance-wise, Falk comes out best. His comic gangster is a pure gem and he should get plenty of offers after this. Sinatra, of course, is smooth and Crosby in a "different" type of role rates a big hand... A lovely assortment of hood types back them effectively.[117]

In his *Hollywood Reporter* article, "'Hoods' Ring-a-Ding B. O. in Clanbake by Sinatra Gang," James Powers was even more enthusiastic:

> *Robin and the 7 Hoods* is the latest outing for The Group— Frank Sinatra, Dean Martin and friends—and it is the best of the collective efforts. ... Two reasons why *Robin* is good are the screenplay by David R. Schwartz and the direction by Gordon Douglas. ...*Robin and the 7 Hoods* is better than its predecessors because there are not so many inside jokes, because there is more story and, with it, new jokes, and because the stars work harder... Sinatra is pleasant in a straight role.[118]

The Actor, on Screen and in Song

The film is a visual treat, with William Daniels' stunning Cinemascope compositions—described by Powers as "giv[ing the film] sparkle and vitality"—contributing to one of the strangest Hollywood films ever made.

Gene Kelly recalled his meetings with Frank following completion of the film:

> I didn't speak to [him] while it was being shot, and our first contact with each other... took place at Mike Romanoff's a few months later. We had a fine time together with no hard feelings on either side. And when he asked me why I walked out on him, I told him the conditions he imposed didn't suit my temperament, which he must have known anyway since we'd done several pictures together, and he knew my working methods and the professional approach I expected everyone around me to have. I was perfectly honest with him and he took my point without any malice.[119]

During the making of *Robin and the 7 Hoods*, Frank recorded three Reprise singles. The first, "Have Yourself a Merry Little Christmas," involved him in a rare overdubbing session on October 13, 1963, when, accompanied by a chorus, he added his vocal to an orchestral track that had been laid down the previous April. On December 3, he cut "Talk to Me, Baby" and "Stay with Me," which was used as the title song for Otto Preminger's 1963 epic *The Cardinal*.

On January 2, 1964, Frank recorded three songs for inclusion on Reprise's patriotic album, *America, I Hear You Singing*, also featuring Bing Crosby and Fred Waring and His Pennsylvanians. "Early American" and an updating of "The House I Live In," arranged by Nelson Riddle, were followed by the Voice's own take on the Andrews Sisters' swinging World War II classic, "You're a Lucky Fellow, Mr. Smith." The following month, he cut two additional numbers, "Let Us Break Bread Together" and, with Crosby, "You Never Had It So Good."

In late January, Frank and producer Sonny Burke developed a concept album of Oscar-grabbing movie songs eventually released with the verbose title, *Frank Sinatra Sings "Days of Wine and Roses," "Moon River" and Other Academy Award Winners*. Though a film-related project, Frank chose not to sing any songs from his previous big-screen efforts.

Henry Mancini and Johnny Mercer's "Days of Wine and Roses," from Blake Edwards' 1962 film, opens the album with a very appealing Nelson Riddle swing. The atmospheric "Moon River," written by the same duo for *Breakfast at Tiffany's* (1961), features a Vince DeRosa French horn solo that adds a warm quality to Frank's longing vocal. Jerome Kern and Dorothy Fields' "The Way You Look Tonight," written for the 1936 Astaire-Rogers classic *Swing Time*, receives Riddle's bouncy medium swing treatment; while "Three Coins in the Fountain" is a remake of the 1954 Riddle arrangement. "In the Cool, Cool, Cool of the Evening," written for Frank Capra's *Here Comes the Groom* (1951) by Hoagy Carmichael and Johnny Mercer, sounds less comfortable for Frank than it did for Bing Crosby; but "Secret Love," in the words of Will Friedwald, "is [the] only reading... that makes the song work with a mature attitude rather than the younger-than-springtime idealism Doris Day originally bagged the Oscar with [in *Calamity Jane* (1953)]."[120]

Another hit for Bing, "Swinging on a Star," written for the Oscar favorite *Going My Way* (1944) by Johnny Burke and Jimmy Van Heusen, is Crosby-ish on the verses, but kicks into Sinatra-Riddle high gear during the choruses. Rodgers and Hammerstein's "It Might as Well Be Spring," from *State Fair* (1945), and "The Continental," from *The Gay Divorcee* (1934), swing along nice 'n' easy before Frank dramatically crescendos into "Love Is a Many-Splendored Thing," giving the album one dose of "Concert Sinatra." The set closes with the version of "All the Way" cut for *Sinatra's Sinatra* the previous year.

Recordings for the *Robin and the 7 Hoods* soundtrack album were done at the time of the film's premiere in April 1964, and the LP was released two months later. Frank originally had commissioned Van Heusen and Cahn to write 14 songs, but only eight were used in the final film. Ten separate numbers were included on the album, including "I Like to Lead When I Dance,"

The Japanese boat, from art director LeRoy Deane's own production photographs for *None But the Brave*.

which Robbo sang to Marian; however, Frank, thinking that the scene slowed Gordon Douglas' pace, cut it from the film. The hard-swinging "My Kind of Town," which was nominated for an Oscar, was the soundtrack's biggest hit. Frank also recorded an additional Reprise single, "I Can't Believe I'm Losing You," during the April 8 session.

Richard Quine's *Paris When It Sizzles*, featuring Frank's ballad "The Girl Who Stole the Eiffel Tower," recorded in March of the previous year, also was released in April. Cowritten by Nelson Riddle, the number plays briefly after star William Holden, who plays screenwriter Richard Benson, mentions the title song, adding, "Maybe we can get Sinatra to sing it."

For years, MGM had planned to make a biopic about the legendary Irving Berlin, but this composer of hundreds of American classics who, like Frank, didn't read music, put the kibosh on the project. Now the studio considered re-teaming their former star with Dean and Bing in "Say It with Music," a tribute to some of Berlin's 3,000-plus melodies, but the production never saw the light.

Howard Koch had to convince Warner Bros. to allow Frank to *direct* his next film, *None But the Brave*, a groundbreaking World War II South Pacific drama told from both the American and Japanese perspectives. Frank again was slated to star *and* produce. Why did the studio have to risk the success of the picture on his neophyte direction when a competent veteran could be hired for $60,000? When *Variety* asked the same question, Koch replied, "Let's wait and see. He's got a chance to prove himself as a director. And you can't direct a picture unless you're there to prepare it. If he makes it, he'll be on his way. And I'm sure he'll make it. I really am."[121] Co-producing with Toho Film of Tokyo (famous for its "rubber monster epics" starring Godzilla and other nuclear-spawned creatures), Warners became the first Hollywood studio to take part in a U.S.-Japanese cinematic collaboration.

Warners had reached an agreement to shoot the film on Kauai land owned by the Kilauea Sugar Company. During a pair of two-week jaunts to Hawaii, production designer and art director LeRoy Deane and his crew spent much of March and April constructing authentic sets to be utilized during a May-June location shoot. To prepare the area for the crash landing of a U.S. plane and the subsequent construction of a Marine camp, roads had to be graded and native plants—palm trees and indigenous shrubs—had to be replaced and enhanced. Huts and wharfs also needed to be built to provide both combatants with bases of operation.

The original story for the film had been a Japanese proposal penned by writer-producer Kikumaru Okuda. Working simultaneously, Katsuya Susaki and John Twist respectively wrote the Japanese and American scenes. On April 6, 1964, Twist delivered the "final change" to the FINAL SCRIPT, dated March 20 (though none of this revision was included in the film).

Though he was directing, producing and acting in a major motion picture, Frank had not forgotten about musical projects. While on Kauai, he phoned Quincy Jones, whom he had worked with briefly when the arranger-musician had conducted his Monte Carlo concert back in 1958. Frank wanted to cut another album with Count Basie and wanted Jones to write the arrangements. "Q" recalled:

> I went over there and he had a flag up over his bungalow in Hawaii. He was directing *None But the Brave*, and he had a flag up with his bottle of Jack Daniels on it. Huge flag! Instead of an American flag, he had a Jack Daniels flag. And that's when we first got to know each other. He had one of the most complex personalities imaginable. We had a great, great chemistry.[122]

While enjoying the exotic atmosphere, Frank nearly drowned while attempting to save the life of Howard Koch's wife, Ruth. After the swimming woman was swept out to sea by a huge breaker, he followed but was quickly carried off course. Then Brad Dexter dove in. Though the young actor was harried by the undertow, he eventually reached Frank, who ordered, "Save Ruth. I'm finished." Dexter wouldn't listen to his "boss," however, and rallied to save both of them.[123] Frank was back in the director's chair the following day.

To help depict his personal statement about the nature of war, Frank intended to make the environment of *None But the Brave* completely convincing. LeRoy Deane and his crew labored to build the most realistic sets possible; and, on June 26, reported that both military camps had been constructed at the cost of $152,550.63, a $10 thousand increase from his estimate of two weeks earlier. In an attempt to economize, Deane previously had sent a memo to Howard Koch, reminding the executive producer that certain items used during the island shoot needed to be shipped back to Hollywood for additional filming.

Working in three different capacities on the film was an enormous challenge for Frank, who, as director, had the additional burden of directing his actors in two different languages, though Japanese dialogue coach Tetsu Nakamura aided immensely. To complete the location work, he was aided by the U.S. Department of Defense, the Marine Corps, the Navy and the Hawaiian National Guard. After wrapping the shoot, Frank admitted:

> I found out that it was in some ways tougher than I had thought. The director has so many things to worry about—pace, wardrobe, the performance... Next time I won't try to perform when I direct...[124]

Getting started posed a special challenge for the aspiring director:

> The toughest thing I had to do on the first day of shooting was to say "print." It took me 10 minutes, because I liked the take but I figured the minute I say "print" I'm on the record... the race is off, it's gone, the horses are running around.[125]

Tommy Sands, who appears as 2nd Lieutenant Blair in the film, recalled:

> I am so proud of having worked with him in the one film he directed. He was absolutely concise. You knew in very few words *exactly* what he wanted—*exactly*—inside and out, and how much he wanted you to move in either direction. He was the best director I ever worked with.[126]

Clint Walker, Sinatra, Brad Dexter and Tommy Sands in Sinatra's only directorial feature film, *None But the Brave*

From the first frame to the last, *None But the Brave* maintains its dual American and Japanese narrative. Not only are the titles presented in both English and Japanese, but the Warners logo itself is first shown in Asian type before dissolving to its native tongue. As the "off the charts" Pacific island comes into view, the voice of a Japanese officer begins to tell the tale. Except for the lieutenant, who occasionally speaks English to the American soldiers, the Japanese always speak their own language, accompanied by subtitles, while the Americans speak English.

Frank admirably creates a realistic atmosphere throughout the film, and, though the perspective inevitably and understandably leans toward the United States, the audience immediately is presented with a Japanese army that is not the group of monsters usually associated with World War II films, but a well-balanced depiction of men who, like the Americans, are fighting for their country.

The final version of the script describes Frank's Francis Maloney as "attached to the Marines, although he is Navy; a raffish, middle-aged corpsman. Drunk or sober, he is a skilled physician and surgeon." Just as this Irish-American pharmacist's mate, the Arkansas mountain boy, the Native American and the African-American (albeit an historical anachronism) have been swept into the maelstrom, the Japanese men, in the words of their CO, are "ordinary men blown together by war." The humanity and intelligence displayed by Kuroki (Tatsuya Mihashi), the Japanese lieutenant, eventually is reflected in the behavior of his comrades. In fact, the screenplay effectively mirrors each of the major American characters with a Japanese counterpart. At one point, Frank powerfully drives home the similarities of both combatants by crosscutting between insubordinate troops in each camp; there are both American and Japanese soldiers who wish to disobey the command, not rashly, to attack their enemy.

The plot of the film is simple: A remote island in the Pacific considered "worthless" by a group of marooned Japanese is suddenly invaded by an American plane shot down by a marauding Zero. When faced with the realities of nature, both sides are forced to cooperate; but after the Americans make contact with a destroyer via a repaired radio, the combatants must fight it out to the last man. Though he has nearly performed a miracle to save a Japanese soldier from gangrene, the Irish medic must look on as he, as well as his comrades, perishes in the service of his country.

One scene in particular powerfully illustrates the futility of war. A boat built by the Japanese is targeted by the American troops, who nearly manage to pirate it out to sea but are foiled by an intrepid soldier who destroys it with a hand grenade. The sequence reaches its dramatic peak when the Japanese carpenter, Leading Private Ando (Shigeki Ishida), who designed the boat, cries out that the craft was his wife, raped by the enemy, just before he is gunned down by Lieutenant Blair. Here, Frank shows us both the Americans who try to survive by stealing the boat and the Japanese who in turn destroy their own means of escape from the island. A subsequent scene depicts the Japanese honoring their men who died trying to save the boat; next to their graves lies an American Marine who was killed while getting a much-needed drink of water at the only spring on the island.

The well-balanced narrative is powerfully represented by the scene in which Maloney saves the life of Hirano (Homare Suguro), the Japanese soldier who in civilian life was a singer and dancer. Kuroki has asked Captain Bourke (Clint Walker) to provide the services of his pharmacist's mate, who reluctantly agrees, having an opportunity to reconnoiter the Japanese camp. At the same time, the Japanese scatter ammunition about, making it look as if they are well supplied. Here Frank expertly intertwines humanism with the realities of warfare.

Not surprisingly, Frank sparks the most memorable scene in the film, giving an unforgettable performance: Understandably nervous, Maloney is very methodical and meticulous, sterilizing the knife and saw (which was used by the carpenter in the construction of the boat) and administering a hypodermic and alcohol to the suffering man prior to amputating his leg. In a very simple, effective gesture, Frank demonstrates his trademark subtle style as Maloney asks God to "don't just look down on me—help me." The scene originally was to include far more distrust from the Japanese soldiers but was softened in a later rewrite; and, as delivered by Frank, who as usual improvised a more economical version of the scripted dialogue, transformed a potentially effective scene into an unforgettable one. The following sequence, depicting a sign figuratively dividing the island between the two combatants, who have called a truce, provides a lighthearted coda to this intense event.

But Frank did not let the film peak with the amputation sequence. Just as the truce is broken by a Japanese "spy" who is examining the American plane, a tidal wave hits the island and both sides again need to cooperate, this time to save all their lives by protecting the spring. When Blair falls from the makeshift dam into the torrent, Kuroki dives in and hauls him to safety, finally earning the formerly hardheaded Marine's respect.

The similarities between the warring commanders, who think similarly throughout the narrative, are visually reinforced by a pair of flashback scenes near the end of the film. After Kuroki tells Bourke and Maloney about the young bride he left behind in Japan, the drunken pharmacist's mate relates the story of his captain's inner anguish: Having refused to marry his girlfriend due to his imminent departure, Bourke is traumatized when she hysterically runs away, straight into a bomb dropped during an air raid.

After the Americans establish radio contact with a U.S. destroyer, they offer the Japanese terms of surrender, but Kuroki replies that he and his men will fight honorably rather than be taken as prisoners of war. Maloney asks Hirano to stay with them, but questions why he worked so hard to save his life when the proud amputee follows his comrades to certain death.

Though the screenplay includes a number of war-film clichés—the multi-ethnic U.S. forces; the boozing, philosophical medical man; the overzealous Marine; the fist fight resulting from insubordination—*None But the Brave* admirably accomplishes its mission of presenting a balanced picture of the conflict, which is explored with some degree of complexity. (More recent war films, including Steven Spielberg's *Saving Private Ryan* (1998), march on with many clichés intact.) The film was the first to show explicitly that, for the most part, the Japanese, too, were everyday citizens thrust into the war; and they also were fighting for love of country and their way of life. At film's end, however, the Americans emerge triumphant (as they did in the real war), simply suffering fewer casualties than the enemy. By the mid-1960s, two decades after the conflict ended, a production such as *None But the Brave* could be made; and though Frank's straightforward direction presents no real innovations, his visual and narrative techniques reflect his overall economical approach to art. The performances are uniformly underplayed much of the time, with the exception of Sands' over-the-top lieutenant and his Japanese counterpart who continually rails against the orders of Kuroki.

Variety's "Whit" was impressed with the dual narrative and technical aspects of the film:

> Sinatra... makes his directorial bow... and is responsible for some good effects in maintaining a suspenseful pace. ...Sinatra appears only intermittently, his character only important in the operation scene, which he enacts dramatically. ...Harold Lipstein's Panavision-Technicolor photography is particularly impressive and Sam O'Steen's editing fast. LeRoy Deane's art direction fills the bill and Johnny Williams' music score provides excellent background. Special effects are credited to E. Tsuburaya, expertly contrived.[127]

Having recently reverted (with some reason) to his early 1940s Sinatra-bashing style, Bosley Crowther declared war on the film in his *New York Times* review:

> If the threat of Frank Sinatra as a film director is judged by his first try on *None But the Brave*, it is clear that there need be no apprehension among the members of the Screen Directors Guild. A minimum show of creative invention and a maximum use of cinema clichés are evident in the staging of this war film...
>
> In putting it all together in a joint production with two Japanese companies, Mr. Sinatra, as producer and director, as well as actor of the secondary role of the booze-guzzling medical corpsman, displays distinction only in the latter job. Being his own director, he has no trouble stealing scenes, especially one in which he burbles boozy wisecracks while preparing to saw off the shivering Japanese's leg. Mr. Sinatra is crashingly casual when it comes to keeping the Japanese in their place.
>
> He has a good deal more trouble with the American fellows. Clint Walker... Tommy Sands... Brad Dexter... and Tony Bill... make over-acting—phony acting—the trademark of the film. With the incredible color and the incredible screenplay of Katsuya Susaki and John Twist, this adds up to quite a fake concoction.
>
> They used to make better war films at Monogram.[128]

Other critics didn't share Crowther's opinion, though Dale Munroe of the Hollywood *Citizen News* pointed out Frank's strengths and weaknesses as an "auteur":

As director, Sinatra proves to be most impressive with his handling of the frequent action sequences which keep the film moving at a fairly rapid pace. The director is least experienced when dealing with scenes which should inspire boldness of purpose. More psychological, intellectual and sociological probing into the private thoughts and acts of the opposing characters would seem to be called for.[129]

Perhaps Kevin Thomas of *The Los Angeles Times* wrote the most balanced review, referring to Frank's direction in a way that equates it with his singing and acting styles:

Provocative and engrossing, the color film is novel... Sinatra's style as a director is straightforward and understated. It is to his credit that he tackled a serious subject on his first try when he could have taken the easy way out with still another gathering of The Clan. ...In front of the camera, Sinatra is in top form as a pharmacist's mate with a wry wit, and gets good performances from Clint Walker as the American commander, a solemn giant who offers a fine contrast to Sinatra, and Tatsuya Mihashi as the very likable Japanese leader.[130]

With *None But the Brave* behind him, Frank made good on his offer to Quincy Jones, hiring him to arrange 10 songs for a second album with the Count Basie band, this time adding a string section. Recorded last on June 9, 1964, the first day of sessions for *It Might as Well Be Swing*, "Fly Me to the Moon" was chosen to open the finished album—for good reason. Originally a Bart Howard waltz titled "In Other Words" and waxed by dozens of singers, including Tony Bennett and Peggy Lee, who apparently suggested the alternate title, this number was destined to become one of the foremost swingers of Frank's career. Jones already had arranged the piece as an instrumental, changing the time signature to 4/4 and increasing the tempo for the Basie band, and now Frank changed it even further by working his improvisatory magic with the lyrics—causing the composer to comment, "[That] normally would have annoyed the shit out of me but didn't because it worked so well."[131] Opening in soft-shoe style with light percussion, the introduction welcomes two notes of Basie's piano, then Frank's full voice and a lightsome flute and guitar, then saxes and brass before the full band kicks in the second time through. It is an absolutely masterful arrangement, building from the first moment to nearly the last (the band drops out to allow Basie his trademark three-note closing riff before Frank adds the final note on "you")—arguably one of the finest written for a Sinatra swinger from any period.

Based on a 1946 French song, "I Wish You Love" is a breezy swing number featuring a punchy Basie bridge and another three-note closer; while "I Believe in You," from Broadway's *How to Succeed in Business Without Really Trying*, recharges the adrenaline level. "More" is the very "cool," jazzy theme from the Italian film *Mondo Cane* (1963), featuring potent punches from the band and silky passages from the string section. The LP strangely segues from the sublime to the ridiculous with the next track, Don Gibson's "I Can't Stop Loving You," which had been a country-R&B hit for Ray Charles two years earlier. As Will Friedwald writes:

Where fellow Italo-American rat-packer Dean Martin could ride forth unembarrassed as a Gucci cowboy in both Hollywood and Nashville, hearing Sinatra attempt that level of material makes one wince the same way as his movie westerns like *Johnny Concho* and *Dirty Dingus Magee* do.[132]

"Hello, Dolly" suits Frank far better, with a fiercely driving Jones arrangement. After a fiery instrumental bridge, the Voice reenters with "Hello, Satch! This is Francis, Louis," singing an entire verse about the legendary trumpeter's recent success with the Broadway hit. Ending the song, Frank cops one of Armstrong's trademarks, singing, "Oh, Yeahhhhhhhh!" "I Wanna Be

Around" had been penned by Johnny Mercer after he was mailed two lines—"I wanna be around to pick up the pieces/When somebody breaks your heart"—and given to Tony Bennett, who cut it in 1962. Frank's version opens with a Basie piano introduction and builds to the band at full steam before halting for the Count's *four*-note closing riff and one last powerful chord. "The Best Is Yet to Come" and "The Good Life" also were songs previously recorded by Bennett, but here given more dynamic arrangements. Burt Bacharach and Hal David's medium swinger "Wives and Lovers," a hit for Jack Jones the previous year, ends the album.

Four days after the Basie sessions were completed, Frank recorded three songs for the Reprise album *12 Songs of Christmas*, returning on June 19 for two more tracks, joining Bing Crosby and Fred Waring and His Pennsylvanians, as he had on *America, I Hear You Singing*. Of Frank's five contributions, Van Heusen and Cahn's "An Old-Fashioned Christmas" is the most refreshing alternative to the typical Yuletide fare. On July 17, he recorded three Reprise singles arranged by Ernie Freeman—"Softly, As I Leave You," "Then Suddenly Love" and "Available"—that apparently were supposed to compete with the Beatles in the charts. "Softly" actually remained on the *Billboard* list for 11 weeks, but Frank enunciating "Hot dog!" on the quasi-rock 'n' roll "Then Suddenly Love" and wedding his vocal style to a Fifties-style 6/8 tempo on "Available" are evidence of his gravitation toward more commercial material as the market moved further toward rock music. An additional track, "Since Marie Has Left Paree," arranged by Billy May, was recorded but left unreleased. The three issued singles provided the foundation of the compilation album, *Softly, As I Leave You*, which also includes three songs—the utterly absurd "Pass Me By," "Emily," the title song for *The Americanization of Emily* (1964), and "Dear Heart"—recorded at an October 3 session and six numbers that had been waxed at earlier Reprise dates.

Following his American-Japanese cinematic experience, Frank switched theaters of operation for his next WWII film, *Von Ryan's Express*, this time an exciting POW drama based on a novel by David Westheimer and filmed in Italy and Spain during August and September 1964. Temporarily leaving his office at Warner Bros. to work for 20th Century-Fox, he was paid $250,000 and guaranteed 15 percent of the gross by Richard Zanuck, son of the legendary Darryl F.

Veteran director Mark Robson, who began his career at RKO helming five innovative thrillers—including *The Seventh Victim* (1944) and *Bedlam* (1946)—for the legendary Val Lewton, and later demonstrated his World War II action-adventure prowess with *The Bridges at Toko-Ri* (1954), also produced the film with Saul David, and William Daniels once again was behind the camera. Up-and-coming composer Jerry Goldsmith was hired to write the atmospheric score (which soon would be "borrowed from," along with visual and narrative elements from the film, for the *Hogan's Heroes* television series), and Frank's pal Brad Dexter was joined in the supporting cast by a distinguished group of international actors including Trevor Howard, Sergio Fantoni, Edward Mulhare, Wolfgang Preiss, Raffaella Carra and a young James Brolin.

Reportedly, while filming in Malaga, Spain, in mid-September, Frank's face was cut by a wine glass when a Cuban actress who had been refused a photo opportunity tossed it at him in a restaurant. Unable to get an apology from the woman because he supposedly refused to make a statement at the local police station, Frank was fined $400, 10 times more than his assailant. When he said that appearing at the station would cut into the film's $25,000-per-day budget, police would not allow him to leave his hotel, and the American ambassador had to persuade him to relent.[133]

Back in L.A., Howard Koch had to inform Frank that he could no longer be his co-producer. Arriving at Fox while Frank was on-camera, dressed as a Nazi officer, Koch was a bit shaky. "Gee, Frank, you've really shot the crap out of that scene," he roughly praised before delivering the blow: "I've been made head of Paramount. I'm afraid I'm going to have to leave."

Nearly shocking his old friend, Frank shouted out to the entire cast and crew that "his boy" had been made a movie mogul.[134] (Their collaboration would continue at Paramount.) A new relationship that blossomed on the Fox set occurred when Frank spotted Mia Farrow, daughter of actress Maureen O'Sullivan and director John Farrow, who currently was starring in the daytime soap opera *Peyton Place*.

Interestingly, Frank had been cast in a film set in an *Italian* POW camp. His introduction as Colonel Joseph Ryan is, like its counterparts in *Young At Heart* and *The Devil at Four O'Clock*, one that reveals his face gradually: Here he is hidden from patrolling Nazis by a group of Italian troops and is seen only when they move away from him. Set in Italy during August 1943, the film depicts Ryan's tribulations both with the enemy *and* his allies, particularly Major Eric Fincham (Trevor Howard), who, being obsessed with breaking out of the camp, withholds Red Cross supplies and medicine from the POWs for potential use after a mass escape. Assuming command of the prisoners as ranking officer, Ryan cuts a deal with the Italian commandant, who has been accused of stealing the Red Cross packages. Revealing where the supplies are hidden, Ryan induces more humane treatment for the POWs, who at first are furious but whistle a different tune after his order to strip and burn their tattered garments results in new, clean clothes for them all.

Frank portrays Ryan as a capable leader who constantly attempts to control his inner emotions—particularly his desire to remain humane in the midst of a savage war—while making the best strategic decisions. His plans often backfire, earning the enmity of the escaped POWs—especially the British—but as the film progresses, his men realize that, like so many of them, this civilian thrust into the war is doing the best job he can. After capturing an enemy train, Ryan, Fincham and the remaining men hold a Nazi officer (Wolfgang Preiss) and young Italian woman (Rafaella Carra) hostage while, dressed as German officers, they make their way toward Switzerland. Some welcome humor alternates with tense and suspenseful action sequences as Ryan and Chaplain Costanzo (Edward Mulhare) enact their finest Nazi impersonations: While the English vicar has studied in Germany and can speak the language, the American colonel must remain silent. (Frank exclaims, "Ya" at one point.)

In classic Sinatra fashion, Frank is most effective when he does very little. During a scene in which Ryan gives a pair of nylons to the Italian woman, he manages to register subtle physical reaction with his back to the camera (much like his favorite Boris Karloff in *The Criminal Code* [1930] and John Wayne in *Red River* [1948]—interestingly both films directed by Howard Hawks). After Ryan is forced to shoot the woman during an attempted escape, Frank reaches his dramatic, but admirably controlled, peak as Fincham tries to console him. Recalling the scene in *Kings Go Forth* in which Frank's Sam Loggins threatens to kill Britt Harris (Tony Curtis), Ryan commands, "Get your hands off me or I'll blow your head off!"

The final half hour of the film involves the Allies' attempts to get the train across the Swiss border. After the Germans bomb the tracks on a railroad bridge in the Alps, the men work frantically to repair them. Following a fierce gun and grenade battle with the Nazis, the surviving men jump aboard the train but the colonel, desperately trying to reach the caboose of Von Ryan's Express, is shot down, his body sprawled between the rails. Although the original version of the screenplay—following David Westheimer's novel—featured Ryan making it to the train, Frank insisted that Richard Zanuck allow him to sacrifice the colonel to give the conclusion a much more dramatic punch.

The Cinema of Sinatra

Robson's pacing is excellent, as is William Daniels' cinematography, perhaps the best he contributed to a Sinatra film. The scenes filmed inside the train car after the escaped POWs are captured by the Nazis are a highlight, with Daniels' beautiful lighting lending the color film a quality that rivals the definition and tonality of black and white. The aerial sequences shot in the Alps are another high point.

Variety's "Whit" praised the film on all levels:

> Mark Robson has made realistic use of the actual Italian setting of the David Westheimer novel in garmenting his action in hard-hitting direction and sharply drawn performances, and producer Saul David provides elaborate values in tome's picturization, lustily scripted by Wendell Mayes and Joseph Landon. ...Sinatra socks over his character strongly and Howard is unusually convincing as the surly British officer... Sergio Fantoni scores brilliantly...
>
> Technical credits are particularly impressive. William H. Daniels' CinemaScope and DeLuxeColor photography is an artistic, outstanding achievement, and art direction by Jack Martin Smith and Hilyard Brown instills the necessary atmosphere. Jerry Goldsmith's stirring music score admirably backgrounds the unfoldment, tightly edited for the most part by Dorothy Spencer.[135]

Abe Greenberg, tuned into the Sinatra style, in the Hollywood *Citizen-News*, wrote:

> As the steely-eyed, curt American officer who takes command as an unpopular chief, Frank Sinatra underplays his role neatly and purposefully where it might easily lead him into an overdramatic trap. ...It's a tough

Sinatra and Deborah Kerr in *Marriage on the Rocks*

assignment, but he makes it believable, even at the finale where he is unwittingly sacrificed in staving off a final Nazi assault on the escape train. ...This is Sinatra at his best as an actor...[136]

On February 28, 1965, CBS included clips from Frank's films in a television special, *Cavalcade of Amateurs*. Having shot *Come Blow Your Horn*, shot and associate produced *Robin and the 7 Hoods* and co-produced *None But the Brave*, William Daniels became a full-fledged producer for "Community Property," later titled *Marriage on the Rocks*. Working with costars Dean Martin, Deborah Kerr and Nancy, Jr., director Jack Donohue began filming on March 8, 1965. Addressing the film's lighthearted depiction of divorce, screenwriter Cy Howard said:

> It shows that divorce accomplishes nothing, that the grass is not always greener on the other side. In the old days when you spoke of divorce you thought of a bad woman. Now kids think nothing of having three sets of grandparents, two Thanksgivings and two Christmases. We have a different set of mores.[137]

Having just finished *The Sons of Katie Elder*, his second film opposite John Wayne, Dino followed up his work on *Rocks* with a three-week stint at the Sands in Vegas and then filmed 10 episodes of his enormously popular television show. He recalled:

> I'll admit...recording sessions are tough—learning and rehearsing the songs. But I don't consider working in movies hard. All that stuff about

actors coming home at night exhausted is a lot of bunk—at least for me. Movie-making—it's a ball, especially in comedies.[138]

Nancy wanted to give her best performance in the film, not only because Frank was her father but also a top Hollywood star: "From our first scene, I stopped thinking of him as my father and concentrated as an actor. We discussed our scenes before shooting them, and Dad's advice helped me considerably."[139]

Frank added, "As far as I'm concerned, I'm doing a scene with an actress, not my daughter. You can't do it honestly any other way."[140]

Ironically, Nancy's own marriage was on the rocks. Tommy Sands had left her, causing a lapse in her ability to perform. Of her sister's temporary return to the family home, Tina noted, "Dad came by after work each day for a week or so, until Nancy felt strong enough to rejoin him on the set."[141]

As part of its advertising campaign, Warner Bros. included large door panels featuring the film's "exotic ingredients": full figure images of the semi-nude blondes "Lola" (the incredible Joi Lansing), "Bunny" (Tara Ashton), "Kitty" (future *Hogan's Heroes* babe Sigrid Valdis) and "Lisa" (Emmy-winning dancer Davey Davison). While working on the film, bombshell Lansing created her own moment of hilarity while having her body makeup applied. Turning this way and that, the actress asked the makeup artist, "Can you give me some cleavage?"

"Can you give *me* some!" the woman replied.[142]

The newspaper ads referred to the film as telling "the story of the tired husband, the bored wife, the happy bachelor with the mad pad and the big switch that began with that go-go girl in a cage!"[143] To top off the campaign, Warners concocted the outrageous idea of having exhibitors set up "Free Marriage Testing Bureaus" in their lobbies, where blonde and brunette "marital researchists" would determine whether bachelors were "ready to wed or…end up with a Marriage on the Rocks."[144]

Excluding *The Kissing Bandit*, this film was perhaps Frank's most ludicrous starring vehicle to date. As advertising executive Dan Edwards, he is considered "boring" and "dull" by his wife of 19 years, Valerie (Kerr), who, while coercing him into a second honeymoon in Mexico, accidentally divorces him and then mistakenly marries his business associate and best friend Ernie Brewer (Martin). The film's cavalier attitude toward divorce—both Edwards children (including Nancy's "Tracy Edwards") repeatedly wish that Ernie was their father so they may experience more freedom—is at turns humorous and sadly reflective of American society. While Frank and Dean both manage to give decent performances amidst this outrageous material, Deborah Kerr is an obvious fish out of water, as is Hermione Baddeley, who portrays Valerie's mother, Jeannie MacPherson, as a clichéd Scotswoman who guzzles Chivas Regal and parades about the house playing Highland bagpipes.

Several scenes suggest Frank's attempts to adjust to 1960s culture. After the divorce debacle, Edwards becomes romantically involved with his daughter's 22-year-old best friend, Lisa (Frank displays his Stan Laurel "collar grab" at one point), and, while suffering through an evening at the "Café A-Go-Go," whines, "I want to go home" as his wife dances with Ernie to the "hip" stylings of Trini Lopez. Unable to clap on the beat, he is tutored by a groovy, longhaired patron; and, during his later period of bachelorhood, he even climbs into Lisa's cage at the café to do a little monkey dancing himself. Variety's "Whit" wrote:

> Sinatra undertakes an entirely different type of role as the sober, middle-aged biz exec who has lost all rapport with his wife, daughter and young son. He, of course, delivers satisfactorily, but comes off second-best to the more sparkling delineations of his two co-stars, who benefit by comedy buildup of their roles.[145]

This time, Bosley Crowther had some reason to trash a Sinatra film (though his *New York Times* review remained unpublished due to a writers' strike):

> *Marriage on the Rocks...* is dedicated to the proposition that Frank Sinatra is dull. For the whole first half of the picture, he is supposed to be that way... And for the second half of the picture, he is dull naturally, since he has to pretend to be a cut-up... It is a foolish and witless piece of nonsense... about the only half-way funny stuff in it is Mr. Martin in a couple of scenes...[146]

During the same week, the low-budget horror film *Beach Girls and the Monster* also hit screens across America. Though *Variety* criticized its mixture of "sex, sadism and suspense," the film's jazzy score was praised.[147] The composer: Frank Sinatra, Jr., who received better reviews than did his father and sister for their latest screen effort.

One unfortunate consequence of *Marriage on the Rocks* prevented Frank from using his vacation home in Acapulco: After seeing the film, an official in the Mexican government ordered customs officials to keep him out of the country. Though he twice had performed there at benefits for Mexican charities, his participation in the scenes set south of the border had seriously offended someone who wanted to throw his weight around. The Mexico City newspaper *Excelsior* reported that Frank "may be allowed back in if he apologizes."[148] Seeking reentry, Frank asked attorney Louis Nizer to negotiate with the government while attending the Acapulco Film Festival. After the affair was settled, Nancy, Jr., wrote:

> [A]s it developed, the Mexican government had not banned Frank Sinatra from the country, although for a long while the petty bureaucrat made it seem so. The minor official based his whole "case" on a couple of scenes in *Marriage on the Rocks*, in one of which an actor says, "Don't drink the water"; in the other there was a reference to quickie marriages and divorces. It was so stupid. And the embarrassment the situation caused my family, especially my father, was hurtful, humiliating, unnecessary.[149]

During the shooting of *Marriage on the Rocks*, Nat Cole mercifully succumbed to lung cancer. Frank—who always had appreciated his music and fortunately jammed with him on occasions—had visited him several times as he wasted away in a Los Angeles hospital. The great jazz pianist and sublime singer was only 44.

To mark the forthcoming milestone of his 50th birthday, Frank collaborated with Gordon Jenkins on *The September of My Years*, an ambitious concept album featuring 13 ballads about growing older. During three sessions on April 13, 14 and 22, and an additional session for the title track on May 27, he cut 15 songs, including two released as Reprise singles. As Chuck Granata notes, "Where programs like *Only the Lonely* and *No One Cares* carry a common theme, they are as much about Sinatra the actor as Sinatra the singer; with *September of My Years*, he *is* the concept."[150]

Van Heusen and Cahn contributed yet another title song for Frank, who, enveloped by Jenkins' string arrangement, opens the album noting his unstoppable approach to "The September of My Years," which have crept up on him almost unnoticeably. "How Old Am I?" the first actual Jenkins composition the two had collaborated on, and "Don't Wait Too Long" are pleasant, lightly swinging love songs; and "It Gets Lonely Early" is another Van Heusen-Cahn "all alone" song, though here not one about a man whose baby has split, but one in his twilight whose family has left the nest. "This Is All I Ask," another Jenkins composition, and Harold Arlen and E. Y. Harburg's "Last Night When We Were Young" are highlights, the latter first recorded by Frank in 1954 and included on the *In the Wee Small Hours* album. The album's first waltz, "The Man in the Looking Glass," written by Bart ("In Other Words") Howard, features the absurd lyric, "How's your sacroiliac today?" quite a bridge to the masterpiece that follows.

Though the Kingston Trio had recorded Ervin Drake's "It Was a Very Good Year" four years earlier, Frank's peerless version eventually would become American classical music, used as a soundtrack in films, television productions and by untold individuals in intimate personal situations through the decades. Recorded on April 22, when CBS shot rare footage of Frank at work in the studio, the song, also released as a single, helped to keep the album on the *Billboard* and *Cashbox* charts for 69 and 48 weeks, respectively, and win several Grammy Awards. Opening with a haunting oboe set against a lightly plucked harp, the song, though running only 4:25, spans the singer's life from 17 to "the autumn" of his years and, as sung with the perfect combination of pensiveness, assurance, dynamics and control by Frank, is akin to a brief musical novel. The verse, "when [he] was twenty-one," featuring the phrasing of the lyric, "It was a very good year for city girls who lived up the stair/With all that perfumed hair/And it caaaaaaaamme undonnnnnnne/When I was twenty-one," is quintessential, unforgettable Sinatra.

"When the Wind was Green," another waltz, using colors as metaphors for the seasons, features another perfect vocal; Rodgers and Hammerstein's *The King and I* classic "Hello, Young Lovers" receives Frank's first reading since 1951; and "I See It Now" is another gaze back to the age of 17 by a man whose years have raced by. Written for the 1962 Broadway show *All American*, "Once Upon a Time" is followed by Frank's third stab at Kurt Weill and Maxwell Anderson's "September Song," an obvious natural to close *The September of My Years* and a dramatic improvement on the 1961 Capitol version. Recorded at the tail end of the April 14 session, the two singles—"Tell Her (You Love Her Each Day)" and "When Somebody Loves You"—arranged by Ernie Freeman as 6/8 pop numbers with chorus, are the musical antithesis of the *September* material.

The April 22 "It Was a Very Good Year" footage was incorporated into *Sinatra: An American Original*, a CBS Reports television documentary hosted by Walter Cronkite. This glimpse of Frank's working methods was only part of an unprecedented move that allowed CBS cameramen to follow him around over a six-month period, filming him at work, mingling with the public and partying with family and friends at Jilly's in New York. Cronkite also shot some interview footage with Frank, but the "Very Good Year" sequences are the high point. Rehearsals, the actual sublime take that made the album, and Frank, down on the studio floor, elbows on knees, tearing up as he listens to the playback, are unforgettable. Another musical highlight is a live performance of "Fly Me to the Moon" with Quincy Jones and Count Basie and his band at a charity concert in Lorton Penitentiary near Washington, DC. One sequence shows Frank and Deborah Kerr shooting a scene for *Marriage on the Rocks*, and ample time is allotted to a June 25, 1965, Summit charity show at St. Louis' Dismas House, named after Father Dismas, a.k.a. "The Hoodlum Priest," that was broadcast in its entirety on closed-circuit TV. Some brief footage of Dean and Sammy doing impressions is included, and Frank delivers superb renditions of "I've Got You Under My Skin" and "You Make Me Feel So Young."

Another media coup, Frank's essay "Me and My Music," appeared in *Life*'s April 23, 1965, issue. Concluding his remarks, he admits that he has achieved every possible professional goal:

> At this stage of my career, I don't have any more mountains left to climb. I have absolutely no desire to do a Broadway show, and that's the only thing I haven't done. I would enjoy rehearsing a show and maybe doing it opening night, but after that the repetition would bore me to death.[151]

The Actor, on Screen and in Song

Chapter 9
Goodbye, Baby, and Amen

He's the kind of guy that, when he dies, he's going up to heaven and give God a bad time for making him bald.—Marlon Brando[1]

Frank makes his mark at Grauman's.

On May 6, 1965, Frank made an atypical move down the road often traveled by his pal Dean when he cut an "Italian" novelty single, "Forget Domani," written for the recently released film *The Yellow Rolls-Royce*. Two months later, he placed his hands and feet into wet cement at Grauman's Chinese Theater In Hollywood; and, in August, he flew to Israel to shoot scenes for *Cast a Giant Shadow*, a film depicting the nation's 1948 fight for independence. On location for three days to play a bomber pilot, he joined star Kirk Douglas, who was cast as David ("Mickey") Marcus, an American Jewish lawyer who became an Israeli hero, Angie Dickinson and (in cameos) John Wayne and Yul Brynner. The screenplay, which ironically opens on "Christmas Day 1947," features pithy dialogue and one scene in which Wayne (incredibly) speaks a bit of Hebrew. Frank does not enjoy as much screen time as do his cameo colleagues, but his "Spence... the pilot [from] New Jersey" serves the heroic strategic function of fooling the attacking Egyptians into believing that seltzer bottles tossed out of the cockpit of his plane are really bombs! Making his final sortie, Vince throws out his machine gun and sprays some seltzer into the sky just before he is shot down—a somewhat ludicrous end for Frank. Producer-director-writer Melville Shavelson said:

> I put in the Sinatra role, which was important, but it might have been better with an unknown playing it. People might have believed it more. All of those things really happened. But having real movie stars in it, made people think it was all phony and *nothing* was true, as if the war itself never happened.[2]

Initially Shavelson called Frank in Rome, informing him that his cameo could be filmed there, but he agreed to play the part only if he could fly to Israel. At an old airport in Tel Aviv, Frank told Shavelson that he would perform the flight himself in a single take. However, after taking off, he returned to the runway. "My insurance," Frank realized. "It isn't any good over here."[3]

Following the shoot, he donated his $50,000 salary to the Frank Sinatra Arab-Israel Youth Foundation in Nazareth, a new organization he had been supporting since his last visit in 1962. Shavelson attended the dedication ceremonies with Frank, who, according to the producer, after witnessing a "12-year-old monologuist who start[ed] telling jokes in Hebrew," left to spend the evening with a "broad in Tel Aviv."[4]

Cast a Giant Shadow was released on March 19, 1966. Many reviewers found the film overlong and ponderous. *Variety*'s "Murf" noted its moments of "complete fiction and fuzzy composites," but was impressed with the technical elements and the cameos: "Sinatra is effective in brief footage, while Brynner...projects a quiet intensity."[5] Having read Ted Berkman's novel closely, Bosley Crowther noted the shortcomings of Shavelson's screenplay—"in attempting to encompass a large part of all the facets of Colonel Marcus' highly complex career, he has come up with a confusing, often superficial biography that leans a good deal on comic or extremely salty dialogues and effects"—and also got in his usual shot at Frank: "Sinatra is a clownish aviator."[6]

However, there were other critics who appreciated the cameo contributions. Clyde Leech, in the Los Angeles *Herald-Examiner*, enthused, "Frank Sinatra, looking all of 28 years old, lights up the screen as a soldier-of-fortune flier," while *Cinema*'s Daniel Davis wrote:

> John Wayne and Frank Sinatra, both playing their usual roles with typical aplomb. ...These two Christian personages help project the hoped-for, moral universality of the issues at stake, at the same time offering the moviegoer that comfortable feeling of international brotherhood—corny, superficially stated, but undeniably heartwarming.[7]

From material recorded at an August 23 Hollywood session, Reprise released two Van Heusen and Cahn singles, the swinger "Ev'rybody Has the Right to Be Wrong (At Least Once)" and ballad "I'll Only Miss Her When I Think of Her," both of which were included with another track, "Golden Moment" and eight others cut at sessions since 1961 on *My Kind of Broadway*, a compilation LP. On October 11 and 21, 1965, two sessions were held to complete *Sinatra: A Man and His Music*, a double-LP featuring 17 previously issued and three newly waxed tracks and narration by Frank. All the songs, including the freshly minted "Come Fly with Me" (the May chart, with updated, "hip" lyrical improvisations), "I'll Never Smile Again" (with the Pied Pipers) and "Love and Marriage" (an October 21 overdub onto an orchestral track cut 10 days earlier), are held together by Frank's informative and tongue-in-cheek recollections of his career, and an audio clip of his Oscar-winning performance in *From Here to Eternity*. Another track cut on October 21, Henry Mancini and Johnny Mercer's "Moment to Moment," was released as a single.

On November 24, NBC broadcast a television version of *A Man and His Music*, a "rare hour of excellence" during which he recalled his career musically with the help of Nelson Riddle and Gordon Jenkins. *The Los Angeles Times* reported that the "one-man performance should have sent 90 percent of the country's singers back to their vocal coaches."[8] Awarded an Emmy and a Peabody Award, the special paralleled its audio version, which won Grammy Album of the Year.

"An album for snuggling rather than wrist-slashing," writes Will Friedwald, comparing Reprise's *Moonlight Sinatra* to Capitol's *In the Wee Small Hours* and *Only the Lonely*.[9] Indeed, this Nelson Riddle-arranged collection of 10 songs dealing with some aspect of the moon—recorded in only two sessions on November 29 and 30, 1965—covers a startling array of musical styles yet is held together by Frank's unfailingly superb performance. Opening in romantic fashion with "Moonlight Becomes You," written by Jimmy Van Heusen and Johnny Burke for Bing Crosby

The Actor, on Screen and in Song

in *The Road to Morocco* (1942), he then warms up a 1932 Kate Smith ballad, "Moon Song," and lends perfect voice to Riddle's orchestral re-invention of Glenn Miller's familiar theme tune, "Moonlight Serenade." An atmospheric high point, Irving Berlin's waltz "Reaching for the Moon," written for a 1931 Douglas Fairbanks film, precedes a Latin-tinged arrangement of another 1930s cinematic number, "I Wished on the Moon," originally sung by Crosby in *The Big Broadcast of 1936*. Johnny Burke and Jimmy Van Heusen's "Oh, You Crazy Moon" is one of the best tracks, a medium swinger featuring sexy trumpet soloing by "Conrad Gozzo or Pete Candoli."[10] "The Moon Got in My Eyes," first sung by Crosby in *Double or Nothing* (1937), also cowritten by Burke (with Arthur Johnston), is a vintage Sinatra-Riddle ballad pairing; while "Moonlight Mood," another Glenn Miller standard, here is given an intimate reading by Frank ("You appear in a ribbon of moo*nnnnnnnnnn*light..."), Bill Miller's piano and the arranger's strings, woodwinds and minimal rhythm section.

"Moon Love," written by Andre Kostelanetz, Mack David and Mack Davis, and first sung by the Voice with the Harry James Band, was inspired by Tchaikovsky's Fifth Symphony; here Frank uses classical-like dynamics when he decrescendos during the final word, "disappears," musically and lyrically drawing a perfect close to the song. Originally cut by Crosby in 1934, "The Moon Was Yellow" here received its third inter-pretation by Frank, who floats effortlessly with long-breath phrasings over Riddle's bossa-nova, flute-tinged arrangement.

For his next album, *Strangers in the Night*, Frank sang "for moderns," a decision that resulted in incredible commercial success though a double-edged musical sword that thereafter grabbed new listeners but compromised his choice of material and, resultingly, the quality of his performances. On this LP, though, as Will Friedwald points out, his performances are "dimin-ished only twice": on the title track and Tony Hatch's "Downtown." Producer Jimmy Bowen saw "Strangers" as a way for Frank to compete in the pop market against the Beatles, which he did by only scant hours before another version by Jack Jones hit the streets, reaching number one in the charts and, months later, racking up Grammy Awards for Record of the Year, Best Vo-cal Performance by a Male, Best Arrangement and Best Engineered Record—although, as one listen will reveal, in the words of Allen Sides—the track "was recorded by Eddie Brackett...[and] sounds pretty lousy. The rest of the album...recorded by Lee Herschberg...sounds terrific."[11] Although Frank already had recorded the nation's foremost versions of its greatest songs—as well as having given his best silver-screen performances—the wider general public finally was catching up, and with an inferior song, to boot, in noticing him. (Perhaps his later artistic output would have benefited if they hadn't; but then a star of his magnitude couldn't simply settle for artistic satisfaction after such commercial success.)

The track is so over-produced that little room is left for Frank's vocal, which, because of his ability to dominate an arrangement, is very competent but fades out as he mocks scat singing: "Dooby, dooby do, do do do de ya, da da da da daaa yiii yaaaaaa..." This ending is further testament that whoever was responsible for this track—which is nearly the sloppiest rhythmically and orchestrally, of any Sinatra song ever waxed—was intent solely on competing with then-current rock fare. However, the next track, "Summer Wind," a German pop song with English lyrics by Johnny Mercer, is one of Frank's "coolest" 1960s songs and his last great collaboration with Nelson Riddle. Retaining the same laid-back swing tempo, the only non-ballad version of "All or Nothing At All," opening and closing with organ and muted brass, apparently an attempt to update his first hit for "moderns," resembles some of his later live rearrangements of earlier hits.

READ THE BOOK!

The breath-taking race for Hollywood's highest award!

THE OSCAR

IN LAVISH COLOR!

SEE THE EXCITING MOTION PICTURE!

The 1920s hit "You're Driving Me Crazy," "modernized" by a few organ riffs, is followed by the truly contemporary title cut from *On a Clear Day (You Can See Forever)*, a blend of classic Riddle, (minimal) R&B organ and a terrific Frank vocal. Also accompanied by the ubiquitous organ, the bluesy swinger "My Baby Just Cares for Me," from the 1928 musical *Whoopee*, though one of the better tracks, is a prime example of the conceptual failure of taking classic stage material, arranging it for a "modern" sound and interspersing it with contemporary songs. Ironically, though one of the most uncomfortable releases of Frank's career, *Strangers in the Night* was the bestselling.

The next track is the most utterly wretched. Never—by the widest stretch of the imagination—a good pop song, even in the mouth of English hit-songstress Petula Clark, "Downtown" is nearly the nadir of Frank's recording career (a few worse tracks would come). As Will Friedwald writes, this number "is so beyond saving that Sinatra can only verbally grimace... as an attempt to win sympathy for having to perform it."[12] Considering the unexpected octave leap in one verse and Jackie Gleason-like groans throughout the track, maybe Frank had slammed back a few Jack Daniels and didn't give a damn. "Yes Sir, That's My Baby," by Walter Donaldson and Gus Kahn, authors of "My Baby Just Cares for Me," brings a little blues redemption, bracketing Frank's warm vocals between Riddle's swinging blend of organ and brass.

Frank contributed a brief cameo to *The Oscar*, which was released in May 1966. A Hollywood insider film about a self-absorbed Best Actor Academy Award nominee, it stars Stephen Boyd, Elke Sommer, Milton Berle, Eleanor Parker, Jill St. John, Ernest Borgnine and Tony Bennett in his only screen role. In 1998, Bennett wrote:

> For years I'd been asked to do films, but since they always wanted me to play an Italian gangster, I just wasn't interested. But in 1965, I was offered a role in...*The Oscar*. ...While Paramount Pictures was in the process of casting the film, producer Clarence Green and director Russell Rouse happened to catch me on television. They thought my personality would translate well to the big screen, so they contacted me to see if I'd be interested in playing Hollywood agent Hymie Kelly. I was. ...It was loaded with great character actors, many of whom had won Oscars for their work in the past...in fact, I was the only unknown quantity. I was thrilled to meet all those wonderful artists.[13]

Playing himself in a scene in which he accepts an Oscar, Frank is joined on screen by Nancy, Jr., in their second cinematic "teaming." Also playing themselves, costume designer Edith Head and gossip columnist Hedda Hopper lend some tinsel-town "realism" to the story.

A black-tie grand premiere hosted by Mike Douglas was held at the Riviera in Las Vegas, and Hollywood trade publications, including *Variety*, had high expectations for the film, but critics found it insufferable. *Films and Filming*'s Richard Davis wrote, "In words that the scriptwriters

themselves might have used, this film deserves to stand as a classic: a classic to all that is shoddy and second rate and cliché-ridden, a grim warning to directors and writers on how not to make a film."[14]

Perhaps some filmgoers thought similarly about Frank's next feature, the high-seas caper *Assault on a Queen*, in which he portrays a small-time skipper who joins a gang of maritime crooks out to heist the Queen Mary with a submarine! Producer William Goetz searched various parts of the world for a workable sub, and after placing a want ad, located a 1935 German U-boat in a New Haven, Connecticut, boat yard, where its owner used it to attract potential customers. Refurbished by a ship repair company, the sub then was transported to Hollywood, where special effects artists "aged" it to look as if it had lain at the bottom of the ocean for 20 years. Filming began on September 20, 1965, and all the *Queen Mary* scenes actually were shot aboard the ship on location at Nassau in the Bahamas.

Signora Virna Pieralisi Pesci, billed as Virna Lisi, was also a great find for the producer. Married to Roman architect Franco Pesci, she was a huge star in Europe at the time, speaking Italian, French, Spanish and English. Of costarring with Frank, she said:

> Frank Sinatra? What is there to say? I watched so many of his movies, and when they came to me and said, "Would you like to work with him?" I literally was speechless. I have so many of his records, and to me he was always a symbol of what I wanted the American male to be. Not what I thought he was, of course, but what I wanted him to be: magnetic, animal, sensuous. That is Sinatra and it happens in his voice when he sings and in his acting when he makes love. Yes, I guess you would say I enjoyed working with him.[15]

Asked how Ms. Lisi stacked up against the starlets of Hollywood, Frank replied, "Virna makes them all look like West Point cadets."[16] Costar Richard Conte admitted that he never would have left Italy if he had seen Lisi there, while Frank, tongue firmly in cheek, added, "If they'd had Virna in the Mafia, I'd never have torn up my membership card."[17]

Also among Goetz's "casting" triumphs was landing the great Rod Serling to write the screenplay. Serling admitted:

> No one had been able to "lick" the Jack Finney book, which was a best seller...It had been tried several ways. But I decided to make it a straight adventure film and it seems to have worked out pretty well. At least Sinatra tells me he's happy with it.[18]

For a scene involving an external fire on the U-boat, special effects technician Irving Kandle blasted a flame thrower outside a porthole. Unfortunately, Kandle miscalculated the trajectory of the fire, searing his face on one occasion and his bum on another. "That is what I call burning the Kandle at both ends," Frank joked.[19]

Following a full day of shooting in the U-boat, Frank, Tony Franciosa, Richard Conte and Errol John stepped outdoors for a break. Sniffing, Conte looked at One-Take Charley and asked, "What smells?"

"Fresh air," replied Frank.[20]

To add convincing sound effects to his fight scene with Alf Kjellin, Frank donned boxing gloves and bashed away at a ham that director Jack Donohue had asked to be hung beside a microphone. Referring to his pork-pounding activities, Frank said, "Probably the first time that a real ham has stood in for an actor."[21]

Paramount encouraged exhibitors to promote a Sinatra quiz among their patrons. Eight questions referring both to his musical and film careers were included, with the studio claiming, "A score of 6-8 rights marks you a dedicated Sinatra follower, 4-5 makes you an average Sinatra devotee and anything less puts you in 'The Beatles' crowd."[22] To appeal to fans of the Summit, Paramount referred to the group of actors as "the pack" in several of the newspaper ads. With the film in the can, Frank guest-starred on ABC's *Sammy and Friends* on February 1, 1966.

From January 26 through February 1, Frank played several dates at the Sands with the Count Basie Band. Produced by Sonny Burke and arranged by Quincy Jones, recordings called "The Man and His Music" were made and edited into a program released as *Sinatra at the Sands*, the first legitimate live Frank Sinatra album. After an instrumental set by the band, the Count inaugurates the Voice's entrance with a furious brass introduction and some trademark piano licks. "How did all these people get into my room?" Frank predictably asks before soaring into a hammering version of "Come Fly with Me" and then leading the band into a half flawless, half comic, version of Gershwin's "I've Got a Crush on You," revealing two sides of his performance style simultaneously and then ending with a Louis Armstrong quote, "Ohhh, yeaahhh." Then he gives no quarter, segueing into "I've Got You Under My Skin," even though not in the best of voice, re-emerging at the end of the bridge again to give up,

> I would sacrifice anything, come what might,
> for the sake of having you near,
> in spite of a warning voice that comes in the night—
> it repeats, it *yells* in my ear—
> Don't you know, you fool,
> there ain't no chance to win—
> Why not use your mentality?
> Wake up, step up to reality.
> A*aaaannnnnn*d each time I do,
> just the thought of you,
> makes me stop just before I begin—
> because I've got you under my skin.
> Yeah, you grab me under my ski*nnnnnn*."

"Here's a very pretty song, a brand new song, as a matter of fact," Frank announces for "The Shadow of Your Smile"—already cut by Tony Bennett—as had "Street of Dreams," though

the Voice had crooned it previously with Tommy Dorsey way back in 1942. On the heels of the closing chord, Bill Miller crawls in to compensate for "the broad fleeing the coop" on Arlen and Mercer's "One More for My Baby," its quiet intimacy then broken by Basie's leading Frank "down the path to righteousness and all that *mother jazz*—in the right tempo" on "Fly Me to the Moon" and a furious "One O'clock Jump" instrumental.

Known as "The Tea Break," Frank opens his nearly 12-minute comic monologue by answering an audience member with "Salute. Good evening, ladies and gentlemen. Welcome to Jilly's West—where the elite meet to eat. And if I rhyme that, this'll be a barn in the morning." Taking predictable shots at his Summit pals, he receives applause when quipping, "I would say that Dean Martin has been stoned more often than the U. S. embassies" and "Sammy Davis wrote a book called *Yes, I Can*. And when I saw that [television] show, I sent a wire and said, 'No, you can't!'"

"You Make Me Feel So Young" opens his second set, followed by a Basie instrumental take on "All of Me," a sparse, string-less arrangement of "The September of My Years" and a rollicking version of "Get Me to the Church on Time." Also devoid of strings, "It Was a Very Good Year" unfortunately is too minimalist to mask Frank's tired voice. He again is somewhat unsure on "Don't Worry 'Bout Me" but, following a rest on Basie's instrumental "Makin' Whoopee!"—accompanied by rattling dishes being bussed from the tables—he returns triumphantly on a superbly swinging arrangement of Rodgers and Hart's "Where or When," which he (and many other singers) previously had recorded in its original ballad form. "Oh, it's boozin' time," he announces before the encore of "Angel Eyes" and "My Kind of Town."

On July 19, Frank and Mia Farrow were married. He told Nancy, Jr., "I don't know, maybe we'll only have a couple of years together. She's so young. But we have to try."[23]

Released on July 27, *Assault on a Queen* is an outlandish film based on the assumption that audiences will empathize with its gang of criminals. The plot involving modern-day pirates who refit a World War II German U-boat they find while searching for sunken Spanish treasure is adventure-film hokum, but Rod Serling's range of characterizations—devil-may-care Mark Brittain (Frank), jealous, arrogant Vic Rossiter (Tony Franciosa) and "his" woman, Rosa Lucchesi (Virna Lisi), stern and confident former Nazi U-boat officer Eric Lauffnauer (Alf Kjellin), practical and hard-working mechanic Tony Moreno (Richard Conte) and Britain's black partner, Linc Langley (Errol John), late of the British Navy—compensate. The Linc character, in particular, adds some depth to the script and reflects Frank's continued interest in racial diversity. When Brittain gives Rossiter his "orders" pertaining to the forthcoming robbery, he adds that Langley will be teaching him a convincing British accent. Following a blunt line of dialogue that wouldn't survive today's political correctness (Linc jests, "Be a good boy and bring the teacher a nice, shiny watermelon"), Brittain explains that Langley is "the only one who speaks *English* English."

Assault on a Queen ends in *Ocean's Eleven* style, with the heist going awry and the "pirates" left without a cent. But rather than a freak occurrence (Bergdorf's cremation in the earlier film) spoiling the stew, here patriotism wins out when Brittain refuses to fire on a U.S. Coast Guard cutter. While the greedy Rossiter is gunned down and Lauffnauer dies in the sub, the likable Brittain, Lucchesi and Langley survive to float into the final fade-out on a rubber raft.

Variety referred to the film as "'Ocean's 6,' or the rat pack goes to sea." "Robe" contributed a long review in which he compared it unfavorably with the earlier Summit feature:

> What *Assault* most lacks, perhaps, is the sense of morality that made the attempt of *Ocean's* motley crew... sympathetic despite their criminal intent. Whereas a casino is more nearly fair game, there's little "humor" in trying to hold up an ocean liner by seriously threatening to torpedo it.
>
> Rod Serling has avoided humor, almost entirely, in his adaptation... but what would be, generally, a wise decision, has resulted in a script that asks for, and gets, little sympathy for the perpetrators. Their actions are exciting but their motives reprehensible and many will feel that their ultimate fate is better than they deserve.
>
> Playing his most overtly criminal character since *Suddenly*, Frank and Virna Lisi were considered "very good in roles that make few demands on their acting ability."[24]

In *The New York Times*, Bosley Crowther missed a chance to take his usual shot at Frank, but Howard Thompson filled in nicely:

> The slick, standard picture... is strictly a celluloid duck, best suitable for those who adamantly believe in Mr. Sinatra or, better still, Santa Claus. ...The star's *Ocean's Eleven*... had it all over this go-round. And with all respect to Duke Ellington, what has a slap-dash, jazzy score to do with the ocean floor?
>
> Even with the Queen Mary ready, willing and able—and what a beautiful babe she is—Mr. Sinatra and his pals have really missed the boat this time.[25]

The New Yorker also printed a similar review, noting that "neither Rod Serling...nor Frank Sinatra and Tony Franciosa, with their respective underacting and overacting, make any constructive contribution to a monotonously inadequate movie about robbing the *Queen Mary*."[26] One of the few critics who liked the film, James Powers, in *The Hollywood Reporter*, wrote, "Sinatra is excellent as the mainspring of the plot. It is the kind of role he does best, sardonic, masculine, sympathetic. He handles the romantic scenes with Miss Lisi with conviction."[27] (Powers' final point is not difficult to understand.)

After Brad Dexter had saved his life in Hawaii two years earlier, Frank promoted him to Executive Vice-President in Charge of Motion Pictures for Sinatra Enterprises. During the summer of 1966, Dexter read Francis Clifford's espionage novel *The Naked Runner* while still in galley-proof form and hired Stanley Mann to adapt it for the screen, a project resulting in a convoluted espionage film that borrows heavily from the superior *Manchurian Candidate*. Using capital from Artanis Productions, the English subsidiary of Sinatra Enterprises, 33-year-old director Sidney J. Furie began shooting on location in London on July 5, 1966. To depict the European travels of Frank's Sam Laker, a former World War II sharpshooter who currently designs furniture in England but is covertly duped by British Intelligence into killing a Soviet agent, Furie filmed in London's Wapping district, at the Houses of Parliament, St. Paul's Cathedral and various locations that doubled for Leipzig, East Germany. Though actual filming behind the "Iron Curtain" was not pursued, Furie hired a photographer in Leipzig to supply him with shots of local people

Belgium poster for _The Naked Runner_

and places that he could use in developing convincing set designs, costumes and props. The fees paid by Artanis to the Centrepoint Building and the Little Angel Marionette Theatre in Islington were turned over to various British charities, including the Royal Cancer Research Fund.

Later scenes set in Copenhagen actually were shot on the real locations in Denmark's capital. One sequence filmed outside the Kastrup Lufthavn airport terminal bewildered an American tourist who, according to Furie, probably didn't "dare use any Danish telephone afterward." The crew had constructed a special phone booth in which Sam Laker was to hear his kidnapped son's voice repeated over and over on a taped message. The phone had been wired to play the message no matter what number was dialed; and when the cast and crew broke for lunch, a man wandered into the booth to make a call. "I tried to catch up with him and explain the booth was only a prop," recalled the director, "but he hurried away, shaking his head and muttering to himself."[28]

When Furie wrapped _The Naked Runner_, Frank returned to the States and, in January 1967, testified at a federal grand jury hearing investigating Mob-controlled casinos in Las Vegas. Four months later, the Italian-American Anti-Defamation League asked him to lead a nationwide campaign to address the stereotyping of Italians in the media. Though some commentators thought him an unwise choice to head such an effort, with his help, the IADL persuaded the producers of _The Untouchables_ series to drop some of the characters' Italian names.

The Naked Runner went into general release on July 7, 1967, and was quickly roasted by the critics. The convoluted narrative—involving Sam Laker's carefully manipulated transformation from innocent businessman to vengeance-ridden killer—fails to convince; and the main reason for his decision to carry out the assassination (devised by the British to look like an East German plot)—the kidnapping and supposed "accidental" death of his son, Patrick (Michael Newport)—is not developed to any extent.

Again, Frank's performance makes a film watchable. Most importantly, he dropped his famous Jersey accent in favor of a carefully enunciated delivery that indicates the character's residence in England. He strictly speaks the King's English and never once resorts to ad-libbing any Sinatra-speak. Even his most dramatic scenes—those involving the reported "death" of his son and the assassination—are underplayed in the classic Sinatra economical style.

Variety's "Murf" criticized the premise but praised Frank's contributions:

> The entire b.o. burden of _The Naked Runner_ will have to be shouldered by Frank Sinatra, who receives little help from other elements of this dreary Sinatra Enterprises programmer... Script premise is dubious, plotting lacks suspense, and climax is unsatisfying. Sidney J. Furie directed in pretentious fashion...
>
> Sinatra, whose personal magnetism and acting ability are unquestioned, is shot down by the script; his limning suggests awareness of futility of the story. ...Furie's direction is inept...[29]

Bosley Crowther again had good reason to criticize a Sinatra film:

> It is curious how Frank Sinatra repeatedly gets himself involved in films about fellows who do violent things with guns—gangsters, soldiers or assassins. He seems to be intensely attracted to stories in which he as the leading character is called upon to kill. ...This time his itch has really got him into a weird, preposterous tale... I couldn't get involved by this picture, no matter how tricky and wild is Sidney J. Furie's direction, nor how diligently Mr. Sinatra plays the sadistically recruited assassin nor how elaborately others play their phony roles.[30]

Films and Filming's Gordon Gow praised, "Sinatra conveys very well, by quiet and interior acting, the demeanor of a man who doesn't much like himself," and Charles Champlin, in *The Los Angeles Times*, noted, "even in... undistinguished material, he commands the screen...," Pauline Kael, in *The New Republic*, thought the film was a waste of Frank's talent:

> [W]hy has Sinatra not developed the professional pride in his movies that he takes in his recordings? ...An implausible, unconvincing spy story without a single witty idea, and the star's role that of an anxious, lifeless mouse. Sinatra wouldn't come on that way to the television audience; why does he have so little regard for the movie audience?[31]

Here, Kael points out the growing gulf between the quality of Frank's recording work and his screen efforts during the mid- to late-1960s. As time would prove, *Von Ryan's Express* became the last great Sinatra film, and most of his subsequent efforts—which were few—were often lifeless, tongue-in-cheek or downright silly. Several factors were responsible for this downturn, not the least of which was the '60s youth culture of sex, drugs and rock 'n' roll in which Frank—along with other performers of his generation—was engulfed. In 1965, he said:

> The biggest complaint I have about a lot of the kids who sing today is that I can't understand what they're saying. If I could only understand some of the words, I might be more interested in what they're doing, but I can't—there's no enunciation, there's no clarity of diction.[32]

That same year, in a lengthy article for *Life* magazine, he wrote:

> The music written today is nowhere as good as it was 10 or 20 years ago. But it's a whole new world. ...Kids want identity and they find their own identity... Sure, there are bad songs... poorly written and they have no melody, but it's another kind of music. There's certainly no harm in it. ...Actual jazz, real good jazz...good music, is dead.
> The era of *cool* jazz is gone. I think it's absolutely dead and buried. If any kind of jazz continues, and I pray it always will, I think it will continue in the sense of what we called in the early '30s "swing." ...I think there'll always be room for the singer...the ballad singer—because I think the world loves a lover, and they love a guy who plays a guitar and sings pretty songs.[33]

Though he primarily remained true to his timeless musical style—aside from occasional, somewhat uncomfortable attempts to "update" his sound for commercial reasons—the film roles that were offered during this period were far inferior to what he had accepted less than a decade earlier. And the simple fact was that Frank was getting older. He no longer looked like Joey Evans; and though he still possessed incredible magnetism, he, like all Hollywood stars, could no longer play characters years younger. But he still had a few entertaining films to come. What did Frank himself say about vehicles like *The Naked Runner*?

> There have been a number of those. But I didn't go looking for them; in most cases. I'm always dying to do comedy. But you can't find them. So when other things come up, you do those instead. I'd also like to do musicals, but who's making musicals any more? I'm always reading, always looking, always talking to people.[34]

Frank cut eight new songs produced by Jimmy Bowen on November 17-18, 1966, for a Reprise follow-up to *Strangers in the Night*, the title cut, "That's Life," having been waxed a month earlier in Hollywood. Opening with bluesy organ, this 6/8 number is a Ray Charles-style R&B semi-rocker with a confident, swaggering vocal by Frank, who made his annoyance musically clear after Bowen had asked him to do another take when the first was perfectly acceptable. Following this interesting opener are a number of primarily forgettable songs that never really groove (due to the arrangements and inferior percussion work): "I Will Wait for You," written for the 1964 Jacques Demy film *The Umbrellas of Cherbourg*, is a stiff medium swinger with superfluous strings and backing vocals; "Somewhere My Love," the theme from *Doctor Zhivago* (1965), is uncomfortably rearranged as a driving swing number; "Sand and Sea" is a lightly shuffling "beach" song; "What Now My Love" swings like a rusty gate; "Winchester Cathedral," in the words of Will Friedwald, "is insipid beyond the call of duty—even for this package"[35]; "Give Her Love" is a Latin-tinged pop song with another saccharine dose of strings and vocal chorus; and "Tell Her (You Love Her Each Day)" is a single cut the previous April. Apparently Frank didn't care for *Man of La Mancha*'s "The Impossible Dream" but recorded it as a favor to Mia. Aside from the title song and the closing number, Andre and Dory Previn's "You're Gonna Hear from Me," a swinger given a respectful treatment by Frank, the overly commercial *That's Life* has little to recommend it.

On November 27, Frank and Mia guested on the CBS game show *What's My Line?* Four days later, he supported a pal on NBC's popular *Dean Martin Show*. On December 7—the 25th anniversary of the bombing of Pearl Harbor—one of World War II's musical icons starred in *Sinatra: A Man and His Music, Part II* on CBS. This time, Nancy, Jr., joined Frank in a musical memory lane again conducted by Nelson Riddle and Gordon Jenkins.

For his next Reprise album, recorded on January 30-31 and February 1, 1967, Frank musically moved light years away from *That's Life*, creating a truly superior, beautiful concept album, one of the great masterpieces of his career. Brazilian bossa nova, a blend of jazz and samba, had begun to influence American musicians during the early 1960s, and though some singers, including Tony Bennett, had dabbled with this "new trend," Frank was the first to create an entire LP dedicated to this exciting new sound. Only 30 years old at the time, Antonio Carlos Jobim had composed several well-known bossa hits (in Portuguese), and Frank thought it would be fascinating to combine new versions of those in English with freshly arranged recordings of some of his favorite Porter and Berlin classics. Together with German arranger Claus Ogerman, the singer and guitarist dynamically teamed for the dreamy and romantic *Francis Albert Sinatra and Antonio Carlos Jobim*.

Frank and Nancy in *A Man and His Music, Part II*

The LP opens with Jobim's most famous song, "The Girl from Ipanema," on which Frank sings with the softest voice since

Sinatra and Jill St. John in *Tony Rome*

Capitol's *Close to You* over a decade earlier. After Jobim adds a vocal in Portuguese, Frank joins in for an effective harmony duet. Will Friedwald writes, "Sinatra is never at a loss for exactly what to do, even when the dynamic options only run the gamut from *piano* to *pianissimo*. While his phrasing is about as far removed from the Basie albums as Rio is from Kansas City, Sinatra is no less of a jazz singer here..."[36]

"Dindi" (pronounced "Jinjee") is sung with such mature mastery, combining dynamics, phrasing and emotion, that, at the age of 51, Frank proved he could reach the passionate heights he had achieved in earlier years, but now with supreme *softness*; this song is simply one of the sexiest ever recorded. For Irving Berlin's "Change Partners," from the Fred Astaire film *Carefree* (1938), on which Jobim was having some problems, Frank asked that Al Viola play the guitar part, though few listeners would be the wiser. A warm flute introduces "Quiet Nights of Quiet Stars (Corcovado)," on which Frank matches his "Dindi" vocal in all its quiet majesty, and "Meditation (Meditacao)," while he opens "If You Never Come to Me" and again vocally duets with Jobim on "How Insensitive (Insensatez)." Porter's "I Concentrate on You" receives a slightly faster tempo accompanied by Jobim's scat-humming, though Frank still is able to maintain his serene dynamics. One of the album's most pleasant surprises is "Baubles, Bangles and Beads," a stylistic 180 from its *Come Dance with Me* predecessor, here as effectively sensual as the earlier version is swaggering (the beads are "noisy" rather than "coo-coo"). A final quiet Jobim song, "Once I Loved," closes the LP, which received three Grammy nominations: Album of the Year, Best Male Vocal Performance and Best Album Notes (by Stan Cornyn). The February 1 session yielded two additional tracks, Johnny Mercer and Doris Tauber's saloon song "Drinking Again" and its antithesis, the single "Somethin' Stupid," a duet with Nancy that reached number one on the *Billboard* and *Cashbox* charts to become his biggest hit of the 1960s.

On April 3, 1967, Gordon Douglas and cinematographer Joseph Biroc began shooting the tongue-in-cheek detective film *Tony Rome* on location in Miami, where Frank acted during the day and performed at the Fontainebleau during the evening. Sixty-five different locations, ranging from flophouses and trailer parks to luxury hotels and mansions, were utilized. Thirty-five vehicles and a crew of 120 were hired to complete the shoot. Joining Frank were *Come Blow Your Horn* costar Jill St. John, Richard Conte, Gena Rowlands and, in cameos, Sinatra pals Rocky Graziano, Mike Romanoff and Shecky Greene. Incredibly, due in part to Frank's one-take nature, Douglas wrapped a full four weeks ahead of schedule. Jilly Rizzo's daughter, Abby, who then was six years old, later recalled:

The Actor, on Screen and in Song

I was on the set of *Tony Rome* in Miami Beach, where we lived on the houseboat *Jilly's Yen* across the street from the Fountainbleau Hotel. I know they filmed scenes at Jilly's South (the go-go dancers). I met Jill St. John and watched them film a wedding. They were going to let me be an extra but I wasn't in wedding clothes.[36]

The musical score was composed and conducted by Billy May. Lee Hazlewood wrote the title song for Nancy Sinatra, and the additional numbers, "Something Here Inside Me" and "Hard Times" were cowritten by May and Randy Newman. The film opens at sea, where Anthony Rome is cruising on his yacht as the younger Sinatra's voice fills the soundtrack. Soon, Tony is shown staring at a bikini-clad woman in the surf, the camera zooming in to a tight close-up of her tush before the scene cuts to a similar shot of a boxer in the ring. This sequence informs the audience that what follows shouldn't be taken too seriously.

The loosely connected, often confusing plot involves Diana (Sue Lyon), the inebriated daughter of a wealthy businessman (Simon Oakland) who is worried about her recent behavior. Recovering a stolen diamond pin she was wearing, Rome discovers that the stones are fake, as are all the rocks currently set in the Kosterman family jewelry, which have been tampered with by the blackmailing ex-husband of Mrs. Kosterman (Gena Rowlands). This main plot is intertwined with several subplots: the murder of Rome's former partner, the seductive activities of self-proclaimed "slut" Ann Archer (Jill St. John) and the misguided activities of the naïve Diana, who, at one point, attempts to seduce Rome.

Frank plays Rome in a relaxed, breezy manner, reflecting the seriocomic tone of the screenplay. There are enough double entendres for two films, along with some (typical for the period) gay bashing and general 1960s "love-in" atmosphere. Frank's usual improvised phrases like "gang of cops," "(he) got croaked in my office," "the creep" and "You know I didn't kill that bum" are blended with such high comedy as, in a scene in which an old lady has lost her cat, "You got a pussy that smiles?" All of this Tony-having-fun and acting like Sinatra business is leavened by Frank's portrayal of the detective as a very ethical character: Several times he resists temptation and does the right thing.

Jilly's South doubles for the Floradora Club, a shady go-go joint where Tony (briefly recalling *The Man With the Golden Arm*) pretends to be a dope addict in order to obtain a pusher's address. And the fact that Shecky Greene (in a convincing performance) turns out to be the murderer is a real gasser. (Greene's father had been a saxophonist with the Tommy Dorsey band during Frank's stint.)

Tony Rome was released November 11, 1967, to a critical consensus on its "lowlife" content. *Variety*'s "Murf" considered it a mixed bag, though he thought it would rake in some dough:

> *Tony Rome* is a flip gumshoe on the Miami scene, and a very commercial blend of tasteful and tasteless vulgarity. A busy heavy-populated script, zesty Gordon Douglas direction and solid Aaron Rosenberg production values add up to a potent first-run b.o. package. ...By fadeout, few will particularly care about the mystery angle... Credit Sinatra's excellent style, and the production elements, for pulling it off.[37]

After airing legitimate critiques of two Sinatra films, Bosley Crowther was back taking potshots:

> Evidently Frank Sinatra is trying to go the Humphrey Bogart route in the role of a private detective... The cryptic Miami Beach gumshoe he plays in this hard-nosed mystery... is such a conscious or unconscious imitation of Mr. Bogart's prototypical Sam Spade... that you'd guess Mr. Sinatra had been spending a lot of time watching *The Late, Late Show*.[38]

How could a critic as experienced as Crowther demonstrate such ignorance of Frank's past film achievements and, moreso, his close friendship with Bogart, to accuse him of preparing for his role merely by watching golden age films noir? True, there is a bit of Bogie in Tony, but how could Frank resist enacting an homage to his hero? Concluding his review, Crowther bemoans, "Mr. Sinatra is nobody's Bogart"—a trite remark, considering that the indelibly unique Bogie is as irreplaceable in Hollywood genre cinema as John Wayne, James Cagney and Boris Karloff. Hollis Alpert, in *The Saturday Review*, wrote, "Frank Sinatra has been a talent in search of a role ever since *The Manchurian Candidate*, and at last... he has found himself one. ...*Tony Rome* is lively and entertaining, and for this we must thank both the capable Mr. Sinatra and the persistent ghost of Mr. Bogart."[39] And while Charles Champlin appreciated the entertainment value—"Sinatra plays the part, or himself, to the hilt, and while this may not convert any Sinatraphobes to the fold, it is likely to delight everybody else"—*Time* echoed Pauline Kael's review of *The Naked Runner*: "It remains one of Hollywood's major myster-ies why a performer who puts so much style into his records so often sabotages his genuine talents in shoddy and ill-chosen movie vehicles."[40]

With their marriage, Sinatra and Farrow became gossip fodder.

After his sublime collaboration with Antonio Carlos Jobim, Frank waxed some pop songs for another Reprise collection, originally titled "Frank Sinatra & Frank and Nancy" but released as *The World We Knew*. To accompany the two additional tracks recorded on the last day of the Jobim project, "Drinking Again" and "Somethin' Stupid," he recorded eight more numbers on June 29 and July 24, 1967, half of which also were issued as singles. "The World We Knew (Over and Over)," featuring Ernie Freeman's overwrought strings and vocal chorus, sounds somewhat like a James Bond movie theme, while James Harbert's "This Is My Love," recorded by Frank in 1959 as "This Was My Love," benefits from an arrangement by Gordon Jenkins, who also did the chart for "Born Free," the theme from the popular 1966 film that Frank probably couldn't avoid. Slightly improving on his "Downtown" shtick, Frank tackles another Petula Clark hit, "Don't Sleep in the Subway," changing the original "darling" to "baby," of course—then moves on to some authentic 1967 pop (brass blended with harpsichord, harmonica and organ) with "This Town" by Lee Hazlewood, who wrote Nancy's mega-hit "These Boots Are Made for Walkin'." "This Is My Song," composed by Charles Chaplin for his final film, the perfectly dreadful *A Countess from Hong Kong* (1967), is Frank's one connection to the comic genius. (Curiously, he did not record Chaplin's "Smile," written for *Modern Times* [1936].) "You are There," a perfunctory, depressing ballad is followed by "Drinking Again" and Frank's third stab at *South Pacific*'s "Some Enchanted Evening," a bombastic H.B. Barnum arrangement.

On September 11, 1967, while gambling at the Sands—which recently had been bought by the increasingly paranoid Howard Hughes—Mia lost $20,000. Trying to win it back, Frank dropped an additional 50 grand in 45 minutes. When his credit was cut off by general manager Edward Nigro, he became enraged and, after yanking the cables from the hotel switchboard—taking Mia in tow—he drove a motorized luggage cart through the lobby. After tossing some chips in manager Carl Cohen's face, he was punched out, losing the caps from two teeth. Soon after, his dentist, Dr. Abe B. Weinstein, flew from Stamford, Connecticut, to a borrowed office in Beverly Hills to replace the caps. On September 23, Frank and the Sinatra children joined Dean and the Martin family for a televised Christmas special. One week later, he recorded Rodgers and Hammerstein's "Younger Than Springtime" for inclusion on his daughter's *Movin' with Nancy* LP.

Frank again teamed with director Gordon Douglas for *The Detective*, a $5.5 million crime thriller based on a popular novel by Roderick Thorp, during the autumn of 1967. Initially, Frank cast Mia as the female lead, but complications arose when she received an even more appealing offer from Roman Polanski to star in *Rosemary's Baby* (1968). Though Frank agreed to stall production to allow for Polanski to shoot Mia's scenes, the difficult director ran over schedule. Frank wouldn't hold off any longer: According to Tina Sinatra, he "had an obligation to the studio...and felt professionally embarrassed in front of his crew."[41] The role eventually went to Lee Remick, who joined an excellent supporting cast including Ralph Meeker, Jacqueline Bisset, Jack Klugman, William Windom and Robert Duvall.

Much of the shoot, which began on October 16, 1967, was done on location at Manhattan's 19th Precinct on East 67th Street, where crowds waited outside all day just to see Frank emerge for a few seconds before disappearing into the back seat of a chauffeured car.

"People forget that when I come here," he told reporters, "I'm coming home. I can walk around New York and nobody bothers me. You can't walk anywhere in Los Angeles, you always have to drive." Referring to the scenes filmed out on 67th, he added, "Of course, we're just shooting little bits of dialogue at a time. It'd be different trying to do a big dramatic scene. You couldn't do *Hamlet* out there."[42]

Another sequence—in which Frank dances with Remick—was filmed in a ballroom at Columbia University. While shooting the studio footage back in Hollywood, Remick occasionally joined him for drinks at the Beverly Wilshire's Oak Bar.

Frank worked closely with veteran cop Johnny Broderick to make his performance as realistic as possible. He recalled:

> I used to chat with him about little idiosyncrasies that they have, and he said, "I never noticed anything."
>
> And I said, "What did you do if you were waiting around?" and he said, "That was the toughest part of the job: waiting to nail somebody."
>
> And I tried to put in all those little things that he told me about. I tried to put it all together.
>
> I was a cop. ...I want you to believe that I am thinking that I am the cop. ...You can do things that you can't do if you're yourself... You're playing a cop with a badge, and the authority... I was always trying to keep a little tenderness in it somewhere...[43]

Set in a gritty urban atmosphere, *The Detective* is a far more serious film than *Tony Rome*. Frank's Sergeant Joe Leland is not a freewheeling Miami Beach P.I., but a New York City cop used to investigating gut-wrenching murders. While the screenplay's homophobic content would be strictly taboo in today's politically correct Hollywood, in 1968 it was a hip sign of the times: Leland discovers the bludgeoned and mutilated corpse of a gay man whose penis has been cut off. Making the rounds of gay hangouts, he eventually obtains a confession from Felix Tesla (Tony Musante), a psychotic homosexual who goes to the chair for his trouble. Later, Leland, who has been uncertain about Tesla's guilt all along, proves that the real killer was Colin MacIver (William Windom), who, ashamed of his bisexuality, subsequently committed suicide. Also troubled by relationships with his estranged wife (Lee Remick) and MacIver's wife, Norma (Jacqueline Bisset), Leland leaves the force after 20 years.

The difference in content and tone between *The Detective* and *Tony Rome* is directly reflected in Frank's two characterizations: While Rome plays the ponies and has a blast staring at women's rear ends, Leland rarely experiences happiness, except in an early flashback sequence when he first meets his lovely (though troubled and nymphomanical) future wife. Leland is strictly an above-board cop, fair and basically unprejudiced: In one scene he punches Detective Mickey Nestor (Robert Duvall) for mistreating "gayboys." In another sequence, Leland is outraged when a black officer (Sugar Ray Robinson) uses Nazi concentration camp methods while interrogating

Sinatra and Jacqueline Bissett in *The Detective*

a *nude* suspect. With half of the precinct "on the take," Leland is the only socially conscious officer in the house. Throughout this dark, often realistic and occasionally unpleasant film, Frank gives one of his toughest, yet—as ever—totally controlled and convincing performances.

Surprisingly, actual violence is kept to a minimum. The first gunshots, fired when Leland defends himself against two assailants, don't occur until 87 minutes have passed. Some atmosphere is again created at Jilly's, remaining undisguised here, where Rizzo actually makes a brief appearance as himself, pouring a drink at the bar.

Referring to the film's "message," screenwriter Abby Mann told critic Vincent Canby, "It's easier to be accepted by our society as a murderer than as a homosexual."[44] However, *Variety*'s ubiquitous "Murf," who claimed that Frank "stars in one of his best performances," noted the flaw in the presentation of this narrative element:

> [A]t the outset... *The Detective* looms as a hot commercial film, though having compromised the main themes of homosexuality and police corruption to an exploitation treatment, rather than exploratory insight. ...Script answers no questions, and even asks them awkwardly. ...Although extremely well cast, and fleshed out with some on-target dialogue (including a multitude of vulgarity which is logically introduced and not forced), Mann's script is strictly potboiler material.[45]

Having visited the set, Vincent Canby wrote the review for *The New York Times*, and agreed with his *Variety* colleague about the exploitative and uneven nature of the film:

> *The Detective* is the kind of film in which Frank Sinatra... drives 40 miles or so out of Manhattan and arrives at a beach house that must—from the looks of the landscape—be in Malibu, Calif.

The Actor, on Screen and in Song

Sinatra seems to be enjoying his role in _The Detective_.

This casual handling of geography epitomizes a film that haphazardly, even arrogantly, mixes the real and the fake. Although it makes some valid comments about contemporary society, it exploits its lurid subject matter in a show-offy, heavy-handed way designed as much to tease as to teach compassion. ...In adapting Roderick Thorp's 600-page novel, which had all the literary grace of a mile-long comic strip without pictures, Abby Mann... left intact...the ironic Thorp message ("It's no worse to be a murderer in our society than a homosexual"), which appears in the corner of the movie like a very small pearl in an artificially irritated oyster.

Mr. Sinatra, whose toupee must be the best that money can buy, has the waxy, blank look of a movie star as he moves through grimly authentic big city settings. ...Lee Remick... simply seems to be movie-star thin in the rather superfluous role of Sinatra's nymphomaniac wife.

There is something particularly disappointing about this awareness of hairpieces, capped teeth and dieted beauty in a movie that wants so hard to reproduce reality.[46]

Unlike Canby, who didn't appreciate Frank's underplaying, Richard Gertner, in the _Motion Picture Herald_, agreed with "Murf": "As for Sinatra, this is his most effective performance in a long time; he acts many scenes with a sharp emotional edge that has been missing in his recent work."[47] And Ray Loynd, in the _Hollywood Reporter_, noted, "Sinatra has honed his laconic, hep veneer to the point of maximum credibility, and his detective Joe Leland is his best performance since _The Manchurian Candidate_."[48]

Frank contributed another fine _A Man and His Music_ performance on November 13, 1967, when NBC paired him with Ella Fitzgerald and Antonio Carlos Jobim, but he stole the show when performing "Ol' Man River" without a partner. In between film, television and recording projects, he again hit the presidential campaign trail, this time for Hubert Humphrey, who became the Democratic candidate after Lyndon Johnson chose not to run for reelection. Frank not only stumped for votes but also became Humphrey's "acting coach," advising him on his TV appearances and teaching him how to play to the camera. Frustrated by Mia's distracting attention to her acting career, he also sought a legal separation, which was reported by the press on November 22.

On December 11, Frank, Dean and Sammy guest starred on Nancy, Jr.'s hour-long television special *Movin' with Nancy*, which also featured Frank, Jr., and Lee Hazlewood. Producer Jack Haley, Jr., who shot the briskly paced variety program at various locations, won an Emmy for his work. On that day and the next—his 52nd birthday—he also recorded a "dream project": a collaboration with Duke Ellington, *Francis A. and Edward K.*, featuring eight songs arranged by Billy May. Though the rehearsals had not gone well, due in large part to the fact that, according to May, "They were all terrible sight readers in that band,"[49] Frank, who was not in the best voice, went ahead with the sessions anyway. "Follow Me," from Lerner and Loewe's *Camelot*, begins what Will Friedwald calls "one of Sinatra's few slow sets not put together entirely of suicide songs... the most erotic of all Sinatra albums... the perfect inspiration for really close slow dancing."[50] Of Frank's singing throughout, Friedwald adds:

> *Francis A.* contains what might be his most concentrated singing. Whether it was the newness of the setting or because he was afraid of missing notes, Sinatra bears down with a supertight intensity. ...For the first time since the '40s he abstains from familiar Frankisms such as "baby" and "jack" and throws in hardly any of his ad hoc lyric alterations. [51]

A hit for its writer, Bobby Hebb, in 1967, "Sunny" is the album's most "commercial" number, though Frank counters this by working in several Billie Holiday-like phrasings and melodic improvisations. The closing 1920s-style muted trumpet riff borrowed from Gershwin's "Summertime" is a highlight. Written by Jule Styne and Stephen Sondheim for the 1959 Broadway show *Gypsy*, "All I Need Is the Girl" features Frank's most relaxed performance on the album.

"Indian Summer," a Victor Herbert melody lent lyrics by Al Dubin, is the album's finest track, a Billy May arrangement Nelson Riddle selected as his favorite, one he wished he had written himself. Even more impressive than Frank's vocal is alto saxophone great Johnny Hodges' ethereal solo. The sole Ellington original on the album, "I Like the Sunrise," written by Duke and his son, Mercer, appealed to Frank's sociopolitical beliefs; a song from Ellington's *Liberian Suite*, it had been composed to celebrate the centenary of the African nation liberated by slaves. "Yellow Days," a 1933 song by Alarcon Carrillo and Alan Bernstein, sounds like vintage Ellington, including sensual ensemble playing and another terrific Hodges solo; and "Poor Butterfly," an even more ancient number (1916), features an energized yet still cautious vocal performance. The only up-tempo swinger on the album, "Come Back to Me," closes the sole collaboration between jazz's greatest composer and popular music's greatest singer.

"'Hoss plays the heavy," trumpeted 20th Century-Fox's publicity for *Lady in Cement*, the second Tony Rome detective thriller, filmed on location in Miami from February 26 through April 6, 1968. As a testament to his television stardom on *Bonanza*, all promotional materials billed Dan Blocker in letters as large as Frank's. It was hoped that droves of moviegoers would turn out just to see the kindly actor play a villain, the ex-con Larry Gronsky.

Fox's pressbook claimed, "Frank Sinatra and company take over Miami for Free-swinging excitement in *Lady in Cement*":

> The scene is Miami, teeming with killers, blackmailers, topless bikinis, girls, cops, cement blocks. And Frank Sinatra is right there in the middle of the action...a private eye who becomes involved with a curvaceous heiress in

Sinatra and Raquel Welch in *Lady in Cement*

the shape of Raquel Welch and an ex-convict played by Dan Blocker, who is making his motion picture debut.[52]

Gordon Douglas and Joseph Biroc again completed a film in record time, shooting at 26 locations over the course of six weeks. As he had done during the *Tony Rome* shoot, Frank again acted during the day and sang at the Fountainebleau in the evening, managing to get his usual four hours of sleep each night.

Appearing in her 13th film, Raquel Welch had not acted in many extended dialogue scenes and had difficulty rehearsing when Frank was present. Gordon Douglas recalled:

> He knew his being around would only make her more nervous, so he dis-appeared to the back of the set. I was concerned how the shooting of this scene would come across. Frank came over to me and said, "Relax, she'll be fine." And to top it all off, he did a little prophesying. "She's also going to be a big star." At that time, I could not see it.[53]

After playing the hard-edged cop Joe Leland, Frank was back in white deck shoes as Rome, enjoying a cruise on his yacht. But this time, while treasure hunting with a pal, he discovers the submerged corpse of a shapely blonde who was fitted with cement overshoes and taken for a ride. The plot here is even more disposable than in the first Rome outing: Hired by Gronsky, a former beau of the drowned woman, Rome becomes embroiled with heiress Kit Forrest (Raquel Welch), a blackout alcoholic, and her guardian, erstwhile gangster Al Mungar (Martin Gabel), who tries to convince her that she committed the murder. Unlike the ending of *Tony Rome*—after solving the case, the P.I. wins the girl before sailing off for the Bahamas. (Of course, Welch's amazing derriere gets the close-up this time.)

Frank again had a field day with the tongue-in-cheek dialogue, strictly a result of high-caliber writing. Having discovered the dead woman, he comments, "She's one blonde I know didn't have more fun," and, later, referring to Kit, he explains, "She likes to hold onto things."

Frank's most obvious bit of improvisation occurs when Rome comments, "I used to know a broad who collected bullfighters," a direct reference to his past trouble with Ava. But the film really becomes self-reflective whenever Dan Blocker is on screen. When first meeting Rome, Gronsky tosses the detective onto a bar like a small bag of potatoes and, later, is shown watching *Bonanza* on television.

Welch provides much of the film's visual appeal, Richard Conte reprises his role as Rome's friend and potential nemesis Lieutenant Santini, and Jilly Rizzo, whose Miami club is prominently plugged in two shots (showing a swizzle stick and sign, respectively), expands his *Detective* cameo: He actually gets to mumble some dialogue while washing his hands in the dressing room where Rome questions a transvestite! Frank's Miami Beach venue, the Fountainebleau, also makes its obligatory appearance, during a scene in which Rome runs into the hotel to elude the "fuzz."

Gordon Douglas matches the casual style of the first Tony Rome film. The underwater footage, staged by former Creature from the Black Lagoon Ricou Browning, is most effective, but the repetitive contemporary musical score by Hugo Montenegro is distracting.

Lady in Cement was released on November 20, 1968. "Murf" was back, again to describe an uneven and exploitative film, and even tossed in some sign-of-the-times, "politically incorrect" sarcasm (which accurately refers to the film's gay-bashing):

> *Lady in Cement...* stars Frank Sinatra as a Miami private eye on the trail of people in whom there couldn't be less interest. ...Strong location production by Aaron Rosenberg and zesty Gordon Douglas direction combine to mitigate a script that relies on violence and swish humor for laughs. ...There's a scene where Blocker beats cop's head against a car window; later, he does in [Steve] Peck for the same effect. Real fun, that. There's a recurring strain of fag humor. All that's missing is for Sinatra to wear a lampshade for a hat, just like they do at far-out swinging parties.[54]

Vincent Canby also returned to comment on Frank's private-eye efforts:

> *Lady in Cement...* is such a perfect blending of material with milieu that the movie's extraordinary vulgarity and sloppiness can almost be cherished for themselves, like widescreen graffiti. ...Unlike The Detective...*Lady in Cement* turns its fakery and garishness into negative virtues that can be appreciated, if not particularly admired.
>
> Mr. Sinatra's Tony Rome, described by one character as the only man he knows who "owns a yacht and eats TV dinners," is much closer kin to Norman Mailer's Lieut. Francis Xavier Pope than (as has been suggested by some critics) to Humphrey Bogart's Sam Spade.
>
> As he has proved in the past, Mr. Sinatra has a very fine and rare talent, but he needs good people to bring it out, like John Frankenheimer in *The Manchurian Candidate* or Ella Fitzgerald and Antonio Carlos Jobim in last year's television special. In *Lady in Cement*, he has no one to bounce off, but since the entire movie is so consistently crude, it doesn't make much difference.[55]

But *The Los Angeles Times'* Charles Champlin again appreciated Frank's characterization:

> Tony Rome is back and, as before, Frank Sinatra has got him down perfectly. Sinatra projects this ex-cop-turned-private-shamus with a time-tested fictional blend of insouciance, cynicism, battered but surviving idealism, wisecracking, courage, libido, thirst and all the more interesting hungers.[56]

The Actor, on Screen and in Song

While in New York, Frank recorded three Don Costa-arranged singles during a session on July 24, 1968: "My Way of Life," "Cycles" and "Whatever Happened to Christmas?" which also was included on a holiday LP release, *The Sinatra Family Wish You a Merry Christmas*. On August 12, he lent his vocals to four additional Yuletide album tracks arranged by Nelson Riddle (and featuring the Sinatra children on the first three): Van Heusen and Cahn's rewritten, tongue-in-cheek "The Twelve Days of Christmas," the songwriting duo's more devotional adaptation of "The Bells of Christmas (Greensleeves)," their original "I Wouldn't Trade Christmas" and Cahn and Jule Styne's "The Christmas Waltz."

On November 11-14, he waxed two Riddle-arranged singles—the ballad "Blue Lace" and the Van Heusen-Cahn swinger "Star!" (which includes a reference to "Jilly's Bar")—and nine additional tracks for the folk-pop LP *Cycles*, so named for the recently released single. "Rain in My Heart" opens the album in turgid fashion, though this number is preferable to the harpsichord-heavy version of Joni Mitchell's "From Both Sides Now," which far too many singers covered during the late 1960s. The lack of melodic and emotional range is on par with the insipidity of the lyrics when delivered by the Voice. The merciful fade-out leads to the even more anemic "Little Green Apples," an overlong, lyrically infantile ballad more suitable for Elvis. "Pretty Colors" is another dirge with harpsichord, this time accompanied by wimpy backing vocals, bracketing "Cycles" with "Wandering," a lightweight but pleasant ballad with one of the album's best vocals. Jimmy Webb's "By the Time I Get to Phoenix" is the first of two ballads made famous by Glen Campbell, here sung very quietly by Frank; "Moody River," a country-pop song previously charted by Pat Boone, is simply awful, with Frank commenting during the fade-out, "I ain't goin' swimmin' in there"; "My Way of Life" is the other single cut in July; and John Hartford's "Gentle on My Mind" is the second Glen Campbell hit, a good folk song suitable to neither Frank's phrasing nor image.

NBC broadcast another one-hour special, this time titled *Francis Albert Sinatra Does His Thing*, on November 28. He sang a superb version of "Lost in the Stars" and joined his special guests Diahann Carroll and the Fifth Dimension for duets. While performing with the Dimension, he donned "hip" 1968 clothing.

During a recording session on December 30, Frank cut only one single, "My Way," originally a French song, "Comme d'Habitude," for which Paul Anka had written English lyrics. Though it charted modestly on both the *Billboard* and *Cashbox* lists, this number eventually became a Sinatra signature. Scholar Leonard Mustazza has pointed out, "Some regard it as an embarrassingly self-congratulatory ode to selfishness; others see it as a factual statement of Sinatra's own indomitability"[57]—while Will Friedwald, referring to the song as "the major mantra, the idee fixe, the recurring motif of Sinatra's career," writes:

> Musically, it's an underwhelming composition…Yet the way he transforms this unpromising source material takes him beyond alchemy and into the realm of sheer magic. Musically, it has no more content than most rock and roll, yet Sinatra pumps it up with the grandeur of an operatic aria…an irresistible piece of theater.[58]

"And now the end is near, and so I face the final curtain" is certainly one of the most depressing lyrics ever to open a song, quite an emotional obstacle for a performer to overcome during a 4:34 piece, yet Frank does it with power countered with a quiet coda when he repeats, "I did it my way."

On January 20, 1969, Frank joined a long list of celebrities—including John Wayne and Richard Nixon—who shocked America by making a television guest appearance on *Rowan and Martin's Laugh In*. But more shocking to Frank was the hospitalization of his beloved father on the 24th. Marty was suffering from heart disease complicated by emphysema and passed away five days later. Nancy, Jr., recalled, "When his father died, something snapped."[59] The following month, planning to record a second album with Antonio Carlos Jobim, he cut 10 songs arranged by Eumir Deodato during three Hollywood sessions but left them unreleased.

On February 18, Frank returned to the studio to record the bulk of the *My Way* album, completing the tracks over three sessions ending on the 24th. A major improvement on *Cycles*, this Don Costa-arranged effort contains an effective and entertaining blend of Sinatra-appropriate styles. The second Sinatra song adapted from *The Umbrellas of Cherbourg*, "Watch What Happens" allows Frank finally to swing once again, delivering a vintage miles behind the beat performance. "Didn't We?" his second stab at Jimmy Webb, is a lovely, sensitive vocal set against an equally tasteful Costa chart. Ray Charles' "Hallelujah, I Love Her So," featuring one of Frank's best blues vocals, is a fine musical contrast to his first interpretation of the Beatles, "Yesterday," which, graced by Costa's lovely chamber-like use of strings, woodwinds and French horn, lyrically suits the Voice very well. "All My Tomorrows," penned by Van Heusen and Cahn for *A Hole in the Head*, is a logical conceptual follow-up that lends the LP a vintage Frank feel, a superb romantic vocal. "My Way" precedes "A Day in the Life of a Fool," originally the Brazilian "Manha de Carnaval," reflecting Frank's interest in bossa nova and blending flawlessly with the other material, making *My Way* the most diverse LP of his career.

"For Once in My Life," a Stevie Wonder hit, charges in like a ram, a bluesy pop song that works very well as a swinger; while "If You Go Away," Frank's first Rod McKuen interpretation, adapted from the French ballad "Ne Me Quitte Pas," adds a tinge of "suicide" to the album—an impression *quickly* dispelled by the closer, his hugely improvised, swingin' comic take on Paul Simon's "Mrs. Robinson," originally written for *The Graduate* (1967), which he opens with "Here's to you, Mrs. Robinson/*Jilly* loves you more than you will know, Whoa, oh, oh." A portent of lyrics to come, this is followed by the likes of "You'll get yours, Mrs. Robinson/Foolin' with that young stuff the way you do" and "How's your bird, Mrs. Robinson?"

On March 19-21, 1969, Frank recorded 11 selections written by pop poet Rod McKuen for a concept album, *A Man Alone*. As he so often does, Will Friedwald provides the ultimate summation of an album:

> McKuen made himself the McDonald's of poetry and got rich marketing his McPoems. One doesn't imagine Sinatra took a lot of convincing to realize it would be worth his while to grab a piece of that action. ...To anyone who considers Whitman, Hart (Lorenz), or Dylan (Thomas, not Bob) their idea of a poet, McKuen offers slim pickings. His music likewise offers little that one would walk away with humming. Yet no Sinatra album has absolutely nothing to recommend it, and even *A Man Alone* has much that is worth hearing. To paraphrase Shaw on Wagner, it's an album of brilliant minutes and excruciating half-hours. ...To put it succinctly, most of the songs are absolutely nothing. ...Didn't Sinatra feel embarrassed reciting this poetry jazz in front of professional studio musicians—real artists and poets—who must have been fighting back the giggles?[60]

Though much of the material is problematic, Frank, in very good voice, delivers a sincere dramatic performance on each Don Costa-arranged piece. The title track is a highlight with a pleasant melody and "lonely" lyrics well suited to his saloon-song tradition. "Night" features one of five blank-verse recitations accompanied by orchestra (the others are the utterly banal "From Promise to Promise," "Empty Is," which also includes a vocal, "Out Beyond the Window" and "Some Traveling Music"), while "I've Been to Town" is a pleasant, lightly swinging number enhanced by Ted Nash's sensual tenor sax. "The Single Man," "The Beautiful Strangers" (described by Friedwald as "a philosophical discourse on broads and hotel rooms."[60]) and "Lonesome Cities" are unmemorable easy-listening fare; while "Love's Been Good to Me," replete with late '60s harpsichord, is the album's most radio-friendly track. A reprise of "A Man Alone" closes

inatra plays cowboys and indians for adults!

Sinatra is

DIRTY DINGUS MAGEE

FRANK SINATRA   GEORGE KENNEDY "DIRTY DINGUS MAGEE"
ANNE JACKSON LOIS NETTLETON · MICHELE CAREY · JACK ELAM

the album. Four days after completing the LP sessions, Frank cut a Reprise single, "In the Shadow of the Moon," for release in Italy.

During the Apollo 11 flight in 1969, NASA's mission control played "Fly Me to the Moon" so often that Frank's performance truly became part of the lunar experience. On August 16, he took part in an all-star tribute to Neil Armstrong, Buzz Aldrin and Michael Collins following their return to Earth. Nancy, Jr., wrote, "One of the great thrills of our lives was hearing Pop singing to us from outer space."[61] Two days later, Frank recorded the single "Goin' Out of My Head," a shaky rearrangement of the Little Anthony and the Imperials hit, and its ballad B-side, "Forget to Remember."

Two months later, the CBS television special *Frank Sinatra, Jr., and His Family and Friends* included a historic musical meeting between father and son shot at Caesar's Palace in Vegas. On November 5, Frank headlined yet another TV special, simply titled *Sinatra*, which blended a few vintage swingers with some more recent pop numbers and a medley of material from the McKuen project. He also hosted a shtick-ridden section poking fun at several of his films, particularly *The Kissing Bandit*, *Johnny Concho* and *The Pride and the Passion*.

Named after a bowling alley in New Jersey, hit bubble-gum group the Four Seasons had been weaned on Frank's music; and in 1969, lead singer Frankie Valli convinced the Voice to record an album of originals by their songwriter Bob Gaudio. Originally planned as a television special, the resulting concept album, *Watertown*, became a further slide into pop mediocrity for Frank. The title track introduces perhaps the least "groovy" Sinatra ever, as an incredibly stiff rhythm section plods its way toward poorly recorded "railroad station" sound effects. The remaining nine tracks offer Frank similarly simple melodies, forcing him to drone his way through the verses, with an occasional dynamic burst on the choruses. Though the ballad "Elizabeth" is a highlight, the album quickly plunges into a lyrical and musical abyss on the dreadful "What a Funny Girl (You Used to Be)" and "What's Now is Now," then reaches its nadir on "She Says," during which Frank trades vocals with a children's choir. "The Train" actually moves along pleasantly, and "Lady Day," a song about Billie Holiday (of whom Gaudio and cowriter Jake Holmes knew nothing), was recorded but left off the original LP release. On November 7, using a Don Costa arrangement, he cut a Reprise single version of the Holiday tribute.

"It's kind of a Western. He's sort of a cowboy" proclaimed MGM's advertising material for *Dirty Dingus Magee*, which was shot on location in Mescal, Arizona, where no highways, telephone lines or modern houses could be found. Here, the town of "Yerkey's Hole" was built by eight studio supervisors and a crew of 70 under the supervision of director-producer Burt Kennedy, who began rolling the cameras on February 24, 1970. Three days later, Frank flew to Washington, DC, to sing at a Nixon tribute to Senator Everett Dirksen.

Referring to *Dingus Magee*'s ludicrous content, Nancy, Jr., claimed that Frank "needed this silliness after Grandpa died."[62] She also admitted, "Though it ranked as one of the worst pictures my father ever made, *Magee* at least provided Dad with a wealth of material for self-deprecating jokes."[63]

Perhaps worse than the waste of a capable cast is the screenplay's constant "ethnic humor" and Frank's unbelievably bad wig. MGM even publicized the fact that his entire wardrobe cost less than $70. Hairdresser Naomi A. Cavin must have been proud of her work. In the pressbook, the studio claimed, "Frank Sinatra, who has the funniest role of his career…in *Dirty Dingus Magee* says he doesn't care how bad his costumes make him look on the screen, as long as they don't make the part look bad."[64] Frank reportedly said:

> As a person, I look pretty bad, but as for the part, I think it's one of the best-looking I've ever had. And it gives me a great opportunity to work with two of the most talented performers in the business, George Kennedy and Anne Jackson. …As far as I'm concerned, being sartorially perfect on the screen doesn't mean a thing. And to me, that's a good sign. It means audiences are becoming much more conscious of good old-fashioned acting and not to be diverted by a lot of glamorous camera tricks to catch the eye. …I'm only interested in what the character does and what happens to him in a real-life way. I'll wear a turban, or a baseball cap, or a miner's helmet if the part is right. I have a tux, but I won't travel—if the role is meaningless.[65]

(Perhaps this explains the wig. After all, "real-life" men do wear ones that are worse.)

Having been away from comedy films for many years, Frank elaborated about the genre:

> [T]he old time comedians like Chaplin, Keaton and Laurel and Hardy… epitomized a lot of situations in which the ordinary fellow was always being pushed around. They were like kids pressing their noses against Christmas store windows and never being able to get the expensive toys inside. They kept reminding people of incidents similar to those in real life. And when one of those comedians threw a pie in the villain's face or placed a well-directed boot in his other end, there probably wasn't a single person in the theatre who didn't visualize himself doing the same thing to a mean boss or somebody else who had been pushing him around for a long time.
>
> After all, comedy isn't too far removed from pathos. And getting down deep into the core of it, what is laughter? Why does a person say, "I laughed until I cried"? Because, laughter is an emotional release, just like tears. In fact, laughter is dry tears.[66]

Character actor Jack Elam was cast as gunfighter John Wesley Hardin. Making his second appearance in a Sinatra film, but actually playing scenes with Frank this time, Elam recalled, "We work[ed] together several pleasant and friendly days. Our greeting each morning was a game of dollar bill liars poker. That's probably the only thing in the world I could beat him at!"[67]

Early in the film, Dingus Magee admits to Hoke Birdsill (George Kennedy) that he is a "part-time ass breaker" for the local stagecoach company, but soon reveals that he also is a low-down thief. After robbing Birdsill of a derby hat and $400, he becomes a legitimate "$10-dollar outlaw" after his mug is printed on a wanted poster. Following his and Anna Hot Water (Michelle Carey), his female "Apache" companion's, stage "holdup," the remainder of the narrative involves the ultimate destination of the stolen loot. Birdsill is named Sheriff of Yerkey's Hole by Mayor Belle Knopps (Anne Jackson), who doubles as madam of the bordello; and after a series of mis-adventures involving the prostitutes, the Apaches, the cavalry and the amorous schoolmarm, he is double-crossed a final time by Magee, who supersedes him as Sheriff and then rides off with the Apache girl and all of Belle's "savings."

Incredibly (according to the pressbook), *Dirty Dingus Magee* received the film industry's first official endorsement from Indians for Truthful Portrayals (IFTP) when president Charlie Blackfeet made a presentation to Burt Kennedy. Blackfeet said:

Outside of this film, which unmasks the long list of Indian clichés with humor and satire, Hollywood's version of the average American Indian in the past has been as artificial as a toupee. Generations of children have grown up with more false impressions than you'd find in a dentist's office.[68]

It's kind of a western.
He's sort of a cowboy.

SINATRA IS
DIRTY DINGUS MAGEE

FRANK SINATRA ... GEORGE KENNEDY "DIRTY DINGUS MAGEE"
ANNE JACKSON ... MICHELE CAREY · LOIS NETTLETON · JACK ELAM

Considering Frank's jet black rug, Blackfeet used an appropriate metaphor, but this statement is nothing more than pure MGM propaganda. The depiction of Native Americans, specifically Apaches, in *Dirty Dingus Magee* is no more inaccurate nor ridiculous than in other films of the era, but it certainly is not, by any stretch of the imagination, a "truthful portrayal!" As Anna Hot Water, Michelle Carey is a white actress adorned with reddish makeup, a long black wig and a buckskin-style outfit—an Old West version of a miniskirt and go-go boots. Her dialogue—"Dingoose...We make bim bam"—is even more ludicrous. The usual clichés are rampant, reaching their apex in the character of "Chief Crazy Blanket," played by white character actor Paul Fix. In one scene, a soldier asks Magee why a white man should be consorting with a female redskin—when in actuality Frank's complexion is far darker than that of the "Indian girl."

The film is strictly a farce, and Frank accepted the role to have a good time, as he had done in earlier productions such as *Ocean's Eleven* and *Sergeants 3*. The white and Chinese characters are also quite absurd, particularly the women, most of whom border on the nymphomaniacal. The double entendres in Tom Waldman, Frank Waldman and Joseph Heller's screenplay are uniformly unsubtle: Belle's reference to the "Little Big Horny," Magee's Freudian admission to Birdsill—after he crawls into bed, mistaking him for Belle—that "every time I take my pants off, you come at me with a gun"; Prudence ("Prude") Frost (Lois Nettleton), the amorous schoolmarm, belying her name by successively bedding down with Magee, Birdsill and Charles Stuart (Harry Carey, Jr.); and, during an Army "Indian drill" used to flush cavalrymen out of the whorehouse, a rooster-toting prostitute's warning to a soldier that he "forgot his cock." The overall level of sophistication is indicated during the first few minutes, when Magee robs Birdsill while the latter is urinating. In the climactic scene, after the bordello is torched by Birdsill, a mangy dog "attempts" to douse the flames by lifting its leg.

Frank's introduction in the opening sequence is actually performed by a stuntman who is bucked off a mule onto a fence that falls apart. Both he and George Kennedy give entertaining performances, as does the reliable Jack Elam, whose outlaw adds yet another level of insane mayhem to the proceedings: John Wesley Hardin's prowess with a firearm is so fierce that he manages to hold off an entire posse with a single six-shooter! The crowning absurdity is the cartoonish musical score by Jeff Alexander.

Variety actually published two reviews of the film, one following the preview and a second after its general release in October 1970. Of the earlier cut, "Murf" wrote:

> *Dirty Dingus Magee* shapes up as a good oater slapstick-satire-burlesque comedy... The comedy varies from unabashedly cornball sight gags to near-satire on the "code of the West." Several double-entendre lines will draw groans—mostly of enjoyment—from less discriminating audiences. ...Kennedy and Sinatra have a great time... The biggest drawback... in its... unfin-

ished format, is director Kennedy's pacing and editing. ...After a promising start, film has virtually ground to a halt by 60 of its previewed 96 minutes; it picks up again (when Elam enters) to a good climax.[69]

Three months later, "Murf" was impressed by the re-edited final cut:

> *Dirty Dingus Magee* emerges in final form as a good period Western comedy... Very good b.o. prospects loom in general situations... The gag sub-plots move along at a good pace, and prominent among the laughs are those generated by Lois Nettleton... and Jack Elam again scores as a slightly befuddled gunslinger.[70]

Roger Greenspun, in *The New York Times*, was closer to the mark:

> Burt Kennedy's *Dirty Dingus Magee*... is a dreadful parody Western that demonstrates once again how objectionable are innuendo and impulse when unaccompanied socially by redeeming sex and violence... seeing [the film] is rather like hearing an interminable traveling-salesman story repeated by somebody who has been told all the elements but doesn't himself get the point.[71]

Only "Murf" had anything good to write about the film. While *The Los Angeles Times'* Kevin Thomas found it "disgusting," Arthur Knight, in *The Saturday Review*, called Frank "bored and uncommitted."[72] Perhaps vying only with *The Kissing Bandit* as his worst film, *Dirty Dingus Magee* became the last feature in which Frank would appear for more than a decade. Sadly, it would become his next-to-last major characterization on the big screen. Though he had considered appearing in "The Little Prince," a Stanley Donen musical to be   based on a 1940s French bestseller and feature a Lerner and Loewe score, the film was never made.

On May 7 and 8, 1970, Frank appeared with the Count Basie Orchestra at London's Royal Festival Hall in a benefit for the Society for Prevention of Cruelty to Children. Prior to his flight to England, the Commissioner of New Scotland Yard contacted the FBI for information about his recent testimony regarding organized crime in New Jersey. The commissioner was worried that it might be improper for Frank to be seen with members of the royal family, but all the fuss was for naught. Again introduced by Princess Grace of Monaco, he gave an outstanding performance that was broadcast as a one-hour television show on November 16.

Frank severed his ties with Caesar's Palace on September 3, 1970, after hotel executive vice president Sanford Waterford drew a gun on him. Having no idea "why Waterman was so frightened," Frank advised, "I hope you like that gun, because you may have to eat it," as Jilly Rizzo "jumped over the desk" and captured the firearm.[73]

In October 1970, Frank recorded additional tracks for the compilation LP *Sinatra and Company*, which includes seven of the 10 songs cut with Antonio Carlos Jobim the previous year: "Drinking Water," "Someone to Light Up My Life," "Triste," "Don't Ever Go Away," "This Happy Madness," "Wave" and "One Note Samba." Although three songs—"Bonita," "Desafinado" and "Song of the Sabia"—were left off the album, the ones that are included indicate why Frank decided not to release them originally: The arrangements by Deodato are inferior to Claus Ogerman's for the earlier masterpiece; and Frank, not in the best voice, has problems hitting or holding some of the notes. The pop numbers taped October 26-29 include "I Will Drink the Wine," Hal David and Burt Bacharach's "Close to You," which had been a hit for the Carpenters earlier in the year, "Sunrise in the Morning," the *Sesame Street* classic "Bein' Green," and two John Denver songs, "My Sweet Lady" and "Leaving on a Jet Plane." The Costa-arranged "Lady Day" recorded the previous autumn closes the album. The October 28 session yielded two singles, "I'm Not Afraid" and George Harrison's "Something," Frank's second Beatles cover.

On November 2, he waxed three songs: two bubble-gum duets with Nancy, "Feelin' Kinda Sunday" and "Life's a Trippy Thing," which were issued in Italy; and the unreleased "The Game is Over." Later in the month, Nixon handlers became concerned that Frank, a former Roosevelt and Kennedy liberal, might not be the best choice for the president to be hanging around with or inviting to perform at official functions. Unlike Scotland Yard, the White House wasn't overly concerned with his "criminal connections," only political ones—but by now Frank, previously rebuffed by the Kennedys and always having enjoyed the company of powerful leaders, had, like Ronald Reagan before him, become more conservative on some issues. On November 18, he guested on Danny Thomas' TV show *Make Room for Daddy*. Six weeks later, he "made room for Ronnie" when he performed live at Reagan's inauguration as Governor of California.

Frank was back at the Academy Awards on April 15, 1971, to receive a special Oscar: the Jean Hersholt Humanitarian Award. In his acceptance speech, he focused on the fact that, while celebrities' acts of charity are recognized by publicity and awards, those of everyday folks don't receive the recognition they deserve:

> If your name is John Doe and you work night and day doing things for your helpless neighbors, what you get for your effort is tired. So Mr. and Mrs. Doe and all of you who give of yourselves to those who carry too big a burden to make it on their own, I want you to reach out and take your share of this, because if I have earned it, so, too, have you.

Two months later, Frank, after announcing his retirement, gave his "final" public performance at a benefit for the Motion Picture and Television Relief Fund. As headliner he followed Sammy, Jack Benny, Don Rickles, Bob Hope and Barbara Streisand. Covering nearly 40 years with 14 songs, he sang "All or Nothing at All," "I've Got You Under My Skin," "I'll Never Smile Again," "The Lady is a Tramp," "Ol' Man River," "My Way," "That's Life," closing with the haunting "Angel Eyes." Journalist Thomas Thompson beautifully captured the coda:

> He had built his career, he said softly, on saloon songs. He would end quietly on such a song. He slipped from his words into "Angel Eyes," surely a song for the short hours. He ordered the stage dressed in darkness, a pin spot picking out his profile in silhouette. He lit a cigarette in midsentence and its smoke enveloped him. He came to the last line. "Excuse me while I... disappear." And he was gone. ...It was the single most stunning moment I have ever witnessed on a stage.[74]

Paramount released Coppola's *The Godfather* March 11, 1972. Prior to Coppola's involvement, Otto Preminger had been approached to produce and direct the adaptation of Mario Puzo's bestselling 1969 Mafia novel. Preminger had sent Frank a copy of the book, asking him if he would be interested in portraying Don Vito Corleone. "I even offered to eliminate the character of the singer, who some people thought was patterned after Sinatra," the director recalled.[75]

In his reply to Preminger, Frank said, "Ludvig, I pass on this."

Frank had never been a fan of the novel. After it was published, many readers assumed that the rise to fame of character Johnny Fontane had been based on Mob participation in helping him nail the Maggio role in *From Here to Eternity*. Though Frank didn't think too highly of Mario Puzo, the author had admitted that the entire incident involving a horse's head placed at the foot of a movie producer's bed was based, not on Columbia's Harry Cohn, but on an old Sicilian folk tale. And, after the release of Coppola's *Godfather*, other individuals claimed that Fontane was based on "another performer" or specifically named Dean Martin as the inspiration. Vic Damone was initially considered to play Fontane, but the part eventually went to Al Martino.

To this day, both printed and electronic publications erroneously list Frank as the model for Fontane—and in the role he reportedly turned down, Marlon Brando won a Best Actor Academy

Italian Prime Minister Giulio Andreotti, Frank Sinatra, Pat and Richard Nixon at the White House.

Award but refused to accept it, due to the way Hollywood had been "treating American Indians." After Brando's surrogate, Satcheen Littlefeather, took the stage to read the absent actor's refusal speech, she was given only 40 seconds by the producer, Frank's erstwhile collaborator Howard Koch. Though liberal Jane Fonda lauded Brando's reaction, Michael Caine said, "If you're going to make a humanitarian gesture, I think a man who makes $2 million a picture should at least give half of it to the Indians."

During spring 1973, President Nixon asked Frank to end his retirement to perform at the White House for visiting Italian Prime Minister Giulio Andreotti on April 17, his first visit since the Kennedy years. "This house is honored," Nixon announced with some nervousness, "to have a man whose parents were born in Italy, who from humble beginnings went to the very top of entertainment: Frank Sinatra." Following the performance, the President added:

> Mr. Prime Minister and all our distinguished guests. I want you to hear this, Frank. Don't leave. Those of us who have had the privilege of being in this room have heard many great performances, and we are always very privileged to hear them, particularly in this room. But once in a while—not always—once in a while there is a moment when there is magic in the room, and a great performer—a great singer, entertainer, is able to capture it and move us all—and Frank Sinatra has done that tonight. We thank him.

On May 10, Nixon wrote a thank-you letter to Frank, mentioning his "graciousness in rehearsing before the members of the White House staff [which] really made their day."[76]

For the first time in nearly three years, Frank recorded material for a new album, during four June sessions in Hollywood. (Two months earlier, he had taped some performances at Goldwyn Studios, but ordered them destroyed.) Completing 11 ballads, eight of which would be included on *Ol' Blue Eyes is Back*, he returned to cut two more on August 20. Though he began the June 4 session with a version of Sonny Bono's suicide song "Bang, Bang," this recording was not issued. *Ol' Blue Eyes* opens with the ballad "You Will Be My Music," the first of four Joe Raposo songs on the LP, indicating that Frank's "comeback" would be a blend of his classic orchestral style and the contemporary pop sound of the pre-"retirement" albums. "You're So Right (for What's Wrong in My Life)" and "Winners" are somewhat more traditionally arranged, but Kris Kristofferson's "Nobody Wins," though lyrically appropriate, recaptures the pseudo-Nashville

The Actor, on Screen and in Song

sound he had attempted a few years earlier. Stephen Sondheim's "Send in the Clowns," from the 1973 Broadway show *A Little Night Music*, transports Frank back a decade, before *Strangers in the Night* began his descent into inferior material, yet his vocal features little dynamic range. Written by John Williams and Paul Williams for the film *The Man Who Loved Cat Dancing* (1973), "Dream Away" fits squarely into the soft-rock mold; while "Let Me Try Again," an attempt to repeat the success of "My Way," was adapted from a French song by Paul Anka (with assistance from Sammy Cahn) and also released as a single. The LP closes with two Raposo contributions: A lament for a changing America that taps into Frank's love of baseball, "There Used to Be a Ballpark" is the haunting high point; while "Noah" surges into a metaphorical miasma.

Beyond reviving his recording career, *Ol' Blue Eyes is Back* also gave Frank a new popular nickname. Continuing the comeback, he appeared in an identically titled NBC television special on November 18, 1973. Joined by his old colleague Gene Kelly, he duetted on "We Can't Do That Anymore," a self-deprecating look at their advancing age, and then performed "Nice 'n' Easy" as the legendary hoofer belied the words they had sung.

The following month, he cut two numbers for single release, placing tongue firmly in cheek for Jim Croce's "Bad, Bad Leroy Brown," which had been a huge hit for the late folk-rocker the previous year, and "I'm Gonna Make It All the Way," an Elvis-style country ballad. Arranged by Don Costa as a rock shuffle with a brass section and female chorus, "Leroy" sets a stilted groove, with Frank improvising, "All the *studs* just call him 'Sir'" and, with his Jersey accent in full force, "Badder than ol' King K*ah*ng," before *barking* at the end.

"While many ponder the future of Metro-Goldwyn-Mayer, nobody can deny that it has one hell of a past," noted "Murf" in the April 17, 1974, issue of *Variety*.[77] Produced and directed by Jack Haley, Jr., *That's Entertainment* celebrated the studio's 50th anniversary with 132 minutes of colorful nostalgia, blending the most memorable scenes from their great musicals with new footage and voice-overs contributed by 11 of their legendary stars, including Fred Astaire, Bing Crosby, Gene Kelly, Peter Lawford, Liza Minnelli, Donald O'Connor, Debbie Reynolds, Mickey Rooney, Jimmy Stewart, Elizabeth Taylor and Frank, who was chosen to open and close the film.

The first voice heard on the soundtrack is Frank's as he notes that MGM produced the first "all talking, all singing, all dancing film ever..." He also is the first star on screen, walking toward the camera through a section of the famous studio backlot. Later clips include Sinatra scenes from *It Happened in Brooklyn*, *Anchors Aweigh*, *Take Me Out to the Ball Game*, *On the Town* and *High Society*. Providing the film's coda, he introduces "MGM's masterpiece," Gene Kelly's ballet sequence from *An American in Paris*.

During May 1974, Frank recorded eight tracks for his next Reprise album, *Some Nice Things I've Missed*, another decidedly mixed bag of pop material—songs that had been chart hits during his brief "retirement"—arranged by Don Costa and Gordon Jenkins. "You Turned My World Around" is a typical early '70s ballad, while Neil Diamond's "Sweet Caroline," with its droning melody, "swings" as ludicrously as "Bad, Bad Leroy Brown" (which, together with its single B-side, "I'm Gonna Make it All the Way," also is included in the collection). Alan and Marilyn Bergman and Michael Legrand's "The Summer Knows," written for the film *The Summer of '42* (1971), is one of the more listenable tracks, but "Tie a Yellow Ribbon Round the Ole Oak Tree," a hit for Tony Orlando and Dawn the previous year, is, in Will Friedwald's words, "the ultimate hymn to the era of platform shoes"[78] and arguably one of the worst pieces of pop drek Frank ever tossed off: Hearing the Voice sing about a "*yella* ribbon," spending "three long *ye-ahs*" in prison, and "the whole *damn* bus" is absurd. The one actual swing number, Floyd Huddleston's prurient "Satisfy Me One More Time" is pure camp indulgence, though perhaps preferable to David Gates' "Bread" ballad "If," rendered even more syrupy by the Jenkins arrangement. Stevie Wonder gets the Costa treatment on "You Are the Sunshine of My Life," which nearly works as a light swinger, and "What Are You Doing the Rest of Your Life?" is another Bergman-Legrand ballad favored by jazz-pop singers.

Howard Cosell announced Frank's next television special in his trademark style, as if it were a pugilistic contest. In fact, Ol' Blue Eyes actually sang in a boxing ring at Madison Square

Garden for *Sinatra: The Main Event*, which was broadcast live from New York on October 13, 1974. Frank had played several dates prior to this extravaganza, backed by Woody Herman's Young Thundering Herd conducted by Bill Miller, and his voice was a bit ragged during the performance. The songs—ranging from the sublime ("I've Got You Under My Skin") to the utterly ridiculous ("Bad, Bad Leroy Brown")—were also marketed on an album release by Reprise, although performances from the Garden, Buffalo, Boston and Philadelphia were edited together to provide a more polished product.

The album includes Cosell's hyperbolic introduction, droning on for three minutes, before Frank offers a rousing, "rest of the broads...wild, knocked-out, coo-coo, groovy" version of "The Lady is a Tramp." Cut together from performances in Philly and New York, "I Get a Kick Out of You" features his comment, "Where do you think Gene Kelly learned how to dance? From me." "Let Me Try Again," also spliced together, is followed by a capable "Autumn in New York," a driving, electrifying "Skin" and a *cat* named "Leroy Brown" (this time the "chick's" name is *Morris*!) After a spectator unbelievably yells, "One more time!" Frank, explaining about "a fellow whose chick split—she grabbed all the money that was laying around, and all the grass, and she left him five gallons of muscatel," rescues the set list with "Angel Eyes." After delivering an enthusiastic, schmaltzy version of "You Are the Sunshine of My Life," he introduces "The House I Live In," offering an updated variation on his 1945 homily:

> This next song is quite personal to me—and I think it is to you....It's a song about this great big, wonderful, *imperfect* country. I say imperfect, because if it were perfect, it wouldn't be any fun trying to fix it, trying to make it work better, trying to make sure that everybody gets a fair shake—and then some.

Frank then closes the set with personalized odes to Chicago and ego, "My Kind of Town" and "My Way."

Between September 24, 1974, and August 18, 1975, Frank cut 13 tracks in Hollywood, but released only four as singles: "Anytime (I'll Be There)," a Paul Anka soft-rock ballad; "The Only Couple on the Floor," another stab at country; "I Believe I'm Gonna Love You," a '70s folk-pop number; and "The Saddest Thing of All." On October 25, 1975, he recorded "A Baby Just Like You" and "Christmas Memories" for a Yuletide single. The following year yielded five more 45-rpm releases, including another performance of "Send in the Clowns," this time an intimate interpretation accompanied only by Bill Miller's piano.

In a seemingly odd pairing that anticipated some of Frank's collaborations on the two *Duets* albums of the 1990s, he threw in his lot with a Colorado folkie when ABC broadcast *John Denver and Friend* on March 26, 1976. Resurrecting his connections with bands from his classic career, he joined the bespectacled one on "All or Nothing at All" with the Harry James Orchestra, "I'll Never Smile Again" with the Tommy Dorsey Band, and "All of Me" with Count Basie. Denver was out of his element throughout, but the presence of Nelson Riddle provided an admirable musical balance.

Frank married for the fourth time—to Barbara Marx, ex-wife of Brother "Zeppo"—on July 11, 1976. Attending the Rancho Mirage ceremony were best man Freeman (*Amos 'n' Andy*) Gosden, Ronald Reagan, Gregory Peck and Kirk Douglas. On January 6, 1977, Dolly Sinatra and her friend Anne Carbone, en route from Palm Springs to Las Vegas, intending to see Frank perform at Caeser's Palace, died when her chartered plane, flying through a terrible storm, crashed into Mt. San Gorgonio. Nancy, Jr., wrote:

> Substantively and symbolically, it was a crucial loss. They'd fought through his childhood and continued to do so until her dying day. But I believe that to counter her steel will, he'd developed his own. To prove her wrong when she belittled his choice of career.

He'd transcended the fame any American entertainer had everachieved. Their friction first had shaped him; that, I think, had remained to the end a litmus test of the grit in his bones. It helped keep him at the top of his game.[79]

Sinatra and Verna Bloom in *Contract on Cherry St.*

The next month, Frank managed to record a single, a ludicrous *disco* version of "Night and Day" backed with Paul Anka's "Everybody Ought to Be in Love." Two subsequent 1977 sessions failed to yield any releasable material, but on April 21, he headlined *Sinatra and Friends*, an ABC special also featuring Natalie Cole, John Denver, Tony Bennett, Loretta Lynn, Robert Merrill, Leslie Uggams and Dean Martin. Prior to his mother's death, Frank had vowed never to act in television films, but now he needed something to distract him from the pain of this tragic loss. Accepting a role as anti-Mafia detective Frank Hovannes in Edward Anhalt's adaptation of Philip Rosenberg's novel *Contract on Cherry Street*—which had been Dolly's favorite book—he developed the Columbia broadcast for Artanis Productions and helped bring aboard top craftsmen like director William Graham and composer Jerry Goldsmith. During production, New York City was hit by a 24-hour blackout on July 13-14, 1977. Though Frank was staying on the 38th floor of the Waldorf-Astoria Towers, he descended the stairs all the way down to street level to work on the film and then climbed up eight flights to the NBC studios to rehearse. After arriving on the set, he received a standing ovation from the cast and crew.

Frank surrounded himself with a fine supporting cast, including Martin Balsam (as Captain Ernie Weinberg), Verna Bloom (as Hovannes' wife, Emily), Martin Gabel and Harry Guardino. Longtime Sinatra pal Henry Silva also played a small role; and, after contributing cameos to *The Detective* and *Lady in Cement*, Jilly Rizzo landed the bit part of "Silvera."

In an interview with *TV Guide*'s Neil Hickey, Frank revealed a major reason for pursuing a silver-screen career:

> I never had any formal training as an actor. I wish I did. I think I was acting without realizing it during all those years I was singing with bands. But acting has always appealed to me. Bing Crosby set such a high example. He once advised me to stay active in every facet of this business—records, movies, TV, nightclubs—so if things aren't going well in one area, you switch to another.[80]

A few days prior to the film's premiere on November 19, Frank guest-hosted *The Tonight Show with Johnny Carson*, telling Ed McMahon, "People say to me, 'How do you feel...any difference in making a movie movie or a TV movie?' And there really is no difference. It's a movie. ...I'm very happy with it."[81]

Frank was universally praised for his portrayal, but the production was considered mediocre by most critics. John J. O'Connor, in *The New York Times*, wrote, "From Mr. Sinatra on down, there are a number of quite good performances wasted in this curious exercise... the birdbrained plot... proves fatal to all concerned."[82] Prior to the movie's premiere, Frank, asked if the movie was made as a pilot for a potential television series, replied, "Absolutely not. I don't want to do that kind of work. It's backbreaking."[83]

Even if the movie had been meant to spawn a series, *TV Guide*'s resident curmudgeon, Judith Crist, made certain that no such possibility remained:

> The Edward Anhalt script begins as 10th-rate *Kojak*, borrows generously from *Police Story* and *The Godfather* and winds up as, quite literally, a bloody mess. It is, at heart, a mealy-mouthed morality tale. ...It's a rich production but why Sinatra chose this brew of murder and mayhem for his TV-movie debut is the only intriguing aspect.[84]

Interestingly, during the late 1970s, when asked by Johnny Carson to name "the highlight" of his career, Frank mentioned, not a particular musical performance or recording, but two films: "Obviously, winning the Academy Award for *Eternity*, and then... being a part of a film called *The Man With the Golden Arm*, which I thought was a milestone in the picture business."[85]

Another milestone Frank wanted to pursue was working with John Wayne on a major film. (They do not share any scenes in *Cast a Giant Shadow*.) In 1977, he revealed that the two former box-office champions were looking for "a real cop story": "I saw Duke recently, and he said, 'What have you read, little fella?' And I said, 'Nothing. What have you read, big fella?' We agreed there was not much around in the way of exciting scripts."[86]

Frank entered a recording studio only once during 1978, a July 17 session resulting in three un-issued tracks. After releasing nearly nothing for two years, Frank and producer Sonny Burke planned *Trilogy*, an ambitious, 3-record set to document the singer's "past," "present" and "future," a project requiring a dozen 1979 recording sessions, utilizing the arrangements of three heavyweight Sinatra collaborators: Billy May, Don Costa and Gordon Jenkins.

After Frank had a falling out with Nelson Riddle, May handled "The Past: Collectibles of the Early Years," which includes seven great standards previously untouched by the Voice. This disc stylistically transports Frank back two decades, opening with a hard-swinging rendition of "The Song is You." "But Not for Me," written for the 1943 film *Girl Crazy*, pairs the mature Sinatra voice with a classic, Dorsey-like sound solidified by trombonist Dick Nash; while trumpeter Charlie Turner beautifully approximates Harry James on "I Had the Craziest Dream," written for *Springtime in the Rockies* (1942) and previously charted by Helen Forrest and the James band. Incredibly, "It Had to Be You," recorded on July 18, 1979, was Frank's first version of the Gus Kahn-Isham Jones standard. Cut nearly 19 years earlier by Frank and Billy for *Ring-a-Ding-Ding!*, Irving Berlin's "Let's Face the Music and Dance" swings hard before closing with a strange Latin coda.

"What the fuck is that on the end there?" Frank reportedly asked May.

"Ah, you'll see," the arranger replied. "You'll like it."[87]

"Street of Dreams" was Frank's fourth recording of the Sam Lewis-Victor Young classic that also had been waxed well by Bing Crosby and Tony Bennett. Frank previously had cut Harold Arlen and Johnny Mercer's "My Shining Hour," written for the Astaire film *The Sky's the Limit* (1943), as a V-Disc, but here provides his only studio recording. The swinging "All of You," written for the Broadway show *Silk Stockings* (1954) [and also featured in the 1957 Astaire-Cyd Charisse film version], lends the obligatory Cole Porter song to the disc; "More Than You Know," from the 1929 stage musical *Great Day!*, adds a vintage ballad previously untouched by Frank; and "They All Laughed," from the Astaire-Rogers film *Shall We Dance?* (1937), in fine Gershwin form, closes "The Past," a refreshing return to true Sinatra land, after a decade of mostly mediocre, market-driven pop material — the sort of songs included in the next *Trilogy* volume, "The Present."

The sessions for "The Present: Some Very Good Years" were held at Columbia's 30th Street Studio in New York on August 20-22, 1979. Peter Allen and Carole Sager's "You and Me (We Wanted It All)" is a weak opener with infantile lyrics, though better than many of Frank's '70s ballads; "Just the Way You Are" reworks Billy Joel's 1977 mega-hit into a light swinger, but the limited melody offers Frank little chance to compete with Costa's arrangement; and his second stab at George Harrison's "Something," here Nelson Riddle's one contribution to the project, is superior to the 1970 Lennie Hayton chart, and includes Frank's improvisation, "But you stick around, *Jack*, it might show." Jimmy Webb's bombastic 1968 art-rock song, "MacArthur Park," previously recorded as a seven-minute epic by actor Richard Harris, was edited considerably by Costa, here merely taking up 2:45 on the LP.

John Kander and Fred Ebb's title song for Martin Scorsese's 1977 bomb *New York, New York*, originally sung by Liza Minnelli, was recorded at the 30th Street Studio but later redone in Los Angeles. Frank had been singing the song live since the autumn of 1978, as part of an overture that also included "Autumn in New York" and other tributes to the Big Apple; but by the time "The Present" was arranged, it had become a hugely popular solo number. The one true swinger on the volume, it builds from start to finish, with Frank soaring over Costa's powerhouse chart. As he continued to perform the song in concert, it—to his satisfaction—became more closely associated with him than even "My Way."

The Bergman-Legrand ballad "Summer Me, Winter Me" also had been performed live before the studio session, and is infinitely preferable to Neil Diamond's "Song Sung Blue," another uncomfortable "swinger" saddled with one of the songwriter's typically droning melodies. Kris Kristofferson's "For the Good Times," the disc's one country number, also droning endlessly, is a bizarre duet with opera singer Eileen Farrell, who sounds just slightly out of place as a "folkie." "Love Me Tender" is Frank's one recording of a song written by Elvis (who adapted the melody of the Civil War song "Aura Lee"), done in the original tempo, rather than the "swinging" arrangement used on his 1960 television summit with the King. The closer, "That's What God Looks Like to Me," is an oddity, to say the least—one that prompted Billy May simply to exclaim, "Oh, shit!"[88]

Gordon Jenkins wrote all the material for "The Future: Recollections of the Future in Three Tenses," recorded in Los Angeles on December 17-18, 1979. The redundant and pretentious title alone foreshadows the disc's content, which Will Friedwald calls "the most spectacular disaster of [Sinatra's] recording career."[89] The performers hired to perform this suite included a full symphony orchestra and chorus, requiring the use of Hollywood's Shrine Auditorium. The project was such a monster that Frank—needing to act the narrative as well as sing the lyrics—had to rehearse for months before it was taped.

The autobiographical "What Time Does the Next Miracle Leave?" opens as the orchestra tunes up and Frank sings, "My name is Francis Albert" and the chorus echoes, "Francis Albert *Sinatra!*" Two minutes into the piece, he then readies himself for traveling to various planets, because, "If they can do it in the movies, why can't I?" After this pinnacle of self-indulgence (as written by Jenkins) fades out, the next section rages in like a horror-film score, welcoming Frank to Venus, where "it will surely be Spring," and then transports him to Pluto, actually Hades, where he asserts, "It's pure hell when your journey ends there. But you can bet your ass, I'll meet a lot of friends there." Then he warp speeds all the way back across the solar system to Mercury and on to Neptune, making one wonder if Jenkins ever looked at an astronomical chart. Finally, Uranus "is Heaven," because they'll meet him at the station with "a cheese and tomato pizza and a little red wine"!

"World War None!" replete with martial percussion and chanting, is Jenkins' simplistic plea for global peace, to be spearheaded by the United States. "The Future" is divided into three sections: the first including a bluesy vocal by Beverly Jenkins and Frank wishing for "a magic wand that I could use"; the second, "I've Been There!" provides "some words of wisdom from a man who's paid his dues"; the third, "Song Without Words," features a lovely soprano vocal by Loulie Jean Norman and some of Jenkins' most moving melodies. The disc then closes with "Finale: Before the Music Ends," during which Frank muses on his current status, a brief segue into saloon style, a thank-you to several classical composers—Schubert, Beethoven, Verdi and Puccini included—and then a *Guys and Dolls*-type diversion about gambling in Vegas! Though the narrative of "The Future" is naïve and often downright insipid, Jenkins—who was, by no means, a lyricist or dramatist—provided several sections of distinguished music, and Frank is in fine vocal form throughout.

When *Trilogy* was released in 1980, the 3-disc set went gold, selling over a half million copies in just a few weeks. Noting that, "at $21 a pop [the sales] added up to a lot of lettuce," Will Friedwald observed:

> That price becomes all the more exorbitant when one considers that people were really paying for just one record, Billy May's "The Past." Most listeners could get through only a track or two of "The Future and probably played "The Present" all the way through once or twice but "The Past" was the disc that rated as essential Sinatra, worth reprising again and again. [90]

Frank returned to feature-film acting on March 10, 1980, a full decade after he had mugged his way through the dreadful *Dirty Dingus Magee*. Opposite Faye Dunaway, he came back in gumshoe mode, for a story far more serious than those depicted in the Tony Rome duo and *The Detective*. Co-executive producing with Elliott Kastner for Artanis and Cinema 7, he worked with director Brian Hutton and screenwriter Mann Rubin, who adapted Lawrence Sanders' grisly crime novel *The First Deadly Sin*. After wrapping the shoot more than two months later on May 23, he performed four nights of live shows at Resorts International in Atlantic City.

Though Frank arguably gives his best screen performance since *Von Ryan's Express*, the plot of *The First Deadly Sin* is simplistic, unconvincing and, at times, unnecessarily lurid. As soon-to-retire New York Precinct 27 detective Edward X. Delaney, he splits his scenes between tracking down Daniel Blank (David Dukes), a psycho serial killer who, for "love," murders his victims with a mountain-climber's "ice axe" (similar to a medieval war hammer but featuring a rounded, downward spike) and hovering over his fatally ill wife, Barbara (Dunaway), who remains bedridden throughout, until she mercifully passes away in the final scene. The entire film is a downer; and the opening sequence, crosscutting between an operation during which one of Mrs. Delaney's kidneys is removed and the first on-screen murder, may turn viewers away before Ol' Blue Eyes even appears. As the killer bludgeons away, the sequence alternates medium close-ups of blood splattering the surgeons' faces.

The supporting cast is quite good, although Dunaway is limited to lying on her back throughout the film. As the coroner, Dr. Sanford Ferguson, James Whitmore contributes his usual convincing performance, and Martin Gabel is splendid as Christopher Langley, an eccentric Metropolitan Museum curator who helps Delaney identify and locate the murder weapon. Gabel's admission to a hardware store clerk (Larry Loonin) that he desires such a weapon "to kill someone" is an effective moment of dark comedy and a highlight of the film. Anthony Zerbe chews the precinct scenery as the one-dimensional "ass kicker" Captain Broughton, and, for viewers who don't blink too quickly, a young Bruce Willis can be seen entering a diner as Delaney leaves. (Willis also stunt doubled as the killer in some long shots.)

Sinatra as Edward X. Delaney in *The First Deadly Sin*

Brian Hutton's pacing is as deadly as the "First Sin," and, even considering Frank's admirable and touching underplaying, the hospital scenes become tedious at midpoint. With its focus on insanity, brutal murder and a patient's wasting away due to what Delaney believes is the ineptitude of Dr. Bernardi (George Coe), whom he assaults in one tense scene, the film is the darkest in Frank's 40-year cinematic career.

For this silver-screen "comeback," Frank received reviews similar to those for his first television film, the high point of an uneven production. But here the violence and gruesome detail of murder and autopsy scenes disgusted the critics. *Variety*'s "Cart," calling Frank "serious... direct... [giving] a decent performance," wrote:

> Pic presents considerable barriers to involvement from the outset, as first few reels consist predominantly of a bloody operation, a violent murder, dialogue conducted over mutilated bodies in an autopsy room and unappetizing hospital scenes. Established tone is therefore distinctly unpleasant, and drama encompassing it isn't sufficiently unusual or compelling to justify such detailed attention to the grim and grisly.[91]

In *The New York Times*, Janet Maslin praised Frank as "tough and credible" following a "return... to the screen after a long hiatus," but also was put off by the gratuitous gore:

> Miss Dunaway... the movie begins with sickenly explicit footage of her surgery. The operation is intercut with footage of Blank... stalking and murdering one of his victims, so that the moment of the murder corresponds with the bloodiest glimpses of the operation. The connection between the two events seems tenuous at best, and the rest of the film does little to link them. The effect is one of sensationalism, nothing more.[92]

On January 19, 1981, Frank headlined the *All-Star Inaugural Gala* on ABC, a star-studded program celebrating Ronald Reagan's ascension to the White House earlier that day. Twenty years earlier, he had accomplished the same feat for JFK, but now gave his all for the opposite side of the political coin, for a president who, like he, had once been an ardent FDR Democrat. He sang "My Kind of Town," "New York, New York" and waxed patriotic on "America, the Beautiful" before performing an ironic parallel to the 1960 Kennedy version of "High Hopes": While paying tribute to the new First Lady, "Nancy (with the Laughing Face)" was transformed into "Nancy (with the Reagan Face)!"

Backed by the Freedom of Information Act and his friendship with President Reagan, Frank obtained the FBI's Sinatra file and petitioned the Nevada Gaming Control Board for a reinstatement of his gambling license. Finding no evidence of illegal activities, the board granted his request. In March of that year, when Reagan was shot in an assassination attempt by John Hinckley, Frank flew to Washington, where he stayed until news of "Ronnie's" recovery was assured.

On April 8, 1981, Frank and Gordon Jenkins began recording tracks for *She Shot Me Down*, a new album of saloon songs titled after the Sonny Bono number he had taped eight years earlier but left unreleased. Following the harsh criticism against "The Future," Frank wanted to collaborate once again with Jenkins, who was seriously ill. Five months later, enough useable takes, featuring a world-weary Frank—lending a perfect tone to a new "suicide" effort—were assembled to complete the LP. "Good Thing Going (Going, Gone)" is a "modern" the-chick-split-the-coop song, written by Stephen Sondheim for the musical *Merrily We Roll Along*; "Hey, Look, No Crying," by Jule Styne and Susan Birkenhead, was edited down for the album (but later released in its haunting entirety); "Thanks for the Memory," written for Bob Hope's first feature film, *The Big Broadcast of 1938*, was revamped lyrically by Leo Robin; and "A Long Night," the melody of which had been written by his friend Alec Wilder in the late '70s, provides an ethereal performance harking back to *Only the Lonely* and *No One Cares*.

"Bang, Bang (My Baby Shot Me Down)" juxtaposes stark, simple lyrics and melody against an elaborate orchestration, featuring one of the most eminently controlled emotive interpretations of Frank's later career. "Monday Morning Quarterback," a Costa original cowritten with Pamela Phillips, is better than its title suggests; "South—To a Warmer Place," featuring another Alec Wilder melody, features a very weary Frank; "I Loved Her," a Jenkins original, combines the usual lush arrangement with mediocre, naïve lyrics; and the medley "The Gal That Got Away/It Never Entered My Mind"—the first half of which had been arranged by Nelson Riddle for a 1956 Capitol single; and the second, a Rodgers and Hart masterpiece—provides a classic Sinatra sound for the closer, kicking into a swaggering swing at the end.

The Man and His Music was back on November 21, 1981, for a one-hour NBC special during which Frank swung a masterful version of "Pennies from Heaven" with Count Basie. Plying the keys with his trademark economical style, Basie was visibly moved by his fellow jazzman's breathtaking behind-the-beat phrasing. The following month, Frank duetted with Don Costa's daughter, Nikki, on "To Love a Child," a Hal David-Joe Raposo single to benefit Nancy Reagan's Foster Grandparents Program.

On November 20, 1982, Frank, joined by his old nemesis Buddy Rich, performed for video cameras during an open-air concert in the Dominican Republic. Produced for cable television, this *Concert for the Americas* was broadcast on the Arts and Entertainment (A&E) network and on PBS. From midsummer 1982 until February 1983, he attempted four recording sessions in New York, but only one single was released, the swinging thank-you note "Here's to the Band," backed by Jule Styne and Susan Birkenhead's "It's Sunday," a unique arrangement in his career—an intimate revelation about mature love accompanied only by Tony Mottola's guitar.

In 1983, Frank contributed a cameo as "himself" to *Cannonball Run II*, stuntman-director Hal Needham's sequel to the immensely popular "good ol' boys smashin' up cars on the road" picture *Cannonball Run*, released two years earlier. Dean and Sammy again were costarring with Burt Reynolds and Dom DeLuise—and since they lent the movie a "Rat Pack" flavor, Needham persuaded Shirley MacLaine, Henry Silva, Alex Rocco and Frank to play small parts. Location filming took place in Darien, Connecticut, Redondo Beach, California, and Tucson, Arizona.

Labeling the entire experience "a disgrace," MacLaine said, "Frank worked only half a day and that was too long for him. He did one take and then left. It looked as though he were never there at all."[93] Appearing in his third "Sinatra film," Jack Elam recalled that he "worked one or two days and I don't think our paths crossed."[94] Frank actually toiled one day on the film, but his fellow actors' various recollections of his participation are a testament to the insignificance of his performance. Hal Needham remembered:

> Even Burt kowtowed to him. But he was very professional. He had his makeup on time, in costume and ready to go. He did his shit and he was gone. …I got along good with him because I gave him the respect he deserved. We liked the fact that he gave all the money he earned to charity.[95]

Of course, the film features satirical references to *The Godfather* and the Mob, including the following families: the Rigatonis, the Fettucinis and the Raviolis. In the United States, it grossed $28.1 million, less than half of the $60 million raked in by its predecessor. *New York Times* critic Janet Maslin wrote:

> Fans of Don Knotts, Jim Nabors, Sammy Davis, Jr., car crashes and trained orangutans may want to celebrate the opening of *Cannonball Run II*… For anyone else, it's a mixed blessing at best. …The fact that [it] isn't much good may not prevent it from becoming this summer's best-loved low-est-common-denominator comedy, if only because of the utter lack of any competition.[96]

One month later, fellow *Times* reviewer Vincent Canby, noting that "12 people [were] in the house," added:

> [S]ince tastelessness didn't hurt the first *Cannonball* film, nor the *Smokey and the Bandit* films… I'm somewhat baffled why the public has turned its back on this one. How is one ever to know when tastelessness will pay off and when it won't? …"The king" is Frank Sinatra, playing himself, and treated with the deference that might be shown a reigning pope, if any pope would consent to do a cameo appearance in a movie of this sort. The director apparently shot Mr. Sinatra all by himself, even in scenes in which he's supposed to be sharing the frame with the other actors.[97]

Frank plays, not "the king," but "The Chairman." Making sure that his right-hand man landed yet another cameo role, he inspired the following comment from *Variety*'s "Loyn": "The film is so inept that the best actor in it is Jilly Rizzo. But he has a great advantage: he's only on screen five seconds."[98]

Sessions for Frank's next album, arranged by Quincy Jones, were held in New York on April 13, 16 and 17, and in Los Angeles on May 17, 1984. Though only one track was cut in the City of Angels, the album was titled *L.A. is My Lady*. Ironically, the title song for this LP was waxed in New York, while his anthem "New York, New York" had been recorded in L.A.!

Jones and his wife, Peggy Lipton (who had costarred in the TV series *The Mod Squad*), cowrote "L.A. is My Lady," which the record label hoped would become a civic anthem much like "New York, New York." Frank's first foray into the "adult-contemporary" jazz genre, this funky song, also released as a single, features him in fine voice; but, even supported by an MTV video, failed to generate expected interest and revenues. It still provides a strong opening for the album, which continues with a collection of standards primarily left out of the Sinatra catalog. "The

Best of Everything," written by the "New York, New York" team of John Kander and Fred Ebb, chugs along nicely; "How Do You Keep the Music Playing?" is the obligatory ballad by Frank's latter-day favorites, the Bergmans and Legrand; "Teach Me Tonight" is a dynamic reworking of the 1953 laid-back swing ballad with new lyrics by Sammy Cahn (noting Frank's film career: "I've played love scenes with a chick or two..."); and Cole Porter's "It's All Right with Me," originally sung by Frank in *Can-Can*, here done initially as a smokin' small-combo jazz number that builds into a full-throttle big-band piece with George Benson on solo guitar.

On his first recording of Kurt Weill, Bertolt Brecht and Marc Blitzstein's "Mack the Knife," Frank pays tribute to all the great versions of the past cut by Bobby Darin, Louis Armstrong and Ella Fitzgerald. The 1931 standard "Until the Real Thing Comes Along" had *six* writers even before Sammy Cahn fashioned new lyrics for this version, a highlight of the album. "Stormy Weather" was Frank's fourth version of the Koehler-Arlen classic, here a bit more inclement because of his somewhat worn voice, but innovative and powerful as it builds into a full-throttle swinger. Written for the 1935 musical *Rose of the Rancho*, "If I Should Lose You" had been recorded by Charlie Parker in 1950, and here swings along nicely, due to Sammy Nestico's masterful chart. Frank had sung the 1933 chestnut "A Hundred Years from Today" for a wartime V-Disc, but here made his first studio recording, another swinging Nestico arrangement. The closer, "After You've Gone," written in 1916 for the Earl Carroll Broadway show *So Long, Letty*, provides an appropriate breakneck tempo, accompanied by Lionel Hampton on vibraphone and another George Benson guitar solo.

To promote *L.A. is My Lady*, a documentary, *Portrait of an Album*, was broadcast during 1984-85. A well-produced profile of the meticulous master at work in the studio, the film shows Frank rehearsing and recording all the songs from the album and interview segments with Quincy Jones, producer Phil Ramone and Marilyn and Alan Bergman.

On October 30, 1986, Frank cut three songs at a Los Angeles session, but only one—laying down a new vocal over the band tracks recorded for the *L.A. is My Lady* "Mack the Knife"—eventually made the grade (released on the 1990 4-CD *Reprise Collection*). Also that year, following surgery to ease the chronic pain of diverticulitis, he flew to Hawaii to make his first dramatic television appearance in nine years, playing a retired police detective in a two-part episode of the popular series *Magnum P.I.* starring Tom Selleck, who recalled:

> I had been a big fan of Frank's for a lot of years. I can't remember where we were at, but Frank said he loved the show and would like to do it, and I didn't take that real seriously until he called. And then he was going through a pretty tough time and had some surgery, and still showed up and did the show and kept his commitment, and Frank Sinatra really doesn't have to do that. There are a lot of ways out, so I was very impressed.
>
> ...The concept for the episode was his idea. He played a New York cop. Someone had killed his granddaughter, and he'd traced the guy to Hawaii.
>
> ...Working with him is real interesting, because Frank has the patience of a saloon singer—and, in his defense, he's ready on the first take. I also produced *Magnum* at the time, and I was very concerned that the show be as good as possible, but Frank had a tendency to want to do one take and say, "That's it, let's move on." And he was always good, but somebody else might not have been.[99]

Having been certified fit by his doctors, Frank insisted on doing some of his own stunts.

The two-part *Magnum* episode was broadcast in February 1987. Later that year, Woody Allen used Frank's Columbia classic "If You Are But a Dream" in *Radio Days*, in a charming, atmospheric scene showing the young protagonist (Seth Green) seeing his first movie at Radio City Music Hall. An earlier sequence in the film shows a Sinatra-like vocalist singing "All or Nothing At All" on a radio program.

On May 13, 1988, Frank consented to a rare, lengthy interview with CNN's Larry King, who previously had spoken with Ol' Blue Eyes on radio. When queried about his film career, Frank admitted that he would consider appearing in another motion picture:

> I keep waiting for somebody to give me something to read. I love making films. ...My daughter Tina, who now is actually working, for me...is now hunting for things for me to do, and if she comes up with something, we'll actually finance the movie ourselves, if we have to.[100]

Bob Hoskins and the Frank singing sword from
Who Framed Roger Rabbit?

On June 6, 1988, Frank, at age 72, made what became his final Reprise studio recording, a Billy May arrangement of Ned Washington and Victor Young's "My Foolish Heart," written for the 1949 film of the same name. Touchstone Pictures released *Who Framed Roger Rabbit?* two weeks later. Directed by Robert Zemekis, the film combines animation and live action starring Bob Hoskins, Christopher Lloyd and Joanna Cassidy. An archival recording of Frank's voice was used for the "Singing Sword" character, nearly qualifying this production

as a "Sinatra film." The following year, director Rob Reiner added Frank's 1979 recording of "It Had to Be You" to Harry Connick, Jr's. score for the film *When Harry Met Sally.*

On December 17, 1990, ABC broadcast a birthday tribute, *Sinatra 75: The Best is Yet to Come*, produced by Tina Sinatra and George Schlatter featuring concert footage, clips and tributes from Frank's friends and colleagues. During a performance at New Jersey's Meadowlands, he received the life-achievement "Ella Award" from the Society of Singers and Composers presented by "The First Lady of Song" herself. Ella then sang "The Lady is a Tramp" with him.

Having missed the collaborations with Frank that Nancy and Frank, Jr., had enjoyed, Tina, for the past four years, had pursued an opportunity to create an homage to her father. Recalling the concept for a 1970s biographical film that never was produced, she mentioned to Frank that a miniseries along the same lines might be successful. As Nancy wrote, "Tina wanted to make a miniseries instead of writing a book because she felt Dad's life lent itself more naturally to a visual rendering than a literary one."[101] He agreed that it was a good idea, and that she should produce it herself. Frank told Larry King:

> That's going to take some time. ...I think she's going to have to do that in sections. There's an awful lot to be done. ...I think we should put on a... well-thought-of hunt for a youngster of 17 or 18 and then move him up, and then use several actors... I think if we do it gently, the audience will buy it, that here he is 17 years old and he's starting out with a dance band...and then with James and Tommy, and then on my own and at the Paramount... that's a lot of work...it's going to be a tough job for her to put together...[102]

Tackling the enormous project, Tina conceived *Sinatra* for Warner Bros., but unsatisfactory scripts and other problems stalled filming until June 1991. A major challenge was finding an actor who could play Frank and lip-synch the classic songs. (The actual Sinatra recordings would be used, along with some new contributions from Frank, Jr., who would provide vocal performances to cover his father's early years. Impressionist Tom Burlinson also contributed some vocals, after failing to land the actual role.) In a discussion with Frank, Tina admitted that she was having difficulty locating a performer who had both "street edge" and "polish." Frank replied, "Then get a polished one, and rough him down." [103] As soon as she met Philip Casnoff, a successful Broadway actor known for his musical roles, she was captivated: "Philip captured my father's *edge*, his essence. As secure as I felt about him, I wanted fresh eyes to see his audition tape. I chose Sidney Poitier, who was blown away. Dad would have a similar reaction."[104]

After other roles were cast—including Gina Gershon as Nancy Sinatra, Sr., Olympia Dukakis as Dolly Sinatra, and Rod Steiger as Sam Giancana—director James Sadwith, armed with an $18.5 million budget (the most spent on a miniseries to date), began shooting in February and worked through the summer of 1992. Though Frank was scheduled to visit the set in April, he called Tina at the last minute to cancel, claiming illness. Then, on May 6, Jilly Rizzo was killed by a drunk driver in a fiery car crash in Palm Springs.

Jilly died on his 75th birthday while driving to visit his girlfriend, Betty Jean, in a Jaguar owned by her neighbor. The man who struck him, a repeat offender without a license and speeding at 85 mph, survived. Rizzo's son Willy recalled:

> My father was the brother that Frank never had. He was a very good father although he was busy most of the time. He took me all over the world, and when he was away—in London, Paris, Rome—I talked to him four or five times a day. "Jilly's the one," Frank used to say. He put dad in those movies—and those songs, "Me and My Shadow" and "Mrs. Robinson."[105]

Frank never recovered from the loss of his beloved friend; and Nancy, Jr., did all she could to console Jilly's children. Abby Rizzo recalled, "Little Nancy is one of the nicest people in, or out, of show business... always has been. She was so kind to me and Kacey the day my dad died. She sat and played a little Barbie game with Kacey to keep her mind off what was going on......and has always kept in touch with us."[106] [Abby's daughter, Kacey, is the granddaughter of Jilly Rizzo and the great-granddaughter of Boris Karloff.]

When production wrapped on the *Sinatra* miniseries, which premiered on CBS in November 1992, Tina admitted that Frank had relived some painful memories while reading the script: "Now that it's done, he's going to have to face it."[107] Tina had worked on it over the course of eight years and was disappointed at her father's response to the publicity, which was considerable. Though Frank had promised to perform with Shirley MacLaine at Radio City Music Hall, where a group of 150 cast and crew members would attend the show, he decided to stay in bed at the Waldorf-Astoria, claiming he had a fever. MacLaine went on without him and Tina was infuriated.

Part one of the four-hour program opens with "That's Life" as Ol' Blue Eyes makes his 1974 "comeback" and then segues to "Hoboken, 1925," where the 10-year-old "Frankie Sinatra" roughhouses with neighborhood boys and sings while perched atop a piano in his parents' saloon and at a Democratic mayoral rally, where he performs "The Star Spangled Banner" in Rudy Vallee style. Soon, he's a teenager striving to become a singer in the Bing Crosby mold, meeting Nancy Barbato, making a fool of himself in a local burlesque show and getting the "Do you wanna be a bum?" treatment from Marty (Joe Santos).

The Rustic Cabin and his stints with Harry James and Tommy Dorsey (Bob Gunton) are covered in some detail. When Frank decides to make it as a solo act, the Dorsey contract dispute is addressed briefly, albeit ambiguously, as is the possibility of his being drafted during World War II. The script is more explicit when dealing with his various romantic affairs, and pulls no punches in scenes depicting the Marilyn Maxwell New Years' Eve bracelet incident, the hot-and-cold relationship with Ava Gardner (Marcia Gay Harden), his introduction to "Lucky" Luciano in Havana and his run-ins with photographers and reporters, including Lee Mortimer and Westbrook Pegler. The first half also includes references to *Las Vegas Nights, Higher and Higher, Reveille with Beverly, Anchors Aweigh, It Happened in Brooklyn, Miracle of the Bells* and *On the Town*. Although *The House I Live In* is not mentioned, Frank's anti-bigotry attitude is depicted in a scene in which he manhandles a hotel clerk who has refused to admit a black member of the Dorsey band.

Part two begins by depicting Frank's "downfall" during the early 1950s, his marriage to Ava and the Maggio role in *From Here to Eternity*. Other films are mentioned in a montage featuring still photographs (in which Casnoff's face is superimposed over Frank's) and titles written on clapboards. The Sam Giancana-JFK connections also are covered, including a scene during which Joseph Kennedy asks Frank to request that the Mob boss swing the West Virginia primary for Jack, or "Chicky Baby" as the Voice calls him. During a Vegas performance by the Summit, Dolly looks at JFK and quips, "Nice Catholic boy. The father—a rum-running son of a bitch." Later scenes show Frank discussing *The Manchurian Candidate* with Kennedy in the Oval Office, Giancana refusing an associate's offer to whack Frank over the administration's "sellout" of the Mob, Frank blowing up at Peter Lawford, and a tearful Frank watching JFK's funeral procession on television. Hank Sanicola's "drop off" in the desert over the Giancana-Cal Neva incident also is dramatized. *Von Ryan's Express* and Frank's courting of and brief marriage to Mia Farrow (and a mention of their aborted film collaboration) are followed by Marty's death and a climactic return to the 1974 comeback.

Sinatra was nominated for nine Emmy Awards, winning for best director and best costume design, and landed the best miniseries Golden Globe. The program also received several positive reviews, but Tina was most concerned with her father's reaction. Though she had sent a personal copy to the Palm Springs estate, the rocky relationship between the children and Barbara Sinatra prevented her from receiving Frank's reply. She revealed: "Dad should have watched *Sinatra* in a safe, supportive environment. Had he viewed it with my mother, I believe that he would have enjoyed every frame... I don't know if he ever saw it all."[108]

The highlight of the miniseries is Philip Casnoff's excellent performance. He not only performs flawless lip-synching to the original recordings but nails Frank's facial expressions, gestures, mannerisms, vocal characteristics and, most impressively, his unique gait while walking on stage and running to improve his breathing capacity. The supporting performances are uniformly impressive, as is the selection of music. The most obvious weakness is the program's total disregard for Sinatra the recording artist: The genius, multiple-take perfectionist studio musician is never shown nor mentioned, thus depriving this portrait of an absolutely essential aspect of his psyche. The Nelson Riddle recordings in general are given short shrift, and his arrangers and conductors during his entire solo career are ignored. Though Frank loved making films, he considered his recordings more important; but, after the Dorsey years, the script focuses on movie-making and live performances exclusively. The only depiction of the classic Capitol studio albums is a montage replacing Frank's faces with those of Casnoff on the familiar covers. While the miniseries is well made and impressively accurate, the narrative omits much of importance and leaves the viewer with no real idea of Frank's true significance as a recording innovator.

During three recording dates in July 1993, Frank, now 77 years old, returned to Capitol to cut 22 new versions of classic Sinatra songs. For an October release, producer Phil Ramone paired Frank's performances with those of 13 popular contemporary singers, who recorded their vocals at separate sessions or telephoned them in via a digital system developed in part by George Lucas' Skywalker Sound. Will Friedwald commented:

> Capitol's PR crew... turned an obvious liability into an asset by ballyhooing the idea that the *Duets* weren't real duets and promoting the set as a techno-logical achievement. (What they were loath to discuss is the degree to which Sinatra's own vocal tracks were tampered with—not only spliced and diced but pitch-altered to improve his fading intonation.)[109]

Duets opens weakly with—"of all inappropriate people"[110]—Luther Vandross on "The Lady is a Tramp," followed by "What Now My Love" with Aretha Franklin, whose over-the-top soul style has nothing in common with anything ever recorded by the Voice. Frank added another dub on top of Barbra Streisand's "I've Got a Crush on You" vocal, creating one of the album's most balanced (yet still dispassionate) offerings; while Julio Iglesias on "Summer Wind" returns the set to its innate awkwardness. Gloria Estefan, on "Come Rain or Come Shine," actually provides one of the most sensitive, stylistically apt duets; but Tony Bennett, seemingly a perfect choice, with his worn, thin voice, detracts from the usually exciting "New York, New York." "They Can't Take That Away from Me" is a highlight, with Natalie Cole (who pioneered the electronic "duet" by adding her own voice to her late father's "Unforgettable" in 1991) effortlessly blending with her "partner." "You Make Me Feel So Young" features Charles Aznavour straining, in Tony Bennett fashion, to hit the notes, but is infinitely preferable to Carly Simon's butchering of an attempted medley of "Guess I'll Hang My Tears Out to Dry"

and "In the Wee Small Hours of the Morning" (during which she sings a second *melody* directly over the one laid down by Ol' Blue Eyes). Frank delivers a fine vocal on "I've Got the World on a String," making Liza Minnelli's unmemorable performance rather superfluous, and is aurally overwhelmed by Anita Baker on "Witchcraft."

Then *Duets* features its true abomination: a massacre of "I've Got You Under My Skin," courtesy of Paul ("Bono") Hewson of the Irish rock band U2, who actually attempts to scat, then groans, over the trombone solo. No words any other author can equal those of Will Friedwald:

> There's no way his rape of the *Songs for Swingin' Lovers* masterpiece can be construed as anything but a sledgehammer attack on Sinatra and everything he stands for. It begins with the rocker moaning along with the Sinatra track as if he were some stoned punker with a karaoke machine...Worse than attempting to sing with Sinatra, which he is completely incapable of doing, the Irish rocker tries to scat alongside him, resulting in nightmarish screams that suggest live animal vivisection.[111]

Though *Duets* could have ended on a high point, "One for My Baby" is rudely interrupted by the tinny, thin tone and technically inept, emotionally dead soprano sax stylings of Kenny G, who also hacks his way through the "All the Way" introduction.

By mid-November 1993, *Duets* had become Frank's most commercially successful record, selling a million copies and climbing to number one on the *Billboard* chart. On October 12 and 14, 1993, Frank cut eight more songs at Capitol for release on *Duets II*, a collection of 14 mostly mediocre numbers. The set opens strongly with Gladys Knight and Stevie Wonder (on harmonica) joining in on a soulful "For Once in My Life," but then slips into the first of its "Frank duetting with a Latin heartthrob" songs, "Come Fly with Me," with Luis Miguel. "Bewitched" is unmercifully mangled by the studio-chewing soul screams of Patti Labelle, whose voice is as out of place as Bono's on the earlier collection; while "The Best Is Yet to Come," with Jon Secada, is the second of the Latin duets. Having attempted to croon and swing with Nelson Riddle a decade earlier, Linda Ronstadt is spiritless on "Moonlight in Vermont," and an ailing Antonio Carlos Jobim also fails to generate much emotion on "Fly Me to the Moon." The Pretenders' Chrissie Hynde nearly enters the Bono zone on "Luck Be a Lady," and Willie Nelson, though no stranger to American standards, sounds ridiculous alongside the Voice on "A Foggy Day." Steve Lawrence and Eydie Gorme, on "Where or When," and Lena Horne, on "Embraceable You," respectively, steer the set in the appropriate direction; but Jimmy Buffett—though having swung lightly a time or two over the years—is stiff and ineffectual on "Mack the Knife." Lorrie Morgan contributes one of the set's most heartfelt and dynamically sensitive performances on "How Do You Keep the Music Playing?/My Funny Valentine," and Frank Sinatra, Jr., swings along with Pop on "My Kind of Town," but the collection returns to unfortunate form on the closer, "The House I Live In," rendered vapid by the nasal tones of Neil Diamond.

On March 1, 1994, Bono presented Frank with the Grammy Legend Award for lifetime achievement. Unfortunately, the U2 frontman's self-indulgent introduction was so verbose that the producer chose to cut to a commercial in the middle of the Voice's acceptance speech. On November 25, CBS broadcast *Sinatra Duets*, a video promotion for the album explaining the "studio magic" that paired Frank with his "partners" who really didn't "duet" with him at all. Included were "A Foggy Day" with Willie Nelson and the turgid music video of the Bono-fied "Under My Skin."

A syndicated *Duets* radio special, hosted and written by Sid Mark and Tony Renaud, also was broadcast to promote the release. Introduced by Barbara Sinatra, the program included recollections from Phil Ramone, co-producer Hank Cattaneo, executive producer Eliot Weisman, arranger-conductor Pat Williams, Gloria Estefan, Tony Bennett, Aretha Franklin, Willie Nelson, Steve Lawrence and Lena Horne. Unfortunately, the performers on the broadcast acted as if they actually sang duets with Frank in the studio, rather than being dubbed on after the fact.

On December 19-20, 1994, Natalie Cole opened for him at Tokyo's Fukuoka Dome. Noticing his tendency to forget the lyrics to standards he had sung for years, Cole recalled:

> Later on, it was reported that [he] had Alzheimer's....Over dinner before the concert, Frank had invited me to fly home with him and his entourage on his private jet. ...Even before the wheels left the runway, however, he was knocking back the Jack Daniels one after the next like there was no tomorrow.
>
> We had been in the air about an hour or so when Frank suddenly looked around at all of us in the cabin and bellowed, "Who the hell are all these people?"
>
> I thought that must be the Jack Daniels talking, and because Frank always was a kidder, my first reaction was to laugh — until I realized that no one else was even smiling. At that point, Frank stood and started going around the room, confronting everyone in turn, getting close up in each face and demanding to know, "Who the hell are *you*?" ...(Although incidents of Frank's erratic and forgetful behavior continued to increase, it was never acknowledged that there was anything wrong with him neurologically...)[112]

> Disappointed with her father's response to the miniseries, Tina asked Frank to appear as himself in a new TV movie, *Young at Heart*, which starred Olympia Dukakis as a Hoboken widow who relies on Sinatra music to survive hard times. Working with her sister, Tina arranged for him to have closely monitored transportation to the set in Toronto. She recalled:

> Dad seemed a foot taller than I'd seen him in years. He was a man at home in this environment; he took command. Though he hadn't read the script, he got the setup from the director and met the actors. He rehearsed his scene with Olympia Dukakis, who'd played his mother in the miniseries. ...[W]e were so well prepared that the whole thing was over in forty minutes — it went by almost too fast. ...Later that night, the director of photography told me that when he took his mark, Dad could tell that he wasn't quite in the right spot. Before the camera operator could make an adjustment, Dad inched into his key light. He knew precisely where he was supposed to be; his instincts were still intact.[113]

Broadcast on CBS on March 12, 1995, this "feel-good" film depicted Frank visiting the widow in its final reel.

During the autumn of 1995, George Schlatter planned to produce an ABC 80th-birthday tribute to Frank, during which past and present singing stars would perform a trademark Sinatra number. Having finally retired due to illness and fatigue, Frank wasn't interested. "Kill it, *please*," he told Tina, who wrote, "My father would willingly sit down and be sung to by very few people in this world, and a fair number of them were dead."[114]

Though there was wrangling within the Sinatra family, Frank agreed to appear at the show's taping, which took place in November. Only two vocalists—Natalie Cole and Tony Bennett—fit comfortably within the Sinatra style, and the remainder were a mixed bag indeed. Though fellow New Jerseyite Bruce Springsteen performed an effective (though strained) "Angel Eyes" and Ray Charles did his own soulful arrangement of "Ol' Man River," many of the performances were downright dreadful, perhaps the worst being two original compositions: U2's "One Shot of Happy, Two Shots of Sad," a terrible (videotaped) attempt to simulate a saloon song, with Bono actually *kissing* the camera lens at one point; and a Bob Dylan number featuring painfully mumbled lyrics that no one (perhaps even the singer) could understand. "Happy birthday, Mr. Frank," the vocally challenged folk legend stammered before leaving the stage. Tina, who sat near Frank's table, recalled, "I could tell that he hated almost every minute of it."[115]

To commemorate this milestone, Capitol released *Sinatra 80th: Live in Concert*, although, with the exception of an unreleased 1993 "My Way" duet with Luciano Pavarotti, the tracks for the album were taken from concerts recorded in 1987-88. In his liner notes, Bill Miller writes, "[Sinatra] is like an actor doing a one-man play telling an intricate, dramatic story with a clearly defined beginning, middle and end."[116] The fact that Frank was 71-72 when the live material was recorded is openly apparent, as his voice is much better than on the *Duets* albums. "You Are the Sunshine of My Love" and "What Now My Love" open the disc energetically before Frank courageously tackles Rodgers and Hart's ballad "My Heart Stood Still." Though he is a little shaky on "What's New," he returns strongly on "For Once In My Life" before referring to David Gates' "If" as "a lovely song." Cole Porter's "In the Still of the Night" and a superb, powerful version of Rodgers and Hammerstein's "Soliloquy" bely Frank's age. "Maybe This Time" is followed by a somewhat restrained "Where or When," which Frank closes with a remarkably sustained final note. Joe Raposo's "You Will Be My Music" precedes "Strangers in the Night," which he perfunctorily polishes off: "I don't even know who the hell these guys are," he comments about the song's writers. The live portion ends with Frank's favorite closers from the period, "Angel Eyes" and "New York, New York." Put simply, the nearly unlistenable "My Way" duet with Pavarotti should have remained unreleased.

On Christmas Day 1995, Dean Martin, aged 78, died of acute respiratory failure. Frank, remorseful that their last collaboration had turned sour, said, "He was my brother. Not through blood but through choice. Our friendship traveled down many roads over the years and there will always be a special place in my heart and soul for Dean."[117]

Battling various illnesses during 1997, Frank was primarily house-bound, watching game shows and films on television. Tina recalled his joy at seeing the 1930 adventure *Trader Horn*, as well as some of his own classics: "My father had never been too interested in watching his own movies, until now. The first one we happened upon was *The Tender Trap*. ...Another time we laughed at *Guys and Dolls*. "He still can't sing," Dad would say, shaking his head at ...Marlon Brando." [118]

On December 15, 1997—Frank's 82nd birthday—the U. S. House of Representatives voted unanimously to award him the Congressional Gold Medal of Honor. "Overwhelmed" as he watched the proceedings on C-SPAN with his family, he said, "I'm just a vocalist who tried to do the best he could."[119]

On Thursday, May 14, 1998, Frank attempted to eat lunch with Barbara on the patio of their Beverly Hills home. In the evening, she left to dine with friends at a local restaurant. During the meal, the maitre d' informed her that her assistant had called, and she excused herself quickly to rush home. Frank, complaining of chest pain, had been taken to the Cedars Sinai emergency room at 9:30 p.m. In true Frank fashion, he attempted to pull out the intravenous tubes but was

cared for by a team of physicians for more than 80 minutes. Before his children—who had not been called—could arrive at the hospital, he looked at Barbara, whispered, "I'm losing" and passed away. The official cause of death was a heart attack.

On Friday, President Bill Clinton, in a written statement, said:

> Sinatra was a spellbinding performer, on stage or on screen, in musicals, comedies and dramas. He built one of the world's most important record companies. He won countless awards, from the Grammy—nine times—to the Academy Award, to the Presidential Medal of Freedom. And he dedicated himself to humanitarian causes. When I became president, I had never met Frank Sinatra, although I was an enormous admirer of his. I had the opportunity after I became president to get to know him a little, to have dinner

with him, to appreciate on a personal level, what fans around the world, including me, appreciated from afar. Frank Sinatra will be missed profoundly by millions around the world. But his music and movies will ensure that "Ol' Blue Eyes" is never forgotten.[120]

Martin Scorsese said:

I'm very saddened… He was an idol of mine, and millions. A great Italian-American, a great American—and a great *actor*, by the way—great, great actor, just alone in films like *Some Came Running* and *Man with the Golden Arm* and *From Here to Eternity*. You know, I'm very, very upset. There will never be another him. You know, he's the idol. He was the original.[121]

Official news of Frank's death didn't break until Saturday, May 16. Of course, most local newspapers across the nation printed headlines trumpeting "He did it his way." Referring to him as "The voice of America," *The Chicago Tribune* credited him for "reinvent[ing] 20th Century popular culture"[122], while *The New York Times* called him "the greatest singer in American pop history… the first modern pop superstar."[123]

For the next several days, remembrances were held across the nation. Frank's star on the Hollywood Walk of Fame and the grounds outside the Beverly Hills home were covered with cards and flowers. On Sunday, hundreds of admirers thronged a public memorial in Palm Springs; and the following evening, Hoboken residents packed a church and sang "My Way." On the eve of the May 20 funeral, a private rosary service was held at Good Shepherd Church in Beverly Hills.

The private funeral service was held for invited guests at Good Shepherd the next afternoon. Joining Cardinal Roger Mahoney, Archbishop of Los Angeles, were eulogists Kirk Douglas, Robert Marx, Gregory Peck, George Schlatter, Frank, Jr., and Robert Wagner. Among the 400 mourners were Tony Bennett, Angie Dickinson, Jack Lemmon, Jack Nicholson, Tony Curtis, Anthony Quinn, Tom Selleck, Sophia Loren, Liza Minnelli, Larry King, Milton Berle, Debbie Reynolds, Mia Farrow and Nancy Reagan. Frank's pallbearers included Steve Lawrence, Don Rickles, Vic Damone and Tom Dreesen. Musical selections included a solo piano arrangement of "Ave Maria" played by Bill Miller and Frank's own "Put Your Dreams Away."

Jerry Lewis didn't attend the funeral, later admitting that the experience would have been "too emotional."[124] Of the two-hour service, Sidney Poitier said, "It was as it should be: extraordinary."[125]

Frank's casket was taken to the Sinatra family vault at Desert Memorial Park in Cathedral City, near Palm Springs, where Dolly and Martin also are interred. The cemetery service was held exclusively for family members.

Shortly before Frank's death, Martin Scorsese and HBO Pictures both announced that "Rat Pack" films were in the works. While Scorsese planned to base his production on Nick Tosches' bestselling Dean Martin biography *Dino: Living High in the Dirty Business of Dreams* (reportedly starring John Travolta as Frank), HBO's small-screen effort would costar Ray Liotta as Frank, Joe Mantegna as Dean, Don Cheadle as Sammy, and Angus McFadyen as Peter Lawford. First televised on August 22, 1998, the latter—often error-ridden—film is a generally well-made and acted effort, but is plagued by the fact that the cable network was unable to use any of the original recordings made by the Summiteers.

Though Sammy and Peter are played convincingly, Mantegna's Martin is a very pale imitation of the dynamic Dino, and Liotta is absolutely miscast as Frank. Not once does he capture any of the Sinatra mannerisms, speech patterns or charisma. His performance is a two-dimensional caricature focusing on Frank's sometimes titanic temper; and the script places an exaggerated emphasis on the Kennedy and Mob material. Sam Giancana (Robert Miranda) is depicted, not as an occasional acquaintance of Frank's, but as a virtual Rat Packer himself, often lurking on the sidelines and actually hanging out with the rest of the pallies during their first scene together.

In an effort to depict the personalities of all the Packers, actor and television writer Kario Salem created contrived dialogue that often is delivered laboriously by Liotta and Mantegna. The singing is even worse, with Michael Dees, Warren Wiebe and Gunner Madsen attempting respectively to imitate Frank, Dean and Sammy. Madsen is the best of the three, with Wiebe literally massacring Dino's terrific version of Van Heusen and Cahn's "Ain't that a Kick in the Head" and Dees never sounding an iota like Ol' Blue Eyes. However, on the occasions that Mantegna actually attempts to sing like Dean, the viewer may be tempted to reach for the mute button on the remote control—as he also may during Liotta's lip-synched climactic performance of "One for My Baby."

Dan O'Herlihy as Joe Kennedy and William Peterson and Zeljko Ivanek as his boys, Jack and Bobby, are fine in their roles. JFK is made to look like the good guy in the triumverate of Massachusetts power, while Bobby is a second-generation version of the manipulating old man, who orders Frank to back down from the Albert Maltz project, persuade Giancana to pressure the West Virginia unions and put the kibosh on Sammy's wedding to Mai Britt. Though these incidents are based on fact, they are operatically overblown.

The only scene showing Frank acting in a film depicts him as One-Take Charley while shooting *Ocean's Eleven* (Lewis Milestone is portrayed by Craig Richard Nelson); and, during the production of this Summit classic—in a distortion of the Lee Mortimer incident—he is shown punching a reporter in a restaurant. The most outrageous image of Frank depicts him at the Palm Springs compound, beating—not the helipad, which is mentioned in most versions of this myth—but the "John F. Kennedy Slept Here" plaque with a sledgehammer! The film's two best Frank sequences involve his agreeing to stand up for Sammy at his wedding and a later scene with Sammy, where the pair are seen working in the studio together (an aspect ignored by the *Sinatra* miniseries).

Although many of the events depicted in *The Rat Pack* are based on real-life incidents, there are dozens of exaggerations and errors added under the guise of "dramatization." Unfortunately, untold viewers who have seen this film believe that these things actually happened. By any stretch of the imagination, these men were not saints, but they also were not cartoon characters *constantly* submerged in a 24-7 sea of booze, brawls, broads and Mob bosses.

While Frank Sinatra the man is no more, his artistry will live on as long as people listen to good music and watch quality films. And future generations will see, not only the productions in which he appeared, but also new motion pictures enhanced by his unsurpassed vocal performances. One in the latter category, featuring the Sinatra-Basie "Fly Me to The Moon" as a score for its ending, is Clint Eastwood's *Space Cowboys* (2000), in which the producer-director costars with Tommy Lee Jones, Donald Sutherland and James Garner. On the small screen, "It Was a Very Good Year" was used to open the second season of HBO's groundbreaking Mob series *The Sopranos* starring James Gandolfini. Frank was mentioned by various characters (including yet another erroneous reference to Johnny Fontane in *The Godfather*) during both the 1999 and 2000 seasons, and Frank, Jr., playing himself, joined an "executive poker game" in the season-two episode "The Happy Wanderer."

While Frank was still on this mortal coil, major Mafia-oriented films, *Goodfellas* (1990) included, usually relied on fellow Italians Tony Bennett, Dean Martin, Vic Damone and Bobby

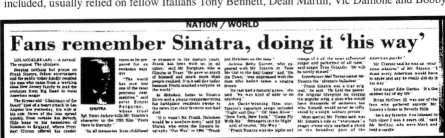

314 *The Cinema of Sinatra*

Darin. Interestingly, director Mike Newell, while preparing research for his exceptional *Donnie Brasco* (1997), revealed:

> We went to…a completely anonymous corner [in New York]… and we went in, and it was full of wiseguys, full of mobsters, and they were drinking. There was a bar. There was a juke box…*huge* juke box. Every one of the records was Frank Sinatra. I checked it. *Truly*, every one of the records was Frank Sinatra.[126]

Johnny Depp, who plays the title character in the film, recalled, "I'm a huge Sinatra fan. You know, I think he's made one of the most important contributions to music of the century."[127]

And, of course, the occasional Sinatra impersonator will rear his head: Joe Piscopo on *Saturday Night Live*; or Toby Huss in the lame military comedy *Down Periscope* (1996), starring longtime Frank fan Kelsey Grammer as an unlikely Navy submarine captain. No impersonations of Frank, nor any tongue-in-cheek references to the original film, can be found in Steven Soderbergh's 2001 remake of *Ocean's Eleven*, starring George Clooney (as Danny Ocean), Brad Pitt, Matt Damon, Don Cheadle, Elliott Gould, Carl Reiner and Julia Roberts (as Tess, an expanded version of Angie Dickinson's Bea). Dickinson is the only Summit performer to make a cameo in this entertaining and suspenseful variation on the 1960 (less serious) caper, here involving the gang of 11 heisting the main vault connected to the Bellagio, the Mirage and the MGM Grand, all owned by Terry Benedict (Andy Garcia), during a major boxing match. The basic plot follows the  original, with new characterizations and a different ending, in which the thieves actually get away with $160 million in cash.

In June 2002, Reprise Records and Turner Classic Movies released *Frank Sinatra in Hollywood*, an ambitious six-CD set produced by Didier C. Deutsch and Charles L. Granata including nearly all of Frank's musical and promotional recordings made for his films. (A few, such as those made for the aborted *Carousel* project, are entangled in copyright restrictions.) Featuring essays by the aforementioned producers, Leonard Maltin, Michael Feinstein, Will Friedwald and Scott Allen Nollen, the box set contains scores of commercially unreleased songs, including all those Frank recorded for the unfinished *Finian's Rainbow* project, and many 1940s and '50s numbers beautifully remixed into stereo from multiple channel orchestral recordings discovered at various archives and studios.

Frank Sinatra is no longer lonely. If you, dear reader, are—while concluding this book, perhaps in the wee small hours of the morning—maybe worrying about the broad or the bum who got away, perchance the one who split with all the bread. Don't grab a glass or stumble down to the local saloon, which is probably closed. Just rouse yourself enough to put on a classic Sinatra platter or picture, and experience the consummate actor at work. You'll be impressed. You'll be moved. You'll sigh and swing. You'll no longer be among only the lonely…

The Films of Frank Sinatra

Major Bowes Amateur Theatre of the Air (October 1935)
Credits: Director and Producer: John H. Auer; Filmed at Biograph Studios, Bronx, New York.
Cast: Jimmy Petrozelli, Patty Principe, Fred Tamburro (The Three Flashes), Frank Sinatra (Waiter/Minstrel Man).

Las Vegas Nights (March 1941)
Credits: Director: Ralph Murphy; Producer: William LeBaron; Screenplay: Harry Clork, Ernest Pagano, Eddie Welch; Original Story: Ernest Pagano; Director of Photography: William C. Mellor; Film Editor: Arthur P. Schmidt; Musical Score: Louis Alter; Musical Arrangements and Direction: Axel Stordahl, Victor Young, Charles Bradshaw, Leo Shuken, Max Terr; Musical Numbers Staged by LeRoy Prinz; Art Directors: Hans Dreier, A. Earl Hedrick; Released by Paramount Pictures; Running Time: 89 minutes.
Cast: Phil Regan (Bill Stevens), Bert Wheeler (Stu Grant), Tommy Dorsey (Himself), Constance Moore (Norma Jennings), Virginia Dale (Patsy Lynch), Lillian Cornell (Mildred Jennings), Betty Brewer (Katy), Hank Ladd (Hank Bevis), Eddie Kane (Maitre D'), Eleanor Stewart (Hat Check Girl), Catherine Craig, Marcelle Christopher, Ella Neal, Jean Phillips (Girls with Bill), William ("Red") Donahue (Guitar Player), Henry Kolker (William Stevens, Sr.), Francetta Malloy (Gloria Stafford), Wanda McKay (Cigarette Girl), Nick Moro (Guitar and Violin Player), Frank Sinatra (Singer in Tommy Dorsey's Band), Frank Yaconelli (Concertina Player), Johnny Clark, Chief John Big Tree.

Ship Ahoy (May 1942)
Credits: Director: Edward N. Buzzell; Producer: Jack Cummings; Screenplay: Harry Clork, Irving Brecher, Harry Kurnitz; Original Story: Matt Brooks, Bert Kalmar, Bradford Ropes; Directors of Photography: Robert H. Planck, Leonard Smith, Clyde De Vinna (retakes); Film Editor: Blanche Sewell; Original Songs: Basil Adam, George Bassman, Margery Cummings, Tommy Dorsey, E.Y. Harburg, Burton Lane, Prince Leleiohaku, Johnny Noble, Walter Ruick, Henry Russell, Percy Wenrich, Ralph Freed, Edward Madden, Ned Washington; Art Directors: Cedric Gibbons, Harry McAfee; Set Decorators: Jack D. Moore, Edwin B. Mills; Costume Designer: Robert Kalloch; Assistant Director: Al Shenberg; Recording Director: Douglas Shearer; Musical Arrangements and Direction: Leo Arnaud, George Bassman, Sy Oliver, Conrad Salinger, George E. Stoll, Axel Stordahl; Choreographer: Bobby Connolly; Released by Metro-Goldwyn-Mayer Pictures; Running Time: 95 minutes.
Cast: Eleanor Powell (Tallulah Winters), Red Skelton (Merton K. Kibble), Bert Lahr ("Skip" Owens), Virginia O'Brien (Fran Evans), William Post, Jr. (H. U. Bennet), James Cross ("Stump"), Eddie Hartman ("Stumpy"), Stuart Crawford (Art Higgins), John Emery (Dr. Farno), Bernard Nedell (Pietro Polesi), Tommy Dorsey (Himself), Philip Ahn (Koro Sumo), Mariska Aldrich (Mother of Waldo), Ernie Alexander (Stagehand), Zita Baca (Bit), Louise Bates (Passenger), Barbara Bedford (Mrs. Loring), Gladys Blake (Secretary), Hillary Brooke (Girl), Baldwin Cooke (Steward), Mary Currier (Secretary), Mark Daniels (Operator), Cliff Danielson (Operator), John Dilson (Doctor Loring), Joe Dominguez (Cart Driver), Ralph Dunn (Grimes), Ziggy Elman (Himself), Martin Garralaga (Hotel Clerk), Bud Geary (Sailor), Henry Guttman (German Sailor), Connie Haines (Herself), Grace Hayle (Pianist), Russell Hicks (Captain C. V. O'Brien), Carol Hughes (Secretary), Arthur Stuart Hull (Passenger), Jerry James (Dancer), Harvey Karels (Dancer), Red Knight (Dancer), Bobby Larson (Waldo, Boy on Boat), Lou Lubin (Steward), Frank Marlowe (Stagehand), Charles Mayon (Dancer), Edmund Mortimer (Passenger), Anne O'Neal (Captain's Wife), Moroni Olsen (Inspector Davis), Nestor Paiva (Felix, a Thug), John Raitt (Sailor), Hal Rand (Dancer), Robin Raymond (Cigarette Girl), Otto Reichow (Waiter), Grandon Rhodes (Lieutenant Commander Thurston), Buddy Rich (Himself), Addison Richards (Agent in Puerto Rico), Julian Rivero (Photographer), Henry Rowland (Operator), Connie Russell (Chorus Girl), Frank Sinatra (Singer in Tommy Dorsey's Band), George Sorel (Headwaiter), Henry Sylvester (Doorman), William Tannen (Flammer), Charles Teske (Dancer), Charles Thomas (Officer), Natalie Thompson (Girl), Mary Treen (Nurse), James Warren (Officer), Bryant Washburn (Officer), George Watts (Hotel Detective), Grant Withers (Waiter), Victor Zimmerman (Officer).

Reveille With Beverly (February 4, 1943)
Credits: Director: Charles Barton; Producer: Sam White; Screenplay: Albert Duffy, Howard J. Green, Jack Henley; Director of Photography: Philip Tannura; Film Editor: James Sweeney; Production Designers: Lionel Banks, Joseph Kish; Assistant Director: Rex Bailey; Musical Director: Morris Stoloff; Released by Columbia Pictures; Running Time: 78 minutes.

Cast: Ann Miller (Beverly Ross), William Wright (Barry Lang), Dick Purcell (Andy Adams), Franklin Pangborn (Vernon Lewis), Harry Anderson (Sgt. Anderson), Bobby Barber (Collins), Count Basie (Himself), the Mills Brothers (Themselves), Barbara Brown (Mrs. Ross), Eddy Chandler (Top Sergeant), Bob Crosby (Himself), Boyd Davis (General Humphrey), Maude Eburne (Maggie), Duke Ellington (Himself), Ernest Hilliard (Mr. Oliver), Jean Inness (Mrs. Oliver), Eugene Jackson (Jackson), Si Jenks (Jenks), Eddie Kane (Medical Officer), Douglas Leavitt (Mr. Ross), Adele Mara (Evelyn Ross), Shirley Mills (Laura Jean), Ella Mae Morse (Singer with Freddie Slack's Band), John T. Murray (Director), David Newell (Sentry), Larry Parks (Eddie Ross), Herbert Rawlinson (Announcer), Jack Rice (Davis), Radio Rogues (Themselves), Irene Ryan (Elsie), Tim Ryan (Mr. Kennedy), Virginia Sale (Mrs. Browning), Walter Sande (Canvassback), Frank Sinatra (Himself), Freddie Slack (Himself), Andrew Tombes (Mr. Smith), Wally Vernon (Stomp McCoy), Doodles Weaver (Elmer), Lee Wilde, Lyn Wilde (Singing Twins).

Higher and Higher (December 1943)

Credits: Director and Producer: Tim Whelan; Executive Producer: George M. Arthur; Screenplay: William Bowers, Jay Dratler, Howard Harris, Gladys Hurlbut; Based on the play by Joshua Logan and Ralph Spence; Director of Photography: Robert De Grasse; Film Editor: Gene Milford; Musical Score: Constantin Bakaleinikoff; Original Songs: Jimmy McHugh, Richard Rodgers, Lorenz Hart, Harold Adamson; Orchestrations: Gene Rose, Axel Stordahl; Vocal Director: Ken Darby; Choreographer: Ernst Matray; Art Directors: Albert S. D'Agostino, Jack Okey; Set Decorators: Claude E. Carpenter, Darrell Silvera; Costume Designer: Edward Stevenson; Released by RKO-Radio Pictures; Running Time: 90 minutes.

Cast: Michele Morgan (Millie Picotte, a.k.a. Pamela Drake), Jack Haley (Mike O'Brien, the Valet), Frank Sinatra (Himself), Leon Errol (Cyrus Drake), Marcy McGuire (Mickey, the Maid), Victor Borge (Sir Victor Fitzroy Victor, a.k.a. Joe Brown), Mary Wickes (Sandy Brooks, a.k.a. Emily Drake), Elisabeth Risdon (Mrs. Georgia Keating), Barbara Hale (Katherine Keating), Mel Tormé (Marty), Paul Hartman (Byngham, the Butler), Grace Hartman (Hilda), Dooley Wilson (Oscar, the Chauffeur), Ivy Scott (Miss Whiffin, the Cook), Robert ["Bob"] Anderson (Announcer at Butler's Ball), Rex Evans (Mr. Green, Victor's Roomate), Edward Fielding (Reverend), Anne Goldthwaite (Debutante), Buddy Gorman (Page Boy), Rita Gould (Rita, Woman Assistant), Harry Holman (Banker), Warren Jackson (Contractor), Daun Kennedy (Bridesmaid) King Kennedy (Mr. Duval), Stanley Logan (Mr. Henry, Hotel Manager), Ola Lorraine (Sarah, Keatings' Maid), Dorothy Malone (Bridesmaid), Shirley O'Hara (Bridesmaid), Elaine Riley (Bridesmaid), Drake Thornton (Bellboy).

Step Lively (June 1944)

Credits: Director: Tim Whelan; Producer: Robert Fellows; Screenplay: Warren Duff, Peter Milne; Based on the Play *Room Service* by Allen Boretz and John Murray; Director of Photography: Robert De Grasse; Film Editor: Gene Milford; Original Songs: Sammy Cahn, Jule Styne; Production Designers: Claude E. Carpenter, Carroll Clark; Art Directors: Albert S. D'Agostino, Darrell Silvera; Costume Designer: Edward Stevenson; Special Effects: Vernon L. Walker; Musical Director: Constantin Bakaleinikoff; Vocal Director: Ken Darby; Choreographer: Ernst Matray; Orchestrator: Glen Rose; Musical Arranger: Axel Stordahl; Released by RKO-Radio Pictures; Running Time: 88 minutes.

Cast: Frank Sinatra (Glen Russell), George Murphy (Gordon Miller), Adolphe Menjou (Wagner), Gloria DeHaven (Christine Marlowe), Walter Slezak (Joe Gribble), Eugene Pallette (Jenkins), Wally Brown (Binion), Alan Carney (Harry), Grant Mitchell (Dr. Glass), Anne Jeffreys (Miss Abbott), George Chandler (Country Yokel), Frances King (Mother), Rosemary La Planche (Louella), Dorothy Malone (Telephone Operator), Frank Mayo (Doorman), Lee Murray (Bellboy), Harry Noble (Father), Shirley O'Hara (Louise), Elaine Riley (Lois), James Bell.

Anchors Aweigh (July 19, 1945)

Credits: Director: George Sidney; Producer: Joe Pasternak; Screenplay: Isobel Lennart; Original Story: Natalie Marcin; Directors of Photography: Charles P. Boyle, Robert H. Planck; Film Editor: Adrienne Fazan; Musical Score: George E. Stoll; Original Songs: Sammy Cahn, Jule Styne; Art Directors: Randall Duell, Cedric Gibbons; Set Decorators: Richard Pefferle, Edwin B. Willis; Makeup: Jack Dawn; Sound Recording Director: Douglas Shearer; Vocal Arranger: Earl K. Brent; Costume Supervisor: Irene; Associate Costume Supervisor: Kay Dean; Choreographer: Gene Kelly; Dance Director: Jack Donohue; Technicolor Director: Natalie Kalmus; Associate Color Director: Henri Jaffa; Camera Operator: Sam Leavitt; Orchestrator: Axel Stordahl; Released by Metro-Goldwyn-Mayer Pictures; Running Time: 143 minutes.

Cast: Frank Sinatra (Clarence Doolittle), Katherine Grayson (Susan Abbott), Gene Kelly (Joseph Brady), José Iturbi (Himself), Dean Stockwell (Donald Martin), Pamela Britton (Girl from Brooklyn), Rags Ragland

(Police Sergeant), Billy Gilbert (Cafe Manager), Henry O'Neill (Admiral Hammond), Carlos Ramírez (Carlos), Edgar Kennedy (Police Captain), Grady Sutton (Bertram Kraler), Leon Ames (Commander), Sharon McManus (Little Girl Beggar), James Flavin (Radio Cop), James Burke (Studio Cop), Henry Armetta (Hamburger Man), Chester Clute (Iturbi's Assistant), Harry Barris (Sailor), Steve Brodie (Soldier), Alex Callam (Commander), Wally Cassell (Sailor), Charles Coleman (Butler), Douglas Cowan (Sailor), Henry Daniels (Sailor), William Forrest (Movie Director), Phil Hanna (Sailor), John James (Sailor), Milton Kibbee (Bartender), Orley Lindgren (Bit), Peggy Maley (Lana Turner Impersonator), Esther Michelson (Hamburger Woman), Garry Owen (Soldier), Milton Parsons (Man with Beard), William ["Bill"] Phillips (Sailor), Renie Riano (Waitress), Sondra Rodgers (Secretary), Ray Teal (Assistant Movie Director), Tom Trout (Sailor).

The House I Live In (1945)

Credits: Director: Mervyn LeRoy; Producer: Frank Ross; Screenplay: Albert Maltz; Original Concept: Frank Sinatra; Musical Director: Axel Stordahl; Released by RKO-Radio Pictures; Running Time: 10 minutes.
Cast: Frank Sinatra (Himself).

All-Star Bond Rally (1945)

Credits: a War Activities-Motion Picture Industry Production for the "Mighty 7th" War Loan.
Cast: Vivian Blaine, Jeanne Crain, Bing Crosby, Linda Darnell, Betty Grable, June Haver, Bob Hope, Harry James and His Orchestra, Faye Marlow, Harpo Marx, Fibber McGee and Molly, Carmen Miranda, Frank Sinatra.

Till the Clouds Roll By (November 1946)

Credits: Directors: Richard Whorf, George Sidney, Vincente Minnelli; Producer: Arthur Freed; Screenplay: Myles Connolly, Jean Holloway; Original Story: Guy Bolton; Story Adaptation: George Wells; Directors of Photography: George J. Folsey, Harry Stradling, Sr.; Film Editor: Albert Akst; Original Music: Jerome Kern; Lyricists: Buddy G. DeSylva, Dorothy Fields, Ira Gershwin, Oscar Hammerstein II, Otto A. Harbach, Lennie Hayton, Edward Laska, Herbert Reynolds, P. G. Wodehouse; Art Directors: Daniel B. Cathcart, Cedric Gibbons; Set Decorator: Edwin B. Willis; Costume Designers: Helen Rose, Valles; Costume Supervisor: Irene; Makeup: Jack Dawn; Hair Stylist: Sydney Guilaroff; Associate Set Decorator: Richard Pefferle; Sound Recording Director: Douglas Shearer; Special Effects: Warren Newcombe; Director of Musical Numbers: Robert Alton; Montage: Peter Ballbusch; Technicolor Director: Natalie Kalmus; Associate Color Director: Henri Jaffa; Music Supervisor and Conductor: Lennie Hayton; Orchestrator: Conrad Salinger; Vocal Arrangements: Kay Thompson; Released by Metro-Goldwyn-Mayer Pictures; Running Time: 137 minutes.
Cast: June Allyson (Specialty), Lucille Bremer (Sally Hessler), Judy Garland (Marilyn Miller), Kathryn Grayson (Magnolia [Show Boat]/Specialty), Van Heflin (James I. Hessler), Lena Horne (Julie [Show Boat]/Specialty), Van Johnson (Bandleader), Tony Martin (Ravenal [Show Boat]/ Specialty) Dinah Shore (Julie Sanderson), Frank Sinatra (Finale Specialty), Robert Walker (Jerome Kern), Gower Champion (Specialty), Cyd Charisse (Dance Specialty), Harry Hayden (Charles Frohman), Paul Langton (Oscar Hammerstein II), Angela Lansbury (Specialty), Paul Maxey (Victor Herbert), Ray McDonald (Specialty), Mary Nash (Mrs. Muller), Virginia O'Brien (Ellie [Show Boat]/Specialty), Dorothy Patrick (Eva Kern), Caleb Peterson (Joe [Show Boat]), William ["Bill"] Phillips (Hennessey), Joan Wells (Sally as a Girl), Lyn Wilde (Specialty), Lee Wilde (Specialty), Stanley Andrews (Bit), Gloria Joy Arden (Showgirl), Wesley Brent (Showgirl), Alma Carroll (Showgirl), Lucille Casey (Showgirl), Ann Codee (Miss Larouche), Bruce Cowling (Steve [Show Boat]), James Darrell (Critic), Ralph Dunn (Moving Man), Dick Earle (Critic), Ed Elby (Critic), Rex Evans (Cecil Keller), Sally Forrest (Dancer), William Forrest (Motion Picture Director), Byron Foulger (Frohman's Secretary), Jane French (Showgirl), Herschel Graham (Critic), Charles Griffin (Critic), William Halligan (Captain Andy [Show Boat]), Russell Hicks (Producer), Reed Howes (Critic), Fred Hueston (Critic), Johnny Johnston (Finale Specialty), Maurice Kelly (Dance Specialty), Charles Madrin (Critic), Mickey Malloy (Showgirl), Matt Mattox (Featured Dancer), Beryl McCutcheon (Showgirl), Leonard Mellen (Critic), Tony Merlo (Critic), Hazard Newsberry (Critic), Lee Phelps (Moving Man), James Plato (Critic), Lee Smith (Critic), Larry Steers (Critic), Ray Teal (Orchestra Conductor), Irene Vernon (Showgirl), Alice Wallace (Showgirl), Esther Williams (Cameo), Larry Williams (Critic).

It Happened in Brooklyn (March 1947)

Credits: Director: Richard Whorf; Producer: Jack Cummings; Screenplay: Isobel Lennart; Original Story: J. P. McGowan; Original Songs: Sammy Cahn, Jule Styne; Non-original Music: Leo Delibes, Wolfgang Amadeus Mozart; Director of Photography: Robert H. Planck; Film Editor: Blanche Sewell; Art Directors: Cedric Gibbons, Leonid Vasian; Set Decorators: Alfred E. Spencer, Edwin B. Willis; Makeup: Jack Dawn;

Sound Recording Director: Douglas Shearer; Choreographer: Jack Donohue; Musical Supervisor and Director: Johnny Green; Musical Arranger: Axel Stordahl; Piano Solos: André Previn; Released by Metro-Goldwyn-Mayer Pictures; Running Time: 104 minutes.

Cast: Frank Sinatra (Danny Webson Miller), Kathryn Grayson (Anne Fielding), Peter Lawford (Jamie Shellgrove), Jimmy Durante (Nick Lombardi) Gloria Grahame (Nurse), Marcy McGuire (Rae Jakobi), Aubrey Mather (Digby John), Tamara Shayne (Mrs. Kardos), Billy Roy (Leo Kardos), Bobby Long (Johnny O'Brien), William Haade (Police Sergeant), Leonard Bremen (Corporal), Bruce Cowling (Soldier), Lumsden Hare (Canon Green), Al Hill (Driver), Raymond Largay (Mr. Dobson), Mitchell Lewis (Printer), William Tannen (Captain), Dick Wessel (Cop), Wilson Wood (Fodderwing).

The Miracle of the Bells (March 27, 1948)

Credits: Director: Irving Pichel; Producers; Jesse L. Lasky, Walter MacEwen; Screenplay: Ben Hecht, Quentin Reynolds, DeWitt Bodeen; Based on the Novel by Russell Janney; Director of Photography: Robert De Grasse; Film Editor: Elmo Williams; Musical Score: Leigh Harline; Original Song, "Ever Homeward": Sammy Cahn, Jule Styne; Art Directors: Ralph Berger, Albert S. D'Agostino; Set Decorators: Harley Miller, Darrell Silvera; Makeup: Gordon Bau, Karl Herlinger; Hair Stylist: Annabell Levy; Production Manager: Fred Fleck; Assistant Director: Harry D'Arcy; Sound: Philip Mitchell, Clem Portman; Special Effects: Russell A. Cully, Clifford Stine; Musical Director: Constantin Bakaleinikoff; Camera Operator: Charles Burke; Choreographer: Charles O'Curran; Wardrober: Renié; Grip: Rod Tolmie; Released by RKO-Radio Pictures; New York Premiere: March 16, 1948; Running Time: 120 minutes.

Cast: Fred MacMurray (William ["Bill"] Dunnigan), Alida Valli (Olga Treskovna, born Olga Trocki), Frank Sinatra (Father Paul), Lee J. Cobb (Marcus Harris), Harold Vermilyea (Nick Orloff, Funeral Director), Charles Meredith (Father J. Spinsky), Jim Nolan (Tod Jones, Reporter), Pataky (Miss Anna Klovna), Philip Ahn (Ming Gow), Frank Ferguson (Mike Dolan, the Director), Frank Wilcox (Dr. Jennings) Robert Bacon (Soldier in "Joan of Arc"), Bobby Barber (Man), Lyle Barton (Woman), Brooks Benedict (Drunken Man), Sedal Bennett (Woman), Oliver Blake (Slenka, the Taxi Driver), George Cathrey (Reporter), George Chandler (Max the Telegraph Operator), Bill Clauson (Bellringer's Son), Lillian Clayes (Woman), Mabel Colcord (Parishioner Witnessing Miracle), Roger Creed (Soldier in "Joan of Arc"), Sidney D'Albrook (Man), Roy Darmour (Reporter), Ned Davenport (Priest in "Joan of Arc"), Bert Davidson (Bob Briggs, Reporter), Pat Davis (Assistant Director), Ted Deputy (Man), Art Dupuis (Man), Al Eben (Miner), Herbert Evans (Nobleman in "Joan of Arc"), Franklyn Farnum (Worshipper), Budd Fine (Man), Jack Gargan (Assistant Director), Fred Graham (Man), Eula Guy (Woman), Maxwell Hamilton (Ray Tanner, Reporter), Mary Henderson (Woman), Clarence Hennecke (Man), Maude Hume (Woman), Perry Ivins (Druggist), Jerry Jerome (Miner), Maxine Johnston (Drunken Woman), Donald Kerr (Man), Paul Lacy (Man), Bertha Ledbetter (Woman), Jack Lindquist (Boy), Sam Lufkin (Man), Duncan MacDonell (Soldier in "Joan of Arc"), David McMahon (Miner), Richard Mickelson (Bellringer's Son), Charles F. Miller (Priest in "Joan of Arc"), Al Murphy (Miner), Dorothy Neumann (Miss Millhouser), Patsy O'Byrne (Woman), Edward Peil, Sr. (Man), David Perry (Miner), Frank Pharr (Bellringer), James Pierce (Soldier in "Joan of Arc"), "Snub" Pollard (Worshipper), Albert Pollet (Man), Alonzo Price (Miner in Bar), Michael Raffetto (Harold Tanby, Harris' Assistant), Jean Ransome (Woman), Marvin Reno (Miner), Quentin Reynolds (Himself, Radio Announcer), Thayer Roberts (Earl of Warwick in "Joan of Arc"), Bob Robinson (Man), Franz Roehn (Cauchon in "Joan of Arc"), Mike Sandler (Reporter), Syd Saylor (Freddy Evans, the Pianist), Marie Scheue (Woman), Dorothy Sebastian (Miss Katie Orwin), Phil Solomon (Man), Jean Spangler (Extra in Church), Ralph Stein (Miner), Tom Stevenson (Milton Wild, Harris' Assistant), Jack Stoney (Miner), Beth Taylor (Worshipper), Ray Teal (Koslick, a Miner), Ken Terrell (Miner), Bob Thom (Reporter), Ray Toone (Man), William Van Vleck (Man), Charles Wagenheim (Mr. Kummer, Hotel Manager), Max Wagner (Baggage Man), Bill Wallace (Reporter), Regina Wallace (Martha), Billy Wayne (Tom ["Tommy"] Elmore, the Choreographer), Mel Wixon (Reporter), Ian Wolfe (Grave Digger).

The Kissing Bandit (November 1948)

Credits: Director: László Benedek; Producer: Joe Pasternak; Screenplay: John Briard Harding, Isobel Lennart; Director of Photography: Robert Surtees; Film Editor: Adrienne Fazan; Musical Score: Earl K. Brent, Nacio Herb Brown, Edward Heyman; Production Designer: Randall Duell; Art Director: Cedric Gibbons; Set Decorators: Jack D. Moore, Edwin B. Willis; Costume Designer: Walter Plunkett; Makeup: Jack Dawn; Hair Stylist: Sydney Guilaroff; Production Manager: Sergei Petschnikoff; Assistant Director: Marvin Stuart; Sound: Wilhelm W. Brockway; Special Effects: A. Arnold Gillespie; Musical Arrangements: Léo Arnaud, George Bradley, Earl K. Brent, Calvin Jackson, Paul Marquardt, André Previn, Conrad Salinger, Albert Sendrey, George E. Stoll, Robert Van Eps; Choreographer: Stanley Donen; Technicolor Consultant: Henri Jaffa; Camera Operator: Al Lane; Released by Metro-Goldwyn-Mayer Pictures; Running Time: 100 minutes.

Cast: Frank Sinatra (Ricardo), Kathryn Grayson (Teresa), J. Carrol Naish (Chico), Mildred Natwick (Isabella), Mikhail Rasumny (Don Jose), Billy Gilbert (General Toro), Sono Osato (Bianca), Clinton Sundberg (Colonel Gomez), Carleton Young (Count Belmonte), Ricardo Montalban (Specialty Dancer), Ann Miller (Specialty Dancer), Cyd Charisse (Specialty Dancer), Edna Skinner (Juanita), Vicente Gómez (Mexican Guitarist), Jose Dominguez (Francisco), Byron Foulger (Grandee), Mitchell Lewis (Fernando), Henry Mirelez (Pepito), Alberto Morin (Lotso), Pedro Regas (Esteban), Julian Rivero (Postman), Nick Thompson (Pablo).

Take Me Out to the Ball Game (April 1949)

Credits: Director: Busby Berkeley; Producer: Arthur Freed; Screenplay: Harry Tugend, George Wells, Harry Crane; Original Story: Gene Kelly, Stanley Donen; Director of Photography: George J. Folsey; Film Editor: Blanche Sewell; Musical Score: Roger Edens; Original Songs: Adolph Green, Betty Comden; Art Directors: Daniel B. Cathcart, Cedric Gibbons; Set Decorators: Henry Grace, Edwin B. Willis; Costume Designers: Helen Rose, Valles; Makeup: Jack Dawn; Hair Stylist: Sydney Guilaroff; Assistant Director: Leslie H. Martinson; Sound: Douglas Shearer; Special Effects: Warren Newcombe; Montage: Peter Ballbusch; Musical Director: Adolph Deutsch; Choreographers: Stanley Donen, Gene Kelly; Assistant Color Director: James Gooch; Technicolor Consultant: Natalie Kalmus; Script Supervisor: Leslie H. Martinson; Vocal Arrangements: Robert Tucker; Released by Metro-Goldwyn-Mayer Pictures; New York Premiere: March 9, 1949; Los Angeles Premiere: April 13, 1949; Running Time: 93 minutes.

Cast: Frank Sinatra (Dennis Ryan), Esther Williams (K.C. Higgins), Gene Kelly (Eddie O'Brien), Betty Garrett (Shirley Delwyn), Edward Arnold (Joe Lorgan), Jules Munshin (Nat Goldberg), Richard Lane (Michael Gilhuly), Tom Dugan (Slappy Burke), Dorothy Abbott (Dancer), Murray Alper (Zalinka), Virginia Bates (Girl on Train), Richard Beavers (Bit), James Burke (Policeman), Ed Cassidy (Teddy Roosevelt), Sally Forrest (Dancer), Douglas Fowley (Karl), Sol Gorss (Steve), Wilton Graff (Nick Donford), Mack Gray (Gangster Henchman), Jackie Jackson (Child), Si Jenks (Sam), Gordon Jones (Senator Catcher), Hubie Kerns (Bit), Henry Kulky (Acrobat), Joi Lansing (Girl on Train), Mitchell Lewis (Fisherman), Esther Michelson (Fisherman's Wife), Eddie Parks (Dr. Winston), Charles Regan (Gangster Henchman), Jack Rice (Room Clerk), Frank J. Scannell (Reporter), Dick Wessel (Umpire).

On the Town (December 30, 1949)

Credits: Directors: Stanley Donen, Gene Kelly; Producer: Arthur Freed; Associate Producer: Roger Edens; Screenplay: Adolph Green, Betty Comden (from their original play); Director of Photography: Harold Rosson; Film Editor: Ralph E. Winters; Musical Score: Leonard Bernstein, Roger Edens; Original Songs: Adolph Green, Betty Comden; Art Directors: Cedric Gibbons, Jack Martin Smith; Set Decorator: Edwin B. Willis; Costume Designer: Helen Rose; Makeup: Jack Dawn; Hair Stylist: Sydney Guilaroff; Associate Set Decorator: Jack D. Moore; Sound: Douglas Shearer; Special Effects; Warren Newcombe; Vocal Arrangements: Saul Chaplin; Technicolor Consultants: James Gooch, Henri Jaffa; Musical Director: Lennie Hayton; Orchestrations: Conrad Salinger; Released by Metro-Goldwyn-Mayer Pictures; New York Premiere: December 8, 1949; Running Time: 98 minutes.

Cast: Gene Kelly (Gabey), Frank Sinatra (Chip), Betty Garrett (Brunhilde Esterhazy), Ann Miller (Claire Huddesen), Jules Munshin (Ozzie), Vera-Ellen (Ivy Smith, a.k.a. "Miss Turnstiles"), Florence Bates (Madame Dilyovska), Alice Pearce (Lucy Shmeeler), George Meader (Professor), Murray Alper (Cab Company Owner), Walter Baldwin (Sign Poster), Bea Benaderet (Working Girl), Eugene Borden (Waiter), Don Brodie (Photo Layout Man), Claire Carleton (Redhead), Hans Conried (Francois, Headwaiter), Lester Dorr (Subway Passenger), Tom Dugan (Officer Tracy, Car 44), Frank Hagney (Policeman), Carol Haney (Dancer in Green), Bern Hoffman (Shipyard Singer), Judy Holliday (Voice of a Sailor's Date), Sid Melton (Spud), William ("Bill") Phillips (Sailor), Dick Wessel (Sailor Simpkins), Robert Williams (Officer, Car 44).

Double Dynamite (December 25, 1951)

Credits: Director: Irving Cummings; Producers: Irwin Allen, Irving Cummings, Jr.; Screenplay: Melville Shavelson; Original Story: Harry Crane, Mannie Manheim, Leo Rosten; Director of Photography: Robert De Grasse; Film Editor: Harry Marker; Musical Score: Leigh Harline; Original Songs: Sammy Cahn, Jule Styne; Art Directors: Albert S. D'Agostino, Feild M. Gray; Set Decorators: Harley Miller, Darrell Silvera; Makeup: Gordon Bau; Assistant Director: James Lane; Sound: Phil Brigandi, Clem Portman; Musical Director: Constantin Bakaleinikoff; Released by RKO-Radio Pictures; Running Time: 80 minutes.

Cast: Jane Russell (Mildred ["Mibs"] Goodhug), Groucho Marx (Emile J. Keck), Frank Sinatra (Johnny Dalton), Don McGuire (Bob Pulsifer, Jr.), Howard Freeman (R. B. Pulsifer, Sr.), Nestor Paiva ("Hot Horse" Harris, the Bookie), Frank Orth (Mr. Kofer), Harry Hayden (J. L. McKissack), William Edmunds (Mr. Baganucci), Russell Thorson (Tailman), William Bailey (Bank Guard), Benny Burt (Waiter), George Chandler

(Messenger), Jack Chefe (Chef), Charles Coleman (Second Santa Claus), Hal K. Dawson (Mr. Hartman) Jean De Briac (Maitre D'), Dickie Derrel (Boy), Joe Devlin (Frankie Boy), Claire Du Brey (Hatchet Faced Lady), Bill Erwin (Man), Jack Gargan (Man), Harold Goodwin (Lieutenant), Dick Gordon (Man), Jack Jahries (Man), Virgil Johanson (Santa Claus), Kermit Kegley (Goon), Harry Kingston (Goon), Mike Lally (Man), Ida Moore (Little Old Lady), Al Murphy (Waiter), Jim Nolan (Detective), Lou Nova (Max), Gil Perkins (Man), Lee Phelps (Detective), Charles Regan (Man), Harry Seymour (Police Sergeant), Billy Snyder (Wire Service Man), Charles Sullivan (Sergeant), Lillian West (Hotel Maid).

Meet Danny Wilson (January 1952)

Credits: Director: Joseph Pevney; Producer: Leonard Goldstein; Associate Producer: Don McGuire; Screenplay and Story: Don McGuire; Director of Photography: Maury Gertsman; Film Editor: Virgil W. Vogel; Art Directors: Bernard Herzbrun, Nathan Juran; Set Decorators: Russell A. Gausman, Julia Heron; Costume Designer: Bill Thomas; Hair Stylist: Joan St. Oegger; Makeup: Bud Westmore; Unit Production Manager: Edward Dodds; Assistant Directors: Frank Shaw, Les Warner; Sound: Leslie I. Carey, Richard DeWeese; Choreographer: Harold Belfer; Musical Director: Joseph Gershenson; Special Photography: David S. Horsley; Dialogue Director: Leslie Urbach; Released by Universal-International Pictures; Running Time: 88 minutes.

Cast: Frank Sinatra (Danny Wilson), Shelley Winters (Joy Carroll), Alex Nicol (Mike Ryan), Raymond Burr (Nick Driscoll), Vaughn Taylor (T. W. Hatcher), Tommy Farrell (Tommy Wells), Donald MacBride (Sergeant), Barbara Knudson (Marie), Carl Sklover (Cab Driver), Jeff Chandler (Cameo), Tony Curtis (Cameo), John Daheim (Gus), Bob Donnelly (Emerson), Tom Dugan (Turnkey), George Eldredge (Lieutenant Kelly), Pat Flaherty ("Mother" Murphy), John Indrisano (Truck Driver), Jack Kruschen (Heckler), Carlos Molina (Bandleader), Bob Reeves, Danny Welton (Joey Thompson).

From Here to Eternity (August 5, 1953)

Credits: Director: Fred Zinnemann; Producer: Buddy Adler; Screenplay: Daniel Taradash, based on the novel by James Jones; Musical Score: George Duning; Original Song: James Jones, Fred Karger; Directors of Photography: Floyd Crosby, Burnett Guffey; Film Editor: William A. Lyon; Art Director: Cary Odell; Set Decorator: Frank Tuttle; Costume Design: Jean Louis; Makeup: Clay Campbell, Robert J. Schiffer; Hair Stylist: Helen Hunt; Assistant Director: Earl Bellamy; Sound: Lodge Cunningham; Boxing Adviser: Mushy Callahan; Technical Adviser: Brigadier General Kendall J. Fielder, Ret.; Stills Photographer: Irving Lippman; Orchestrator: Arthur Morton; Musical Director: Morris Stoloff; Lyricist: Robert Wells; Released by Columbia Pictures; Running Time: 118 minutes.

Cast: Burt Lancaster (First Sergeant Milton Warden), Montgomery Clift (Private Robert E. Lee ["Prew"] Prewitt), Deborah Kerr (Karen Holmes), Donna Reed (Alma Burke [Lorene]), Frank Sinatra (Pvt. Angelo Maggio), Philip Ober (Captain Dana ["Dynamite"] Holmes, Company Commander), Mickey Shaughnessy (Corporal Leva, Supply), Harry Bellaver (Private Mazzioli), Ernest Borgnine (Staff Sergeant "Fatso" Judson, Stockade Sergeant of the Guard), Jack Warden (Corporal Buckley), John Dennis (Sergeant Ike Galovitch), Merle Travis (Sal Anderson), Tim Ryan (Staff Sergeant Pete Karelsen), Arthur Keegan (Treadwell), Barbara Morrison (Mrs. Kipfer, Owner of New Congress Club), Claude Akins (Sergeant Dhom), Vicki Bakken (Suzanne), Margaret Barstow (Roxanne), Willis Bouchey (Lieutenant Colonel), John Bryant (Captain G. R. Ross, New Company Commander), Mary Carver (Nancy), John L. Cason (Corporal Paluso), Mack Chandler (Bit), John Davis (Bit), Elaine DuPont, Don Dubbins (Private Friday Clark), Moana Gleason (Rose, Waitress in Enlisted Mens Club), Robert Healy (Soldier), Douglas Henderson (Corporal Champ Wilson), James Jones (Bit), Robert Karnes (Sergeant Turp Thornhill), Manny Klein (Trumpet Player), Edward Laguna (Bit), Weaver Levy (Bartender), William Lundmark (Bill), Freeman Lusk (Colonel Wood), Tyler McVey (Major Stern), Kristine Miller (Georgette, Lorene's Roommate), Patrick Miller (Bit), Robert Pike (Major Bonds), Allen Pinson (Bit), George Reeves (Sergeant Maylon Stark), Joe Roach (Bit), Fay Roope (General Slater), Delia Salvi (Billie), Louise Saraydar (Bit), Alvin Sargent (Nair), Joseph D. Sargent (Bit), Joan Shawlee (Sandra), Angela Stevens (Jean), Brick Sullivan (Military Guard), John Veitch (Bit), Guy Way (Bit), Norman Wayne (Bit), Robert J. Wilke (Sergeant Henderson), Jean Willes (Annette), Carleton Young (Colonel Ayres), Carey Leverette.

Suddenly (October 7, 1954)

Credits: Director: Lewis Allen; Producer: Robert Bassler; Screenplay: Richard Sale; Director of Photography: Charles G. Clarke; Film Editor: John F. Schreyer; Musical Score: David Raksin; Art Director: Frank Paul Sylos; Set Decorator: Howard Bristol; Costume Designer: Jack Masters; Makeup: Willard Buell; Hair Stylist: Lois Murray; Production Manager: Charles R. Hall; Assistant Director: Hal Klein; Sound: Joseph

Edmonson; Sound Editor: Delmore Harris; Special Effects: Louis DeWitt, Jack Rabin, Herman E. Townsley; a Libra Production; Released by United Artists Pictures; Running Time: 77 minutes.

Cast: Frank Sinatra (John Baron), Sterling Hayden (Sheriff Tod Shaw), James Gleason (Pop Benson), Nancy Gates (Ellen Benson), Kim Charney (Peter ["Pidge"] Benson III), Willis Bouchey (Dan Carney), Paul Frees (Benny Conklin), Christopher Dark (Bart Wheeler), James Lilburn (Jud Kelly), Kem Dibbs (Wilson), Clark Howat (Haggerty), Charles Smith (Bebop), Paul Wexler (Slim Adams), John Beradino (Trooper), Richard Collier (Ed Hawkins), Roy Engel (First Driver), Ted Stanhope (Second Driver), Charles Wagenheim (Kaplan), Dan White (Burge).

Young at Heart (January 1955)

Credits: Director: Gordon Douglas; Producer: Henry Blanke; Screenplay: Lenore J. Coffee, Julius J. Epstein; Story Adaptation: Liam O'Brien, based on the novel by Fannie Hurst; Director of Photography: Ted D. McCord; Film Editor: William H. Ziegler; Musical Score: Ray Heindorf; Art Director: John Beckman; Set Decorator: William Wallace; Makeup: Gordon Bau; Assistant Director: Al Alleborn; Sound: Charles David Forrest; Leslie G. Hewitt; Special Effects: Hans F. Koenekamp; Technicolor Consultant: Philip M. Jeffries; Piano Solos: André Previn; Wardrobe:Howard Shoup; an Arwin Production; Released by Warner Bros. Pictures; Running Time: 117 minutes.

Cast: Doris Day (Laurie Tuttle), Frank Sinatra (Barney Sloan), Gig Young (Alex Burke), Ethel Barrymore (Aunt Jessie Tuttle), Dorothy Malone (Fran Tuttle), Robert Keith (Gregory Tuttle), Elisabeth Fraser (Amy Tuttle), Alan Hale, Jr. (Robert Neary), Lonny Chapman (Ernest Nichols), Frank Ferguson (Bartell), Marjorie Bennett (Mrs. Ridgefield), Ivan Browning (Porter), Celeste Bryant (Little Girl), Cliff Ferre (Bartender), Joseph Forte (Reverend Johnson), John Maxwell (Doctor), William McLean (Husband), Grazia Narciso (Fat Man's Wife), Barbara Pepper (Wife), Robin Raymond (Girl), Tito Vuolo (Fat Man), Harte Wayne (Conductor).

Not as a Stranger (1955)

Credits: Director and Producer: Stanley Kramer; Screenplay: Edna Anhalt, Edward Anhalt; Based on the novel by Morton Thompson; Director of Photography: Franz Planer; Film Editor: Frederic Knudtson; Musical Score: George Antheil; Production Designer: Rudolph Sternad; Art Director: Howard Richmond; Set Decorator: Victor A. Gangelin; Costume Designers: Joe King, Don Loper; Hair Stylist: Esperanza Corona; Makeup: Bill Wood; Production Manager: John Burch; Assistant Director: Carter De Haven, Jr.; Sound: Watson Jones, Earl Snyder; Technical Advisers: Josh Fields, Marjorie Lefevre, Morton Maxwell; Script Supervisor: John Franco; Orchestrator: Ernest Gold; Production Assistant: Sally Hamilton; Dialogue Director: Anne P. Kramer; Camera Operator: F. Bud Mautino; Company Grip: Morris Rosen; Conductor: Paul Sawtell; a Stanley Kramer Production; Released by United Artists Pictures; Running Time: 135   minutes.

Cast: Olivia de Havilland (Kristina Hedvigson), Robert Mitchum (Lucas Marsh), Frank Sinatra (Alfred Boone), Gloria Grahame (Harriet Lang), Broderick Crawford (Dr. Aarons), Charles Bickford (Dr. Dave Runkleman), Myron McCormick (Dr. Snider), Lon Chaney, Jr. (Job Marsh), Jesse White (Ben Cosgrove), Harry Morgan (Oley), Lee Marvin (Brundage), Virginia Christine (Bruni), Whit Bissell (Dr. Dietrich), Jack Raine (Dr. Lettering), Mae Clarke (Miss Odell), William Vedder (Carlisle Emmons), John Dierkes (Bursar), Nancy Kulp (Hypochondriac Woman), Harry Lauter (Harry, Radio Technician), Jerry Paris (Medical Student), Harry Shannon (Patient), Carl ("Alfalfa") Switzer (Unexpected Father), Herb Vigran (Salesman), Will Wright (Patient With Cigar), King Donovan.

The Tender Trap (November 1955)

Credits: Director: Charles Walters; Producer: Lawrence Weingarten; Screenplay: Julius J. Epstein, based on the play by Max Shulman and Robert Paul Smith; Musical Score: Jeff Alexander; Original Song: Sammy Cahn, Jimmy Van Heusen; Director of Photography: Paul C. Vogel; Film Editor: John D. Dunning; Art Directors: Cedric Gibbons, Arthur Lonergan; Set Decorators: Jack D. Moore, Edwin B. Willis; Costume Designer: Helen Rose; Hair Stylist: Sydney Guilaroff; Makeup: William Tuttle; Assistant Director: Joel Freeman; Musical Conductor: Jeff Alexander; Technicolor Consultant: Charles K. Hagedon; Released by Metro-Goldwyn-Mayer Pictures; Running Time: 111 minutes.

Cast: Frank Sinatra (Charlie Y. Reader), Debbie Reynolds (Julie Gillis), David Wayne (Joe McCall), Celeste Holm (Sylvia Crewes), Jarma Lewis (Jessica), Lola Albright (Poppy), Carolyn Jones (Helen), Howard St. John (Mr. Sayers), Joey Faye (Sol Z. Steiner), Tom Helmore (Mr. Loughran), Willard Sage (Director), Marc Wilder (Ballet Actor), Jack Boyle (Audition Dancer), James Drury (Eddie), Madge Blake (Society Reporter), Leonard Bremen (Cab Driver), Gil Harman (TV Announcer), Gordon Richards (Doorman), Benny Rubin (Mr. Wilson), Reginald Simpson (Stage Manager), Frank Sully (Doorman), Dave White (Cab Driver), Wilson Wood (Elevator Boy), Hugo Haas.

Guys and Dolls (November 3, 1955)

Credits: Director: Joseph L. Mankiewicz; Producer: Samuel Goldwyn; Screenplay: Joseph L. Mankiewicz, Ben Hecht; Based on the play by Abe Burrows and Jo Swerling; Original Story: Damon Runyon Abe Burrows; Original music: Jay Blackton, Frank Loesser; Director of Photography: Harry Stradling, Sr.; Film Editor: Daniel Mandell; Production Designer: Oliver Smith; Art Director: Joseph C. Wright; Set Decorator: Howard Bristol; Costume Designer: Irene Sharaff; Hair Stylist: Annabell; Makeup: Ben Lane; Assistant Director: Arthur S. Black, Jr.; Sound: Roger Heman, Sr., Fred Lau, Vinton Vernon; Special Photographic Effects: Warren Newcombe; Musical Conductor: Jay Blackton; Orchestrators: Alexander Courage, Skip Martin, Nelson Riddle, Albert Sendrey; Musical Adaptations: Cyril J. Mockridge; Technicolor Consultant: Alvord Eiseman; Choreographer: Michael Kidd; a Samuel Goldwyn Production; Released by Metro-Goldwyn-Mayer Pictures; Running Time: 150 minutes.

Cast: Marlon Brando (Sky Masterson), Jean Simmons (Sarah Brown), Frank Sinatra (Nathan Detroit), Vivian Blaine (Miss Adelaide), Robert Keith (Lieutenant Brannigan), Stubby Kaye (Nicely Nicely Johnson), B. S. Pulley (Big Jule), Johnny Silver (Benny Southstreet), Sheldon Leonard (Harry the Horse), Danny Dayton (Rusty Charlie), George E. Stone (Society Max), Regis Toomey (Arvide Abernathy), Kathryn Givney (General Cartwright), Veda Ann Borg (Laverne), Mary Alan Hokanson (Agatha), Joe McTurk (Angie the Ox), Kay E. Kuter (Calvin), Stapleton Kent (Mission Member), Renee Renor (Cuban Singer), Barbara Brent, Jann Darlyn, Madelyn Darrow, June Kirby, Larri Thomas (Goldwyn Girls), Franklyn Farnum, Sam Harris (Spectators at Song and Dance Number), Earle Hodgins (Pitchman), John Indrisano (Liverlips Louie), Matt Murphy (The Champ), Frank Richards (Man with Packages), Julian Rivero (Cuban Waiter), Harry Tyler (Max the Waiter), Harry Wilson (Man in Barber Shop), Tony Galento, Joe Gray.

The Man with the Golden Arm (December 1955)

Credits: Director and Producer: Otto Preminger; Screenplay: Walter Newman, Lewis Meltzer, Ben Hecht; Based on the novel by Nelson Algren; Musical Score: Elmer Bernstein; Director of Photography: Sam Leavitt; Film Editor: Louis R. Loeffler; Production Designer: Joseph C. Wright; Set Decorator: Darrell Silvera; Costume Designer: Mary Ann Nyberg; Hair Stylist: Hazel Keats, Helene Parrish; Makeup: Ben Lane, Bernard Ponedel, Jack Stone; Production Manager: Jack McEdward; Assistant Directors: James Engle, Horace Hough; Sound: Jack Solomon; Music Editor: Leon Birnbaum; Lighting Technician: Jack Almond; Titles: Saul Bass; Technical Adviser: Jack Entratter; Script Supervisor: Kathleen Fagan; Wardrobe: Joe King, Adele Parmenter; Camera Operator: Albert Myers; Key Grip: Morris Rosen; Assistant to Producer: Maximilian Slater; Assistant editor: Tony de Zarraga; a Carlyle Production; Released by United Artists Pictures, Running Time: 119 minutes.

Cast: Frank Sinatra (Frankie Machine), Eleanor Parker (Zosch Machine), Kim Novak (Molly), Arnold Stang (Sparrow), Darren McGavin (Louie), Robert Strauss (Schwiefka), John Conte (Drunky), Doro Merande (Vi), George E. Stone (Sam Markette), George Mathews (Williams), Leonid Kinskey (Dominiwski), Emile Meyer (Bednar), Jerry Barclay (Junkie), Leonard Bremen (Taxi Driver), Paul E. Burns (Suspenders), Harold ("Tommy") Hart (Kvorda), Shelly Manne (Himself), Frank Marlowe (Antek), Joe McTurk (Meter Reader), Ralph Neff (Chester), Ernest Raboff (Bird-Dog), Frank Richards (Piggy), Shorty Rogers (Himself), Charles Seel (Proprietor), Martha Wentworth (Vengie), Will Wright (Lane).

Meet Me in Las Vegas (February 1956)

Credits: Director: Roy Rowland; Producer: Joe Pasternak; Screenplay: Isobel Lennart; Musical Score: Nicholas Brodszky, Johnny Green, George E. Stoll, Sammy Cahn; Director of Photography: Robert J. Bronner; Film Editor: Albert Akst; Art Directors: Cedric Gibbons, Urie McCleary; Set Decorators: Richard Pefferle, Edwin B. Willis; Costume Designer: Helen Rose; Hair Stylist: Sydney Guilaroff; Makeup: William Tuttle; Assistant Director: George Rhein; Special Effects: Warren Newcombe; Music Coordinator: Irving Aaronson; Technicolor Consultant: Charles K. Hagedon; Choreographers: Eugene Loring, Hermes Pan; Orchestrators: Skip Martin, Albert Sendrey; Recording Supervisor: Dr. Wesly B. Miller; Vocal Supervisor: Robert Tucker; Released by Metro-Goldwyn-Mayer Pictures; Running Time: 112 minutes.

Cast: Dan Dailey (Chuck Rodwell), Cyd Charisse (Maria Corvier), Agnes Moorehead (Miss Hattie), Lili Darvas (Sari Hatvani), Jim Backus (Tom Culdane), Oscar Karlweis (Lotzi), Liliane Montevecchi (Lilli), Cara Williams (Kelly Donavan), George Chakiris (Young Groom), Betty Lynn (Young Bride), Pete Rugolo (Conductor), John Brascia (Specialty Dancer), John Harding (Worried Boss), Benny Rubin (Croupier), Jack Daly (Meek Husband), Henny Backus (Bossy Wife), Jerry Colonna (Himself), Paul Henreid (Pierre), Lena Horne (Herself), Frankie Laine (Himself), Pier Angeli (Cameo), Peter Lorre (Cameo), Debbie Reynolds (Cameo), Jeff Richards (Cameo), Frank Sinatra (Cameo), Jerry Velasco (Piano Player Accompanying Lena Horne), Hank Worden (Bit), Mitsuko Sawamura, Roscoe Ates, Billy Dix.

The Actor, on Screen and in Song

Johnny Concho (July 1956)
Credits: Director: Don McGuire; Producer: Frank Sinatra; Associate Producer: Henry W. Sanicola; Screenplay: Don McGuire; Original Story, "The Man Who Owned the Town": David P. Harmon; Musical Score: Nelson Riddle; Director of Photography: William C. Mellor; Film Editor: Eda Warren; Casting: Lynn Stalmaster; Art Director: Nicolai Remisoff; Set Decorator: G.W. Berntsen; Costume Designer: Gwen Wakeling; Makeup: Ernest J. Park, Bernard Ponedel; Assistant Director: Emmett Emerson; Titles: Saul Bass; Assistant Editor: Tony de Zarraga; a Kent Production; Released by United Artists Pictures; Running Time: 84 minutes.
Cast: Frank Sinatra (Johnny Concho), Keenan Wynn (Barney Clark), William Conrad (Tallman), Phyllis Kirk (Mary Dark), Christopher Dark (Walker), Dorothy Adams (Sarah Dark), Claude Akins (Lem), Harry Bartell (Sam Green), Joe Bassett (Bartender), Willis Bouchey (Sheriff Henderson), Jean Byron (Pearl Lang), Wallace Ford (Albert Dark), Leo Gordon (Mason), Wilfred Knapp (Pearson), Robert Osterloh (Duke Lang), Howard Petrie (Hegelson), John Qualen (Jake), Dan Russ (Judge Tyler), Ben Wright (Benson).

High Society (July 1956)
Credits: Director: Charles Walters; Producer: Sol C. Siegel; Screenplay: John Patrick; Based on the play *The Philadelphia Story* by Philip Barry; Musical Score: Cole Porter; Director of Photography: Paul Vogel; Film Editor: Ralph E. Winters; Art Directors: Cedric Gibbons, Hans Peters; Set Decorators: Richard Pefferle, Edwin B. Willis; Costume Designer: Helen Rose; Hair Stylist: Sydney Guilaroff; Makeup: William Tuttle; Assistant Directors: Arvid Griffen, Hank Moonjean; Sound: Wesley C. Miller; Special Effects: A. Arnold Gillespie; Musical Director: Johnny Green; Associate Musical Director: Saul Chaplin; Technicolor Consultant: Charles K. Hagedon; Orchestrators: Nelson Riddle, Conrad Salinger; Choreographer: Charles Walters; Released by Metro-Goldwyn-Mayer Pictures; Running Time: 107 minutes.
Cast: Bing Crosby (C. K. Dexter-Haven), Grace Kelly (Tracy Samantha Lord), Frank Sinatra (Mike Connor), Celeste Holm (Liz Imbrie), John Lund (George Kittredge), Louis Calhern (Uncle Willie), Sidney Blackmer (Seth Lord), Louis Armstrong (Himself), Margalo Gillmore (Mrs. Seth Lord), Lydia Reed (Caroline Lord), Gordon Richards (Dexter-Haven's Butler), Richard Garrick (Lord's Butler), Hugh Boswell (Parson), Barrett Deems (Louis' Drummer), Edmond Hall (Louis' Clarinetist), Paul Keast (Editor), Richard Keene (Mac), Billy Kyle (Louis' Pianist), Ruth Lee (Matron), Arvell Shaw (Louis' Bassist), Reginald Simpson (Uncle Willie's Butler), Helen Spring (Matron), Trummy Young (Louis' Trombonist).

Around the World in Eighty Days (October 17, 1956)
Credits: Directors: Michael Anderson, Sidney Smith (documentary sequence); Producer: Michael Todd; Associate Producers: Kevin McClory, William Cameron Menzies; Screenplay: James Poe, John Farrow, S. J. Perelman; Based on the novel *Le Tour du monde en quatre-vingts* by Jules Verne; Musical Score: Victor Young; Director of Photography: Lionel Lindon; Film Editors: Howard Epstein, Gene Ruggiero; Casting: Frank Leyva, William White; Production Design: Ken Adam; Art Directors: James W. Sullivan, Ken Adam; Set Decorator: Ross Dowd; Costume Designers: Laure Lourie, Miles White; Hair Stylist: Edith Keon; Makeup: Gustaf Norin, John O'Gorman, Robert J. Schiffer, Yamada; Production Manager: Percy Guth; Assistant Directors: Dennis Bertara, Lew Borzage, Farley James; Second Unit Director: Kevin McClory; Second Unit Assistant Directors: Ronald R. Rondell; Property Master: Thomas Erley; Sound: Fred Hynes, Joseph I. Kane; Sound Editor: Theodore Bellinger; Music Editor: Charles Clement; Special Effects: Lee Zavitz; Stunts: Reginald C. Armor, Jr., Paul Baxley, Jerry Brown, Bob Burrows, Dick Crockett, Don Cunningham, Mario Dacal, Bob Folkerson, Bob Gordon, Sol Gorss, Joseph Goss, Tex Holden, Charles Horvath, Ace Hudkins, Alexander Jackson, Bert LeBaron, Boyd ("Red") Morgan, Charles Mosley, Eddie Parker, Gil Perkins, Walter Pietila, Allen Pinson, George Ross, Frosty Royce, Danny Sands, Audrey Saunders, Raymond Saunders, Russell Saunders, Clint Sharp, George Spotts, Buddy Van Horn, Dale Van Sickel, Frank Vincent, Bill White, Jr., Louis Williams, Bud Wolfe; Lyricists: Harold Adamson, Kurt Feltz, Gösta Rybrant; Titles: Saul Bass; Technical Advisers: C. R. Beard, Koichi Kawana, Schuyler A. Sanford; Stand-ins: Wanda Brown, Antonio Gutiérrez, Esteban Gutiérrez, Les Raymaster, Ed Scarpa, Virginia Whitmire, John Zuniga; Second Unit Directors of Photography: Ellis W. Carter, Stanley Horsley, William N. Williams; Stills Photographer: Robert D. Christie; Animated Titles Director: William T. Hurtz; Titles Animator: Shamus Culhane; Orchestrators: Sidney Cutner, Leo Shuken; Choreographer: Paul Godkin; Executive Secretaries: Richard Hanley, Midori Tsuji; Camera Operators: Graham Kelly, Harry Mimura; Unit Manager: Frank Kowalski; Executive Assistant: Samuel Lambert; Wardrobe Manager: Robert Martien; Researcher: Ann Perls; Assistant to Producer: Michael Todd, Jr.; Technical Consultant: Edward Williams; a Michael Todd Production; Released by United Artists Pictures; Running Time: 178 minutes.

Cast: David Niven (Phileas Fogg), Cantinflas (Passepartout), Shirley MacLaine (Princess Aouda), Robert Newton (Inspector Fix), Finlay Currie (Whist Partner), Robert Morley (Ralph), Ronald Squire (Reform Club Member), Basil Sydney (Reform Club Member), Noel Coward (Hesketh-Baggott), John Gielgud (Foster), Trevor Howard (Fallentin), Harcourt Williams (Hinshaw), Martine Carol (Tourist), Fernandel (Coachman), Charles Boyer (Monsieur Gasse), Evelyn Keyes (Flirt), José Greco (Dancer), Luis Miguel Dominguín (Bull-fighter), Gilbert Roland (Ahmed Abdullah), Cesar Romero (Ahmed Abdullah's Henchman), Alan Mowbray (Consul), Cedric Hardwicke (Sir Francis Gromarty), Melville Cooper (Steward), Reginald Denny (Police Chief), John Carradine (Col. Proctor Stamp), Ronald Colman, Charles Coburn, Peter Lorre, George Raft, Red Skelton, Marlene Dietrich, Frank Sinatra, Buster Keaton, Tim McCoy, Joe E. Brown, Andy Devine, Edmund Lowe, Victor McLaglen, Jack Oakie, Beatrice Lillie, John Mills, Glynis Johns, Hermione Gingold, Ava Gardner, Keye Luke, Mike Mazurki, Jack Mulhall, Philip Van Zandt, Dick Wessel (Cameos), Edward R. Murrow (Narrator), A. E. Matthews (Club Member), Casey MacGregor (Engineer), Shep Houghton (Specialty Dancer), Michael Trubshawe (Man Betting at Lloyd's), Abdullah Abbas, Leo Abbey, Charles Abraham, Dinah Ace, Rosemarie Ace, Boyd Ackerman, Panchita Acosta, Ronald Adam, Frances Adams, Jesse Adams, George Agawa, David Ahdar, Richard Aherne, Philip Ahn, Benny Ahuna, Fred Akahoshi, Carlos Albert, Gladys Alden, Fred Aldrich, Emil Alegata, Kurpan Ali, Lorey Allen, Sally Alonzo, Lupe Alvarado, Dick Ames, August Angelo, William Angelo, Ernest Aquilar, Ed Arbogast, Gene Ardell, Danny Aredas, Ray Armstrong, Ray Arnett, Larry Arnold, Russell Ash, Eula Asher, Gertrude Astor, Edward Astran, George Atsumo, Besmark Auelua, Aggie Auld, Irene Austin, Roy Aversa, Kaz Awai, Sande Aziko, Walter Bacon, Rama Bai, Al Bain, Leah Baird, Benjie Bancroft, Ralph Bara, Dick Barber, Bertha Barbier, Beverly Barker, Olga Barone, Salvadore Barroga, Robert Barry, Merril F. Bates, Mary Ellen Batten, E. Baucin, Angelina Bauer, Brandon Beach, Elena Beattie, Eugene Beday, Ivan Bell, Helen Benda, Eleanor Bender, Norma D. Bernhart, Alfred Berumen, Audrey Betz, Ongyue Big, Bobby Birchfiel, Cathy Ann Bissutti, Richard Bissutti, George Blagoi, Tina Blagoi, Eumenio Blanco, Oscar Blanke, Rosemary Blong, George Bloom, Phil Bloom, William Bloom, Toni Bond, Paul Bordman, Olga Borget, Danny Borzage, Hazel Boyne, Virginia Bradley, Mario Bramucci, Kahala Bray, John Breneman, Ernst Brengt, Kenneth Brischof, Mildred Brown, Wanda Brown, George Bruggeman, Phyllis Brunner, Helen Bruno, Guy Buccola, Joan Buckley, Al Buen, Jane Burgess, Ted Burgess, Betty Burns, Bob Burrows, Paul Busch, Boyd Cabeen, Eugene Cahn, Allen Calm, Ann Cameron, Joyce Cameron, John Carboni, Fred Carpenter, Mick Carr, Kit Carson, Dick Carter, Gordon Carveth, Danny Casabian, Marlene L. Caspari, Perta Castneda, Steve Cavalieri, Bert Cefali, Frank Ceniceros, Dorothy Chan, Douglas Chan, Eugene Chan, Jowe Chan, Lum Chan, Mary Chan, Ronald Chan, Spencer Chan, Suey Chan, Wong Hing Chan, Pauline Chang, Irene Chapman, Jack Chefe, Huaplala Cherie, Dick Cherney, Fon Chillson, May Chinn, Nina Chirva, Noble ("Kid") Chissel, Lee Chon, Margarite Chow, Beulah Christian, Elaine Leemoi Chu, Howard M. Chueng, Kui Sau Chui, Wong Chun, Bing Yee Chung, Jane Chung, Sue Fawn Chung, Martin Cichy, Michael Cirillo, Richard Dale Clark, Mary Lou Clifford, Walter Clinton, Bud Cokes, Louise Colombet, Anthony M. Conde, Kathy Connors, Connie Conrad, Miguel Contreras, Chabling Cooper, Jean Corbett, Wilson Cornell, Dolores Corral, Bárbara Correa, Bill Couch, Theresa Courtland, Lynne Craft, Paul Cristo, Catalina Cruz, Stuart W. Culp, Dorothy Curtis, Max Cutler, Gloria Dadisman, Ruth Dalbrook, Roy Damron, Anita Louise Dano, Edmund Dantez, Lawrence Daquila, Theresa Darling, Eddie Das, Richard Date, Serafin Davidoff, Jack Davidson, Jack Davies, Jack Davis, Robert Dayo, Louise De Carlo, Denise De Lacey, Rod De Medici, Angelo De Meo, Gabriel De Valle, Joe DeAngelo, Gloria DeWerd, Angela DeWitt, Gloria Dea, Diana Deane, John Deauville, Helen Dee, Deena, George Deere, Douglas Degioia, Maria Deglar, John Delgado, Maria Delgado, La Verne Dell, Jack Delrio, Rosita Delva, Emory Dennis, Gill Dennis, Harry Denny, Kathleen Desmond, Lala Detolly, Maya Kaur Dhillon, Marilyn Dialon, Sterling Dillard, James Dime, Franklin Dix, Edward Gary Dodds, Dolores Domasin, Robert Dominguez, William Dominguez, Barbara Donaldson, William Donnelly, Diane Dorsay, Julie Dorsey, Joe Dougherty, Al Dowling, Dan Dowling, Jack Downs, Fanny Drabin, Morris Drabin, Barbara Drake, Helene Drake, John Drake, Dewey Drapeau, Joe Draper, Alfonso Du Bois, Darren Dublin, Harry Duff, Arthur Dulac, Robert Dulaine, Gordon Dumont, Charles Dunbar, Renald Dupont, Larry Duran, William Duray, Minta Durfee, Andre K. Duval, Heidi Duval, Bob Dyer, Everett L. Eddy, Ina Edell, Michka Egan, Jerry Elliott, Jack Ellis, Richard Elmore, John Eloff, Calvin Emery, Ronald Eng, Helen Enriquez, Frank Erickson, Maude Erickson, Madge Erwin, Miguel Esquembre, Marcello Estorres, Bob Evans, Harry Evans, Joe Evans, Henry Faber, F. W. Fahrney, James Fakato, Antonio Farfan, Franklyn Farnum, Amir Farr, Margaret Farrell, Joseph C. Fay, Adolph Faylauer, Art Felix, Tony Fillion, Walter Findon, Sam Finn, John Fioff, Carlo Fiore, Bess Flowers, Ray Flynn, Charles Fogel, Gene Foley, Clarence Fong, Richard Fong, Yut Man Fong, Raymond Fontes, Otto Forrest, Helen Foster, Harold Francis, Jess Franco, Oscar Freeburg, Milton Freibrun, Wilma Friedman, John Fritz, Shilia Fritz, Ben Frommer, Virginia Fuentes, Janice Fujinani,

Koshihiro Fukdo, Jay Fuller, Sumi Funo, Curt Furburg, John Furukawa, M. Furukawa, Yoneka Furukawa, Carol Ann Gainey, Michael Gainey, Juliana Galic, Al Gallagher, Elias Gamboa, Charles Garcia, Diana Garrison, Robert Garvin, Mark Gates, Edward Gee, June Gee, Toc Yee Gee, Wong Kim Gee, Wayne Geer, Anita Gegna, Carine A. Generaux, John George, Myers George, Jay Gerard, Rudolph Germane, Curley Gibson, Elaine Gilbert, Joe Gilbert, Leon Gill, H. D. Gin, Njon Tuey Gin, Stephen Ginn, Jr., May Ginn, Noreen Ginn, Kay Ginoza, Wong Git, Howard C. Glasson, Mary Ellen Gleason, Betty J. Glennie, Joseph Glick, June Glory, Albert Godderis, Joe Gold, Roy Goldman, Angela Gomez, Mar Suey Gong, Quon Gong, Soledad Gonzales, Alex Gonzalez, Charles Gonzalez, James Gonzalez, Armando González, Carmelita González, Fernando González, Allen Goode, Alora Gooding, Verne Goodrich, Lee Teu Gook, Dick Gordon, Eve Gordon, Ruth Gordon, Mickey Gotanda, Oxy Goto, Violet Goulet, William Graeff, Jr., Ann Graeff, Betty Graeff, Rita Graeff, Joan Graffeo, Herschel Graham, Grace Grant, Valeri Gratton, Donald Gray, Eleanora Norina Greco, Suzanne Greco, David Greene, David Greenwood, Dolly Grey, Karla Gribbel, B. Pat Groom, Vic Groves, Edward Grubb, Kit Guard, Edward A. Guerra, Jesus Guerra, Tenmana Guerra, Marilyn Gustafson, Paul Gustine, Georgina Gutierrez, Edward Ha, Herman Hack, Robert Haines, Betty Hall, Stuart Hall, Chick Hannon, Maria Haro, Silver Harr, Sam Harris, Louis Hart, James Hasagawa, George Hashimoto, Gus Hashimoto, Al Haskell, Lauren Hastings, William Hayden, Frank Heaney, Charles Heard, Shirley Heart, Bonnie Henjum, Charles Hennecke, Clarence Hennecke, Robert Hennes, Lars Hensen, George Hickman, Charles Hicks, George Higa, Sue Hikawa, Jimmy Hing, Yoshio Hiraga, Kimiko Hiroshige, Hiroshi Hisamune, Fun Ho, Harlan Hoagland, Lee Yuen Hock, Yoshyo Hohamura, Tex Holden, Stuart Holmes, Syd Holtby, Yee Jock Hom, Kenny Homabe, Midori Homano, Lee Kim Hong, Janice Hood, Hans Hopf, James Horan, John Hoskin, Ken Hovey, Gladys Howe, Lee Yuen Hoy, Madelon Hubbard, Clyde Hudkins, Jr., Warren Huff, Tom Humphrey, Frank Hunt, S. Iguchi, Yoneo Iguchi, Joe Iino, Taruko Ikari, Kazuo Ikida, Kay Imamura, Omaru Imazaki, John Impolito, David Inez, Vi Ingraham, Leona Irvin, Merrill C. Isbell, Yoshio Ishibashi, Tom Ishikura, Ray Ishimatsu, Kinuko Ann Ito, Roy Iwaki, Jacqueline Jackler, Diane Jackson, Marjorie Jackson, Allen Jaffe, Charles James, Idell James, Robert James, Mary Jan, Sushila Janadas, Gerald Jann, William Janssen, Dolly Jarvis, Michael Jeffers, Joan Jerrae, Robert Jewett, Dee Ho Joe, Edgar W. Johnson, Leroy Johnson, Dick Johnstone, Todd Joko, Freda Jones, Joanne Jones, Myra Jones, Sallie Jones, Winfield Jones, Madge Journeay, Raymond Joyer, S. S. Jung, Fred Kajikawa, Gee Toy Kam, Yukimi Kamaka, Joe Kameshita, Stanley Kamijama, Ken Kane, Madelynne Kane, Mary Kane, Morris Kaneshire, Mamie Karaki, Harvey Karels, Bo Peep Karlin, Harumi Kashaka, Ken Kato, George Katsuhiro, George Kawashima, Tak Kawashima, Sugar Willi Keeler, Valentine Kekipi, Jodi Kelley, Joan Kelly, Fannie Kennerly, Jack Kenney, Eleanor Kent, Johnny Kern, Joseph Gee Key, Al Kikume, Allan Kila, John Kim, Anita King, Brian King, Grace King, Judith A. Kinnon, Ken Kinoshita, Shinya Kito, Max Kleven, Marlene Kloss, Frank Kneeland, William J. Kolberg, King Kong, Bob Konno, James Kono, Harry Koshi, Katy Koury, Akira Koyama, Tom Koyama, Gladys Kress, Paul Kruger, Jack Krupnick, Jo Ngau Kum, Ann Kunde, Roy Kuochi, Wally Kushinaejo, Wallace Kusumajo, George Kuwashige, Sumiyo Kuwashige, Jeung Lai Kwong, Richard LaMarr, June LaVere, Lita Laceman, Paul Lacy, Clyde Ladd, Jeanne Lafayette, Webster Lagrange, Laura Lamb, Connie Lamont, Alfredo Landa, Cherokee Landrum, Frank Lane, Warren Lane, Frances Lara, Manuel Laraneta, Jean Larson, Lydia Latzke, Gustave Lax, Park Lazelle, B. M. Lee, Bik Yuk Lee, Esther Ying Lee, Fee Loon Lee, Foo Lee, Gee Sho Lee, Harold Lee, Jack Lee, Margaret Lee, Nelson Lee, Ng Jung Lee, Norman Lee, Richard Goon Lee, Teng Kem Lee, Tommy Lee, Virginia Lee, Charles Legneur, Lewellyn Lem, Christopher Leng, Marian Leng, Marrilee Leng, Jeanne Lennox, Frank Leonard, Peggy Leonard, Rita Leonard, Johnny Leone, Rose Leong, Harry Leroy, Lillian Leroy, Carl M. Leviness, Mabel Lew, Shirley Lew, William H. Lewin, John Lewis, Eleanor Lexaber, James Leyton, Baron James Lichter, Amelia Liggett, David Lim, Gin Lim, Sing Lim, Geraldine Lindsay, Quong Ling, Yee Suey Ling, King Lockwood, Dale Logue, Kwong You Loo, Tu Duck Look, Caroline Lopez, Richard Lopez, Robert Loraine, Marie Loredo, Billy Louie, Donald Louie, James Louie, Marygold Louie, Wilbert Louie, Louise Loureau, Harry Lowe, Jr., Wai Lue, Cop Lum, David Lum, Pauline Lum, Marco López, Bessie Ma, Bruce MacCallister, Duncan MacDonell, Michael Macey, Ann Macomber, Celeste Madamba, Ralph Madlener, T. Maeshiro, Roy Maeua, Guadelope Malasig, Cy Malis, Shoji Malyama, Tela Mansfield, Max Manues, Joseph Marievsky, Ramon Marintz, Joseph Mariunsky, Johnny Marlin, Rena Marlin, Sandee Marriott, Gloria Marshall, Joseph Marsico, Rickey Martin, Thomas F. Martin, Carlos Martinez, Mary D. Mascari, Rudy Masson, Nita Mathews, Peter Mathews, John Matsutani, Mack Mauda, Dorothy May, George Mayon, Ila McAvoy, Angelita McCall, David O. McCall, Glenn McCarthy, Frank McClure, Frank McComas, Robert McCrady, Robert F. McElroy, Donald McGuire, Bob McGurk, Lanie McIntyre, Sylvia McKaye, Dorcas McKim, Rowena McNamara, William Meada, Rudolph Medina, Russell Meeker, Marie Melish, Ann Merman, Tommy Merrill, Sam A. Mides, Harold Miller, Frank Mills, Bob Milton, Tom Mishimoto, Lennie Mitchell, Tameo Mitsunaga, Mary Miyaji, Henry Miyamoto, Helen Miyarahara, Luther Mizukami, Irene Mizushima, Sam Mizushima, King

Mohjave, James Mohlmann, Jr., Joe Molina, William Monahan, Maria Monay, Marion Monsour, Beverly Mook, Lee Kai Moon, Earl Moore, Zelinda Mora, Ralph Moratz, Ernesto Morelli, Mike Morelli, Linda Moreno, Clive Morgan, Patricia Morgan, Evelyn Moriarty, Thomas Morita, Shiegeyo Moriyama, Patricia Morris, Charles Morton, Shirley Motonada, Kai Motowaki, Man Ho Moy, Thomas Mullen, Inez Murakami, Jan Murakami, Sol Murgi, Joe Murphy, Tessie Murray, Thomas Murray, Mike Musso, Stevie Myers, Satya Nanda Nag, Frank Nagai, Hiro Nakado, Kico Nakado, Kisabaro Nakado, Tsunesuki Nakado, Joe Nakai, Charles Nakamura, Mary Nakamura, Fred Nakano, Kay Nakashihma, Ken Nakasoni, Frank E. Naley, George Nardelli, Aurora Navarro, Myra Nelson, Augie Neves, Stewart Newmark, H.,B. Newton, Irving Fig Newton, Ngai Foo Ng, Woo Shee Ng, Charles Nickum, William Nind, Keiko Ninura, Shizuko Nishida, Bob Nishihar, Ray Noda, Lynn Noe, Joseph Nordon, Anton Northpole, Barry Norton, Faye Michael Nuell, Daniel Núñez, Jack Perrin, Bob Reeves, Buddy Roosevelt, John Fox Stone (Extras), Walter Fitzgerald, Hung Choy Shih, Joseph Garcio, Robert McNulty, Frank Baker, Alex Ball, Bernie Gozier, John Benson, Leon Bouvard, R. Brodie, Donald Brown, Ollie Brown, Theona Bryant, J. W. Burr, Robert Cabal, Patrick Cargill, Al Cavens, Fred Cavens, Neil Collins, Cecil Combs, Louis Cortina, Campbell Cotts, Ashley Cowan, Roy Darmour, Anna De Linsky, Amapola Del Vando, Leslie Denison, Clint Dorrington, Joan Dyer, Mitchell Dylong, Elaine Earl, Ed Edmonson, Carli Elinor, Felix Felton, Duke Fishman, Frances Fong, Raoul Freeman, Tommy Fujiwara, Fernando García, Israel García, Harry Gilette, Arthur Gould-Porter, Ralph Grosh, Sei Jeri Groves, Cameron Hall, Chuck Hamilton, Mahgoub Hanaf, Maria Hanson, Doc Harnett, Chester Hayes, David B. Hughes, Roddy Hughes, Paul King, Walter Kingsford, Ben Knight, Frederick Leister, Freddie Letuli, Weaver Levy, Richard Loo, Joan Lora, Manuel López, N. Macowen, D. Ellsworth Manning, Dewey Manning, Harry Mayo, Lorion Miller, Bob Okazaki, Manuel París, James Porter, Satini Pualoa, Amando Rodriguez, Frank Royde, George Russell, Jim Salisbury, Sohi Shannon, Bill Shine, Bhogwan Singh, Alvin Slaight, Fred O. Sommers, Owen Kyoon Song, Janet Sterke, Ward Thompson, Frank Vessels, Jr., Al Walton, Richard Wattis

The Pride and the Passion (June 1957)
Credits: Director and Producer: Stanley Kramer; Screenplay: Edna Anhalt, Edward Anhalt, Earl Felton; Based on the novel *The Gun* by C. S. Forester; Musical Score: George Antheil; Director of Photography: Franz Planer; Film Editors: Ellsworth Hoagland, Frederic Knudtson; Production Designer: Rudolph Sternad; Art Directors: Fernando Carrere, Gil Parrondo; Costume Designer: Joe King; Hair Stylist: Grazia De Rossi; Makeup: John O'Gorman, Bernard Ponedel, José María Sánchez; Production Manager: Stanley Goldsmith; Production Supervisor: Ivan Volkman; Assistant Directors: Alfonso Acebal, Isidoro M. Ferry, José María Ochoa; Supervising Assistant Director: Carter De Haven, Jr.; Property Master: Art Cole; Sound: Joseph de Bretagne; Sound Effects: Walter Elliott, Bates Mason; Special Effects: Maurice Ayers, Willis Cook; Titles: Saul Bass; Associate Cameraman: Manuel Berenguer; Military Advisor: Luis Cano; Script Supervisor: John Franco; Production Liaisons: Eduardo García, Fernando Navarro, Augustin Pastor, Hank Werba; Musical Conductor: Ernest Gold; Dialogue Supervisor: Anne P. Kramer; Camera Operator: Fred Mandl; Animal Coach: Bob Miles; Choreographer: Paco Reyes; Company Grip: Morris Rosen; Chief Gaffer: Don Stott; Locations: Toledo, Spain; a Stanley Kramer Production; Released by United Artists Pictures; Running Time: 132 minutes.
Cast: Cary Grant (Anthony), Frank Sinatra (Miguel), Sophia Loren (Juana), Theodore Bikel (General Jouvet), John Wengraf (Germaine), Jay Novello (Gallinger), José Nieto (Carlos), Carlos Larrañaga (José), Philip Van Zandt (Fidal), Paco El Laberinto (Manolo), Julián Ugarte (Enrique), Félix de Pomés (Bishop), Carlos Casaravilla (Leonardo), Juan Olaguivel (Ramón), Nana DeHerrera (María), Carlos De Mendoza (Francisco), Luis Guedes (French Soldier), Bernabe Barta Barri (Xan das Bolas), Alfonso Suárez.

The Joker Is Wild (August 1957)
Credits: Director: Charles Vidor; Producer: Samuel J. Briskin; Screenplay: Oscar Saul; Based on the book *The Life of Joe E. Lewis* by Art Cohn; Musical Score: Harry Harris; Original Songs: Walter Scharf, Sammy Cahn, Jimmy Van Heusen; Director of Photography: Daniel L. Fapp; Film Editor: Everett Douglas; Art Directors: Roland Anderson, Hal Pereira; Set Decorators: Sam Comer, Grace Gregory; Costume Designer: Edith Head; Hair Stylist: Nellie Manley; Makeup: Wally Westmore; Assistant Director: Charles C. Coleman; Sound: Charles Grenzbach, Harold Lewis; Choreographer: Josephine Earl; Special Photographic Effects: John P. Fulton; Orchestrators: Jack Hayes, Nelson Riddle, Leo Shuken; Musical Director: Walter Scharf; an A.M.B.L. Production; Released by Paramount Pictures; Running Time: 126 minutes.
Cast: Frank Sinatra (Joe E. Lewis), Mitzi Gaynor (Martha Stewart), Jeanne Crain (Letty Page), Eddie Albert (Austin Mack), Beverly Garland (Cassie Mack), Jackie Coogan (Swifty Morgan), Barry Kelley (Captain Hugh McCarthy), Ted de Corsia (Georgie Parker), Leonard Graves (Tim Coogan), Valerie Allen (Flora), Hank Henry (Burlesque Comedian), Eric Alden (Doorman at the Copacabana), Don Beddoe, Wally Brown,

The Actor, on Screen and in Song

Paul Bryar, Mary Treen (Hecklers), John Benson (Mug), James Cavanaugh (Straight Man), James Cross (Jack), Joseph Donte, Paul Gary, Ralph Montgomery, Billy Snyder (Men in Hotel Suite), Dick Elliott (Man Shaving), Ruby Fleming (Girl), Ned Glass (Johnson), Kit Guard (Doorman at the Valencia), John Harding (Allen), Maurice Hart (Squawk Box Voice), Bill Hickman (Mug), Paula Hill (Burlesque Girl), Harold Huber (Harry Bliss), Walter Woolf King (Mr. Page), Lucy Knoch (Girl), Oliver McGowan (Judge), Dennis McMullen (Photographer), Sid Melton (Runner), Frank Mills (Florist Truck Driver), George Offerman (Elevator Starter), William Pullen (Letty's Husband), Mabel Rea (Chorus Girl), Paul Salata (Mug), Harriette Tarler (Burlesque Girl), Sophie Tucker (Herself), Ned Wever (Doctor Pierson), Eric Wilton (Butler), Robert Asquith, Bill Baldwin, Sr., Russ Bender, Billie Bird, Fred Catania, Joe Gray, Larry Knight, Ned Le Fevre, Arthur Lewis, Leon Martin, Arturo Petterino, David Siegel.

Pal Joey (October 25, 1957)
Credits: Director: George Sidney; Producer: Fred Kohlmar; Screenplay: Dorothy Kingsley; Based on the play byJohn O'Hara; Musical Score: George Duning, Nelson Riddle; Original Songs: Richard Rodgers, Lorenz Hart; Director of Photography: Harold Lipstein; Film Editors: Viola Lawrence, Jerome Thoms; Art Director: Walter Holscher; Set Decorators: Louis Diage, William Kiernan; Costume Designer: Jean Louis; Hair Stylist: Helen Hunt; Makeup: Ben Lane, Robert J. Schiffer; Assistant Director: Arthur S. Black, Jr.; Sound: Franklin Hansen; First Assistant Camera: Albert Bettcher; Technicolor Consultant: Henri Jaffa; Recording Director: John P. Livadary; Orchestrator: Arthur Morton; Choreographer: Hermes Pan; Musical Director: Morris Stoloff; an Essex-George Sidney Production; Released by Columbia Pictures; Running Time: 111 minutes.
Cast: Rita Hayworth (Vera Simpson), Frank Sinatra (Joey Evans), Kim Novak (Linda English), Barbara Nichols (Gladys), Bobby Sherwood (Ned Galvin), Hank Henry (Mike Miggins), Elizabeth Patterson (Mrs. Casey), Leon Alton (Printer Salesman), Robert Anderson (Policeman), Maurice Argent (Tailor), Tol Avery (Detective), Rita Barrett (Stripper), Eddie Bartell (Barker), Steve Benton (Electrician), Barry Bernard (Anderson), Gail Bonney (Heavyset Woman), Sue Boomer (Secretary), Paul Cesari (Pet Store Co-Owner), George Chan (Chinese Pianist), Sydney Chatton (Barker), Nellie Gee Ching (Chinese Dancer), Jane Chung (Flower Lady), Jean Corbett (Dancer), Oliver Cross (Bit), Giselle D'Arc (Maid), Judy Dan (Hat Check Girl), Jules Davis (Red-Faced Man), George De Normand (Bit), Helen Elliot (Travelers' Aid), Franklyn Farnum (Person), Elizabeth Fenton (Chinese Dancer), Michael Ferris (Tailor), Bess Flowers (Person), George Ford (Electrician), Allen Gin (Chinese Drummer), Everett Glass (Pet Store Owner), Bob Glenn (Sailor), Connie Graham (Stripper), Bobbie Jean Henson (Stripper), John Hubbard (Stanley), Ellie Kent (Carol), Cheryl Kubert (Girl Friend), Pat Lynn (Chinese Dancer), Ramon Martinez (Headwaiter), Mara McAfee (Sabrina), Henry McCann (Shorty), Raymond A. McWalters (Army Captain), Joe Miksak (Barker), Ernesto Molinari (Tony the Chef), Robin Morse (Bartender), Jean Nakaba (Chinese Dancer), Al Nalbandian (Barker), George Nardelli (Headwaiter), Bek Nelson (Lola), Ilsa Ostroffsky (Stripper), Hermes Pan (Choreographer), Roberto Piperio (Waiter), Edith Powell (Stripper), Jack Railey (Hot Dog Vendor), Robert Rietz (Boy Friend), Hermie Rose (Bald Club Owner), James Seay (Livingston), Howard Sigrist (Sidewalk Photographer), Jo Ann Smith (Stripper), Genie Stone (Girl), Frank Sully (Barker), Betty Utey (Patsy), Pierre Watkin (Mr. Forsythe), Frank Wilcox (Colonel Langley), Frank Wilimarth (Sidewalk Artist), Andrew Wong (Chinese Club Owner), Lessie Lynne Wong (Chinese Dancer), Barbara Yung (Chinese Dancer), Isabel Analla.

Kings Go Forth (June 1958)
Credits: Director: Delmer Daves; Producer: Frank Ross; Screenplay: Merle Miller; Based on the novel by Joe David Brown; Musical Score: Elmer Bernstein; Director of Photography: Daniel L. Fapp; Supervising Editor: William B. Murphy; Casting: Lynn Stalmaster; Production Designer: Fernando Carrere; Costume Designer: Leah Rhodes; Makeup: Bernard Ponedel; Production Manager: Richard McWhorter; Assistant Director: Edward O. Denault; Property Master: Darrell Silvera; Orchestrators: Jack Hayes, Leo Shuken; Musicians: Red Norvo (vibraphone), Pete Candoli (trumpet), Richie Kamuca (tenor saxophone), Jimmy Weible (guitar), Red Wooten (bass), Mel Lewis (drums); a Frank Ross-Eton Production; Released by United Artists Pictures; Running Time: 109 minutes.
Cast: Frank Sinatra (1st Lieutenant Sam Loggins), Tony Curtis (Corporal Britt Harris), Natalie Wood (Monique Blair), Leora Dana (Mrs. Blair), Karl Swenson (Lieutenant Colonel), Anne Codee (Madame Brieux), Edward Ryder (Corporal Lindsay), Jacques Berthe (Jean-François), Pete Candoli (Musician), Marie Isnard (Old Woman with Wine), Red Norvo (Musician).

Some Came Running (December 1958)
Credits: Director: Vincente Minnelli; Producer: Sol C. Siegel; Screenplay: John Patrick, Arthur Sheekman; Based on the novel by James Jones; Musical Score: Elmer Bernstein; Original Song: Sammy Cahn, Jimmy

Van Heusen; Director of Photography: William H. Daniels; Film Editor: Adrienne Fazan; Art Directors: William A. Horning, Urie McCleary; Set Decorators: Henry Grace, Robert Priestley; Costume Designer: Walter Plunkett; Makeup: William Tuttle; Assistant Director: William McGarry; Technicolor Consultant: Charles K. Hagedon; Sound: Franklin Milton; Locations: Hanover and Madison, Indiana/Milton, Kentucky; Released by Metro-Goldwyn-Mayer Pictures; Running Time: 127 minutes.

Cast: Frank Sinatra (Dave Hirsh), Dean Martin (Bama Dillert), Shirley MacLaine (Ginny Moorhead), Martha Hyer (Gwen French), Arthur Kennedy (Frank Hirsh), Nancy Gates (Edith Barclay), Leora Dana (Agnes Hirsh), Betty Lou Keim (Dawn Hirsh), Larry Gates (Professor Robert Haven French), Steven Peck (Raymond Lanchak), Carmen Phillips (Rosalie), Connie Gilchrist (Jane Barclay), Ned Wever (Smitty), Jan Arvan (Club Manager), George Brengel (Ned Deacon), John Brennan (Wally Dennis), George Cisar (Hubie Nelson), Chuck Courtney (Hotel Clerk), Roy Engel (Sheriff), Don Haggerty (Ted Harperspoon), Anthony Jochim (Judge Baskin), Paul Jones (George Huff), Donald Kerr (Dr. Henderson), Harold Lakeman (Extra), Len Lesser (Dealer), William Lockridge (Bus Driver), Denny Miller (Dewey Cole), Frank Mitchell (Waiter), Janelle Richards (Virginia Stevens), Ric Roman (Joe), Marion Ross (Sister Mary Joseph), William Schallert (Al), George E. Stone (Slim), Albert T. Viola (Guitarist), Geraldine Wall (Mrs. Stevens), Dave White (Bus Driver), Diane Signore, John Wurtz (Extras), Joe Gray.

A Hole in the Head (July 15, 1959)
Credits: Director and Producer: Frank Capra; Executive Producer: Frank Sinatra; Screenplay: Arnold Schulman, based on his play; Musical Score: Nelson Riddle; Original Songs: Sammy Cahn, James Van Heusen; Director of Photography: William H. Daniels; Film Editor: William Hornbeck; Art Director: Eddie Imazu; Set Decorator: Fred M. MacLean; Costume Designer: Edith Head; Hair Stylist: Helene Parrish; Makeup: Bernard Ponedel; Production Manager: Joe Cook; Assistant Directors: Jack R. Berne, Arthur S. Black, Jr.; Sound: Fred Lau; Orchestrator: Arthur Morton; Locations: Cypress Gardens and Miami Beach, Florida; a Sin-Cap Production; Released by United Artists Pictures; Running Time: 120 minutes.

Cast: Frank Sinatra (Tony Manetta), Edward G. Robinson (Mario Manetta), Eleanor Parker (Eloise Rogers), Carolyn Jones (Shirl), Thelma Ritter (Sophie Manetta), Keenan Wynn (Jerry Marks), Eddie Hodges (Ally Manetta), Joi Lansing (Dorine), Connie Sawyer (Miss Wexler), James Komack (Julius Manetta), Dub Taylor (Fred the Clerk), George DeWitt (Mendy Yales), Benny Rubin (Mr. Diamond), Ruby Dandridge (Sally), B. S. Pulley (Hood), Joyce Nizzari (Alice, Jerry's Secretary), Pupi Campo (Master of Ceremonies), Emory Parnell (Sheriff), Bill Walker (Andy the Handyman), Robert Williams (Cabby).

Never So Few (December 1959)
Credits: Director: John Sturges; Producer: Edmund Grainger; Screenplay: Millard Kaufman; Based on the novel by Tom T. Chamales; Musical Score: Hugo Friedhofer; Director of Photography: William H. Daniels; Film Editor: Ferris Webster; Art Directors: Addison Hehr, Hans Peters; Set Decorators: Henry Grace, Richard Pefferle; Costume Designer: Helen Rose; Hair Stylist: Sydney Guilaroff; Makeup: William Tuttle; Assistant Directors: Hank Moonjean, Robert E. Relyea; Special Effects: Robert R. Hoag, Lee LeBlanc; Technicolor Consultant: Charles K. Hagedon; Sound: Franklin Milton; Musical Conductor: Charles Wolcott; Locations: Burma, Sri Lanka, Thailand; a Canterbury Production; Released by Metro-Goldwyn-Mayer Pictures; Running Time: 124 minutes.

Cast: Frank Sinatra (Tom Reynolds), Gina Lollobrigida (Carla Vesari), Peter Lawford (Captain Grey Travis), Steve McQueen (Bill Ringa), Richard Johnson (Captain Danny De Mortimer), Paul Henreid (Nikko Regas), Brian Donlevy (General Sloan), Dean Jones (Sergeant Jim Norby), Charles Bronson (Sergeant John Danforth), Philip Ahn (Nautaung), Robert Bray (Colonel Fred Parkson), Kipp Hamilton (Margaret Fitch), John Hoyt (Colonel Reed), Whit Bissell (Captain Alofson), Richard Lupino (Mike Island), Aki Aleong (Billingsly), Ross Elliott (Dr. Barry), James Hong (Ambassador), Leon Lontoc (Laurel), Maggie Pierce (Nurse), George Takei (Soldier in Hospital), William Smith.

Can-Can (March 9, 1960)
Credits: Director: Walter Lang; Producer: Jack Cummings; Associate Producer: Saul Chaplin; Screenplay: Dorothy Kingsley, Charles Lederer; Based on the play by Abe Burrows; Musical Score: Nelson Riddle; Original Songs: Cole Porter; Director of Phorography: William H. Daniels; Film Editor: Robert L. Simpson; Art Directors: Jack Martin Smith, Lyle R. Wheeler; Set Decorators: Paul S. Fox, Walter M. Scott; Costume Designer: Irene Sharaff; Makeup: Ben Nye; Hair Stylist: Myrl Stoltz; Assistant Director: Joseph E. Rickards; Sound: W.D. Flick, Fred Hynes; Technicolor Consultant: Leonard Doss; Styling Consultant: Tony Duquette; Titles: Tom Keogh; Choreographer: Hermes Pan; Vocal Supervisor: Robert Tucker; a Suffolk-Cummings Production; Released by 20th Century-Fox Pictures; Running Time: 130 minutes.

Cast: Frank Sinatra (François Durnais), Shirley MacLaine (Simone Pistache), Maurice Chevalier (Paul Barriere), Louis Jourdan (Philipe Forrestier), Juliet Prowse (Claudine), Marcel Dalio (Andre, Headwaiter), Leon Belasco (Arturo, Orchestra Leader), Nestor Paiva (Bailiff), John A. Neris (Photographer), Jean Del Val (Judge Merceaux), Ann Codee (League President), Geneviève Aumont (Secretary), Eugene Borden (Chevrolet), Carole Bryan (Gigi), Charles Carmen (Knife Thrower), Barbara Carter (Camille), Peter Coe (Dupont, Policeman), Marcel De la Brosse (Plainclothesman), Nicole Desbrosses (Jane Earl), Renee Ruth Earl (Julie), Laura Fraser (Germaine), Renee Godfrey (Dowager), Jonathan Kidd (Recorder), Edward Le Veque (Judge), Vera Lee (Gabrielle), Ambrogio Malerba (Apache Dancer), Maurice Marsac (Bailiff), Alphonse Martell (Butler), Lisa Mitchell (Fifi), Wanda Shannon (Maxine), Wilda Taylor (Lili), Darlene Tittle (Giselle), Lili Valenty (Dowager), Marc Wilder (Adam).

Ocean's Eleven (August 10, 1960)
Credits: Director and Producer: Lewis Milestone; Associate Producer: Henry W. Sanicola; Screenplay: Harry Brown, Charles Lederer; Original Story: George Clayton Johnson, Jack Golden Russell; Musical Score: Nelson Riddle; Original Songs: Sammy Cahn, James Van Heusen; Director of Photography: William H. Daniels; Film Editor: Philip W. Anderson; Art Director: Nicolai Remisoff; Set Decorator: Howard Bristol; Costume Designer: Howard Shoup; Makeup: Gordon Bau, Robert J. Schiffer; Production Manager: Jack R. Berne; Assistant Director: Ray Gosnell, Jr.; Sound: M. A. Merrick; Titles: Saul Bass; Titles Director: William T. Hurtz; Production Assistant: Dick Benedict; Orchestrator: Arthur Morton; Locations: Las Vegas, Nevada; a Dorchester Production; Released by Warner Bros.; Running Time: 127 minutes.
Cast: Frank Sinatra (Danny Ocean), Dean Martin (Sam Harmon), Sammy Davis, Jr. (Josh Howard), Peter Lawford (Jimmy Foster), Angie Dickinson (Beatrice Ocean), Richard Conte (Anthony Bergdorf), Cesar Romero (Duke Santos), Patrice Wymore (Adele Ekstrom), Joey Bishop (Mushy O'Connors), Akim Tamiroff (Spyros Acebos), Henry Silva (Roger Carneal), Ilka Chase (Mrs. Restes), Buddy Lester (Vince Massler), Richard Benedict (Curly Stephans), Jean Willes (Mrs. Bergdorf), Norman Fell (Peter Reimer), Clem Harvey (Louis Jackson), Hank Henry (Mr. Kelly), Lew Gallo (Jealous Young Man), Robert Foulk (Sheriff), Red Skelton (Himself), George Raft (Jack Strager), Murray Alper (Deputy), Don ("Red") Barry (McCoy), Marjorie Bennett (Customer), Rummy Bishop (Castleman), Nicky Blair (Gangster), Paul Bryar (Cop), Laura Cornell (Honeyface), John Craven (Cashier), Ronnie Dapo (Timmy), West Gale (Red Cap), Gregory Gaye (Freeman), Hoot Gibson (Roadblock Deputy), Joe Gray (Barber), John Holland (Man), John Indrisano (Texan), William Justine (Parelli), Sparky Kaye (Riviera Manager), Forrest Lederer (Sands Manager), Pinky Lee (Himself), Shirley MacLaine (Tipsy Girl), Charles Meredith (Mr. Cohen), Tom Middleton (TV Newscaster), Anne Neyland (Dolores), Red Norvo (Vibraphonist), Steve Pendleton (Major Taylor), Carmen Phillips (Hungry Girl), Louis Quinn (DeWolfe), Shiva (Snake Dancer), Joan Staley (Helen), Barbara Sterling (Girl), George E. Stone (Proprietor), Jerry Velasco (Harmonica Playing Garbage Man).

Pepe (December 1960)
Credits: Director and Producer: George Sidney; Associate Producer: Jacques Gelman; Screenplay: Claude Binyon, Dorothy Kingsley; Original Story: Sonya Levien, Leonard Spigelgass; Based on the play *Broadway Magic* by Leslie Bush-Fekete; Musical Score: Johnny Green, Maria Teresa Lara, André Previn, Dory Previn; Director of Photography: Joseph MacDonald; Film Editors: Al Clark, Viola Lawrence; Production Designer: Ted Haworth; Set Decorator: William Kiernan; Costume Designer: Edith Head; Sound: James Z. Flaster, Charles J. Rice; First Assistant Camera: Albert Bettcher; Musical Supervisor: Johnny Green; Choreographers: Eugene Loring, Alex Romero; a G.S.-Posa International Films Production; Released by Columbia Pictures; Running Time: 195 minutes.
Cast: Cantinflas (Pepe), Dorothy Abbott (Girl), James Bacon (Bartender), Steve Baylor (Parking Attendant), Stephen Bekassy (Jewelry Salesman), Lela Bliss (Dowager), John Burnside (Parking Attendant), Michael Callan (Dancer), Steve Carruthers (Bit Part), James Cavanaugh (Dealer), Dan Dailey (Ted Holt), Shirley DeBurgh (Dancer), William Demarest (Movie Studio Gateman), Carol Douglas (Waitress), Bonnie Green (Dancer), Hank Henry (Manager), Joe Hyams (Charro), Shirley Jones (Suzie Murphy), Kenner G. Kemp (Bit), Ernie Kovacs (Immigration Inspector), David Landfield (Announcer's Voice), Suzanne Lloyd (Carmen), Jeanne Manet (French Woman), Matt Mattox (Dancer), Carlos Montalbán (Rodriquez, the Auctioneer), Margie Nelson (Patron), Jay North (Dennis the Menace), Francisco Reiguera (Priest), Freddie Roberto (Cashier), Billy Snyder (Bit Part), Vicki Trickett (Lupita), Ray Walker (Assistant Director), Jim Waters (Bit Part), Robert Williams (Immigration Officer), Joey Bishop, Billie Burke, Maurice Chevalier, Charles Coburn, Richard Conte, Bing Crosby, Tony Curtis, Bobby Darin, Sammy Davis, Jr., Ann B. Davis, Jimmy Durante, Jack Entratter, E. E. Fogelson, Zsa Zsa Gabor, Judy Garland, Greer Garson, Hedda Hopper, Don Jaun, Peter Lawford, Janet

Leigh, Jack Lemmon, Dean Martin, Kim Novak, André Previn, Donna Reed, Debbie Reynolds, Carlos Rivas, Edward G. Robinson, Jane Robinson, Cesar Romero, Frank Sinatra, Bunny Waters (Cameos).

The Devil at Four O'Clock (October 18, 1961)

Credits: Director: Mervyn LeRoy; Producers: Mervyn LeRoy, Fred Kohlmar; Screenplay: Liam O'Brien; Based on the novel by Max Catto; Musical Score: George Duning; Director of Photography: Joseph F. Biroc; Film Editor: Charles Nelson; Production Designer and Art Director: John Beckman; Set Decorator: Louis Diarge; Makeup: Ben Lane, Robert J. Schiffer; Production Manager: Milton Feldman; Assistant Directors: Carter De Haven, Jr., Floyd Joyer; Sound: Charles J. Rice, J. S. Westmoreland; Special Effects: Willis Cook; Musical Conductor: Arthur Morton; Locations: Lahaina, Maui, Hawaii; Released by Columbia Pictures; Running Time: 126 minutes.

Cast: Spencer Tracy (Father Matthew Doonan), Frank Sinatra (Harry), Kerwin Mathews (Father Joseph Perreau), Jean-Pierre Aumont (Jacques), Grégoire Aslan (Marcel), Alexander Scourby (The Governor), Barbara Luna (Camille), Cathy Lewis (Matron), Bernie Hamilton (Charlie), Martin Brandt (Doctor Wexler), Louis Merrill (Aristide), Marcel Dalio (Gaston), Tom Middleton (Paul), Ann Duggan (Clarisse), Louis Mercier (Corporal), Michele Montau (Margot), Nanette Tanaka (Fleur), Tony Maxwell (Antoine), Jean Del Val (Louis), Moki Hana (Sonia), Warren Hsieh (Napoleon), William Keaulani (Constable), "Lucky" Luck (Captain Olsen), Norman Wright (Fouquette), Robin Shimatsu (Marianne), Momi Blackburn (Hawaiian Girl), Eugene Borden (Citizen), Earl D'Eon (Radio Operator), Max Dommar (Grellou), Janine Grandel (French Woman), Guy Lee (Tavi), Ma Ma Loa (Dancer), Michael Mancuso (Hawaiian Boy).

Sergeants 3 (February 12, 1962)

Credits: Director: John Sturges; Producer: Howard W. Koch; Screenplay: W. R. Burnett; Musical Score: (original) Billy May, Johnny Rotella; (non-original): Franz Steininger; Director of Photography: Winton C. Hoch; Film Editor: Ferris Webster; Assistant Director: Terry Morse, Jr.; an Essex-Claude Production; Released by United Artists; Running Time: 112 minutes.

Cast: Frank Sinatra (Mike Merry), Dean Martin (Sergeant Chip Deal), Sammy Davis, Jr. (Jonah Williams), Peter Lawford (Sergeant Larry Barrett), Joey Bishop (Roger Boswell), Henry Silva (Mountain Hawk), Ruta Lee (Amelia Parent), Buddy Lester (Willie Sharpknife), Phillip Crosby (Corporal Ellis), Dennis Crosby (Private Page), Lindsay Crosby (Private Wills), Hank Henry (Blacksmith), Dick Simmons (Colonel William Collingwood), Michael Pate (Watanka), Alzamora (Caleb), Richard Hale (White Eagle), Mickey Finn (Morton), Sonny King (Corporal), Eddie Little Sky (Ghost Dancer), Rodd Redwing (Irregular), James Waters (Colonel's Aide), Madge Blake (Mrs. Parent), Dorothy Abbott (Mrs. Collingwood), Walter Merrill (Telegrapher), Mack Gray (Bartender), Joe Gray.

The Road to Hong Kong (April 1962)

Credits: Director: Norman Panama; Producer: Melvin Frank; Screenplay: Melvin Frank, Norman Panama; Musical Score: Robert Farnon; Original Songs: Sammy Cahn, James Van Heusen; Director of Photography: Jack Hildyard; Film Editors: Alan Osbiston, John C. Smith; Production Desiger: Roger K. Furse; Art Directors: Syd Cain, William Hutchinson; Set Decorator: Maurice Fowler; Makeup: David Aylott; Assistant Director: Bluey Hill; Sound: A. G. Ambler, Chris Greenham, Red Law; Special Effects: Jimmy Harris, Garth Inns, Curly Nelhams, Ted Samuels, Wally Veevers, Choreographers: Jack Baker, Sheila Meyers; Titles: Maurice Binder; Animators: Bob Godfrey, Keith Learner; Filmed at Shepperton Studios, Middlesex, England; a Melnor Films Production; Released by United Artists; Running Time: 91 minutes.

Cast: Bing Crosby (Harry Turner), Bob Hope (Chester Babcock), Joan Collins (Diane), Dorothy Lamour (Herself), Robert Morley (The Leader), Felix Aylmer (Grand Lama), Roger Delgado (Jhinnah), Walter Gotell (Dr. Zorbb), Peter Madden (Lama), Robert Ayres (American Official), Alan Gifford (American Official), Robin Hughes (American Official), Bill Nagy (Agent), Guy Standeven (Photographer), John McCarthy (Messenger), Simon Levy (Servant), Mei Ling (Chinese girl), Katya Douglas (Receptionist), Julian Sherrier (Doctor), Frank Sinatra, Dean Martin, David Niven, Peter Sellers, Jerry Colonna, Zsa Zsa Gabor, Dave King (Cameos), Irving Allan, Harry Baird (Nubians), April Ashley, Camilla Brockman, Victor Brooks, Edwina Carroll, John Dearth, Lier Hwang, Jacqueline Jones, Jacqueline Leigh, Lena Margo, Michel Mok, Roy Patrick, David Randall, Yvonne Shima, Sein Short, Diane C. Valentine, Sheree Winton, Michael Wynne, Zoe Zephyr.

The Manchurian Candidate (October 24, 1962)

Credits: Director: John Frankenheimer; Producers: George Axelrod, John Frankenheimer; Executive Producer: Howard W. Koch; Screenplay: George Axelrod, John Frankenheimer; Based on the novel by Richard Condon;

Director of Photography: Lionel Lindon; Editor:Ferris Webster; Musical Score: David Amram; Production Designer: Richard Sylbert; Set Decorator: George R. Nelson; Costume Design: Moss Mabry; Makeup: Ron Berkeley, Jack Freeman, Bernard Ponedel; Hair Stylists: Gene Shacove, Mary Westmoreland; Second Unit Director: Joseph C. Behm; Property Master: Arden Cripe; Assistant Art Director: Philip M. Jeffries; Music Editor: Richard Carruth; Sound Mixer: Joe Edmondson; Sound Effects Editor: Del Harris; Sound Re-recordist: Buddy Myers; Music Recordist: Vinton Vernon; Photographic Effects: Howard A. Anderson; Special Effects: A. Paul Pollard; Dialogue Coach: Thom Conroy; Costumer: Wesley Jeffries; Assistant Film Editor: Carl Mahakian; Operative Cameraman: John Mehl; Script Supervisor: Amalia Wade; Locations: New York, Los Angeles; an M. C. Production; Released by United Artists; Running Time: 116 minutes.

Cast: Frank Sinatra (Bennett Marco), Laurence Harvey (Raymond Shaw), Janet Leigh (Rosie Chaney), Angela Lansbury (Raymond's Mother), Henry Silva (Chunjin), James Gregory (Senator John Iselin), Leslie Parrish (Jocie Jordon), John McGiver (Senator Thomas Jordon), Khigh Dhiegh (Dr. Yen Lo), James Edwards (Corporal Alvin Melvin), Douglas Henderson (Colonel), Albert Paulsen (Zilkov), Barry Kelley (Secretary of Defense), Lloyd Corrigan (Holborn Gaines), Madame Spivy (Female Berezovo [Nightmare]), Joe Adams (Psychiatrist), Frank Basso (Photographer), Mary Benoit (Woman in Lobby), Whit Bissell (Medical Officer), Nicky Blair (Silvers), Merritt Bohn (Jilly), Nick Bolin (Berezovo), Burton (Convention Chairman), Evelyn Byrd (Party Guest), Lana Crawford (Party Guest), Ray Dailey (Page Boy), Mimi Dillard (Mrs. Melvin), Joan Douglas (Woman in Lobby), Estelle Etterre (Woman in Lobby), Mickey Finn (Reporter), Bess Flowers (Gomel), Lee Tung Foo (Man in Lobby), John Francis (Haiken), Paul Frees (Narrator), Ralph Gambina (Man in Lobby), Joe Gray (Soldier), Tom Harris (F.B.I. Man), Maggie Hathaway (Woman in Lobby), Maye Henderson (Chairlady), Sam ["Kid'"] Hogan (Man in Lobby), Harry Holcombe (General), John Indrisano (Reporter), Miyoshi Jingu (Miss Gertrude), Rita Kenaston (Woman in Lobby), Helen Kleeb (Chairlady), Lou Krugg (Manager), John Lawrence (Grossfeld), Richard LePore (Private Ed Mavole), Tom Lowell (Private Bobby Lembeck), Mike Masters (F.B.I. Man), Marquita Moll (Soprano), Reggie Nalder (Gomel) Frances E. Nealy (Woman in Lobby), Karen Norris (Secretary), Richard Norris (Reporter), Julie Payne (Party Guest), Robert Riordan (Presidential Nominee Benjamin K. Arthur), Anna Shin (Korean Girl), Ray Spiker (Policeman), Irving Steinberg (Freeman), William Thourlby (Little), Raynum K. Tsukamoto (Man in Lobby), Jean Vaughn (Nurse), James Yagi (Man in Lobby), Anton von Stralen (Officer).

The List of Adrian Messenger (May 1963)

Credits: Director: John Huston; Producer: Edward Lewis; Screenplay: Philip MacDonald; Based on the novel by Anthony Veiller; Director of Photography: Joseph MacDonald; Film Editor: Hugh S. Fowler; Musical Score: Jerry Goldsmith; Art Directors: Alexander Golitzen, Stephen B. Grimes, George C. Webb; Set Decorator: Oliver Emert; Makeup: Bud Westmore, John Chambers, David Grayson, Nick Marcelino; Hair Stylist: Larry Germain; Unit Production Manager: Richard McWhorter; Assistant Director: Tom Shaw; Second Assistant Director: Terry Morse, Jr.; Sound: Waldon O. Watson, Frank H. Wilkinson; Music Supervisor: Joseph Gershenson; Assistant to the Director: Gladys Hill; Double for Kirk Douglas: Jan Merlin; Photographer (Europe): Edward Scaife; a Joel Production; Released by Universal-International Pictures; Running Time: 98 minutes.

Cast: George C. Scott (Anthony Gethryn), Dana Wynter (Lady Jocelyn Bruttenholm), Clive Brook (Marquis of Gleneyre), Kirk Douglas (George Brougham), Robert Mitchum (Jim Slattery), Frank Sinatra (Gypsy), Burt Lancaster, Tony Curtis (cameos), Gladys Cooper (Mrs. Karoudjian), Herbert Marshall (Sir Wilfrid Lucas), Jacques Roux (Raoul Le Berg), John Merivale (Adrian Messenger), Marcel Dalio (Max), Bernard Archard (Inspector Pike), Tony Huston (Derek), Alan Caillou (Inspector Seymour), Constance Cavendish (Maid), Tim Durant (Hunt Secretary), Bernard Fox (Lynch), Paul Frees (Various Voices), Eric Heath (Orderly), Delphi Lawrence (Airport Stewardess), Mona Lilian (Proprietress), Joe Lynch (Cyclist), Stacy Morgan (Whip Man), Barbara Morrison (Nurse), Richard Peel (Sgt. Flood), Noel Purcell (Countryman), Jennifer Raine (Student Nurse), Anita Sharp-Bolster (Mrs. Slattery), Anna Van Der Heide (Stewardess), Nelson Welch (White), Ronald Long Carstairs, John Huston.

Come Blow Your Horn (June 5, 1963)

Credits: Director: Bud Yorkin; Producers: Norman Lear, Bud Yorkin; Executive Producer: Howard W. Koch; Screenplay: Norman Lear; Based on the play by Neil Simon; Director of Photography: William H. Daniels; Film Editor: Frank P. Keller; Musical Score: Nelson Riddle; Original Songs: Sammy Cahn, Jimmy Van Heusen; Production Designers/Art Directors: Roland Anderson, Hal Pereira; Set Decoration: Sam Comer, James W. Payne; Costume Designer: Edith Head; Makeup: Wally Westmore; Special Effects: Paul K. Lerpae; Orchestrator: Gil Grau; Locations: New York; an Essex-Paramount-Tandem Production; Released by Paramount Pictures; Running Time: 112 minutes.

Cast: Frank Sinatra (Alan Baker), Lee J. Cobb (Harry R. Baker), Molly Picon (Mrs. Sophie Baker), Barbara Rush (Connie), Jill St. John (Peggy John), Tony Bill (Buddy Baker), Dan Blocker (Mr. Eckman), Phyllis McGuire (Mrs. Eckman), Herbie Faye (Waiter), Romo Vincent (Rudy, the Barber), Charlotte Fletcher (Manicurist), Greta Randall (Tall Girl), Joyce Nizzari (Snow Eskanazi), Phil Arnold (Clothing Store Tailor), Warren Cathcart (Willie, the Dry Cleaner), James Cavanaugh (Shoe Salesman), George Davis (Hansom Cab Driver), Vinnie De Carlo (Maxie, the Bookie), Frank Hagney (Man), John Indrisano (Taxi Driver), Dean Martin (The Bum), Jack Nestle (Hampshire House Desk Clerk), Barbara Pepper (Mildred), Eddie Quillan (Elevator Boy), George Sawaya (Man), Grady Sutton (Clothing Store Manager), Carole Wells (Eunice).

4 for Texas (December 25, 1963)

Credits: Director and Producer: Robert Aldrich; Associate Producer: Walter Blake; Executive Producer: Howard W. Koch; Screenplay Robert Aldrich, W. R. Burnett, Teddi Sherman; Director of Photography: Ernest Laszlo; Film Editor: Michael Luciano; Musical Score: Nelson Riddle; Art Director: William Glasgow; Set Decorator: Raphael Bretton; Costume Designers: Charles E. James, Norma Koch, Joyce Rogers; Makeup: Robert J. Schiffer; Production Supervisor: Jack R. Berne; Assistant Directors: Tom Connors, Jr., David Salven; Second Unit Director: Oscar Rudolph; Property Master: John Orlando; Sound Mixer: Jack Solomon; Special Effects: Sass Bedig; Stunts: John Indrisano, Chuck Roberson, Marvin Willens; Script Apprentice: Adell Aldrich; Second Unit Cameramen: Joseph F. Biroc, Burnett Guffey, Carl E. Guthrie; Script Supervisor: Robert Cart; Orchestrator: Gil Grau; Dialogue Supervisor: Robert Sherman; Locations: Mojave, California; a Sam Company Production; Released by Warner Bros. Pictures; Running Time: 124 minutes.

Cast: Frank Sinatra (Zack Thomas), Dean Martin (Joe Jarrett), Anita Ekberg (Elya Carlson), Ursula Andress (Maxine Richter), Charles Bronson (Matson), Victor Buono (Harvey Burden), Edric Connor (Prince George), Nick Dennis (Angel), Richard Jaeckel (Pete Mancini), Mike Mazurki (Chad, Zack's Bodyguard), Wesley Addy (Winthrop Trowbridge), Marjorie Bennett (Miss Emmaline), Virginia Christine (Elya Carlson's Maid), Ellen Corby (Widow), Jack Elam (Dobie), Jesslyn Fax (Mildred), Fritz Feld (Fritz, Maitre d' at Orlando's), Percy Helton (Jonas Ansel, Railroad Agent), Jonathan Hole (Head Waiter on Riverboat), Jack Lambert (Monk), Paul Langton (Beauregard), Grady Sutton (Bank Clerk), Ralph Volkie (Spindrift Survivor), William Washington (Bill Williams), Dave Willock (Alfred), Larry Fine, Joe DeRita, Moe Howard (Painting Deliverers), Arthur Godfrey (Mr. Godfrey), Keith McConnell, Teddy Buckner and His All-Stars, Michele Montau, Maidie Norman, Bob Steele, Mario Siletti, Eva Six, Abraham Sofaer, Michael St. Angel, Max Wagner, Yaphet Kotto.

Robin and the 7 Hoods (June 24, 1964)

Credits: Director: Gordon Douglas; Producer: Frank Sinatra; Associate Producer: William H. Daniels; Executive Producer: Howard W. Koch; Screenplay: David R. Schwartz; Director of Photography: William H. Daniels; Film Editor: Sam O'Steen; Musical Score: Nelson Riddle; Original Songs: Sammy Cahn, James Van Heusen; Production Designer/Art Director: LeRoy Deane; Set Decorator: Raphael Bretton; Costume Designer: Don Feld; Makeup: Gordon Bau, Robert J. Schiffer; Supervising Hair Stylist: Jean Burt Reilly; Assistant Directors: David Salven, Lee White; Second Assistant Director: Michael Daves; Sound Directors: Everett A. Hughes, Vinton Vernon; Musical Numbers Staging: Jack Baker; Dialogue Supervisor: Thom Conroy; Orchestrator: Gil Grau; Script Supervisor: Dolores Rubin; a Claude-Essex-Warner Bros. Production; Released by Warner Bros. Pictures; Running Time: 123 minutes.

Cast: Frank Sinatra (Robbo), Dean Martin (Little John), Sammy Davis, Jr. (Will), Bing Crosby (Allen A. Dale), Peter Falk (Guy Gisborne), Barbara Rush (Marian Stevens), Victor Buono (Sheriff Alvin Potts), Hank Henry (Six Seconds), Robert Foulk (Sheriff Glick), Allen Jenkins (Vermin Whitowski), Jack La Rue (Tomatoes), Robert Carricart (Blue Jaw), Joseph Ruskin (Twitch), Phil Arnold (Hatrack), Harry Swoger (Soupmeat), Bernard Fein (Charlie Bananas), Richard Bakalyan, Sonny King, Phillip Crosby, Al Silvani (Robbo's Hoods), Harry Wilson, Joe Brooks, Roger Creed, Richard Sinatra (Gisborne's Hoods), Caryl Lee Hill (Cocktail Waitress), Mickey Finn (Bartender), Dick Simmons (Prosecutor), Chet Allen, John Delgado, Joe Gray, Boyd ("Red") Morgan, John Pedrini, Tony Randall, Al Wyatt (Hoods), Eve Bernhardt (Woman), Linda Brent (Derelict), Hans Conried (Mr. Ricks), Thom Conroy (Butler), Billy Curtis (Newsboy), Anne D'Aubray (Woman), Jerry Davis (Boy), Ronnie Dayton (Bit Part), Paul Frees (Radio Announcer), Chris Hughes (Jud), Joey Jackson (Butler), Barry Kelley (Police Chief), Larry D. Mann (Workman), Maurice Manson (Dignitary), Jo Ann March (Woman), Carolyn Morin (House Girl), Ed Ness (Lawyer), Manuel Padilla, Jr. (Boy), Leslie Perkins (Woman), Edward G. Robinson (Big Jim), Milton Rudin (Judge), Sig Ruman (Hammacher), Diane Sayer ("Booze" Witness), Frank J. Scannell (Lawyer), Mark Sherwood (Boy), Aldo Silvani (Guard), Bill Zuckert (Jury Foreman).

None But the Brave (February 1965) [Japanese title: *Yusha Nomi*]

Credits: Director and Producer: Frank Sinatra; Producer (Japan): Kikumaru Okuda; Associate Producer: William H. Daniels; Executive Producer: Howard W. Koch; Screenplay: John Twist, Katsuya Susaki; Original Story: Kikumaru Okuda; Director of Photography: Harold Lipstein; Film Editor: Sam O'Steen; Musical Score: John Williams; Art Directors: LeRoy Deane, Haruyoshi Oshita; Set Decorator: George James Hopkins; Makeup: Gordon Bau, Shu Uehara; Wardrobe: Hiroshi Maruyama; Assistant Directors: David Salven, Koshiro Uchiyama; Sound: Stanley Jones; Special Effects: Tsuburaya Eiji; Dialogue Coaches: Thom Conroy, Sataru Nakamura, Masao Mera; Music Supervisors: Morris Stoloff, Kenjiro Hirose; Technical Adviser: Kazuo Inoue; Art Adviser: Haruyoshi Oshita; Script Supervisor: Mitsushige Tsurushima; Locations: Kauai, Hawaii; a Sinatra Enterprises-Toho-Tokyo Eiga Production; Released by Warner Bros. Pictures; Running Time: 106 minutes.

Cast: Frank Sinatra (Chief Pharmacist Mate), Clint Walker (Captain Dennis Bourke), Tommy Sands (Second Lieutenant Blair), Brad Dexter (Sergeant Bleeker), Tony Bill (Air Crewman Keller), Sammy Jackson (Corporal Craddock), Richard Bakalyan (Corporal Ruffino), Rafer Johnson (Private Johnson), Jimmy Griffin (Private Dexter), Christopher Dark (Private Searcy), Don Dorrell (Private Hoxie), Phillip Crosby (Private Magee), John Howard Young (Private Waller), Roger Ewing (Private Swensholm), Richard Sinatra (Private Roth), Laraine Stephens (Lorie), Tatsuya Mihashi (Lieutenant Kuroki), Takeshi Kato (Sergeant Tamura), Homare Suguro (Lance Corporal Hirano), Shigeki Ishida (Leading Private Ando), Kenji Sahara (Corporal Kato), Mashahiko Tanimura (Private Tauda), Toru Ibuki (Private Arikawa), Ryucho Shunputei (Private Okunda), Hisao Dazai (Private Tokumaru), Susumu Kurobe (Private Goro), Takashi Inagaki (Private Ishii), Kenichi Hata (Private Sato).

Von Ryan's Express (June 23, 1965)

Credits: Director and Executive Producer: Mark Robson; Producer: Saul David; Screenplay: Wendell Mayes, Joseph Landon; Based on the novel by David Westheimer; Director of Photography: William H. Daniels; Film Editor: Dorothy Spencer; Musical Score: Jerry Goldsmith; Art Directors: Hilyard M. Brown, Jack Martin Smith; Set Decorators: Raphael Bretton, Walter M. Scott; Makeup: Ben Nye; Hair Stylist: Margaret Donovan; Unit Production Manager: Harry Caplan; Assistant Director: Eli Dunn; Second Unit Director: William Kaplan; Assistant Art Directors: Ed Graves, Lou Korn; Sound: Carlton W. Faulkner, Elmer Raguse; Sound Effects: Walter Rossi; Sound Editor: Don Stern; Special Effects: L.B. Abbott, Emil Kosa, Jr.; Second Unit Cameraman: Harold Lipstein; Orchestrator: Arthur Morton; a P-R Production; Released by 20th Century-Fox Film Corporation; Running Time: 112 minutes.

Cast: Frank Sinatra (Colonel Joseph L. Ryan), Trevor Howard (Major Eric Fincham), Raffaella Carrà (Gabriella), Brad Dexter (Sergeant Bostick), Sergio Fantoni (Captain Oriani), John Leyton (Orde), Edward Mulhare (Captain Costanzo), Wolfgang Preiss (Major Von Klemment), James Brolin (Private Ames), John Van Dreelen (Colonel Gortz), Adolfo Celi (Battaglia), Vito Scotti (Italian Train Engineer), Richard Bakalyan (Corporal Giannini), Michael Goodliffe (Captain Stein), Michael St. Clair (Sergeant Dunbar), Ivan Triesault (Von Kleist), John Daheim (American Soldier), Domenick Delgarde (Italian Soldier), Horst Ebersberg (German Pilot), Barry Ford (Ransom's Batman), Brian Gaffikin (English voices), Donald F. Glut (Extra), Jacques Stanislawski, Gino Gottarelli (Gotrz's Aides), Joe Gray (Prisoner), Peter Hellman (Pilot), Robert ("Buzz") Henry (American Soldier), Walter Linden (German Captain), Eric Micklewood (Ransom), John Mitory (Oriani's Aide), Ernesto Molinari (Italian Tailor), Benito Prezia (Italian Corporal), Michael Romanoff (Italian Nobleman), Bob Rosen (POW Who Opens Sweat Box), James Sikking (American Soldier), Brad Stevens (German Sergeant), Al Wyatt, Jr. (American soldier).

Marriage on the Rocks (September 24, 1965)

Credits: Director: Jack Donohue; Producer: William H. Daniels; Screenplay and Original Story: Cy Howard; Director of Photography: William H. Daniels; Film Editor: Sam O'Steen; Musical Score: Nelson Riddle; Original Songs: Bobby Hart, Trini López, Bill Barberis, Teddy Randazzo, Bobby Weinstein; Art Director: LeRoy Deane; Set Decorators: Arthur Krams, William L. Kuehl; Costume Designer: Walter Plunkett; Makeup: Gordon Bau; Sound: Dan Wallin; Choreographer: Jonathan Lucas; an A-C/Sinatra Enterprises Production; Released by Warner Bros. Pictures; Running Time: 109 minutes.

Cast: Frank Sinatra (Dan Edwards), Deborah Kerr (Valerie Edwards), Dean Martin (Ernie Brewer), Cesar Romero (Miguel Santos), Hermione Baddeley (Jeannie MacPherson), Tony Bill (Jim Blake), John McGiver (Shad Nathan), Nancy Sinatra (Tracy Edwards), Davey Davison (Lisa Sterling), Michel Petit (David Edwards), Trini López (Himself), Joi Lansing (Lola), Darlene Lucht (Bunny), Kathleen Freeman (Miss Blight), Flip

Mark (Rollo), DeForest Kelley (Mr. Turner), Sigrid Valdis (Kitty), Byron Foulger (Mr. Bruno), Parley Baer (Dr. Newman), Nacho Galindo (Mayor), Hedley Mattingly (Mr. Smythe), Reta Shaw (Saleslady at Saks).

The Oscar (February 1966)

Credits: Director: Russell Rouse; Producer: Clarence Greene; Screenplay: Harlan Ellison, Clarence Greene, Russell Rouse; Based on the novel by Richard Sale; Director of Photography: Joseph Ruttenberg; Film Editor: Chester W. Schaeffer; Musical Score: Percy Faith; Production Designers: Arthur Lonergan, Hal Pereira; Set Decorators: Robert R. Benton, James W. Payne; Costume Designer: Edith Head; Makeup: Wally Westmore; Special Effects: Paul K. Lerpae; Choreographer: Steven Peck; a Greene-Rouse Production; Released by Paramount Pictures; Running Time: 119 minutes.

Cast: Stephen Boyd (Frankie Fane), Elke Sommer (Kay Bergdahl), Milton Berle (Kappy Kapstetter), Eleanor Parker (Sophie Cantaro), Joseph Cotten (Kenneth Regan), Jill St. John (Laurel Scott), Tony Bennett (Hymie Kelly), Edie Adams (Trina Yale), Ernest Borgnine (Barney Yale), Chris Alcaide (Ledbetter), Army Archerd (Reporter at Press Conference), Jean Bartel (Secretary), Ed Begley (Grobard), Walter Brennan (Orrin C. Quentin), Broderick Crawford (Sheriff), John Crowther (Wally), John Dennis (Sid), James Dunn (Network Executive), Ross Ford (Lochner), Jean Hale (Cheryl Barker), Edith Head (Herself), John Holland (Stevens), Bob Hope (Guest), Hedda Hopper (Herself), Peter Lawford (Steve Marks), Peter Leeds (Bert), Merle Oberon (Guest), Walter Reed (Pereira), Eddie Ryder (Marriage Broker), Frank Sinatra (Himself), Nancy Sinatra (Herself), Jack Soo (Sam), Douglas Evans.

Cast a Giant Shadow (March 30, 1966)

Credits: Director and Screenplay: Melville Shavelson; Producers: Melville Shavelson, Michael Wayne; Based on the book by Ted Berkman; Director of Photography: Aldo Tonti; Film Editors: Bert Bates, Gene Ruggiero; Musical Score: Elmer Bernstein; Casting: Lynn Stalmaster; Production Designer: Michael Stringer; Art Director: Arrigo Equini; Costume Designer: Margaret Furse; Makeup: Robert J. Schiffer; Second Unit Director: Jack N. Reddish; Mechanic: Avraham Leibman; Stills Photographer: Bob Penn; Locations: Israel, Italy; a Batjac-Llenroc-Mirisch Company Production; Released by United Artists Pictures; Running Time: 141 minutes.

Cast: Kirk Douglas (Colonel David ["Mickey"] Marcus), Senta Berger (Magda Simon), Angie Dickinson (Emma Marcus), Frank Sinatra (Spence Talmadge), Yul Brynner (Asher Gonen), John Wayne (General Mike Randolph), James Donald (Major Safir), Stathis Giallelis (Ram Oren), Luther Adler (Jacob Zion), Topol (Abou Ibn Kader), Ruth White (Mrs. Chaison), Gordon Jackson (James MacAfee), Michael Hordern (British Ambassador), Allan Cuthbertson (Immigration Officer), Jeremy Kemp (British Immigration Senior), Sean Barrett (British Immigration Junior), Michael Shillo (Andre Simon), Rina Ganor (Rona), Roland Bartrop (Bert Harrison), Robert Gardett (General Walsh), Michael Balston (1st Sentry), Claude Aliotti (2nd Sentry), Samra Dedes (Belly Dancer), Michael Shagrir (Truck Driver), Frank Latimore, Ken Buckle (U.N. Officers), Rodd Dana (Aide to General Randolph), Robert Ross (Aide to Chief of Staff), Arthur Hansel (Officer), Hillel Rave (Yaakov), Shlomo Hermon (Yussuf), Vera Dolen (Mrs. Martinson), Michael Douglas (Jeep Driver), Gary Merrill (Pentagon Chief of Staff), Dan Sturkie (Parachute Sergeant).

Assault on a Queen (June 1966)

Credits: Director: Jack Donohue; Producer: William Goetz; Associate Producer: William H. Daniels; Screenplay: Rod Serling; Based on the novel by Jack Finney; Director of Photography: William H. Daniels; Film Editor: Archie Marshek; Musical Score: Duke Ellington; Costume Designer: Edith Head; Underwater Camera Operator: Owen Marsh; Orchestrator: Van Cleave; a Seven Arts-Sinatra Enterprises Production; Released by Paramount Pictures; Running Time: 106 minutes.

Cast: Frank Sinatra (Mark Brittain), Virna Lisi (Rosa Lucchesi), Val Avery (Trench), Leslie Bradley (3rd Officer), Lawrence Conroy (Junior Officer), Richard Conte (Tony Moreno), Reginald Denny (Master-at-Arms), Anthony Franciosa (Vic Rossiter), Arthur Gould-Porter (4th Officer), Errol John (Linc Langley), Alf Kjellin (Eric Lauffnauer), Ronald Long (2nd Officer), Murray Matheson (Captain), Lester Matthews (Doctor), Gilchrist Stuart (1st Officer), John Warburton (Bank Manager), Barbara Morrison.

The Naked Runner (July 1967)

Credits: Director: Sidney J. Furie; Producer: Brad Dexter; Screenplay: Francis Clifford, Stanley Mann; Director of Photography: Otto Keller; Film Editor: Barrie Vince; Musical Score: Harry Sukman; Art Directors: William Alexander, Peter Proud; Musical Director: Morris Stoloff; Locations: London, Copenhagen; an

Artanis-Sinatra Enterprises Production; Released by Warner Bros. Pictures; Running Time: 101 minutes.
Cast: Frank Sinatra (Sam Laker), Peter Vaughan (Slattery), Derren Nesbitt (Colonel Hartmann), Nadia Gray (Karen), Toby Robins (Ruth), Inger Stratton (Anna), Cyril Luckham (Cabinet Minister), Edward Fox (Ritchie Jackson), J. A. B. Dubin-Behrmann (Joseph), Michael Newport (Patrick Laker).

Tony Rome (November 10, 1967)
Credits: Director: Gordon Douglas; Producer: Aaron Rosenberg; Screenplay: Richard L. Breen; Based on the novel by Marvin H. Albert; Director of Photography: Joseph F. Biroc; Film Editor: Robert L. Simpson; Music Score: Billy May; Original Songs: Lee Hazlewood, Randy Newman; Casting: Joe Scully; Art Directors: Jim Roth, Jack Martin Smith; Set Decorators: Walter M. Scott, Warren Welch; Costume Designers: Moss Mabry, Elinor Simmons, Malcolm Starr; Makeup: Ben Nye; Gaffer (Miami): Al Reiners; Script Supervisor: Dolores Rubin; Locations: Miami Beach, Florida; an Arcola Production; Released by 20th Century-Fox Film Corporation; Running Time: 110 minutes.
Cast: Frank Sinatra (Tony Rome), Jill St. John (Ann Archer), Richard Conte (Lieutenant Dave Santini), Gena Rowlands (Rita Kosterman), Simon Oakland (Rudolph ["Rudy"] Kosterman), Jeffrey Lynn (Adam Boyd), Lloyd Bochner (Vic Rood, Drug Pusher), Robert J. Wilke (Ralph Turpin, Hotel House Detective), Virginia Vincent (Sally Bullock), Joan Shawlee (Fat Candy), Richard Krisher (Donald Pines), Lloyd Gough (Jules Langley, Thug), Babe Hart (Oscar, Thug), Rocky Graziano (Packy), Elisabeth Fraser (Irma), Shecky Greene (Catleg, a.k.a. John Fields), Jeanne Cooper (Lorna Boyd), Harry Davis (Ruyter, Dutch Jewler), Stanley Ross (Sam Boyd), Sue Lyon (Diana Pines), Tiffany Bolling (Photo Girl), Templeton Fox (Mrs. Schuyler), Robert ("Buzz") Henry (Nimmo), Deanna Lund (Georgia McKay), Jilly Rizzo (Card Player), Michael Romanoff (Sal, Maitre d' Hotel), Joe E. Ross (Bartender at Paradise Club), Linda Dano.

The Detective (May 28, 1968)
Credits: Director: Gordon Douglas; Producer: Aaron Rosenberg; Based on the novel by Roderick Thorp; Director of Photography: Joseph F. Biroc; Film Editor: Robert L. Simpson; Musical Score: Jerry Goldsmith; Art Directors: William J. Creber, Jack Martin Smith; Set Decorators: Walter M. Scott, Jerry Wunderlich; Costume Designers: Donald Brooks, Moss Mabry; Assistant Director: Richard Lang; Assistant Cameraman: Thomas Del Ruth; Script Supervisor: Dolores Rubin; Locations: New York; Released by 20th Century-Fox Film Corporation; Running Time: 114 minutes.
Cast: Frank Sinatra (Detective Joe Leland), Lee Remick (Karen Leland), Ralph Meeker (Curran), Jack Klugman (Dave Schoenstein), Horace McMahon (Captain Tom Farrell), Lloyd Bochner (Dr. Wendell Roberts), William Windom (Colin MacIver), Tony Musante (Felix Tesla), Al Freeman, Jr. (Robbie), Robert Duvall (Nestor), Pat Henry (Mercidis), Patrick McVey (Tanner), Dixie Marquis (Carol Linjack), Sugar Ray Robinson (Kelly), Renée Taylor (Rachael Schoenstein), James Inman (Teddy Leikman), Tom Atkins (Harmon), Jacqueline Bisset (Norma MacIver), Ted Beniades (Reporter), Mark Dawson (Desk Sergeant), James Dukas (Medical Examiner), Jan Farrand (Karen's Friend at Theatre), Don Fellows (Reporter), Tom Gorman Prison Priest), Sharon Henesy (Sharon), Richard Krisher (Matt Henderson), Paul Larson (Reporter), Earl Montgomery (Desk Clerk), Peg Murray (Girl at Party), Lou Nelson (Procurer), George Plimpton (Reporter), Frank Raiter (Tough Homosexual), Jilly Rizzo (Bartender), Jose Rodriguez (Boy in Police Station), Arnold Soboloff, Philip Sterling (Reporters), Peter York (Decent Boy).

Lady in Cement (October 1968)
Credits: Director: Gordon Douglas; Producer: Aaron Rosenberg; Screenplay: Marvin H. Albert, Jack Guss; Based on the novel by Marvin H. Albert; Director of Photography: Joseph F. Biroc; Film Editor: Robert L. Simpson; Musical Score: Hugo Montenegro; Art Director: LeRoy Deane; Set Decorators: Walter M. Scott, Jerry Wunderlich; Costume Designer: Moss Mabry; Makeup: Layne Britton, Daniel C. Striepeke; Assistant Director: Richard Lang; Special Effects: L. B. Abbott, Art Cruickshank; Stager, Underwater Sequences: Ricou Browning; Gaffer: Al Reiners; Script Supervisor: Dolores Rubin; Locations: Miami Beach, Florida; an Arcola-Millfield Production; Released by 20th Century-Fox Film Corporation; Running Time: 93 minutes.
Cast: Frank Sinatra (Tony Rome), Raquel Welch (Kit Forrest), Richard Conte (Lieutenant Dave Santini), Martin Gabel (Al Mungar), Lainie Kazan (Maria Baretto), Dan Blocker (Waldo Gronsky), Pat Henry (Rubin), Steve Peck (Paul Mungar), Virginia Wood (Audrey), Richard Deacon (Arnie Sherwin), Frank Raiter (Danny Yale), Peter Hock (Frenchy), Alex Stevens (Shev), Christine Todd (Sandra Lomax), Mac Robbins (Sidney, the Organizer), Tommy Uhlar (The Kid, Tighe Santini), Rey Baumel (Paco), Pauly Dash (MaComb), Andrew Jarrell (Pool Boy), Joe E. Lewis (Himself), Shirley Parker (Red), Jilly Rizzo (Himself).

Dirty Dingus Magee (November 1970)

Credits: Director and Producer: Burt Kennedy; Associate Producer: Richard E. Lyons; Screenplay: Tom Waldman, Frank Waldman, Joseph Heller; Based on the story "The Ballad of Dingus Magee" by David Markson; Director of Photography: Harry Stradling, Jr.; Film Editor: William B. Gulick; Musical Score: Jeff Alexander; Original Song: Mack David; Art Directors: George W. Davis, J. McMillan Johnson; Set Decorators: Robert R. Benton, Chuck Pierce; Costume Designer: Yvonne Wood; Makeup: Layne ("Shotgun") Britton; Hair Stylist: Naomi Cavin; Unit Production Manager: John W. Rogers; Assistant Director: Al Jennings; Second Assistant Director: Lynn Guthrie; Sound: Hal Watkins, Bruce Wright; Stunts: Jerry Gatlin, Ron Nix; Locations: Mescal, Arizona; Released by Metro-Goldwyn-Mayer Pictures; Running Time: 91 minutes.

Cast: Frank Sinatra (Dingus Magee), George Kennedy (Herkimer ["Hoke"] Birdsill), Anne Jackson (Belle Nops), Lois Nettleton (Prudence Frost), Jack Elam (John Wesley Hardin), Michele Carey (Anna Hot Water), John Dehner (Brigadier General George), Henry Jones (Reverend Green), Harry Carey, Jr. (Charles Stuart), Paul Fix (Chief Crazy Blanket), Don ("Red") Barry (Shotgun), Mike Wagner (Stage Driver), Terry Wilson (Sergeant), David Burk, David S. Cass, Sr., Tom Fadden (Troopers), Mae Old Coyote, Lillian Hogan, Florence Real Bird, Ina Bad Bear (Old Crones), Marya Christen (China Poppy, Belle's Maid), Mina Martínez, Sheila Foster, Irene Kelly, Diane Sayer, Jean London, Gayle Rogers, Timothy Blake, Lisa Todd, Maray Ayres, Carol Andreson (Belle's Girls), Willis Bouchey (Ira Teasdale), Grady Sutton (Corporal, the General's Orderly), Morgan Justin.

That's Entertainment (April 1974)

Credits: Director, Producer and Screenplay: Jack Haley Jr.; Executive Producer: Daniel Melnick; Musical Score: Henry Mancini; Directors of Photography: Allan Green, Ennio Guarnieri, Ernest Laszlo, Russell Metty, Gene Polito; Film Editors: David E. Blewitt, Bud Friedgen; Unit Production Managers: William R. Poole, Wally Samson; Assistant Directors: Claude Binyon, Jr., Richard Bremerkamp, David Silver; Sound Re-recording Mixers: Lyle J. Burbridge, William L. McCaughey, Aaron Rochin, Harry W. Tetrick, Hal Watkins; Music Editor: William Saracino; Visual Effects: Robert R. Hoag, Jim Liles; Assistant Film Editors: Ramon G. Caballero; Ana Luisa Corley Pérez, Abe Lincoln, Jr., Todd C. Ramsay; Head Film Librarian: Mort Feinstein; Music Supervisor: Jesse Kaye; Apprentice Editors: George Nakama, Michael J. Sheridan; Released by Metro-Goldwyn-Mayer Pictures; Running Time: 127 minutes.

Cast: Fred Astaire, Bing Crosby, Gene Kelly, Peter Lawford, Liza Minnelli, Donald O'Connor, Debbie Reynolds, Mickey Rooney, Frank Sinatra, James Stewart, Elizabeth Taylor (Hosts/Narrators), June Allyson, Kay Armen, Ray Bolger, Virginia Bruce, Jack Buchanan, Leslie Caron, Carleton Carpenter, Cyd Charisse, Maurice Chevalier, Joan Crawford, Virginia Dale, Vic Damone, Jimmy Durante, Deanna Durbin, Buddy Ebsen, Nelson Eddy, Cliff Edwards, Clark Gable, Judy Garland, Cary Grant, Kathryn Grayson, Virginia Grey, Jack Haley, Jean Harlow, Bernadene Hayes, Lena Horne, Lottice Howell, Van Johnson, Allan Jones, Louis Jourdan, Buster Keaton, Howard Keel, Charles King, Lorraine Krueger, Bert Lahr, Mario Lanza, Jeanette MacDonald, Joan Marsh, Tony Martin, Douglas McPhail, Ann Miller, Robert Montgomery, Dennis Morgan, Jules Munshin, Fayard Nicholas, Harold Nicholas, Margaret O'Brien, Eleanor Powell, Jane Powell, Ginger Rogers, Paula Stone, Russ Tamblyn, William Warfield, Esther Williams.

Contract on Cherry Street (November 19, 1977)

Credits: Director: William A. Graham; Producer: Hugh Benson; Executive Producer: Renée Valente; Teleplay: Edward Anhalt; Based on the novel by Philip Rosenberg; Director of Photography: Jack Priestley; Film Editor: Eric Albertson; Musical Score: Jerry Goldsmith; Casting: Shelley Ellison; Art Director: Robert Gundlach; Set Decorator: Leslie Bloom; Costume Designer: John Boxer; Makeup Supervisor: Mike Maggi; Unit Production Manager: Hal Schaffel; Assistant Director: Ralph S. Singleton; Sound Editor: Don Crosby; Music Editor: Erma E. Levin; Sound Editor: Steve Olson; Sound Mixer: James Sabat; Score Mixer: Dan Wallin; Special Effects: Tony Parmelee; Location Coordinator: Paul Ganapoler; Technical Adviser: Sonny Grosso; First Assistant Camera: Gary Muller; Casting Supervisor: Al Onorato; Locations: Hackensack, New Jersey, New York City; an Artanis-Columbia Pictures Television Production; Broadcast by NBC; Running Time: 145 minutes.

Cast: Frank Sinatra (Deputy Inspector Frank Hovannes), Martin Balsam (Captain Ernie Weinberg), Jay Black (Tommy Sinardos), Verna Bloom (Emily Hovannes), Joe De Santis (Vincenzo Seruto), Martin Gabel (Baruch Waldman), Harry Guardino (Ron Polito), James Luisi (Al Palmini), Michael Nouri (Lou Savage), Marco St. John (Eddie Manzaro), Henry Silva (Roberto Manzaro), Richard Ward (Jack Kittens), Addison Powell (Bob Halloran), Steve Inwood (Fran Marks), Johnny Barnes (Otis Washington), Lenny Montana (Phil Lombardi),

Murray Moston (Richie Saint), Robert Davi (Mickey Sinardos), Nicky Blair (Jeff Diamond), Estelle Omens (Flo Weinberg), Raymond Serra (Jimmy Monks), Sol Weiner (Paul Gold), Bill Jorgensen (Himself), Jimmy Boyd (Gallagher), Carmine Foresta (Saladino), Sonny Grosso (Rhodes), Dan Hannafin (Menneker), Randy Jurgensen (Al Jenner), Michael Stroka (Mike Farren), Ruth Rivera (Cecelia Benitez), Anna Berger (Mrs. Moore), Richard Corley (Desk Clerk), Mitchell Jason (Leo Goffman), Johnny Smash (Bartender at Cop's Bar), Louise Campbell (Admissions Nurse), Jilly Rizzo (Silvera), Gil Frazier (Bodyguard), Neil Elliot (Medic #1), Tucker Smallwood (Bus Driver), Phil Rubenstein (Deli Clerk), Robert Davis (Rabbi), Michelle Mais (Secretary), Keith Davis (Jamie Lenox).

The First Deadly Sin (October 3, 1980)
Credits: Director: Brian G. Hutton; Producers: George Pappas, Mark Shanker; Executive Producers: Fred C. Caruso, Elliott Kastner, Frank Sinatra; Screenplay: Mann Rubin; Based on the novel by Lawrence Sanders; Director of Photography: Jack Priestley; Film Editor: Eric Albertson; Musical Score: Gordon Jenkins; Casting: Louis DiGiaimo; Production Designer: Woods Mackintosh; Set Decorator: Robert Drumheller; Costume Designers: Theoni V. Aldredge, Gary Jones; Makeup: Mike Maggi; Hair Stylist: Joseph Paris; Unit Production Manager: Fred C. Caruso; DGA Trainee: Penney Finkelman Cox; First Assistant Director: Joe Napolitano; Second Assistant Director: Lewis Gould; Props: Howard Duff; Scenic Artist: Sante Fiore; Construction Grip: Lou Gallo; Chief Carpenter: Gilbert Gertsen; Carpenter: Harry Lynott; Assistant Props: Ray Murphy; Assistant to production Designer: Ray Recht; Scenic Chargeman: Bruno Robotti; Property Master: Walter Stocklin; Set Dressers: Hans Swanson, Morris Weinman; Chief Construction Grip: Joe Williams, Sr.; Boom Operator: Ed Abele; Sound Mixer: John H. Bolz; Pre-recording/Re-recording Mixer: Jack Cooley; Music Editor: Donald Harris; Sound Recordist: Peter Ilardi; Sound Editors: Ron Kalish, Sandy Tung; Assistant Sound Editor: Linda Shamest; Sound: Magno Sound; Score Mixer: Dan Wallin; Assistant Film Editors: Eric L. Beason, Thomas Seid; Studio Coordinator: Stefanie Brooks; Assistant Location Manager: Marc Epstein; Best Boy: James Fitzpatrick; Technical Consultant: Charles Garabedian; Transportation Coordinator: James Giblin; Second Assistant Camera: Michael Green; Costumer: Richard Hershey; Location Manager: A. Kitman Ho; Script Supervisor: Maggie James; Technical Consultant: Floyd Katske; Key Grip: Jack Kennedy; Dolly Grip: Bill Lowry; Production Office Coordinator: Shirley Marcus; Executive in Charge of Production: Stanley Mark; Production Assistants: Kevin McNeely, Roger Joseph Pugliese, Marina Spinola, Jeffrey Thomas; Gaffer: Charles Meere; Stills Photographer: Randy Munkacsi; Assistant Production Coordinator: Bruce Patterson; Assistant Camera: Richard Reis; Unit Publicist: Jay Remer; Apprentice Film Editor: Cathy Rose; Assistant Auditor: Marianne Scanlon; Wardrobe Supervisor: Teresa Alba Schipani; Technical Consultant: Arthur Schultheiss; Camera Operator: William H. Steiner; Personal Assistant to the Director: Donna Stevenson; Stand-in: Bruce Willis; Locations: New York; an Artanis-Cinema 7 Production; Released by Filmways; Running Time: 112 minutes.
Cast: Frank Sinatra (Edward X. Delaney), Faye Dunaway (Barbara Delaney), David Dukes (Daniel Blank), George Coe (Dr. Bernardi), Brenda Vaccaro (Monica Gilbert), Martin Gabel (Christopher Langley), Anthony Zerbe (Captain Broughton), James Whitmore (Dr. Sanford Ferguson), Joe Spinell (Charles Lipsky), Anna Navarro (Sunny Jordeen), Jeffrey DeMunn (Sergeant Fernandez Corelli), John Devaney (John Rogers), Robert Weil (Sol Appel), Hugh Hurd (Ben Johnson), Jon DeVries (Calvin Samtell), Eddie Jones (Officer Curdy), Victor Arnold (Officer Kendall), Frank Bongiorno (Nick), Reuben Green (Bill Garvin), Tom Signorelli (Carl Lucas), Richard Backus (Walt Ashman), Frederick Rolf (Judge James Braggs), Carol Gustafson (Matron), Michael Ingram (Bernard Gilbert), Bill Couch (Albert Feinberg), Larry Loonin (Hardware Salesman), Denise Lute (Sports Clerk Girl), Robert Cenedello (Night Doorman), Sherman Jones, Nick Caris, Bruce McLane (Detectives), Scott Palmer (Lab Technician), David Vaszuez, Ramón Franco (Boys on Bus), Leila Danette, Rosalyn Braverman (Women on Steps), Ramona Brooks, Sophia Sopher, Billi Vitale, Nan Whitehead (Hookers), Chico Kasindir, Paul M. Hunt, Dadi Pinero, Riki Colon (Street Kids), Nick DeMarinis (Taxi Driver), Henry E. Bradley, Jay Hargrove (Maintenance Men), Don Jay (Policeman), James Hayden (Young Policeman), Deborah Howell, Lydea Meléndez, Iliana Barsann, Pearl Franklin, Ellen Weiss, Theta Tucker (Nurses), David Gideon, Floyd Katske (Doctors), Vanessa Pesce, Vivian Oswald (Kids), Gloria Sauve (Prisoner), Bruce Willis (Man Entering Diner as Delaney Leaves).

Cannonball Run II (June 29, 1984)
Credits: Director: Hal Needham; Producer: Albert S. Ruddy; Executive Producer: André E. Morgan; Screenplay: Harvey Miller, Hal Needham, Albert S. Ruddy; Director of Photography: Nick McLean; Film Editors: William D. Gordean, Carl Kress; Musical Score: Al Capps; Casting: Jane Feinberg, Mike Fenton; First Assistant Director: Tom Connors; Second Assistant Directors: Jan DeWitt, John Peter Kousakis; Assistant Property Master: Richard Baum; Boom Operator: Donald L. Bolger; Music Editor: Nancy Fogarty;

Supervising Sound Editor: Don Hall; Supervising Music Editor: Jim Henrikson; Sound Mixer: C. Darin Knight; Sound Re-recordists: Gregg Landaker, Allen L. Stone, Bill Varney; Stunts: Dean Raphael Ferrandini, Alan Gibbs, Andy Gill, Diane Kay Grant, Conrad E. Palmisano, Ronnie Rondell, Jr., Thomas Rosales, Jr.; Negative Cutter: Donah Bassett; Camera Operators: Ray Delamotte, Michael Genne, Michael D. O'Shea; Administrative Assistant: Tom Ellison; Aerial Sequences Coordinator: Ray Lykins; Video Operator: David J. McGraw; Pilot: Fred S. Ronnow; Key Grip: Tim Ryan; Assistant to Director: Kathleen M. Shea; Special Vehicle Effects: Frank Welker; Locations: Darien, Connecticut; Redondo Beach, California; Tucson, Arizona. Released by Warner Bros. Pictures; Running Time: 96 minutes.

Cast: Burt Reynolds (J. J. McClure), Dom DeLuise (Victor Princie/Captain Chaos), Dean Martin (Jamie Blake), Sammy Davis, Jr. (Fenderbaum), Jamie Farr (The Sheik), Telly Savalas (Hymie Kaplan), Marilu Henner (Betty), Shirley MacLaine (Veronica), Susan Anton (Jill), Catherine Bach (Marcie), Foster Brooks, Sid Caesar, Louis Nye (Fishermen), Jackie Chan (Jackie), Tim Conway (CHP Officer), Tony Danza (Terry), Jack Elam (The Doc), Michael V. Gazzo (Sonny), Richard Kiel (Arnold), Don Knotts (CHP Officer), Ricardo Montalban (King), Jim Nabors (Private Homer Lyle), Molly Picon (Mrs. Goldfarb), Charles Nelson Reilly (Don Don Canneloni), Alex Rocco (Tony), Henry Silva (Slim), Frank Sinatra (Himself), Joe Theismann (Mack), Mel Tillis (Mel), Shawn Weatherly (Dean's Girl), Abe Vigoda (Caesar), Dale Ishimoto (Japanese Businessman), Arte Johnson (Pilot), Chris Lemmon (Young CHP), George Lindsey (Cal), Doug McClure (The Slapper), Jilly Rizzo (Jilly), Dub Taylor (Sheriff), Fred Dryer (Officer in Highway Patrol Car), Hal Needham (Man With Cowboy Hat), Branscombe Richmond (Biker), Frank O. Hill.

Notes

Introduction

[1]*Live with Larry King*, 13 May 1988.

[2]Will Friedwald, *Sinatra!: The Song is You* (New York: Scribner, 1995), p. 18.

[3]Tina Sinatra, with Jeff Coplon, *My Father's Daughter: A Memoir* (New York: Simon and Schuster), p. 160.

[4]Pete Hamill, *Why Sinatra Matters* (Boston: Little, Brown and Company, 1998), p. 69.

[5]Julie Harris, Letter to Scott Allen Nollen, 5 May 1996.

[6]Friedwald, *The Song is You*, p. 22.

[7]Friedwald, *The Song is You*, p. 110.

[8]Steven Petkov and Leonard Mustazza, eds., *The Frank Sinatra Reader* (New York: Oxford University Press, 1995), p. 95.

[9]*Live with Larry King.*

[10]Hamill, p. 94.

[11]Friedwald, *The Song is You*, p. 19.

[12]Friedwald, *The Song is You*, p. 26.

[13]Friedwald, *The Song is You*, p. 67.

[14]Friedwald, *The Song is You*, p. 27.

[15]Friedwald, *The Song is You*, p. 148.

[16]Friedwald, *The Song is You*, pp. 146-147.

[17]Frank Sinatra, "Me and My Music," *Life*, 1965, pp. 101-102.

[18]Friedwald, *The Song is You*, p. 139.

[19]Charles L. Granata, *Sessions with Sinatra: Frank Sinatra and the Art of Recording* (Chicago: A Cappella Books, 1999), p. 14.

Chapter 1

[1]*Variety*, 11 October 1918, p. 45.

[2]Richard Schickel, *D.W. Griffith: An American Life* (New York: Simon and Schuster, 1984), p. 270.

[3]Nancy Sinatra, *Frank Sinatra: An American Legend* (Santa Monica, CA: General Publishing Group, Inc., 1995), p. 18.

[4]Nancy Sinatra, *Frank Sinatra: An American Legend*, p. 20.

[5]J. Randy Taraborelli, *Sinatra:Behind the Legend* (Secaucus, NJ: Carol Publishing Group, 1997), p. 12.

[6]Hamill, p. 74.

[7]Hamill, p. 82.

[8]Hamill, pp. 88-89.

[9]Nancy Sinatra, *Frank Sinatra: An American Legend*, pp. 20-21.

[10]Nancy Sinatra, *Frank Sinatra: An American Legend*, p. 21.

[11]Nancy Sinatra, *Frank Sinatra: An American Legend*, p. 21.

[12]Nancy Sinatra, *Frank Sinatra: An American Legend*, p. 22.

[13]Taraborelli, p. 19.

[14]Frank Sinatra, *Life*, p. 86.

[15]Hamill, p. 94.

[16]Nancy Sinatra, *Frank Sinatra: An American Legend*, p. 25.

[17]Nancy Sinatra, *Frank Sinatra: An American Legend*, p. 27.

[18]Nancy Sinatra, *Frank Sinatra: An American Legend*, p. 25.

[19]Taraborelli, p. 23.

[20]Nancy Sinatra, *Frank Sinatra: An American Legend*, p. 32.

[21]Taraborelli, p. 25.

[22]Nancy Sinatra, *Frank Sinatra: An American Legend*, p. 35.

[23]Jack Lawrence, "All or Nothing At All," *Harry James and his Orchestra featuring Frank Sinatra: The Complete Recordings* (Columbia Legacy CD 66377), p. 21.

[24]Nancy Sinatra, *Frank Sinatra: An American Legend*, p. 39.

[25]Nancy Sinatra, *Frank Sinatra: An American Legend*, p. 42.

[26]Nancy Sinatra, *Frank Sinatra: An American Legend*, p. 42.

[27]Nancy Sinatra, *Frank Sinatra: An American Legend*, p. 43.

[28]Friedwald, *The Song is You*, p. 78.

Chapter 2

[1] Frank Sinatra, *Life*, p. 99.

[2] Nancy Sinatra, *Frank Sinatra: An American Legend*, p. 42.

[3] Friedwald, *The Song is You*, pp. 79-80, 85.

[4] Friedwald, *The Song is You*, p. 84.

[5] Frank Sinatra, *Life*, p. 86.

[6] Frank Sinatra, *Life*, pp. 86-87.

[7] Granata, p. 13.

[8] Will Friedwald and William Ruhlmann, *Tommy Dorsey, Frank Sinatra: The Song is You* (RCA 66363 2/4), p. 24.

[9] Nancy Sinatra, *Frank Sinatra: An American Legend*, p. 43.

[10] Nancy Sinatra, *Frank Sinatra: An American Legend*, p. 43.

[11] Nancy Sinatra, *Frank Sinatra: An American Legend*, p. 44.

[12] *Variety*, 26 March 1941.

[13] *Variety*, 26 March 1941.

[14] Friedwald and Ruhlmann, p. 10.

[15] Nancy Sinatra, *Frank Sinatra: An American Legend*, p. 50.

[16] *Variety*, April 1942.

[17] Friedwald and Ruhlmann, p. 59.

[18] Nancy Sinatra, *Frank Sinatra: An American Legend*, p. 50.

[19] Nancy Sinatra, *Frank Sinatra: An American Legend*, p. 50.

[20] Nancy Sinatra, *Frank Sinatra: An American Legend*, p. 51.

[21] *Variety*, April 1943.

[22] *New York Times*, 24 April 1943, p. 17.

[23] Will Friedwald, "The Complete Columbia Sessions," *The Columbia Years, 1943-1952: The Complete Recordings* (New York: Columbia Records, 1993), p. 38.

[24] Will Friedwald, "Sinatra! The Visual Factor," *Frank Sinatra in Hollywood* (New York and Burbank, CA: Reprise Records-Turner Classic Movies Music, 2002), p. 59.

[25] *Variety*, 15 December 1943.

[26] Gene Ringgold and Clifford McCarty, *The Films of Frank Sinatra* (Secaucus, NJ: Citadel Press, 1993), p. 36).

[27] Ringgold and McCarty, p. 36.

[28] Tom and Phil Kuntz, eds. *The Sinatra Files: The Secret FBI Dossier*, p. 21.

[29] *Variety*, June 1944.

[30] *The New York Times*, 27 July 1944, p. 14.

[31] Ringgold and McCarty, p. 41.

[32] Nancy Sinatra, *Frank Sinatra: An American Legend*, p. 59.

Chapter 3

[1] Nancy Sinatra, *Frank Sinatra: An American Legend*, p. 61.

[2] Nancy Sinatra, *Frank Sinatra: An American Legend*, p. 61.

[3] Clive Hirschhorn, *Gene Kelly: A Biography*. Chicago: Henry Regnery Co., 1974, p.145.

[4] *TV Guide* (Vol. 25, No. 47/Nov, 19, 1977), p. 16.

[5] Nancy Sinatra, *Frank Sinatra: An American Legend*, p. 62.

[6] Frank Sinatra, "Foreword," in Clive Hirschhorn, *Gene Kelly: A Biography*, p. 11.

[7] Hirschhorn, p. 145.

[8] Frank Sinatra, in Hirschhorn, p. 11.

[9] Hirschhorn, p. 145.

[10] Hirschhorn, p. 145.

[11] Nancy Sinatra, *Frank Sinatra, My Father* (New York: Pocket Books, 1986), pp. 103.

[12] Nancy Sinatra, *Frank Sinatra, My Father* (New York: Pocket Books, 1986), pp. 67-68.

[13] "Tunesmiths 'Sing,' *New York Times*, 12 October 1947.

[14] Stephen M. Silverman, *Dancing on the Ceiling: Stanley Donen and His Movies* (New York: Alfred A. Knopf, 1996), p. 71.

[15] Taraborelli, p. 70.

[16] Anthony Tollin, *Starring Frank Sinatra and Friends* (Schiller Park, IL: Radio Spirits, 2000), p. 24.

[17] John Howlett, *Frank Sinatra* (Philadelphia: Courage Books, 1980), pp. 38-39.

[18] *Variety*, 18 July 1945.

[19] *New York Times*, 21 July 1945.

[20] Ringgold and McCarty, p. 44.

[21] Nancy Sinatra, *Frank Sinatra: An American Legend*, p. 66.

[22] Nancy Sinatra, *Frank Sinatra: An American Legend*, p. 60.

[23] Ringgold and McCarty, p. 47; Taraborelli, p. 78.

[24] Nancy Sinatra, *Frank Sinatra: An American Legend*, p. 69.

[25] Goddard Lieberson, *Frank Sinatra Conducts the Music of Alec Wilder* (Sony Music Special Products A 4271).

[26] Will Friedwald, "The Complete Columbia Sessions," p. 62.

[27] Nancy Sinatra, *Frank Sinatra: An American Legend*, p. 73.

[28] Patricia Seaton Lawford, with Ted Scharz, *The Peter Lawford Story* (New York: Carrol and Graf Publishers, Inc., 1988), p. 99.

[29] Silverman, pp. 78-79.

[30] *Screen Actor*, October 1946.

[31] *New York Times*, 6 December 1946.

[32] *Sinatra: 80 Years My Way* (ABC Television, 14 December 1995).

[33] Ringgold and McCarty, p. 50.

[34] Robert C. Ruark, letter to Westbrook Pegler, 14 March 1947.

[35] Hamill, p. 145.

[36] Hamill, p. 146.

[37] Tony Bennett, with Will Friedwald, *The Good Life* (New York: Simon and Schuster, Inc., 1998), p. 90.

[38] *Variety*, March 1947.

[39] *Variety*, March 1947.

[40] Ringgold and McCarty, p. 53.

[41] Ringgold and McCarty, p. 53.

[42] *New York Times*, 14 March 1947.

[43] Howlett, p. 49.

[44] Glenn Neville, press release "H23-'16, April 9, 1947."

[45] Associated Press, 9 April 1947.

[46] Chicago *Herald-American*, 14 April 1947.

[47] Kuntz, pp. 31-32.

[48] "As Pegler Sees It," King Features, 26 April 1947.

[49] "As Pegler Sees It," 26 April 1947.

[50] Nancy Sinatra, *Frank Sinatra: An American Legend*, p. 80.

[51] Hamill, p. 139.

[52] E.J. Kahn, Jr., "What Will Sinatra Do Next?" *Look*, 5 August 1947.

[53] Kahn, p. 59.

[54] Friedwald, *Columbia Complete Recordings*, p. 72.

[55] *Screen Album*, Fall 1947, p. 21.

[56] Lee Mortimer, letter to Westbrook Pegler, 1 September 1947.

[57] Nancy Sinatra, *Frank Sinatra: An American Legend*, p. 84.

[58] Nancy Sinatra, *Frank Sinatra: An American Legend*, p. 81.

[59] "As Pegler Sees It," King Features, 10 September 1947.

[60] "As Pegler Sees It," King Features, September 1947.

[61] "As Pegler Sees It," King Features, 9 September 1947.

[62] Kuntz, p. xviii.

[63] Kuntz, p. 40.

[64] Nancy Sinatra, *Frank Sinatra: An American Legend*, p.

[65] Nancy Sinatra, *Frank Sinatra: An American Legend*, p.

[66] Friedwald, "The Complete Columbia Sessions," p. 86.

[67] Tina Sinatra, p. 19.

[68] *Variety*, 3 March 1948.

[69] Ringgold and McCarty, p. 56.

[70] Nancy Sinatra, *Frank Sinatra: An American Legend*, p. 84.

[71] Nancy Sinatra, *Frank Sinatra: An American Legend*, p. 85.

[72] Silverman, p. 92.

[73] Silverman, p. 88.

[74]Silverman, p. 95.

[75]*Frank Sinatra: A Tribute* DVD.

[76]Nancy Sinatra, *Frank Sinatra: An American Legend*, p. 87.

[77]Hamill, pp. 48-49.

[78]Silverman, pp. 84-85.

[79]*Variety*, 17 November 1948.

[80]*New York Times*, 19 November 1948; Ringgold and McCarty, p. 58.

[81]Ringgold and McCarty, p. 59.

[82]Hamill, p. 138.

[83]Nancy Sinatra, *Frank Sinatra: An American Legend*, p. 87.

[84]Nancy Sinatra, *Frank Sinatra: An American Legend*, p. 90.

[85]*Variety*, 9 March 1949.

[86]Hirshhorn, p. 168.

[87]Friedwald, *Columbia Complete Recordings*, p. 93.

[88]Hirshhorn, p. 180.

[89]Silverman, p. 113.

[90]Silverman, p. 116.

[91]Silverman, pp. 116-17.

[92]Friedwald, *The Song is You*, p. 341.

[93]Hirschhorn, p. 182.

[94]Nancy Sinatra, *Frank Sinatra: An American Legend*, p. 54.

[95]Taraborelli, p. 111.

Chapter 4

[1]*Frank Sinatra: Off the Record*, 1965.

[2]*Columbia Complete Recordings*, p. 102.

[3]Nancy Sinatra, *Frank Sinatra: An American Legend*, p. 95.

[4]Nancy Sinatra, *Frank Sinatra: An American Legend*, p. 93.

[5]Nancy Sinatra, *Frank Sinatra: An American Legend*, p. 96.

[6]*Columbia Complete Recordings*, p. 109.

[7]Nancy Sinatra, *Frank Sinatra: An American Legend*, p. 97.

[8]Friedwald, *Columbia Complete Recordings*, p. 113.

[9]Friedwald, *Columbia Complete Recordings*, p. 114.

[10]Friedwald, *Columbia Complete Recordings*, p. 114.

[11]Friedwald, *Columbia Complete Recordings*, pp. 115-116.

[12]Friedwald, *Columbia Complete Recordings*, p. 118.

[13]Nancy Sinatra, *Frank Sinatra: An American Legend*, p. 99.

[14]Nancy Sinatra, *Frank Sinatra: An American Legend*, p. 99.

[15]*Variety*, 7 November 1951.

[16] *New York Times*, 26 December 1951, p. 19.

[17]Ringgold and McCarty, p. 70.

[18]Nancy Sinatra, *Frank Sinatra: My Father*, p. 321.

[19]*Variety*, 16 January 1952.

[20]*New York Times*, 27 March 1952, p. 34.

[21]Wanda Hale, "'Meet Danny Wilson' on Paramount Screen," 27 March 1952.

[22]Howlett, p. 54.

[23] Ethan Mordden, *The Hollywood Musical* (New York: St. Martin's Press, 1981).

[24]Nancy Sinatra, *Frank Sinatra: An American Legend*, p. 104.

[25]Nancy Sinatra, *Frank Sinatra: An American Legend*, p. 105.

[26]Ed O'Brien, with Robert Wilson, *Sinatra 101: The 101 Best Recordings and the Stories Behind Them* (New York: Boulevard Books, 1996), p. 34.

[27]Friedwald, *Columbia Complete Recordings*, p. 124.

[28]Friedwald, *Columbia Complete Recordings*, p. 124.

Chapter 5

[1]Friedwald, *The Song is You*, p. 199.

[2]Nancy Sinatra, *Frank Sinatra: An American Legend*, p. 106.

[3]John Howlett, *Frank Sinatra* (Philadelphia: Courage Books, 1980), p. 67.

[4] Nancy Sinatra, *Frank Sinatra: My Father*, p. 96.
[5] Nancy Sinatra, *Frank Sinatra: An American Legend*, p. 107.
[6] *Frank Sinatra In Concert at the Royal Festival Hall* laserdisc (Reprise, 1971).
[7] Nancy Sinatra, *Frank Sinatra: An American Legend*, p. 105.
[8] Freedland, p. 194.
[9] Freedland, pp. 188-89.
[10] Nancy Sinatra, *Frank Sinatra: An American Legend*, p. 109.
[11] Nancy Sinatra, *My Father*, pp. 97-98.
[12] Freedland, p. 199.
[13] Nancy Sinatra, *Frank Sinatra: An American Legend*, p. 111.
[14] Friedwald, *The Complete Capitol Singles Collection*, p. 12.
[15] Friedwald, *The Complete Capitol Singles Collection*, p. 19.
[16] *New York Times*, 10 May 1953.
[17] Freedland, p. 196.
[18] Howlett, p. 71.
[19] Nancy Sinatra, *Frank Sinatra: My Father*, p. 98.
[20] Britt, p. 83.
[21] Taraborelli, p. 160.
[22] Britt, p. 84.
[23] *Variety*, 29 July 1953.
[24] Ringgold and McCarty, p. 79.
[25] Leonard Mustazza, *Ol' Blue Eyes: A Frank Sinatra Encyclopedia* (Westport, CT: Greenwood Press, 1998), p. 328.
[26] Nancy Sinatra, *Frank Sinatra: An American Legend*, p. 112.
[27] Nancy Sinatra, *Frank Sinatra: An American Legend*, p. 114.
[28] Tina Sinatra, p. 27.
[29] Britt, p. 86.
[30] Nancy Sinatra, *Frank Sinatra: An American Legend*, p. 11.
[31] O'Brien, p. 54.
[32] Stephen Bogart, *Bogart: In Search of My Father* (New York: E.P. Dutton, 1995). p. 54.
[33] Nancy Sinatra, *Frank Sinatra: An American Legend*, p. 11.
[34] Bogart, p. 10.
[35] *New York Times*, 9 May 1954.
[36] *New York Times*, 9 May 1954.
[37] *Variety*, 8 September 1954.
[38] *New York Times*, 8 October 1954, p. 27.
[39] Ringgold and McCarty, p. 83.
[40] A. E. Hotchner, *Doris Day: Her Own Story* (New York: William Morrow and Company, Inc., 1976), p. 145.
[41] Hotchner, p. 146.
[42] Hotchner, p. 147.
[43] Hotchner, pp. 147-48.
[44] Hotchner, p. 147.
[45] Hotchner, pp. 148-49.
[46] James Kotsilibas-Davis, *The Barrymores: America's Royal Family in Hollywood* (New York: Crown Publishers, 1981), p. 282.
[47] Hotchner, p. 149.
[48] *Variety*, 15 December 1954.
[49] *New York Times*, 20 January 1955, p. 35.
[50] *Variety*, 15 June 1955.
[51] *New York Times*, 2 July 1955, p. 24.
[52] *Variety*, 15 June 1955.
[53] *New York Times*, 2 July 1955, p. 24.
[54] Ringgold and McCarty, p. 90.
[55] Freedland, p. 249.
[56] *Frank Sinatra Memorial* DVD (Passport Video 9011, 1999).
[57] Pete Welding, *In the Wee Small Hours* compact disc liner notes (Capitol Records 4 96988 2).
[58] Nancy Sinatra, *Frank Sinatra: An American Legend*, p. 120.

[59]Freedland, p. 225.

[60]Nancy Sinatra, *My Father*, pp. 111-112.

[61]*New York Times*, 4 November 1955, p. 26.

[62]Nancy Sinatra, *Frank Sinatra: An American Legend*, p. 124.

[63]*Tender Trap* pressbook, p. 2.

[64]*Tender Trap* pressbook, p. 3.

[65]*Variety*, 2 November 1955.

[66]Ringgold and McCarty, p. 94.

[67]*New York Times*, 12 November 1955, p. 23.

[68]Nancy Sinatra, *Frank Sinatra: An American Legend*, p. 124.

[69]*TV Guide*, 30 May 1998.

[70]Nancy Sinatra, *Frank Sinatra: An American Legend*, 123.

[71]Nancy Sinatra, *My Father*, p. 105.

[72]Otto Preminger, *Preminger: An Autobiography* (New York: Doubleday and Co., 1977), p. 111.

[73]Preminger, p. 111.

[74]Preminger, p. 111

[75]Hamill, p. 29.

[76]Preminger, p. 111.

[77]Preminger, p. 110.

[78]Preminger, p. 112.

[79]Willi Frischauer, *Behind the Scenes of Otto Preminger* (London: Michael Joseph, Ltd., 1973), p. 141.

[80]Preminger, pp. 112-13.

[81]Preminger, p. 113.

[82]Peter Harry Brown, *Kim Novak: Reluctant Goddess* (New York: St. Martin's Press, 1986), p. 72.

[83]Brown, p. 73.

[84]Taraborelli, p. 188.

[85]Taraborelli, p. 188.

[86]Preminger, p. 156.

[87]Al Young, *John Coltrane: Coltrane for Lovers* compact disc liner notes (The Verve Music Group 314 549 361-2).

[88]*Frank Sinatra Memorial* DVD.

[89]Preminger, p. 113.

[90]*Variety*, 12 December 1955.

[91]*New York Times*, December 1955.

[92]Ringgold and McCarty, p. 104.

[93]Ringgold and McCarty, p. 104.

[94]*Variety*, 8 February 1956.

[95]Nancy Sinatra, *Frank Sinatra: An American Legend*, p. 125.

[96]Nikki Harmon, letter to Scott Allen Nollen, 17 February 2000.

[97]Harmon.

[98]*Variety*, 11 July 1956.

[99]*New York Times*, 16 August 1956, p. 30.

[100]Ringgold and McCarty, p. 111.

[101]Bennett, p. 139.

[102]Friedwald, *The Song is You*, p. 203.

[103]Freedland, p. 229.

[104]Freedland, p. 229.

[105]Friedwald, p. 45.

[106]Nick Caruso, Jr., discussion with Scott Allen Nollen, 7/20/01.

[107]Freedland, p. 230.

[108]Nancy Sinatra, *Frank Sinatra: My Father*, p. 113.

[109]*Variety*, 18 July 1956.

[110]*New York Times*, 10 August 1956, p. 9.

[111]Nancy Sinatra, *Frank Sinatra: An American Legend*, p. 126.

Chapter 6

[1]*New York Times*, 10 February 1957.

[2]Pete Welding, *Close to You* compact disc liner notes (Capitol Records 4 96991 2).

[3]Friedwald, *The Song is You*, pp. 242-43.

[4]Friedwald, *The Song is You*, pp. 328-29.

[5]*New York Times*, 13 May 1956.

[6]Howlett, p. 95.

[7]Howlett, p. 95.

[8]Taraborelli, p. 192.

[9]*New York Times*, 10 February 1957.

[10]Howlett, p. 95.

[11]Nancy Sinatra, *Frank Sinatra: An American Legend*, p. 265.

[12]*Variety*, 26 June 1957.

[13]Ringgold and McCarty, p. 127.

[14]*New York Times*, 29 June 1957.

[15]Nancy Sinatra, *Frank Sinatra: An American Legend*, p. 128.

[16]*Variety*, 24 October 1956.

[17]*New York Times*, 18 October 1956.

[18]*New York Times*, 10 February 1957.

[19]Nancy Sinatra, *Frank Sinatra: An American Legend*, p. 135.

[20]Freedland, p. 251.

[21]*New York Times*, 10 February 1957; Nancy Sinatra, *Frank Sinatra: An American Legend*, p. 135.

[22]*Frank Sinatra Memorial* DVD.

[23]*Frank Sinatra Memorial* DVD.

[24]Freedland, p. 252.

[25]*Variety*, 28 August 1957.

[26]*New York Times*, 27 September 1957.

[27]Nancy Sinatra, *Frank Sinatra: An American Legend*, p. 128.

[28]Bogart, p. 77.

[29]Nancy Sinatra, *Frank Sinatra: An American Legend*, p. 138.

[30]Pete Welding, *Where Are You?* compact disc liner notes (Capitol Records 4 96993 2).

[31]Friedwald, *The Song is You*, p. 341.

[32]*New York Times*, 10 February 1957.

[33]*Pal Joey* laserdisc jacket (Columbia laserdisc).

[34]*Pal Joey* laserdisc jacket.

[35]Britt, p. 108.

[36]Taraborelli, p. 204.

[37]*Variety*, 11 September 1957.

[38]*New York Times*, 28 October 1957.

[39]Nancy Sinatra, *Frank Sinatra: An American Legend*, p. 138.

[40]Tina Sinatra, p. 37.

[41]Nancy Sinatra, *Frank Sinatra: An American Legend*, p. 138.

Chapter 7

[1]Nancy Sinatra, *Frank Sinatra: An American Legend*, p. 185.

[2]Friedwald, *Jazz Singing*, p. 333.

[3]Friedwald, *Jazz Singing*, p. 338.

[4]Nancy Sinatra, *Frank Sinatra: My Father*, p. 127.

[5]*New York Times*, 6 January 1958.

[6]Nancy Sinatra, *Frank Sinatra: An American Legend*, p. 136.

[7]Nancy Sinatra Lambert, letter to Scott Allen Nollen, December 1997.

[8]O'Brien, p. 93.

[9]*Variety*, June 1958.

[10]*New York Times*, 4 July 1958, p. 15.

[11]Ringgold and McCarty, p. 142.

[12]Pete Welding, *Frank Sinatra Sings for Only the Lonely* compact disc liner notes (Capitol Records 4 96996 2).

[13]Friedwald, *The Song is You*, p. 249.

[14]Nancy Sinatra, *Frank Sinatra: An American Legend*, p. 141.

[15]*Variety*, 24 December 1958.

[16]Nick Tosches, *Dino: Living High in the Dirty Business of Dreams* (New York:Dell Publishing Co., 1999), p. 317.

[17]Freedland, p. 52.

[18]*Frank Sinatra: Off the Record*, 1965.

[19]Lawrence Quirk and William Schoell, *The Rat Pack: The Hey-Hey Days of Frank and the Boys* (Dallas: Taylor Publishing Company, 1998), p. 159.

[20]*Variety*, 24 December 1958.

[21]*New York Times*, 23 January 1959.

[22]Ringgold and McCarty, pp. 146-148.

[23]Freedland, p. 257.

[24]Freedland, p. 258.

[25]Nancy Sinatra, *Frank Sinatra: My Father*, pp. 125-26.

[26]Nancy Sinatra, *Frank Sinatra: An American Legend*, p. 141.

[27]Pete Welding, *Come Dance with Me* compact disc liner notes (Capitol Records 4 96997 2).

[28]Welding, *Come Dance with Me*.

[29]*Variety*, 20 May 1959.

[30]*New York Times*, 16 July 1959.

[31]Ringgold and McCarty, p. 153.

[32]Nancy Sinatra, *Frank Sinatra: An American Legend*, p. 130.

[33]Sammy Davis, Jr., *Hollywood in a Suitcase* (New York: William Morrow and Company, Inc., 1980), pp. 88-89.

[34]Freedland, p. 259.

Chapter 8

[1]Freedland, p. 68.

[2]Freedland, p. 263.

[3]Freedland, p. 264.

[4]O'Brien, p. 106.

[5]*Variety*, 16 March 1960.

[6]*New York Times*, 10 March 1960.

[7]James Spada, p. 213.

[8]Tosches, p. 336.

[9]Davis, *Hollywood in a Suitcase*, p. 85.

[10]Lawford, p. 100.

[11]Davis, *Hollywood in a Suitcase*, p. 84.

[12]Freedland, p. 287.

[13]Spada, p. 215.

[14]Lawford, p. 112.

[15]Davis, *Hollywood in a Suitcase*, p. 84.

[16]Davis, *Hollywood in a Suitcase*, ps. 86, 87.

[17]*Ocean's Eleven* DVD.

[18]Pete Welding, *Nice 'n' Easy* compact disc liner notes (Capitol Records 4 97000 2).

[19]Sammy Davis, Jr., *Yes I Can* (New York: Farrar, Straus and Giroux, 1965), p. 499.

[20]*Ocean's Eleven* DVD.

[21]*Variety*, 10 August 1960.

[22]*New York Times*, 11 August 1960.

[23]*New York Times*, 10 February 1960.

[24]*New York Times*, 21 March 1960.

[25]Note to Westbrook Pegler, March 1960.

[26]*New York Times*, 27 March 1960.

[27]*New York Times*, 9 April 1960.

[28]Tina Sinatra, p. 68.

[29]Lawford, p. 119.

[30]*New York Times*, 9 April 1960.

[31]Lawford, p. 120.

[32]Nancy Sinatra, *Frank Sinatra: An American Legend*, p. 147.

[33]Nancy Sinatra, *Frank Sinatra: An American Legend*, p. 149.

[34]Nancy Sinatra, *Frank Sinatra: An American Legend*, p. 157.

[35]*New York Times*, 3 November 1960.

[36]*New York Times*, 3 November 1960.

[37]Tina Sinatra, pp. 68-69.
[38]Nancy Sinatra, *Frank Sinatra: An American Legend*, p. 150.
[39]Nancy Sinatra, *Frank Sinatra: An American Legend*, p. 151.
[40]Tina Sinatra, p. 77.
[41]Granata, p. 157.
[42]*Come Swing with Me*, CD booklet.
[43]O'Brien, p. 118.
[44]Freedland, p. 289.
[45]Tosches, pp. 345-346.
[46]Freedland, p. 290.
[47]Davis, *Hollywood in a Suitcase*, p. 87.
[48]*Variety*, September 1961.
[49]Ringgold and McCarty, p. 174.
[50]*New York Times*, 19 October 1961, p. 39.
[51]Kuntz, p. 181.
[52]Pete Welding, *Point of No Return* compact disc liner notes (Capitol Records 4 97004 2).
[53]Friedwald, *The Song is You*, p. 383.
[54]*The Manchurian Candidate* DVD.
[55]*The Manchurian Candidate* DVD.
[56]*The Manchurian Candidate* DVD.
[57]Tina Sinatra, p. 82.
[58]*The Manchurian Candidate* DVD.
[59]*The Manchurian Candidate* DVD.
[60]*The Manchurian Candidate* DVD.
[61]*New York Times*, 11 February 1962.
[62]*The Manchurian Candidate* DVD.
[63]*The Manchurian Candidate* DVD.
[64]*The Manchurian Candidate* pressbook, p. 8.
[65]*The Manchurian Candidate* DVD.
[66]*The Manchurian Candidate* DVD.
[67]*The Manchurian Candidate* DVD booklet.
[68]*The Manchurian Candidate* DVD.
[69]*The Manchurian Candidate* DVD.
[70]Tina Sinatra, p. 79.
[71]*The Manchurian Candidate* DVD.
[72]*The Manchurian Candidate* DVD.
[73]*The Manchurian Candidate* DVD.
[74]*The Manchurian Candidate* DVD.
[75]*The Manchurian Candidate* DVD.
[76]*The Manchurian Candidate* DVD.
[77]*The Manchurian Candidate* DVD.
[78]*The Manchurian Candidate* DVD.
[79]*The Manchurian Candidate* DVD.
[80]*The Manchurian Candidate* DVD.
[81]*The Manchurian Candidate* DVD.
[82]*The Manchurian Candidate* DVD.
[83]*The Manchurian Candidate* DVD booklet.
[84]*Variety*, 17 October 1962.
[85]*New York Times*, 25 October 1962, p. 48.
[86]Ringgold and McCarty, p. 187.
[87]*Live with Larry King*, 13 May 1988.
[88]Friedwald, *The Song is You*, p. 399.
[89]Nancy Sinatra, *Frank Sinatra: An American Legend*, p. 166.
[90]Willy Rizzo, discussion with Scott Allen Nollen, 20 July 2001.
[91]Friedwald, *The Song is You*, p. 404.
[92]Friedwald, *The Song is You*, p. 405.
[93]Friedwald, *The Song is You*, p. 405.
[94]Kuntz, pp. 172-180.

[95]Freedland, p. 300.
[96]Freedland, p. 302.
[97]Freedland, pp. 100-101.
[98]Freedland, p. 301.
[99]Granata, p. 171.
[100]Granata, p. 171.
[101]Friedwald, *The Song is You*, p. 328.
[102]Freedland, p. 302.
[103]*Come Blow Your Horn* pressbook, p. 9.
[104]Freedland, p. 302.
[105]*Variety*, December 1963.
[106]*Variety*, December 1963.
[107]Quirk and Schoell, p. 234.
[108]Jack Elam, letter to Scott Allen Nollen, 7 January 1998.
[109]Nancy Sinatra, *Frank Sinatra: My Father*, p. 173.
[110]Nancy Sinatra, *Frank Sinatra: My Father*, p. 173.
[111]Hirschhorn, p. 277.
[112]Milliken to Howard Koch, inter-office memo, Warner Bros., 25 October 1963.
[113]Howard Koch to Milliken, inter-department memo, Sinatra Enterprises, 30 October 1963.
[114]Nancy Sinatra, *Frank Sinatra: An American Legend*, p. 177.
[115]*Robin and the 7 Hoods* shooting schedule, Warner Bros, 1963.
[116]Bill Zehme, *The Way You Wear Your Hart: Frank Sinatra and the Art of Livin'* (New York: Harper Collins, 1997), p. 188.
[117]*Daily Variety*, 24 June 1964, p.3.
[118]*Hollywood Reporter*, 25 June 1964, p. 3.
[119]Howlett, p. 277.
[120]Friedwald, *The Song is You*, p. 263.
[121]Freedland, p. 315.
[122]Granata, pp. 169-170.
[123]Freedland, p. 315.
[124]Howlett, p. 133.
[125]Petkov and Mustazza, p. 96.
[126]*Frank Sinatra Memorial* DVD.
[127]*Variety*, 10 February 1965.
[128]*New York Times*, 25 February 1965, p. 24.
[129]Ringgold and McCarty, p. 202.
[130]Ringgold and McCarty, p. 203.
[131]Friedwald, *The Song is You*, p. 411.
[132]Friedwald, *The Song is You*, p. 412.
[133]Freedland, p. 317.
[134]Freedland, p. 318.
[135]*Variety*, 19 May 1965.
[136]Ringgold and McCarty, p. 207.
[137]*Marriage on the Rocks* pressbook (Warner Bros. Pictures, 1965), p. 2.
[138]*Marriage on the Rocks* pressbook, p. 4.
[139]*Marriage on the Rocks* pressbook, p. 3.
[140]*Marriage on the Rocks* pressbook, p. 4
[141]Tina Sinatra, p. 107.
[142]*Marriage on the Rocks* pressbook, p. 3.
[143]*Marriage on the Rocks* pressbook, p. 18.
[144]*Marriage on the Rocks* pressbook, p. 5.
[145]*Variety*, 22 September 1965.
[146]*New York Times*, 1965.
[147]*Variety*, September 1965.
[148]Associated Press, 1965.
[149]Nancy Sinatra, *Frank Sinatra: My Father*, p. 212.
[150]Granata, p. 175.
[151]Frank Sinatra, *Life*, p. 104.

Chapter 9

[1]*Who Tribute: Frank Sinatra, His Life, His Way* (Time Inc. Magazine, 1998).

[2]Freedland, p. 322.

[3]Freedland, p. 323.

[4]Freedland, p. 324.

[5]*Variety*, 30 March 1966.

[6]*New York Times*, 31 March 1966, p. 43.

[7]Ringgold and McCarty, ps. 214, 215.

[8]*Los Angeles Times*, 25 November 1965.

[9]Friedwald, *The Song is You*, p. 263.

[10]Friedwald, *The Song is You*, p. 26.

[11]Granata, p. 181.

[12]Friedwald, *The Song is You*, p. 265.

[13]Bennett, p. 185.

[14]Ringgold and McCarty, p. 218.

[15]*Assault on a Queen* pressbook (Paramount Pictures, 1966), p. 2

[16]*Assault on a Queen* pressbook, p. 4.

[17]*Assault on a Queen* pressbook, p. 4.

[18]*Assault on a Queen* pressbook, p. 3.

[19]*Assault on a Queen* pressbook, p. 4.

[20]*Assault on a Queen* pressbook, p. 3.

[21]*Assault on a Queen* pressbook, p. 4.

[22]*Assault on a Queen* pressbook, p. 4.

[23]Nancy Sinatra, *Frank Sinatra: An American Legend*, p. 199.

[24]*Variety*, 22 June 1966.

[25]*New York Times*, 28 July 1966, p. 23.

[26]Ringgold and McCarty, p. 222.

[27]Ringgold and McCarty, p. 222.

[28]*The Naked Runner* pressbook (Warner Bros. Pictures, 1967), p. 3.

[29]*Variety*, 5 July 1967.

[30]*New York Times*, 20 July 1967, p. 30.

[31]Ringgold and McCarty, p. 226.

[32]*Frank Sinatra: Off the Record.*

[33]Frank Sinatra, *Life*, p. 101.

[34]*TV Guide*, p. 16.

[35]Friedwald, *The Song is You*, p. 425.

[36]Friedwald, *The Song is You*, p. 428.

[36]Abby Rizzo, letter to Scott Allen Nollen, 26 June 2001.

[37]*Variety*, 8 November 1967.

[38]*New York Times*, 16 November 1967, p. 58.

[39]Ringgold and McCarty, p. 230.

[40]Ringgold and McCarty, p. 230.

[41]Tina Sinatra, p. 119.

[42]*New York Times*, 18 October 1967.

[43]*Live with Larry King*, 13 May 1988.

[44]*New York Times*, 18 October 1967.

[45]*Variety*, 17 May 1968.

[46]*New York Times*, 29 May 1968.

[47]Ringgold and McCarty, p. 234.

[48]Ringgold and McCarty, p. 234.

[49]Friedwald, *The Song is You*, p. 304.

[50]Friedwald, *The Song is You*, p. 307.

[51]Friedwald, *The Song is You*, p. 307.

[52]*Tony Rome* pressbook (Twentieth Century-Fox Film Corporation, 1967), p. 4.

[53]Nancy Sinatra, *Frank Sinatra: An American Legend*, p. 205.

[54]*Variety*, 24 October 1968.

[55]*New York Times*, 21 November 1968, p. 41.

[56]Ringgold and McCarty, p. 237.

[57]Mustazza, p. 98.

[58]Friedwald, *The Song is You*, p. 447.

[59]Nancy Sinatra, *Frank Sinatra: An American Legend*, p. 210.

[60]Friedwald, *The Song is You*, p. 438.

[61]Nancy Sinatra, *Frank Sinatra: An American Legend*, p. 212.

[62]Nancy Sinatra, *Frank Sinatra: An American Legend*, p. 214.

[63]Nancy Sinatra, *Frank Sinatra: An American Legend*, p. 216.

[64]*Dirty Dingus Magee* pressbook (Metro-Goldwyn-Mayer Pictures, 1970), p. 4.

[65]*Dirty Dingus Magee* pressbook, p. 4.

[66]*Dirty Dingus Magee* pressbook, p. 5.

[67]Elam.

[68]*Dirty Dingus Magee* pressbook, p. 4.

[69]*Variety*, 21 July 1970.

[70]*Variety*, 28 October 1970.

[71]*New York Times*, 19 November 1970, p. 42.

[72]Ringgold and McCarty, ps. 239, 240.

[73]Nancy Sinatra, *Frank Sinatra: An American Legend*, p. 215.

[74]Nancy Sinatra, *Frank Sinatra: My Father*, p. 223.

[75]Preminger, p. 113.

[76]Kuntz, p. 226.

[77]*Variety*, 17 April 1974.

[78]Friedwald, *The Song is You*, p. 466.

[79]Nancy Sinatra, *Frank Sinatra: My Father*, p. 257.

[80]*TV Guide*, 19-26 November 1977, p. 14.

[81]Tina Sinatra, p. 77.

[82]Ringgold and McCarty, p. 243.

[83]*TV Guide*, 19-26 November 1977, p. 14.

[84]"This Weeks Movies," *TV Guide*, p. A-7.

[85]Tina Sinatra.

[86]*TV Guide*, 19-26 November 1977, p. 14.

[87]Friedwald, *The Song is You*, p. 313.

[88]Friedwald, *The Song is You*, p. 478.

[89]Friedwald, *The Song is You*, p. 356.

[90]Friedwald, *The Song is You*, p. 476.

[91]*Variety*, 22 October 1980.

[92]*New York Times*, 24 October 1980, p. C10.

[93]Freedland, p. 396.

[94]Elam.

[95]Freedland, p. 396.

[96]*New York Times*, 29 June 84, p. C14.

[97]*New York Times*, 29 July 1984.

[98]Ringgold and McCarty, p. 248.

[99]*Frank Sinatra Memorial* DVD; *TV Guide*, 30 May-5 June 1988.

[100]*Live with Larry King.*

[101]Nancy Sinatra, *Frank Sinatra: An American Legend*, p. 316.

[102]*Live with Larry King.*

[103]Tina Sinatra, p. 220.

[104]Tina Sinatra, p. 221.

[105]Willy Rizzo.

[106]Abby Rizzo, letter to Scott Allen Nollen, 26 June 2001.

[107]Nancy Sinatra, *Frank Sinatra: An American Legend*, p. 316.

[108]Tina Sinatra, p. 227.

[109]Friedwald, *The Song is You*, p. 506.

[110]Friedwald, *The Song is You* p. 506.

[111]Friedwald, *The Song is You* p. 508.

[112]Natalie Cole, written with Digby Diehl, *Angel on My Shoulder: An Autobiography* (New York: Warner Books, Inc., 2000), pp. 288-90.

[113]Tina Sinatra, pp. 242-243.

[114]Tina Sinatra, p. 246.

[115]Tina Sinatra, p. 247.

[116]Bill Miller, *Sinatra: 80th Live In Concert* compact disc liner notes
(Capitol Records CDP 7243 8 31723 20).

[117]Freedland, p. 422.

[118]Tina Sinatra, p. 265.

[119]Tina Sinatra, p. 269.

[120]*All Politics* (Birmingham, England), 15 May 1998.

[121]*Sinatra: A Tribute* CD (BDD Audio), 1998.

[122]*Chicago Tribune*, 16 May 1998, p. 1.

[123]*The New York Times*, 16 May 1998, p. 1.

[124]*Frank Sinatra Memorial* DVD.

[125]*Frank Sinatra Memorial* DVD.

[126]*Donnie Brasco* DVD.

[127]*A Tribute* CD.

Bibliography

Primary Sources
Writings by Sinatra
"Me and My Music." *Life*, Vol. 58, No. 16; 23 April 1965.

Interviews and Reminiscences
Caruso, Nick Sr. Discussion with Scott Allen Nollen, Willy Rizzo and Nick Caruso, Jr., Chicago, Illinois, 20 July 2001.
Caruso, Nick Jr. Discussion with Scott Allen Nollen and Willy Rizzo, Chicago, Illinois, 20 July 2001.
Dickinson, Angie. *Ocean's Eleven* DVD.
Frankenheimer, John. *The Manchurian Candidate* DVD.
Karloff, Sara Jane. Discussion with Scott Allen Nollen, Hollywood, California, November 1996.
Kelly, Grace. "Live at the Royal Festival Hall" *Reprise Collection* laserdisc.
Lansbury, Angela. Telephone discussion with Scott Allen Nollen, 17 July 1996.
Rizzo, Abby. Discussion with Scott Allen Nollen, July 2002.
Rizzo, Willy. Discussion with Scott Allen Nollen and Nick Caruso, Jr., Chicago, Illinois, 20 July 2001.
Sinatra, Frank. Interview with Edward R. Murrow, 14 September 1956.
Sinatra, Frank. *Pal Joey* DVD.
Sinatra, Frank. Interview with Walter Cronkite, 1965.
Sinatra, Frank. Interview with Larry King, 13 May 1988.
Sinatra, Frank Jr. *Ocean's Eleven* DVD.
Sinatra, Frank Jr. *Robin and the 7 Hoods* DVD.

Letters and Memos
Bernhardt, Milt. Letter to Scott Allen Nollen, 1999.
Elam, Jack. Letter to Scott Allen Nollen, 7 January 1998.
Harmon, Nikki. Letter to Scott Allen Nollen, 17 February 2000.
Harris, Julie. Letter to Scott Allen Nollen, 5 May 1996.
Mortimer, Lee. Letter to Westbrook Pegler, 1 September 1947.
Rizzo, Abby. Letter to Scott Allen Nollen, 26 June 2001.
Ruark, Robert C. Letter to Westbrook Pegler, 14 March 1947.
Sinatra, Nancy. Letter to Scott Allen Nollen, 16 December 1997.

Press Releases
Neville, Glenn. Press release H23-'16, 9 April 1947.

Scripts
Schwartz, David. *Robin and the 7 Hoods*. Annotated by Leroy Deane. Warner Bros. Pictures, Inc. Final, 15 October 1963, and Revisions, 22 October 1963, 23 October 1963, 24 October 1963, 25 October 1963, 29 October 1963, 31 October 1963, 6 December 1963.
Twist, John, and Katsuya Susaki. *None But the Brave*. Annotated by Leroy Deane. Artanis Productions/ Warner Bros. Pictures. Final, 20 March 1964, and Revisions, 23 March 1964, 24 March 1964, 6 April 1964, 22 May 1964, 29 May 1964.

Studio and Production Company Documents
"Cast and Crew from Tokyo Eiga Co.," *None But the Brave*. Warner Bros. Pictures, Inc., 17 March 1964.
Deane, LeRoy. Production No. 480, *None But the Brave*, "Set 21—All Location Shots," annotations and notes. Warner Bros. Pictures, Inc., 14 April-14 May 1964.
Deane, LeRoy. Set Construction, *None But the Brave*. Warner Bros. Pictures, Inc., 12 June 1964.
Deane, LeRoy. Set Construction, *None But the Brave*. Warner Bros. Pictures, Inc., 26 June 1964.
Deane, LeRoy. Set Construction, *Robin and the 7 Hoods*. Warner Bros. Pictures, Inc., 5 November 1963.
Deane, LeRoy. Set Cost, *Robin and the 7 Hoods*. Warner Bros. Pictures, Inc., 6 December 1963.
Deane, LeRoy. Set Cost, *Robin and the 7 Hoods*. Warner Bros. Pictures, Inc., 13 December 1963.
Deane, LeRoy, to Howard Koch. Inter-Office Communication, *None But the Brave*. Warner Bros. Pictures, Inc., 7 May 1964.
Koch, Howard W., to Carl Milliken, Jr. Inter-Department Communication, *Robin and the 7 Hoods*. Sinatra

Enterprises, 30 October 1963.

Koch, Howard W., to Charles Greenlaw. Inter-Department Communication, *Robin and the 7 Hoods*. Sinatra Enterprises, 10 March 1964.

Koch, Howard W., to Charles Greenlaw. Inter-Department Communication, *Robin and the 7 Hoods*. Sinatra Enterprises, 17 March 1964.

Koch, Howard W., to Leroy Deane. Inter-Department Communication, *Robin and the 7 Hoods*. Sinatra Enterprises, 4 October 1963.

Milliken, Carl, Jr., to Howard W. Koch. Inter-Office Communication, *Robin and the 7 Hoods*. Warner Bros. Pictures, Inc., 25 October 1963.

Nilson, E. F., to Robert S. Irving. Construction Estimate, *None But the Brave*. Artanis Production Corp./ Warner Bros. Studio, 9 March 1964..

None But the Brave. Shooting Schedule. Warner Bros. Pictures, Inc., 8-23 June 1964.

None But the Brave. Staff and Crew List. Warner Bros. Pictures, Inc., 1964.

Robin and the 7 Hoods. Shooting Schedule. Warner Bros. Pictures, Inc., 31 October-24 December 1963.

Government Records

Kuntz, Tom, and Phil Kuntz, ed. *The Sinatra Files: The Secret FBI Dossier*. New York: Three Rivers Press, 2000.

Memoirs

Bennett, Tony, with Will Friedwald. *Tony Bennett: The Good Life*. New York: Simon and Schuster, Inc., 1998.

Bogart, Stephen. *Bogart: In Search of My Father*. New York: E.P. Dutton, 1995.

Cole, Natalie, written with Digby Diehl. *Angel on My Shoulder: An Autobiography*. New York: Warner Books, 2000.

Davis, Sammy Jr. *Hollywood in a Suitcase*. New York: William Morrow and Company, Inc., 1980.

Davis, Sammy Jr. *Yes I Can*. New York: Farrar, Straus and Giroux, 1965.

Preminger, Otto. *Preminger: An Autobiography*. New York: Doubleday and Co., 1977.

Sinatra, Nancy. *Frank Sinatra: My Father*. New York: Pocket Books, 1985.

Sinatra, Nancy. *Frank Sinatra: An American Legend*. Santa Monica, CA: General Publishing Group, Inc., 1995.

Sinatra, Tina, with Jeff Coplon. *My Father's Daughter*. New York: Simon and Schuster, 2000.

Pressbooks and Program Books

Assault on a Queen pressbook. Paramount Pictures, 1967.

Can-Can program book. Twentieth Century Fox Film Corporation, 1959.

Come Blow Your Horn pressbook. Paramount Pictures, 1963.

The Detective pressbook. Twentieth Century-Fox Film Corporation, 1968.

Dirty Dingus Magee pressbook. Metro-Goldwyn-Mayer Pictures, 1970.

The Manchurian Candidate pressbook. United Artists Pictures, 1962.

The Naked Runner pressbook. Warner Bros. Pictures, 1967.

The Tender Trap pressbook. Metro-Goldwyn-Mayer Pictures, 1955.

That's Entertainment pressbook. Metro-Goldwyn-Mayer Pictures, 1974.

Documentary Films, Video and Audio Programs

Frank Sinatra: A Tribute. BDD Audio CD, 1998.

Frank Sinatra Memorial. Passport Video DVD, 1999.

Frank Sinatra: Off the Record, CBS, 1965.

Frank Sinatra with All God's Children, 1962.

Newspapers, Trade Papers, Magazines and Websites

"Actor Dean Martin Dies at 78," CNN Website, 25 December 1995.

"As Pegler Sees It," King Features, 1947.

Canby, Vincent. "Post-Mortem on Flops," *New York Times*, 29 July 1984.

Chicago *Herald-American*, 14 April 1947.

"Clinton Reacts to Frank Sinatra's Death," *All Politics*, Birmingham, England, 15 May 1998.

Crist, Judith. "This Weeks Movies," *TV Guide*, 19-25 November 1977, Vol. 25, No. 47.

Crowther, Bosley. *New York Times*, 14 March 1947.

Hale, Wanda. "'Meet Danny Wilson' on Paramount Screen," 27 March 1952.

Hickey, Neil. "What a Swell Party This Was," *TV Guide*, 19-25 November 1977, Vol. 25, No. 47.

Hollywood Reporter, 1941-1974.

Kahn, E.J. Jr. "What Will Sinatra Do Next?" *Look*, 5 August 1947.

Los Angeles Times, 1941-1974.

New York Times, 1941-1974.

Powers, James. "'Hoods' Ring-a-Ding B. O. by Sinatra Gang," *Hollywood Reporter*, 25 June 1964.

"Private Funeral Held for Sinatra," CNN Website, 20 May 1998.

"The Private World and Thoughts of Frank Sinatra," *Life*, Vol. 58, No. 16; 23 April 1965.

"Program for Funeral of Frank Sinatra," CNN Website, 20 May 1998.

"Remembering Frank Sinatra," *TV Guide*. Volume 46, Number 22, 30 May 1998.

"Robin and the Seven Hoods," *Daily Variety*, 25 June 1964.

"Sinatra in Sands Fracas," *New York Times*, 13 September 1967.

Screen Album, Fall 1947, p. 21.

"Tantrum Gets Frank Punch in the Mouth," *Chicago Tribune*, 13 September 1967.

Tresniowski, Alex, and Richard Lacayo. "A Swinger with Swagger," *People Weekly*, Volume 49, Number 21, 1 June 1998.

"Tunesmiths 'Sing'," *New York Times*, 12 October 1947.

Variety, 1941-1984.

Who Tribute: Frank Sinatra, His Life, His Way. Time, Inc., Magazine Company, 1998.

References on Sinatra's Career

Mustazza, Leonard. *Ol' Blue Eyes: A Frank Sinatra Encyclopedia*. Westport, Connecticut: Greenwood Press, 1998.

Secondary Sources
Biographies

Britt, Stan. *Sinatra: A Celebration*. New York: Schirmer Books, 1995.

Brown, Peter Harry. *Kim Novak: Reluctant Goddess*. New York: St. Martin's Press, 1986.

Freedland, Michael. *All the Way: A Biography of Frank Sinatra, 1915-1998*. New York: St. Martin's Press, 1997.

Frischauer, Willi. *Behind the Scenes of Otto Preminger*. London: Michael Joseph, Ltd., 1973.

Hamill, Pete. *Why Sinatra Matters*. Boston: Little, Brown and Company, 1998.

Hirschhorn, Clive. *Gene Kelly: A Biography*. Chicago: Henry Regnery Co., 1974.

Hotchner, A. E. *Doris Day: Her Own Story*. New York: William Morrow and Company, Inc., 1976.

Howlett, John. *Frank Sinatra*. Philadelphia: Courage Books, 1980.

Kotsilibas-Davis, James. *The Barrymores: The Royal Family in Hollywood*. New York: Crown Publishers, 1981.

Lawford, Patricia Seaton, with Ted Scharz. *The Peter Lawford Story*. New York: Carrol and Graf Publishing, Inc, 1988.

Quirk, Lawrence J., and William Schoell. *The Rat Pack: The Hey-Hey Days of Frank and the Boys*. Dallas: Taylor Publishing Company, 1998.

Silverman, Stephen M. *Dancing on the Ceiling: Stanley Donen and His Movies*. New York: Alfred A. Knopf, 1996.

Taraborelli, J. Randy. *Sinatra: Behind the Legend*. Secaucus, NJ: Carol Publishing Group, 1997.

Tosches, Nick. *Dino: Living High in the Dirty Business of Dreams*. New York: Dell Publishing Co., 1999.

Books About Sinatra's Music

Granata, Charles L. *Sessions With Sinatra*. Chicago: A Cappella Books, 1999.

Friedwald, Will. *Sinatra! The Song Is You*. New York: Scribner, 1995.

O'Brien, Ed, with Robert Wilson. *Sinatra 101: The 101 Best Recordings and the Stories Behind Them*. New York: Boulevard Books, 1996.

Books About Vocal Jazz

Friedwald, Will. *Jazz Singing*. DeCapo, 1996.

Books on the Musical Genre

Mordden, Ethan. *The Hollywood Musical.* New York: St. Martin's Press, 1981.

Compact Disc Liner Notes

Friedwald, Will, with Mitchell Zlokower. "Songs for Swingin' Singles: An Appreciation," *The Complete Capitol Singles Collection.* Capitol Records C2724383808922.

Friedwald, Will. "The Complete Columbia Sessions," *The Columbia Years, 1943-1952: The Complete Recordings.* New York: Columbia Records, 1993.

Friedwald, Will, and William Ruhlmann. *Tommy Dorsey, Frank Sinatra: The Song Is You.* RCA 66363 2/4.

Lawrence, Jack. "All or Nothing At All," *Harry James and his Orchestra featuring Frank Sinatra: The Complete Recordings.* Columbia Legacy CD 66377.

Lieberson, Goddard. *Frank Sinatra Conducts the Music of Alec Wilder.* Sony Music Special Products A 4271.

Maltin, Leonard, and Charles L. Granata, Didier C. Deutsch, Will Friedwald and Scott Allen Nollen. *Frank Sinatra in Hollywood.* New York and Burbank, CA: Reprise Records-Turner Classic Movies Music, 2002.

Miller, Bill. *Sinatra 80th: Live in Concert.* Capitol Records CDP 7243 8 31723 2 0.

Pignone, Charles. *Robin and the 7 Hoods.* Artanis Entertainment Group ARZ-104-2.

Tollin, Anthony. *Starring Frank Sinatra and Friends.* Schiller Park, IL: Radio Spirits, 2000.

Welding, Pete. *Close to You.* Capitol Records 4 96991 2.

Welding, Pete. *Come Dance with Me.* Capitol Records 4 96997 2.

Welding, Pete. *Come Swing with Me.* Capitol Records 4 97001 2.

Welding, Pete. *Frank Sinatra Sings for Only the Lonely.* Capitol Records 4 96996 2.

Welding, Pete. *In the Wee Small Hours.* Capitol Records 4 96988 2.

Welding, Pete. *Nice 'n' Easy.* Capitol Records 4 97000 2.

Welding, Pete. *Point of No Return.* Capitol Records 4 97004 2.

Welding, Pete. *Where Are You?* Capitol Records 4 96993 2.

Young, Al. *John Coltrane: Coltrane for Lovers.* The Verve Music Group 314 549 361-2.

Filmography

Ringgold, Gene, and Clifford McCarty. *The Films of Frank Sinatra.* Secaucus, NJ: Citadel Press, 1993.

Index

Numbers in **boldface** indicate photographs.

Abbott, Bud 32, 52
The Abbott and Costello Show (radio show) 52
"Ain't That a Kick in the Head?" (song) 211, 212
Albert, Eddie 157-158
Albright, Lola 127-128, **128**, 130, **131**
Aldrich, Robert 11, 244-245
Algren, Nelson 132
"All My Tomorrows" (song) 192, 220, 289
"All of Me" (song) 50, 96, 274, 297
"All or Nothing At All" (song) 23, 32, 54, 270-271, 294, 297, 305
The All-Star Bond Rally (1944 film) 51
"All the Way" (song) 155-156, 159, 173, 243, 309
Allen, Fred 21, 33, 50, 58
Allen, Lewis 55, 112, 114
Allen, Woody 305
"Almost Like Being in Love" (song) 69
"Always" (song) 64
"American Beauty Rose" (song) 90, 220
Anchors Aweigh (1945 film) 43-50, **43**, **44**, **47**, **48**, 51, 52-53, 54, 59, 62, 68, 69, 78, 82, 88, 89, 165, 296, 307
Andress, Ursula 244-245
Andrews Sisters 23, 51, 162, 254
"Angel Eyes" (song) 11, 177, 274, 294, 297, 311
"April in Paris" (song) 174
Arlen, Harold 38, 52, 60, 72, 90, 105, 110, 118, 125, 182, 219, 266, 273-274, 299
Armstrong, Louis 15, 32, 52, 61, 74, 121, **143**, 144, 146-147, 162, 260
Around the World in 80 Days (1956 film) 154-155, **154**
Assault on a Queen (1966 film) 271-275, **272**, **274**,
Astaire, Fred 15, 42, 43, 53, 192, 236, 238, 279, 296
"Autumn in New York" (song) 74, 174, 296, 300
"Autumn Leaves" (song) 163

Bacall, Lauren 54, 111-112, 147, 162, 171
Bailey, Pearl 74
Ball, Lucille 70, 234, 246
Barton, Charles T. 32
Barrymore, Ethel 118-119, 164
Basie, William ("Count") 32, 125, 238-239, 256, 260-261, 267, 273-274, 303, 314
"Baubles, Bangles and Beads" (song) 192, 279
Beau, Heinie 192
"Begin the Beguine" (song) 23
Ben Gurion, David 237
Benedek, Laslo 80, 81
Bennett, Tony 15, 65-66, 89, 94, 141, 260-261, 271, 273, 278, 297, 299, 309, 310, 313, 314
Benny, Jack 31, 50, 69, 77, 87, 89, 99
Berkeley, Busby 11, 78-79, 203
Berlin, Irving 30, 60, 61, 75, 119, 192, 217, 255, 278, 279
Bernstein, Elmer 135-136, 149, 175, 177, 179, 189
on Sinatra 135-136
"The Best is Yet to Come" (song) 261, 309
"Bewitched" (song) 166, 167, 173, 241, 309
The Big Minstrel Act (1935 film) 21
Bill, Tony 239, 242, 259
"The Birth of the Blues" (song) 99, 170
Bishop, Joey 198, 205-206, **206**, 216, 218
Bisset, Jacqueline 282, **283**
"Blame It On My Youth" (song) 148
Blocker, Dan 242, 285, 287
Bloom, Verna **298**
"Blue Moon" (song) 217
"Blue Skies" (song) 61
"Body and Soul" (song) 74
Bogart, Humphrey 53, 54, 111-112, 130, 147, 162, 176, 180, 198, 242, 252, 280-281
on Sinatra 111
Bond, Ward 244
Borgnine, Ernest 104, 271
on Sinatra 104

Brando, Marlon 12, 112, 126-127, **126**, 132-133, 166, 187, 295
on Sinatra 126, 268
Broadway Bandbox (radio show) 32, 33, 34, 38
"Brooklyn Bridge" (song) 66, 69
Brown, Lawrence 64
Brynner, Yul, 268-269, **269**
Burke, Johnny 28, 50, 72, 86, 91, 148, 182, 220, 254, 270
Buono, Victor 244-245, **245**, 252
on Sinatra 244-245
Burns and Allen Show (radio show) 37, 51, 63
"But Beautiful" (song) 72
Butterfield, Billy 91

Cagney, James 19, 126, 164, 208, 281
Cahn, Sammy 27, 40, 44, 48, 50, 51, 52, 60, 66, 67, 69, 71, 81, 91, 94, 110, 118, 127, 129, 131, 136, 138, 155, 156, 162, 173, 174, 175, 177, 185, 188, 189, 192, 197, 219, 220, 226, 238, 241, 242, 252, 261, 266, 269, 288, 289, 295, 305, 314
on Sinatra 44
Can-Can (1960 film) 201-204, **202**, **204**, 305
Cannonball Run II (1984 film) 303-304
Capone, Al 250-251
Capra, Frank 11, 76, 190-197
Carney, Harry 64
Carousel (Broadway show) 52, 60, 241
Carousel (1955 film project) 124, 315
Casnoff, Philip 306-308
Cast a Giant Shadow (1966 film) 268-269, **269**, 299
"C'est Magnifique" (song) 203
Chaney, Jr., Lon 123
"Change Partners" (song) 279
Chaplin, Charles 16, 17, 46, 70, 281, 291
Charisse, Cyd 81, 138
Charles, Ray 63, 260, 278, 289, 311
The Charlie McCarthy Show (radio show) 51

"Cheek to Cheek" (song) 192

Chevalier, Maurice 201-204, **204**, 220

"Chicago" (song) 155, 173

Clift, Montgomery 11, 13, 46, 103-108, **107**, **108**, 123, 187

Clinton, Bill 311-312

Clooney, Rosemary 91, 243

Close to You (album) 148-149, 278

Cobb, Lee J. 239, 242

"The Coffee Song" (song) 60, 219

Cohn, Harry 54, 100, 102, 105, 164-165

Cole, Nat ("King") 64, 77, 81, 105, 173, 177, 208, 218, 237, 266

Cole, Natalie 297, 309, 310

Comden, Betty 78, 83

Come Blow Your Horn (1963 film) 239-243, **240**, 264, 279

"Come Blow Your Horn" (song) 242

Come Dance with Me (album) 191-192, 279

Come Fly with Me (album) 173-174, 221

"Come Fly with Me" (song) 174, 269, 273, 309

Come Swing with Me (album) 220

"Come Rain or Come Shine" (song) 91

The Concert Sinatra (album) 241-242

Condon, Richard 226, 231

Conte, Richard 210, 272-273, 279, 287

Contract on Cherry Street (1977 TV film) 298-299, **298**

Costa, Don 288, 289, 296, 299, 303

Costello, Lou 32, 52

Coward, Noel 50, 224, 237

on Sinatra 201

Crosby, Bing 11, 15, 19, 20, 21, 23, 25, 26, 28, 30, 31, 32, 34, 36, 37, 38, 42, 43, 51, 52, 54, 59, 60, 69, 73, 77, 89, 91, 99, 110, 111, 112, 141, 142-147, **143**, **145**, **146**, 148, 162, 174, 203, 208, 230, 236, 243, 246, **248**, 250, 252-254, 255, 270, 296, 298, 299

Crosby, Bob 30, 32, 42

Curtis, Tony 98, 175, **176**, 178-182, **179**, 243, 262, 313

D'Amato, Paul ("Skinny") 108, 217, 238

Dana, Leora 178, 180, 181, 188, 189

Daves, Delmer 11

Davis, Sammy Jr. 71, 130, 138, 162, 198, 205-214, **205**, **206**, **209**, 218, 225, 238, 239, 243, 246, 248-253, **248**, 273, 274, 285, 303-304, 314

on Sinatra 205, 206-207

"Day By Day"(song) 220

Day, Doris 73, 84, 99, 115-121, **119**, 254

on Sinatra 116-118

"Day In, Day Out" (song) 110, 192

Deane, LeRoy 248, 255-256

DeHaven, Gloria 39-41, **39**, **41**, 43, 50

DeMille, Cecil B. 42, 152, 154

The Devil at Four O'Clock (1961 film) 217, 222-224, **223**, 261

The Detective (1968 film) 281-284, **283**, **284**,

Dickinson, Angie 205, 207-208, **207**, 268, 313

on Sinatra 207-208

Dietrich, Marlene 154, 162

DiMaggio, Joe 132, 162

"Dindi" (song) 279

Dirty Dingus Magee (1970 film) 260, 290-293, **290**, 301

Disney, Walt 49, 122

Donen, Stanley 11, 49, 62, 66, 78-79, 80, 84-85, 99, 293

"Don't Worry 'Bout Me" (song) 274

Dorsey, Jimmy 142

Dorsey, Tommy 11, 12, 15, 24-31, 52, 58, 86, 91, 125, 133, 139, 163, 171, 174, 273, 297, 306, 307, 308

on Sinatra 28

Double Dynamite (1951 film) 81, 89, 94-95, **95**,

Douglas, Gordon 11, 247, 253, 254, 279, 281-282, 286-287

Douglas, Kirk 243, 268-269, **269**, 297, 313

Duets (album) 308-309

Duets II (album) 309-310

Durante, Jimmy 38, 62, 66, **67**, **68**, 141, 208, 218

Duvall, Robert 282

Edison, Harry ("Sweets") 125, 148

Eisenhower, Dwight D. 72, 78, 105, 214

Ekberg, Anita 244-245

Elam, Jack 245, 291-293

on Sinatra 245, 291

Ellington, Edward Kennedy ("Duke") 32, 64, 161, 175, 236, 275, 285

"Embraceable You" (song) 209

Entratter, Jack 91, 208

Evans, George 31, 53, 62, 70, 84, 89

"Ever Homeward" (song) 77

"Everybody Loves Somebody" (song) 74, 175

The Execution of Private Slovik (novel) 214

The Execution of Private Slovik (aborted film project) 214-216

Falk, Peter 248-250, 252

Fame and Fortune (radio show) 27

Farnon, Robert 237

Farrow, Mia 261, 274, 281-282, 313

Finian's Rainbow (1954 film project) 122, 315

The First Deadly Sin (1980 film) 301-302, **302**

Fitzgerald, Ella 15, 28, 122, 162, 208, 224, 284, 287, 306

"Five Minutes More" (song) 60, 220

"Fly Me to the Moon" (song) 260, 267, 274, 290, 309, 314

Flynn, Errol 16, 78, 91, 140, 250

"A Foggy Day" (song) 109, 171, 219, 309, 310

Ford, John 52, 100-102, 196, 226, 244

4 for Texas (1964 film) 243-245, **245**

Francis A. and Edward K. (1967 album) 285

Francis Albert Sinatra and Antonio Carlos Jobim (album) 13, 278-279

Frank Sinatra Conducts the Music of Alec Wilder (album) 59

Frank Sinatra Conducts Tone Po-

ems of Color (album) 149

The Frank Sinatra Show (radio show) 38, 52, 58, 59, 71

The Frank Sinatra Show (TV show) 91, 92, 93, 99

Frank Sinatra in Hollywood (compact disc box set) 315

Frank Sinatra with All God's Children (1962 film) 236-237

Frankenheimer, John 11, 227-229, 231-234, 287
on Sinatra 227

Freed, Arthur 78-79, 83, 84-85, 99

From Here to Eternity (novel) 100, 105

From Here to Eternity (1953 film) 10, 11, 12, 13, 16, 100-110, **101**, **102**, **107**, **108**, 112, 115, 120, 123, 133, 164, 180, 192, 201, 214, 269, 299, 307, 313

"From Here to Eternity" (song) 136

Gable, Clark 20, 46, 63, 77, 81, 100

Gardner, Ava 69, 71, 81, 87, 89-91, 92, 93, 95, 96, 98, 100, 108, 115, 123, 150-151, 165, 171

Garfield, John 78, 116-117, 120, 132

Garland, Judy 15, 54, 58, 71, 78, 81, 83, 99, 111, 130, 226

Garrett, Betty 79, 82-83, **82**, 84-85, **84**, **87**
on Sinatra 79

Gates, Nancy 112, **114**, 185, 188, 189

Gershwin, George 44, 50, 60, 74, 109, 161, 171, 209, 221, 236, 238, 285

Gershwin, Ira 38, 44, 50, 60, 74, 109, 161, 171, 209, 221, 236, 238

Giancana, Sam ("Momo") 108, 217-219, 237-238, 239, 245-246, 307, 308, 313-314

"The Girl from Ipanema" (song) 278

Gleason, James 42, 113

The Godfather (1972 film) 294-295, 304

"The Good Life" (song) 261

Goodman, Benny 15, 23, 31, 32

"Goodnight, Irene" (song) 91

"Goody, Goody" (song) 236

Grahame, Gloria 66, 122-124, **122**

Grant, Cary 20, 64, 150-154, **150**, **153**, 164, 225
on Sinatra 151

Grayson, Katherine 46, **48**, 62, 66, 67-68, **67**, 71, 74-75, 78, 80

Green, Adolph 79, 83

Greene, Shecky 279-280

"Guess I'll Hang My Tears Out to Dry" (song) 11, 61, 177, 309

Guys and Dolls (1955 film) 126-127, **126**, **127**, 246, 311

Hackett, Bobby 74

Haines, Connie 28, 30

Hammerstein, Oscar 50, 52, 60, 63, 82, 83, 92, 124, 161, 176, 241, 243, 267, 281

Hardy, Oliver 46, 129, 161, 221, 291

Harmon, David P. 139
on Sinatra 139

Harmon, Nikki 139

Hart, Lorenz ("Larry") 36, 44, 52, 59, 74, 90, 95, 109, 125, 148, 149, 155, 161, 164, 166, 168, 177, 189, 217, 220, 221, 274, 311

Harvey, Laurence 46, 227-228, **228**, **229**, **230**, 233-234

Hawkins, Coleman 64

Hawks, Howard 262

Hayden, Sterling 112-114, **114**

Hayworth, Rita **164**, 165-171

Hecht, Ben 76-77

Hefti, Neil 236, 238

"Hello, Dolly" (song) 81, 260

"Hello, Young Lovers" (song) 92, 267

Herman, Woody 296-197

"High Hopes" (song) 194, 197, 218, 220

High Society (1956 film) 142-147, **143**, **144**, **145**, **146**, 148, 149, 296

Higher and Higher (1943 film) **34**, **35**, 36-37, **37**, 38, 74, 307

Hodges, Eddie **190**, **193**, 194-196

Hodges, Johnny 64, 236, 285

Hoffa, Jimmy 224

Holden, William 78

A Hole in the Head (1958 film) 11, 190-197, **190**, **193**, 239, 289

Holiday, Billie 28, 55, 162, 290

Holm, Celeste **128**, 130, 142-146
on Sinatra 142

Hoover, J. Edgar 16, 70, 74

Hope, Bob 27, 28, 38, 51, 54, 59, 60, 69, 70, 91, 99, 141, 153, 176, 202, 230

Horne, Lena 15, 63, 208, 310

The House I Live In (1945 film) 16, 54-59, **57**, **58**, 60, 63, 75, 180, 192, 214, 217, 307

"The House I Live In" (song) 55, 254, 297, 309

House Un-American Activities Committee (HUAC) 54

"How Deep Is the Ocean (How High Is the Sky)" (song) 60, 96, 98, 209

Howard, Trevor 261-263, **263**

Humphrey, Hubert 285

Huston, John 11, 162, 243

Hutton, Betty 52

Hutton, June 86, 96, 119

"I Believe" (song) 66, 67, 69

"I Concentrate on You" (song) 64, 279

"I Could Write a Book" (song) 95, 166, 168, 173

"I Cover the Waterfront" (song) 163

"I Didn't Know What Time It Was" (song) 166

"I Fall in Love Too Easily" (song) 49, 51

"I Get a Kick Out of You" (song) 109, 171, 236, 296

"I Got It Bad (And That Ain't Good)" (song) 161

"I Love Paris" (song) 202, 208, 246

"I Only Have Eyes for You" (song) 238, 246

"I Wanna Be Around" (song) 260

"I Won't Dance" (song) 239

"I'll Never Smile Again" (song) 26, 28, 58, 269, 294, 297

"I'm a Fool to Want You" (song) 11, 92, 163

"I'm Beginning to See the Light" (song) 236

"I'm Gonna Sit Right Down and Write Myself a Letter" (song) 111, 238

"The Impossible Dream" (song) 278

"In the Blue of the Evening" (song) 31

In the Wee Small Hours (album) 10, 124-125, 141, 270

"In the Wee Small Hours of the Morning" (song) 125, 243

"It All Depends on You" (song) 86, 90

It Happened in Brooklyn (1947 film) 62, **63**, 66-69, **67**, **68**, 69, 88, 175, 296, 307

"It Was a Very Good Year" (song) 267, 274, 314

"It's Only a Paper Moon" (song) 90

"It's the Same Old Dream" (song) 66-67, 69

"I've Got a Crush On You" (song) 74, 96, 98, 209, 273

"I've Got the World on a String" (song) 105, 309

"I've Got You Under My Skin" (song) 12, 141-142, 161, 171, 219, 243, 267, 273, 294, 309, 310

James, Harry 12, 13, 23-24, 25, 32, 51, 93, 220, 236, 297, 306, 307

"Jeepers Creepers" (song) 111

Jenkins, Gordon 10, 52, 149, 162, 163, 171-173, 177, 182, 266-267, 270, 278, 281, 296, 299, 300, 303

Jobim, Antonio Carlos 13, 16, 278-279, 281, 284, 287, 289, 293, 309

Johnny Concho (1956 film) 139-141, **140**, 141, 142, 144, 149, 260, 290

"Johnny Concho Theme" (song) 139

Johnson, Lyndon B. 285

The Joker is Wild (1957 film) 10, 11, 155-161, **156**, **159**, **160**, 166, 171, 173

Jolson, Al 11, 42, 160

Jones, Carolyn **128**, 130, 190-197, **190**

on Sinatra 190

Jones, James 100, 105

on Sinatra 105

Jones, Quincy 256, 260, 267, 273-274, 304-305

Jones, Shirley 124, 208

"Just In Time" (song) 189

"Just One of Those Things" (song) 111, 117, 118, 121, 171, 204

Karloff, Boris 11, 63, 120-121, 177-178, 180, 226, 262, 281, 307

Kaye, Stubby **127**

Keaton, Buster 30, 46, 154, 291

Kelly, Gene 11, 42, 43-49, **43**, **47**, **48**, 51, 53, 62, 63, 66, 74, 78-79, **79**, 82-88, **82**, **84**, **86**, **87**, 89, 100, 115, 164-165, 203, 246-247, 295, 296

on Sinatra 246-247, 252-253

Kelly, Grace 100-102, 142-147, **143**, **144**, **146**, 237, 293

on Sinatra 101-102

Kennedy, Robert 215, 219, 230, 314

Kennedy, John F. 8, 115, 208, 211, 213, 214-215, 217-219, 225, 227, 230, 235, 242, 246, 249-250, 294, 308, 313-314

Kern, Jerome 38, 44, 50, 60, 63, 161, 176, 236, 254

Kerr, Deborah 103, 264-265, **264**, 267

King, Martin Luther Jr. 181, 220

Kings Go Forth (1958 film) 10, 11, 98, 175-176, **176**, 178-182, **179**, 188, 200, 226

The Kissing Bandit (1948 film) 71, 72, 73, 74, 75, 78-81, **78**, 80-81, 88, 95, 265, 290, 293

Kramer, Stanley 11, 115, 122-123, 149-154, 197, 214

Kruschev, Nikita 202-203

L.A. is My Lady (album) 304-305

"L.A. is My Lady" (song) 304

Lady in Cement (1968 film) 285-288, **286**,

"The Lady is a Tramp" (song) 161, 166, 168-169, 170, 171, 246, 294, 296, 306

"The Lamplighters Serenade" (song) 30

Lancaster, Burt 102-108, **108**, 176, 243

on Sinatra 103-104

Lang, Charles 117-118

Lansbury, Angela 234

Las Vegas Nights (1941 film) 27-28, 29, 36, 307

"Last Night When We Were Young" (song) 266-267

"Laura" (song) 74, 163

Laurel, Stan 46, 68, 83, 129, 161, 169, 171, 221, 265, 291

Lawford, Peter 62, 66, **67**, **68**, 198, 204-214, **206**, 216, **222**, 230, 246, 296, 308

on Sinatra 205

"Lean Baby" (song) 103

"Learnin' the Blues" (song) 125, 239

Lee, Peggy 15, 175-176, 203, 224, 260

Leigh, Janet 228-229

LeRoy, Mervyn 11, 54, 60, 217

Levant, Oscar 148

Lewis, Jerry 95, 162, 176, 187, 313

Lewis, Joe E. 155-161

Life with Luigi (radio show) 80, 91

Lisi, Virna 272-275, **272**, **274**

on Sinatra 272

The List of Adrian Messenger (1963 film) 243

Lollobrigida, Gina 198-200, **199**

"Lonesome Road" (song) 161

Loren, Sophia 150-153, **150**, **153**

on Sinatra 151

Lorre, Peter 138, 154

"Lost in the Stars" (song) 62, 241

"Love and Marriage" (song) 131, 269

"(Love Is) The Tender Trap" (song) 129, 132, 171, 238

Luciano, Charles ("Lucky") 64-65, 69, 108

"Luck Be a Lady" (song) 126, 243, 246, 309

Lugosi, Bela 125-126

"Lush Life" (song) 178

"Mack the Knife" (song) 305, 309

MacLaine, Shirley 154, 183-189, **183**, **186**, **188**, 198, 201-204, **202**, **204**, 205, 303-304, 307

MacMurray, Fred **75**, **76**, 76-77

Magnum P.I. (TV show) 305

Major Bowes and His Original Amateur Hour (radio show) 20-21

"Makin' Whoopee" (song) 142, 274

Maltz, Albert 54-55, 214-216, 314

"Mama Will Bark" (song) 92, 93, 95, 99

A Man Alone (album) 289-290

The Man with the Golden Arm
(1955 film) 10, 11, 16, 132-
138, **134**, **137**, **138**, 144,
158, 166, 180, 184, 224,
280, 299, 313
"The Man with the Golden Arm"
(song) 136
The Manchurian Candidate (1962
film) 11, 16, 115, 226-236,
228, **229**, **230**, **232**, 239,
275, 281, 284, 287
Mancini, Henry 254, 269
Mankiewicz, Joseph L. 11, 126
Marriage on the Rocks (1965 film)
264-267
Martin, Dean 12, 50, 64, 74, 95,
130, 182-189, **183**, **186**,
205-214, **205**, **206**, **209**, 220,
222, 226, 230, 238, 243,
244-246, **245**, 248-253, **248**,
255, 260, 264-265, 268, 278,
281, 285, 294, 297, 303,
311, 313, 314
Marx Brothers 39, 297
Marx, Groucho 94-95, **95**, 99
Marx, Harpo 51
Maxwell, Marilyn 53, 71
May, Billy 10, 149, 173-174, 177,
189, 191-192, 220, 239, 243,
280, 285, 299, 300, 306
Mayer, Louis B. 41, 45, 62, 69,
84, 88
McQueen, Steve 198-199
"Me and My Shadow" (song)
239, 307
"Mean to Me" (song) 74
Meet Danny Wilson (1952 film)
92, **93**, 96-99, 111
Meet Frank Sinatra (radio show)
91, 92
Meet Me in Las Vegas (1955 film)
138-139
Melcher, Marty 117
Mercer, Johnny 38, 52, 60, 72,
110, 118, 141, 163, 182,
209, 224, 236, 254, 260,
269, 274, 279, 299
"Mighty Lak' a Rose" (song) 50
Milestone, Lewis 11, 205-206,
213
on Sinatra 206
Miller, Ann 81, 84-85, **84**, **87**
Miller, Glenn 28, 236, 270
Miller, Mitch 89-91, 92, 95, 108
Mills Brothers 21, 32
Minnelli, Vincente 11, 182-189,
197
The Miracle of the Bells (1848

film) 70, 72-76, **75**, **76**, 307
Mitchum, Robert 115, 122-124,
122, 207, 243
Monroe, Marilyn 132, **157**
Montalban, Ricardo 81
"Moon River" (song) 254
"Moonlight in Vermont" (song)
174
Moonlight Sinatra (album) 270
"More" (song) 260
Morgan, Michele **34**, **35**, 36, **37**
Mortimer, Lee 54, 69-72, 307,
314
Movin' with Nancy (1967 TV
show) 285
"Mrs. Robinson" (song) 289,
307
Munshin, Jules **79**, **82**, 83-87,
84, **86**, **87**
"My Funny Valentine" (song) 109,
166, 169, 171, 309
My Kind of Broadway (album)
269
"My Kind of Town" (song) 252,
254, 274, 303, 309
"My Shining Hour" (song) 38,
299
My Way (album) 289
"My Way" (song) 288, 294, 300,
311

Naish, J. Carroll 80, 91
The Naked Runner (1967 film)
275-278, **276**, 281
"Nancy (With the Laughing
Face)" (song) 50, 51, 54,
59, 243
"Nature Boy" (song) 77
Never So Few (1959 film) 198-
200, **199**, 204
Newman, Paul 131
Nice 'n' Easy (album) 208-209,
216
"Nice 'n' Easy" (song) 208-209
"Nice Work If You Can Get It"
(song) 161, 238
Nichols, Loring ("Red") 52
"Night and Day" (song) 21, 30,
32, 35, 43, 52, 74, 161, 225
The Night Club (1935 film) 21
"The Night We Called It a Day"
(song) 30, 74
"A Nightingale Sang in Berkeley
Square" (song) 237
Nixon, Richard 214, 218, 288,
290, 295
No One Cares (album) 10, 197,
266, 303

None But the Brave (1965 film)
11, 16, 255-260, **255**, **257**,
264
Norvo, Red 122, 179
Not as a Stranger (1955 film) 115,
122-124, **122**
"Not as a Stranger" (song) 125,
203
Novak, Kim 134-137, **137**, 166-
171, 208, 242
on Sinatra 134

Ocean's Eleven (1960 film) 204-
214, **205**, **206**, **207**, **209**,
210, 215, 275, 292, 314
"Oh, Look at Me Now" (song)
28
Ol' Blue Eyes is Back (album)
295
Ol' Blue Eyes is Back (1973 TV
show) 295
"Ol' Man River" (song) 11, 35,
41, 51, 52, 61, 63-64, 241,
284, 294, 311
"On the Sunny Side of the Street"
(song) 220
On the Town (1949 film) 47, 66,
82, 84-88, **84**, **86**, **87**, 163,
296, 307
On the Waterfront (1954 film)
112
"One for My Baby (And One
More For the Road)" (song)
16, 72, 117, 118, 121, 171,
182, 274, 309
Only the Lonely (album) 10, 177-
178, 182, 266, 270, 303
"Only the Lonely" (song) 11
The Oscar (1966 film) 271
Our Town (1955 TV show) 131,
203
"Over the Rainbow" (song) 52

Pal Joey (1957 film) 11, **14**, 95,
164-171, **164**, **165**, **167**, 173,
174, 242
Paley, William S. 58
Parker, Charlie ("Bird") 135,
305
Parker, Eleanor 135, 190-197,
190, 271
on Sinatra 190-191
Pegler, Westbrook 65, 66, 70, 73,
74, 214-216, 307
"Pennies from Heaven" (song)
238, 303
Peterson, Oscar 122
Pichel, Irving 76

"Please Be Kind" (song) 238, 246

Poitier, Sidney 218, 306, 313

Porter, Cole 12, 21, 23, 60, 64, 81, 90, 109, 111, 125, 141-142, 161, 201-202, 217, 219, 225, 236, 243, 246, 278, 279, 305

Portrait of an Album (1984 TV show) 305

Preminger, Otto 11, 132-138, 163, 197, 214, 224, 254, 294
on Sinatra 133-134

Presley, Elvis 11-12, 80, 216, 288, 296, 300

The Pride and the Passion (1957 film) 149-154, **150**, **153**, 158, 200, 201, 290

Prowse, Juliet 203, 208, 230

"Put Your Dreams Away" (song) 52, 175, 243, 313

Puzo, Mario 294

Raft, George 208, 212

The Rat Pack (1998 TV film) 313-314

The Rat Pack Live at the Sands (album) 246

Reagan, Ronald 63, 70, 294, 297, 302-303

Reed, Donna **101**, 103, **108**, 110, 208

Reflections (radio show) 31, 34

Reveille with Beverly (1943 film) 32, 36, 307

Reynolds, Debbie 127-130, **128**, 138, 208, 243, 296, 313
on Sinatra 127

Rich, Buddy 24, 25, 29, 32, 64, 96, 246, 303

Riddle, Nelson 10, 12, 30, 103, 105, 109, 111, 115, 125, 130-131, 132, 139, 141-142, 148-149, 155, 161, 162, 168, 170-171, 175, 177, 189, 191, 208-209, 212, 216, 217, 219-220, 241, 242, 243, 252, 254, 255, 269-270, 278, 285, 299, 300, 308

Ring-a-Ding-Ding! (album) 219-220, 221, 299

Rizzo, Abby 9, 279-280, 307

Rizzo, Jilly 9, 139, 227, 238, 239, 267, 274, 279-280, 283, 287, 288, 289, 293, 298, 304, 307

Rizzo, Willy 9, 238, 307

The Road to Hong Kong (1962 film) 230

The Road to Victory (1944 film) 43

Robeson, Paul 63

Robin and the 7 Hoods (1964 film) 8, 12, 16, 246-254, **248**, **249**, **251**

Robinson, Earl 55

Robinson, Edward G. 19, 190-197, **190**, **193**, 208, 214, 239, 248

Robson, Mark 11, 261-263

Rocky Fortune (radio show) 108, 109-110, 111

Rodgers, Richard 36, 44, 52, 59, 60, 74, 82, 83, 90, 92, 95, 109, 124, 125, 148, 149, 155, 161, 164, 166, 177, 189, 217, 220, 221, 241, 242, 243, 267, 274, 281, 311

Romero, Cesar 205, 208, 211

Roosevelt, Franklin Delano 38, 54, 69, 74, 294, 302

Rowan and Martin's Laugh In (TV show) 288

Rowlands, Gena 279-280

Rush, Barbara 239, **240**, 242, 248

Russell, Jane 89, 94-95, **95**

Sacks, Emmanuel ("Manie") 30, 31, 34, 38, 40, 81, 89, 94, 95, 176

Saint, Eva Marie 131

"Same Old Saturday Night" (song) 130, 203

Sands, Tommy 256, **257**, 259, 265

Sanicola, Henry ("Hank") 21, 28, 34, 71, 93, 95, 103, 125, 139, 171, 189, 237-238, 308

"Saturday Night (Is the Loneliest Night of the Week)" (song) 51, 192

Scott, George C. 243

Scorsese, Martin 300, 313

Screen Actors Guild (SAG) 63

"The Second Time Around" (song) 243

"Send In the Clowns" (song) 163

The September of My Years (album) 266-267

"The September of My Years" (song) 266, 274

"September Song" (song) 63, 110, 267

Sergeants' 3 (1962 film) 221-222, **222**, 292

Serling, Rod 272-273, 275

"The Shadow of Your Smile" (song) 273

Shavelson, Melville 268-269

She Shot Me Down (album) 303

"She's Funny That Way" (song) 33, 38, 92, 96, 97, 209

Ship Ahoy (1942 film) 29, 36

Shore, Dinah 52, 58, 59, 70, 88, 183, 243

Sidney, George 11, 43, 49, 165
on Sinatra 45-46, 169

"Silent Night" (song) 64

Silva, Henry 126, 205, 228, 298, 303

Silvers, Phil 50, 54, 62

Simms, Ginny 59, 88

Sinatra, Frank
and Academy Award wins and nominations 60, 110-111, **110**, 160, 192, 294
and allegations involving the Mafia 16, 31, 64-66, 92, 102-103, 108, 213, 245-246, 276, 293, 294
and 4F military status 38, 42, 54
and *The Godfather* 294-295
birth 17
charity work 73, 236-237, 268, 275-276, 293, 303
childhood 18-19
comic techniques 46, 68, 158, 169
death 311-312
education 18-19
gambling investments 109, 237-238, 245-246, 281, 303
health problems 90, 310
on acting 13, 298
on "Count" Basie 238
on Dean Martin 311
on *Dirty Dingus Magee* 291
on discrimination and racism 18, 55-56, 59
on films 10, 20, 52-53
on Gene Kelly 42
on his personal problems 89, 100, 175, 187
on his success 25, 148, 267
on his vocal techniques 26
on Italian stereotypes 80
on jazz 277
on Marlon Brando 126, 311

on other vocalists 15-16, 20
on Prohibition 18
    on *Sinatra* miniseries 306
    on *The Detective* 282
on the Mafia 18, 31, 65, 92
on *The Man with the Golden Arm* 135
on *The Manchurian Candidate* 235, 236
on Tommy Dorsey 24, 25
on *None But the Brave* 256
on winning the Academy Award 110
reputation as "One-Take Charley" 46, 85, 126, 133, 150-151, 193, 201, 205, 207-208
sociopolitical beliefs 16, 17, 41, 42, 54-59, 60, 70, 75, 137, 180, 198-199, 214-218, 285, 296, 302-303, 307
suicide attempts 93, 95
use of jive talk/"Sinatra-speak" 109, 144, 174, 203
Sinatra, Anthony Martin (father of FS) 17-19, 74, 93, 290, 313
Sinatra, Barbara Marx (fourth wife of FS) 297
Sinatra, Franklin ("Frank, Jr.") 38, 182, 250, 266, 309, 313, 314
Sinatra, Nancy Barbato (first wife of FS) 20, 64, 74, 77, 89, 93, 94, 110, 250, 307
Sinatra, Nancy (daughter of FS) 27, 52, 53-54, 80, 99, 130, 139, 177, 216, 218, 246, 248, 264-265, 271, 274, 278, 279, 281, 285, 290-291, 294, 297, 306
Sinatra, Natalie Garavente ("Dolly") (mother of FS) 17-19, 74, 84, 93, 99, 297-298, 307, 313
Sinatra, Tina (daughter of FS) 10-11, 77, 109, 171, 215, 218, 239, 306-308, 310-311
Sinatra (1992 TV miniseries) 306-308
Sinatra: A Man and His Music (album) 269
Sinatra: A Man and His Music (1966 TV show) 269-270
Sinatra: A Man and His Music, Part II (1967 TV show) 278
Sinatra and Company (album) 293-294

Sinatra and Swingin' Brass (album) 236
Sinatra at the Sands (album) 273-274
Sinatra-Basie: An Historic Musical First (album) 238-239
Sinatra 80th: Live in Concert (album) 311
Sinatra Sings Great Songs from Great Britain (album) 237
Sinatra: The Main Event (album) 8, 296-297
Sinatra: The Main Event (1974 TV show) 296-297
Sinatra's Sinatra (album) 243, 254
Sinatra's Swingin' Session (album) 216-217
Sing and Dance with Frank Sinatra (album) 90, 216
Siravo, George 90, 109, 111
Skelton, Red 29-30, 63, 81, 212
Smith, Keely 243
Softly, As I Leave You (album) 261
"Soliloquy" (song) 60, 124, 241-242, 311
Some Came Running (1968 film) 10, 182-189, **183**, **186**, **188**, 214, 313
Some Nice Things I've Missed (album) 296
"Someone to Watch Over Me" (song) 50, 60, 117, 118, 119
"Somethin' Stupid" (song) 279, 281
"The Song is You" (song) 30, 35, 74, 189, 191, 299
Songs By Sinatra (radio show) 38, 58, 69
Songs for Swingin' Lovers (album) 12, 141-142, 161, 171, 173, 217, 309
Songs for Young Lovers (album) 109, 111, 204
St. John, Jill 239, 242, 271, 279-280, **279**
Stafford, Jo 15-16, 24, 27, 243
"Stardust" (song) 23
"Stars Fell on Alabama" (song) 161
Step Lively (1944 film) 39-41, **39**, **40**, **41**, 47
"Stella By Starlight" (song) 66
Stordahl, Axel 24, 28, 30, 31, 33, 34, 38, 40, 51, 52, 55, 61,

69, 74, 86, 94, 103, 105, 110, 115, 148, 163, 175, 220
Strangers in the Night (album) 8, 270-271, 278
"Strangers in the Night" (song) 270, 311
Strayhorn, Billy 178
"Street of Dreams" (song) 273, 299
Sturges, John 11, 225
Styne, Jule 40, 48, 51, 60, 61, 66, 67, 69, 81, 91, 94, 110, 118, 173, 175, 220, 285, 288
Suddenly (1954 film) 10, 16, 112-115, **113**, **114**, 117, 120
"Summer Wind" (song) 8, 270-271, 308-309
"Sweet Lorraine" (song) 64
Swing Easy! (album) 74, 111, 121
A Swingin' Affair (album) 30, 161, 168, 171, 173
"Swinging on a Star" (song) 155, 254

Take Me Out to the Ball Game (1949 film) 78-79, **79**, 82-83, **82**, 85, 88, 89, 296
Taylor, Elizabeth 52
The Tender Trap (1955 film) 11, 127-130, **128**, **131**, 144, 147, 239, 242, 311
"That Old Black Magic" (song) 60, 96
"That Old Feeling" (song) 209
That's Entertainment (1974 film) 296
That's Life (album) 278
"That's Life" (song) 278, 294
"(The Theme From) New York, New York" (song) 8, 300, 303, 304, 309, 311
"There's a Flaw in My Flue" (song) 148-149
"These Foolish Things" (song) 51, 60
"They Can't Take That Away from Me" (song) 109, 171, 236, 309
"Three Coins in the Fountain" (song) 110, 111
Three Stooges 244
Till the Clouds Roll By (1946 film) 11, **60**, **61**, 63-64
"Time After Time" (song) 66, 69, 70
To Be Perfectly Frank (radio show) 109

Tolson, Clyde 70
The Tonight Show with Johnny Carson (TV show) 298-299
Tony Rome (1967 film) 279-281, **279**, 282
Torme, Mel 36, 173
Tracy, Spencer 147, 196, 208, 217, 222-224, **223**
Trilogy (album) 38, 299-301
Truman, Harry S. 72
Turner, Lana 53

Valli, Alida **75**, **76**, 76-77
Van Heusen, James ("Jimmy") 28, 50, 72, 86, 91, 111, 118, 129, 131, 136, 141, 143, 148, 155, 174, 177, 185, 188, 189, 192, 197, 219, 220, 226, 241, 242, 246, 253, 254, 261, 266, 269, 270, 288, 289, 314
Vaughan, Sarah 15
Vera-Ellen 84-84, **84**, **87**,
"The Very Thought of You" (song) 237
Vidor, Charles 11
Viola, Al 64
The Voice (album) 60
Von Ryan's Express (1965 film) 8, 261-264, **262**, **263**, 277, 308

Walters, Charles 99, 130, 144
Warner, Jack 117, 213, 246
Waterman, Sanford 293
Watertown (album) 290
"The Way You Look Tonight" (song) 38, 254
Wayne, David 128-130, 242
Wayne, John 70, 176, 216, 227, 262, 264, 268-269, **269**, 281, 288, 299
Webster, Ben 236
"Weep They Will" (song) 132
Welch, Racquel, 286-287, **286**
Welles, Orson 74, 91
"When Your Lover Has Gone" (song) 51, 125, 171
"When You're Smiling" (song) 96, 216
"Where Or When" (song) 52, 189, 274, 311
"White Christmas" (song) 51, 118
"Why Try to Change Me Now?" (song) 99
Wilder, Alec 34, 59, 163, 303

Wilder, Billy 76
Williams, Esther 78, **79**, 82-83, **82**
"Willow Weep for Me" (song) 178
"Witchcraft" (song) 170, 216, 220, 243
"Without a Song" (song) 28
Wood, Natalie 175, 178-182, **179**
The World We Knew (album) 281
"Wrap Your Troubles in Dreams" (song) 111

Yorkin, Bud 239-240, 242
on Sinatra 239-240
"You Make Me Feel So Young" (song) 141, 171, 274, 309
"You'd Be So Nice to Come Home To" (song) 161
"You'll Never Walk Alone" (song) 74, 241
Young, Lester 238
Young at Heart (1955 film) 10, 115-121, **116**, **119**, **121**, 125, 158, 169, 204, 247, 261
Young at Heart (1994 TV film) 310
"Young at Heart" (song) 109, 110, 243
Your Hit Parade (radio show) 32, 50
"You're a Lucky Fellow, Mr. Smith" (song) 254

Zinnemann, Fred 100, 103-105, 197

27377374R00196

Made in the USA
Lexington, KY
08 November 2013